THE HISTORY OF THE DRAINAGE OF THE FENS, CALLED BEDFORD LEVEL • VOLL (ESQ.)

Publisher's Note

The book descriptions we ask booksellers to display prominently warn that this is an historic book with numerous typos or missing text; it is not indexed or illustrated.

The book was created using optical character recognition software. The software is 99 percent accurate if the book is in good condition. However, we do understand that even one percent can be an annoying number of typos! And sometimes all or part of a page may be missing from our copy of the book. Or the paper may be so discolored from age that it is difficult to read. We apologize and gratefully acknowledge Google's assistance.

After we re-typeset and design a book, the page numbers change so the old index and table of contents no longer work. Therefore, we often remove them; otherwise, please ignore them.

Our books sell so few copies that you would have to pay hundreds of dollars to cover the cost of our proof reading and fixing the typos, missing text and index. Instead we let most customers download a free copy of the original typo-free scanned book. Simply enter the barcode number from the back cover of the paperback in the Free Book form at www.RareBooksClub.com. You may also qualify for a free trial membership in our book club to download up to four books for free. Simply enter the barcode number from the back cover onto the membership form on our home page. The book club entitles you to select from more than a million books at no additional charge. Simply enter the title or subject onto the search form to find the books.

If you have any questions, could you please be so kind as to consult our Frequently Asked Questions page at www.RareBooksClub.com/faqs.cfm? You are also welcome to contact us there. General Books LLC™, Memphis, ___., 2012.

❦ ❦ ❦ ❦ ❦ ❦ ❦ ❦

r
THE
HISTORY OF THE DRAINAGE
OF THE
GREAT LEVEL OF THE FENS,
CALLED
Bedford Level;
WITH THE
CONSTITUTION AND LAWS
OP THE
BEDFORD LEVEL CORPORATION.
By SAMUEL WELLS, Esq.,
REGISTER OF THE COnroBATION.
VOL. 1.
LONDON
for
BY K, PHENIiY, LAW BOOESELLER, 17, FLEET-STREBT.
W. Pople, Printer, v, Chancery Lane.
r TO THE MOST NOBLE 08 JOHN DUKE OF BEDFORD, o o GOVERNOR i -OF THE 'HONORABLE THE CORPORATION OF THE GREAT LEVEL OF THE FENS, f COMMONLY CALLED THE BEDFORD LEVEL, !Tf)iiJ Volume *it (WITH HIS GRACE'S PERMISSION) ItiaiU tlutifuUji antt rerfpectfullj)* Brttcatett, IS THE FONDLY-CHERISHED HOPB
THAT
THE HOUSE OF RUSSELL WILL COHTINUB TO EVINCB THE SOLICITUDE AND INEXTINOUI8HABLE ZEAL, IN SUPPORT OF *THE RIGHTS AND INTERESTS OF THE FENS,* WHICH HAV.B SO PREKMINENTLY MARKED THE CONDUCT OF ITS ILLUSTRIOUS PREDECESSORS.

196134 PREFACE length the author is enabled to submit to the Board, the Corporation, and the Country, the completion of his Work upon the Bedford Level. It is the duty of an Historian to collect facts, to record events, to reason upon them with accuracy, and faithfully to transmit the result for the benefit of posperity is less important. He has merely to collect and arrange passing events, to furnish evidence of their authenticity, and leave his readers to form their own conclusions. The following work may be considered as partaking of both of these descriptions of literary labour.

The changes among the Members of the Corporation, and other persons interested in the property of the Level, are of daily occurrence; and it frequently happens, that the Board (many of whom, at the-time of their election, are totally unacquainted with the nature of their office) are greatly at a loss to understand the several subjects from time to time presented to their attention.

The collection of laws relative to the corporation of the Bedford Level, compiled by the late register, Charles Nalson Cole, Esq., being out of print, and a work comprising the varied information embraced by this complicated subject being in constant requisition, the Author deemed it incumbent upon him, particularly considering his appointment in the corporation, to endeavour to give a detail of the several plans of the drainage of the Fens, and the origin of the laws, and at the same time to offer a few remarks on the characters of the persons to whom the execution of those laws was originally confided. He has also attempted to describe and explain the numerous works connected with the general drainage of the Fens, the means of their support, and the improvement effected by time and circumstances, in a country little known in proportion to its extent, and its importance to the general interests of the kingdom at large.

The early history of the Fens will ever be involved in obscurity; nor would the most diligent search amidst the libraries of antiquaries, the scarce chronicles of religious houses, the early records of public offices, or the obsolete statutes and common law proceedings of the realm, lead to any satisfactory result. The most rigid investigation would terminate only in conjecture. That many very valuable documents were lost at the time of the dissolution of monasteries (much interested in the Fens), in the reign of Henry the Eighth, and in the destructive fire of London, in the reign of Charles the Second, is beyond all doubt.

The records of the Fen Office relate exclusively to the transactions of the adventurers, subsequent to the proceedings of the first undertaking by Francis Earl of Bedford, under the Lynn law, passed in 1631.

Two hundred years have elapsed since the first undertaking of the drainage by that illustrious nobleman; and a period of scarcely less duration, since the unparalleled exertions of William Duke of Bedford, his incomparable son and successor. The author marvels much that so many ages should have passed away without producing any history of the great and good names of these noblemen, embracing, as such a memoir necessarily would do, anecdotes of persons the most eminent, and of times the most interesting, in the annals of their country.

Partially to attempt the task has, however, devolved upon the Author; and if he has not brought to his performance a lofty genius, or an erudite mind, he has at least omitted nothing that elaborate research could discover, or unwearied industry achieve; no diligence has been spared in examining the works of historians, and documents, both public and private, coeval with the times, circumstances, and events, of which he treats; nor has he shrunk from labour or exertion when he had the least hope of finding aught that might elucidate his subject, or even afford entertainment to the reader: yet may he exclaim, in common with other and more elaborate and valued writers, that the chief unhappiness accompanying researches of this kind, is the impossibility of totally avoiding mistakes, and guarding against misconceptions. By those only who have been engaged in similar undertakings, can the toil and anxiety attendant upon a literary production be duly appreciated. And when the Author states, that the following sheets have been composed at moments when his professional and official avocations (the neglect of which would justly entail upon him the charge of inattention to the interests of those, whom every sentiment of gratitude should induce him never to neglect,) divided his attention, he hopes to disarm the severity of criticism, and to experience the indulgence of his friends:—alas! he has no means of averting the hostility of his enemies.

As an indispensable accompaniment to the work, the Author has published a Map of the Bedford Level and the adjacent country. Its beauty and accuracy reflect the greatest credit upon those who were intrusted with its execution. *As a* specimen of that class of engraving it is almost unequalled. There is no other Map extant which comprehends at one view the whole of the Bedford Level, the contiguous districts, and their modern alterations and improvements.

. When the Author published the prospectus of his intended work, he knew little of the time it would consume, or the extent and cost of the production. His pecuniary sacrifices have perhaps been beyond what the interests of his children justified him in incurring. Be this as it may; at least he leaves to those children an ex- ample of the industry and exertions of an affectionate parent.

As the work possesses particular claims to the attention of the owners and occupiers of property within the Level and its vicinity, the Author trusts he may indulge the hope of receiving the patronage and support of the Board, the Corporation, and his brother fen-men in general; should he be disappointed, it would ill become him to complain; particularly when he recurs to the.unfortunate fate of so many illustrious authors, In a word, he has performed what he conceived to be a public duty; and, at any rate, receives that "which no man taketh from him," the approbation of his own heart.

. *Fen-Office,* 6, *Serjeantf Inn, Fleet Street,*

%th April, 18JO.

TABLE OF CONTENTS.

CHAPTER I.

The Great Level.—Extent.—Counties.—Parishes or Places.

—Quantities of Land.—Natural Rivers.—Their outfalls
to sea, and Navigation.----*Poge* 1

CHAPTER II.

Causes of Inundation.—Upland, Downfall, and Tidal
waters.—Tides in general.-... 44

CHAPTER HI.

Original state of the Great Level.—State during the time
of the Ancient Britons.—On the arrival of the Romans.—

Works erected during their Government.—Departure of
the Romans.—State of the Fens under the Saxons.—At
the Conquest.------54

CHAPTER IV.

State of the Great Level from the Conquest to the Reformation.—John of Gaunt's design.—Growing power of the

Church.—Countess of Richmond. 69

CHAFFER V.

State of the Great Level during the reign of Queen Elizabeth.—Commission of Sewers, 13 and 20 Eliz.—John

Earl of Bedford.—Meeting of Commissioners of Sewers.

—Lord Burghley.—General drainage act.—Death of

Queen Elizabeth.—Accession of James I.— Sir Cornelius

Vermuyden.—Commissions, and State of the Level
during the reign of James I.—Accession of Charles I.
Page 78

CHAPTER VI.

State of the Great Level under Charles I.—The Lynn law.

—The indenture of fourteen parts.—Charter of Incorporation.—Its dissolution.—St. Ives law.—Engagement of

Sir Cornelius Vermuyden.—The King's harsh conduct.

—Reversal of the St. Ives law.—Noble conduct of the

Earl of Bedford, and his death.-106

CHAPTER VII.

Oliver Cromwell.—Character of William, Earl and afterwards first Duke of Bedford.—Their conduct with
regard to the Great Level.----134

CHAPTER VIII.

State of the Great Level under the Commonwealth.—The
Pretended act.—Progress of the works.—Distinction
between "the Participants," "the Adventurers," and
"the Company."—Transactions with Sir Cornelius Vermuyden.— Distresses of the Company; and generosity
of the Earl of Bedford 146

CHAPTER IX.

Division of the Great Level.—The North, Middle, and
South Level.—Their respective works of Drainage, &c.
—Commission of Adjudication.—Proceedings with reference to the South Level.—Employment of the Scotch
Prisoners.------*Page* 193

CHAPTER X.

State of the South Level.— Employment of Dutch Prisoners.
—Proceedings relative to the second and last adjudication.—Completion of drainage 246

CHAPTER XI.

Petitions.—Accession of Cromwell. —Ordinance or act of
state.—Sir Cornelius Vermuyden's death.—His scheme
of drainage.—The government of the company established.-------2/9

CHAPTER XII.

State of the Great Level under the Protectorate continued.
—Disapproval of Sir Cornelius's scheme.—Westerdyke
consulted.—Opinions of Badeslade, Labelye, Seaford,
Elstobb, and Smith.—Account of Romney Marsh.—
Adoption of laws and customs of,— Laws, system of
government, and officers of the Great Level.—Death of
Cromwell.-___..._ 290

CHAFFER XIII.

Causes of the restoration.—Situation of the Earl of Bedford, his participants, and adventurers.—Desertion of St.
John.—Lord Gorges.—The Earl of Bedford's return to
parliament.—The restoration.—State of the Level.—
First temporary act.—The Earl of Bedford's petition,
and order thereon.—Second temporary act.—King's proclamation.—Commission of sewers — The state of parties in the Great Level.—Further parliamentary proceedings.—The general drainage act.-*Page* 323

CHAPTER XIV.

Continued exertions of William Earl of Bedford.—At-
. tempts to ahridge the power of the commonalty of the
corporation.—The project defeated.— Court of appeal.—
Proceedings-of the corporation.— Colonel Dodson's design.—Sandy's cut.—Further application to parliament.
—The tax act passes.— Its utility.— The clause for general inclosures throughout the Bedford Level considered.—The clause repealed by the statute of James.—
The death and character of William Earl of Bedford.
389

CHAPTER. XV.

Phenomena of the Fens.—The soil.— Nature of turf.—Plants
and natural productions.—Opinion of De la Pryme.—
System of drainage.—Mills and steam engines.—Mode
of cultivation.—Decoys.—The Meers.-417

CHAPTER XVI.

Boundary of the Bedford Level.— Constitution of the corporation.— Distinction between corporations by statute
and by charter.— Constituent parts of the corporation.—
Since that part of the work which treats of the drainage of the Fens by mills and steam engines was printed, the author has been favored with the following particulars relative to the
The select body, from the foundation to the last election.
—The election of the corporation.— Their power to purchase, hold, and dispose of lands.— Their corporate assemblies.—Meetings of the select body.—Corporate documents.—Evidence.-*PclSe*

CHAPTER XVII.

Officers of the corporation.—How appointed.—Their election.—Salary.—Duties.—Regulations on the death of
.. the Register.—List of persons who, from time to time,
have held the several offices under the corporation.
539

CHAPTER XVIII.

General commissions of sewers.— Provisions as to sewers
works in the Bedford Level.—Lynn Law.—Charter.—
Saint Ives Law.—Pretended act.—General drainage act.

powers of the engine recently erected, near the great hank of
the One Hundred Feet River, for the drainage of Littleport
Fen.

Wheel *yift.* Sin.; 32 feet main circumference; ladle, *3ft.*
4in. wide; 5 feet dip.

Mean velocity of the ladle at«highest head, 226 feet per
minute.

Ditto, lowest head, 339 feet per minute.

Area of ladle, *16ft.--,* superficial.
A tunnel one foot square, and 22G feet long, will hold as many cubic feet of water. To pass the whole length in one minnte,
would be 1,356 gallons; by increasing the area of this tunnel to the area of the ladle, *16ft. --,* 22,148 gallons will be

discharged against the highest head. A tunnel of one foot square, and 339 feet long, will pass 2034
gallons in one minute; by increasing its capacity to the area of the ladle, it will then discharge 33,242 gallons every minute against the lowest head.—This the engine will perform.

—The select body of the corporation appointed commissioners of sewers.—System of puddling.—Advice of
Lord Tenterden.-... *Page* 584

CHAPTER XIX.
Registration of Deeds-----593

CHAPTER XX.
Parliamentary proceedings.—Standing orders as to Drainage bills.—Notices to be given.—Resolutions of the
board of the Bedford Level corporation.—Duties of the
Register, as to bills before parliament.—Reservation
clauses.-,_--__ 603

CHAPTER XXI.
Particulars of the 95,000 acres of Adventurers' lands.—
The Cut Land Roll.—Turf Act.—The revenues of the
corporation.—The annual taxes.—The arrcar roll.—Particulars of the lands charged with each sort of tax.—
Amount of tax in each Level.—Public houses.—Tolls.
—Hermitage sluice, and Bridge toll.—Banks and fish-
cries.—Cottages, and regulations thereof.—The expenditure of the corporation.—Barrier Banks.—Minor
banks.—General orders for expenditure.—Extra expenditure.—The debt of the corporation.—First and second
Bond act.—Payment of interest.—The Fen Office.
612

CHAPTER XXII.
Division of the Three Levels.—The North Level: its
several ancient and modern works of drainage, and in-
termit economy.—Thorney Church, and Crowland Abbey.
—Private Acts.—Kinderley's Cut.—Tidd and Newton
act.—Nene Bridge and Outfall.—Lord William Bentincke.—The intended improvement in the North Level
drainage.-*Page* 060

CHAPTER XXIII.
The Middle Level.—Boundary.—Its three divisions.—
Their boundaries.—Early dissentions between Drainage
and Navigation.—River Nene Act.—Tongs Drain.—Sir
Thomas Hare's transaction.—Wisbech Canal act.—
Ashlin's sluice.—Middle Level and Barrier Banks acts.
—Works generally in the Middle Level.—Private Tolls.
692

CHAPTER XXIV.
The South Level, and its boundary.—Corporation works.—
The Washes.—The Wash Sluices, and Cradge Bank.—
St. John's Eau.—Denver sluice.—Labelye's scheme.—
Doctor Mawson, Bishop of Ely.—The Suspension
Bridge.-... 727
0
ERRATA.
Page 72, lines 13 and 19, for " Halloft," read "Haltoft." 94, 18, for " refused," read " desired." 136, 18, for " nunneries," read "religious bouses." 137, 25, for " this," read " that." 181, note, for "he was afterwards created," read "he afterwards succeeded to the title of." 279, chapter xi, line 3, dele " Romney Marsh." 448, line 10, for " presented," read " prevented." i 496, line 15, the asterisk annexed to the name of Lord Viscount Townsbend, should be made to refer to the Earl of Sandwich (first line of page 497). 503, note, line 15, for "Baronet of Stradbrooke," read " Earl of
Stradbrooke." 504, note, line 1, for " Cumington Castle," read " Coimington Castle." 506, note, line fi, for " Pyndele," read " Tyudale." 51G, line 18, second column, for " deceased," read "resigned." 695, 21, for" waded," read " *rotated."* 70S, 28, for " Button," read "Sailers." 713, 11, the word " act" omitted." 733, 18, for " New Bedford Level," read " New Bedford River."

The reader is requested to mark the errors iu the print.

CHAPTER T. THE GREAT LEVEL. *Extent.— Counties.—Parishes or Places.—Quantities of Land.—Natural Rivers.—Their Outfalls to Sea, and Navigation.*

The Great Level of the Fens comprises several districts not forming-part of the *Bedford Level.* This last appellation was first given to the country under the jurisdiction of the corporation, by the title to the General Drainage Act, passed the loth Car. II.; it was previously designated the *Great* App. 383. *Level.* The Bedford Level contains upwards of A?p. 367. 300,000 acres of fen land, and extends itself over a surface exceeding twenty square miles. The districts without the limits of the Bedford "Level are known by the names of South Holland, Deeping Fen, Lindsey Level, and East and West Wildmore Fens, in the county of Lincoln; Marshland, Bardolph, and Downham Fens, in the county of Norfolk; Wisbech Hundred, Waldersey and Coldham, in the Isle of Ely. All other fen lands, (except some small part drained by the river Nar, or Sandrigham Eau, in the county of Norfolk,) are comprised within the precincts of the Bedford Level. The Bedford Level and the

Vol. i. B whole of the foregoing districts are respectively bounded by the highlands of the counties of Norfolk, Suffolk, Cambridge, Huntingdon, Northampton, Lincoln, and the Isle of Ely.

PARTICULARS *Of Fen Lands, in and near the Bedford Level, according to Hayward's Survey, in* 1635-0. App. 141. N. B. The places printed in Italics are not within the Bedford Level.

Norfolk
Denver----
Ford ham----
Roxham----
Deerliam and Wereham-----
Wretton and Stoke-
Norwold----

Methwold---
Southery----
Hilgay----_
Feltwell----
Hockwold and Wilton
1,610 0 0 576 0 0 281 1 0 879 0 0 1,458
1 0 1,227 0 0 8,394 2 0 3,309 2 20 5,908
1 20 8,162 2 0 4,202 3 20

The total number of acres enumerated above amounts to about 311,000.

Natural rivers. There are eight principal rivers, formed by nature for conveying to sea great part of the upland waters of the before mentioned and some adjacent counties: viz. the Glen or Glean, Weiland, Nene, Cam, (united near Cambridge with the Grant,) Great Ouze, Mildenhall or Lark, Brandon or Lesser Ouze, and Stoke or Wissey. There is also the river above noticed, which enters at the port of Lynn, called the Nar, or Sandringham Eau.

outfalls to sea. These rivers have three several outfalls to sea; namely, Boston, in the connty of Lincoln, Wisbech, in the Isle of Ely and county of Cambridge, and Lynn Regis, in the county of Norfolk. They may be considered the main arteries of the fens. Most of them were originally united by connecting streams, forming themselves, at different situations, into large estuaries: these acting at periods of pressure as natural depositories, gave time, until Nature was relieved, for the passage of the floods of the one or the other to their outfalls to sea. Art has changed these currents; and had not the works of Nature been indelible, no traces would now be left to record the wide distinction between the works of the Creator and those of his feeble creatures.

In order to form a proper understanding of the original state of the fens, and of the immense influx of water from the uplands, previous to the drainage, it becomes necessary to describe those rivers, from their source to their entrance into the fens, and thence to their outfalls to sea. The *vast* quantity of water brought into the level surface of the fens, (many miles distant from the outfalls,) must at all times have occasioned great inconvenience and injury to the lands through which it passed: this inconvenience (with other attendant circumstances) ultimately led to those works of drainage, which it is the more immediate object of the author to develop.

River Glen.

The river *Glen* or *Glean* has its rise (by tradi-GienorGic»n. tion) at Little Glen, a village near Leicester. If this ever was the fact, all trace of it is now quite gone, as that river is intersected in many places by the Oakham and Melton Canal. The more modern opinion is, that its source commences in or near the parish-of Holywell, in the county of Lincoln, and passes through several parishes, until it reaches the turnpike road from Peterborough to Lincoln, at Kate's Bridge, three miles south of Bourn, from which point to its termination at the reservoir, (where it enters the river Welland, about five miles below the town of Spalding,) it is embanked on both sides.

The river Glen is navigable for vessels or lighters, of about fifteen tons burthen, from the Reservoir upwards to Kate's Bridge, or near thereto; but the chief traffic is between the Reservoir and a place called Tongue-head, where the Bourn Eau navigation branches off to Bourn in a northwest direction. This branch of the Glen is most copiously supplied with water, and many intelligent persons have suggested the practicability of supplying the port of Boston, (so deficient in this most useful necessary of life,) with ample streams from its abundant springs.

The river Glen itself affords, by means of numerous tunnels, a bountiful supply of excellent water to the lands on each side of its banks.

After its junction with the Welland, it runs with that river to Fosdyke, Stow, and onwards to the outfall at Boston Deeps.

The Glen has no connection with the Drainage of the Bedford Level, beyond that which arises from its waters being mingled with those of the river Welland; nor has it any remarkable features of natural or artificial beauty, except the fine and extensive domain of Grimsthorpe Castle, near Bourn. That branch of the river which proceeds from Bourn contributes greatly to adorn this magnificent seat, the property of Lord Gwydir. . Sol The several Acts of Parliament relating to

Deeping Fens, and the bank and road of the river Welland, contain clauses affecting the river Glen;. as also do the Acts for inclosing the commons of Spaldhig, Pinchbeck, Cowbit, and other commons in Kesteven, Holland, and River Welland.

River fFelland. The Welland finds its source at a place near Sibertoft, amidst a gentle range of hills between Lutterworth and Harborough, and divides Northamptonshire from Leicestershire, Rutland, and Lincolnshire, in a direction mostly to the northeast. It then turns directly north, and taking in some petty streamlets, comes at length to Market Deeping, and St. James Deeping, where it enters the fens, and burthens them with all the waters and downfalls of part of Northamptonshire, Lei-, cestershire, Rutland, and Lincolnshire; whence passing to Crowland, it there divides itself into two branches, the one leading by the Old South Eau to Clow's Cross, and so by Guyhirn towards Wisbech; the other to Spalding and Surfleet, where receiving the waters of the river Glen, it passes on in an united stream to Fosdyke, Stow, and thence into Boston Deeps.

The several Acts of Parliament alrea'dy alluded App. *soi.* to, in the account of the river Glen, apply also to the river Welland.

The Welland is stated by some writers to derive its name from the Saxon word *Vealland,* which signifies bubbling, boiling, raging. But this has been discredited, because, in fact, the river does not boil and rage, but glides along with a comparatively smooth surface. It must, however, be confessed, that there is so great an affinity between *Vealland* and Welland, that we ought to consider of some defence for an etymology that cannot with reason be altogether rejected. It may, therefore, be conjectured, that the river was perhaps more rapid previous to the formation of locks for the purposes of navigation, and of dams for the convenience of mill work; and consequently, that the term was then more appropriate in the winter's swell, and in occasional floods.

The spring-head is under the parlour window of the Parsonage House, at Sibertoft, about four miles beyond Hnrborough, and feeds two or three ponds in the garden.

This river, being less than the Nene, does not equal it in the beauty of its course; yet it traverses a fine plain between Harborough and Rockingham, distinguished by some bold hills, and well sprinkled with villages. Carlton, the mansion of Sir John Palmer, covers one of the eminences. The church having of late years been handsomely rebuilt, in the Gothic style of Architecture, acids to the beauty of the scene; while on the opposite hill, in Leicestershire, Mr. Nevill's old collegiate house of Holt displays itself. Near this mansion is found a celebrated mineral water. Rockingham Castle also, the ancient seatof Lord Sondes, overlooks the Welland from its high terrace, backed by a finely wooded park; andas the'river approaches Rutland, the vale contracts itself, the hills becoming higher, one of which is" crowned with the lofty spire of Uppingham Church. The great forest of Rockingham covers all the Northamptonshire side with its abundant woods, being formed into large ridings, to embellish the various fine seats con tuincd within its confines; among which Doughton, Dean Kirby, and Dray ton are the principal. Advancing with the Welland, the two high towers of Colly Weston and Easton, with the venerable ruins of Wothorp, mark the Northamptonshire termination of the vale; and the spire of Ketton, amidst the meadows of Rutland, is another object of attraction. The numerous steeples and towers of Stamford rise in almost collegiate grandeur to grace the entrance of Lincolnshire; and the princely pile of Burghley, appearing itself a town, in the midst of its highly ornamented territory, adorns the Northamptonshire bank. Majectic avenues of old trees, and almost numberless young plantations, cover the encircling eminences, within which all the art of Browne has been happily expended, and the highest powers of architecture and painting have been bestowed to decorate this splendid domain of the House of Burghley. The Welland soon afterwards sinks into the fens of Lincolnshire, below the two Deepings, and. passing near the grand monastic ruin of Crowland Abbey, arrives at Spalding, built after the Dutch fashion, like Wisbech; soon after which it reaches the sea.

It would be improper to omit to notice in this Crowland place the famous bridge at Crowland (or Croyland, as Gough calls the town); it is a curiosity worthy of attention, more from the singularity of its form than of its size, or any difficulty in its construction. According to some writers, it was erected so long since as the year 942; according to others, in the reign of Edward 1st. Gough, the antiquary, considered this bridge the greatest curiosity in Britain, if not in Europe. It is of a triangular form, rising from three segments of a circle, and meeting at a top. It seems to have been built under the direction of the Abbots, rather to excite admiration, and furnish a pretext for granting indulgences and collecting money, than for any real use; for though it stands in a bog, and must have cost a vast sum, yet it is so steep in its ascent and descent, as to be almost impassable to carriages or horsemen.

Nene. The river Nene, by means of a stream called the

Catwater, formerly united itself at this bridge with the river Welland, both meeting under the great arch; and these forming one river, flow thence through Spalding into the sea, in the course before mentioned. The bridge itself has three fronts, three ways over it, and three ways under it.

The Chater joins the Welland at Ketton, rising in the forest of Liffield,on the borders of Leicestershire. The Guash also falls into it a little before Stamford, forming in its passage the pleasant vale of Catmose, in which the town and spire of Oakham, encircled by numerous villages, are proudly overlooked by the late Earl of Winchelsea's elevated palace of Burley-on-the-hill, the court yard of which is the most splendid in England. Both these rivers traverse the whole of the little county of Rutland, moving chiefly in an eastward'direction.

The river Welland was famous for a fish called the Stickleback, which is seldom more than two inches long, and could, one would think, easily find support in any water; yet it is obliged to colonize, and leave its native fens in search of new habitations. Once every seventh or eighth year amazing shoals of these fish appear in the river near Spalding, and come up the stream, forming one great column. They are supposed to collect in multitudes insonie of the fens, until, on account of the extraordinary accumulation of their numbers, they are periodically obliged to migrate. An idea may be formed of their abundance from the circumstance, that a man employed by a farmer to take them for the purpose of manuring his grounds, obtained, for a considerable time, four shillings a day for selling them at a halfpenny a bushel.

In the 13th year of Queen Elizabeth, an Act was passed for making the river Welland navigable from Stamford to the sea. This act, says the amiable and intelligent author of the History of Stamford, was passed, on the application of the aldermen, burgesses, and commonalty of Stamford, stating that their town, which had formerly been inhabited by many opulent merchants, whose wealth had been increased by the navigation of the river Welland, and its connection with Boston, Lynn, and other parts, was then gone to great ruin and decay from the prejudice done to the navigation, by the erection of mills between Deeping and Stamford, and the consequent divisions of the stream of the river from its ancient course. And Goldsmith's History of the Earth, Vol. iii. p. 414.

commissioners at a general session of the Commissioners of 17 jac."' Sewers, holden at Stamford, on the 23d of August, and the 10th of September, in the 17th year of King James the First, by that Act of Parliament it was enacted and decreed, that it should be lawful for the aldermen and burgesses of Stamford, and their successors, to make a river or new cut, of such breadth and depth as they should think fit, for the passage of boats, barges, lighters, and other vessels, from the north side of the river Welland, from the east end of the town of Stamford and Hudd's Mill, across the river called Newstead River or the Wash, and thence through Uffington, Tallington, West Deeping, Market Deeping, and past Market Deeping Corn Mill, to rejoin the ancient course of the river, and thence, in the course before stated, unto the outfall to sea, at Boston Deeps. The aldermen and burgesses, and their successors, were enabled to make such locks, sluices, and other works, as were necessary for the navigation, the expense of which undertaking was then estimated at 2000/. The Commissioners of Sewers also ordained, as this work Corporation of was undertaken at the expense of the corporation and their friends, that the aldermen and burgesses, and their successors, should receive for all boats, &c., passing through each lock, "such a competent consideration as should be fit and convenient, proportioning the same according to the burthen of the said vessels."

King James the first, by his grant, confirmed the proceedings of the Commissioners of Sewers; and, willing that the aldermen and burgesses, and their successors, should receive towards their expenses in the execution of the work, and the continual maintenance of the same, a competent recompense, ordained that they and their successors should, immediately after the new work was passable, demand *3d.* a ton for all vessels passing to Toiu. and fro upon the river or new cut at every lock, without accounting to the Crown for what they should receive; and he granted to the aldermen and burgesses, and their successors, the fishery of Fishery. the new river or cut.

In 1663, the corporation of Stamford demised the navigation from Stamford to the Welland at Deeping, to one Daniel Wigmore, one of the aldermen, for 80 years, at *2d.* a year; and at the expiration of that term, a further demise for 80 years was granted by the corporation to Charles Halford, Esq., the representative of Wigmore, on the payment of 100/., under a stipulation contained (as it is said) in the former lease. The property of the navigation next came into the hands of Mr. Feast; afterwards into those of Edward Buckley, Esq.; and a lease has since been.granted to Mr. Thomas Smith, by whose heirs it is still retained. The iniquity, continues the historian of Stamford, attending this grant, is self-evident; inasmuch as a public trust was perverted into private emolument; and even if it could be sustained in a court of law, it would undoubtedly be censured in a court of equity.

At a meeting held at Stamford, in the year 1809, a plan was proposed, to form an effective navigable communication between Stamford, Oakham, Peterbrough, and Boston. But this plan was never carried into effect; for however beneficial it might have proved to the town of Stamford and the upland counties, it would have proved, it is supposed, any thing but advantageous to the towns of Lynn and Wisbech, by destroying the traffic in sea coal, the chief commodity of these places, and by bringing the pit coal of Derbyshire, Nottinghamshire, and perhaps Yorkshire, into the heart of the fens, now solely supplied with that most essential necessary of life, by the ports of Lynn, Wisbech, and Boston.

On the navigation from Hudds Mill below Stamford to the lock at East Deeping inclusive, a distance of nine miles and a half, there are twelve locks, which are of a capacity to receive vessels of seven feet beam only. No vessels of greater burthen than 15 tons are navigable from Stamford to Spalding, and goods are usually brought up to Stamford in a gang of four lighters, of from seven to thirteen or fourteen tons burden, not carrying together more than from 36 to 42 tons. The voyage from a place called the Scalp, through Spalding to Stamford, being about-'50 miles, is usually performed in three or four days. Sea coal and timber are the chief articles of merchandize.

River Nene. The Nen, Nene, or Nine , (for this river bears Nene. all these appellations,) rises in two branches, north and south of Daventry, at a place called Catesby, in Northamptonshire, and pursues an eastern direction to Northampton, where it turns more towards the north, through one of the pleasantest vales in that county; from Wandsford (Wandsford in England!!) its course is again more eastward to the city of Peterborough, near which place it enters the fens in this fenny flat, and divides itself into sundry branches, one of which passes through Standground Sluice and Horsey Bridge into Whittlesey Mcer, (a branch also proceeding upwards to Yaxley); thence by Ramsey under Bodsey Bridge, by the side of Ramsey Meer to Benwick, March, Upwell, and Outwell, to Saiter's Lode, where it unites with the river Ouze, and passes to the outfall below Lynn. Another branch (called Whittlesey Dike) passes from Standground Sluice through Whittlesey, forming a junction with the preceding course at Floods Ferry, between Benwick and March. The upland waters being denied entrance into the fens by the erection of Standground Sluice, proceed from Peterborough through artificial rivers, The River is said to take its name from the circumstance of its deriving its source from "nine" springs or rivulets. VOL. I. C namely, Moreton's Leam, and the rivers called Hill's Cut and Smith's Leam (of which more particulars hereafter), to Guyhirn, and thence in one united stream to Wisbech. This river divides Lincolnshire from Norfolk, as it advances below Wisbech, to form the Wash of Cross Keys, terminating in the great gulf, where the river Ouze formerly also discharged its waters. There was another branch not far from Peterborough, called the Muscatt Water, running through the bounds of Thorney, afterwards forming the streams called Knarr Lake, the Wride, and South Eau, and again uniting below Wisbech.

The first part of this river runs through a delightful country, and its character is that of a gentle but full stream, flowing in placid beauty amidst enamelled meadows, through a tract abundant in towns, villages, and fine seats. Northampton, one of the most elegant and ornamented county towns in England, graces its early course; and its banks as far as Wellingborough are lined with elegant mansions, among which Castle Abbey presents a conspicuous figure. This county abounds in villages, and handsome spires start up in every quarter. It is also distinguished by large forests: that of Rockingham is the most considerable, covering almost all the space from the Welland to the Nene, near Thrapston and Oundle on the latter river. Wandsford has a long bridge connecting the north road. Of this bridge is related a romantic story, of a man having flouted, in consequence of a summer flood, down the river, from the higher districts of Northamptonshire, on a haycock, on which he was sleeping, and being stopped by its arches: his surprise on awaking, and his extraordinary preservation, form the interesting part of the tale. Many think it altogether fabulous, though it has given a sign to an excellent inn on the Huntingdonshire side of the bridge, the property of his Grace tlie Duke of Bedford, who has considerable possessions iu the neighbourhood. The country afterwards becomes far more level, though yet distinguished by a range of green meadows and some elevated grounds on the Northamptonshire bank, where Lord Fitzwilliam's fine old seat of Milton covers a long waving ridge with its well-arranged plantations. Soon afterwards, the majestic pile of Peterborough Cathedral exalts itself above its city with great grandeur; below which the Nene becomes lost in those immense fens which cover the extensive Level beyond the city. Those fens are interspersed with large pools of water, of which Whittlesea Meer and Ramsey Meer are the greatest. These fens and meers are plentiful in wild fowl: those rare and delicate birds, called the Ruff and Ree, are found here, and are trained with considerable expense and difficulty. Wisbech may be called wubech. the port of the River Nene; it is singularly constructed, after the manner of towns in Holland, the broad muddy channel of the river, from Guyhirn, occupying the centre. The ancient channel of the river Ouze, from Littlepool Bridge, formerly flowed somewhat northward, through the fens, and emptied itself below the town; thus finally uniting the waters of both rivers, and so proceeding to the outfall, at a place called Crab Hole. The river Nene was first attempted to be made navigable from Northampton to Peterborough, in 12 Anne. e twelfth year of the reign of Queen Anne: but n Goo. 2, c. the attempt failing, another act passed, 11 Geo.

19. IF. c. 19, for making the former act more ef fectual; by which certain commissioners were appointed to put the several powers thereby given into execution; and further powers were eo 3 c also given by a subsequent statute, 34 Geo. III.

M. c. 84, particularly respecting the setting out of proper halingways. The property of the navigation is vested (under the control of the commissioners) in private individuals. From Northampton to Thrapston Bridge forms the first division; and from that place to Peterborough the second: the latter was till lately the property of the elder branch of the respectable and opulent family of the Squires, who have long resided in the city of Peterborough, where they have been, and still are, deservedly honoured and esteemed. The navigation of the river *Nene* from Standground Sluice through the fens to Saiter's Lode will be considered in a future part of this work, in relation to its connection with the general drainage of the Bedford Level. The navigation of the river from Peterborough, through Hill's Cut and Smith's Leam to Guyhfrn, (whence it proceeds to Wisbech,) is under the management of trustees acting under the authority of the Honorable the Corporation of the Bedford Level, having power to take haling tolls, not only to reimburse the sums already expended in improving the navigation, but for keeping the same in a proper state during the existence of that authority.

The river from Guyhirn is simply called (says Colonel Watson, the able and industrious historian of the town of Wisbech,) "The Great River;" and is now become of considerable importance for the purposes of navigation, forming a communication with the upland country. Wisbech is situated on both sides of the "Great River," over which is a handsome stone bridge, erected by the respectable corporation of Wisbech, chiefly out of their corporate funds. It Wisbech was commenced in the year 1758, and completed in 1760. The Honorable the Corporation of the Bedford Level contributed 300/. towards the construction. The old bridge was of wood, and totally inadequate to the discharge of flood waters. The present building forms an elliptical arch of seventy-two feet span. It is repaired by the corporation of Wisbech, to which liability they did not submit until it was investigated and established by the decision of a court of law.

The tides, continues the same author, come with Tides, great velocity up the river, and flow many miles beyond Wisbech. The resistance, by the influx of the tides meeting the ebb waters, is called the *Hygre* or *JEgar,* which rushes in with considerable impetuosity about the time of either of the equinoxes. At every new nnd full moon, the spring titles flow about 8 feet. and laid out. The stream itself *is* but stagnant; yet it adds something to the peculiar traits of the landscape, with its several handsome stone bridges: nor do the fronts of the colleges, as they appear in succession, intermixed with thick groves, any where shew themselves to such advantage. The area in front of Clare Hall, and the magnificent new buildings of King's College, with its superb chapel, (matchless in that species of Gothic architecture which has been called "*the improved*") added to the fine buildings lately erected by Trinity and St. John's Colleges, exhibit one of the most striking displays in England. The waters of the Cam'are augmented by those of Bottisham, ,....,. ,,,,,,,,, Swaftham, three several rivers arismg amiust the Chalk Hills, Rcacu on the south-east of Cambridge, running through the fens, and called Bottisham, Swaffham, and Reach Lodes, entering the Cam through sluices, between Clayhithe and Upware, soon after which, the river arrives at Harrimecr. From this latter place are seen the proud pile and towers of Ely Cathedral, finelyelevated on the level just beyond the junction of the ancient branch of the Ouze, called the West River, (from the Hermitage, near Earith,) with the Cam, from Essex and Cambridgeshire.

A dreary tract of marsh accompanies these united rivers to Denver Sluice, near Downham Market in Norfolk; nor does the country much improve afterwards. The estuary (previously to the making of the Eau Brink Cut) was very considerable, and the exit of those rivers is splendid where the flourishing port and great external and internal trade of Lynn present a crowd of vessels wafting their commerce, through the; enterprize and industry of its wealthy and highly respected merchants, to both hemispheres.

The river Cam is navigable from the town of Cambridge to Lynn. From Cambridge to Clayhithe Sluice, the navigation is regulated by two i Anno, c. ii. statutes passed 1 Anne, c. 11, and 53Geo. III. c.

53Geo.3. c. 214. By the first act, eleven Conservators are to 214. be appointed; three to be nominated by the chancellor of the university of Cambridge, or his deputy, and the heads of the colleges of that university for the time being, or in their absence, by their deputies, or the major part of them; five by the justices at their general quarter sessions of the peace for the county of Cambridge, (such persons being noways interested in any of the lands and soil lying on or near the said river;) and three by the mayor and aldermen of the town of Cambridge for the time being, or the major part of them. The navigation is under the management and control of those conservators. The following persons in the present year, 1829, fill these situations:

For the county (The. Earl of Hardwickc.

The Rev. George Jenyns.
_ / Henry Adeane, Esq.
I R. G. Townly, Esq.
I Peter Allix, Esq.
Alderman Purchase. For the borough--
Alderman Coe.
I Mr. Ingle.

By the stat. 1 Anne, certain tolls are imposed on all vessels navigating that part of the river under the control of the conservators; and by the 53 Geo. III. the conservators have power to make bye laws. Their funds are said to be iu a flourishing state.

In consequence of the erection of the new cast iron bridge at Cambridge (by public subscription) an increased water way of several feet is given to the passage of the upland waters, as well as by the great improvements in progress by the commissioners, under an act passed 8 Geo. IV. for improving the drainage of that part 8 Geo.4. of the Bedford Level called the South Level. South L«vei. There can be little doubt that the conservators will find themselves under the necessity of making considerable improvements, both as regards the depth of the river and the capacity of the sluices between Clayhithe (including the sluice) and the town of Cambridge; or probably of removing some of the sluices, the continuance of which it is thought will be rendered unnecessary, should the bed of the river be made of sufficient depth to correspond with the improvements below. The navigation of the river from Clayhithe Sluice to Littleport Bridge, is under the direction and control of the commissioners appointed by the act passed 8 Geo. IV. for improving the drainage of the South Level, who have authority to impose a tonnage toll.

The river from Littleport bridge to Denver Sluice is called the Ten Mile River. It is not known at what period the ancient course of the old river was diverted from its outfall by Wisbech into its present channel to Lynn.

River Ouze. The *Ouze* traverses a very considerable part of the midland counties of England, rising in two branches not far from Brackley and Towcester, on the borders of Northamptonshire and Oxfordshire, whence its course is eastward, a little inclined to the north, through Buckinghamshire, joined at Newport Pagnell by a small stream from Ivinghoe on the south: it descends, by many windings towards the south, to reach the town of Bedford, and afterwards becomes navigable to Lynn and Cambridge. It is joined by the Hyee from Wooburn, and the navigable river Ivel from Shefford to Biggleswade, in Bedfordshire, the Ivel uniting with it at or near Tempsford Bridge: hence it pursues its original direction through the market town of St. Neot's to the borough of Huntingdon; thence, through the fine meadows of Godmanchester, Hartford, and Hemingford, to the populous and opulent market town of St.Ives, flowing onwards through fertile meadows until it enters the Bedford Level near Over Cote, and so proceeds to Earith, where it unites with the artificial river cut by the Adventurers, called the Hundred Feet River, running in a straight line to Denver Sluice, and again unites with another branch of the river which passes through the Hermitage Sluice, (called the West River,) fertilizing the luxuriant commons of Willingham, Cottenham, Rampton, and Streatham, (so famous for their rich dairies,) to Harrimeer, where it receives the waters of the Cam and the Grant, and passes near the city of Ely, through Littleport bridge, and thence to Denver Sluice; and then forms the great river Ouze. Near Littleport bridge the Ouze receives the waters of the Lark, or Mildenhall river, and somewhat lower down, the waters of the Brandon, or Lesser Ouze. Another branch (now quite grown up) formerly proceeded from Earith by Chatteris Ferry, and This river is crossed by a Bridge called Aldreth High Bridge, which connects the county of Cambridge and the Isle of Ely. The bridge is repaired by the owner of lands in Haddenham parish, which lands in the year 1766 were the property of Mr. Micah Coulson. In early times, this was the only entrance into the Isle of Ely, and was much contested during the time William the Conqueror laid siege to that place. The bridge is approached by a celebrated causeway, called Aldreth Causeway; which was heretofore repaired by certain parishes and individuals within the Isle, but is now wholly neglected. united with the river Nene at Benwick, and so found its course anciently to Wisbech, where it mingled its waters with those of the river Nene. Another arm once branched out near Littleport, and passing through Elm, united also with the Nene at Wisbech; but both those branches are now nearly grown up, though still forming the boundary line in many places between the Isle of Ely and the counties of Norfolk aud Huntingdon.

The following Document is extracted from Cole's MSS. "A coppy of the places and length, where towns, people, and places arc oblidged to repair of Aldreth Causeway.

Poles or F
Roods. eet.

Doddington parish (begins at Aldreth end)--20 —

Mr. Castle, now Mr. Goftbrd------ 20 March parish, with the heads and coffens of the
leam bridge------30 —

Whittlesea bridge 30 —

Mr. Castle, now Mr. Coulson, Cheesmonger of
Peterborough------15 —

Chatterice parish, Deep Whells, coffens and heads, and their part of Causeway---7 —

Thomas Castle Esq., beyond deep wheel,--15 —

Tidd St. Giles parish 7 —
Leverington do.-----12 —
Wisbech do. 12 —

Elme parish, causeway with Mr. Coulson of Peterborough's Pole-bridge, heads and coffens and other parts interfere, Elm Causeway 33 feet-12 —

Lord Hardwick for Hintin----40 —
Newton parish..----9 —
William Drury Esq., now Farrin--2 —

Stuntney parish------11 —
Haddenham end------8 —

Ralph March Esq. for the manor of Gray's 2 — the manor of Che well's-3 —

Heads and coffens of high bridge to Mr. Coulson 5 —
"Chains 60 1 3$

The Ouze neither gives nor receives much beauty, the great tract through which it passes including some of the least interesting districts in England. Its course is uniformly dull and unimportant to Buckinghamshire, nor is it at all an object of ornament from the princely territory of Stowe, which abounds in grand scenes and buildings, rather too artificially disposed, as well as too numerous.

The Hyee, which meets it a little below Bedford, Hyce. passes near the Duke of Bedford's noble domain of Wooburn Abbey; and the Ivel flows north-lTclward from its rise in the Chalk Hills near Baldock, to Biggleswade and Tempsford, through a dull tract of country.

The Ouze does not much improve as it traverses the counties of Bedford and Huntingdon, though it adds some consequence to their capitals, being there navigable. The old mansion at Hinchinbrook, formerly a priory, afterwards the property of the Cromwells, and now of the Earls of Sandwich, presents a feature of some beauty, as do the grounds of the author of this work, at Hartford near Huntingdon.

The upland waters of the River Ouze (as already stated) empty themselves near Earith into an artificial river, cut by the adventurers for draining the Bedford Level, called the "One
Hundred Feet River," which being straight, and open to the daily flow of the tides from Lynn, becomes liable to be silted up, unless a sufficient scour can be obtained by as strong an ebb current as possible from the waters of the Ouze. The state of the latter river is, therefore, of essential importance to the Bedford Level Corporation, and may justify the author entering upon a short historical account of the origin of its navigation, and the persons and public bodies now empowered or compelled to take active steps in its preservation and improvement.

The navigation of the River Ouze appears to have been first undertaken by one Arnold Spencer, under the authority of letters patent, granted to sc»r. i. nim and his assigns in the third year of the reign of King Charles the First. By subsequent letters 14 Car. i. patent, (14 Car. I.,) the Crown granted to the said Arnold Spencer, the only and absolute use and benefit of all and singular the water carriage in and upon the river, from St. Jves to St. Neots, and so far as the same is made navigable higher up, for ever.

Spencer paid an annual fee farm rent to the Crown of $6l$. 13s. 4d., and was bound to repair all the bridges, locks, and works, made by him or his assigns upon the course of the river; but whether this payment is now continued is not known to the author.

It is probable that Arnold Spencer was unable to complete the work he had undertaken, for we 16 &i7Car.2. find an act passed, 16 & 17 Car. II. c. 12, enabling other persons to moke the river navigable, under the authority and control of certain commissioners, being justices of the peace in those counties through which the river has its course.

Under this authority and control, the parties owning the right of receiving the tolls for the navigation of the river must, it is presumed, even at this period, act in the performance of the duties imposed upon them.

Grants from the Crown in earlier, and perhaps better times, were never conceded without the performance by the party benefited of some corresponding advantage to the public; and although the doctrine of " Resumption," has been long out of fashion, in these more degenerate days, there can be no doubt, that if the parties beneficially interested in the profits of the tolls of the navigation, neglect.or refuse to do that which the grant imposes, the law would compel a specific performance of the original contract.

Many persons are, doubtless, ignorant of the Godmanchester existence of a public body, called the Corporation of Godmanchester, although of antiquity so considerable that it traces its origin to the time of King John. Tradition states that King James the First, upon his journey from Scotland to London, upon his accession to the Crown of England, was met, upon passing through the borough, by this corporation and the inhabitants, with a procession of some hundreds of ploughs.

Godmanchester is a place of great extent, as regards its agricultural lands, as well as its extensive meadow grounds and open commons. Great part of the two latter being liable to be overflowed by the waters of the river Ouze, extensive power is vested in this corporation for the regulation of the commons.

It does not appear what was the fate of those who became adventurers, under the act of 16 & 17 Car. I.: they were, probably, like other undertakers both of ancjent and modern times, unable to complete their contract, and became utterly Ashley's con-ruined. Be this as it may, it seems that one tract, 1689. Henry Ashley, of Gray's Inn, Esq., was the owner of the navigation in the year 1689, having succeeded his father in the property. In that year, the bailiffs, assistants, and commonalty of the borough of Godmanchester, conveyed to this Henry Ashley. Esq., for the consideration of 120/., the fee simple of a piece of ground in Godmanchester, called the "Mill Holts," with the reservation of certain rights and privileges to the corporation; and, in this deed, is the following very important provision: "And moreover, that it shall and may "be lawful to and for the miller of the said God"manchester Mills, for the time being, and in his "default or omission, for such person or persons, "officer or officers, as shall be thereupon appointed "by the bailiffs of Godmanchester for the time "being, for ever hereafter, upon every *likelihood "and appearance of any flood or outrage of water,* "to set open, and keep open, or else to take off the "gates of the aforesaid sluices; and also the gates "of the sluices in and near Hough ton; and also the "gates of the sluices in and near the Mill of Hem"mingfordGrey,in the said county of Huntingdon, "and lay them upon the lands by the siile of the "said sluices, until the water be fallen and the "flood well abated."

The possession of this power is of essential consequence, not only to the drainage of the meadows and commons adjoining the River Ouze, but also to the quick passage of the upland waters to sea. The stream of the River Ouze, at ordinary times, is not rapid, and its course is rendered more unequal, or rather impeded, by the number of watermills with which it is (if the expression may be used) much incumbered. The interest of the landowners, and the interest of the millers are, at times of high water, or the expectation of high water, any thing but reciprocal; hence mutual complaints have arisen, and probably will arise, until some equally beneficial remedy be devised: the millers contending that the gates of the sluices are drawn at too early a period, while the land-owners, on the other hand, complain that their lands are destroyed by the great and unnecessary heads of water held up by the millers. This state of things has, unfortunately, led to litigation, and must continually lead to similar consequences, unless all parties interested in drainage and navigation, as well as in the mills, will concur in some general improvement, which, it is apprehended, may be accomplished by calling into activity the powers vested in the commissioners named in the statute 16 & 17 Car. II. , and the provisions of a subsequent statute, to be presently noticed, 6 Geo. I; or should these statutes not afford the means of carrying into effect Vol. i. D some general plan and arrangement, satisfactory to all parties, recourse should be had, either to the ancient common law redress, a commission of sewers, or the more modern practice—an application to the legislature.

No alteration appears to have taken place in the rights, powers, and interests of the several parties, until the sixth year of the reign of King Geo. I., when an Act was passed for preserving and improving the navigation of this river, which is stated in the recital to have become so shallow, at or near St. Ives, and other places *in the county of Huntingdon,* that by reason thereof, and of the decay of a certain work *formerly* built, and standing in the said river below St. Ives, commonly called St. Ives Staunch, boats and lighters could not pass up the said river to St. Ives, *muck less higher up* the said river, as they used to do. By this act, Henry Ashley, Esq., the then proprietor of the river, and who had succeeded to this property from his father, was authorized "to repair, amend, meliorate, and improve the passage thereof for boats, &c. within the *county of Huntmgdon,* and to make the same better and more perfectly navigable from a place called Hollywell-f-, in the said county, to every such other place or places higher up the stream of the river, and within the said county." This Act authorized Mr. Ashley to erect a staunch and other works at or near St. Ives (which were accordingly completed); and at the same time, gave power to the magistrates of the county in sessions, to settle the amount of any damage that the lord of the manors or landholders of St. Ives and Fenny Stanton might sustain by the erection of such staunch: and in order to reimburse Mr. Ashley for the additional charges of erecting the same staunch and other works, he was to receive an additional toll. Considerable fears appear to have been App. 7-2. entertained, even at that period, of the effects of the staunch so to be erected; in consequence of which, a kind of court of conservancy was created by the Act, consisting of six justices of the peace for the county of Huntingdon, and six Commissioners of Sewers within the Great Level of the Fens, to be annually appointed in manner directed by the act; and, when we consider the state of the river, it is greatly to be lamented, that the jurisdiction and powers, given as well by the 16 and 17 Car. II. as by 6 George I., are not (and there is no doubt they legally may be) carried into immediate effect.

It does not appear when this staunch was originally built, but, it is presumed, it was made under the authority of the 16 & 17 Car. 2. f The jurisdiction of the Bedford Level Corporation ends at the foot of the Highlands near this place.

The conveyance of 1689, before alluded to, and also the act of 6 George I., vested great powers in the corporation of Godmanchester, as to running the waters, and regulating the sluices; and, considering the extent and value of their commons and meadows, it was very proper that such powers should have been so vested, as they were not very likely to be abused. The corporation having no political motives, would (unlike those corporations which lend and bend themselves to the Moloch of the day) be indisposed to be swayed by improper or interested motives in the due execution of the responsible duties committed to their charge. The rights, privileges, and usages of the ancient corporation of Godmanchester, for prevention of the overflowing of the lands of the inhabitants, are fully and unequivocally reserved by this Act; and it is to be hoped that sufficient industry, talent, and perseverance, will be found in that body to justify the public in looking forward with confidence to their active exertions and cooperation, to accomplish that improvement in the state of the river, and the drainage of the lands adjoining, which must appear so obviously necessary, even to the most superficial observer.

The necessary steps ought without loss of time to be taken, in order to render effective all the dormant but legal powers now vested in the justices of the counties of Huntingdon and Bedford, the corporation of the Bedford Level, and the ancient corporation of Godmanchester. It will be conceded to the author of this work, that since he has had the honor of holding the important situation of Register, he has done all in his power to rouse the parties to an active discharge of the duties imposed upon them. Ouzc below Returning now to the lower end of the river

Denver sluice.

Ouze, between Denver Sluice and the port of Lynn, it should not be omitted to state, that the navigation of this part of the river is under the management of certain commissioners, appointed by an act passed in the 30th Geo. III., three of which commissioners are to be nominated annually, at the April meeting, under the common seal soceo.3. of the corporation of the Bedford Level. This App' is sometimes, but not always, attended to; and as the rights and privileges of the corporation may suffer by disuse, it is to be regretted that this power is not uniformly exercised. Twice only, since the first election of the present Register, has the appointment of commissioners taken place at the general April meeting of the corporation. The subject of the improvement of the lower end of this river, by the Eau Brink Cut, will be hereafter mentioned in the history of the origin and completion (perhaps we should rather say, the progress) of that important work.

There are five bridges over the river, between Ouzo Bridges. Denver Sluice and the harbour of Lynn; namely, Downham, Stow, Magdalen, St.Germains, and Eau Brink; some of these bridges are by no means in the state required for the increased celerity which recent improvements are likely to give to the passage of the waters to the outfall. It may be proper, as lawyers say, to put them upon record, although the consideration of their present and future state must be reserved for that part of this work, which treats of the Eau Brink Cut. It may, however, be mentioned, that sanguine hopes are entertained, that some, if not all of these bridges, will soon be so altered, that no impediment will arise to those improvements which are now in progress, and, it is expected, will be ultimately completed.

Before this cursory review of the natural rivers emptying their waters through the fens is completed, we must not neglect to notice the rivers Lark, Brandon or Lesser Ouze, and the Wissey; all of which have their outfall to sea, through the harbour of Lynn, by the river Ouze.

The. Lesser Ouze, or Brandon River. This river has its source at Lopham, in the The Lesser

Ouzo, or county of Norfolk; and passing through the towns of Thetford and Brandon, (at which latter place it divides the counties of Norfolk and Suffolk,) continues its course through the fens to its outfall into the river Ouze, between Littleport and Southery, in the county of Norfolk, at a place called Brand Creek.

The history of the navigation of this river, or at least, a considerable part of it, is rather curious, and proves that the anxiety of persons of distinction to oblige corporations, existed at a period when political servility was not (to use the memorable remark made by the late Lord Colchester, when speaker of the House of Commons,) as notorious as the sun at noon day.

By an act passed in the 22d year of Car. II., the 22 Car. 2. mayor, burgesses, and commonalty of Thetford, were empowered, under the superintendence and control of certain commissioners, to make this river navigable from a place called Whitehouse, beneath Brandon Ferry, to Thetford, and to receive certain tolls from persons navigating along the river; but the corporation being at that time " *not at all in a condition to execute the work"* the Right Honourable Henry Earl of Arlington undertook its execution, and the tolls were subsequently assigned to him. His lordship's only child, Isabella, married and survived the most noble Henry, Duke of Grafton; and after the decease of the Duke, her Grace *very kindly* released to the corporation of Thetford all her right and interest in these tolls. Mutual feelings of gratitude and good-will appear to have existed between the noble house of Fitzroy and the worthy corporation, up to the present period. The corporation of Thetford seem to have expended considerable sums in making navigable that part of the river under their control; but it was in later times discovered, that the inhabitants of the town of Brandon, and persons carrying goods to and from thence, had all along received the benefit and advantage of the navigation of the river from Whitehouse up to Brandon, and paid no toll, although the boats passing between these places could not often get to Brandon without the assistance of the sluices and staunches erected between Thetford and Brandon.

In order, therefore, to obviate this evil, and put the whole line of river between Thetford and Whitehouse, (near Brandon Ferry,) into a proper sooco. s. state, an act was passed, 30 Geo. III. c. 1(56, vesting the tolls of the river in the mayor, burgesses, and commonalty of Thetford, who are by that act appointed and continued undertakers for making, improving, and *completing* the navigation of the river, and authorized to take *to their own use and uses,* the several tolls specified in such act.

It has certainly been said, that the navigation and general condition of this river are by no means in that perfect state of " *completion'* contemplated by the Act. This must, however, have arisen from the insufficiency of the funds, or the "condition of the corporation," to carry its provisions into effect. Considering the way in which the public funds of political corporations are too often appropriated, illiberal persons might, without due inquiry, attribute some blame to the Corporation; but when we consider their great personal respectability, no doubt ought to be entertained that they are fully able to prove that all has been done that could be done. It is not for mortals to command success; nor is it of importance to the more immediate object of this work to pursue the inquiry: it is left, if necessary, to persons more peculiarly interested; although it may not be improper to observe, that in case the Corporation neglect their duty, certain commissioners are empowered to receive and apply the tolls in such works as are in the opinion of those commissioners neglected by the Corporation.

It will probably be necessary to refer to the state of both of the last-mentioned rivers, when the subject of the Eau-Brink Cut is considered, in a future part of this work.

River IVissey.,

This river also rises in the county of Norfolk, above Stoke Ferry, through which place it runs, and, after crossing the turnpike road between Ely and Downham, in the town of Hilgay, empties itself a short distance below that place into the Ouze.

It is only partially navigable above Denver Sluice, and is under no other legislative regulation than that of commissioners appointed for carrying into execution an Act passed in 1814, for draining and preserving certain fen lands in the parishes of Stoke Ferry, Northwold, Wretton, Wereham, West Dereham, Roxham, Ford ham, Denver, Downham Market, Wimbotisham, and Stow Bardolf, in the county of Norfolk. By the provisions of this act, the commissioners, when they shall judge it necessary, are to "widen, rode, or crab" the River Wissey, between Stoke Bridge and Hilgay Creek's End; and the same is to be done at the sole costs and charges of the owners and occupiers of the land lying within the boundary described in that act. The commissioners have also the power of receiving tolls from persons passing along the north bank of this river; such tolls to be applied only in the repairs of that bank.

There are several small brooks and lodes which also bring the upland waters into the fens; but RIVER WISSEY. we have already, ii is feared, been too prolix and tedious. It was, however, impossible to convey a full knowledge of the causes ofjthe original inundation of the fens, without particularizing the several natural rivers, with their sources and tributary streams. We must now proceed to consider, what other causes contributed to the general inundation of the Great Level. — This inquiry will form the subject of the next chapter.

Causes of Inundation.— Upland, Downfal, and'

Tidal Waters.— Tides in general.

Having in the previous Chapter laid down the course of the several natural rivers with their tributary streams, and the means by which the upland waters are conveyed into and through the

Great Level of the Fens; it will naturally suggest itself to the reader, that when the beds of the rivers were overflowed, the waters would spread themselves over the adjoining surface, and there remain, until in process of time they found their way to the several outfalls at sea. But had there been no other causes of inundation than those arising from the influx of the upland water, such inundation would have been both partial and temporary; partial, according to the quantity of water, and the different periods when brought down by each river; temporary, inasmuch as the floods would seldom be very large during the summer months; and would consequently permit cultivation, although at short intervals. But the

Great Level had to encounter other, and, in one respect, much more important enemies. The downfal rains poured their waters upon the smooth

and porous surface of the fens, amidst the already Dowufai waaccumulated burthen from the uplands; but the greatest addition was the daily flux and reflux of the tides, driving their vast billows from the Ger-Tidaiwaters. man Ocean, through the harbours of Lynn, Wisbech, and Boston, into the defenceless and already overburthened Level. Those waters would naturally overflow, to a considerable distance, the surface of a flat country, and the constant recurrence of the tides prevent the regular dis-App. p.63—72. charge of the floods, collected from the upland and downfal waters. Such must have been the natural consequences. It will be seen hereafter, at what different periods this unhappy state of things excited the attention of the ingenious, the industrious, the enterprising, or the patriotic.

Before we proceed further in this inquiry, a few remarks relative to the subject of the flux and reflux of tidal waters may, it is hoped, be considered a venial digression. The Author of this Work has frequently, and more particularly in his early days, found some difficulty in understanding the theory of tides; and there are few persons interested in Fen affairs, who will deny the advantage of being well acquainted with this subject. The discussion may, indeed, appear superfluous to the more experienced reader, and practical fen man; but it should be remembered, that men, like nations, rise and fall, flourish and decay; and that the instruction of youth is never beneath the genius of the wisest of mortals.

We are all aware of the consummate talent of 0l70'?the

Aristotle.

Kepler.

Galileo.

Descartes.

the immortal Newton; of his knowledge

of the sun and the planets; it might also be said, his intercourse with Heaven itself. To his vast and comprehensive mind we are indebted for settled and durable principles of science. Let us follow him into the world of waters—through the depths of the ocean. Let us inquire, by what power or cause it is, that this vast liquid body rises and falls alternately, twice a day, in a manner so constant and regular.

The ancients beheld in the tides one of the greatest mysteries of nature, and were utterly at a loss to account for them. Aristotle, the great oracle of antiquity, is represented to have thrown himself into the sea, from his inability to explain their motions; and when he was in India, with Alexander the Great, it is said, that he wanted to follow the tide in its reflux, to ascertain the termination of its course. The story is sufficiently absurd; but not more ridiculous than the following, related of Kepler. This great man, in one of his reveries, considered the earth as a living being, and thought the flux and reflux of the sea, were the effect of its respiration; men and other creatures, he considered to be insects which fed upon this animal; bushes and trees, the bristles on its back; and the water of seas and rivers, a liquid which circulated in its veins.

Galileo, Descartes, and even Kepler, have, however, expressed themselves more philosophically upon "this subject; but the first who clearly pointed out the cause of the phenomenon, and shewed its agreement with the effects, was Newton. To a genius like his, enterprise and discovery were second nature. The moon, he presently saw, was the principal agent which produced these motions; and by applying his new principles of geometry and attraction, he soon shewed the manner in which they were effected. To follow him through all his calculations and inquiries would be difficult, and foreign to our purpose. Not to insist, therefore, upon abstruse investigations, which are intelligible only to mathematicians and philosophers, we will begin by describing the most obvious facts, and afterwards shew their conformity with the theory he has established.

The ocean, it is well known, covers more than The Ocean. one half of the globe; and this large body of water is found to be in continual motion, ebbing and flowing alternately, without the least intermission. What connexion these motions have with the moon, we shall see as we proceed; but at present, it will be sufficient to observe, that they always follow a certain general rule: for instance, if the tide be now at high watermark in any port or harbour which lies open to the ocean, it will presently subside, and flow regularly back, for about six hours, when it will be found at low water mark. After this, it will again gradually advance for six hours, and then again retreat in the same time to its former situation; rising and falling in succession twice a day, or in the space of about twenty-four hours.

The interval between its flux and reflux is, however, and Low not precisely six hours, but exceeds that period by about eleven minutes; so that the time of high water does not always happen at the same hour; but is about three quarters of an hour later every day, for thirty days, when it again recurs as before:—for example: if it be high water at Lynn to-day at noon, it will be low water at eleven minutes after six in the evening; and consequently, after two changes more, the time of high water the next day will be at about three quarters of an hour after noon; the day following, it will be about half an hour after one; the day after that, at a quarter past two; and so on for thirty days, when it will again be high water at noon, the same as on the day the observation was first made; and this exactly answers to the motion of the moon: she rises every day about three quarters of an hour later than upon the preceding one, and by moving in this manner round the earth, completes the revolution in about thirty days, and then begins to rise again at the same time as before.

To make the matter still plainer, suppose at Wisbech it is high water at three o'clock in the afternoon upon the day of the new moon; the following day, it will be high water at three quarters of an hour after three; the day after that, at half an hour past four; and so on, till the next new moon, when it will again be high water exactly at three o'clock, the same as before: and by observing the tides continually at the same place, they will always be found to follow the same rule; the time of high water, upon the day of every new moon, being exactly at the same hour; and three quarters of an hour later every succeeding day.

Such a perfect harmony of motions as is here pointed out, could not possibly arise from the mere recurrence of fortuitous causes, or the uncertain operations of blind chance, as many sceptical philosophers affect to believe. On the contrary, the flux 'and reflux of the tides are in such exact conformity with the motion of the moon, that, independently of all mathematical considerations, we should certainly be induced to look to her as their primary cause. The tides are not, however, solely affected by the moon, but by the combined forces of the sun and moon; or, properly speaking, there are two tides, a solar tide, and a lunar, which have a joint or opposite effect, according to the situation of the bodies which produce them. When the actions of the sun and moon conspire together, as at the time of the new and full moon, the flood becomes more considerable; and in this case they are called springtides. But when one tends to sprmj tides, elevate, whilst the other tends to depress the waters, as at the moon's first and third quarters, the effect will be exactly the contrary: the flux and reflux, instead of being augmented as before, will now be diminished; and they are then called neap tides. Ne"Plldc8

The effects of the disturbing forces of the sun and moon depend, likewise, upon their respective distances from the earth, as well as upon their particular situations; for the less the distances VOL. I. E are, the greater will be their effects; and, therefore, in winter, when the sun is nearer to the earth, the spring tides will be greater than in summer, when that luminary is more remote; and the neap tides, on that account, will be less. For a like reason, as the moon moves in an elliptical orbit round the earth, and is nearer to us sometimes than at others, the tides will, at those times, be greater, and at the opposite points of her orbit, less. Some variations, likewise, take place in consequence of the different declinations of the sun and moon at different times; for if either of these celestial bodies were at the pole, it would occasion a constant elevation, both there and at the opposite one, and a constant depression at the equator: so that, as the sun and moon gradually decline from the equator, they lose their effect, and the tides become less; and when they are both in the equator, the tide of course becomes greater. These are the principal phsenomena of the tides; and where no local circumstances interfere, the theory and facts will be found to agree. But it must be observed, that what has been here said, relates only to such places as lie open to large oceans. Thus, it is high water at Plymouth about the sixth hour; at the Isle of Wight, about the ninth hour; and at London Bridge, about the fifteenth hour, after the moon has passed the meridian. There are also great variations in the heights of the tides, according to the situation of coasts, or the nature of the straits through which they have to pass. Thus, the Mediterranean and Baltic Seas have very small elevations, while at the port of Bristol, the height is sometimes forty feet; and at St. Malo's, it is said to be near a hundred.

One great privilege of genius seems to be that of considering difficult subjects in a point of view which renders them more simple and perspicuous, and enables the mind to follow them with ease, and fully to comprehend their various intricacies and relations. This facility of conception was possessed by Newton in the highest degree: he always knew, in every case which required investigation, the proper mode of resolving the question. The Newtonian theory of tides has not, however, been established without encountering the most strenuous opposition-f-. And here, we cannot avoid noticing the ingenious, but fanciful ideas, of one of the most amiable of men and elegant of writers;;, who attempts to introduce a new theory of tides, from the effusion of the polar ices. It is sufficient, says this interesting author, to admit the alternate effusions of the polar ices, (which it is impossible to call in question,) to explain, with the greatest facility, all the phenomena of the tides, and of the currents of the ocean. These phsenomena present, in the journals of navigators the most enlightened, a perpetual obscurity, and a multitude of contradictions, as often as such navigators persist in ascribing the causes of them to the constant pressure of the moon and of the sun upon the equator, without paying attention to the alternate currents from the poles, which direct their courses to the equator, and the counter currents, which, returning towards the poles, produce tides; and to the revolutions which winter aad summer effect on those two movements.

Monsieur Bernardin Saint Pierre is ingenious-, but he has not *quite* overturned the Newtonian theory. It is time, however, to conclude this long discussion, which, as it arises from a desire to impart instruction upon a subject connected greatly with the fens, it is hoped the candid reader will readily pardon.

The rise of the tides at Lynn, and the state of high and low water mark at Denver Sluice, will be shewn under the Chapter which treats of the origin, progress, and (would the author could add!) the completion, of the Eau Brink Cut, and works arising out of that important measure.

It has already been stated, that at every new and full moon, the tides flow about eight feet at Wisbech; and there is no great difference in that respect between that port and the ports of Lynn and Boston.

Thus have been brought before the reader the original causes of the general inundations of the fens; namely, the upland waters conveyed by the natural rivers; the downfal of rain waters; and lastly, the flux and reflux of the tides.

We will now proceed briefly to state what was the situation of the fens in consequence of this continual inundation, or (to use a word usually adopted in older times) this surrounding of the low lands within the Level, and at what periods this important subject of drainage became mutter of serious consideration.

Original state of the Oi-eat Level.— State during the time of the indent Britons—On the Arrival of the Romans.— Works erected during their Government. —Departure of the Romans.— State of the Fens under the Saxons.—At the Conquest. original state It must be apparent to every reader who has attentively perused the foregoing Chapters, that, from the earliest period, the whole Great Level of the Fens must have been one vast bay, subject to inundation from natural causes; and in. ages long before the commencement of history, which is but the record of those who are of yesterday, and know nothing, the waters of the ocean mingled with those of the heavens, and the springa of the earth passed over the whole of what was then in its most extended sense, "The Great Level of the Fens."

History itself has left very scanty materials from which any correct opinions can be formed, with respect to the period at which this important country was first attempted to be reclaimed from the waters, and brought into cultivation.

The ancient Britons were a brave and hardy During the i i i -i« time of the race, totally unacquamted with the arts of civih-Ancient Bri zation, neither distinguished for their superior knowledge, nor their gentleness or orderly habits of life. They were truly the children of nature. Indeed, the man most closely resembling the ancient Briton, is the daring poacher of modern days. His life is staked on projects of hazard, and his heart is prepared, no matter whether by a fancied or real progressive system of individual wrongs, for any desperate enterprize. It was therefore unlikely that these rude beings should attempt any improvement or alteration in the natural state of the country. The undisturbed inhabitants of a vast tract, wild and uncultivated, abounding in game, studded with extensive lakes, and generally adapted to the sports of the field, must inevitably be less refined and less tractable than those who are not urged by similar temptations to brave the hazards which attend general and nocturnal depredation. The undrained and uncultivated state of the fens, presented endless inducements to marauding and plunder, particularly as it was improbable that any considerable proprietor was resident within its boundary. Such a mode of life would, doubtless, engender a most lawless spirit. The manners and feelings of nations endure in a greater or less degree for generations; and it may not be an overstrained deduction, that this ungovernable disposition, these unrestrained habits, this predatory mode of life, continued for after ages, and, perhaps in part occasioned the violence with which the natives of these regions opposed, in more modern times, the persons who undertook to drain and reclaim the fens from the watery element.

All writers seem to concur in opinion, that no attempts were made to drain the fens by the Britons, who. were called the ancient "Gyrvii;" 'Gyr,' in English, signifying the same as ' Palus,' in Latin, viz. a deep fen.

At this distance of time, and in the absence of all authentic records, we can only conjecture what was the actual state of the fens at the period of the arrival of the Romans, which took place under Julius Caesar, in the fifty-fourth year before the birth of Christ. We have a right to consider the Level one vast, wild morass, perpetually, indeed daily, subject to inundation, with only small detached patches of cultivated soil, inhabited by persons of the most rude and laborious habits. As no evidence appears upon record, that the ancient Britons made any progress in improving and draining the country, and as the influx of the upland waters, the downfal from the heavens, and the daily recurrence of the tides still existed, (as they had done from the beginning of the world,) the statements of many authors must be considered extremely improbable, that the Romans, on their arrival in Britain, found the fens, and particularly the Great Level, " the greatest part, a sound, fruitful soil, covered with woods and trees;" or, that it followed,

"that the "greatest part of this country had remained

"*wit/tout any hurtful annoyance occasioned by* "*the natural rivers passing through it,* from the "time of the retreat of the water at the general "deluge, to the time when the Romans entered "the Island." It is impossible, from the operations of nature, that the Great Level of the Fens could have arrived at any state of cultivation and improvement without the assistance of art It remains to be seen, whether, in after times, the agency of art was judiciously applied by those, who, at different periods, undertook the drainage of the country.

The arrival of the Romans occasioned entirely Arrir»iofthe ., *f* ., Romans.

new measures m the management of the country. Although flushed with conquests, they came clothed with all the principles of civilization; and, with all their faults, they were certainly a wonderful people. Like all other invaders and conquerors, they were in general tyrannical and oppressive, and exercised their recently acquired power with unreasonable severity. In other respects, however, they may be said to have been eventually real benefactors to many, if not to all the countries and nations which they subdued, by furnishing the means of greatly improving those countries and nations, and by introducing amongst their people the rudiments of useful knowledge, habits of industry, and the refinements of more polished life. Britain was not reduced without numerous struggles; evincing on the part of the inhabitants those virtues, which it is to be hoped will for ever adorn the character of their posterity—courage, perseverance, and love of country. The native warriors were unable to withstand the repeated attacks of veteran legions accustomed to the improved arts of war; and at length the Romans became the indisputable masters of the country.

Soon after Britain became reduced, and made a part or province of the Roman Empire, the Romans began to view the fens as a very important part of their acquisition. Whether they ever formed any systematic plan for a general drainage of the fens, cannot now be ascertained. Their designs were doubtless of a most gigantic nature, as the remnants of their works, still extant, sufficiently evince; but the lapse of ages has so mutilated and destroyed the unity of these works, that nothing but conjectures can be formed as to their original purposes or extent. To the present generation of fen men, any inquiry of this nature would lead to no practical result, however interesting such an investigation might be to the antiquary. Considering, however, that the Romans were the *first undertakers* of the drainage of the Great Level, it will be proper to take a cursory view of the works which still remain, and are reputed to have been the result of their plans and labours.

The Romans had an extended line of fortifications upon the entire southern boundary of the Fens, remains of which are still discernible; and in many places, the entire plan may be clearly traced. The first of this kind, will be found at a place called Horsey, in the parish of Standground, near Peterborough; and another, of very considerable dimensions, still called " the Bulwarks," at Earith, in the county of Huntingdon. Bodsey and Worlick, in the parish of Ramsey, in the same county, were unquestionably Roman stations; and similar situations occur in the parish of Willingham, in the county of Cambridge: and as these positions were chiefly upon, or near the entrances of rivers, and upon the skirts of the highland bordering upon the Fens, they were doubtless erected to preserve the possession of that extensive tract of country, and the. works of drainage and improvement, which had been begun, and were probably completed. It is, however, matter of surmise, at what period of time these earth works were first constructed, and now perhaps incapable of solution; but they are manifestly of very early origin. On the retreat of the native Britons before the conquering arms of the Romans, stations and military establishments were formed, as occasion might require, or convenience suggest, not only for the purpose of giving facility and despatch to transition, and to ensure a regular communication, but to operate as a constant check upon the daring and intrepid spirit of our British ancestors, who disputed with gallant and becoming, but fruitless bravery, the hostile march of their inveterate foes. The curious in matters of this kind, are invited to a view of these proofs of the exertions of this extraordinary people.

Many banks or mounds of earth, still called Roman banks. "Roman banks," are to be found in various parts of the fens, particularly in the vicinity of Wisbech; and Dugdale mentions a long road or causeway made of gravel, about three feet in thickness, and in breadth sixty feet, extending in length twenty-four miles across the fen, from Denver in Norfolk, near Salter's Lode, over the Great Wash to Cheerk (now called Creek) in the hamlet of March, thence to Eldernell, near Whittlesey, and so to Peterborough. At various places, the remains of this stupendous undertaking may even now be easily traced.

cm Po-Dykc. The Old Po-Dyke, for the drainage of Marsh land, and the banks which originally defended that extensive country from the irruptions of the sea, were assuredly the works of the Romans; but that which remains in the most perfect state, and the uses of which are available even at the present

Cmt. or Con day, is the Carr, or Corr Dyke. It is said to be the "' last of the Roman military works. Most writers have stated, that it commenced at the River Nene, just below Peterborough, namely, at Horsey, before mentioned; but this is an error: it begins at Bodsey, also before mentioned, continues its course through the fens, dividing the counties of Cambridge and Huntingdon, to Horsey, and thence, after crossing the river Nene, proceeds, until it joins the river Welland, which it also crosses, and may be now traced, not only to the city of Lincoln, but in the opinion of the late eminent engineer, John Rennie, Esq., to the river Trent, at Torksey. That part of this dyke which extends from Bodsey to Horsey, is sometimes said to have been constructed by King Canute, by tradition the inhabitant of Bodsey House,

whose motive for this work is reported to have had its origin in the circumstance of that monarch having been in great danger when crossing Whittlesey Meere. This statement must be considered erroneous; or, at any rate, this branch, sometimes called Oakley Dyke, must in that case have been *added* to the Old Carr Dyke, commencing at the fortification near Horsey. The modern purposes of this dyke will be considered in future remarks upon that part of the Bedford Level, called " the North Level. "

It is but justice to state, that historians are not agreed upon the point, that the Fens were actually drained by the Romans; nor is the fact at all material at this distance of time, as far as any practical good is concerned. It is matter of curiosity, and is left to the more elaborate researches of the scholar and the antiquary. It cannot, however, be denied, that the fens must have been in a very dismal state before the arrival of the Romans; and, without doubt, their exertions wrought a mighty and most happy change in the face of the country: and it would be monstrous to suppose that this most active, industrious, and ingenious people, would have continued, as they did, in full possession of Britain forfive hundred years, and yet take no steps to improve a country, which, if left in its original condition, must have been a perpetual source of trouble and annoyance.

About the beginning of the Fifth Century, Departure of
'tbcRomuns.
the Roman Empire having been weakened and greatly impaired in the western parts, by ConStantine removing the imperial seat from Rome to Constantinople, a resolution was taken utterly to abandon the island. This memorable event, which put an end to the Roman Empire in Britain, is placed by some historians in the year A.d. 422, 422; by others a few years later. Repeated attacks from their barbarian neighbours, the Picts and the Scots, at length induced the Britons to resort to a measure for their preservation, of all others the most infamous and degrading, namely,

by soliciting the protection of a foreign nation. To whatever unhappy state unprincipled governors or pernicious laws may reduce a country, no circumstances can justify calling for the interference of foreigners, which must invariably terminate in the most complete and abject subjugation. The Britons solicited the assistance of the Saxons, by whose aid, it is true, the former overcame their invaders; but these crafty Saxons, having obtained a footing in the island, and perceiving the exuberant richness of the land to which they had been invited, became desirous of finally accomplishing its possession.

The Britons and the Saxons being much engaged in continual quarrels and wars, it is likely, that after the Romans deserted the island, their labours were neglected, the banks no longer upheld, or the drains kept open; and that the whole Level again became a fen, and shallow lake, the haunts of fishermen, or the retreat of marauders and banditti. England is, undoubtedly, greatly indebted to hep Saxon ancestors for the foundation of many of her finest institutions and dearest privileges: nor will the labours of the illustrious Alfred ever be effaced.

In the Ninth Century, the frequent and almost unintermitted invasions of this kingdom by the Danes, introduced the greatest disorder and confusion in the state, and reduced it to the brink of ruin. War, and its necessary attendants, rapine and destruction, desolated the land. In the midst of these public calamities, it pleased Providence to raise to the throne the immortal Alfred, worthily surnamed " The Great." The vigorous measures he pursued to rescue his country from the hands of its barbarous invaders, and to raise it to a proud pre-eminence in arts, in sciences, and in legislative greatness, deserve the highest encomiums. Harassed as he was, in continual wars, during his whole reign, of nearly thirty years, he never ceased to exert his utmost endeavours to restore religion and learning, to promote commerce, to cultivate and improve the fine and elegant arts. His court was the resort of learned men of all professions, as well of foreign nations, as of his own subjects.

But whatever might have been the beneficial effects arising from the legislative talents of our Anglo-Saxon ancestors, it must be admitted, that no testimony is left, no record discovered, no historian found, to prove that any attempt was made by the Anglo-Saxons either to restore or preserve the works of the Romans, or even to commence any plan for the general drainage of the Fens. It is not necessary, for the purpose of this work, to enter into any minute details of the government of the Anglo-Saxons, their wars with the Danes, or their final extinction by the defeat and death of Harold at the battle of Hastings, by the victorious Normans, under the command of the Duke of Normandy, commonly called William the Conqueror; an event that effectually changed the whole face of affairs, and introduced an entirely new era, as well as a formidable revolution in the rights of persons and of property.

All great events, all violent convulsions, all sudden reformations in countries and in governments, have their partizans and their opponents; and historians too often become the humble followers of the one or the other party: hence arises the difficulty of ascertaining the truth, or arriving at sound conclusions. Fortunately, it is not important for the purposes of this work, to ascertain whether the Norman Conquest (or *acquisition only,* as some writers pretend) was productive, or otherwise, of those principles and those measures which tend to the general happiness of all classes of the community. Bute of the The state of the Fens, in the absence of all

Fens at the

Conquest. authentic records, must be considered at this period as most deplorable. Doubtless Ely, and many little tracts which had the advantage of elevation, were at that time literally islands. Several of these in early times became the retreat of the religious. Ely, Ramsey, Thorney, Crowland, Spinney, and others, rose into celebrated abbeys, and by the industry, zeal, and ability of their inhabitants, first began to restore the works of the Romans. It is said, that the Abbot of Ely successfully resisted for some time all the efforts of the Norman Conqueror to p.102. subdue the Isle of Ely, although it eventually fell under the dominion of the invaders in the reign of Henry the First. During the continuance of these wars between the Abbot of Ely and the Conqueror, it seems unlikely that any steps should be taken to promote the drainage of the fens: indeed, until the reign of King Stephen, historians preserve a profound silence upon this subject, although very full and elaborate accounts of the origin, progress, and termination of the attempts to obtain possession of the Isle of Ely, will be found in Dug-Du&daie, P. dale's History of Embanking and Draining of the Fens.

However improbable it may be that any steps A. D. were taken for the drainage of the fens during the reigns of William the Conqueror, William Rufus, or Henry the First, yet it certainly appears that in the succeeding reign of King Stephen, most material improvements took place. Henry of Huntingdon, who lived in that reign, describes the fens as a very pleasant and agreeable country to the eye, watered by many rivers which run through it, diversified with many large and small lakes, and adorned with many woods and islands. It is undeniable, that Whittlesey Meer was in existence and well known at the time of the Conquest, it being mentioned in the Survey of the Kingdom taken in the year 1086, and contained in the celebrated »omes(iay Domesday Book, "that the Abbott of Ramsey book.

'had one ship or vessell upon Whittlesey "Meer."

William of Malmsbury also, who lived to the first year of Henry the Second, has praised the state of that part of the Level called Thorney, near Ely, in the most glowing language. He represents it as a paradise; the very marshes abounding in trees, whose length without knots, emulated the stars. "The plain there (says he) "is as level as the sea, which, with the flourish"ing of the grass, allureth the eye, and *so* "smooth that there is nothing to hinder him "that runs through it; neither is there any tt waste place in it; for in some parts there are "apple-trees, in others vines, which either "spread upon the grounds, or run along "poles."

Making every allowance for the florid colouring of the above picture, it is manifest, that the Level, in the times of the above writers, must have been in a very flourishing condition, and superior to its state a few centuries afterwards, when the fens were again covered, and the inhabitants of many islands in danger of perishing for want of food. Lord Chancellor Bathurst. ciareimju.

. 'Orvm, 12 Uco. in giving judgment in a tithe suit, states, but 3-

without quoting any authority, "that about

"three centuries after the Conquest, the Isle of

"Ely was one of the most fertile countries in

"England until the floods broke in; but when

"this occurred, antiquaries differ."

From what cause arose so fatal a reverse, whether from some great convulsion of an earthquake, or from the ordinary course and progress of nature, can by no means be determined; nor have those who have addressed themselves to this subject of inquiry, left any satisfactory information by which the doubt may be solved; but certain it is, that these accounts of the early state of the Level, were, amongst others, an inducement to the subsequent undertaking, to recover and drain it. By some it was urged, that attempts for this purpose were made so early as the reign of Edward the First; but no well attested records, no settled plans of operation have been discovered until the reign of Richard the Second. Leaving the labyrinth of conjecture, let us now proceed to the more sure path of documentary testimony.

improvement of the rivers affected by the outfalls at Lynn and Wisbech, although, from the great lapse of time, the records are lost or mislaid.

John of Gaunt was the fourth son of that illustrious monarch King Edward the Third. He resided at Bolingbroke Castle, in the county of Lincoln, upon the borders of the fena. He was App.37. Duke of Lancaster, which Duchy then held, and now continues to enjoy, considerable property within the Great Level: he was also appointed Regent during the minority of his ill-fated nephew, Richard the Second. Being of an ardent and enterprising character, it was most probable he would direct his attention to the cultivation and improvement of so vast a tract of country, in which he was personally interested, and would also receive the concurrence and assistance of the Church, which at this period had attained great power and valuable possessions within the fens, by the establishment of rich abbeys at Ramsey, Crowland, Thorney, and elsewhere. Even had any general design of improvement been contemplated, it was necessarily abandoned or deferred, John of Gaunt being obliged to quit the country, to which he returned only a few years before his death, in 1390, when Richard the Second conn's-. cated all his extensive estates to the use of the crown, to which they have ever since continued annexed. Nothing appears to have been attempted in the reigns of Henry the Fourth and Fifth. In the reign of Henry the Sixth commerce and speculation began to exercise a more active influence over the minds of men. Efficient measures were adopted to convert these energies to beneficial practical purposes.

Base and degenerate must be that English heart which does not glow with pride and admiration at the achievements of the gallant, brave, and generous Edward Prince of Wales, who, by the glorious victories of Poictiers, of Cressy, and of Calais, placed upon his father's brow the crown of France, hailing him king of that vanquished country: base and degenerate must be that English heart which does not heat with indignation against those pusillanimous statesmen who, in modern days, *voluntarily* surrendered that title, the rich legacy of our heroic ancestors, foolishly at the same time retaining the motto, *Dieu et man droit,* assumed by the illustrious King Edward, as he placed the glittering diadem of France around his brow. Compare (and blush for the age in which we live) the noble and Christian conduct of the heroic Prince of Wales to his vanquished enemy, the King of France, with that adopted in later times by a heartless set of puny statesmen towards the deserted and betrayed Napoleon, Emperor of France. The surrender of the Islands of Guernsey and Jersey would not in the least surprise me, if England, fallen England, continue in its present abject and degraded state, both at home and abroad. —1829. Early in this reign, a statute was passed, pre-6 H. 6 —U27. scribing a form of all commissions that should thereafter issue throughout the entire realm, wherein directions and powers were given to Ramsey, in the county of Huntingdon, was called " Ram"sey the rich." The abbot was a temporal peer, and sat in the House of Lords as Buron of Bronghton, in the county. The Abbey is said to have been possessed of the whole of the manors within the Hundred of Hurstingstone, in that county, except those of King's Ripton, Somersham, and Bluntisham Stockings.

those who were to be employed therein, to make and ordain all necessary and convenable statutes and ordinances for the salvation and conservation Magn» charta, of the sea banks and marshes, and the parts adMPEdfii.c.'4. joining1 thereto. Several acts of Parliament had 21 Rfc!u'.c'2' Deen previously passed, for avoiding all annoy4'Hen. iv. ances and obstructions in navigable rivers, but c. ll-this is the first Statute in any way concern ing drainage, although there can be no doubt that commissions of sewers had been previously issued, under the sanction and authority of the common law. Immediately after the passing of this act, Gilbert Halloft, one of the Barons of the Exchequer, and a resident in the neighbourhood of Well, in the Isle of Ely, procured a commission for draining and settling that part of the country, and accordingly proceeded to make laws, which were then, and still are, known by the name of Hal loft's Commission. In a future part of the work, this subject of commissions of sewers will be more maturely considered, when the author treats of the powers and authorities of the Bedford Level Corporation, in their capacity of commissioners.

History has left no traces of any design of draining by Margaret, Countess of Richmond, (mother of Henry VII.) Hondius must, therefore, have been in error in asserting that such an attempt had been made by her. Morton, consecrated Bishop of Ely in 1478, was politically connected with the Countess, having, with the aid of the Duke of Buckingham, been mainly instrumental in accomplishing the marriage between Henry VII. with Elizabeth, one of the co-heiresses of the house of York. Although of mean birth, Morton was a man of consummate talent; and he may be deemed the first person who projected and carried into effect any definite design of drainage. At considerable expense, he executed a work of singular utility for draining the fens and extending navigation, by making a App.69. cut of forty feet in breadth and four feet in depth, from Peterborough to Guyhirn, which yet bears the name of the New Leam, or Morton's Leam; cam. Brut. 294 412 he also continued the same to Wisbech, and by other cuts, made, it is said, a new outfall to sea. He attempted other works of drainage; but it is supposed, that their completion was prevented by the disastrous war that raged through the kingdom between the houses of York and Lancaster. Dugdale, in his History of Embanking, does not afford any very detailed information relative to the extent of the works executed or contemplated by this eminent prelate. Bishop Morton unfortunately introduced the system of straight cuts and artificial rivers, a system which was never afterwards abandoned, and which the reader will ultimately find to have been productive in after-times of the most fearful consequences.

There can be no doubt, that from this period to that of the Reformation, the charge of preserving the rivers and drains within the Great Level fell principally upon the Church, whose possessions had greatly augmented in almost every part of the Great Level.

Whatever steps may have been taken at this period for scouring out and-deepening the several rivers and drains within the Level, for carrying the waters to the outfall, the principles of embanking appear to have been quite disregarded; indeed, with the exception of the imperfect work of Bishop Morton, and of commissions of sewers being issued from time to time (under the provisions of the statute 6 Hen. VI.) for the improvement of particular districts within the Level, no remains are to be found of any settled plan of draining.

It has already been stated, that the power and possessions of the church had greatly increased by the establishment of monasteries. The church has, at all times, and in all countries, been scrupulously tenacious of its rights and privileges. The troubled state of the country during the reign of Henry VII., notwithstanding the rising power of the church, may account for the absence of any recorded proceedings for draining or improving the Great Level; but no doubt can exist, that at this period neither the government nor the church entirely lost sight of the advantage that might be derived from a careful regard to the improvements of the several rivers and drains affecting their particular interests.

In the early part of the reign of Henry the Eighth, the affairs of the kingdom became more settled; and it followed, that attention would - naturally be paid to those objects that must in themselves enhance the value of property, and, consequently, promote the benefits of drainage and of navigation. In the twenty-third year of 2311. e. c. s. that reign was passed a general act concerning commissions of sewers, the provisions of which act continue in force, and are the ground work for all proceedings of commissions of sewers at the present day. This act, however, gives no power to make *new* drains, or to erect and maintain *new* banks.

The dissolution of monasteries was effected a few years after this act was passed; property changed hands; liabilities connected with that property were neglected or destroyed; and it was, says Sir William Dugdale, in his History of Embanking and Draining, a long received opinion, as well by the borderers upon the fens as others, that the total drowning of the Great Level at this tinae, was, for the most part, occasioned by the neglect of putting the laws of sewers into due execution. Before the dissolution of monasteries, the passage of the waters was kept with cleansing, and the banks in better repair, chiefly through the care and costs of the religious houses.

It does not appear, that any serious endeavour Dugdaie, 375. had been made, even by the clergy, to render the fens other than summer lands. Many, doubtless, were the attempts by individuals, for the better draining of their particular lands, by opening and scouring such petty drains and sewers as might conduce to the more speedy dissipation of the vast spreadings of water in the summer season; but wholly to disperse them was impossible, until the perfect opening and cleaning of their natural outfalls, which the daily flowing of the tides had so completely choked up, could be accomplished.

The.Statute of Sewers was remedial only: — Much more extensive powers were required to bring into operation a general plan of draining and embanking the Great Level of the Fens.

The Reformation did not take place suddenly. The opinions of Luther had, it is true, been promulgated abroad and at home; and, as sagacious and penetrating minds will always be found to foretell great changes and great events, it was clearly predicted that some important alteration 27 Hen.a. was approaching. The first act for the dissolution of smaller monasteries was passed in the siHcu.s. 27th year of this reign; and three years.afterwards, the act which dissolved the greater monasteries; by which acts the reformation became complete; great part of the property passed into the hands of laymen, while no inconsiderable portion was again placed in the possession of those who became members of the reformed church.

The Reform-The Reformation formed a new sera in the history of the world, and was one of those mighty revolutionary occurrences which leave a most extensive and lasting effect on the affairs and destinies of mankind. But men have been greatly divided ever since in their ideas and judgments con atioii.
cerning it. While some have hailed it as a most happy, admirable, and glorious event, fraught with Heaven's choicest blessings; it has been denounced by others, and even by a large class of the inhabitants of Christendom, as an exceedingly unfortunate, pernicious, and execrable event. It is quite foreign to the plan or design of this work to enter in the least into this disputed point: enough to know, that a considerable part of the property within the Great Level of the Fens became, through the bounty of the Crown, the property of individuals; while that which was still continued in the possession of the reformed Church, was subject to regulations far different from those which existed in the time of the monasteries.

The passing of the General Sewers Act was unquestionably an important measure, although it led to no practical results within the Great Level, either during the reign of this monarch, or of his successor, Edw. VI, or of Queen Mary.

CHAPTER V. *State of the Great Level during the reign of Queen Elizabeth.— Commission of Sewers,* 13 *and* 20 *Eliz. —John Earl of Bedford. —Meeting of Commissioners of Sewers.—Lord Burghley.— General Draining Act.— Death of Queen Elizabeth.—Accession of James I.—Sir Cornelius Vermui/den. —Commissions, and State of the Level during the Reign of James I.—Accession of Charles I.*

Accession of Queen Elizabeth succeeded to the throne of betii. England the 17th of November, 1558. Although commissions of sewers appear to have been issued during the short reign of Edward VI, nothing effectual had yet taken place for draining the Great Level of the Fens. The reign of this illustrious princess may be properly fixed upon as the period in which the Great Level began to be immediately considered as a public concern. Many causes united to produce this effect. Learning had been heretofore chiefly confined to the MonksUpon the dissolution of monasteries, literature became more widely diffused. The very struggles that had so recently convulsed the country, both as to the succession of the Crown, and the re-establishment of the monastic church, led to serious inquiries. Those inquiries induced reflection; reflection gave birth to knowledge, and knowledge to power. Commerce and Navigation had now sprung up, and were making rapid strides towards that perfection they have since attained. Hence arose a more enlarged intercourse with foreign nations, particularly with Flanders, Holland, and the Low Countries.

In 1572,—15 Eliz., —took place the massacre of 15/2. Saint Bartholomew, when all the Huguenots were most inhumanly butchered, and by this most sanguinary and atrocious event all the protestants of Europe were thrown into the utmost astonishment. In consequence of the persecutions of the Duke D'Alva, and the subsequent murder of the Huguenots, great numbers of ingenious and industrious foreigners fled, and settled themselves in divers parts of England. They were kindly received by the Protestant Queen, and enjoyed the protection of her government. It is natural to suppose that these foreigners, in their choice of residence, would principally resort to that part of England which most assimilated itself to the country from which they had been obliged to fly. Hence, we find considerable numbers settling in the Northern part of the Great Level, in the neighbourhood of Wisbech, Whittlesey, and Thorney. It will be subsequent';/ seen, tvnt this colonization was in after-times, i.y similar disastrous and political circumstances, greatly promoted.

Hitherto no steps had been taken during this reign, for recovering the Great Level from its inundated and forlorn condition. It is supposed that the intimate connection which existed between Holland and England at this time, engendered a belief, founded on experience, that if expenditure and industry had recovered from the sea sufficient land whereon to erect a great repub lie, less expense and industry would be required to recover from the sea lands which they were well aware had been usurped by the sea.

Those foreigners who had settled in the fens, (now their adopted country,) without doubt, felt great anxiety to forward any improvement that might better their condition. Divers applications were made to the government, for the purpose of obtaining commissions of sewers for cleansing the outfalls, and leading the waters to sea. The government exactly understood how valuable so large a tract of land, if recovered, would be to the kingdom at large, and how easily its natural richness and fruitfulness, added to its peculiar situation, might be made subservient to all the purposes of commerce.

A.d. 1570. A commission of sewers, with very limited powers, had already issued in the thirteenth

A.d. 1177. year of Elizabeth: but one of a more extend

£0 Elia. J ed, though still partial nature, was afterwards granted in the 20th of Elizabeth, the object of which was, the drainage of the fens about Clow's Cross, in that port which is now called the North Level. This commission was directed to Sir Thomas Cecil, Sir William Fitzwilliams-f-, Sir Edward Montagu, and Sir Henry Cromwell, Knights, Robert Sapcote, Robert Wingfield, William Hunstone, Edmund Hall, Robert Bcvill, Vincent Skinner, and John Mountsteving, Esqrs. It is rather singular, that, although Francis, then Earl of Bedford, was in possession of the Lordship of Thorney, with several thousand acres of fen land, a great proportion of which would be affected by the success or failure of this commission, the name of Russell is not found in it: probably, as it appears to have been issued to " Knights" and "Squires" only, the Earl of Bedford was considered of too elevated a rank to be joined in an undertaking of this kind. Its interests were, perhaps, committed to the management of Mr. Sapcote, into whose family the first Earl had previously married. It does not seem that the Russell family took any very active part in the administration of public affaire during the reign of Queen Elizabeth. John, first Earl of Bedford, (so created by Edward VI.,) had very considerable grants from the crown at the time of the dissolution of monasteries, was a great favourite at the court of King Henry VIII., and made one of the council to Edward VI. Strange to say, notwithstanding his lordship had benefited so largely by Protestant King Henry, he was retained by Catholic Queen Mary in his office of Privy Seal, and was actually selected as ambassador, and sent to Spain to escort into England Philip II., the husband of Queen Mary, whose grandfather had in the reign of Henry VII. first introduced him (the Earl of Bedford) to the English Court. He died in 1558.

Son of Sir William Cecil, first Lord Burghley, and Prime Minister to Queen Elizabeth. f Ancestor of the present venerable and benevolent Earl Fitzvvilliam. Sir William was an *eltre* of the famous Cardinal Wolsey, whom (much to his honor) he did not desert in adversity. Sir William was one of the favourites of the Court of 'Henry VIII., and partook largely of the grants that were made to court favourites at the time of the dissolution of monasteries. He was Lord Justice of Ireland in 1560, and Lord Deputy from 1571 to 1575. His grandson was created the first Baron Fitzwilliam. % Youngest son of Honry I., Earl of Manchester, and founder of the present branch of the Montagu family, now seated at Hinchinbrook, near Huntingdon. He was the father of Sir Sydney Montagu, who was elected M. P. for the county of Huntingdon in 1640; but was expelled the House of

Commons, 3d September, 1612, for refusing to take an oath which the House had framed for its members: "That they

"would lire and die with their general the Earl of Essex."

Sir Sydney was the father of Sir Edward Montagu, who had the address to bring over the whole fleet to submit to

King Charles II.; for which service he was created Earl of Sandwich. He was a brave and gallant sailor, and in that capacity an honor to his country.—He filled the important office of Lord High

Admiral, and fell nobly fighting, not paltry borough battles, but those of his country, at the great sea engagements against the Dutch, off Southwold Bay,— 20th May, Itt72.

§ John, first Earl of Bedford, married Ann, daughter and heir of Guy Sapcotc, Esq.

VOL. I. G
But to return to the commission. Seven dis-Dugfi»ic, p. tinct articles of inquiry were drawn up for the consideration of the commissioners, and to each of which they were to make a distinct return. The Meeting commissioners. commissioners sat at Peterborough on the 9th June Dngd.p. 375. in the same year, and there empannelled certain jurors, viz., six for each of the counties of Northampton, Lincoln, Huntingdon, and Cambridge, who made their regular presentments, subjoining thereto not only an estimate of the works proposed, but also the names of all the towns and lands contributory and chargeable towards the same, and the names of the treasurer and surveyors for each county. Notwithstanding this progress, nothing in reality was achieved; nor indeed does it appear that any part of the intended plan was carried into execution. The disease affected the whole body; and this being a remedy calculated to cure a part of it only, was as successful as the like kind of application would prove in the human constitution: it might occasion hope for a time, but could not possibly produce any beneficial effect, or attain the end it was designed for. Similar consequences had resulted from the partial attempts made by John Morton, Bishop of Ely, before Ante, P. 73. alluded to, and subsequently from the endeavours of Chief Justice Popham, the Londoners, and others. Had the sums lavished upon these crude and fruitless undertakings, been bestowed upon one united and well digested scheme, they would have gone far towards accomplishing a general and effectual improvement. Alas! the same errors have been adopted in much later times; and there is reason to fear, that even yet, but little probability exists of their being totally renounced.

Whatever opinions historians or statesmen may have entertained of the policy or character of Jueen Elizabeth, it must be admitted by all, that she made choice of most able and consummate statesmen to wield the energies of her government. These were certainly times of wisdom. Men did not make one blunder the foundation whereon to build another. It was not an age of experiments: a mistake at once set them right. No more commissions of the kind above adverted to issued during this queen's reign.

Lord Burghley. Sir William Cecil, afterwards Lord Burghley, resided upon the confines of the Fens, having built the splendid mansion of Burghley House, near Stamford; and founded the pre'sent noble family, of which the Marquess of Exeter is now the head. A mind like Burghley's could not behold without regret the deplorable state of the Fens, or feel otherwise than desirous that such an extent of country should be made available to General Drain-the general benefit of the commonwealth. After A.gD.ci6oo. the failure of the commission granted to his son Sir Thomas Cecil and others, no advance was made till the 43d year of this reign, when the. 34. first statute was passed, proposing a general plan for draining the whole Great Level; and indeed it was "so general," that it comprehended all the marshes and drowned lands in England. The reader's attention will hereafter be more.. i particularly drawn to the provisions of this most important statute, which, in truth, is the basis (coupled with ulterior proceedings) of the titles to all the adventurers' lands within the Bedford Level. The provisions of the statute are too general; but they are still in force. It is supposed that this act of Parliament was prepared under the advice of Lord Burghley; but, his death occurring in 1598, no opportunity was offered to him of bringing it before the Legislature. It does not appear to have been carried into execution, although it has been said, that great expectations were conceived of its consequences by those who interested themselves in the design: probably those expectations were destroyed by the death of the queen, which oc-Death of Queen curred in the year 1602, about two years after A. 0.11)02. the enactment.

The letter of the law, it is true, was left, but that spirit which was to fulfil the object in contemplation, terminated with the death of this singular but illustrious princess, whose memory (however grievous her errors) ought ever to be endeared to the hearts of Englishmen by the recollection of the foundation she laid of that naval superiority, hitherto preserved by Great Britain, over all the countries in the world; a superiority, which the author of this work hopes will, under Divine Providence, continue as long as the name of England shall endure.

Accession of
James I.
A.D. *1602.*

Queen Elizabeth was succeeded by James I. of England, but VI. of Scotland; thus uniting in his person the crowns of both kingdoms. The recent Act of Parliament for the general drainage of the Fens, and the general attention that had been excited in the late reign by their distressed states rendered this subject familiar to almost all men. The character of the king at once guaranteed that this matter would be no longer neglected. King James was a grave and prudent prince; and, in many instances, of a noble and patriotic spirit. Historians relate, that the ideas which he entertained of his own transcendent abilities, induced him to believe that he understood all kinds of learning, human and divine; all kinds of business, as well that which was transacted in the cabinet, as that which was carried on by the labourer in the field: be this, however, as it may, the king had filled the throne of England but for a short period, before he directed his extensive and active mind to the important work of reclaiming the Great Level. The crown at this period (independently of the possessions of the Duchy of Lancaster) had acquired vast estates within the Great Level, recently much increased by the alienation that had taken place by Heton, Bishop of Ely, in the latter part of the last reign. Amongst other properties, the crown, at the

Hut. of the 7.

Church of Ely, accession of King James, by the alienation of that prelate, was seised of the manor and soak of Somersham, with the demesne lands, the park, meadows, pastures, and free chases, thereto be longing; the manors of Fenton, Blnntisham, Colne, Earitli, and Pidley, in the county of Huntingdon; the manors of Streatham, Wilburton, Haddenham, Littleport, Doddington with Benwick, and March, in the isle of Ely; and the manors of Feltwell and Hockwold, in the county of Norfolk. These several manors lying within, and indeed forming a very large proportion of the Great Level, would naturally attract the attention of a prince recently arrived from so poor a country as Scotland; particularly as the fens, when drained and improved, would offer such tempting rewards to the shoals of hungry dependents who had accompanied him into England. No people in the world are so well acquainted with the principles of emigration as the Scotch, the Jews excepted. Great similarity appears in the habits, manners, and indeed occupations, of these two races of people. The Scotch, like the Jews, are wanderers all over the world. Both are hucksters and pedlers; both are devoted to the acquisition of wealth; both industrious, crafty, and scheming. The Jews have no country: the Scotch, it is true, have a " local habitation and a name;" but while love of country is ever in their mouths, (and may have existence in their hearts,) they lose no favourable opportunity of forsaking that country for the most distant parts of either hemisphere. There is no doubt that king James took a personal interest in accomplishing the work of drainage. Speaking of the Great Level, he is reported to have made the right royal declaration, that " he

"would not suffer any longer the land to be "abandoned to the use of the waters." The success which had attended the labours of the inhabitants of the Low Countries, assuredly kept the attention, not only of the King, but of the Publie, alive to the possibility of converting, as the Hollanders had done, this extensive fenny and watery country into solid and productive ground.

That many plans were in agitation, even during the last reign, for effecting partial drainages, may be collected from the words of the statute 36, 20 Eliz., which speaks of " Undertakers;" and those plans were probably still under consideration upon the accession of James I. to the throne of England. In the second year of his reign, the King, by letters directed to the commissioners of sewers for the isle of Ely, and counties of Norfolk, Suffolk, Cambridge, Huntingdon, Northampton, and Lincoln, bearing date at Westminster the llth July, encouraged their proceedings in the work of drainage, expressing his ieadiness to allow a part of his own lands so to be recovered, to be rated towards the charge of the work, in the same proportion as his subjects should be rated; and he signified to them, that he had appointed certain persons to take a view of the Fens, and to treat and contract with as many lords and commoners as they might, touching the premises, desiring likewise the commissioners to be aiding to the persons so appointed by his Majesty. Certain limits of country were set forth in the commission; and Mr. Atkyns, an eminent surveyor of App. 71.72. that day, well acquainted with the Fens, was employed to ascertain the nature of the soil. After the inquiry, a return was made to the Privy Council, and many subsequent proceedings took place, in all of which the King greatly interested himself. It appears also by the Journals of the House of Commons, that on the 18th of February, 1605, a bill was introduced, "for draining of "certain fen and low grounds within the isle of "Ely and country adjoining, subject to hurt by "surrounding, being 300,000 acres at the "least," and read the first time. It was however rejected upon the third reading; the numbers being, With the Yeas,.. 93 With the Noes.. 116

Another bill of a similar nature was introduced Jonmais, immediately afterwards, and shared the same fate. Sir John Peyton, bart., then M. P. for the county of Cambridge, appears to have taken a very active part against both these bills; and an anecdote is mentioned in Cole's MSS., preserved in the British Museum, that the baronet was called into the lobby of the House, during the discussion, to the Lord Westmoreland, who was a very considerable proprietor of land in the Great Level, and was offered a considerable sum if he would support the bill; but this he declined, in a manner at once dignified and patriotic.

...

Journal, 1607. Although the general bill of drainage failed, better success attended one of a more limited nature. On the llth of June, 1607, Sir Robert Wingfield brought up the report of what was then called the " Little Bill," for the draining of 6000 acres of surrounded land. Upon the second reading, a proviso, and some alterations in the title, were offered, which were, upon the question, agreed to be added; and ou the 22d of June, 1606, the bill passed, and was sent up to the House of Lords, by whom the same was also passed; and it finally received the royal assent. Thus was enacted the statute for draining the country of Waldersea, being the first local district act for improving the state of the Fens. It will be

App.p.39. found fully set out in the Appendix, and deserves the attention of the reader for its extreme brevity, in comparison with the prolixity of more modern legislation. By this act, Francis Tindal, Esq., Henry Farr, and John Cooper, gentlemen, undertook to drain certain lands, (the boundaries of which are set forth in the act,) called and named the ring of Waldersea and Coldham, in the isle of Ely: for which undertaking the adventurers agreed to receive "two-thirds" of the lands so to be drained. The work was completed:—at least, the parties had the recompense. One provision in this act merits the serious consideration of fen-men; namely, that clause which provides that the two-thirds so allotted for drainage *should not be liable to the payment of tithes for seven years after the timejixed for completing the drainage.* Unfortunately, this wholesome precedent has been generally lost sight of in after-times; although Equity would certainly say, that, the lands being improved at great cost to the proprietors, it would be but fair that they who reap so great a share by such improvement, should contribute in some proportion to the benefit received. This principle, however, has been recently recognized, and indeed, acted upon, in a statute passed for improving the drainage of that part of the Great Level called the South Level. No alteration took place in the drainage of Waldersea, until a short time waidcncaAct, 9 Gco. 4. C. P.

since, when a more improved and general system was adopted, and is now in progress.

A multiplicity of commissions issued during this reign, and a variety of disputes arose between the fen owners and occupiers, and the commissioners. Orders were sent from the Privy Coun- VidesirO nu'iit Edmoml s cil for carrying on particular works: letters were Rep. App.ss, 60 written by the King himself to the undertakers: expensive views were taken of the Great Level: Dugdaic, ssa. a general dissatisfaction arose amongst all parties concerned: much was attempted, and little executed. Displeased at last with those whom he had employed, and to make amends for the long and continued disappointment the conductors concerned had experienced, the King himself most graciously condescended to become the undertaker of this great work, for which he was to receive 120,000 acres of the Great Level, to be set out by metes and bounds.

In order to carry this work into effect, his Majesty invited over from the Low Countries a personage, who subsequently became of no mean consideration and importance in the affairs of the Fens, Sir Cornelius Vermuyden. Not much is urs"-. known of this singular man. He was a Zea

App. 341. lander, the son of Giles Vermuyden, by Sarah his wife, daughter of Sir Cornelius Workendyke. His parents lived at Saint Martin's Dyke, in the Isle of Tholen, near the mouth of the Scheldt. He was, therefore, born and brought up in a country, similar in some degree to the Fens, and where the triumph of the art of embanking and draining had been most complete, and the practice of it constituted half the occupation of the Inhabitants. But the first exertions of this very extraordinary man, did not take place within the Greal Level of the Fens. It is said, that pri nee Henry, eldest son of James I. making a progress to York, hunted at Hatfield Chase , near Doncaster, and was entertained by one Portington of vJe Hunter's One of the principal proprietors of Hatfield Chace, is John Walbank Childers, Esq., of Cantley Hall, near Doncsater, and one of the Conservators of the Bedford Level Corporation. The mother of Mr. Childers is still living: she is the daughter, and one of the three co-heiresses of Sampson, last Lord Eardley. His lordship was for many years a Bailiff of the Bedford Level Corporation, and, having very large property in the North and Middle Levels, took an anxious part in fen affairs. His lordship, from the moment he came into possession of these estates, was always ready, either with his purse, or by his personal exertions, (being a very regular attendant at the board,) to forward every measure for the improvement of the Bedford Level; nnd that in times of great pecuniary diffi J. History of

Tudworth. Vermuvden was in the suite of this ionc»ster.

Miller's ilis pnnce; and hence, it is conceived, arose the de-tory of Donsign of draining those Levels. Having obtained a neia Prime's *c i c* ii *ir* History of grant from the crown of all its property, Vermuyden entered into the prosecution of that great undertaking with all the confidence which a knowledge of what had been executed in Holland, and a natural genius for vast designs, could inspire. His own command of capital was perhaps scarcely adequate to the object in contemplation; but he was supported by many of his countrymen, particularly by Sir Philibert Vernatti, the Volkenburgh family, the Vampeerens, Abram Vernatti, Andrew Bocean, and John Corsellis.

Some of these foreigners embarked with Vermuyden in this design, and subsequently, in the scheme for draining the Great Level, with the intention of abandoning their own country, and becoming permanent residents upon lands somewhat resembling those they proposed to relinquish. Others considered the speculation as a means of employing capital; and to these it was of importance to find tenants who would cultivate the kmd redeemed. This, it appears, was not matter of difficulty. The state of Holland and the Low Countries, both political and religious, was such, that (as already mentioned) there were numbers of persecuted parties, who would gladly avail themselves of the asylum, which a country like England presented.

It is well known, that a series of the most cruel persecutions awaited all who refused to embrace the doctrines of Calvin; and hence appears to have originated the variety of names of French derivation down to the present day, amongst those who reside in the Fens. These inhabitants of the Low Countries are described to have been a harmless and industrious people, who pursued in peace their agricultural avocations, while the great participants were involved in all the troubles which we have described. De la Pryme, whose ancestor was one of the adventurers, says, that for a time they lived like princes; but it is to be feared that the misfortunes and losses of the superiors would shed an influence over the tenantry. They lived in most parts in single houses, dispersed through the newly recovered country.

The Reverend Abraham De la Pryme was born at Hull. He was the son of Matthew De la Pryme, who emigrated from the city of Ipres, in Flanders, during those cruel religious persecutions under the Duke d'Alva. Matthew settled, with many others of his unfortunate countrymen, in the Level of llatliclcl Chaw,

It had, however, ceased to be of importance. A small colony quickly adopts the language, as well as the manners of the people with whom they are in the habits of daily intercourse. But the colony itself became sadly reduced, and the deserted places in the Level were occupied by native Englishmen. Families pass away more rapidly, than persons, who have never adverted to the fact, can well imagine. How few families in the middle class of life are found on the same site, down to the fourth generation! I am told, that, in Lincolnshire, the names of Bruyme and Egar, and others, still exist. There are also the Dd la Prymesor Prymes; but they quitted the Levels. In the Great Level, arc still found the Descovvs, and the La Plas, and others. Nor have these foreigners qg left many memorials of themselves. How interesting and affecting a narrative would Abraham De la Pryme, the antiquary and philosopher of the Levels, have produced, had he lived to perfect his admirable design of giving a complete history of this singular colony! We read with peculiar pleasure the simple and touching inscription on the monument of Matthew De la Pryme, in the Church at Hatfield, near Doneaster, in Yorkshire. Vermuyden's plan did not give satisfaction; but he exerted his utmost to satisfy the country. He employed many workmen, at a higher rate of wages than had been known before; he strenuously endeavoured, as far as lay in his power, without incurring a ruinous expense, to relieve the people who had suffered from the change he had effected. He was supported by the court. On the 26th of January, 1629, he received the honor of knighthood; and on the 8th of February, in the same year, he took a grant from the crown, of the whole of Hatfield Chace. Soon afterwards, Sir Cornelius withdrew from that work, having sold his lands, and left its completion to other participants. It is generally supposed that he was solicited by King James to render his assistance in the gigantic project of draining the Great Level.

About the time he began his operations at Hatfield Chace, (1626,) Sir Cornelius took to wife Catherine, daughter of All Saints Lapps, of London. By her he had five children; namely, Cornelius, John, Sarah, Catherine, and Adriane. No other Rush. Mem. trace is left of these children than that it appears, there was in the parliament army commanded by Fairfax, a Colonel Vennuyden, who resigned his commission a few days before the battle of Nazeby, having, as he alleged, special reasons requiring his presence beyond the seas, whence he probably never returned.

Although frequent mention will be made hereafter of this most singular person, in developing the subsequent history of the drainage of the Great Level, it may be as well to state in this place, that his ultimate destiny is wrapped in uncertainty. In 1642, he published his celebrated discourse, touching the drainage of the fens. In 1654, he joined in a conveyance of lands in Hatfield Level; and, in 1656, he appears in the journals of the House of Commons as a petitioner. After this date, no information can be found respecting him. Probably, he died soon after, and, it is feared, in circumstances which are too frequently the lot of persons who engage in large speculations. The author of a pamphlet on the state of Hatfield Level, says, that at last "this know-nothing died, miserably "poor, in the south." In truth, he shared the unfortunate fate of the first adventurers in the Great Level, all of whom, with the exception of Francis Earl of Bedford, were completely ruined; and even his Lordship's circumstances were much impaired, he being compelled to sell many valuable estates to defray the enormous expenses incurred in the first ineffectual work of drainage.

VOL. I. H

Before we proceed to a further consideration of the means employed to effect a general drainage of the Great Level during this reign, it may not be uninteresting to take a short view of the state of Flanders and Holland, from which Sir Cornelius Vennuyden had unfortunately derived that knowledge of artificial drainage, which he in after-times made applicable to the purposes of improving the Great Level. It may be well to understand the difference that existed between those countries and the Great Level.

In Flanders, hardly any natural river is to be discovered, that freely empties itself into the sea, except the Scheldt. This river is strongly embanked wherever it is necessary, more especially towards its mouth, where the land lies lowest of all; and the tide is suffered to run up into it without any hinderance, several miles beyond Antwerp, which city is at a considerable distance from the sea. All the other rivers, not only the natural ones, but their canals, or artificial rivers, many of which (but not all) run above the soil of the adjacent lands throughout the year, are strongly embanked, for which purpose they have indeed plenty of good materials at hand in most places: moreover, all these inland rivers are sluiced, to keep out the sea; and their extensive navigation, much greater than that in the Feus, is chiefly performed by haling with horses, and locks are erected wherever it is necessary to change the levels of those rivers or canals, without any considerable stop or obstacle to their boats and vessels; and as to draining, the waters of the lands are conveyed by common tunnels through the banks, when and wherever the surface of the waters in the rivers will permit it; and where not, they are raised by engines, chiefly windmills, into those rivers, and thence to sea at very low water, through either breast-gates, which then open themselves and shut again as the tide falls or rises, or through common drawdoors, which men, appointed and paid, watching day and night the flow and ebb of tides, lift up and let down again at proper times.

In Holland and the neighbouring provinces, the situation of the lands is still less favorable. The most considerable river is the Maese, which brings down with it to the sea part of the Rhine. This river is strongly embanked, and the tide runs up freely into it several leagues, not only above Rotterdam, but above Dort. without interruption; but all other rivers, either natural or artificial, are not only embanked, and the banks maintained at a national charge, but the sea is kept out of them by locks, breast-gates, or draw-doors, through which an almost incredible inland navigation is performed, as in Flanders: but what distinguishes the case of Holland from Flanders is, that in the former the lands in general lie so low as to be always under the surface of the rivers and the sea; and the soil is to the full as bad and as moorish as the ground in the worst part of the Fens. All these difficulties, patience, steady industry, and good regulations, have surmounted. The banks are strong and well made, by a mixture of divers substances, and by being fortified with timber and brick-work where necessary; but being deprived, in most places, of the advantage of having the land waters drained into cuts and canals by the common methods of valves or tunnels, because of the very low situation of the lands, in respect to the surface of those rivers and canals; the Hollanders keep their lands drained by the help of engines, principally windmills, well made, properly situated, and their number suited to the water they are to throw out; and it is common in those countries, to see three or four windmills playing one to another; so that the water is raised over a perpendicular bank, sometimes twelve or fourteen feet in height.

The obvious difference between those countries and the Great Level, will be sufficient to account for the extravagant outlay, and irretrievable misfortunes that have occurred; and to prove, that the adoption of principles and plans, however judicious and successful in the one country, were utterly inapplicable to the other.

But to return to the plans of drainage which were attempted during the reign of James I. Previously to the King's becoming the undertaker, two several attempts were made to drain certain lands near Upwell, in the county of Norfolk and Isle of Ely; the one by Sir John Popham, (chief justice of the King's Bench,) and the other by certain undertakers, called at this period " the Londoners," no record of their names being left. Both these plans failed, notwithstanding each party had the assistance of two of the most able and scientific fen men of that time (Mr. Atkyns and Mr. Hunt). The plan of Lord Chief Justice Popham is still worthy of remembrance, on account of the river bearing his name being, at the present moment, used for the drainage of that part of the Great Level called the Middle Level. Some remains of a river cut by the Londoners, and still called "Londoners' Lode," may be traced in the Fens of Upwell, particularly near the residence of William Lee, Esq., a veryopulent and influential fen man-f-.

This plan, which is called "double lifts," has been adopted in many places in the fens. Several steam engines having been recently erected, with great advantage, it is thought, that in progress of time, the use of windmills will be exploded.

The obloquy and hatred which the undertakers met with from the mass of the people, may be accounted for, in a great measure, by the natural dislike which the poorer commoners have shewn to inclosures at all times, and in all parts of the kingdom. The improvement of a country, totally desolate, and almost valueless, and the fan Vide App. p. 71, for a very able report, made by Mr. Atkyns, to Andrews, then Bishop of Ely.

t The reader is referred to Dugdale's History of Draining and Embanking, and Badesdale's work on the Fens, for more detailed particulars of these commissions. cied improvements which have marked the progress of avarice and ignorance, in more modern times, are widely different. From the former, naturally spring the sources of industry, plenty, and comfort; while the reward of the latter, by cutting off the resources of industry, and the App.519. pride of independence, invariably work a woeful change in the moral habits and manners of a population previously obedient, industrious, and benevolent.

What would have been the consequences of the undertaking entered into by King James, must now be left to conjecture, no one executive step having ever been taken; and such is the strange reverse of human affairs, that at the time the King was meditating how to obtain a new country, as it were, for his subjects, he was withdrawn from that design, to recover an old kingdom for his own family, from which they had been expelled. The ill-timed ambition, and strange politics of Frederick, Elector Palatine, who married the Princess Elizabeth, (daughter to King James,) induced him to accept the crown of Bohemia; but for one year's reign, he afterwards paid as a price his electoral dominions, out of which he was driven, through revenge, by the Emperor of Germany. He applied to his fatherin-law. In those, as well as in modern times, the same unhappy propensity existed in the English nation, to interfere in the dissensions of other kingdoms. Alas! Nations and princes never profit by experience: woeful indeed have been the consequences of this wretched policy. The attempts of King James to recover the Palatinate for his son-in-law, and other political embarrassments which attended him during the rest of his reign, entirely extinguished his zeal as an adventurer for the improvement of the fens.

From this time, nothing seems to have been Am-wiun oi attempted for the relief of the Level, until the 5th year of King Charles I., when, at a session of 5 «-.«. sewers, held at Huntingdon, upon the 6th of January, it was decreed, that a tax of six shillings per acre should be laid upon all the marsh fenny waste, and surrounded grounds, in order to the general drainage; notwithstanding which decree, no part of this tax was paid, nor was there any prosecution of that work.

The importance of the drainage seems never to have been entirely lost sight of, after the statute passed in the 20th of Elizabeth; and consequently, at another session of sewers, held at King's Lynn, upon the 1st of September in the ensuing year, the « Car. u commissioners then present, being 46 in number, made a contract with Sir Cornelius Vermuyden, for draining the Great Level; and for his recompense therein, he was to have 95,000 acres of the surrounded lands. At no period were Englishmen willing that foreigners should become the masters of any part of the soil of Britain. The Fen men partook of this virtuous feeling, and were greatly dissatisfied with the contract thus entered into with an alien. It was finally abandoned; and the country found a friend and protector in the illustrious Francis, Earl of Bedford. By his benign influence, fostering care, and munificent protection, the foundation was laid for those laws, those institutions, and those measures, which it now becomes the duty of the author to develop and explain, being the original proceedings which really gave rise to the present Corporation of the Bedford Level.

CHAPTER VI. *State of the Great Level under Charles L—The Lynn Law.— The Indenture of Fourteen Parts. — Charter of Incorporation. — Its dissolution.— St. Ives Law.—Engagement of Sir Cornelius Vermuyden. — The King's harsh conduct.— Reversal of the St. Ives Law. —Noble conduct of the Earl of Bedford, and his death.*

A Great majority of the inhabitants of the Fens were utterly hostile to a general drainage of the Great Level. This, upon consideration, will not appear strange. The project would have had the effect of changing their habits, their manners, and their pursuits; and above all, would ultimately have led to a spoliation of a great portion of their property. The massacre of Saint Bartholomew, and the accession of King James, had spread over the country (particularly the Fens) a vast herd of foreigners. Fen men have never lacked sagacity, although they may not have evinced an extraordinary degree of foresight: however, they possessed sense enough to perceive, that if these destitute refugees and Scotchmen were to be fed and clothed, it must be done at the expense of some proportion of their property. Moreover, it cannot be denied, that the proceedings of the commissioners of sewers, basking in and flourishing under the sunbeams of royalty, were exceedingly arbitrary: but fen men were doomed to submit. When, therefore, the people found these commissioners of sewers had actually concluded a treaty with Sir Cornelius Vermuyden, an alien and a foreigner, in the anguish of despair, they threw themselves upon the protection of Francis, then Earl of Bedford, who was the owner of 20,000 acres of land in and near Thorney and Whittlesey, in the Isle of Ely; and in the language of App. p-ioi. the Lynn law, " became humble suitors to the "Earl for so great and noble a work, so much "concerning the whole country, and his lord"ship iii his own particular; and that he would "be the undertaker thereof; which motion, pro"ceeding so freely from the country, and being "seconded by all the commissioners present, "his lordship yielded unto, and did agree to "undertake the said work."

The application to the Earl of Bedford was both wise and politic. He was a man of a noble and finely gifted mind; he stood high in the councils of his sovereign; was the owner of extensive fen possessions; and, above all, was the friend and neighbour of the *ten* men. A more striking instance of self-devotion to the wishes of the people, and the real benefit of the state, appears not upon the records of history. The call of country is magic to a patriot's ears: it is heard only to be obeyed. The Earl of Bedford saw before him the brightest prospects. Hope dawned over a dreary waste; and in the.ardour of his Imagination, he beheld a new world arise, to crown his efforts, and enable him to deserve from posterity a monument of unceasing gratitude und admiration. Alas! human hopes and expectations are too often futile, and are sometimes ultimately entomhed in the grave of experience. Could the noble-minded Earl of Bedford have foreseen the mortifications he was to endure, the obstacles against which he was to contend, the tremendous pecuniary sacrifices he was to make, the base ingratitude destined to be his ultimate and only public reward, while his last hours were to be embittered by the most poignant domestic affliction, his generous spirit would have quailed, his righteous purposes would have paused upon the threshold of hope, and the great work of drainage have fallen either into the hands of an alien and adventurer, or been procrastinated until, in after-times, Providence should raise up to the succour and support of the fen men, a patron and a benefactor, as noble and disinterested as the illustrious Francis Earl of Bedford.

The contract with the Earl is usually called the TheLynnLaw. Lynn Law, and is dated the 13th January, 1630. 13 Jan. 1630. Its authority was founded upon a commission issued by the Crown: it was ratified and confirmed by the power and jurisdiction of the commissioners of sewers, and ultimately enrolled in the High Court of Chancery; yet was it inoperative in itself to the extent required, as will be presently shewn, although it must be considered to have been in u great degree the foundation of all the laws relative to the Corporation of the Bedford Level.

It is not necessary to set forth the minute particulars of the contract between the commissioners of sewers, the country, and the noble Earl. The reader's labour will, however, be repaid by giving these particulars his careful perusal and attention, and by reference to the APP. P. gs. law itself, which is fully set forth in the Appendix to this work. Suffice it to say, that the contract embraced all the requisite parties. The Earl was to have 95,000 acres of the drained lands for his satisfaction, on account of the expense and hazard consequent upon such a work; of which 95,000 acres, 40,000 acres were to be appropriated for continuing and preserving the work, and 12,000 acres allotted to the Crown.

It will naturally become a subject of inquiry, what power the crown or the commissioners of sewers had to sever and alienate this great proportion of the property of others; and how the same could become a vested fee in the Earl and his assigns.

App. p. 20. By the statute 23 H. 8, c. 5, s. 9, it is enacted,

"That the same laws, ordinances, and decrees, to "be made and ordained by the said commissioners "(of sewers), or six cf them, by authority of the "said commission (from the Crown), shall bind as "well the lands, tenements, and hereditaments, of "the King our Sovereign Lord, as all and every "other person and persons, and their heirs, for "such their interest as they shall fortune to have, "or may have, in any lands, tenements, or here"ditaments, or other casual profit, advantage, or "commodity, whatsoever they be, whereunto the "said laws, ordinances, and decrees, shall in any "case extend, according to the true purport, "meaning, and intent of the same laws."

The proceedings of the commissioners of sewers would have been totally ineffectual without this provision; but as the greater part of the Level consisted of very extensive open commons, a difficulty still arose as to the power of enforcing a "division of any proportion thereof; and this difficulty, coupled with the natural aversion of the owners to any such division, was the main cause of retarding so long some general plan of drainage and improvement. The genius of Queen Elizabeth, or of her government, saw and remedied this evil. By the General Drainage Act, passed in the 43rd year of her reign, App. p. 35. it is enacted, "That the lord or lords, as "well bodies politic or corporate, or any other "person or persons whatsoever, of all and "every the wastes and commons aforesaid; "and the most of the commoners for the "particular commons, and likewise the own' ers, and such as have or shall have inte"rest in any several surrounded ground, lying "within or near the same, *may contract or "bargain for part of such commons, wastes, and "severaLs aforesaid,* with such person and per"sons which will undertake the draining and "keeping dry perpetually the several wastes "and commons of that quality; whicli con

"tract and bargain, and conveyances thereupon "made, shall be good and available in law to "all constructions and purposes, against the '" said lords of the said soil, and owners of "severals, and their heirs, successors, and as"signs; and all the commoners, as such, as shall "or might have common or interest there after"wards, according to contracts, covenants, pro"visions, and agreements in those conveyances, "to be specified; and for so much of such com"mons, wastes, or severals, as shall be so con"tracted or conveyed, to hold and enjoy in "severalty to such person or persons, his or their "assignee or assignees, as shall or have under"taken the same, in such manner and form as "his or their estates or interests are or shall be, "by or upon such contracts or agreements, by "such conveyance limited and appointed."

The commissioners of sewers, the proprietors of fen lands, and the Earl of Bedford, having united under the King's commission, the contract being duly enrolled in the High Court of Chancery, became an effective law, aided by the provisions of the two statutes last mentioned; and ultimately vested the 95,000 acres, when set out, in the Earl, his participants, and their respective assigns.

Whether the noble Earl, at the time of undertaking the general drainage, intended to manage the whole concern himself, and from his own resources, is not ascertained; if he did so intend, he was afterwards induced to alter that determination, probably, somewhat alarmed at the enormous sums that must necessarily be required to carry on so stupendous an undertaking. When it was known, that the Earl of Bedford had liecome the undertaker of the work, the greatest hopes were entertained of its success. It was seen, that, independently of his exalted rank and his political importance, he had a fortune to support the expense, a spirit capable of surmounting any difficulties, and that he who enjoyed the good opinion of all men, would, by endeavouring to make them think well of each other, reconcile their jarring interests. The whole country having promised their assistance, the Earl looked around for proper associates in this noble work, and in the following year, thirteen A.d. icsi. persons of rank and fortune proposed themselves as joint adventurers. The terms of their agree-Tin-indenture of fourteen ment are contamed in a deed, which is called, p«ru. the Indenture of Fourteen Parts.

These matters being arranged, the adventurers App. p. in. cast the whole land into twenty parts or lots, each lot consisting of 4000 acres, whereof the Earl was to have two shares or lots; Oliver, Earl of Bullingbrooke, one; Edward, Lord Gorges, one; Sir Robert Heath, Knight, one; Sir Miles Sandys, Knight and Baronet, two; Sir William Russell, Knight and Baronet, two; Sir Robert Bevill, Knight and Baronet, one; Sir Thomas Tyringham, Knight, two; Sir Philibert Vernalt, one; William Sames, LL. D., one; Anthony Hamond, Esq., two; Samuel Spalding, Gent., one; Andrew Burrell, Gent., one; and Sir Robert Lovett, 409. Knight, one. Dugdale states, that the Earl of Bedford reserved three shares, which would make up the full number stipulated; but this was not the fact. Nineteen shares only were taken in the first instance; but other persons subsequently joined in the undertaking.

By this indenture, the Earl and his participants did covenant with each other, to expend the sum of five hundred pounds for each lot or share; and on failure, the defaulters, after ten days' notice, were to be wholly excluded from taking any benefit of the premises, and were also to lose, and for ever be debarred from having or demanding, all or any such sum or sums of money, as by any such person or persons should have formerly been paid or disbursed for and towards the said work.

This agreement being settled and concluded, the Earl and his participants began the work; although, it should be stated, soon after the execution of the agreement, several of the participants assigned over certain proportions of their respective shares.

In order to carry off the superfluous waters, wherewith the Level was so much annoyed, from causes already stated, the Earl and his associates caused the following several channels to be made, viz.: 1. Bedford River, (now called the Old Bedford River,) extending from Earith to Salter's Lode, 70 feet wide, and 21 miles in length.
2. Sam's Cut, from Feltwell, in Norfolk, to the River Ouze. 3. A cut near Ely, now called Sandy's or Sandall's Cut, 2 miles long, and 40 feet wide. *4.* Bevill's Leam, being a cut from Whittlesey Meere, to Guyhirn, about 10 miles in

length, and 40 feet in breadth. 5. Morton's Leam, before mentioned, was now Ante, p. 73, made. 6. Peakirk Drain, 10 miles in length, and 17 feet in breadth. 7. New South Eau, from Crovvland to Clow's Cross. 8. Hill's Cut, near Peterborough, about 2 miles in length, and 50 feet in breadth. 9. Shire Drain, from Clow's Cross to Tyd, and so on to the Sea.

Besides these cuts and drains, they caused two sluices to be made at Tyd, upon Shire Drain, to keep out the tides; and also a clow at Clow's Cross, for the fresh water; and likewise a great sasse, at the end of Well Creek, where it empties itself into the River Ouze, at a place called Salter's Lode; also another stone sluice at the mouth of the Bedford River, near Salter's Lode, to keep out the tides; and another sluice at Earith, in the county of Huntingdon, to keep out the land floods; but above all (says Dugdale), that great Dugd.P. «i«. stone sluice below Wisbech, at the Horseshoe, which cost about eight thousand pounds, to hold the tides out of Morton's Leam.

The utility of these works will be more particularly referred to, when the present state of the VOL. I. I

Three Level (into which the Great Level was afterwards divided) is considered.

charter of The work proceeded rapidly; unanimity, incorporation. 8piritf anc judgment, constituted the character of the adventurers; the success appeared equal to what such characters promised; but the Earl and his participants, having now expended very large sums in commencing and carrying on the foregoing works, and the royal favor still shining upon this chosen band, who were enterprising at their own expense, and at extreme hazard, for the happiness of thousands, became naturally very anxious to obtain every legal protection, especially as it was part of the original contract, App. p. 103. that the Commissioners of Sewers "should unite "with the Earl in becoming humble suitors to his "Majesty, to incorporate the Earl, and such as "he should associate unto him, into one body "corporate or politic, to have continuance for "ever." Application was accordingly made in the proper quarter; and, in the 10th year of his reign, A. D. 1637. King Charles the First granted to the Earl and his App. p. i20. adventurers, acharter of incorporation. This charter is a signal proof of the desire of the King to forward the work of drainage; indeed it was policy so to dp, considering that the Crown was to be benefited to the extent of 12,000 acres, out of the 95,000 to be allotted to the Earl, under the provisions of the Lynn Law. Many valuable privileges are conferred by the charter, to the particulars of App. p. 123. which the reader *is* referred. Former letters patent are also mentioned, but no record of any such documents can be now discovered, nor indeed is it material at this distant period. This Charter (however beneficial its provisions) con-.*f* tained within itself the seeds of its own disso-its Jissoiutio». hit ion; and the Corporation thereby appointed, was eventually dissolved for want of due succession of its component parts; but many of the provisions are still available, and would be evidence as to the recognition of any right or privilege claimed by the present Corporation.

A corporation aggregate is dissolved, when Ey.i, 2,ns. by accident it is rendered incapable of continuing its corporate succession but it has been solemnly decided, that a new charter does not merge or extinguish any of the ancient privileges, but the new corporation inay use them Eyd, 1.2'1. as before. For instance, this charter grants to the Earl of Bedford, lord of the manor of Thorney, his heirs and assigns, a weekly market, and two annual fairs, with reasonable tolls, &c. These markets and fairs are still held; and no doubt can exist, that this charter is in full operation in law, in support of any right connected with the establishment and continuance of these markets and fairs. Again, the corporation are thereby empowered, for maintenance of the works, to take certain tolls for the pas-App. 137, is. sage of all horses and carts passing over the bridges then newly erected; also for any boat passing under such bridges; and also for every boat passing through any of the sluices erected by the corporation: notwithstanding its dissolution, the charter would be evidence in support 6f any of these tolls. A veiy important priApp.p.138. vilege is also conferred by this charter: "That.» "the governor, bailiffs, and commonalty of the

"society, and every of them, and their suc"cessors, shall not be put as constable, receiver, "bailiff, *or other officer,* of us, our heirs, or successors, without the liberties of the pre"cincts of the Fens;" and doubts may reasonably arise, whether any person, being a member of the select body of the present corporation, can be compelled to serve the office of high sheriff; and whether this charter might not be pleaded in bar of *aprcemunire.* But however extensive were the privileges thus conferred— privileges which it well became the Crown to grant, because they were bestowed upon those who deserved them; yet it must be evident, that, although King Charles had every disposition to stretch to the utmost extent the prerogatives of the Crown, this great undertaking required not only a fostering care, but powers beyond those the Crown had the means of conferring; if required, the power of taxation, and sale of lands in default of payment. Parliament alone could invest the Earl and his coadjutors with these ample means of raising the necessary funds for the prosecution and completion of the work. It appears very evident, that an application to A loa the legislature was contemplated by the Lynn Law, it being particularly stipulated in the offer of the 12,000 acres to the King. Probably, the Earl discovered an indisposition in Parliament to entertain the bill; or perhaps, the divisions and troubles that were now fast hastening to a complete subversion of the government, might render such an application hopeless. Certain it is, that no such application was made.

In order to carry the contract into effect, the General survey. commissioners of sewers caused a general survey of all the fen lands within the Great Level to be made by one Hayward, who appears to have been a surveyor of skill and eminence in those days; and in the year 1637 this survey was delivered in upon oath. It is even now a very valuable, as well as curious and interesting document, and will be found fully set forth in the Appendix.

App. p. m.

Warmed by the beams of royal sunshine, and animated by the cheering prospect of ultimate success, the Earl and his participants proceeded with vigour and spirit, notwithstanding the great expense and risk of the undertaking. The drainage was to have been completed within six years from the date of the Lynn Law; but it must be obvious to every one in the least acquainted with the locality of the Great Level, that if all the works projected by the adventurers (and which have been already set forth) had been completed, they would have been perfectly inadequate to the great end proposed; although it should be always recollected, that the contract with the Earl was, that the Great Level should be made "summer lands" only. However imperfect or incomplete the plan, the commissioners thought fit, at a session of sewers, held at St. Ives, in the county of Huntingdon, on the 12th of October, in the 13th year of the reign of King Charles I., (after personal perambulation and view,) to adjudge and declare, that the Earl of Bedford had at his own costs and charges, and with the expense of great sums of money, drained the said fenny and low grounds, according to the true intent of the Lynn Law; and therefore to allot and set out the 95,000 acres, out of the several and respective lordships, manors, towns, parishes, precincts, fens, and places of the said Great Level. His Majesty's surveyor-general assisted in the work. A schedule of the lands thus set out was framed by the commissioners, and returned into the Court of Chancery, and the Earl and his friends fully expected to be put into possession of what they had so dearly earned; but no such good fortune befel them. This law of sewers will be found fully set forth in the Appendix; and, notwithstanding what afterwards took place, now makes a material part of the present

A.d. 1637.

iTcsLaw. at Ah. p 210.

constitution of the Bedford Level Corporation; and the schedule of the particulars of the 95,000 acres (commonly called the Adventurers' Lands) is nearly an accurate description of the land that is now enjoyed by those claiming under the Earl and his participants, subject to the necessary taxes at this time imposed, for maintaining and securing the works for the preservation of the Great Level. It is singular, however, that this law does not set out specifically, or indeed take any notice of the 12,000 acres agreed to be allotted to the King. The moral, as well as political influence of the Earl of Bedford, must have been very great, to have induced the commissioners of sewers to make this most extraordinary adjudication. It appears scarcely to be justified upon any defined rule of law or equity. The contract was evidently incomplete; but perhaps the commissioners felt for the painful situation in which the adventurers were placed, by the heavy and continued outlay of money required to carry on the works, and were therefore induced to pass the St. Ives Law, so that possession might be given of the 95,000 acres, and the Earl and his companions be thereby enabled to sell or mortgage their respective lots, in order to provide the necessary funds. More probable reasons for this extraordinary act of the commissioners do not present themselves. All this, however, was unavailable: misfortune, disappointment, and oppression, were soon to fill to the brim the cup of misery which these patriotic citizens were ultimately doomed to drain to the very dregs.

The great influence of the Earl of Bedford's good name had induced the people to consent, reluctantly indeed, to the project of a general drainage; their hostility was rather in abeyance than finally destroyed. Unhappily, steps were taken by the Earl, which again awakened it to all its EiMpipornpntof pristine vigour. Strange as it may appear, the Sir Cornelius i, b ...'. Earl was induced to take mto his service the very person Sir Cornelius Vermuyden) to whom the country had always shewn the greatest aversion, and with whom they declined entering into any contract whatever. Vermuyden and Westerdyke (both Dutchmen) presented plans to the Earl, the former of which was unfortunately adopted, and Vermuyden appointed the conductor of the works. No records remain of the plans of the latter. One inducement might have operated upon the feelings of the Earl of Bedford, and have been an inducement to him to accept Vermuyden's services. He had been in the employ of King James; was well acquainted with the country; and probably had in his possession not only the requisite materials for carrying on the works, but also at his command great numbers of workmen who first followed him from Holland, and had been afterwards engaged in the drainage of Hatfield Chace. Whatever were the reasons that weighed upon the mind of the Earl, and regulated his conduct in this respect, the result was most unprosperous. It afforded a ground for discontent. That opposition, which only slumbered, was now roused, and repeated complaints were addressed to the King in Council, as will appear from the following document:

There was this day at the Board his Matie beinge prsent severall petic'ons of complaints concerninge the Fenn businrs one in the name of the Lord Bp of Ely and of the Deane and Chapter of Ely one other in the name of some justice of peace of Norff: Suff: and Cambridgeshiere and a third in the name of the Inhabitants of Over Wivlingham & Cottenham in the County of Cambridge All wch. petic'ons havinge beene considered of and debated in the prsence of many of the parties and of his Matle" Surveyor Generall of his Lands his Matie did declare that the decree whereby the Fenns are adjudged drayned shall in noe wise be impeached as to the judgement of Dreyninge But that the petic'ons and complaints concerninge the inequallitye of Allottm" by the decree of Wisbich especially of the Church of Ely and the Land of the Colledges in Cambridge shal bee referred to the ComTM whoe made that decree and to his Mulics Surveyor Gen"11 to be ordered and established by them or such of them as shal be present at the next Meetinge as they shall thinke reasonable and that the sett out and Allottm' of the Drayners parts shall p'ceede speediely and effectually wteout interrupc'on by those complaints or any other And that if any disturbance shall happen the Dreyners shall have the imediate assistance of the Boord for the suppressinge and punishinge of the same And his Matle doth further declare that he disliketh that comp'lts of this nature should be made except there be ground for them and cannot but reprehend the Complayners But especially his Matlc will be very sensible if any of those whoe are trusted by his Matie wth the governm' of the Countrey shal bee found for any Interest or by respects to be stirrors or inciters of Complaints whereby the peace of the Country may be disturbed as soe great good a worke put in danger or shall sciently forbeare to doe their duties and endeavoᵀᴹ to prevent And therefore his Malle and the Boord having received good information that Castle Esqr one of the Justices of peace of the County of Hunt: hath in this way miscarryed himselfe have Ordered that he shal bee discharged of the Comission of the peace and sent for upp by a Messenger to answere his misdemeanor.

Will: Beeceer."

It appears, therefore, that the Earl and his companions still retained the favour of their Sovereign; but they were soon fated to experience a sad reverse. Those who are the least acquainted with the annals of England are not to be informed that resolution was by no means characteristic of King Charles the First. At this distance of time it is almost impossible to ascertain correctly what were the real motives which induced his Majesty to withdraw his protection and countenance from the Earl of Bedford and his enterprising colleagues. His disposition, from whatever cause it arose, became entirely changed. At this period, the legislative branch of the constitution began to assume an attitude very different from any former parliament of England. The extent of the royal prerogative became the subject of general discussion. The Earl of Bedford was known to be hostile to the rapid strides the King was making towards the establishment of absolute government. But he had too plentiful a fortune to desire a subversion of the government itself. Pym and Saint John were wholly devoted to the Earl, through whose influence the latter was made solicitor-general. Perhaps the uncourtier like conduct of the Earl raised a prejudice in the King's mind, and induced the alteration of sentiment that unfortunately took place. Others consider that it was owing to the pressing exigencies of his Majesty's private finances, and that his unpopular treasurer, the Bishop of London, thought the measure which his Majesty afterwards took with regard to the drainage, would have the effect of retrieving those finances. The King might also have taken offence at the passing of

Tin" King's liarsh conduct to the adventurers.

the Saint Ives Law, without the acknowledgment of his right to the 12,000 acres. Whatever might have been the cause, the effect was equally injurious. The King, who, by his charter, had expressed his highest approbation of the proceedings of the Earl and his participants, and granted them the most extensive privileges for carrying on their undertaking, *in* less than four years, by the most cruel proceedings, persecuted these very men he had so kindly protected, to the ultimate ruin of the undertaking, and the destruction of the private fortunes of most of those who had with so much spirit engaged in so formidable a speculation. It has often been remarked, and with great truth, that a party inclined to create a quarrel is not often at a loss to procure the means.

The King and his Council now listened with greedy ears to the numerous complaints that were continually arriving from the Fens, many of which it cannot in justice be denied were founded in truth. It is impossible to deny that the contract of the Earl was yet *re infectd*. The most disheartening difficulties had arisen, not only as regarded the work of drainage, but also from those who were interested in the navigation of the country. The Earl and his joint adventurers had unfortunately become deeply indebted to Sir Cornelius Vermuyden, and indeed to almost all the men employed upon the works. Some of the adventurers, (amongstwhom was the Earl himself,) had conveyed, even previously to the adjudication of the Commissioners of Sewers at St. Ives, many thousand acres to Sir Cornelius Vermuyden, in liquidation of, or rather as security for, the sums so due and owing. Doubtless, the Commissioners of Sewers had a most arduous and difficult duty to perform; they were in truth between the horns of a dilemma: if, on the one hand, they had refused to adjudicate the drainage complete, and set out the 95,000 acres as the recompense thereof, the company would have been unable to find adequate funds for executing the contract, and the immense sums already expended would have been totally lost; while, on the other hand, by setting out and dividing the 95,000 acres before the contract was completed, great hostility and discontent amongst the proprietors, and the commoners in particular, would of course have been engendered, and would have been considerably augmented by the interference and complaints of those interested in the navigation, who were at all times inimical to the undertaking.

The Earl of Bedford was no longer one of the King's advisers, or had influence in his councils: he was now (to use the expression of those times) one of the governing voices in the House of Lords. His manly spirit could ill brook the base ingratitude of those whose welfare he had promoted at the hazard of his fortune. The King and his Council proceeded. A Commission of Sewers was directed to officers and servants of the Crown,and those whom the Court had obliged; and to these persons, entirely unacquainted with the business, and as little interested in the event of it as strangers could be, was entrusted the charge of examining into the proceedings of the Earl and his companions. These commissioners met at April, Huntingdon, on the 12th April, 1639. Before they set out, they were instructed in their business, which waa to traverse the whole of what the Saint Ives Law had done not above six months before. The commissioners who met at St. Ives, understanding the nature of the work, unbiassed in their opinions, determined the contract to be complete, and decreed the Earl of Bedford and his adventurers to be entitled to the recompense they adventured for. These Court Commissioners, ignorant of the first principles of draining, fixed as to their judgments before they inquired, were todeclarethe work to be incomplete, and put the Earl and his adventurers under such difficulties as should make them relinquish the undertaking, and throw the whole advantage resulting from it into the hands of the Crown. Well as they might have been tutored before they set out, yet such was the opinion entertained of them by their employers, that on the 9th of April, three days before they met, a letter bearing date on that day, was addressed to them by the high treasurer, the Bishop of London, to confirm them in their good purpose; and for fear this should not have the desired effect, on the 13th, which was the day after they met, the King himself condescended to write to them, and the royal signet was prostituted to the purposes of oppression and injustice. It appears by these letters, that the King had been much enlightened within the compass of three days, and he knew that to be a fact before examination, which these commissioners were to make a fact after their investigation. In these letters the King declared, that since the Lord Treasurer had sent his despatches, he was perfectly well satisfied that the Earl of Bedford had not drained the country, and offered himself to be the undertaker of the work. If the Lord Treasurer's letters warmed the commissioners in their purpose, they glowed at this strange but royal mandate of his Majesty. They commenced their labours with the greatest zeal and ardour, not by halves, but went roundly through the whole business. They began, in op-Rereiai of tiio position to the Saint Ives Law, to arraign the Earl of Bedford's conduct; they determined that the work was incomplete and defective; they adjudged the Earl and his adventurers not to have performed their contract, and therefore, not entitled to their recompense, in the manner it had been contracted for; and, with scandalous adulation, extolling his Majesty's great goodness in offering to undertake the work, they most meanly accepted his proposals, with a free will offering of 57,000 acres more, for his princely care of this distressed country. To oppress the Earl and his colleagues, they imposed an arbitrary tax of 30 shillings an acre on the 95,000 acres, amounting in the whole to 142,500/., well knowing, that, however able the Earl of Bedford might be to advance his share of that sum, the circumstances of the rest of the adventurers, many of whom had been ruined by the expenses already incurred, were by no means capable of defraying such a tax; and that, if they had been so, it could not, on any principle of calculation, have been prudent to advance it on these terms. They declared his Majesty the undertaker of the work, and returned to London with all the self approbation that attended an ignorance of the consequences of their conduct. Such knight-errants, in so arduous a service, could not but receive the highest approbation from their employers, his Majesty and the Lord Treasurer.

The part the Earl of Bedford took in that transaction was worthy of his character; the nobleness of his nature scorned an attention to other business when the happiness of individuals was an immediate object; when he could employ himself in attempting to procure and establish the prosperity of a whole kingdom. And such was his object while the business of this Court Commission was carried on. King Charles, ever since his accession to the throne, had taken all opportunitiesof shewing that his ideas of government were very dissimilar to those of his subjects, who, well understanding the first principles of the constitution, saw what government should and ought to be. He had treated parliaments as only ministers of his authority; had dissolved them, when they assumed to themselves the exercise of any of those powers with which they were armed by the wise policy of the constitution; and ventured of himself even to levy money without their concurrence or interposition. AH these causes, and several others well known in history, had been long combining to light up that general flame which afterwards broke out. The Earl of Bedford stood foremost on all occasions to contend for that true political liberty which the privilege of the constitution ought to confer. A friend to the prerogative of the crown, as part of the constitution, he constantly opposed all excesses which arose from its being carried beyond its bounds, as encroachments dangerous to the liberties of the subject, and at the same time destructive of that prerogative itself. It was to him, that on all great occasions the eyes of good men were turned. The business of this court commission was transacting at a time when the fire was first kindled in Scotland; there, a rebellion was actually begun, and the country was in arms. The fatal consequences of this no one could predict; but they were, as could not but be foreseen, of the highest import to the nation. From this time to his death the Earl was wholly employed in a constant and watchful attention to whatever might concern the happiness of these kingdoms. The Great Level, therefore, engaged no part of Ins care. The golden dreams of his Majesty and his High Treasurer, of the resources that might be drawn from undertaking the drainage of the country, could never have been realized; but the general confusion and distraction which soon followed, prevented them from making any of those experiments for which the zeal of the commissioners had paved the way. What afterwards happened to the King was a scene of warfare and imprisonment: he lost his kingdoms, and with them his life. Amidst these great and weighty concerns, the project in which he had been so earnest to engage seems to have been totally forgotten. The works completed by the Earl of Bedford and his adventurers at so great an expense, decayed; their drains were getting choked up; and the whole undertaking was hastening into as distressful a condition as it had been in before they embarked in it.

The King, entering accordingly upon the undertaking, began the following works: 1. A bank was made on the south side of Morton's Leain. extending from Peterborough to Wisbech, ami a navigable sasse, a sluice at Standground, and also a like bank on the north side of that leam. 2. He caused a new river to be cut between the stone sluice at the Horseshoe and the sea, below Wisbech, of 60 feet in breadth, and about 2 miles and a half in length, with banks on both sides. 3. And lastly, he placed a sluice in the marshes below Tidtl, Duipd. p. 415. upon the outfall of Shire Drain, which afterwards was swallowed up in the quick sands.

These works, however, were not completed: the King had more important affairs to engage, his attention; and, it seems, nothing more was done in the work of drainnge.

Francis Earl of Bedford departed this life, of the small pox, the 9th of May, 1611. He was undoubtedly a man of great and noble mind, capable of generous notions, and of extended philanthropy: he lived in times of great difficulty, and was desirous of moderate courses: his fault (and who amongst the greatest is exempt from fault?) was a certain degree of irresolution, which carried him into violent proceedings if his advice were not submitted to; and, therefore, many who knew him thought his death not unseasonable, as well to his fame as to his fortune; and that, while it might rescue him from some possible guilt, might also be the means of preserving him from those terrible misfortunes which men of all.conditions, in those perilous times, could scarcely avoid. The Earl of Bedford was indeed a good, as well as a great man; but while his public virtues command our admiration, his private sorrows excite our regret. He was the victim of disappointed hopes, lacerated feelings, and bitter ingratitude. He beheld his own, and the fortunes of his patriotic participants, fruitlessly wasted; his anxious desires for the public good frustrated; and last, not least, bis domestic comforts annihilated, The Earl had been mainly instrumental in supplanting King

James's creature and favourite, Carr, afterwards Earl of Somerset, and introducing in his place Villiers, subsequently Duke of Buckingham. The infamous character and conduct of the Countess of Somerset, are too well known to need repetition. She and her husband, driven fro n the presence of their Sovereign, and expelled from the society of their equals, retired into privacy. Unfortunately, William, the Eaii's eldest son, afterwards created first Duke of Bedford, in whose future conduct and prospects his unhappy father beheld the only chance of reparation for his own wrongs, accidentally saw, and became enamoured of Ann, the only daughter and sole heiress of the Ear and Countess of Somerset; and, notwithstanding every persuasion and entreaty of his family and his friends, ultimately became her husband. The Earl was so strongly averse to this alliance, that he gave his son leave to choose a wife out of any other family in the kingdom. Opposition usually stimulates desire, and the young couple's affections were only increased. At length, it is said, the King interposed, and sending the Duke of Lennox to urge the Earl to consent, the match was brought about. It must be acknowledged, that the Earl of Somerset acted a noble part. He stood disgraced before the world, and was reduced to poverty, perhaps in a great measure owing to the political conduct of the father of the man who now sought to woo and to win his daughter. The Earl of Somerset sold his house at Chiswick, his plate, jewels, and furniture, to raise a fortune for his daughter of twelve thousand pounds, (which the Earl of Bedford demanded,) saying, that, since her affections were settled, he chose rather to ruin himself than make her unhappy. A splendid alliance with the opulent and noble house of Russell, had also its inducement. It is but justice to add, that the lady proved worthy of the union she had formed. It is even said,that she *was* ignorantof her mother's dishonour till accidentally informed of it. There was issue by this marriage seven sons and three daughters. The second, but eldest surviving son, was the celebrated Lord Russell, executed upon a charge of high treason, in the reign of King James the Second. bad somewhat abated this hostility; but it was not destroyed. Sir Cornelius Vermuyden, whom the Earl unfortunately employed as conductor of the works, had inundated the country with foreign labourers, whom he had called over to his assistance from Holland;—a step he was probably compelled to adopt, from the disinclination of the labourers in the Fens to execute any employment under this obnoxious foreigner. Perpetual disputes and bickerings took place; the Level was in a very feverish and unsettled state, partaking of the general aspect of the country at large. However inimical Fen men were to the drainage, they could not but admire the generosity and disinterestedness of Earl Francis. When, therefore, they beheld him the victim of the base ingratitude of the Sovereign whom he bad served, under whose protection he and his participants had squandered to little orjio purpose such enormous wealth; and when they found withal that Monarch attempting to increase his own resources from the wreck of their, ruined fortunes, it was natural that their original hostility should break out, and the link, the sacred link, between the governor and the governed, become weakened,—indeed we may say, severed.

To conclude: the deep and everlasting debt of gratitude and affection which will ever be due from fen men to the memory of Francis Earl of Bedford, has hitherto been cheerfully acknowledged, and proved by the constant election of his successors to the important and highly honorable office of Governor of the Bedford Level Corporation, of which he was undoubtedly the founder.

The persons interested in the navigation had been opposed throughout to the drainage, and no doubt beheld this deranged state of things with considerable gratification; inasmuch as all dissensions would most probably have the effect of delaying, if not of preventing, that dreaded project. In times of difficulty every triflingcircumstance augments the embarrassment, and excites the uneasiness of government. The state of the Fens was any thing but satisfactory to the King and his advisers.

At this critical moment appeared upon the stage of public life the most extraordinary man that this or any other country has ever produced, oiirer Oliver Cromwell, subsequently Lord Protector

Cromwell. of Engiandj Wa8 jineally descended from the family of Thomas Cromwell, Earl of Essex, Vicar General of England, and prime minister in the reign of Henry VIII. The sister of Essex became the wife of Morgan Williams of Llanisher, in the county of Glamorgan. Sir Richard Williams, the issue of this marriage, obtained, like many other courtiers of that day, very extensive grants of nunneries, at that time dissolved, and, amongst others, of the nunnery of Hinchinbrook, and the rich abbey of Ramsey, both in the county of Huntingdon. Sir Richard had a sou named Oliver, whose s,econd son Robert was the father of the Protector. Cromwell was a man of great virtues, was fervent in his patriotism, and earnestly devoted to the best interests of mankind. He had a frame of mind which no complication of difficulties could inspire with a doubt of his power to conquer them. The fertility of his conception, like the intrepidity of his spirit, was incapable of being exhausted. He was a man raised up by events for the times in which he commenced his public career. Cromwell was undoubtedly a most accomplished statesman, Ob well as a skilful soldier. So many memoirs and histories of this eminent character however exist, that it would be an useless waste of time again to repeat what has been so often told. The subject is indeed foreign to the purpose of this work. Suffice it to eay, that the town of Huntingdon had the honour of being his native place, and that the record of his birth still remains in the register of the parish church of All Saints in that borough.

Oliver Cromwell took the most prominent part Misconduct in opposing, and effectually, the infamous commistu'e Great Level, sion issued by King Charles, and which sat at Huntingdon, the 12th of April, 1639. This was the commencement of his brilliant career. His manners, his zeal, his perseverance, and his undaunted bravery, excited the admiration of his fellow Fen men, and finally subdued those effeminate courtiers whom the Crown had most unadvisedly employed to harass and to plunder the Level. The town of Cambridge, being deeply interested, was very much opposed to the drainage of the Fens; and consequently, as Cromwell had defeated the plan by his courage and vigilance, he became extremely popular in this place; and ultimately represented it in Parliament. Although a decided enemy to the infamous project of King Charles, yet, as will be seen hereafter, when he had acquired political power, he was foremost in promoting those measures which led in the result to the completion of the scheme of a general drainage.

The Earl of Essex, the commander of the parliamentary forces, appointed Cromwell governor of the Isle of Ely ; in which situation It is not generally known, that the third title borne by the King of England, is that of " Marquis of the Isle of Ely.' For reasons not very apparent, this title has been omitted in the different editions of the peerage, for some few years past. The author of this work has not only stated this circumstance that it might reach "the highest quarter," but he has ineffectually endeavoured to obtain its re-insertion. The title of Marquis has been erroneously supposed to have been conferred for the first time by Richard II., that monarch having created his great favourite Richard de Vere, Earl of Oxford, "Marquis of Dublin." The style Marquis, Marchio, or Marisco, took its origin from the person having the care or government of the marshes or frontier provinces. The origin of the title of Marquis, or Marisco, of the Isle of Ely, otherwise the great Lordship of Marisco, in Norfolk and Cambridgeshire, is of much greater antiquity than the time of Richard II. Its origin and history may not be uninteresting:

Geoffrey deMontmorency, sometimes styled "the rich," was the second son of Herve" de Montmorency, Grand Butler of France, and came into England in the time of William the Conqueror. Being appointed Chamberlain to the Conqueror' daughter-in-law, Matilda, the wife of Henry I., that monarch granted to Geoffrey de Montmorency the lordship of Thorney, in the Isle of Ely, (now the property of his Grace, John Duke of Bedford, under a grant from the Crown, upon the dissolution of monasteries in the reign of Henry VIII.,) and other manors. Herve", the brother of this Geoffrey, was constituted the first Bishop of Ely, in the year 1108. At this period, (the Isle having previously submitted to King William,) Geoffrey obtained the grant of the great Lordship of Marisco, in Norfolk and Cambridgeshire, along with the *hereditary* governorship of the Isle of Ely; which last dignity his descendants continued to hold until the Fourteenth Century, and from that be doubtless acquired that knowledge of the country, which enabled him ultimately to lend his aid to its regeneration.

Connecting all these circumstances, it is not improbable that the fatal catastrophe which befel King Charles the First, was primarily occasioned by his base ingratitude to his friend and counsellor, Earl Francis; by his nefarious attempt to raise an unconstitutional tax upon the Fens; and by the state of insubordination which consequently existed in the country. Above all, when we reflect that these events gave " pomp and circumstance" to a man like Cromwell, the opinion entertained in the Fens can be considered neither unjust nor unreasonable-Let us close this long digression.

Francis Earl of Bedford was succeeded by his character of *i i* TTT'ii-i *A. i* "" William, Earl, eldest son William, whose apparently unpro-afterwards first pitious marriage has been already mentioned, This nobleman, following the footsteps of his

Great Level.

period until the Fifteenth Century, (when the title of Marquis became formally recognized by patent of creation,) they bore the title or name of " De Marisco." In the year 1379, William, then Lord de Marisco, sold the great Lordship of Marisco to Thomas de Cockfield and to Henry de Lczignan, or Lusignan. How long it continued in the possession of these persons is unknown; but there can be little doubt that it became ultimately forfeited to the Crown, (in which the title now remains,) during some of those political convulsions which afterwards took place. Some persons have erroneously considered that the Isle of Ely *ia* a county palatine: it is not so. The bishop exercises *jura regalia* within its limits; but he exercises this right only in subjection to the Crown. father, continued to give his support to the Long Parliament: indeed, for some time, he acted a very distinguished part in the military proceedings of these extraordinary times. Earl William was a man of very considerable attainments, and of the most amiable and benevolent principles; but he also unfortunately inherited from his father the same unhappy habit of irresolution,—a habit which ultimately led to his political disappointments, and his final retirement, during the Commonwealth, from public life.

Coke, Selden, Hampden, Pym, Vane, St. John, and Cromwell, were the men who, by their extraordinary talents and intellectual energies, so greatly contributed to produce that state of things which conduced to the establishment of the Commonwealth. With these men should be associated such of the principal of the nobility of the land, as, from the beginning of the civil war, took part against the absolute measures attempted to be established by the Crown and its advisers. Amongst these illustrious names, we find that of William Earl of Bedford. A. D. 1642. In 1642, at the same time were raised seventyfive troops of horse, consisting of sixty men each, the chief commanders of which bore the appellation of Colonel. These troops appear to have been raised at the sole expense of their respective colonels. The Earl was one of this patriotic band; he was the second officer in the army, being general of horse under the Earl of Essex; and was engaged at the battle of Edghill,—a battle which concluded without any decisive advantage to either party.

The principal defect in the character of William Earl of Bedford, (his great irresolution,) could not fail, in times so perilous, to display itself. Soon after the battle of Edghill, the Earl was induced, by the persuasions or example of the Earl of Northumberland, the first nobleman in the kingdom, and of the Earls of Holland and Clare, to entertain what under a regular government would be called treasonable designs against his employers: he finally stole off unperceived, with the Earls of Holland and Clare, to the King's quarters. The Earl of Northumberland retired, with leave, to his house, at Petworth, in Sussex, there to remain till he should see whether he could negotiate a secure peace with the parliamentary party; in which if he failed, he determined to follow the others to the general rendezvous of the King at Oxford.

Historians have given no clew by which any determined opinion can be formed of this strange act of tergiversation and desertion. A good citizen should be extremely slow in abandoning the cause of his lawful sovereign; but when he beholds the people, driven by repeated wrongs to resist despotism and oppression, and embarks with them in one common cause, equal justice demands constancy and firmness to those who have engaged in an enterprize always.attended in the first outset (whatever may be the result) with great hazard and personal danger. The Earl might have grown weary of a war, into which he had, perhaps, hastily entered, urged as well by private feelings of anger and mortification, as by the recollection of the wrongs of his deceased father. There is no doubt that the Earl and his noble compeers had been discountenanced at Court, and saw no hopes of being elevated in that sphere to the summit of their expectation. Perhaps they were induced by their ambition or their vanity to throw themselves into the opposite party, but afterwards discovered their mistake. They saw things going further than they had intended, and a spirit rising in the nation, which their more aristocratic habits might not enable them to comprehend, and which they felt themselves incompetent to control. In such a conjuncture, it must have been evident, that talents and real worth would raise every one to his due consideration and influence; and that high birth, and a copious rent-roll, would prove comparatively unavailing. To the Earl, the contemplation of these prospects could not be agreeable: he had too great a stake in the country not to tremble at events which might establish a government solely democratical. By whatever motives, however, he was actuated, the result of this unhappy secession was most unfortunate. He thereby lost the confidence and devotion of the popular party, and failed to acquire either the countenance or gratitude of the sovereign,

Under whose banners he had now voluntarily enrolled himself.

The conduct of the King in this transaction was even more unaccountable than that of the Earl and his followers. Surely this was a moment that demanded the utmost forbearance, good humour, and condescension on the royal part: but in no instance did the folly and obstinacy of the Court shew itself so conspicuously. One of the main characteristics of the unfortunate Charles was, that he never did any thing in a gracious manner; and it was quite natural that the courtiers who attended him, should be kindled into a flame at the very thought that the persons who for a considerable time had been their active opponents, should now come over, when the cause of their enemies appeared desperate, and share in honors, emolument, and favor, clarendon, equally with those who had borne the brunt of 329'. 'P' the day. All was selfishness and narrowness of soul in the royal camp. If these earls had been well received and countenanced, it would have been a signal for all who were tired of the parliament, or wanted firmness of mind to ad-Godwin. here to the public cause through good and evil events, that upon a shew of repentance, they might be assured of forgiveness. Let us haste to the termination of this unhappy event. Bitterly must the Earl have felt that the fatal step he had taken was irrecoverable, and that if he returned to the parliament it would still be impossible for him to recover their confidence. Notwithstand

A. D. 1643. ing these feelings, the treatment he received was so intolerable that he resolved to quit the King's quarters. He returned towards the capital, and, journal of after a short quarantine, was permitted, *in ap*

Lords—Nov. 6. 1 ' *f pearance,* to resume his former station. The lmk was however broken. Confidence once destroyed is seldom restored, even in the ordinary affairs of life; but never when the high behests and solemn destinies of a country are at issue. The Earl of Bedford sat no more in the Long Parliament; nor during the existence of the Commonwealth did he take any part in public affairs. He retired into private life, residing chiefly at his seat at Thorney Abbey, within the precincts of the Great Level. It is but justice to the government of that period, and as a proof of the excellent character of this exalted nobleman, to state, that, without any solicitation whatever, he was restored to that part of his estates, lying in the county of Devon, which had been sequestered during his secession to the cause of the King. Whatever may have been the effect of this defection upon the political and public character of the Earl, the result was eminently favourable to the best interests and welfare of the Fens, as it enabled him to become in bis retirement, the friend, the adviser, and the promoter of that general system of drainage, which ultimately took place under the legislative enactment of the Long Parliament, and which might not have occurred had the Earl continued engaged in all the turmoil and feverish anxiety of an active citizen and a devoted statesman.

Many readers, it is feared, will consider these long historical notices as foreign to the purpose of the work. It is hoped, however, that they will be found upon reflection to be perfectly relevant and necessary. The development of the subject can only be understood by shewing the actual causes, however apparently extraneous, which first retarded, and ultimately led to the general drainage of the country, as well as the position of persons and parties who prevented or promoted the undertaking.

CHAPTER VIII. *State of the Great Level under the Commonwealth.— The Pretended Act.—Progress of the Works.— Distinction between "The Participants? "The Adventurers" and " The Company. "— Transactions with Sir Cornelius Vermuyden.—Distresses of the Company; and generosity of the Earl of Bedford.*

The Earl of Bedford retired from public life, taking no further part either in the proceedings of the government established by the long parliament, or in the protectorate established by Cromwell. Although his brother, Colonel John Russell, joined in the unsuccessful conspiracy against Cromwell, called the "Sealed Knot," it does not appear that the Earl was in the least implicated in the affair. Many of the conspirators were tried and executed, and Colonel Russell was committed to the Tower, but was never brought to trial. Neither the government of the long parliament, nor that of the Protector, can be considered as determined persecutors. They possessed, in a great degree, all the attributes of strength. They were respected at home, and uni versally feared abroad. Not only were their armies victorious, but they had organized a most formidable and successful navy. The long parliament had immortalized itself by the enactment of those navigation laws, which more degenerate legislators and sciolistic quacks have in modern times dared to abrogate. And, unlike our own days, there was no Tory administration requiring for the justification of its public character the forensic aid of a Whig Malthusian Attorney General. The wisdom and firmness of the Parliament at once excited admiration and commanded respect.

Whatever might have been the feelings of the Earl as to the principles of the government itself, he saw that it had all the appearance of stability, and acted accordingly. Indeed, it was impossible for him in his retirement, not to reflect upon the wretched state of those who had been the companions of his noble father, as well as upon the injurious and fatal consequences resulting to the Great Level, from the decay and abandonment of those works of drainage, upon which such heavy sums had been so fruitlessly squandered. His benevolent and compassionate nature looked down with sympathy and hereditary kindness upon the distresses of the mined adventurers and their miserable country. His residence at Thorney daily reminded him of past events; and at length finding, as already stated, an evident sta Sir James Scarlett.

bility in the government, he declared a disposition to countenance and assist the adventurers. Readily were his offers embraced. Such of the original adventurers as were left, or their representatives, as well as the other parties who had now become interested in the completion of some general scheme of drainage, united with the Earl in an application to the then Parliament, for its sanction and support. Too much foresight, and too much public feeling prevailed in that assembly, to neglect so favorable an opportunity, well appreciating, as they did, the importance of the measure, and the advantage likely to accrue to the commonwealth from its execution. 2d Aug. 1645. On the 2d August, 1645, a petition was presented to the House, and committed to Mr. Solicitor Sir Anthony Irby, Mr. Maynard, Lord Grey, Sir Henry Vane, jun., Sir Edward Partheriche, Mr. Ellys, Sir

Thomas Wodehouse, Mr. Recorder, and Mr. Rigby. The committee were instructed to consider the petition, and to prepare and bring in an ordinance for settling and perfecting the works of drainage in such manner as should be "most agreeable to justice, most "advantageous to the public, and most con"ducive to the safety of the Level." The bills brought into Parliament were at that time so designated. The petitions for all bills of drainage are now referred to a select-committee, prior to their introduction into Parliament.

This committee had power to send for parties, witnesses, papers, and records; and, on the 16th of August following, an ordinance was brought in "For draining the Great Level extending itself into the counties of Northampton, Norfolk, Suf"folk, Lincoln, Cambridge, Huntingdon, and the "Isle of Ely;" it was read the first time, and (after the reading of a general petition from the adventurers) the ordinance was read a second time, and committed unto Mr. Pelham, Mr. Trenchard, journals of Lieut.-General Cromwell, Mr. Scawen, Sir Roger common!. North, Sir Edward Partheriche, Mr. Maynard, Sir John Burgoyne,Mr. Dennis Bond.Sir JohnTrevor, Colonel Montagu, Mr. Rigby, Sir Dudley North, Sir Robert Pye, Sir Thomas Walsingham, Mr. Lemmon, Lord Grey, Mr. Whitelock, Mr. Grinston, Sir Thomas Trenchard, Sir Peter Wentworth, Mr. Gerard, Sir William Spring, Sir Norton Knatchbull, Mr. Henry Darlcy, Mr. Recorder, Mr. Reynolds, Mr. Blackiston, Sir John Danvers, the burgesses of the University of Cambridge, and the knights and burgesses of the several counties within the Level. The committee were " to hear the several counties, "and all parties interested; to examine, and, "as near as they can, agree and reconcile all "differences and receive any petitions that shall "be tendered to them;" and were also empowered "to send for parties, witnesses, papers, and re"cords;" and it was also ordered by the House, that "no person who was himself an adven"turer should be of the committee."

The committee assembled "on the 20th of May, 1646; letters were ordered to be written to the sheriffs of the adjoining counties, to the bailiffs of the isle of Ely, and also to the mayors of Cambridge and Lynn, requiring them to give notices to the inhabitants that the ordinance was referred to such committee; and a sub-committee was also chosen, to examine what interest and title the Earl of Bedford and his participants had to the draining of the Great Level, and what money had been expended therein, and to report both the title and accounts to the general committee.

On the 1st of June following, Mr. Trenchard reported from the sub-committee the interest of the Earl of Bedford in the draining of the Great Level of the Fens, by producing and reading the Lynn Law, passed in 1630, and which, it appears, was the only document delivered to the committee in support of the interest and title of the Earl and the adventurers. It was also reported, that the Earl had delivered in to the subcommittee the following brief of his disbursements in the business of the Fens.

"A Collec'on of all the generall somes of moneye layd owte by the Earle of Bedford &c. in ye busines of drayning the Greate Levelle of the Fennes from the 10th of July 1631 until the 10th of August 1638 together wth a computac'on what the single interest of cache some according to the time of forbearance cometh unto after the rate of 8 p1 cent as followeth (viz1.)

'The Moneyea payd.
"10,000/6.
10,000
07,000
10,000
05,000
10,000
10,000
10,000
08,000
03,600
02,400
05,000
02,000

The times when.
10 July 1631
8 Maye 1632 9 Octob: 16:12
23 March 1632
20 Maye 1633
10 Novem: 1633
10 Maye 1634
10 Novem: 1634
10 Maye 1635
30 Novem: 1636
loFcbrua: 1636
6 April 1637 7 March 1637

The totall of 1 93,000/ft. The totall of interest 1
Money es paid/ _ for those Moneyes I
The totall of both somes 127.170M.

"There is also yet owing by the AdvTM for works &c. alreadie donne above 00,4000/6."

The grand committee then gave notice, that they were ready to receive any petitions that persons might desire to submit to their consideration; and forty-eight distinct petitions were presented to the committee, from sundry persons and places within the Great Level and its vicinity, generally complaining of the injury that would be occasioned to navigation, and of the inutility of the scheme to the lands of the petitioners.

After numerous previous meetings, the grand committee assembled on the 6th of November, 1646, when two points were put in issue: 1st, whether the work of draining the Great Level were feazible or not; 2dly, if feazible, whether beneficial to the commonwealth. Upon these two points both the adventurers and petitioners were to examine witnesses, upon interrogatories exhibited from the Court of Chancery. The examinations upon these interrogatories were delivered on the 19th of January following to the committee; and after much debate, and hearing of counsel on all sides, on the 22d November, 1647, the committee

"Resolved upon the question:

"1st, That the committee is of opinion, that "a great part of the Great Levell of the Fennes "may bee drained."

"Resolved upon the question,

"2nd, That this committee is of opinion, that "this drayning will be profitable to the Common"wealth."

The committee, having come to these conclusions, proceeded to the consideration of the several provisions to be inserted in the ordinance. Sir John Danvers and others were appointed to view the several maps of the Fens, and compare them with the boundaries of the Great Level then read, and to report their opinion the next sitting, concerning the boundaries; aiid at the same meeting it was "Resolved, that 95,000 "acres within the Levell shall be sett out for the "forbearing the charge of draining and main"taining the works from tyme to tyme."

At subsequent meetings the boundaries were finally settled, and the names of the commissioners inserted in the ordinance, for the purpose of "acting and seeing that all things were done App.p. ssi. "according to the ordinance." These commissioners had power to adjudge when the said Level should be drained, or any part thereof; and they were to be empowered, "whensoever 30,000 acres "or more were adjudged by them to be drayned, "to allot and set out to the adventurers a pro"portionate part, according to the former allot"ments, answerable to that part adjudged by "the commissioners to be drained."

Onthe23d of December, 164 7, the several amendments were read and voted, as they were reported from the sub-committee, and directed to be reported to the House; the names of commissioners were also read, but not voted, being referred to the consideration of the House.

The grand committee then adjourned for a fortnight; but they do not appear to have met again until the 8th of May, 1649; nor were any steps taken in the mean time: indeed, the civil war now raged with great fury between the King and the parliament, which necessarily engrossed the exclusive attention of the incipient government of the Commonwealth.

The year 1648 was probably the most critical period of this eventful struggle. Never had England been so thoroughly convulsed; never had war and insurrection spread their ramifications so widely throughout all parts of the kingdom. In fine, King Charles perished on a scaffold, Execution of ,. King Charles. erected in the open street, opposite the present remains of the Palace of Whitehall, on Tuesday, aoth Jan. 1549. the 30th of January, 1640, having been tried and condemned only on the Saturday preceding-. Thus triumphed the men who founded the Commonwealth of England, and who, doubtless, intended by this violent and daring act, to teach a lesson, that no person, however high in station, and however protected by the prejudices of his contemporaries, must expect to be criminal against the welfare of the state, and the happiness of the community, without receiving, sooner or later, his just retribution and punishment.

To proceed: the grand committee for settling the ordinance of drainage had not been dissolved. They appear to have reassembled; and on Thursday the 8th of May, 1649, Mr. Reynolds, one of the Committee, reported the amendments of the ordinance, which amendments were twice read; and the question being propounded, that the said journal of ordinance be re-committed, and the question

House of Com-,.,,,...

bemg put, that that question be now put; it passed in the House with the affirmative; and the main question being put, it was

"Resolved that the said ordinance for draining "the Great Level be re-committed unto Sir John "Danvers, Mr. Reynolds, Lord Howard, Colonel "Hutchinson, and others, or any five of them; "and all that will come to have voices, and to "meet the then next Wednesday, in the after"noon, at the Exchequer Chamber; and the said "ordinance to be brought in that day se'nnight; "and the especial care thereof was referred to "Mr. Reynolds;" at which meeting the said ordinance was read; and the commissioners' names added, as they were particularly voted in order, for reporting to the House; and the amendments passed the committee.

On the 16th of the same month, Mr. John Goodwyn, in the absence of Mr. Reynolds, was by order of the House appointed to report the said amendments the next day, which he accordingly did; and, upon debate, the same report was ordered to be engrossed.

On the 29th of May, 1649, the Act " for "draining the Great Level of the Fens extending "itself into the Counties of Northampton) Nor"folk, Suffolk, Lincoln, Cambridge, Huntingdon, "and the Isle of Ely, or some of them," was that day read the third time, and, upon the question, passed, and ordered to be printed and published.

Thus passed the first specific act of Legislation App. p. 367. for the general drainage of the Great Level. This The Pretended ordinance, is called "The Pretended Act," as were all other Acts passed during the period of the Commonwealth, which were not re-enacted upon the restoration of Charles the Second.

The Ordinance (as it was called) was prepared by the celebrated Oliver Saint John, and bears internal evidence of the ability, discernment, and foresight of that highly gifted scholar and statesman. No legislative decree ever received more serious investigation and elaborate inquiry, both by the Committee and the House itself. The interests of all parties underwent the strictest scrutiny before the Committee, and were subsequently fully discussed by the House. The Parliament (which was, in truth, the Government) was placed in a very critical situation. Their power was newly acquired, and it was evidently their interest to reconcile existing differences, rather than revive old grievances. They felt that a boon was due to the Earl of Bedford and those companions who had shared in the losses and misfortunes of his noble father; but they wercalso conscious that the work of drainage was by no meanspopular throughout the whole of the Great Level. The plans both of Francis Earl of Bedford and the late King, as far as they were developed, seemed greatly to affect the state of the natural rivers, and consequently the interests of navigation -, and hence arose great hostility from the University and Town of Cambridge, (the latter of which was represented by Lieutenant-General Cromwell,) the ports of Lynn and Wisbech, the city of Peterborough, the towns of Huntingdon, Saint Ives, Saint Neots, Bedford, Bury Saint Edmunds, Thetford, and many other places. Nor could Parliament avoid perceiving that considerable difficulty would arise, in the execution of the provisions of the Act, between the conflicting claims and disputes of those who, in consequence of the abandonment of the works, had re-entered upon the lands set out to the adApp.236,253. venturers by the Saint Ives Law of Sewers, and those who claimed under that law. Again, owing to the impoverished state of many of the original adventurers, their lands had been seized, cither by mortgagees, assignees, or creditors, and a great part had been totally abandoned in despair. These things did not escape the penetration either of Saint John or of the Parliament. A court of judicature, or rather of appeal, consisting of the most eminent App. p. statesmen and lawyers of the day, was created by the Act, with power not only to protect the interests of navigation, and to settle contested claims, but also to adjudge when the Level should be properly drained according to the contract, and to give possession to the Earl and his participants and adventurers, of the proportion to which they were consequently entitled.

From this time, the undertaking proceeded with wonderful success; although it will be presently shewn, that, by the passing of this Act, nearly all the works of drainage now existing, and indeed the country itself, were placed in a regular progress towards that degree of perfection which they have since attained; yet the Act itself is not at this period an available law. It would, perhaps, be admitted as evidence (in the same manner as the charter before mentioned) in explanation or support of any right, custom, or usage, sought to be established or continued by the Corporation of the Bedford Level. Probably, no ill effects have arisen, or will arise, from specific enactments being no longer valid. Be this however as it may, the reader is entreated to peruse the document with attention: in truth, it will be impossible for him to follow the course of the author, or become master of the very important subjects humbly endeavoured to be narrated in this work, without a careful and diligent perusal of all the documents which are so frequently referred to, and fully set out in the Appendix.

Under the protection and encouragement of this Act, the Earl and his colleagues, and the subsequent adventurers, advanced with the work. But before we arrive at the result of their labours, let us inquire somewhat briefly into their preliminary proceedings.

This important act passed the House between ten and twelve in the morning; and immediately afterwards, some of the participants and adventurers assembled, and the same was read over; after which it was instantly desired that the Earls of Bedford and Arundel should attend Lieut.-General Cromwell and Commissary Ireton the following morning at seven o'clock, to return "thankful acknowledgements." This circumstance evinces that Cromwell had used all his influence in promoting the measure of drainage. On the following morning the adventurers met at the Lord Whitelock's house, near Temple Bar, bis Lordship being one of the keepers of the Great Seal of England, and also a commissioner appointed by Government. At the meeting were present; — The Earl of Bedford, Sir Miles Sandys, Sir Thomas Thynne, Mr. Edward Russell, Mr. Hewley, Mr. Crane, Mr. Latch, Mr. Gorges, and Mr. Jenyns, who agreed to pay, and did then contribute, "forty "shillings a piece for disbursements of the "clerks' fees of the Parliament for passing and "engrossing the act;" and they also appointed to meet every Monday, Wednesday, and Friday, in the week, at the same place (on which days only it may be observed, the Fen Office is now open to the public, otherwise than by the courtesy of the Register). It appears by the subsequent proceedings of the adventurers, that the whole expense of obtaining the act, amounted to 98*l*. 16. *8d.*; which sum, even in the first instance, was advanced by the Earl of Bedford, and subsequently repaid.

Certainly a very great alteration has since taken place in the hours of meeting of the House of Commons, and a like alteration in the fees paid upon passing private acts of parliament: an alteration, it is true, but, all will agree, by no means an improvement. The present amiable and venerable Earl of Hardwicke, with that alacrity and anxiety which he always evinces in the service of the Fens, kindly made an ineffectual attempt in the House of Lords, in the Sessions of 1828, (by appointment of a committee to inquire into the subject,) to correct the evil arising from the multiplication of parliamentary fees. His lordship however found that the principle of "not interfering with vested inte"rests" was too powerful for his kind and patriotic exertions. He is not the less entitled to the thanks of the country.

The persons who had originally united with Francis Earl of Bedford, and became parties to the indenture of fourteen parts, and their

App.p. 124. heirs, were called "The Participants;" and the persons who subsequently adventured for a share App. p. s-8. of the twenty lots into which the 95,000 acres were divided, were styled "Adventurers;" and fl' tn's reason we find the terms " Participants" and "Adventurers." During the execution of the woɪ'ks under the provisions of the pretended act, ti)e Earl, and the participants and adventurers, were called "The Company." As yet they had not assumed the title of a corporation, although, singularly enough, they are so styled (by antiApp p. 106. cipation) in the Lynn Law.

The Company, soon after the act was passed, appointed five officers to conduct their concerns, namely,—a treasurer, an cxpenditor, a clerk, a director, and a comptroller; denning at the same time their respective duties and remuneration.

It appears that the Company had by no means agreed upon any specific plan of drainage, although they felt a great desire that the works which had been begun by Francis Earl of Bedford, should be made available to any scheme which should be ultimately decided upon. Sir Cornelius Vcrmuyden had become possessed of a large proportion of the 95,000 acres, set out by the Saint Ives Law of Sewers; he had also invited persons of consideration from Holland, who had likewise become proprietors; and he had his legions of workmen, and quantities of materials already prepared: but above all, the country was his debtor. Sir Cornelius was an incubus, a night-mare, which, it will be hereafter seen, the Company vainly endeavoured to shake off. When King Charles undertook the drainage in 1639, he commanded divers persons expert in such adventures to give their advice how the Level might be made "winter grounds?" it being concluded and understood, that the contract with Francis Earl of Bedford extended no further than to make the lands "summer grounds." Sir Cornelius delivered to his Majesty the plan, which will be found in his "Discourse-f-," and to which the reader is particularly referred. Other plans of drainage were also delivered to the Company; but, however solicitous they were to disengage themselves from the trammels of this foreigner, the attempt was ultimately found to be unavailing. Their first application was therefore made to Sir Cornelius; and on the 3d of June 1649, the question of recompense was considered; " when seven of the ad"venturers agreed to give him 4000 acres, and "other seven agreed to give 2000 acres, the "Earl of Bedford only dissenting, being for "three thousand acres; but yet afterwards, to "turn the scale, he consented to 4000 acres." It *ia* said to have been his Majesty's intention, had his plan of a general drainage of the Fens been fully effected, to erect a palace at Manea in the Isle of Ely, (standing upon an eminence,) and to change the name of that place to " Charlemont." † This discourse was ordered to be printed and circulated by the Grand Committee of the Fens.

App. p.sso.

VOL. I. M

At the next meeting of the Company, Sir Cornelius promised to shew his design to such five of the adventurers as the major part of the Company should appoint; but, prior to this being done, the Earl of Bedford acquainted the adventurers with a discourse between him and a Dutchman, relative to the better completion of the works of draining. No name is mentioned: probably it was Westerdyke, who had been previously invited from Holland to advise upon the plan suggested in Vermuyden's Discourse, and was subsequently called in by the Company. It was afterwards agreed, that "any person that "would speak towards the advancement of the "work of drainage, *(in the presence of Sir Cor"nelius Vermuyden,)* should be at liberty to "speak their minds, and should be heard by the A.D. 1649. "adventurers." Soon after this determination, Lieut.-Colonel Dodson (of whom more hereafter) delivered in a design for " setting a sluice "in the river Ouze, and effecting the work of "drainage *by new rivers, and not by banks:"* and it was determined that his design should be subsequently taken into consideration. This probably was the origin of the erection of Denver Sluice, and the cutting of St. John's Eau, particularly as Colonel Dodson was afterwards employed under Sir Cornelius in the execution of the works. On the 19th of June 1649, a large meeting of the Company took place in the Middle Temple Hall, at which were present—

Sir Miles Sandys, Mr. Latch,
Sir Edward Partheriche, Mr. Jenyns,
  Mr. Georges, Mr. Bradley,
  Mr. Fountayne, Mr. Thurlow, (for Mr. Henley, Lord St. John,)
  Mr. Crane, Mr. Spalding,
  Mr. Ingram, Mr. Annesley.

"Sir Cornelius Vermuyden came and delivered "in to the adventurers his ultimate answer in "writing, by way of replication to the adven"turers' answers to his demands formerly given "in, which were read over to the adventurers; "and thereupon they resolved to lay it by, and "enter upon some other business for the present, "and they agreed to propound to the Lordes "what theire sense is thereupon; and further, "that they thought it not fit to depend upon Sir "Cornelius Vermuyden any longer, but make "choice of some other to goe on with this sum"mer's worke, beginninge on the north side of "Bedford River. But yet the Adventurers did "then expresse, that they would determyn no"thing therein themselves, untill they received "the Lordes' concurrence;" and ordered, that "Sir Edward Partheriche, and Mr. John Foun"tayne, to-morrow morning attend the Lordes "for theire direction therein." 163

The following appear to have been the demands of Sir Cornelius Vermuyden: 1. "That when the workes have cost 90000M " from henceforward to bee accompted, then if "more expended, Sr Cornelius Vermuyden is to "pay his part pro rata 4000 acres." 2. "That Sr Cornelius Vermuyden is, and "stands freed of all taxes layd heretofore and "such taxes as from henceforward are layd to be "freed thereof also untill 90000 bee raised." 3. "That after the judgm' of such parts where"in the 4000 acres lye, Sir Cornelius Vermuyden "shall enjoy the same; but he shall have nocon-vey"ance thereof in toto onely for so much as there is "adjudged p. rata and in respecte of which part "the particip-3 have out of the remayninge 90000 "acres." 4. "The Taxes to bee layd out in this yeare "to be 5. the acre, in the next yeares 1650 & "1651 the rest of what the worke will cost, and "the worke is not to bee retarded nor delayed "but to goe on speedily." 5. "That the Comp-trollments touching the "directions may bee so lymitted that it shall "not bee in prejudice to Sir Cornelius in re-spect "of his 4000 acres or otherwise; and that he "shall be freed of the charges and taxes towards "any worke in vaine made, nor bee prejudiced "for the retarding the worke for want of going on "as it should." 6. "The Landes sett out in Fassett and Yax"ley to bee parcell of the 4000 acres, and the re"maynder beinge about 2300 acres to be sett "out indifferently out of the lands sett out in the "severall places of Peterborough Soake. " 7. "The *WOOL* to bee paid mee this tyme "with my convenience." 8. "That hereof may be made articles in due "forme of Lawe."

These demands of "Sir Cornelius Vermuyden "were answered perticular-ly as followetjb:" 1. "As to the first; it was agreed unto as to "the drayninge." 2. " As to the 2d; hee shall be freed of Taxes ' as in respect of the 4000 acres recompense "and onely freed of that as to the makinge of "the workes, not to the repay res after adju"dicatlon of any part. And if hee enjoy the "4000 acres, then any benefitt or recompence "that may bee had or obtayned in respect of "dreyninge or melioration in Crowland, Deep"inge, Ellow, Holland, the North side of Wis"bich, or in any other parts adjacent to the "Level shall come intirely to the adventurers "participants and theire assignes." 3. "To the 3rd; when any proportion of "Land is sett out and adjudged to the adven"turers and participants hee shall have his "equall proportion in that part answerable to "80,000 acres in the whole to be indifferently "sett out; And that no grant made by Sr Cor"nelius of the 4000 acres or any parte thereof "untill the whole Levell be dreyned shall bee "valid or effectuall nor the parties trusted to "make any such Assurance to any Grantee; "And that after the whole Levell is adjudged "dreyned hee shall not passe away above 2000 "acres untill Ten Yeares after the said Adju"dicac'on." 4. "To the 4th; that the Compaine will from "tyme to tyme raise such Taxes as shall be "requisite for carrying on and perfecting of the "worke, and without any delay as concerning "themselves in point of interest." 5. "That no Comptrollm' shall bee made of "any worke designed by Sr Cornelius without "consent of 11 of the adventurers and parti"cipants at least, whereof the Earle of Arundell, "Earle of Bedford, Lord Chiefe Justice S« John, "Mr. Henley, and Mr. Castell, or three or more "of them, to bee of the number; whereby Sr "Cornelius Vermuyden may bee fully satisfied "that there shall bee nothing done therein to "his prejudice in perticuler or to the prejudice "of the Company in generall." 6. "The sixth is answered in the former, "whereby it is resolved to bee indifferently sett "out through the whole Levell equal wth the "adventurers and participants." 7. "To the 7th; that he shall have 300/. att "present and the residue thereof to bee paid by "20/. a month duringe the continuance of the "worke." 8. "To the 8th; that this agreement shall bee "entred as an order of the adventurers and "participants wch is the best security wee can "give and wch shall bee fiwrthw entred as "soone as the designe shall bee approved by the "Earle of Bedford, Lo: Chiefe Justice Sl John, "and Mr. Henley; And if the Lord Chiefe Justice "S' John cannot be prevayled wth to spare to "do it then to desire the Earle of Arundell "to undertake it with the Ea: Bedford and Mr. "Henley."

To these answers of the Company Sir Cornelius Vermuyden replied;— 1. " If the worke bee done substantially as "I intend expect no lesser charges for your "desired Comptrollm' would still call out 'ex"pend not soe nmch, doe not such a worke so "great and so substantiall,' and perhaps a dry "season concurringe you might have it adjudged "and afterwards I might be forced (if not prov"ing sufficient for the floodes) to remake it "and draw mee to contribute upon p'tence of "meyntenance besides the discreditt of the "worke; therefore excuse me to become contri"butory till 90000lb be expended." 2. "The first part is answered in the former; "and as to melioration I pretend nothinge there"in but for to give directions for the dreyninge "in other places. I desire to reserve it to my"selfe in regard you refuse to give mee 5000 "acres upon which I first offerd it." 3. " Upon my proportion of land, and Avhere "it shall lie I stand upon my former note in regard "it lies most convenient for the rest of my estate, "and to have it conveyed accordingly; for I desire "no conveyance in toto pr rata; and for not havinge "power to dispose of my lands I am contented to "keepe 2000 acres for five yeares after the adju"dication, but as to the rest I desire to bee free, "although my present resolutions are not to part "with any part of it neither now nor hereafter. "But under faror I desire to bee Mr of my owne." 4. " I have answered in my note for those taxes ' will be requisite to speed the worke for the "benefitt of all." 5. "To say it shall bee noe prejudice is no ar"gument and my experience is such that in case "you should comptroll I am sure it will bee and "therefore I stand upon yr owne offer which is "that if in case any worke by you comptrolled ' prove ineffectual yet I should enjoy my recom"pence and not be charged with those works." 6. "Is partly answered in the 3ri. And Whereas "some doe objecte that my proportion will be "betterdrcynedthan the rest, I answer it isimpos"sible by reason it lies further from the fall; and "further the land is not to be adjudged but by a "whole Level, and therefore if it be not a general "dreyninge I cannot enjoy my proportion." 7. " I agree to 300/. present and the rest to be "paid by 507. a moneth." 8. " I expect to have it under yor hands and "scales in due forme of Law as also entred in "yor Booke and this is your owne offer. As for "nay designe after wee are agreed I will discover "it to the Earle of Bedford and my Lord S' John "wch is needlesse in regard you take eleven to "comptroll from tyme to tyme although my ex"perience is so well knowne that under favor it is "frivolous, and I cannot hut much wonder that "you put mee to replication having hitherto "prosecuted your busines so long freely without "any stipulation with care travell and charge, and ' withall considering that many desired recom"pense I become a joint adventurer only you con"tribute for me but 4000 acres. And so upon "that small advantage I recover your lost estates, "and gaine to the commonwealth a great and vast "country."

The Earl of Bedford and Lord Chief Justice St. John concurred with the Company in rejecting the demands of Sir Cornelius, and several ineffectual attempts were made to employ other persons. Soon afterwards, the Company appear to have repented of this determination: for on the 29th of the same month of June, it appears, that the adventurers then present (consist iug of the Earl of Bedford, Sir Edward Partheriche, Mr. Annesley, Sir Thomas Thynne, Sir C. Vermuyden, Mr. Henley, Mr. Fountayne, and Mr. Bradley,) took into consideration " the necessity of having an able director "for the worke. Upon debate it was thought fitt "and resolved to make some propositions to Sr ' Cornelius Vermuyden in order to a new "agreement with him if he shall think fitt to

"meete at Peterborough the 4th of July next and "will there treat and agree with the company "meeting there." 1. "To give him 4000 acres for his recompense "for perfecting the worke wth such quallifications "as shall be thought fitt and agreed." 2. "That hee shall have his proportion of 4000 "acres in such parts of the Levell as shall be ad"judged dreyned, according to the proportions "that 4000 acres beareth to 95,000 acres in the "whole." 3. "That hee shall have Three hundred thyrtye "threepoundes six shillinges and eight pence paid "for 3 yeares together, the said some to bee paid "to him at the beginninge of each yeare." 4. " To lymitt the charge of the worke to "95,000lb in the whole." 5. "That if the perfecting of the worke ex"ceede 95,000'b then hee to have but 3000 acres"And if it exceed 100,000lb to have"

There appears to be a hiatus in the order.

The company still evinced considerable caution, indeed, great reluctance to enter into any contract with Sir Cornelius; for on the 24th of the ensuing July, appear the following entries: —

"Resolved that if the adventurers shall here"after agree with Sr Cornelius Vermuyden for "4000 acres, that hee shall not dispose of any part "thereof untill the adjudication of the whole "95,000 acres. And that hee shall not dispose of "above a moytye of the 4000 acres for 7 yeares "after adjudication."

"Resolved and agreed that if the charge of "dreyninge the great Levell of the Fennes shall "exceede the some of 90,000lb then Sir Corne"lius Vermuyden shall become an Adventurer "and pay all taxes for the 4000 acres propor"tionable to the rest of the 95,000 acres untill "the charge of dreyninge amounts unto 100,000'b; "And if the charge thereof shall exceede the "some of 100,000lb then it shall bee at the choice "of S' Cornelius Vermuyden whether he will "become an adventurer and pay all taxes for "the 4000 acres proportionable to the rest of the "95,000 acres from the tyme of the passing of "the Acte of Parliament or loose his recom"pense."

"Sir Cornelius Vermuyden refused to proceede "upon theis propositions and resolves."

"Ordered that upon Saturday the 4th of Au"gust next shall bee a general 1 meetinge of all "the adventurers at Peterborough to counte"nance the worke and settle the same in such a "way as shall bee most conducinge to the good "of the worke in general: To which purpose most "of the Adventurers have agreed and promised "to meete at the place aforesaid (viz1) Earle of "Bedford, Mr Georges, Sr Edward Partheriche, Mr "Robert Henley Senr, Mr Latch, Mr Fountayne, Jphn Fountayne Esq. was a Serjeant at law, and maternal ancestor of the present Richard Fountayne Wilson, Esq. M. P. for the county of York, who still retains very large possessions in the Bedford Level and its vicinity.

"Mr Thomas Jenyns, and Mr Andrew Hen"ley. And it is further ordered that l'res "shall be written to all adventurers that are "absent thereby givinge them notice of this "order and desire their meetinge to bee ac"cordingly at the place aforesaid, And the "Clarke to subscribe the names of all the adven"turers present to every letter."

On the 24th of August following it was finally agreed, "that Sir Cornelius should bring in a par"ticular design and not a general design which "was to be put down in writing under his hand "that so he may not vary from it without the "adventurers' consent; that he should be appoint"ed only to direct the works but not to appoint "any officers; that Lieut' Colonel Dodson, not"withstanding the agreement with Sir Cornelius, "should still be employed as an assistant under "him if he should so think fit; and that Sir Cor"nelius should have a copy of certain proposi"tions made to him by the company in order to "such agreement with him; and also he may have "a Copy of the Act of Parliament (if he please) "delivered to him, upon both of which he might "take advise with his counsel." Thomas Jenys Esq. was the ancestor of the Reverend George Leonard Jenyns, of Bottlsham Hall, near Cambridge, now one of the bailiffs of the Corporation, and chairman of the board, whose vigilant attention to the duties of that important situation, entitles him to the thanks of the country. From the earliest period of any settled plan for the drainage of the Level, the ancestors of Mr. Jenyns have taken most active parts, and have tilled many of the most responsible offices of the Company and of the Corporation.

The company and Sir Cornelius, however, had by no means arrived at any definitive conclusion; for, on the llth of September, he proposed that the particulars in dispute should be referred to the Lord Chief Justice Saint John.

Other matters of the most serious and painful nature now engaged the attention of the Company. They were harassed by the introduction of a bill into Parliament, by Mr. Weston, a rela- App. P. 388. tive of the Earl of Portland, who was the grantee from King Charles of 2000 acres in the Level, part of the 12,000 acres agreed to be given to the App.p. io». Crown, by the provisions of the Lynn Law; but which (together with 10,000 acres remainder of the 12,000 acres) had been omitted altogether in the pretended Act, the whole of the 95,000 acres being thereby vested in the Earl and the trustees, without any reservation whatever.

Soon after this period, Mr. Weston requested to be admitted an adventurer for the 2000 acres, and to have a conveyance thereof from the trustees named in the act, undertaking, at the same time, to pay all arrears and all future taxes; to which request the company acceded. In a short time, the remaining 10,000 acres were sold, and conveyed by the company to different persons. Although the whole 95,000 acres were allotted by the Act to the Earl of Bedford, his participants and adventurers, yet, as soon as the Commonwealth saw the drainage making favor able progress, they made a demand of 3000 acres for the benefit of the state; the company, however, stoutly resisted this unjust and illegal claim, declaring their determination to abandon the undertaking, rather than comply with the demand, which was ultimately relinquished. Upon the restoration, and under the provisions of the General Drainage Act, the 10,000 acres were ApP. P. 390. restored to the Crown, and are now enjoyed by its grantees or assignees.

A. D. 1649. Not only does this claim relative to the 2000 acres appear to have been an annoyance to the adventurers, but they also suffered the greatest embarrassment for want of money to carry on the works then in hand. On the 12th of September are the following entries in the orderbooks of the Company:

"In regard the busines of the 12,000 acres is "not settled whereby many are discouraged to "adventure any moneys and some of the ad"venturers to bring in their Taxes whereby the "worke cannot proceed, It is ordered that the "workmen be paid and forthwith dismissed "until further orders."

"Forasmuch as a present supplie of moneye is "wantinge to satisfie the workmen's wages for "this weeke the Earle of Bedford offered to pay "in the arreares of his second payment in case "Mr. Henley and Mr. Isaac Jones would doe "the like for theires which was accordingly "agreed unto and undertaken both by Mr. An"drew Henley and Mr. Isaac Jones; Whereupon

"terday night after and the workmen still con"tynued noe fault c;m be objected against the "Company for it. Your Letter mentions not "what debt is already contracted to the work"men whome the Company expect be forthwith "dismistand the debt certified hither that order "may be taken for the satisfying of it, Andjn "the meane tyme noe further debt increased or "charged upon the Company untill the business "be setled in parliament and further orders "from them for it which otherwise they appre"hend will be very prejudicial to them. The "Company doe not understand by your Letter "whether the 200/. you borrowed have cleared "all with the workmen or how much will clear "all with them, which they desire to know "speedily. Concerning the 400"' according to "your desire was furnished the last Week which "they apprehended would have cleared all to "the end of that week when the order of dis"mission was sent. As concerning Mr. Prowle "the Gentlemen present make noe doubt but "the Company when they meete will take his "paines into consideration, and in the meane "tyme desire you to supply him with some "money for his present occasions and leave the "further disposal of him at present to your dis"cretion, and desire to knowe from you wherein "hee may be further usefull to the company. "This being that I had in command at present I "subscribe myselfe "Middle Temple, "Yr affectionate servant

"21 SeptM649." "G. S."

X1C To my worthie friends Co" Rob' Castle and Lieften' Colo" Dobson or either of them, these &c."

Difficulties appear to have multiplied, and nothing but the prudence,the unwearied attention, and continued generosity of the Earl of Bedford, aided by the consummate talent and perseverance of Lord Chief Justice St. John, (whose exertions were also unremitted,) could have saved the design from ultimate ruin. On the 27th of September, appear the following entries:

"Whereas divers persons which have no interest "in any of the Adventure Lands belonging to the "Great Levells of the Fens have formerly in' truded themselves into the general meetings ' and consultations of the adventurers and parti"cipants, and thereupon have divulged divers "matters contrary to the true meaning of the "Company and to their great disadvantage. It is "therefore ordered that from henceforth noe per: son or persons whatever that is not an adven' turer or participant doe sitt amongst the adven"turers whilst they are in consultation. But the ' clerke or his deputie is to give them notice of "this order to the intent they may forthwith "withdraw."

"Whereas some of the Company is informed "that Sir Cornelius Vermuyden hath prepared a "petic'on against the adventurers which he in"tends to have read in parliament, a copie "whereof.cannot as yet bee obtayned; And that "Sir Cornelius Vermuyden (as it is alsoe iii VOL. I. N

"formed) hath written to a member of parlia"ment that the Company intends to prejudice "the navigac'on to King's Lynne; It is therefore "ordered, that the agreement wth Sr Cornelius "Vermuyden be from henceforth suspended; And "Mr Henley and Mr Jenyns is desired to conferre "with the said member of parliament and reporte "the contents of Sr Cornelius Vermuyden's letter "to the Company at their next meeting; And "any adventurer thatknowes of any artist which "may be usefull for the effecting of the worke of "dreyninge is desired to present his or their "names to the Company, that soe hee or they may "be treated with as there shal be occasion."

"Whereas the passing of the Act for Mr Weston's "2000 acres hath hitherto bene delayed to the "great prejudice of the Company; And forasmuch "as the speedy passing of the said Act will be of "great advantage to the whole Company, It is "therefore ordered, that the care thereof be "comitted to the discretion of Mr Henley for "the gratifying of such as shal be assistant to the "speedy passing thereof."

"Ordered that everi Adventurer be faithfull "to each other and not devulge any order of the "Company but to such of the Adventurers and "Participants as shal be conformable to the "orders of the Company. Also the Clerke and "Deputy Clerke is ordered not to disclose any "of the Orders to any person or persons that is "not an Adventurer or Participant, and likewise "conformable to the orders of the Company."

The distresses of the Company still encreased; A. D. ie». for, at a meeting held on the llth of October following, the following entries were made:—

"The Company being in debate of raysing "moneye to pay the 450lb due to the workmen, "have ordered the clerke to write several Ir'es "to the adventurers under-written to paye in "their arreares of both payments of the taxe of "2. 6d. pf acre according to the effect of the "letter following (viz').

"At a meeting of the Adventurers on the llth "of this moneth, I was commanded by them to "acquaint you they have lately received letters "from Colo"

Castle and Leiften' Colo" Dodson, "that for want of moneye to pay the workmen "they fall into mutinies and seize upon the offi"ccrs and threaten to cary them away and cut "them in peeces in case they have not speedy "payment; And that divers of the Adventurers "have already paid both their payments of the taxe "of 2. Rrf. pr acre, and some more; They there"fore desire you, for the preventing of this great "mischiefe, to preserve the reputac'on and honor "of the Company speedily to make payment to "the Treasurer of your proportion of the said

"taxe in arrere, which is as they conceive.
"This is that which was given
"in command
"Your Servant,
"By them to" "G. S."

No doubt can exist, that Sir Cornelius VerihDyden was at the bottom of all the intrigues that operated so greatly to the disadvantage of the Company; and that, observing their reluctance to his appointment, he threw every obstacle in their way. The struggle of the adventurers demands both sympathy and admiration. But turn which way they would, escape from this inexorable Dutchman was hopeless. Accordingly, on the 27th of October, at a numerous meeting, consisting of the Earl of Bedford, Sir Miles Sandys, Sir Thomas Gardiner, Sir Edward Partheriche, Sir Thomas Thynne, Mr. Henley, Sen', Mr. Ingram, Mr. Fountayne, Mr. Isaac Jones, Mr. Crane, and Mr. Carill, the following order was passed:

"It was putt to the question, whether Sir Cor"nelius Vermuyden should be the director or not, "and resolved in the affirmative."

"Whereas upon the 11th of September last Sir "Cornelius Vermuyden proposed to the Com"pany that the particulars in difference between "them and him might be referred to the conside"ration of the Lord Chiefe Justice St. John; "It is now ordered that his Lordship be desired "to take the same into his consideration, by "whose order the company are content to be "bound, soe as Sir Cornelius Vermuyden in "convenient tyme enter his consent in the "clerke's booke to be likewise bound there"by." Ancestor of the present Marquess of Bath, created on the 16th December, 1682, Uarou Thynne of Warminster, Wilts, and Viscount Weymouth.

' Sir Cornelius Vermuyden is to have notice "of this Order."

Again, on the 26th November, Mr. Gorges, one of the adventurers, was ordered to confer with Sir Cornelius, that he might bring in his final demands to the company on Thursday then next, that the business between him and the company might be brought to a conclusion; but on that day, Sir Cornelius not having entered his consent to the reference to the Lord Chief Justice, according to the order, both parties were considered at liberty; but five of the adventurers were ordered to attend his lordship upon the difference still existing between the company and Sir Cornelius: and on the 7th of December, Sir Cornelius delivered in his final demands in writing, from which he would not recede, which the company declared to be unreasonable, in regard that Sir Cornelius refused to undertake the work upon any certainty, or to deliver any particular design, or to be subject to any control.

Sir Cornelius was well acquainted with the extent of his power over those with whom he was dealing so cavalierly. The treaty being once more abandoned, several propositions were made to, and considered by the adventurers, the particulars of which may not be uninteresting.

"Mr. Hamond proposeth to the Company, that "for 30,000'b a gentleman will give caution of "4000'b for the dreyning of that part of the "Great Level which lyeth betweene Bedford "River and Welland, according to the Act of "Parliament. Whereupon the Company have "ordered that Mr. Hamond, Mr. Marsham, and "Mr. Latch, treate with the gentleman touching "the same and to know his lowest demands and "the utmost caution hee will give for the per"fonnance thereof; And alsoe the severall works "hee intends to make and the dimensions of "them, together with the tyme when he will "finish them and the places where, with all other '" circumstances conducing to the worke, and "report it to the Company at their next meet"ing to-morrowe at 2 o'clocke in the after"noone."

"Sir Edward Partheriche proposeth to the "Company that for 30000lb to be paid at "King's Lynne, Wisbich, or Peterborough, by "5000'b p. Mensem, the first payment to be "made on the 10th day of January next, beside "what moneyes are already disbursed, and "makeing use of sach tymber and materialls "as are already bought, hee will undertake to "dreyne the north part of the Great Levell of "the Fenns lying betweene Bedford River and "Welland, and within one yeare next ensuing so "performe the same worke according to the act "of parliament fitt for judgement. And hee will "give caution of 4000lh to perform the same. "To effect which hee hath delivered in his designe "in writing of such workes as hee conceaves neces"sary. And he is content to adde thereunto a "sufficient in-drayne to the north bank of Bed"ford river, and to make the south part as well as "the north, if the said Sir Edward Partheriche be "chosen Director of the worke on the south "side."

"And whereas it was alleadged that the worke "must be made slighte to spare money for the un"dertaker's proffitt, Sr Edward Partheriche offers "that for the consideration of 1000lb hee will un"dertake to perfect the said worke for 30000lb to "be paid vt. sup. (accompting the moneys already "disbursed since the passing of the act of parlia"ment to be part thereof). And hee will deliver "an accompt to the company for all the money "that shal be disbursed in the said worke and "restore the moneys unexpended to the company. And in case the charge of the said worke beside "what is already disbursed as aforesaid shall ex"ceede 26000'b, then Sir Edward Partheriche is "content to accept of 500lb for his recompence. "And if the same shall exceede 30000'b beside "the moneys already disbursed, then hee is "willing to loose his whole reward."

"Ordered that if any other man will propose "or tender to the Company any other way or "designe for the dreyning of the Great Levell or "any parte thereof, and upon what conditions hee "will undertake the same, the Company will take "the same into consideration."

"Mr Henley declaring that there were several "propositions of Sir Cornelius Vermuyden and "others to be considered of, Sir Cornelius being "present declared to the Company that hee ut"terly disclaymed to medle or have any thing to "doe with the dreyning of the fenns, and that hee "came only as an adventurer."

Mr. Henley had been appointed Treasurer to the Company, upon the resignation of the Earl of Bedford. He was evidently a person of great influence in other respects with the country, and had always evinced a marked partiality towards Sir Cornelius, conceiving, probably, that his great apparent wealth best enabled him to carry the work into execution: finding, therefore, that matters were likely to take a turn unfavourable to the interests of Sir Cornelius, on the 10th of December, he made the following proposition j— ff Mr. Henley offers to the Company, that if Sir "Cornelius Vermuyden be Director of the worke "he will engage 4000 acres which hee hath "already and 4000 acres which hee hath and will u purchase, that Sir Cornelius shall with or under "the charge of 109,700lb to the Company, "(viz.) 33,900lb for the north part of Bedford "River, and 76,200Ih for the south side thereof, "doe the worke according to the act of parlia"ment, otherwise he will loose his 8000 acres; "And that the Company shall have that pro"portion of the defaulters' lands at the same "rate which hee hath already purchased it at "towards Sr Cornelius his 4000 acres recom"pence, and that hee will before the worke bo "finished, purchase so much more of the do"faulters' lands as shall make up the said pro"portion full 4000 acres for Sir Cornelius his "recompence, which the Company shall like"wise have at the same rate it shal be pur"chased at."

"And Sir Cornelius demands 1000lb to be ' paid to him, as was formerly resolved by the "Company."

"Mr. Henley offers that if any man will prof pose a better bargaine and more advantageous ' to the Company than this, that it may be "accepted and taken into consideration."

"Sir Cornelius demands over and above 270"" ' per annum for one surveyor and fovver over"seers during the contynuance of their imploy"ment".

"Ordered that Mr. Gorges, Mr. Henley, Mr. "Latch, and Mr. Hamond, peruse the propo"sitions and estimate of Sir Edward Parthe"riche and Sir Cornelius Vermuyden, and con"sider which may be most essential and ad"vantageous to the Company, and tomorrow at "10 o'clock to report their opinions to the Com"pany."

"Mr. Henley offers to pay the taxes for the "8000 acres which he proposes to engage if Sir ƒ Cornelius Vermuyden be the director during "the worke, and will lose both land and taxes "if Sir Cornelius do not perform the work aa "hce shall undertake it."

"Mr. Henley is content Sir Cornelius shall "have his fifth lott, and he will accept of the "4000 acres which he hath and is to purchase "in lieu of it soe as he may enjoy the said "4000 acres and may receive I0000lb from the "Company for the said fifte lott in case hee "cannot enjoy the 4000 acres which hee hath "already and is to purchase as aforesaid, "and "Mr. Henley desires to be defended from suite "touching the same/'

"Mr. Dodson offers to engage 1000lb to make "a river from the outfall at the Horse-shoe to "Murroe Gate 50 feet wide for 5500lb, with "banke sufficient to secure the country, and "to repaire the same worke for 7 years after "the same shal be made; And for200lb more hee "will undertake to pay for all the lands which "shal be purchased for the said worke."

"Sir Cornelius Vermuyden offers to dreyne the "south parte of the Levell for that proportion of "land that is to be sett out to the Adventurers "as their recompense on that side of the Level."

"Sir Cornelius excepts in the 4th article, ex"emptions of lands, charges of commissioners' "meetings, solicitations, suits, and officers' sala"ries."

"Resolved to meet tomorrow morning at nyne "o'clock, and then or in the afternoone to cou"sider whoe shall be the director of the worke "of dreyning, and upon what terms it shall be "undertaken; And if the same cannot be agreed "by consent then to putt it to the vote for a

"conclusion, and nothing else to be treated on or "debated untill the director be chosen."

"12lh Decr. Anno Dom: 1649. "Ordered, that notice be forthwith given or "lefte in writing at the several habitations or "lodgings of the Adventurers following, desiring "their meetinge at two o'clocke in the after"noone, to agree upon a director of the worke "(viz.)

"Sir Cornelius Venmiyden was desired by the "Company to deliver in his ultimate demands. "In pursuance whereof he delivered in his de"mands in writing written with his owne hand."

"Whereupon the Company desired that Sr Cor"nelius Vermuyden should sett down what workes "he would undertake to do on the North part of "the Levell and the dimensions of them, and at "what rates and for what rewards."

"Sir Cornelius answered that he would doe "such workes as shall be sufficient to make the l(land fitt for judgement; And as to the dimeu"sions he saith he can only give it here in the "generall, for that there may be occasion to vary "upon the place; And for the rate of that worke "he proposeth 33000lb at the utmost, and saith "it may peradventure be dope for 2 or 3000lb "lesse. Yet he refuseth to undertake the same for "33,000lb. And for his reward hee demands "1000lb, and the proportionable part of 4000 "acres which he formerly demanded for the "whole worke, which he computed to be 2400 "acres."

"In pursuance of an Order made at the last "meeting, the Company upon reading the several "propositions and demands of Sir Cornelius Ver"muyden and Sir Edward Partheriche, insisted "upon the chosing of the director; And the "question being put, whether Sir

Cornelius Ver"muyden or Sir Edward Partheriche should be "the director of the works, the major part of the "Company declared themselves for Sir Edward "Partheriche, as followeth particularly (viz'.)" of which, and of the adjoining parish of Stretham, he was Lord of the Manor, and had granted to him by the Charter of Incorporation (1634), the privilege of holding a weekly market and two annual fairs at the latter parish. He was the common ancestor of the present Marchioness of Downshire (Baroness Sandys in her own right), and of Sir Edward Bayntum Sandys, Bart,, of Missenden Park, in the county of Gloucester.

"Sir Miles Sandys,
"Sir Tho-Thynne,
"SirTho'Gardiner,
"Mr. Hamond,
"Mr. Latch,
"Mr. Carill,
"Mr. Dodson,
"Mr. Williams,
"Mr. Browne,
"Mr. Allen,
"Mr. Lukins,
"Mr. Bradley,
  "Mr. Henley,
"Mr. Ingram,
"For Sir Edward
Partheriche.
"For Sir Cornelius
Vermuyden."

"Alsoe the Company unanimously agreed to "proceed in the woi'ke of drayning according to "the latter of the twoe propositions of Sir Ect"ward Partheriche of the 8th Decr instant, *"nemine contradicente."* "Ordered that Colo" Castle, Mr. Hamond, "Mr. Marshall, Mr. Latch, or Mr. Jenyns in his "stead, and Mr. Crane, or any twoe of them, be "desired by the Company to be constantly upon "the works to husband the same for their best "advantage, and that there shal be an allowance "of 4Ob p. mensem for such twoe of the Ad"venturers as shal be upon the place (viz1.) 20Ib "a peece for soe long as there shal be occasion "for their residence there."

"13lhDecr. 1649.
"Ordered, that the papers which Sr Cornelius "Vermuyden demands from the Company be "forthwith ent'red into the Journal Book and "restored to Sr Cornelius."

Vermuyden being once more rejected, the adventurers were again compelled to seek for aid in carrying on the works; and accordingly we find the following letter, addressed to the Earl of Norwich:

"May it please your Lopp.

"The Adventurers in the Great Levell of "the Fenns have this day mett and have been Goring Earl of Norwich. This title became extinct in the year 1672. It was afterwnrds granted to a branch of the noble house of Howard, and becoming extinct in the year 1778, was again granted to the Duke of Gordon, who, in the year 1784, was created Earl of Norwich, in consequence of his descent from Lady Elizabeth Howard, eldest surviving daughter of Henry Earl of Norwich, whose title had become extinct in

"informed of your Lordpp« honorable regard to "the Company and well wishing to the worke; "And that yor Lopp upon conference with some "of the Company hath been pleased to expresse "that you would bring in from beyond the Seas "persons of estates and artists to advance the "worke, have commanded me to signifie to yor "Lopp that the Company is nowe absolutely "broken off with Sr Corneylius Vermuyden as "to the direction of the works, and have made "choice of Sir Edward Partheriche to be their "director, whoe hath undertaken to doe such "works as in the opinion of the Company will "dreyne one hundred and fowerscore thousand "acres or thereabouts within the space of one "yeare, and that they shall friendly receive "strangers whoe are men of estates, whoe may "have good bargains for their money, and alsoe "men of skill in works of this nature, whoe may "have good rewards for their paines; In which "perticuler as the occasion requires they desire "yor Loppe speedy answere. This being all I "have in command I crave leave to remayne

"Yor LoppB most humble Servant

"Middle Temple, "George Smith,
"14 Dec'. 1649. "Clerke to the Company."

The noble Earl does not appear to have taken any notice of this application. The agreement between Sir Edward Partheriche and the Company was prepared; but on the 22d Dec. it was oi'dered, that Sir Edward Partheriche be desired to declare to the Company on the following day, whether he would adhere to the latter of his two former propositions or not, or whether he would not undertake the draining1 of the north part of the Level, unless he undertook the whole. To this proposition, it seems, that no answer was returned by Sir Edward: he was unable to cope with the wily and indefatigable Dutchman. On the 1st Jan. 1650, the following very curious entries were made:

"Sir Cornelius Vermuyden offers to demon"strate to the Earle of Bedford, the Lord Chiefe "Justice S' John, Sr Miles Sandys, Sr Edward "Partheriche, Mr Henley, and Mr Latch, that Sr "Edward Partheriche his designe is destructive to "the worke of dreyning in divers perticulers; "Whereuppon it is ordered, that to morrowe "morning at nyne of the clocke Sir Cornelius "Vermuyden demonstrate the same accordingly "in writing; And the said Earle, the Lord Cheife "Justice, and the rest of the Gentlemen before "mentioned, are desired by the Company to re "ceave the same and to declare their sense there"uppon to the Company; And Mr Carill and Mr "Jenyns were presently desired to acquaint the "Lord Cheife Justice herewith and to desire.his "Lopp to be p'sent at the demonstration thereof."

"2nd Jany 1650,
"Ordered, that Sr Edward Partheriche, Mr Hen"ley, and Mr Latch, do consider of the nomination "of nyne of the adventurers and participants as "are most fitt for the management of the whole "worke of dreyning on the behalfe of the Com"pany, and of all such powers and circumstances "as shal be requisite to enable them thereunto; "And they are desired to deliver their sense "touching the same to the Com-

pany as soone as "may be."

"10th Jan 1650.

"Ordered that the nyne adventurers hereafter "named or any five of them shall have full power "for the management of the whole worke of "dreyning accordinge to the order of the second of "January instant; But as to the setting of taxes, "selling of land, and takeing of acco'8, it is to "be done as formerly if this order had not bene "made."

"Ordered that the fower grand days in the "yeare, viz. Candlemas day, Assension day, Mid"summer day, and All Saints day, are appointed "dayes for a generall meeting of the whole Com-"pany at nyne of clocke in the forenoone, where-"by they may receave an acco' from the nyne "Adventurers or some of them by the appoint"ment of five at the least that are chosen for the "management of the whole worke of dreyning, of "all their proceedings; And if any of the Grand "dayes fall upon the Lord's day then such meet"ings are appointed the next day following."

"Ordered that everie adventurer and parti"cipant enter in the clerke's booke by CandleVol. i. o
' mas day next at his perill the place in London "where and the partie with whome hee will "have notice lefte upon any occasion touching "the proceedings in the worke of dreyning of "the Great Levell of the Fenns, to the intent "he may be advertised thereof from tyme to "tyme. And all the adventurers and parti"cipants are to take notice hereof at their pe"rills, whoe are to be concluded by the orders "of the rest of the Company."

"24th January 1650.

"A draught of Articles of Agreement betweene "the Company and Sir Cornelius Vermuyden "touching his being director of the worke of "dreyning was read, and upon the reading "thereof assented unto and agreed as well by "the Company as by Sir Cornelius Vermuyden; "Whereuppon it is ordered that the said ar"tides shal be ingrossed and the com'on seale "of the Company put to one parte thereof by "Mr. Henley Treasurer to the Company, and to "be delivered to Sir Cornelius Vermuyden, the "said Cornelius Vermuyden sealing and deli"vering the other parte thereof to the use of "the Company."

"25th January 1050.

"The Articles of Agreement betweene the "Company and Sir Cornelius Vermuyden being' "ingi;ossed accordjng to a former order, the "clerke in Mr. Henley's absence is ordered to' "put the com'oa scale of the Company thereunto, "and to enter one parte thereof in the booke "of Entries."

"According to a clause in the Articles of "Agreement betweene the Company and Sr "Cornelius Vermuyden, the said Sr Cornelius "Vermuyden declared his designe to the Com"pany for their approbation; and upon debate "and consideration thereof, his designe was ap"proved of in the generall, being conceaved "by the Company present a probable way to "*effect* the worke of dreyning according to the "Act of Parliam'."

Thus finally triumphed Sir Cornelius Vermuyden; and the consequences of his victory are felt at the present period. The reader will not, perhaps, complain that he has been so long detained by the consideration of these proceedings; they are essentially important, inasmuch as the plan adopted under them occasioned the works of drainage extant even at this day. We will now proceed to consider what particular works were executed under this contract; and then discuss, not only the merits of the plan itself, but the opinions entertained thereon by persons of skill and science; and submit at the same time some biographical notices of those eminent and exalted personages who were united with William Earl of Bedford in this arduous undertaking.

CHAFFER IX. *Division of the Great Level.— The North, Middle,*
and South Level.—Their respective works of
Drainage, 8$c. Commission of Adjudication.—
Proceedings with reference to the South Level.—
Employment of Scotch prisoners.
Division of the It is necessary, before we describe the works ultimately executed under the plan finally adopted by the Company, to state, that Sir Cornelius Vermuyden had partitioned the Level into three

App. p.349. divisions: the North, the Middle, and the South; by which names they are distinguished and known at the present day; and will presently be distinctly and separately noticed with reference as well to their respective boundaries, as their internal works of drainage. Each of these Levels has its particular rivers, banks, works of drainage, and outfalls to sea.

North Level The exertions of the Company appear to have been first directed to the drainage of that part of the Level which had more particularly engaged the attention of the original Adventurers. The lands lying between the Welland River and Morton's Leam were called the North Level. The former river the Company defended by a bank, beginning at Peakirk, running to Crowland, and onwards to Brotherhouse, there uniting it with Holland Bank, which bank (as all the great banks generally were) was made seventy feet broad at the bottom, and eight feet in height. The waters of the river Nene, descending from Northamptonshire, were also restrained by a like bank extending from Peterborough to Guyhirn. The natural drains, such as Shire Drain, &c., were scoured out and opened. The outfall by Shire Drain, and the sluice at Tyd St. Giles, continued the same. The sluices that had been set in the marshes, at an expense of 25,000/., were all lost and abandoned. The Company also made some very judicious improvements in the navigation from Wisbech to Peterborough, by forming a river, now called Smith's Leam, as a continuation of Hill's Cut, made by Francis Earl of Bedford.

The Company also defended the Middle Level Middle Level from the overflowing of the Northamptonshire waters, (a sasse or sluice having been previously erected at Standground,) by a large bank from Standground to Guybirn, where it unites with the great Waldersea bank. This bank was raised, chiefly upon the foundation of that which had been originally begun by Bishop Morton, and was subsequently continued by King Charles the First. The waters of the river Ouze were restrained by a great bank, extending from the high lands of Over in the county of Cambridge, near Over-Cote, to the Hermitage near Earith, where a navigable sasse or sluice Was erected, to tnro the upland flpods out of their natural channel, by Ely, into a new river cut by the Company, called the New Bedford, or One Hundred Feet River, (parallel with the Old Bedford River, cut by Francis Earl of Bedford,) commencing a short distance below the great bridge over the old river Ou?e, near the Hermitage, and running thence in a nearly straight line to the great sluice at Denver, in the county of Norfolk. The earth coming out of this river was laid on the south side thereof, and formed into a bank of threescore feet wide jjt the bottom, ten at the top, and eight feet in height. Another great bank was also made on the north side of the Old Bedford River, thus leaving a very large space of land, containing upwards of 5000 acres, called the Washes, for the floods " to bed in," to use the quaint expression of Sir Cornelius Vermuyden.

The Company also cut or completed several artificial rivers; viz. Vermuyden's Eau, or the Forty Feet Drain, extending from Welch's Dam to the River Nene, near Ramsey Meer; Hammond's Eau near Somersham, in the county of Huntingdon; Stonea Drain, near March, in the Isle of Ely; Moore's Drain, or the Twenty Feet Rivev, also in the parish of March; Thurlow's Drain, or the Sixteen Feet River, extending from the Forty Feet to Popbam's Eau; and Conquest Lode, leading to Whittlesey Meer, and dividing the parishes of Yaxley and Farcett, in the county of Huntingdon.

They also cut a new river, called the Tong's Drain, or Marshland Cut, without the boundary of the Great Level, in order to obtain a quicker passage for the floods than could be procured by the circuitous course by Well Creek and Salter's Lode; sluices being placed at both ends of the drain. Considerable improvements were made in Whittlesey Dike, Popham's Eau, and the Old River Nene.

In order to turn the tidal waters into the One Hundred Feet River, as well as to prevent the upland floods reverting up the Ten Mile River towards Littleport, that great bone of ancient and modern contention,—Denver Sluice, was erected.

Some trifling embankments only were made, south Level (beyond the great bank already mentioned) for the protection of the South Level against the upland waters descending by the Cam, and also the Mildenhall, Brandon, and Stoke Rivers.

The greatest work intended for the benefit Downham, or

Saint John's of the South Level, was the cuttmg ot a large Eau. river, of one hundred and twenty feet wide, and ten feet deep, extending from near Denver Sluice to Stow Bridge, for the conveying away with greater facility the flood waters descending from the several rivers within the Sooth Level.

All the artificial rivers cut by the adventurers bore the name of some influential member of the Company. This river was intended to have been called "St. John's Eau," in compliment to Lord Chief Justice St. John; but it appears by the following entry in the Order Book of the Company, that this honor was declined by his Lordship:—

"25th April, 1651.

"Mem: That a letter be written to Sir Cor"nelius Vermuyden upon the motion of Mr. 'Thurlow on behalf of the Lord Chief Justice "Saint John, that the name of "Saint John "Eau" may be spared and some other name be "given thereunto." It was ultimately called "Downham Eau," from its vicinity to that place.

Sluices were also erected at both ends of this river.

Two new sluices were erected at Salter's Lode, and at the mouth of the Old Bedford River, for the purposes of drainage and navigation, and the prevention of the influx of the tidal waters into the Middle Level; and a dam was made across the old Bedford River, called Welch's Dam, (a person of that name being then employed as one of the surveyors of the Company,) to turn the waters of the Forty Feet into the Old Bedford River, or to the outfall near Salter's Lode, by which dam the upper part of the Old Bedford River to Earith became abandoned, and has been since used only for the purpose of private and district drainages.

Divers small drains were also cut, such as Grunty Fen Drain, near Streatham, in the Isle of Ely, and others;—Reach, Swaffham, and Bottisham Lodes were scoured out, straightened, and enlarged; and most of the works begun by Francis Earl of Bedford were completed .

The Company also set out the following public ways, bridges, and forelands.

One highway from South Eau Bank to the North Bank of Morton's Leam, by the adventurers' grounds in Sutton Fen, by Gold Dike, of 30 feet wide.

A highway of 60 feet wide, leading from Whittlesey to Upwood Hards, and to run through the Fens of Whittlesey, Ramsey, and Upwood.

Another highway of 40 feet wide from the Stedds, where it crosses and meets with the former at Bevill's Leam, unto Ramsey, along by Delphe's Dike and the lotted high grounds of Ramsey, called Michwood.

A way upon Vermuyden's Eau Bank, leading from Bedford Drain through the Fens of Byall, or BalstaffFen, Doddington, Chatteris, and Ramsey, and from Vermuyden's Eau up to Ramsey Town, as should be found most convenient.

One way, leading from Warboy's Wood to Vermuyden's Eau, of 60 feet wide, called Puttock's Drove, through the Fens of Wistow, Ramsey, and Warboys, and so to be continued to Copholder Bank, on the outside of the Adventurers' Dike of

Dikeamoor, and where Dikeamoor is parted by a cross line, to lead on that way to BenwickTown.

One way, leading from Mepal to Chatteris Hards, commonly called Ireton's Way, through the Fens of Mepal and Chatteris, and so up through the common to the highway of Chatteris.

One way, leading from Marsh to Whittlesey, of 40 feet wide, by the bank of Ransom Moor, adjoining to Burrow Moor, and so through West Fen and Whittlesey Fen to the Gravel near the Cotes, and so to Whittlesey.

One way, from Morton's Leam South Bank, along Shaw's Dike, to cross the highway that leads from Whittlesey to Doddington, and to be continued so far that all the lot lands in West Fen might have passage that way unto Vermuyden's Eau Way.

One way, leading from Upwell to Honey Hards, and so through the Fens of Upwell, Doddington, and Chatteris.

A way crossing the former from Wimblington to Manea, by the bank called Stonea Bank, and so by Oxwillow Lode to the bridge upon the Were Dike, near Bedford Drain.

One way, leading from the bridge upon Well Creek, upon London Lode Bank, to Calsy Dike, through the Fens of Upwell.

One way, from Friday Bridge, along by Elm Leam, through Elm Common and Creek Fen, unto March Stream.

. Another way, upon the bank from Eastwood over to Stonea, and so on upon the cross bank to Binnamoor, and thence through Binnamoor to meet with the highway that goes by Elm Leam to Friday Bridge.

One highway upon Waldersea Bank, from the Chain to Hobb's House, and so along the Cross Bank to Guyhirn.

One other way, upon Coldham Bank, and so along the drain that now goeth that way on the north side thereof.

A highway from Peakirk to Guyhirn, to be made along the drain that now goeth that way on the north side thereof.

Copholder Bank, to be a common highway for the adventurers.

A highway in Somersham over the corner of the fourth lot into the second, if there should be need, which may be seen upon the place; the rest were to have passage by the highway then already made, and by such lands as should be found needful.

A way between Wenney Farm and Langwood Fen, and those lands there between the 8, 2, 3, and 12 lots, to a bridge to be made over the Forty Feet Drain next or through Mr. Russell's land in Byall Fen, for Witcham men to come to their mead-lands, as should be thought most convenient by the surveyor.

On the South Side of Bedford River.
A highway of 40 feet wide from Southery Town to Feltwell, leading through Southery and Feltwell Fens.

Another way of 30 feet wide, leading to Brandon River from the former, betwixt the Severals of Sir Thomas Woodhouse and Felt well Mow Fen, and by the adventurers' grounds in Feltwell Severals.

A highway of 40 feet wide, passing from the Ouze to Littleport, Chaire, and so along by the adventurers' dikes of Whelpmoor and Burnt Fen, up by Shippey Farm, Beggar's Lode, and Mildenhall Fens, up to the high grounds of Mildenhall, and to the nearest and most convenient highway there.

Two ways, meeting with the former, of 30 feet wide, one in Whelpmoor, betwixt the 6th lot and the adventurers' pieces in Whelpmoor, abutting upon the Ouze. Another near Undley, crossing Pope's Lode to Lakenheath Severals, in such sort that every piece there might be way'd out.

A highway from Ely Middle Fen along by the river to Prickwillow, and from thence along by the River Ouze to the end of Mildenhall River, and up by that river unto Isleham.

A highway from Littleport to Southery Ferry, and so through Mr. Skipwith's grounds to the Great Sasse at Saiter's Lode, and Dam upon the Ouze, and to Downham Bridge, along the Old Ouze, 60 feet wide.

The bank of Sir Edward Partheriche to be continued to Crouchmoor for a highway.

A way leading from Welney to Littleport Causey, in Westmoor, of 60 feet wide.

A way from Pyemoor Plain to Downham in the Isle, to answer the way from Manea, upon Oxwillow Lode, of 60 feet wide.

A highway from Wicken to Reach Lode, of 30 feet wide, along by the adventurers' grounds.

A convenient way to be set out for the adventurers' proportions about Burwell and Reach.

A droveway from Mepal to Welch's Dam, of 60 feet wide, by the south bank of Bedford Drain, which bank was to be reserved for planting of wood for preservation of the north bank.

A highway to be made along by the drain that conies from Fordham Brook to Prickwillow.

For Forelands, North Side.
Between Croyland and Peakirk, 60 feet to be set out for a foreland next to the bank in the Wash, the dike anciently made along the bank not to be accounted.

The foreland between Croyland and Brotherhouse to be at the inside of Porsand, where none was to be had at the outside.

From Guyhirn to Peterborough, on the North Side.
A foreland of 60 feet to be made on the Wash side, the Old Dike not accounted, until they come at the firm clay ground, and there to leave it.

From Guyhirn to Eldernell and the High ground also 60 feet foreland on the Wash side.

From thence to the Hards of Whittlesey 60 feet foreland at the inside to be taken.

A foreland of 60 feet wide to be made, from the foot of the north bank of the Wash, by Bedford Drain, which foot of the bank was to be continued three feet over the dike that was to be filled up, and this to be continued from Welch's Dam to Salter's Lode, which dike was to be 12 feet in Ihe top, and so to continue proportionably until it should be 20 feet at the outfall into Ouze.

From Mepal upwards to Earith, also a foreland of 60 feet, to be lockspitted out, as afores.iid, below Mepal.

On the South Side.
The Company were to take from or near Swasesey Hards to Mepal, and thence unto Salter's Lode, on the inside of the south bank, 60 feet foreland, the Weredike not accounted, excepting the hard lands near Mepal.

Upon the several rivers of Grant, Mildenhall, Old Ouze, Brandon, and

Stoke, on each side of the said rivers next the bank, 60 feet foreland to be set out at the outside thereof, and where there was no place wide enough at the outside, then to be taken at the inside of the banks beyond the Were-dike.

Additions by Sir Cornelius Vermuyden.
A way to join unto Yaxley Drove-way, for the most convenience of their lands and the town.

A way to Fassett, and along the Division Dike of the adventurers' lands set out in Fassett.

A way to strike up to Whittlesey by one of the highways set out in Whittlesey, going to the Commons of Fassett.

A way to go from the said lands to the high way that goeth to Upwood, which might be done by or along Underwood's Drain, or otherwise as the surveyor should see most convenient, by Bevill's Leam, highway, or otherwise.

Many of these highways are now lost by disuse; others are become parochial roads; and the rights of the corporation in many of them entirely neglected.

Bridges.
One bridge over the New River, called Bedford River, at Sutton Gault.

One other bridge over the said New River at Mepal Town.

One other bridge over the said New River, near Oxwillow Load.

And one other bridge over the said New River at Welney Town.

Also one other bridge over Bevill's Leam, leading from Whittlesey to Ramsey, now called Pon's Bridge.

i
These immense works were not carried Oh without considerable interruptions and temporary delays, sometimes occasioned by failure of pecuniary resources, sometimes by want of the requisite number of labourers, and at others by hostile appeals to the commissioners of adjudication appointed by the act. These appeals were generally foi injuries done to the navigation, or claims for damage sustained by individuals or towns during the progress of those works. Again and again was the Earl of Bedford compelled, not only to pay his taxes in advance, but also to join in giving security for sums borrowed, and to make advances of money to many of the participants. His liberality was unbounded, his perseverance astonishing, his attendance unremitted. His lordship had evidently acquired, not only a complete knowledge of the subject, but also the habit of conducting the business of the Company, and of amalgamating the discordant materials of which the meetings were too often composed. In his endeavours to carry into execution this most arduous and patriotic undertaking, he enjoyed for some time the co-operation and concurrence of the Earl of Arundel, which concurrence, however, did not long continue; and, amidst other mortifications, the Earl of Bedford was doomed to witness the desertion of his noble friend and fellowlabourer in this great cause. On the 19th of April, 1651, the Earl of Arundel sent his agent to a meeting of the Company, to inform them, not only of his intention to pay no more taxes, but that the Company might dispose of his land as they thought fit; and soon afterwards the whole of the lands belonging to the Lord Arundel, amounting to 5900 acres, were sold to William Stephens, of the Middle Temple, Esq., for the sum of three Henry Frederick, Earl of Arundel and Surrey: he was summoned to parliament in the life-time of his father, as Haron Mowbray. His lordship married Elizabeth, eldest daughter of Esme Stuart, Earl of March, afterwards Duke of Lennox shillings and nine-pence per acre, and the Earl took no further interest in the work of drainage. About the same time, Sir Thomas Thynne, the ancestor of the present Marquess of Bath, also retired from the Company. Whatever might have been their motives for withdrawing from this perilous undertaking, it doubtless helped to multiply the difficulties of the Company, at that period in a woeful state of pecuniary distress. The Lord Chief Justice Saint John still adhered firmly to the cause; and without his skill, legal advice, and determined perseverance, that cause would probably have been entirely abandoned.

Let us here pause to put upon record some particulars of this highly gifted individual—one, to whose memory the Great Level of the Fens owes, even at this distant period, the tribute of unbounded respect and gratitude. Francis Earl of Bedford was a man of great discernment of character; he was proud of cultivating talent, and of fostering genius. He must himself have been possessed of no small calibre of mind to have discerned the merits and become the protector of Pym and of Hampden, as well as the patron of Saint John.

Oliver Saint John was a near relative of the Earl of Bullingbrooke, one of the parties to the App. p. in. Indenture of Fourteen Parts; and a family alliance existed with the house of Russell. Under these circumstances it is probable that Francis Earl of Bedford became acquainted with those rare abilities, which were afterwards so essential to the suc Vol. i. p cess of a cause so near and dear to his (St. John's) early patron. In the year 1630, Oliver Saint John was admitted a student of Lincoln's Inn. He was the eldest son of Oliver Saint John, of Cavenham, in Bedfordshire. Being attached to the cause of liberty, he was soon (through the influence of his noble patron) raised to consequence, having, under his auspices, been elevated to the situation of Solicitor General. It is said, that the King, upon learning that Saint John had connected himself with the parliamentary leader, vainly attempted to conciliate and win him over to the royal cause. Saint John was appointed one of the Parliamentary Commissioners of the Great Seal; then Attorney General; and upon the death of Lord Chief Justice Banks, he was constituted Lord Chief Justice of the Common Pleas. He held situations under the Commonwealth through all the revolutions. He was of the council of state in the years 1649, and 1650. He was fixed upon by the parliament to go into Holland, as ambassador from the Commonwealth, after the murder of Dorislaus. This embassy proved ineffectual, and Saint John, after an absence of a few months, returned to England.

In all probability, his journey into Holland extended his knowledge of those works of drainarft, in the progress of which he still continued to taKe a most active and prominent part. It must be confessed, however, that he deserted his patrons at the restoration of King Charles the Second; and was perhaps too justly accused of ingratitude by the friends of the Commonwealth. Although this desertion presents an unfortunate blot in his escutcheon, yet his memory ought ever to be cherished; and he himself must ever be entitled to the highest praise and gratitude, as the projector of the Act of Navigation, the real foundation of the naval greatness of England; the principles of which have been recently most sacrilegiously overturned by vain sciolists and theorists, unfotunately backed by a House of Commons neither returned by, nor sympathizing with, the feelings and wishes of a brave and generous nation .

The English government had in rain attempted to cement an intimate commercial union with the republic of the United Provinces. Saint John's embassy had proved a complete failure. Having now received every kind of contumely and affront, the parliament determined to adopt such proceedings as they conceived must be conducive to the welfare and prosperity of their country, without being restrained by any tender regard to the interest of their neighbour Commonwealth. Both states were obviously commercial. The Dutch possessed a country of little produce, and could scarcely subsist, certainly could not become opulent, but through the medium of trade. Great Britain was an island with many ports, and every convenience for shipping. She could not defend herself from the ambition or insolence of her neighbours, hut by means of her navy. At the same time, her soil was fertile, and her manufactures prosperous. The two countries were therefore, in the common construction, rivals. Such, very properly, was the opinion of the English statesmen. They desired, in the first place, a perfect union of interests. But if that could not be effected, they looked, in the next place, to whatever could render their commerce flourishing, and their navy powerful.

The assistance of Saint John was important to William Earl of Bedford, not only from his high judicial rank and character, but from his natural influence with the commissioners of adjudication and appeal established by the act. Those commissioners held their sittings with great regularity; receiving with attention all complaints; deciding with much caution, and the utmost impartiality; counsel were heard at considerable length; the most eminent men at the bar were

It was, doubtless, this train of ideas that led to the Act of Navigation, which was prepared by Saint John, and was brought into Parliament by that able and acute stateman Uulstrod Whitlocke. The more Saint John had reason to be dissatisfied with his late adventure to Holland as a statesman, the more determined he seemed to persist in the occupation. He was a man of much subtlety of invention, and great resources of ingenuity and refinement; but all these advantages had been lost by the perverse turn the Dutch negotiation had taken. He resolved not to be finally judged by that unfortunate specimen, but in some way to shew himself to (he world for what he was intrinsically worth. We owe, therefore, in some degree, to the miscarriage of Saint John's embassy to Holland, the strenuousness and energy of his subsequent labours.

The famous and immortal Act of Navigation was brought into Parliament the 5th of August, 1651, and received its final sanction on the 9th of October following. The provisions of this law were, that no produce of any of our colonies should be brought into this country, but in ships, the property of England or its colonies; and that no produce or manufacture of any part of Europe, should be brought here, but in ships, the property of England, or of those countries respectively of which the goods were the proper produce nnd manufacture.
retained on both sides; and the court seemed to attract general attention. Nor can this be matter of surprise, when we consider that this court was composed of the most distinguished and learned men of lhat very enlightened period of English history.

But to return to our subject.—The works proceeded with rapidity, and without any material interruption, although not without occasionally encountering the collision of conflicting interests. The commissioners of adjudication were indefatigable in their attendance; constant attention was given to the numerous petitions presented to them; and their decisions appear, upon the whole, to have given satisfaction. At length the period arrived when the Earl and the other adventurers thought they had made such progress in the drainage, as entitled them to call upon the commissioners for an adjudication, and the consequent allotment of a proportionate part of the 95,000 acres which had been already set out by the Saint Ives Law, but under which law no legal possession had been given. The commissioners cheerfully entertained the application, and took immediate steps to ascertain whether they could, with an honest and consistent discharge of a great public trust, comply with the request. They appointed a special court to be held at Wisbech, and directed the Company not only to attend the meeting, but also to give previous notice to all the towns included in that part of the Great Level which was stated to have been drained, of such intended meeting, in order that the commissioners might hear if any complaints yet existed against the proceedings of the Company. The commissioners also desired the Company to be prepared with evidence to prove the completion of the contract, as far as they required adjudication. The following proceedings prove that the commissioners proceeded with great caution and circumspection, and cannot be otherwise than interesting to many readers of this work.

"Die Veneris, 28 die Febr. 1650.

"Comission" present in the Middle Temple "Hall:

"Lo: Com'. Whitelocke,., Keepers

"Lo: Comr. Lisle, J Great Seal.

"Sr John Danvers, "Mr. Eltonhed (one of "Mr. George Goodwyn. the Welch judges),

"Mr. Henrie Darley, "Mr. Steele, Recorder

"Col. VaL Walton, of London." "S'

John Trevor,

"Whereas the Adventurers for dreyning of "the Great Levell of the Fennes acquainted "the comissioners at their meeting this day "in the Middle Temple Hall, that they had "(at their great costs and charges) dreyned

"Some little confusion and error may perhaps occur at thia period as to dates, arising from the circumstance of the year then commencing on the 25th of March.

"a rreat part of the said Levell, viz.: That

"part thereof lyeing on the North side of Bed

"ford River; and thereof they desired that

"the Com" would by such meanes as they in

"their wisdomes shall thinke fit, satisfie them

"selves, to the end that they may adjudge the

"same dreyned, and give the Adventurers pos "session of their severall proportions within App. 375,375.

"the said part of the Levell alleadged to be

"dreyned as aforesaid, according to the intent

"of the said acte: Whereupon and upon read

"inge of that part of the said acte, the said

"Comissionrs thought fitt and did agree to

"adjourne their meeting to Wisbich, and from

"thence to Peterborough; To the end they

"myght both by view and by examination of

"witnesses upon oath, satisfie themselves of

"the truth of what the Adventurers alleadged;

"And accordingly doe adjourne unto Wisbich

"the 21st of March next, and from thence

"they doe agree to meete at Peterborough on

"the 24th of the same month; And did like

"wise order, that notice should be given to

"the country of the said two severall meet

"ings; And did likewise issue forth two

"warrants under their hands and scales, for

"the attendance at such respective meetings."

The lords commissioners arrived at Wisbech on the day appointed, and at the first meeting and session the following lords were present:

"Lord Comr Whitelocke, " William Leman,

"Lord Comr Lisle, "John Sadler,

"Sir John Trevor, "Edward Eltonhed,

"Sir John Bouchier, "Jeremiah Whitchcott."

"Talbott Pepis, Recorderi of Cambridge,'

This meeting was held at the Schoolhouse in Wisbech. Several petitions were presented to the lords commissioners, and the respective parties heard thereon; after which they adjourned to meet at Peterborough, on the 24th day of March.

commission at "At a meetinge and session of the lordes and

Peterborough.,........

other coimssioners, m pursuance or the acte "of parliament for dreyninge the great Levell of "the Fennes, by adjournment, held at Peterburgh, "24th of March, 1650:

"ComTM present at the Towne Hall at Peterburgh."

"Lo: Comissr Whitelocke, "Mr. Talbott Pepis,

"Lo: Comissr Lisle, Recr of Cambridge, 1

"Sr John Trevor, "Mr. Leman,

"Sr John Bouchier, « Mr. Sadler, J "Mr. Whitchcott."

"Edward Lyons (after the acte of parliament "read over) made oath, that on 10th March in"stant, he gave notice of the comissioners' meet"inge at Wisbech, 21, and at Peterborough, 24th

"March instant, unto 31 parishes hereafter fol"lowinge, viz'.,

Chartris,

Somersham,

Conington,

Glayton and Holme,

Stanground,

Glinton,

Peterburgh,

Crovvland,

Outwell,

Caldicott,

Warboys,

Wood wal ton,

Upwell,

Upwood,

El me,

"Mepoll,

"Wisbich,

"Stilton,

"Fassett,

"Ramsey,

"March,

"Doddington,

"Peakirke,

"Whittlesey Sl Maries,

"Whittlesey S' Andrews,

"Denver,

"Sutton in Holland,

"Salterie,

"Eye,

"Sutton in the Isle,

"Names of the witnesses examined this day, "whose depositions are enrolled in Chauncery, "are as followeth:

"Wm. Stringer, "John Turner,

"George Glapthorne, "Robert Margeram,

"Thomas Measure, "Robert Burton."

"The said lords and other comissioners doe "adjourne to meete againe in the Towne Hall of "of Peterborough aforesaid, to-morrow morning, "being the 25th of this instant March."

"ComissionTM present in the Towne Hall at "Peterborough, on Tuesday, the 25th of March, "1651;

"& John Trevor, "Mr. Leman,

"Mr. Talbott Pepis, i "Mr. Eltonhed, Rec' of Cambridge/ "Mr. Sadler,

"Mr. Whitchcott."

"Names of the witnesses examined this day, "whose depositions are enrolled in Chauncery, "are as followeth, viz1.,

"George Glapthorne, "Jonas Moore, "Ro. Burton, "John Turner,

"Nich. Palmer, "Tho. Saundy,

"John Rayner, "Geo. Preston,

"John Man, "Wm. Caterell,
"Wm. Collins."
"The said comissioners doe adjourne to meete "againe in the Minster Church at Peterborough "forthwith."
"Comr present in the Minster Church at "Peterborough, on Tuesday, being 25th of March, « 1651;
"Lo: Com" Whitelock, "Mr. Leman,
"Lo: Comr Lisle, "Mr. Sadler,
"Sr John Trevor, "Mr. Eltonhed,
"Sr John Bouchier, "Mr. Whitchcott.
"
"Mr. Talbott Pepis,
Recorder of Cambridge,/
"Upon hearing many petitions, Mr. Attorney "Hall, Attorney Genl of the Dutchie, of counsell M with the Earl of Bedford, his adventurers and "participants, humbly moveth, That in regard it "appeared to the comTM, by their owne view and "cleere testimony of witnesses, that all that part "of the Levell, lyeing on the north-west part of "Bedford River, conteyninge one hundred and "seaventy thousand acres, or thereabouts, was "dreyned according to the acte of parliament in "that behalfe, at the charges of the said Earle, "his adventurers and participants, which had "cost them above 170,000/., that the said com" "would proceed to adjudge the same dreyned "accordingly, and to give seizen and possession "to the sayd Earle, Edward Russell, Robert appp"Henley , and Robert Castell-f, EsqTM, and their "heires, upon the trust in the acte of parliament, "of their proportion of the 95,000 acres, lyeing "within the part of the Levell dreyned, which "was heretofore sett forth in October, in the 13th "yearc of the late King Charles: Whereupon the "comTM doe order to advise thereon, and do ad"journe from hence presently to the signe of the "Angell, in Peterborough, where they will fur"ther heare what can be said on either side."

"Comissioners present at the signe of the "Angell, in Peterborough, the '25th March, 1651.
style, and title of Sir William.Russell, of Chippenhani, in the county of Cambridge. The patent bears date 16th Jan. 1629-30. This dignity was conferred upon him for his many years' services as Treasurer of the Navy. Sir Edward Russell was buried at Chippenham. The estate was afterwards purchased by the Earl of Orford, then became the residence of George Montgomery, 'Esq., and is now in the possession of a very elegant and hospitable family of the name of Tharpe. Robert Henley, Esq. , was ancestor of Baron Henley, afterwards created Earl of Northington, (Lord High Chancellor of England,) which title became extinct in the year 1787. t Robert Castell, Esq., was the owner of a very considerable estate at Glatton, in the county of Huntingdon. He was the maternal ancestor of that branch of the Sherard family, which hus for many years resided in the county of Huntingdon; the present representative of which family is Castell Sherard, Esq., who occasionally resides at Godmanchester. In the event of the death of the present Earl of Harborough without male issue, the ancient Irish barony of " Leitrim" will descend to Mr. Sherard, the earldom and English honours becoming extinct. The family still are, or lately were, the owners of the estate at Glatton.

"Lo: Com' Wbitelocke, "Mr. Leman,
"Lo: Com' Lisle, "Mr. Eltonholt,
"Sir John Trevor, "Mr Sadler,
"Sir John Bouchier, "Mr. Whitchcott"
"The sayd comiTM, upon their owne view and App.P.srs. "testimony of witnesses, are satisfied, and doe "adjudge that above 30,000 acres of the said "Great Levell of the Fennes, viz'., All that part "of the Great Levell, lyinge on the north-west "part of the Bedford River, and conteyning "170,000 acres, or thereabouts, are dreyned ac"cording to the true intent and meaning of the "said acte of parliament."
"The sayd Comissioners, according to the App. p 376. "power given to them by the said acte of par"liament, doe give unto William Earle of Bed"ford, Edward Russell, Robert Henley, and "Robert Castell, Esqrea, and their heirs (upon App. p. 372. "such trusts as are mentioned in the said acte "of parliament) seizen and possession of his "and their proportions of the 95,000 acres, "lyinge within the quantity of acres adjudged "dreyned as aforesaid, as the same have here"tofore byn sett forth in October, in the I3th "yeare of the raigne of the late Kinge Charles, "To be holden of the mannor of East Green"wich by fealty onely, in free and common "soccage, and not otherwise, Subjecte never"theles and lyable to such alterations, burthens, "recompences, and powers, as in the said act "are expressed."

"It is ordered, that an instrument be pre"pared, conteyning the aforesaid adjudication, "and delivery of seizen and possession, accord"ing to the true intent of the aforesaid ad"judtcation, seizen, and possession, whereto the "Comrs will put to their hands and scales; "And that one part thereof may be enrolled "ui Chauncery for safe custody, and the other "part remaine with the Earle of Bedford, his "adventurers and participants; It is ordered, "that a warrant bee drawne according to the App. p. 381. "power given them by the sayd acte of par"liament, directed to the several Sheriffs, and "all other officers and ministers of the respec"tive countyes in which the sayd Fenn "Grounds doe lye, to require them to be "aydinge and assistinge according to the true "intent of the said acte of parliament, to be "signed and sealed by the said Commissioners."

"It is ordered by the said ComTM, that care "be taken that such depositions and exami"nations as are taken in writinge by the Co"missioners, may be enrolled in Chauncery for "safe custody."
"The said Commissioners present doe ad"journe to meete againe at the signe of the "Angell in Peterborough aforesaid, at 9 o'clocke "to-morrow morning, being the 26th of March, "1651."
"Comissioners present at the Angell, in "Peterborough, on Wednesday, 26th of March, "Lo: Comr Whitelocke, "Mr. Recorder Pepis,
"Lo: Comr Lisle, "Mr. Eltonhed,
"Sr Jo: Trevor, « Mr. Sadler,
"Sr John Bourchier, "Mr. Whitchcott.
"
"Mr. Leman, ,
"Names of the witnesses examined

this day, "whose depositions are enrolled in Chauncery, "are as followeth, viz'.,

"Algernon Peyton, "Wm Palmer, "Edvd Bellamy."

"The said Comissioners, in pursuance of "their former order, did sett their hands and "seales to an Instrument or Acte of Adjudi"cation, consisting of seven skins of parch"ment, which is to be enrolled in Chauncery, "for safe custody; And alsoe the said Com"issioners did then and there, in pursuance of "the said order, sett their hands and seales "to a warrant, directed to the several sheriffs "of the respective countyes to be ayding and "assisting according to the intent of the said "acte of parliament, a true coppie of which "warrant followeth in theis words, viz'.:

"Bulstrod Whitlocke and John Lisle, two Adjudication. "of the Lords Commissioners of the Great "Scale of England, Sr John Bourchier, Knl, "Sr John Trevor, Kn, Talbott Pepis, Esq., Wil"Ham Leman, Esq., John Sadler, Esq., Edward "Eltonhed, Esq., and Jeremiah Whitchcotb

"Esq., Comissioners amongst others by an "Acte of this present Parliament, for dreyning "the Great Levell of the Fennes, extendinge it"selfe into the countyes of Northampton, Nor"folke, Suffolke, Lincolne, Cambridge, and "Huntingdon, and the Isle of Elie, or some "of them, to doe and acte as by the said acte "of parliament is appointed, To the severall "Sheriffes for the tyme being of the said severall "countyes of Northampton, Norfolke, Suffolke, "Lincolne, Cambridge, and Huntingdon, and "to all other officers and ministers of all and "every the said respective countyes, greeting; "Wee have, according to the powers given us "by the said acte of parliament, after our "owne view, and upon full hearinge of all pe"titions and objections offered, and examination "of witnesses upon oath, touching the dreyning "of the said Great Levell of the Fennes, at a "session held by adjournment at Peterborough, "in the said countye of Northampton, the 24th "day of March, 1650, adjudged all that part of "the said Great Levell of the Fennes lying on "the north-west part of Bedford River to be "dreyned in such sort as by the acte of parlia"liament is appointed to bee dreyned; amount"inge in the whole to One hundred and seventy "thousand acres or thereabouts; and in further "pursueance of the powers given to us by the "said acte of parliament, have by an instrument "indented under our hands and scales, given "unto William Earle of Bedford, Edward Rus"sell, Esq'., Robert Henley, Esqr., and Robert "Castle, Esqr., and their heires, upon the trusts "in the sayd Acte of Parliament expressed, seizen "and possession of fiftie-eight thousand two "hundred acres one rood and fifteen perches "particularly expressed in the said instrument "indented, lyinge within the said bounds of the "said Great Levell, parcell of ninety-five thou"sand acres heretofore sett forth in October in "the thirteenth yeare of the reign of the late "King Charles, To be holden of the manner of "East Greenwich in fee and common soccage "by fealty only, subject and lyable nevertheless "to such alternate burthens powers and recom"pences as by the sayd Acte of Parliament the "same are subjecte and lyable unto: And there"fore by virtue of and according to the autho"rity given us by the sayd Acte of Parliament "Wee hereby will and comand you and every "of you to be ayding and assisting in all and "singular the premises as you will answer the "contrary at your perills. Given under our "hands and scales at Peterborough the 26th "day of March, Anno d'ni accordinge to the "English accompt 1651."

"B. Whitlock, (l. s.) "Wm: Leman,
"Jo: Lisle, (l. s.) "Jo: Sadler,
"Jo: Trevor, "Edw: Eltonhed,
"Jo: Bourchier, "Jer: Whitchcott."
"Tal: Pepis, VOL. I. Q

This Act of Adjudication, and the depositions of the witnesses, were subsequently enrolled in the High Court of Chancery.

The Earl of Bedford and several of his participants attended the meetings of the Lords Commissioners of Adjudication, both at Wisbech and at Peterborough. The attainment of this adjudication was of the utmost importance to the interests of the Company. It proved the feasibility ef the measure; it gave confidence to the proceedings; it reinvigorated those whose efforts had slackened in despair, and whose hearts had sickened with hope deferred. In short, it placed the undertaking upon a firm and stable system, by giving to the several adventurers a legal title, and a positive possession of the several lands included within the limits of such adjudication. Much, however, still remained to be accomplished. Nothing had been done towards perfecting the drainage of the South Level; and the works already executed in the other Levels required constant care and perpetual expense. The Earl of Bedford did not relax in his exertions. It was the peculiarity of his character, in proportion to the multiplicity and magnitude of the difficulties by which he was surrounded, to possess energy of his mind, to contend with, and to vanquish them. What pen can do justice to the virtuous efforts, and the extraordinary exertions of this amiable and benevolent nobleman? Why has his memory, and the memory of his noble father, slumbered for ages, unnoticed in the silent tomb? Was there no pen able and willing to record an imperishable testimony of their patience, their perseverance, and their philanthrophy?— Statues ought to have been erected to their memories in every town and village within the Great Level; and parents should have taught their children to lisp in gratitude the names of these incomparable noblemen, the firm, the persevering, the watchful guardians and benefactors of a country regenerated by their unceasing exertions.

Immediately after the adjudication, the Earl Proceedings of Bedford called a general meeting of the Com-to the soutu pany, to take into consideration the state of the South Level, and the best mode of draining the same; at which meeting it was agreed, after some serious debates, that Sir Cornelius Vermuyden should present to the Company a specific plan, which he accordingly did; and the execution of the works was entrusted to his care, as director general. This plan will be more fully detailed in the progress of this work. The projected scheme of drainage advanced at first but slowly. Great difficulties arose in collecting the taxes imposed by the Company. Persons interested in the navigation between Cambridge and Lynn abated nothing of their original hostility to the measure, and the great mass of the people still continued adverse to a general drainage: hence, considerable inconvenience was experienced from the inability of the Company to procure a sufficient number of workmen. Another cause, besides disinclination in the people, doubtless occasioned this inability; namely, the existence of a very heavy debt to the poor labourers, as well on account of the proceedings of Francis Earl of Bedford, as of those of the King. In the year 1651, a petition was actually presented to the Company, and to the Commissioners of Adjudication, by upwards of 500 labourers, praying the payment of 5000/. then in arrear to them, and which it appeared continued undischarged, in consequence of one of the adventurers (Mr. Latch) having misapplied a very large sum, which ought to have been appropriated to the payment for certain works executed by these unfortunate petitioners. This circumstance, no doubt, added to the general dissatisfaction, and distrust of the honour and pecuniary means of the Company.

In the year 1650 was fought the memorable battle of Dimbar, when the whole Scotch army, commanded by Leslie, was completely overthrown by the consummate skill and bravery of Cromwell and his courageous and enthusiastic soldiers. It is said that three thousand Scotch were killed, and ten thousand taken prisoners. These prisoners were sent into England, and distributed in various towns. Some of the adventurers suggested, that, as their progress was impeded by the want of workmen, it would be highly desirable to employ a proportion of these Scotch prisoners in prosecuting the designs of the Company; and, accordingly, a successful application was made for this purpose to the government. The following proceedings, relative to this singular negotiation, may not be unentertaining to the reader.

"1 October, 1651.

"Memor: That Mr. Fountayne and Mr. Hen"ley are desired to take a view of the Scotch "prisoners, and to entertayne so many of them "as are willing to bee employed in the service of "the Compie on the workes, and to advise with "my Lord S' John w' is fitt for the Clomp1 to doe "theirin, and what condic'ons the Compie shall "bee bound unto."

"11 Octor. 1651.

"The Comple havinge lately recd an order from "the Counsell of State for imployinge of the "private Scotch prisoners in the workes of drayn"ing, did order that a letter bee written unto "my Lord Chiefe Justice Saint John as fol'loweth."

"May it please y' Lordshipp. "The greatest part of all our tyme this weeke "and the last hath been spent in contriving "which way wee might best dispose of such of "the Scotch prisoners in Totchill Fields as "were able to worke, and the State should "please to entrust us with, for preventing theire "runninge away, or acting any thinge preju"diciall to the present Government, and keeping "them at worke: To that ende, wee did resolve and propose to become petitioners to his ex"cellencye the lord generall, that hee would bee "pleased to appoint some person in nature of "a provost marshall to whome the Companie "would allow a reasonable salary for his "service to take the care of them, and prevent "their straglinge, and punish the offender; "and wee intended to have clothed them all in a "white habite, or some other colour, with cappes "of a different colour, whereby they might bee "known from Englishmen; and lay a charge upon "our overseers and officers in the workes, if any "of them were absent from theire workes, or "did oppose the established government, to give "present notice to the provost marshall, who "had the charge of them, to apprehend and pun"ish them as the state or his excellencye should "please to directe. And wee did hope that they "might have byn brought into so good discipline "as, receiving a fitting reward from us for theire "labour, they might have had just cause to blesse "God for the parliamentary mercy to them. By "an order from the counsell of state, of the 10th "of this instant, we understand that security is "required to pay *5l.* for every man (exceedinge "10 in a 100"), which shall goe beyond Trent, or "which shall act any thinge prejudicial to the "state, which is an engagement the companie "are fearefull to enter into for persons of theire "qualitye and condition; and therefore, unless "the state shall be pleased to take off the secuK rityе by theire order required, and accept other "said proposalls, which, as wee conceive, is all wee "cann safely doe, wee dare not meddle with "them, which wee thinke our duty to make "known to your lordshipp, beinge very sorry for "your lordshipp's trouble in this busines, for "which, as wee have just cause, wee shall ever "acknowledge your lordshipp's favor intended to "the companie herein, and expressed upon all "occasions both to the companie in generall and "to your lordshipp's most humble servants,

"John Fountayne, "John Latch, 'iiih Oa

"Robert Henley, "Roger North,

"John Trencbard, "Thomas Alleyn."

"14«Octor. 1651.

"Mr. Say, Mr. Trenchard, Mr. Henley, Mr. "Fountayne, and Mr. Latch, or any two of them, "are desired to wayte on his excellency the lord "generall, to obteyne a warrant for the delivery "of the Scotch prisoners, for the use of the com"panic, according to the order of the counsell "of state, and to make the best contract they can "tout-hinge the said prisoners, and with least "prejudice to the Companie, and to procure "the delivery of the said prisoners at Erith if "they can."

"Mr. North, Mr. Trenchard, Mr. Fountayne, "and Mr. Bradley, Mr. Henley, and Mr. Traf"ford, or any two of them, are desired to take a "list, and view and make choice of such of the "Scotch prisoners as they shall conceive fitt for

"the service of the Companie, in order to the "sendinge of them to the

Fennes."

"Memorand: To imploy the Scottish prisoners "first for securing the adjudged part from the "country, and to perfect the general! workes "of the Companie on the north side of Bedford "river, before they bee imployed on the south "side."

"Whereas the counsell of state have thought "fit, by their order of 13th October, 1651, to "appointe such Scottish prisoners as are fitt and "able to worke to be sett on worke by the Com"panic in the workes of the Fennes. And "whereas Major Miller, Major of Colonell Baxter's "regiment, hath recommended one John Johnston "for a person very fitt to receive and take the "care of the said Scottish prisoners according to "the said order. It is therefore ordered, that the "said John Johnston doe reeceive the said Scot"tish prisoners, and hee is to take care that the "said Scottish prisoners, or any of them, doe not "depart or absent themselves contrary to the "said order; but cause them to bee sett on worke "in such sort as the Companie, or five or more of "them, or their officers in the Fennes, shall from "tyme to tyme directe; and for his paynes hee "shall receive a fitting sallary, to bee paid him "by the receivor or expenditor for the Com"panie, for which this order shall bee theire "warrant."

"15th October, 1651.

"Ordered, that Thomas Bunbury and Hugh "Famham or one of them do receive at Erith "one hundred and sixtie six Scotch prisoners "from Corporall Foster, for the use and service "of the Companie of Adventurers for dreyninge "of the Great Levell of the Fennes, and to give "a receipt for so many as he shall receive, not "reckoning women or boys, hee or they giving "security to Gualter Frost, Esqr, Secretary to "the Counsell of State, accordinge to an order "of the Counsell of State of the 13th of Octo"ber 1651."

"Ordered, that Thomas Bunbury and Hugh "Farnham, or such as shall receive the Scotch "prisoners from Corporall Foster to the use and c service of the Company, shall be disposed and "imployed in the workes of dreyninge as An"thony Hamond, John Thurlow, and John "Walker, Esqrt", or any of them, shall directe "and appointe."

"Ordered, that all the officers of the workes "in the Great Levell of the Fennes shall use "their best endeavours to prevent all or any of "the Scotch prisoners nowe sent down from "goinge beyond Trent without the leave of those "that shall bee authorized by the Counsell of "State or the Adventurers for dreyninge the "said Great Levell in pursuance of the order "of the Counsell of State of the 13th of October K 1651."

"Ordered, that John Kelsey be overseer in "chiefe of all the Scotch prisoners; And wherein "hee shall find any thing amiss or defective in "them or any of the workes of the whole Levell, "to endeavour the amendment; And forthwith "to certifie the Companie the truth of the same; "And for his sallary hee shall receive and have "ten shillings sixpence a weeke for the yeare "ensuing, to begin from this daie, whereof hee "shall hare nyne shillinges paid unto him weeke"ley or nionthley as hee shall desire, and the "rest at the yeare's ende."

"It is ordered, that the clarke of the Companie "do once every month certifie to the Councell "of State the number of the Scottish prisoners, "and what decrease there is of them eyther by "death or otherwise; And all the officers of the "Companie, in case of absence or death of any "of them, are forthwith to certifie the same to ' the olarke of the Companie; and however "once every month to certifie the Company "what number of Scottish prisoners are upon "the works."

"Ordered, that Mr. Jessop, receiver of the Com"panic, do pay or cause to be paid all such some "or somes of money as have or shaH be expended "and layd out in order to the going down of the "Scottish prisoners as shall be set down in wriC"inge, and allowed by Robert Henley and John Fountayne Esq"3."

"Ordered, that 666 yards of white kersey, not "exceed inge the rate of *2s.* or *2s. 3d.* the yard, "bee contracted for, which is to bee made use "of in makinge clothes for the use and service "of the Scottish prisoners now sent downe into "the Fennes; And Co" Samuel JoneSj one. of the "members of the Companie, is desired to contract "for the same for the best advantage to the "Companie; whereupon the Companie allowinge "thereof, Mr Jessop the receivr is to make "payment accordingly."

"Memorand: That Mr Bradley is desired to "make enquiry of the price of cappes, which "are to be bought and sent downe for the use "and service of the Scottish prisoners, lately "sent downe upon the workes."

"Memor: That Mr Trenchard is hereby con"tended, and doth agree to be responsible for "one William Cristen, and Mr Trafford doth the "like for one William Worley, two of the Scot"tish prisoners; and they doe undertake that the "said prisoners shall be ready at the disposal "of the Companie whensoever they shall think "fitt."

"Ordered, that a letter be written, and sent "downe to Mr. Hamond and Mr. Thurloe, &c., ' with copies of the several orders made this day, "whereby they may be acquainted with the "proceedings of the Companie as touching the "goinge downe of the Scottish prisoners to be "imployed in the workes of the Fennes."

"IfV October, 1651. "It is ordered by the Companie of Adventurers "for dreyninge the Great Levell of the Fennes, "that the bearer hereof, Thomas Bunbury, doe "with all convenient speede repay re to Yorke, "and apply himself to the comander of the "guard of the Scottish prisoners there, and to "desire to see them drawne forth, and thereby "to informe himselfe how many able persons "there are of them hayle and sound, without "wives, and willinge and accustomed to labour; "and forthwith to return the Companie acco1 "thereof by the first post; that according to an "order of the Councell of State in that behalfe "of the 13th October, 1651, the Companie may "provide for the disposal of such of them at "Peterburgh as are fit for theire service."

"Ordered, that Thomas Bunbury doe receive "them at Peterburgh, and give security as hee "hath done for those att Totchill Fields."

"Ordered, that a letter be written to Sr Will"1 "Allanson to desire him to write to the Com"missioners at York, to send to Peterburgh all "such Scottish prisoners as Thomas Bunbury "shall allow of, and certifie the tyme when they "shall bee there."

"Ordered, that Mr. Walker, one of the mem"bers of the Companie, bee desired to goe downe "to Yorke, there to exercise power of comptroll "over Thomas Bunbury, in the choice of the "Scottish prisoners, and that none bee chosen "but men hayle and sound of bodie, and able "and fitt for labour."

"22d October, 1651.

"Proposition beinge made for some gratuity "to bee given to Corporall Foster, and the con"voy that went downe with the Scottish pri"soners; whereupon the Companie ordered, that "theire receiver do give them fortie shillings as "a gratuity from them."

"Motion was made that the Companie would "entertayne some Scottish prisoners that are "now at Nottingham, and they shall be deli"vered at Erith, without any charge to the "Companie."

"Memor: Mr. Trenchard is desired to treat "with some man to provide shoes for the service "of the Scottish laborers, some to be of 12, some "13, and some of 14 sizes."

"Ordered, that Mr. Fountayne, Mr. Henley, "senr, Mr. Latch, and Mr. Brown, or any two "of them, are desired to meete to-morrow morn"inge, and then agree for the sending down of "cappes, for the service of the Scotch laborers, "and at what rates and prices, and to conclude "and agree for the same."

"23rd Octor. 1651.

"Ordered, that Mr. Jessop, receiver of the "Companie, do pay all such several bills of "expences as are to bee paid for and towards the "provision of clothes, shooes, and other neces"saryes, for the service of the Scotch prisoners "imployed in the workes; the said several "bills beinge first approved of and signed by

"Robert Henley and John Fountayne, Esqres; " and this order shall be the receiver's war"rant."

"5th November, 1651.

' *A* question beinge put, whether or not the "Company will have any more Scotch worke"men imployed on the workes, it was resolved in ; the affirmative."

"Another question beinge also put, how many "more shall be imployed, it was resolved there "should bee as many more imployed as will "make up those now imployed a thousand "Scotch workemen."

"14th Nor. 1651.

"Upon reading a letter from Mr. Walker, at Yorke, of the 1 Ith ins'., it is ordered, that a letter "gbe sent unto him as followeth, (viz.)

"Sir, "Your letter from Yorke, of the 11th inst'., the "Companie received the last night, and upon "reading thereof thought it not necessary to "write more unto you than onely to refer you to "theire former letters, wherein they signified "their resolutions of havinge as many of the "Scotch prisoners at Yorke as are fitt for theire "service; and that you should do your best to put "the charge of conducting them to Peterbargh, "or at least some part thereof, upon the country; "and likewise to delay the receivinge of them as "long as you could, without endangering the "totall loosinge of them. They intreat you to "pei-sue the instructions you received in theire "said former letters, and tymely to give them "notice when the Scotts will bee at Peterburgh. "For shooes and stockins wee know not how to "avoyd the providinge of so many as are neces"sary, and wholly leave it to your discretion to "manage it for the best advantage of the Com"panic. For the allowance in theire march you "must do it as cheape as you can. Those that "went from hence were allowed *4d.* per diem, "and 20. over for the whole number, but wee "are informed that was too little; wee take no "care of money for you, in regard your letter "sales you may bee furnished by Mr. Berry, "whose bill the Companie will take care to pay "forthwith. This being all in charge, I rest, "Sir,

"Your humble Serv'.,
R. H."

"19'" Nov., 1651.

"There is an order of Parliament made this"daie, that it is death without mercy for any of "the Scotts which run awaie, and it is now print"ing, and it shall be sent you by the next; and "the Company expect that Kelsey and the pro"vest marshall, John Stan, take care for retaking "such as are or shall run away, that justice may "bee done."

"24th November, 1651.

"Ordered, that 500 copies of the order or re"solve of parliament, made, the 19th November "last past, touching the Scottish prisoners, bee "forthwith printed at the charge of the Com"pany, and they are to be dispersed all over the "Levell, and fixed upon some convenient place "in every towne, to the intent that justice may "bee done, and marshal 1 law executed upon all "such Scotch prisoners as are taken runninge "away, in pursuance of the order of parliament. "And Mr. Jessop is to pay a marke for printing "the said order; and this shall bee his discharge."

"8th December, 1651.

"Ordered, that Mr. Moore, the surveyor, shall "have four Scotts prisoners allowed for to assist "him in rowing and carryinge the chayne, and "other imployment, in order to the surveyingeof "the Fennes; and Mr. Walker is to give direc"tiona, that so many of the Scotch prisoners be "drawne out for the service aforesaid. And when "the said Mr. Moore hath noe other imployment "for them, they are to return to the other workes "again."

".Memol": The Company do agree, that on "Monday come fortnight next, so many of the "members of the Company as are willinge may "then, if they please, take into consideration "the entertaynment of the Scotch prisoners for "theire private occasions."

"24th December, 1651.

"Ordered, that every private man whatsoever "that desires to have his land hassacked by the "Scotts shall henceforward allow unto the Com"pany six shillings an acre for every acre so "hassacked. And in regard Mr. Henley does "offer six shillings an acre for every acre of "his owne adventure land as shall be hassacked "by the Scotts, it is further ordered by the "Company, that Gabriell Ellyott his servant doe "imploy so many of them as by Mr. Hamond "shall be thought necessary to be forthwith "sett a worke and imployed in hassacking Mr. "Henley's owne Adventure Landes."

"31" December, 1651.

"Memor: to get 500 Scotch prisoners from "Durham to bee sent to Lynne according to "the order lately made at the Counoell of "State."

"Ordered, that the Scotts that are not yet fur"nished with clothes bee forthwith provided for "here according as the other Scotch prisoners "were, and at the like rates."

"9 January, 1651.

"Whereas there are severall Scotch prisoners "that are destitute of shirts sutes and stockings, "and are now imployed on the workes: It is "ordered that 256 shirts be forthwith bought, "and 128 sutes and stockings provided at the

Vol. i. R

"charge of the Company; And it is further "ordered that Mr. Henley and Mr. Thurloe, or "any one of them, be desired to sign the parti"cular bills that shall be brought in touchinge "the premisses; whereupon Mr. Jessop, receiver "of the Company, or in his absence Mr. Dalton, "is forthwith to pay the respective bills."

"Ordered, that Mr. Saye be desired to speake "with Sir Arther Hazlerigge touchinge the 500 "Scotch prisoners now att Durham, and to de"sire him to give warrant to Mr. Walker, one "of the members of the Company, who is desired "to take the paines to goe downe to Durham "to have them delivered at Lynne for the ser"vice of the Company; in which imployment "the Company desire him to follow the same "course as hee did in the choice of the prisoners "at Yorke."

"Metnor: That the clerk of the Company "forthwith repayre to the secretary of the Coun"sell of State, and take out the order of the "Counsell for the Scotch prisoners at Durham "to be imployed on the workes, and to deliver it "to Mr. Saye."

"Ordered, that my Lord S'John, or whom his "Lordship shall name, shall have power to choose "twenty Scotch prisoners out of the number of "those that lately came from Yorke to bee im*tf*ployed by himselfe in his owne perticuler "affayres as his owne servants, and accordingly "to provide for them for clothes and otherwise; "And his Lordship is likewise to paie to the "Company so much money as it cost them to "bring the said twenty prisoners from Yorke "to Peterburgh. And his Lordship is hereby "desired to give order that a certificate be made "to the Counsell concerninge the said prisoners "in such manner as the Company are obliged "to doe."

"13 February, 1651.

"Ordered, that the 156 shirts, and 128 sutes "and stockins, now provided by Mr. Henley "for the Scotts imployed on the works, in pur"suance of an order of the 9th Jan. last, bee "forthwith sent down to Mr. John Crane, of "Cambridge, and from thence to Mr. Hamond, "att Wilburton, who is desired to dispose thereof "as hee shall see cause."

"23 February, 1651.

"Ordered, that all such Scotch prisoners as "are now imployed in the workes of the Great "Levell of the Fennes, shall be divided amongst "the Company of Adventurers, according to the "twenty lotts or shares; and lotts are to bee "drawne for them. And it is further ordered,

"that Mr. Hamond be desired to take care to "see there bee an equall and indifferent division "made, according to the aforesaid twenty lotts "or shares."

"6th May, 1652. "Ordered, that upon the certificate of Mr.

Qutcrc, 256? Thus in original document.

"Kelsey, and of such other person as the super"intendants shall from tyme to tyme appoint, "touchinge the number of Scotts upon the musters, and the moneys due for theire lodginges, ' Mr. Latch, the comptroller, may from tyme "to tyme issue his warrant to the expenditor for "payment of such proportion of money to or "for the Scotts, as hath byn usually allowed "them formerly for their paie, as also of such "moneys as shall be so certified to be due and "oweing for their lodgings."

The Scotch prisoners continued to labour upon the works of the drainages until the political arrangements between the two countries enabled them to return home. Many, however, settled in the Fens, and were the origin of most of the Scotch families and names that now exist within the Great Level. They were, and still are, excellent workmen; inoffensive in their manners; in their habits, sober, industrious, and indefatigable. Within the last half century, Scotch labourers were accustomed to come into the fens to assist in gathering the harvest. The proceedings of a "liberal" Parliament did not at that period transport the wealth of England, torn by ruthless taxation from its industrious and too confiding inhabitants, to be expended in Caledonian canals without vessels, highland roads without travellers, harbours and docks without shipping and without commerce. The forty " independent" Scotch members did not at that period watch with such unceasing zeal and intense anxiety the progress of an "appropriation bill," which now annually disgraces the statute book. Scotland has possessed, nay, still possesses, brave soldiers, erudite statesmen, inspired poets, and eminent historians. Who ventures to doubt these self-evident truths? Yet the author of this work (perhaps from a too overweening love of England) feels that the Scotch nation, by their petty huckstering, their continued practice of emigration, their subserviency to "the pow"ers that be," have lost those chivalrous and ennobled sentiments that exalt one nation above another; and have placed themselves far, very far inferior to the genius, the high-mindedness, and the patriotic energies of the most favoured of all countries—England, ever beloved England! No more. The indulgent reader will pardon this digression.

CHAPTER X. *State of the South Level.—Employment of Dutch Prisoners.—Proceedings relative to the second and last Adjudication.— Completion of Drainage.* state of the Notwithstanding the crude remarks of Elstobb, South Levtl.

in his meagre History of the Bedford Level; and notwithstanding the elaborate, though more acrimonious observations of Badeslade, in his History of Drainage; the author of this work is slow to credit that the South Level was, at the period of the general drainage, in that state of security and cultivation which those authors would induce us to believe. Elstobb's book lacks as well industry and science, as originality. Badeslade's pen was dipped in party gall, and his efforts (directed by hired patrons) tended only to degrade and to destroy the works of the adventurers. Dugdale, in his laboured and valuable compilation, (it is no more,) offers no opinion as to the state of the country at this period; and closes his researches (as to the Great Level of the Fena) with the proceedings under the Pretended Act passed in 1649.

If the South Level was ever in the flourishing state described by some authors, it must have been at a period when that branch of the river Ouze, running from Earitli by Chatteris Ferry, to its junction with the river Nene, was in full operation, and from which great relief must have been derived. Since that branch of the river became decayed, the South Level must have been continually surcharged with vast quantities of upland waters, descending by the West river, the Ouze, Cam, Grant, Lark, Brandon, and Wissey. The banks of these rivers were composed of very light and porous earth, and the lower part of the Level had to encounter in all its rivers, the daily recurrence of the tides, which at that period flowed up as high as Harrimeer in the Grant, and also forced themselves a considerable distance up the minor rivers.

At the time of the general drainage, the South Level was in a very desolate condition: the cutting of the New Bedford, or One Hundred Feet River, rendered some immediate and effectual steps absolutely necessary. William Earl of Bedford had not a particle of self-interest in the composition of his noble nature. Although he had obtained an adjudication, and the consequent legal possession of that part of the Level in which his own personal interests were concerned, he did not, on that account, relax in his exertions. His object was to complete the drainage of the entirety of the Level. The cutting of the New Bedford, or Hundred Feet River, had quieted the hostility of those interested in the navigation of the river Ouze above Saint Ives; but it had awakened that of the merchants of Lynn and Cambridge, and had added to the opposition always evinced to the measure of drainage by the inhabitants of the towns immediately adjoining the West River, between the Hermitage and Harrimeer. Petition after petition was presented by these disappointed parties to the commissioners of adjudication; the Company became involved in enormous legal expenses; and nothing but the perseverance of the Earl, and the influence, weight, and ability of Saint John, could have averted the most fatal consequences.

Most of the Scotch labourers had returned to their native country. The works were now being carried on through a hostile district, and a very serious riot broke out at Swaffham Buibeck, in the county of Cambridge, which was only quelled by military assistance. The Company found great difficulty in procuring labourers competent in number to conduct the affairs of drainage. Succour, however, was unexpectedly at hand.

The author cannot avoid paying a tribute of respect to the unceasing exertions of his friend Samuel Ftckering Bealee, Esq., of Cambridge, in promoting those measures and principles which tend to cement a purniancnt union between drainage and navigation: an union of interest which ought never to have been disunited.

The government of the Commonwealth made A. D. less, the most vigorous exertions to restore the honour of their country, and to humble the Dutch, by Navnim-tory whom they had been recently defeated. By their OTCrtheDut:hindefatigable efforts that brave and distinguished naval commander Blake was enabled to take the sea with 80 ships of war; and on the 18th of February, 1652, he fell in with Admiral Trump, the bold and skilful commander of the Dutch fleet, with an equal number of ships of war, and two hundred merchantmen under his convoy. It was a day glorious to Old England. Blake's recollection of his recent disaster with the enemy, (under the most adverse circumstances,) doubtless stimulated his efforts, and called all his energies into action. Indeed, nothing more seems to have been necessary to the English commander than a force approaching to an equality with the enemy, to secure the most auspicious results. The battle commenced off the Isle of Portland, and was continued for three days, both sides displaying the most determined bravery. In the close, however, it was found, that we had taken or destroyed seventeen or eighteen of the Dutch ships of war, with the loss of only one of our own vessels, which was sunk, after being emptied of as many of its crew as were left alive. Thirty of their merchantmen were captured; and thirty or forty more were destroyed. In a word, this battle, the last fought under the government of the Commonwealth, secured to this country by far the most complete of the many naval victories achieved by our gallant seamen during the Dutch war. A vast number of Dutch prisoners were sent to England.

Thuriowe. Thurlowe, soon after his return from Holland, quitted the service of Saint John, having been from a youth in his employment. He had constantly attended the meetings of the Company, and having become possessed of a considerable quantity of adventurers' lands, he naturally took much interest in the progress and completion of the work of drainage; nor was he ignorant of the difficulties under which the Company laboured. He had now attained a degree of importance in the government, being the principal Secretary of State. The Dutch prisoners proved a heavy charge to the government; and it struck Thuriowe, that their habits might render them useful in forwarding the Company's undertakings. He accordingly wrote a letter, containing proposals for the employment of a certain number upon the works; and an agreement was entered into for 500 prisoners. An order was passed for providing them with spades and shovels for work, with huts for lodging, and with such other accommodations as were thought fit and necessary. The Dutch prisoners were of essential service in forwarding the works of drainage; and they continued to labour until the treaty of peace, in 1654, restored them to their native land.

Proceedings to.
obtain the 2nd By great exertion, and at a sad pecuniary and last adjiidi-.-_' c«uon. sacrifice, the works appear to have made great progress. On the 3d FebT, 1652, it was ordered, that the Earl of Bedford, Sir Gilbert Gerard, Colonel Walton, Sir Edward Partheriche, Sir John Potts, Mr. Latch, Mr. Gorges, Mr. Fountayne, Mr. Edward Russell, Mr. Henley, Senr, Mr. Andrew Henley, Mr. Saye, Mr. Trenchard, Mr. Thurloe, Colonel Sydney, Colonel Castell, and Mr. John Russell, or any six or more of them, be desired to attend the Lord Chief Justice Saint John, to the intent that they may confer together, and consider of all things preparatory towards the obtaining an adjudication on the south side of Bedford River. The committee reported, " that "his lordship having many urgent occasions "could not therefore appoint a sett tyme of meet"inge at the present." On the 10th of February following, the committee were desired again to attend the Lord Chief Justice, to know "what "tyme his lordship can dispense with his occa"sions to appoint a tyme of meeting to conferre "with the committee formerly named, in order to an adjudication, who reported hii£ fcurdship "would not be at leisure until aflerthe terme." On the 12th of the same month, the committee were again desired to wait upon his lordship for the same purpose, who appointed the then next Thursday, on which day the following proceedings took place. Some discrepancy will arise as to dates: the reader should recollect that at this period the year commenced on the 25th of March.

"Thursdaie, 17th of Febr. 1652. "Adventurers p'sent,

"Mr. Henley, Senr, "Mr. Browne,
"Mr. Trafford, "Mr. Hampson,
"Sr Gilbert Gerard, "Capt Blackwall, "SrCorneliusVermuyden, " Mr. Wm. Smith,
"Mr. Trenchard, "Coll. Sam. Jones,
"Mr. Longe, "Mr. Walker,
"Mr. Hamond, "Mr. Buffkin,
"Mr. Holman, "Mr. Holworthy,
"Mr. Spaldinge, "Coll. Walton,
"Mr. Sam. Smith, "Corn. Vermuyden,
"Mr. Thurlowe, "Sr Edw. Partheriche,
"Mr. Say, "Mr. B. Arthur,
"Mr. Can-ill, "Mr. Neale,
"Mr. Bradley, "Mr, Henry Fenn,
"Mr. Draper, "Mr. W. Crane, "Sf John Potts."

"Memorand: Sir Cornelius Vermuyden, on "the daie of the date hereof, in performance of "the coutracte made with the Comple as Director "of the works, does hereby declare, that the works "concerninge the whole remaynder of the Great "Levell of the Fennes unadjndged are now "finished, so as the same remaynder is fitt for "an adiudicac'on, within the true meaninge and "intenc'on of the acte of parliam'."

"A question was put whether or noe the "Compnle all p'sent shall demand an adjudic'n."

"The question was whether that question "should bee put or noe: It was resolved in the "affirmative."

"The former question beinge put, whether or "noe the Compnle shall att p'sent demand an "adiudicac'on; It was resolved in the affirma"tive."

"Another question was put, whether or noe "the Company shall demande judgm' of the "com" att theire meetinge on Satterday next: "It was resolved in the affirmative, *nullo contra"die"."*

'The committee appointed to consider of all "things p'paratory to the obtaininge an adiudi"cac'on made theire report to the Comp", that "the severall brookes and rills, at the south side "of the Bedford River, hereafter followinge, are "sufficient to carry away the waters to their "proper outfall, viz',

"Okington brooke falls into Willingham Mere, "and so into the old channell of Ouze a little "below the Hermitage by Willingham Gravell."

"Cottenham brooke falls by a particular "dreyne into the old channell of Ouze by Sut"ton's Coate."

"Botesham brooke falls into Bottesham Load "and so into the River of Grant below Clayhithe "by a sasse at the head; and if Grant bee too "high at Clayhithe, that falls into Reach Lode, "and falls out below at Upwere."

"Swafbam brooke comes down by a Load into "the River of Grant, against Waterbeach, and a "sasse at the head; and if the Grant bee there

I

"high, then it falls into Reach Load, and falls "into Upwere."

"Reach brooke goes along in a navigable "Load to Upwere, with a sasse at the head, and "there emptieth itselfe into Grant."

"Harwell brooke falls into Reach Loade, and "so goes out at Upwere."

"Wickam hath noe brooke, but the water "that falls goes into Reach."

"Fordham brooke goes, part of it beinge a "mill-water, into Soham Mere, the superfluitye "goes by a cut of 16 feet through Soham and "Isleham comons, and falls into Mildenhall "river att Prickwillow, and so into Ouze. The "water of the said Soham Mere goes by Barway "Lode, and falls into the river of Ouze by tun"nells, a little above Elie over against Thet"ford."

"Freckenham brooke comes downe above Isle"ham, and falls into Mildenham River between "the banckes."

"Earswell brooke, or Bener's Loade, is part of "it, to fall into Brandon river, and the other "part of it by Pope's Lode dividing the comons "of Lackingheath from the severalls, and to fall "into Depney Lode, into the highway att Ship."pey Corner, and soe into Ouze at Littleport "Chavie, if necessary to preserve navigation; in "Earswell brooke it may be done by a sasse, "where the said brookes fall into Brandon "River."

"A Load that comes from Lackingheath feildes,

"and falls into Brandon River,

through a ton"nell, about five miles below Brandon."

"The brooke of Feltwell is received into "Sams his Cutt, and so falls into Ouze nere the "mouth of Stoake river."

"Methwold brooke falls into Stoake river, "betweene banckes of its owne in his proper "channell, and the upper part of the said brooke "hath about 200a of receptacle."

"The rills of Dereham and Wereham are car"ryed away by a new dreyne that falls into "Stoake river, about a mile below Helgay."

"Grunty Fen and Downham West Fenne do "issue theire waters at Littleport, by a peculiar "dreyne, and a sasse att the ende thereof."

"Ordered, that Mr. Fountayne, Mr. Adams, "Mr. Marsham, Mr. Culpepper, Mr. Can 11, Mr. "Will"1 Smith, Mr. Hamond, Mr. Say, Mr. "Henley, Senr, Sr Cornelius, Mr. Wm Weston, "and Mr. Trafford, are named a committee, and "they, or any two of them, are desired to attend "the commissioners in the Middle Temple Hall, "on Satterday next, at two o'clocke In the after"noone, in order to the demanding adjudication "on the south side of Bedford river, not yet "adjudged dreyned; And this committee are "desired to meete on Satterday next, in the "forenoone, to take the same into their con

"siderac'on."

' .

"Satterdaie, 19th of Febr: 1652. "Adventurers present,

"Ea: of Bedford, "Mr. Henley, Senr,

"Mr. Gorges, "Mr. Wm. Crane,

"Mr. Trenchard, "Sr Corn: Vermuyden,

"Mr. Hamond, "Mr. Bradley,

"Mr. Say, "Mr. Browne, "Mr. Henry Henne, "Mr. W. Smith,

"Sr John Potts, "Mr. Sam: Smith,

"Mr. Vermuyden, "Mr. Holman."

"Resolved upon the question, "That the commissioners bee desired to goe "downe into the Levell and give their judgment "of the lands on the south side of the Bedford "river."

"Resolved also upon the question, "That the com" bee desired to take theire "journey the 21st of March next, and appoint a "meeting and session to be held at Elie, 24th of "March next."

"Aftcrnoone. "Adventurers present, "Mr. Henley, Senr, "Sr John Potts,

"Mr. Carill, "Sr Corn: Vermuyden,

"Mr. Hamond, "Mr. Wm. Smith,

"Mr. W. Weston, "Mr. Vermuyden."

"Ordered, that the members above named, or "any two of them, be desired to take into con

"sideration all things for accommodation of the "com" in theire journey into the Levell, and like"wise all other matters concerninge the adjudi"cation; and they are desired to meet on Mpn"day next, att nyne o'clocke in the forenoone. "

"Ordered, that there bee 100 printed papers "made ready, to be reade *in* all churches through"out the whole South Levell, givinge notice of "the tyme and place of meetinge of the comis"sioners in order to an adjudication; and the "receivior is to paye unto the printer five shil"lings and fower pence for his paines in printinge "the same."

"Mondaie, 21 Febr: 1652. "Adventurers present, "Mr. Henley, senr, "Mr. Gorges, "Mr. Wm. Smith, "Sr Edw. Partherick,

"Capt. Blackwall, "Mr. Holman,

"Sir John Potts, "Mr. Henry Henne,

"Mr. Hamond, "Mr. Samnell,

"Mr. Carill, "Mr. Culpepper."

"Mr. Henley, senr, Mr. Say, Mr. Fountayne, "Mr. Wm. Smith, Mr. Carill, Mr. Adams, Mr. "Marcham, or any two of them, are desired forth-. "with to prepare drafts of the judgment that is ' to bee had at Elic, and to advise with counsell "therein, and so to order the same as it may be "engrossed and made readye to be sealed against "the meetinge of the comissioners att Elie, "against the 24th of March next, a paper draft VOL. I. S

"whereof is to be brought into the Companie by "this day se'nnight; and this comittee are de"sired to meete de die in diem, at 9 a clocke in "the forenoone, and 3 o'clocke in the after"noone, untill the same be fully finished; and "this comittee are hereby impowered to call to "theire assistance what counsell wilTplease, and "as'many of the,,Companie as thinke fitt are "desired to bee present."

"Mr. Wm. Smith and Mr. Oxenbridge are "desired to attend my Lord Cheife Justice St. "John to know if his, lopp will be pleased fto "countenance the judgment by his presence at "Elie, 24th of March next, and make returne "to the Company by three o'clocke in the "afternoone."

"Ordered, that Sr Cornelius Vermuyden, Mr. "Hamond, and Mr. Moore, the surveyour, be "desired to pr'pare, by way of schedule, a note "of all the complaints whatsoever concerning "the dreyninge of the Levell, eyther for cutting "through lands, and those that want satisfac"tion for the same, or for bridges, or for any "other thinge that they shall finde to bee an ob"jection against the proceedings of the Com"panie, and endeavour by all means to give the "country satisfaction therein; and to that pur"pose they are desired, by way of breviate, to "describe theire reasons in the margent of the "said note or schedule, eyther for or against "the said objections."

"Wednesdaie, 23rd of Febr: 1652. "Adventurers present,

"Ea. of Bedford, «Lo.Ch. JusticeS John,

"Mr. John Russell, "Sr Gilb' Gerard,

"Mr. Henley, sen'. "Mr. Hamond,

"Mr. Say, "Mr. Carill,

"S'CorneliusVermuyden, " Mr. Gorges,

"Mr. Vermuyden, "Sr John Potts,

"Mr. Trenchard, "Mr. Marcham,

"Mr. Culpepper, "Mr. Holman. "Mr. Browne,

"Ordered, that a letter be drawne by Mr. ' Jessop, to bee sent to the Lord Whitelocke, to "invite his low to favour the Companie by be"inge present att the meeting of the comTM at "Elie, the 24 of March next, and they will "take care and provide all necessary and con"venient accommodations for his lordshipp and "his attendants, w letter is as followeth: "My lord,

"It hath pleased the com" appointed by acte "of parliament for dreyninge the Great Levell "of the Fennes, (upon a representation made by "the adventurers touchinge the state of theire ' workes, and theire prayinge of a judgment for "the remaynder of the Levell not already ad "judged dreyned,) to adjourn theire meetinge to "Elie, on Thursday the 24th of March next com"ing, in order to the informinge of themselves "by view, examination of witnesses, or otherwise, "how the workes are advanced on the south

"side, and thereupon to doe further accordinge "to the powers given by the sayd acte. Your "lordshipp was pleased at the passing of the last "judgment to affoard your presence, and to take "much paines for the just satisfaction both of "the country and adventurers, whereof both have "received the fruite, and for that do owe a very "great acknowledgment; and because we hope "the issue of this meetinge will bee the obteyn"inge an adjudication for the south side of the ' Levell, (as by the justice of your lordship and "the other com" is allready granted for the "" north side,) wee doe offer to y low our earnest "suite, that if your health and occasions will "permit, your lopp will please to favour the Com"panie, and the publique service therein con"cerned, with your companie and presence at.' that meetinge. For your lordshipp's and at"tendants' accommodation, wee shall provide "and dispose of coaches and other conveniences " in such sort as you shall direct, and some of "the Company will allso bee ready to wayte upon " your Iopp to the place. By your lordshipp's "concession of this our request, you will very '" much obleige, as all persons concerned in the " Levell, so in a particular manner,

"Your low's very affectionate and
"humble servants,
"Bedford, "Richard Gorges,
"Rob' Henley, sens ' W. Say,
"Jn Potts, "Anth: Hamond,
u.Jn Marcham, "John Carill." "23"1 Febr, 1652."

"Fridaie, 25 of Febr: 1652. "Ordered, that the solicitor attend Mr. Jef' frey Palmer, Mr. Latch, and Mr. Archer, to "desire they would bee pleased to meete the "Companie to-morrow, about ten o'clocke, to "conferre together about drawinge up the ad"judication."

"Satterdaie, 26'b of Febr: 1652.
"Mr. Jeffrey Palmer, Mr. Latch, and Mr. "Archer, did, according to the request of the "Companie, by theire solicitor, attend the Com"panie this dale to advise and conferre touching "the next adjudication."

"Ordered, that Mr. Jessop, the receiver of the ' Companie, be desired to paie unto Mr. Jeffrey "Palmer, Mr. Archer, and Mr. Latch, beinge of "counsell with the Companie, the sum of fortie "shillinges a peece for theire advise in drawinge "up the judgment."

"Mondaie, 7»h of March, 1652." "Mr. Henley, Coll: Jones, Mr. Hampson, Mr.. "Walker, and Mr. Staunton, or any three of "them, are desired to examyne the perticuler of "the acte of adjudication, and to meete to"morrow by eight of the clocke."

"Thursdaie, 10th of March, 1652." "Adventurers present,

"Mr. Henley, sen% "Mr. W. Weston,
"Mr. Trafford, "Mr. Bradley,
"Mr. Adams, "Mr. Holman,
"Mr. Sheriffe Underwood, " Mr. Jessop, "Coll: Wm. Smith."

"Ordered, that all such Adventurers as give "in theire names betweene this and Mondaie "next, shall have accommodation with horses "or coaches att the Com panic's charge as they "shall thinke fitt. And Mr. Henley is to have an "allowance from the Companie for his charges "of a horse-litter in going downe with the "com"."

"Ordered, that Mr. Jessop bee desired to goe "downe with the lords com" the 21st of March "instant, and he is to carry downe with him 200/., "and to take up at Cambridge 400/. more; and in "case there will necessarily be required a further "sum, the expenditor is to provide the same. "And Mr. Jessop is to issue all such other sum "and sums of money as are needfull to bee ex"pended and layd out here in towne, besides the "said journey."

"Ordered, that Mr Bradley, one of the mem"bers of the Companye, bee desired to husband "the affayres of the Companye in theire journey "to and from the Levell to their best advantage, "and to overlooke the several bills upon the way, "which are to be brought unto him by Anthony "Spencer; and hee is to underwrite every such "bill, that such and such moneys are to bee paid; "whereupon it shall bee a sufficient warrant to "the receivour to pay and discharge the same."

"Ordered, that a letter bee written to Mr. "Moore the surveyor, to desire him to provide "14 of the best lodginges for the lords and "other comTM att Elie, and likewise for theire "attendants; and also 16 good lodginges for "the adventurers, together with necessary ac"comodation for theire servants, and such other "lodginges as Mr. Moore shall conceive neces"sary. It is desired (if possible may bee) that "Mr. Poveye's house may bee a reception for "the lords com"."

"Ordered, that 100 warrants for sumoninge "witnesses, signed by the comisTM att theire last "meetinge, be forthwith printed, at the charge of "the Companie; Mr. Jessop is to pay 5. for "the printing, and eight pence for the paper."

"Memo: That Mr. Moore the surveyour be "sure to have ready the mappes for the lords "comTM at their meeting att Elie."

"Ordered, that Mr. Hamond, in the absence "of Mr. Latch and Mr. Walter S' John, doe ex"ercise the office of comptroll, and signe war"rants for payinge the workmen that are in "arrere, that there may bee no just cause of com"plaint by any workmen for not paying theire "due wages; and such warrants so signed shall "be a sufficient discharge to the expenditor for "the issuinge money accordingly. A copie of "this order is to be sent to Mr. Hamond, and "another to Mr. Expenditor."

"15th of March, 1652. "Adventurers present,

"Mr. Marsham, "Mr. P. Arthur,
"Sr John Potts, "Mr. Henley, sen',
"Mr. Bradley, "Mr. Trafford,
"Mr. Doctor Fryer, "Mr. W. Weston. "

"The persons of the Companie hereunder named "are desired to wayte upon the lords and other "comTM, whose names are also entred in a paper "of this day, delivered to Mr. Holman:".

"Coll: Walton, "Mr. W. St. John, "Mr. Henley, senr, "Mr. Latch, "Sr Edw. Partheriche, "Mr. Trafford, "SrJohnPotts,and hisSonne, "Mr. Holman,
"Mr. Wm. Smith, "Mr. Bradley,
"Mr. Hy. Henne, "Mr. Jessop,
"Mr. Fountayne, "Mr. Walker,
"Mr. Adams, "Mr. B. Arthur, "Mr. Browne."

"Ordered, that as many other members of the "Company as please to meete the *com* at Elie, "24th of March instant, shall, during the session "there, have horse-meate and man's meate at the "charge of the Companie."

"Ordered, that there be forthwith provided a "sumpter-horse and trunkes, with appurtenances "thereunto belonging, for the carriage of all "deeds, evidences, and writings of the Companie, "as they shall conceive are necessary to bee car"ryed downe: And Mr. Jessop is to take notice "hereof, and issue out monyes for the charge "thereof accordingly."

"Ordered, that the com" attendants, as also "the adventurers and theire servants, that are "desired to goe downe into the Levell, and the "officers of the Companie, shall have particularly t(allowed from the Companie, for horses that shall "be hyred, after the rate of 2. and 6*d. a* day, be"sides borse-meate, untill the session bee ended, "and theyre return to London: And the receiver ': of the Companie is to take notice thereof, and 'paie the same accordingly; and this shall bee his "warrant in that behalfe."

"Thursdaie, 17th of March, 1652. "Adventurers present,
"Mr. Edw. Russell, "Mr. John Potts,
"Mr. Henley, sen', "Mr. Adams,
"Mr. Say, "Mr. Henry Henne,
"Mr. Holworthy, "Sr Edw. Partherich,
"Mr. Gilb'. Gerard, "Mr. B. Arthur,
"Mr. Holman, "Mr. Alexand: Jones."

"Ordered, that Mr. Thurloe be desired to pro"cure a letter from the Lord Gen11 Cromwell, to "require his troops quartered at Elie or there"abouts to meete the comTM on Wednesday next, "and accompany them to Elie."

"Afternoone: "Adventurers present,

"S' John Potts, "Mr. Trenchard,
"Mr. Henley, senr, "Mr. Henry Henne,
"Mr. Trafford, "Mr. Sheriffe Underwood."

"Ordered, that a letter be written to Mr. "Moore, the surveyor, as followeth:
"Mr. Moore,
"The lords and others contynue theire resolu"tions of goinge towards Elie on Monday next; "and because it will bee of much importance to "have them and the adventurers well accomo"dated with lodginges, towards which a good "advantage will bee given by a tymely provision "in that behalfe; the Companie have comanded "me, by way of addition to their former order, "to desire you speedily to take up and secure for "their service all the convenient lodginges in that "towne that can be had; and that they may be "most properly applyed to the persons that are "to goe downe, accordinge to theire respective "quallityes, theire names are in a paper enclosed. "Mr. Holman, a member of the company, is de"sired to goe from hence to-morrowe, so as they "hope he will not fail to bee at Elie on Monday "next for the purpose aforesaid: In the meane"tyme your owne speciall care is desired herein; "and as there shall bee occasion, you will call in "the helpe and care of Mr. Tench, if hee bee "thereabouts, or of such other person as you "shall see cause to imploy for furtherance of this "service. Having performed the comands en"joyned me, I rest, "J. H. &c."

"Ordered, that Mr. Holman, one of the mem"bers of the Company, bee desired to goe be"fore the com", and provide lodginges and "accomodation both for the comTM and adven"turers, whose names are sett downe in a paper

"herewith delivered unto him: And for all "such accomodations satisfaction shall be given "by a member of the Company appointed for "that purpose at Stevenidge, St. Ives, and Elie. "And the Companie doe desire the owners of "private howses, as well as inne keepers, to "give what accomodation and respect they can."

"Satterdaie, the 19th of March, 1652.

"Afternoone:
"Adventurers present,
"Mr. Henley, senr, "Sr John Potts,
"Mr. Henne, "Mr. Sheriffe Underwood,
"Mr. Adams, "Mr. Wm. Weston,
"Mr. Thurloe, « Mr. Walker."

"Ordered, that Mr. Jessop, the receiver of the "Company, be authorized to issue out and paie "all such sum and sums of money, as well in "towne as out of towne, in order to the journey "to Elie, touchinge an adjudication, as hee shall "conceive necessary to bee layd out and ex"pended for the purpose aforesaid, takinge an "acquittance for every sum as shall be paid, "and placing the same to his acco', which shall "be a sufficient discharge to the said receiver."

"A letter from the Lord Generall to Cap "Hunter, or the officer in cheife of his excel"lencye's troope, to attend the lords comTM to "Elie, and soe to wayte upon them untill theire "returne to London being read,—"

"Mr. Glapthorne, cheife bayliffe in the Isle, "was by the Company desired to write to the "said Cap' Hunter to meet the com" at Erith "bridge, with his troope, about 10 o'clocke on "Wednesday morning next, signifyinge that ' att the same tyme and place hee himselfe would "be there with his deputie and bayliffes to "attend the com"."

"Which letter, with the generall's enclosed, "was sent by Mr. Arundell, who was directed "to make haste to deliver the same, together "with a letter to his deputie and bayliffes, and "give ace1 to the Comple att theire meetinge "att St. Ives."

The lords commissioners of adjudication left London on the 21st of March, 1652, and proceeded by way of Stevenage to St. Ives, and from thence to Earith, where their lordships embarked, attended by several of the Company, and their servants. They advanced down the New Bedford River to Stow Bridge, and from thence viewed the work of St. John's Eau, and the several sluices near thereto, and thence proceeded to Ely, where they arrived in the evening of the 23d of the same month.

The two following days the lords

commissioners were much occupied in hearing and determining a great number of petitions from various parts of the South Level, relative to the works of drainage performed by the adventurers. Sir Cornelius Vermuyden was also desired to read over to the lords and other commissioners his design for draining the South Level, which was done, and is as follows:

"The designe in what manner the South "Levell of the Fennes is dreyned, humbly pre"sented to the right honorable the lordes and "others comnr3 nominated in the late acte of "parliament, at Elie, the 24th day of March, "1652, by Sr Cornelius Vermuyden, Knight, "director of the workes:"

"The Great Levell of the Fennes extendinge "itselfe into the six countyes named in the said "acte of parliament, is now divided by banckes "into 3 Levells, namely, the North Levell, the "Middle Levell, and the South Levell, so called "from theire respective situations, whereof the "two former are already adjudged dreyned by "the law of Peterborough, bearing date the "24th day of March, 1650, and are so far im"proved, that there are about 40,000 acres at "this time sowne with cole seede, wheate, and '' other winter graine, besides innumerable quan"tityes of sheepe, cattle, and other stocke, where "never had byn any before, and not surrounded "since the adjudication, being now 2 yeares "past."

"The South Levell, whereupon your lord"ships' judgment is now humbly demand"ed, is devided from the Middle Levell by "streight banckes and a great river, which "runneth from Erith, in the county of Hun"tiogdon, to a place called Saiter's toade, in "the county of Norfolke, about one and twenty "miles, and extends itself eastward and south"ward to the high lands of Norfolke and Suf"folke, and westward upon the high lands of the "county of Cambridge, conteyninge by esti"mation about one hundred and thirty thou"sand acres of land. " i

"Though this South Levell be watred by 5 "rivers which runn through it, and did here"tofore occasion the surrounding thereof, name"ly, the river of Ouze, the river of Grant, the "river of Mildenhall, the river of Brandon, and "the river of Stoake, all mentioned in the said "late acte of parliament; yet it is generally "knowne that the overflowinge of the said "Levell was occasioned chiefly by the river of "Ouze, which is a very great water in the tyme "of floodes cominge downe from Newport Pag_ "nell, Bedford, and the parts adjacent, and did "discharge itselfe into this great body of the "Fennes, by reason, first, that the old channel "of the Ouze was insufficient for such a water, "havinge neither breadth nor depth propor"tionable, beinge in many places not above "oue foote and two foote deepe under soyle, "as namely, at Willingham Gravell, Twenty"pence, and Stretham Gravdl; secondly, be"cause the said river of Ouze ran in a circular "course to the fall goinge upon the south of "Elie, above twenty miles about, whereby the fall "was lessened, and havinge noe sufficient banckes "to keep in the water, it must of necessity over"spread the Levell; especially, which is the 3rd "and last reason, because the.said water coming "to Harrimeer and Elie there mett with the "river of Grant, which came from Cambridge, "and the tydes from sea, which checked his "course, and forced him over the surface of "the Fennes, filling the other 4 rivers also, "which all fell also into that channell with "theire water, and checkinge theire course to "the sea, also did occasion theire putting over "of theire water upon the Levell, though not "' in so great proportion."

"Theis being the undoubted causes of the "inundation of this country, I did conclude "with myselfe that the best way of dreyning"would be, First, to take of the river of Ouze "from its old channell, and in a shorter and "straiter Jyne to the fall, so that it should runn but twenty miles or thereabouts to come "to Salter's Loade, whereas it ran above fortie "before, which I have done by addinge a large "bancke of fiftie and sixtie foote in the seate, "and 9, 10, and 12 foote high, drawn from "the high land of Over, above Erith, to Salter's "Loade aforesaid, on the south side of the said "river, called New Bedford River, to restrayne "it from overflowing this South Levell, leavinge "a large wash betweene that and the north "bancke, being half a mile over where it is "broadest, in the fashion of that which runs "from Peterborough to Guyhirne, between the

"other two adjudged Levells; onely to satisfie "the demaudes of some who desired to con"tynue navigation with small boates in the "old channell of Ouze, from Erith towards "Cambridge, I made a navigable sasse att "Erith, upon the said Old River of Ouze, ft to preserve that navigation: Secondly, I "thought it necessary to shutt out the tydes "from cominge the old way up to Harri"meer, by a dam made over the Old Ouze, "nere Salter's Loade, leavinge to the tyde the "new channell aforesaid, and the whole wash to "play over, and the rather, because the outfall "would bee the better preserved, and the towne "of Lynne should have no cause to complain "that any damage should come to theire haven "by the reason of this dreyninge, placing a "double sasse nere the said dam of twenty"fowerfoote water-way, with fresh water-doors, "thereby to bee able both to hold in and lett goe "the water, as there should bee occasion, and "preserve the navigation from Cambridge."

"This divertion of the Ouze and of the tydes "beinge made, doth plainely demonstrate, that "the old channell of the Ouze will receive the "waters of the fower lesser rivers aforesaid, viz': "Grant, Mildenhall, Brandon, and Stoake; and "least it might bee objected, that duringe the "stop the tyde makes, which is about 4 hours in "12, the said 4 lesser rivers of Grant, Mildenhall, "Brandon, and Stoake, would swell upwards, "and overflow the sovle of the Fennes, for want "of banckes, I did judge it convenient to cause "the rivers upwards to bee imbanked with suf"fi"cient banckes, leaving proportionable recepta"cles betweene the said banckes for any sudden "downfall that might happen to plash over for a "while."

"And because some doubt might bee

made "that the said double sasse att Salter's Loade "would not bee capable to vente the waters of "the said 4 lesser rivers, and the downfall, as "likewise that the fall there was not sufficient in "tyme of land floodes, I did direct a new dreyne "of 114 foote wide, and 6 footc deepe, to be «' made from the said dam over the old Ouze, near "Salter's Lode, on the east side of the said river, "through the land of Denver, Downham, and "Stow, beyond Stow Bridge, about 4 miles in "length, fenced with great banckes on either side, "and 3 large sluices placed att the lower ende of "the said dreyne of 24 foote water-way a peece, "where the water into Ouze hath a better fall by. " 6 foote and a halfe, and runs sooner and longer "than at the said double sasse, nere Salter's "Loade, that there might bee noe question but "that the said fower rivers would bee sufficiently "provided for. And yet, least whilst I was "dreyninge I might not prejudice the navigation "from Cambridge to Salter's Loade, and so to "Lyn, in regard the tydes were stopt out att "Salter's Loade, and the old channel I of Ouze, "nere to Elie bridge, exceedinge large and "spatious, and very shallow, by reason whereof VOL. I. T c the navigation formerly, in dry tymes,and upon "all neape tydes in summer, was obstructed, I "caused a water gage to bee sett upon the said "river, nere Elie, at a place called Rassell Hill, "to keep up the water att a gage, and then "made a little cutt by about a myle in length, "sufficient for boates to passe att all tymes, and "which is fedd with water sufficient from Grant "river to supply it, by reason of the narrowness "now it is of, so that the navigation is now bet"ter, and more certaine than formerly."

"And allthough theis great workes are those "onely directed by the acte of parliament, yet I "have made divers other little workes to convey "both little brookes, and also the downfall in the "said South Levell."

"This beinge the sum of my designe for the "dreyninge of the South Levell, according to "the intent of the late acte of parliament, I am "ready to prove by witnesses, that the workes "here mentioned are well and sufficiently per"formed att the exceedinge greate cost of the "Earl of Bedford, and his adventurers and parti"pants, and now the whole Levell is entirely "dreyned, and there is not, besides the meres "pooles and lakes which are excepted, and not "to bee dreyned within the intention of the said "acte, any part of the said Levell undreyned, "more than the washes and receptacles, which "doe not exceede 12,000 acres, whereas the acte "gives liberty for 15,000 acres."

"Theis workes have approved themselves suf"ficient, as well by the great tyde about a month "since, which overflowed Marshlande banckes,and "drowned much ground in Lincolnshire and other "places, and a flood, by reason of a great snow, "and rayne upon it followinge soon after, and yet "never hurt any part of the whole Levell; and "the view of them, and the consideration of what "hath byn formerly said, proves a cleere dreyn"inge according to the acte."

"If any thing shall bee with reason objected "against the said dreyninge, I am ready to answer "the same, and. as I hope to your lordshipps' "satisfaction; and make it appear to your lord"shipps that the designe is perfecte, well exe"cuted, and every way sufficient for the intended "dreyninge, without prejudice to navigation in "the said rivers and parts adjacent."

"I presume not to say more of the workes, least "I should bee accompted vaine glorious; all. "though I might truly affirme that the present or "former age have done nothinge like it for the "generall good of the nation. I humbly desire "that God may have the glory, for his blessing ' and bringing to perfection my poore endeavours, "at the vast charge of the Earle of Bedford and "his participants;

"And humbly submit all to your "Loppl§ judgment,

"Corn: Vermuyden."

"The certificate of Mr. Jonas Moore, surveyour "of the receptacles taken in by the brookes, and "appointment of the director, Sr Cornelius Ver"muyden, that they doe not exceede the quan"tityes follow!nge, viz'., *a. r. p.* "The Wash of Stoake River 400 00 00

"The Wash of Brandon River-800 00 00

"The Wash of Mildenhall-400 00 00

"The Wash of New Ouze-5800 00 00

"The Wash of Neane--3500 00 00

"The Wash nere Elie--10000000

"The Wash of Grant--0200 00 00 12,100 00 00 "Jonas Moore." Tie second On the 26th day of March, 1653, the Com adjudication. pany were summoned to the presence of the lords commissioners of adjudication, of whom were present,

"Lo: Comr Whitelocke, "Mr. Bacon,

"Lo: Comr Lisle, "Mr. Lowry,

"Sr John Bouchier, "Sr Henry Mildmay,

"Mr. Henry Darley, "Mr. Browster,

"Mr. Talbott Pepys, "Mr. Eltonhead."

The following adventurers were also present,

"Ea: Bedford, "Mr. Trafford,

"Sr Ed: Partherick, "Mr. Hampson,

"Mr. Henley, "Major Blake,

"Mr. Hamond, "Mr. Hoi man,

"Mr. W. Crane, "Ll. Coll: Underwood,

"Mr. Adams, "Mr. Browne,

"Mr. Jo: Arthur, "Mr. Dey,

"Mr. B. Arthur, "Mr. Potts,

"Mr. Jo: Russell, "Mr. Bland,

"Mr. W. Smith, "Mr. Lane,

"Capt. Blackwall, "Mr. Bradley,

"Mr. Henry Henne, "Mr. Jessop."

The instrument referred to in the foregoing orders was read over, signed and sealed by the necessary parties, and then delivered to the Earl of Bedford. His lordship received the important document kneeling. It had been previously arranged by the Company that a general thanksgiving should take place, in humble gratitude to Heaven for the completion of the work; and the celebrated Hugh Peters, chaplain to the Lord General Cromwell, had been requested by the Company to preach the sermon on this occasion. Upon rising from his recumbent posture, therefore, the Earl requested the lords commissioners would give their presence at the church, to which their lordships instantly acceded.

On the following day the ceremony took place in the cathedral church in Ely, and was attended by the lords commissioners of adjudication, their officers and suite, as well as by the Earl of Bedford, and others of the company of adventurers, their officers and servants, and a vast concourse of other persons.

Reader! does not your heartthrob with fine emotions in viewing even in imagination so imposing a scene? Behold this truly Christian nobleman, and his indefatigable companions, after all their toils, their disappointments, and their misfortunes, bending in humble gratitude and adoration at the altar of their Maker, and offering up their prayers and thanksgivings for that protection and those mercies which had at length enabled them to accomplish a work so beneficial in its effects, and so important to the welfare of the kingdom at large! The ceremony ended; the business of the commission at Ely closed; and that night William Earl of Bedford slept soundly upon his pillow.

al inns in the lots and numbers of the adventurers' lands, which in modern days have rather puzzled some of the possessors. The commissioners, in the first instance, generally directed a reference of the point in controversy to indifferent persons, chosen by each party, with power to issue a commission out of the High Court of Chancery for the examination of witnesses. The referees made their report, accompanied with the depositions; which report was subsequently considered and finally disposed of by the commissioners of adjudication. The matter of these petitions is too voluminous for insertion in this work; but they would form a volume of deep interest to the antiquary, and to the reader, who, from local connection with the subject, or literary curiosity, might feel desirous of becoming acquainted with all the minute circumstances attending the drainage of the Great Level.

The first meeting of the commissioners of adjudication took place on the 10th day of July, 1650, and the last upon the 5th day of December, 1654. Many readers will perhaps suppose, that the Earl of Bedford, having thus fulfilled his contract, and having fortunately obtained the adjudication of the commissioners, would suspend his labours and solicitude. Far, far otherwise. Alas! When were the exertions and anxieties of William Earl of Bedford to terminate? He might now exclaim with the Trojan General, " Italia, O Italia!" He might behold, that he was not yet destined to enjoy in peace and security the promised land.

Soon after the adjudication, an event occurred Accession of

Cromwell.

which astonished the nation, Europe, and the civilized world,—the violent dismissal of the long parliament by Cromwell, and his immediate assumption of the supreme government. True it is, that the genius, the valour, and the success of Cromwell, had mainly assisted in supporting the Commonwealth; but this event entirely changed the nature and principles of the government. It effected a complete revolution.

The Earl of Bedford was not an idle spectator of a change in public affairs which might operate so injuriously to the interests of the Level, if not render invalid those measures that had been pursued, and we may add, completed, under the sanction and authority of a government which had now ceased to exist. Foresight, vigilance, and activity, were the characteristics of this incomparable nobleman. He instantly perceived, that advantage might be taken by the enemies to the drainage (of whom alas! there were too many) of the course of those numerous changes incidental to the establishment of a new dynasty, to invalidate the proceedings transacted under the sanction of the Commonwealth, unless the most prompt and efficient measures should be taken, to give to these proceedings the protection, as well as the confirmation, of the new government.

Although the Earl of Bedford appears to have taken no part whatever in the public affairs of this most eventful period, Cromwell was too keen an observer, and too good a judge of human nature, not to estimate truly the Earl's character for high integrity, determined perseverance, and almost unexampled philanthropy. What was the Earl's opinion of the personal character or political conduct of Cromwell, we have no record by which we can form an accurate opinion. Each party appeared actuated by a similar disposition to confirm the adjudication. Accordingly, an ordinance or act of state was passed by the Protector and his council, and subsequently confirmed (as were many other acts of the Commonwealth) by the Parliament, (which assembled on the 17th day of September, 1656,) by an act passed the 22d day of June, 1657.

The ordinance itself is an important document, as it affords an illustration of the legislative proceedings of that important period.

Ordinance, or "*An Ordinance for the Preservation of the*

Act of S.,l,.

' Oliver, Lord Protector of the Commonwealth "of England, Scotland, and Ireland, and the "dominions and territories thereunto belonging, "To all whom these presents shall come, greet"ing. Whereas, by an act of parliament, en"tituled 'An act for the draining of the Great "Level of the Fens, extending itself into the "several counties of Northampton, Norfolk, Suf"folk, Lincoln, Cambridge, and Huntingdon, "and the Isle of Ely, or some of them,' William "Earl of Bedford, participants, and adventurers, "are thereby empowered to drain the said Level, "which is done accordingly, and so adjudged; "and to have for their recompence the propor"tion of ninety-five thousand acres, which is "also set out and assigned: In and by which "act there is not a full remedy made and pro"vided to enforce the payment of taxes, which "shall be laid out and assessed, in order to the "preserving of the said Level: For remedy "whereof, and also for providing of all ways "and means conducing to the preservation there"of, be it ordained and established, by his "highness the Lord Protector, with the con"sent of his council, That upon any tax or "taxes to be made or laid, in pursuance of the "said act, that it shall and may be lawful for "any person or persons, by any warrant under "the hands and seals of any five or more of the "said adventurers or participants of the said "ninety-five thousand acres, (having five hun"dred acres a-piece,) not only to distrain upon "the said lands, which are or shall be in arrear "for such taxes, but in case of non payment "by the space of thirty days after the tax so "in arrear, to sell the distress, or distresses so "taken, and the moneys arising by such sale "or sales, to be employed as well to the sa"tisfying of such arrears of taxes, as to the pay' ment of two shillings in the pound for the "taxes so in arrear, to the use of the said Earl, "participants, and adventurers, their heirs and "assigns, for defraying charges occasioned in "and about such distresses and sales, rendering

"always the surplusage upon such sales, above "the said arrear taxes, and two shillings in the "pound aforesaid, if any be, to the owner of "the distresses demanding the same; and where "no sufficient distress or distresses shall be "found, after the said thirty days, when any "person shall come to distrain for such taxes "in arrear, Be it ordained by the authority "aforesaid, that in such cases it shall and may "be lawful to and for the said William Earl "of Bedford, participants, and adventurers, their "heirs and assigns, or any five or more of them, "having the said proportion of five hundred "acres a-piece, to lay any mulct or penalty for ' non-payment of taxes so made or laid as afore"said, not exceeding the sum of three shillings "and four pence in the pound for the taxes "unpaid, and as well for the said taxes as pe"nalty, to enter, seize, and sequester the lands "so in arrear for want of taxes, to and for the "use of the said Earl, participants, and adven"turers, their heirs and assigns, and the rents "and profits of the said sequestered lands to "receive without accompt, until the said taxes "and penalties shall be satisfied and paid.'

"And be it further ordained and established "by the authority aforesaid, that the said Wil' liam Earl of Bedford, participants, and adven"turers, their heirs and assigns, or any five or "more of them, having the said proportion of

"five hundred acres, shall and may use and "exercise the same, and the power for the "making, repairing, and amending of any banks, "dams, sluices, sasses, drains, or other works, "made or to he made out of the compass and "boundaries of the said Great Level, as they "or any five of them, do or may use or exercise "in the repairing or amending of any banks, "dams, sluices, sasses, drains or works, within "the compass of the said Levell."

"And be it further ordained and established "by the authority aforesaid, that if any person "or persons shall unlawfully cut, cast down, "burn, or destroy, or other act do for the de"stroying of any bank, dam, sluice, sasse, drain, "or other work, made or to be made, which "doth or shall conduce to the draining of the "said Level, that in such cases, the commis"sioners in the said act named, or such as "shall from time to time be nominated in their "rooms by act of parliament, or under the "Great Seal of England, according to the said "act, or any three or more of them, upon "complaint and proof made before them of such "unlawful burning, casting down, cutting, or "destroying, or other act doing for destroying "as aforesaid, award double damages to the "said Earl, participants, and adventurers, their "heirs and assigns, to be levied by distress and "sale of the offender's goods, and to be imployed "for and towards the maintenance of the said "works; and for want of sufficient distress, to "commit such offender or offenders to the House "of Correction, there to remain until satisfac

"tion be made and given of the said damages "so awarded; And if such cutting, burning, "casting down, or destroying, shall be perverse "and malicious, the offenders therein shall be "adjudged felons, and be proceeded against, "and suffer such pains and punishments as "those who shall perversely or maliciously cut "the new Podick bank in Marshland, in the "county of Norfolk; provided that all and every "such offender be prosecuted within four months "next after the offence committed."

"And be it further ordained and established, "that the said commissioners, or any three or "more of them, are hereby impowered and au"thorized to hear, adjudge, and determine, all "matter and things for and concerning the dis"turbing the possession or possessions of any "adventurer, or participant, in the said ninety"five thousand acres, or any part thereof, their "or any of their heirs or assigns, as also for and "concerning all ways and passages used or be"longing to any part or parcel thereof; and upon "judgement and determination given therein, "then to commit to the common gaol all such "person and persons who shall not be conform"able thereunto, there to remain until a con"fortuity and obedience shall be given; and the "sheriff and all other officers and ministers of "justice, and such as shall be concerned, are "hereby required to be aiding and assisting to "the said commissioners in what they shall do, "or command to be done or executed by vertue

' of this ordinance; and all and every person and "persons concerned, or to be concerned by this "ordinance, or which shall do any thing in exe"cution of the same, may upon any action, suit, "or information, plead the general issue, and "upon any issue joyned may give this ordinance "in evidence, which shall be of equal force and "validity as if the same had been especially "pleaded; and all judges, justices, jurors, and "others, are so to accept the same. Provided "that this ordinance, or any thing therein con"tained, shall not extend, nor be construed to "extend, to invalidate any covenant, contract, "or agreement, made by the said adventurers "with the purchasers of any part of the ninety"five thousand acres, or among themselves, con"cerning the taxing, not taxing, or the manner "of taxing, of or concerning any part of the "ninety-five thousand acres."

"And be it further ordained or established, "that if any person or persons of a forein nation, "in league and amity with the commonwealth, "being protestants, shall become purchaser or "farmer of any lands, part of the said ninety-five "thousand acres, the said person or persons, "their heirs, executors, and administrators, (as "to the said lands, and the rents, profits, and "proceeds of the same, and all suits touching "the same,) shall be accounted free denizens "of this commonwealth, and enjoy the like pri"viledges and advantages for descent to their "children, dower to their wifes, and otherwise, as

"denizens of this commonwealth ought to "enjoy."

Let us digress shortly to a subject not altogether uninteresting, before we notice the proceedings of the Earl after obtaining the foregoing ordinance and act of state.

D«tii of sir *c*. It has been already stated, that Sir Cornelius VermuyJen continued to be the director general of the works in the South Level. He docs not seem to have been greatly benefited by the appointment, or for his general services in the Level. He became involved in pecuniary difficulties with the Company, whose meetings he appears to have attended for the last time upon the 4th of February, 1655, having been previously ordered to account for a considerable sum received bv him *tt* for expediting the works of drainage; but failing to do so, part of his land was sequestered, to answer the demand. Whether this circumstance induced his retirement, or whether, having arrived at a " good old age," he was removed from the turmoil and troubles of this world, must remain doubtful: no record remains of his ultimate destiny: but it is conjectured that this most extraordinary man died between the 4th of February, 1655, and the 12th of March following, as his son (who had previously attended with great regularity the meetings of the Company) was absent from the several meetings during that period. Thus terminated, rather ignobly, the life of a man of no ordinary vigour of mind. Posterity offers him no tribute of respect. It is the misfortune of the race of the present day that they are called upon to correct the errors of their predecessors. Sir Cornelius Vermuyden was the fatal origin of these errors. His son appears to have possessed a considerable quantity of adventurers' land, which he had purchased for arrears of taxes. He attended the meetings of the Company until the restoration, after which, on the second election of the board (1663), he was chosen as Conservator; but he never attended. His land was conveyed to strangers, and no further record of him, or of any other branch of his family, is now to be found.

CHAPTER XII. *State of the Great Level under the Protectorate, continued. — Disapproval of Sir Cornelius s Scheme. — JVesterdyke consulted.—Opinions of Badeslade, Labelye, Leaford, Elstob, and Smith. —Account of Romney Marsh.—-Adoption, of Laws and Customs of,—Laws, System of Government, and Officers of the Great Level.— Death of Cromwell.*

The scheme " propounded" by Sir Cornelius Vermuyden, and unfortunately adopted in all the different attempts of drainage, did not receive the entire approbation either of ancient or modern days. Sir Cornelius had unluckily drawn his conclusions from his knowledge of Holland and Flanders. These countries were utterly dissimilar to the Great Level of the Fens. The former were recovered from the sea, to which the lands were contiguous. The latter was many miles distant from the ocean, to which it had never yielded, except to the partial flux and reflux of the tides. The error of Sir Cornelius originated in a great neglect of the outfalls to sea, for the improvement of which no plan whatever was carried into execution. The Great Level *was* an extensive plain, through which four natural rivers had regular and continued currents; namely, the Welland, the Nene, the Ouze, and the Grant; each of these rivers effecting a junction with tributary streams. Surely, the obvious course was to scour out, widen, deepen, and straighten these rivers and adjoining streams, and embank their sides, partly with the earth arising from the excavation, and partly with earth of a stronger substance, which might have been readily obtained in the vicinity, surrounded as the Great Level was by chalk and strong clay land. Having thus improved the internal drainage by natural means, Sir Cornelius ought to have turned his attention to widening or compressing (as the case might require) the line of rivers out of the Level, in their course to the outfall; and further relief might have been given, by making a receptacle at the foot of the high lands, in the nature of a catch-water drain for the upland waters at the time of pressure, as recently recommended by the late John Rennie, Esq. Instead, however, of pursuing plans so evidently beneficial, thus aiding and improving the works of nature, Sir Cornelius completely altered the face of the Level, by abandoning in many cases the natural rivers, and cutting straight drains through porous soils, which, for want of a continual current, soon closed up again; and as one error occasioned another, sluices were erected, and endless unnecessary works executed, at an expense much beyond what would have been required had the system been confined to a natural instead of an artificial plan of drainage. The best intentioned persons are unfortunately liable to error. No doubt can justly be entertained of Bishop Morton's solicitude to benefit the Great Level; but, alas! we must not shrink from the truth: he it was who first introduced the system of cutting straight artificial rivers; he it was who abandoned nature and resorted to art, by the erection of Standground Sluice, thereby first establishing the principle of diverting the ever active currents of natural rivers. King James, as well as King Charles the First, continued the system, as did Francis and William Earls of Bedford, unquestionably induced thereto by an anxious desire to avail themselves, each in his turn, of the immense sums that had been previously expended by their respective predecessors.

William Earl of Bedford had indeed his misgivings of Vermuyden's system being founded in "absolute wisdom;" and in 1652, his lordship moved the Company that Barance Westerdyke, an eminent Dutch engineer, should be called over to give his opinion of the plan being then prosecuted in the Level. Westerdyke accordingly came to England, and took a general view of the

Level, and of the works then already executed, as well as of those at that time in progress. His opinions were not favorable to the plan; but it was too late to think of any alteration. To those who have had the least experience in the practice of engineering it will certainly create no surprise, that Westerdyke should dissent from the plan of drainage then sanctioned by Vermuyden. Probably, had Vermuyden been called upon to give his opinion of any scheme suggested by Westerdyke, he would have differed in like manner from Westerdyke, as Westerdyke himself did from Vermuyden. No doubt can ex-, ist that engineers are men of science, of industry, and utility. The works erected throughout the kingdom under the superintendence of Telford, of Walker, of the two Kennies, of Mylne, and of many others, are splendid monuments of their genius, their taste, and their skill. But it is to be lamented, that the province, or rather the practice of engineers, so frequently leads them to "agree to disagree." It might be well perhaps if in many cases they were ignorant of their employers.

An anecdote will best illustrate the author's opinion upon this subject. Two persons disputed about a matter of fact, namely, the base and altitude of Saint Paul's Cathedral; each supporting his opinion by a wager of one hundred guineas. Engineers were employed by both parties, and having viewed the building, and taken sections, they reported the result to their employers. The difference being considerable, an umpire became necessary, who, having also viewed and taken sections, reported in favor of the correctness of the one engineer, as to the base, but disagreed with the other as to the altitude: in fine, the wager could not be decided. Both parties had however to pay each engineer fifty guineas, and to be content to live the remainder of their days in conjecture only of what was the actual base and altitude of Saint Paul's Cathedral.

To return to our subject. It plainly appears from what Westerdyke relates in the brief of his observations of what passed between him and Sir Cornelius, and his pretended demonstration, that neither of them was master of so much theory as to be able to determine what water-way would be sufficient at Denver for the land waters, whatever knowledge or practice these two gentlemen may be allowed to have enjoyed in other matters. The opinion and advice of Westerdyke came too late, and consequently no alteration took place in the plans pursued by Vermuyden. It may, however, be interesting briefly to advert to the opinions of authors as to the ruinous effects which they considered were produced by the system of artificial rivers and sluices.

End. p. 101. "The only reason (says Badeslade) why the Fens were at all drowned in the winter, at the time of the undertaking for a general drainage, was, that proper drains were not made to convey the waters of the Level into the main stream (viz. the river Ouze); and also because the river itself was, from Huntingdon to Ely, generally foul and overgrown with weeds, and stopped with weers; and against Ely, as in other parts, made shallow by gravels and fords. Had they been removed (as the Lord Popham and others proposed) for the readier passage of the waters in times of floods, it was at that time believed the Fens would not have been hurtfully overflowed by the waters of the Ouze. This shews that the Fens cannot be drained, unless the principal river, which is the Ouze, be made so wide and deep as to be capable of passing through it to sea the waters descending from the high countries." "Nature (continues the same author), in the compass of a few hundred years, made the river Ouze very wide and deep, compared with the dimensions it was of before Wisbech waters had their course by Lynn Harbour, and continued to enlarge it in width and depth by degrees, until Denver Sluices were erected cross it, beneath the mouths of all the rivers that have their outfall to Lynn; which sluices, hindering the tide from flowing into its ancient receptacles, and the river, haven, and channel to seaward being thereby deprived of their wonted stock of back water to scour out the silt or sand in their reflux which the tide brings up in the flux, they were soon choked with the said silt and sand; so very soon, that Lynn, Cambridge, and the inhabitants of the adjacent parts were thoroughly convinced the said sluices were the cause thereof. And, for our part, we can't help being of opinion, that if Denver Sluices had not been erected, nature would herself, by this time, have made the river Ouze and outfall to Lynn so wide and deep, that there would have been room for the fen waters to pass to sea in winter time; and that the fens, with proper drains to convey their downfall waters into Ouze, would have been perfectly exiccated, especially if art had been used to assist nature by embankments, not to contradict her by sluicing her waters."

Although Badeslade's book is undoubtedly a work of great merit, and the production of a scholar and a man of science; yet must his opinions be viewed with considerable jealousy, and by no means adopted as infallible. For instance, in the foregoing opinions he purposely omits the additional scour the great river received below Denver Sluice, by the upland waters passing down the New Bedford River. In short, Badeslade wrote for a purpose; and his opinions generally squared with those of his employers. Dugdale's History of Draining and Embanking, and Badeslade's History of the Navigation of Lynn, will always be considered standard works, without a knowledge of which no one can be considered thoroughly acquainted with the History of the Great Level of the Fens, or the principles of drainage and navigation.

Other writers, however, upon these important subjects, have offered opinions worthy of some notice. In the year 1745, Charles Labelye, a native of Switzerland, the architect of Westminster Bridge, took a view of the Fens, and reported his opinion to the Corporation of the Bedford Level. Labelye was evidently a man of acute observation and considerable skill. His report evinces great judgment, and his opinions are entitled to the highest respect. He expresses himself exceedingly averse to the artificial plans pursued by Vermnyden. The same may be said of Leaford, of Elstob, and of Smith, who have respectively made reports at different times as to the state of the Great Level. It is, however, unnecessary to dwell longer in this place upon these matters. The die was cast; and it is the province of fen men of the present day to rectify the errors of their predecessors.

The final adjudication of the commissioners having been obtained by William Earl of Bedford, his participants, and adventurers, and possession taken of the 95,000 acres, and the new government of Cromwell having confirmed all the proceedings under the act of 1649, the contract was completed. The zeal, the industry, and perseverance of the Earl did not on that account relax. He had long foreseen the necessity of some steps being taken for the constant care and preservation of the immense works that had been executed at such an enormous expense.

The meetings of the Company had been very irregular. Many persons obtruded themselves without any right to be present. The qualification directed by the act had not been adhered to; neither had the officers and servants employed on the works any regular authorities to whom they could refer in cases of difficulty. The constant attendance of the Earl and of Lord Chief Justice Saint John greatly tended to preserve order and decorum, amidst so many jarring and discordant interests. The Earl, previously to the adjudication, expressed a desire, that as soon as that desirable event should occur, some steps should be taken by the Company for forming a permanent system of government.

A. D. 1652. On the 22d of February, 1652, it was ordered,

"that the Earl of Bedford, the Lord Chief Jus"tice Saint John, Mr. Fountayne, Mr. Thurloe, "Mr. Adams, Mr. Hammond, Mr. Gorges, Mr. "Henley, senior, Mr. Say, Sir Cornelius Ver"muyden, Mr. Marcham, and Mr. Carill, should "be a committee; and they, or any three of them, "were desired to advise with counsel, and take "into their consideration what was fit to be of"fered to the Company, for the ordering, govern"ing, and regulating of the works after the next "adjudication; and the committee was to con"sider all things conducive thereto."

This committee took great pains. The act of

ApP. P. 374, 1649 authorized " William Earl of Bedford, par 3/3.

"ticipants, and adventurers, his and their heirs "and assigns, each of them having two hundred "acres a piece of the said 95,000 acres, or any "five or more of them, *after the said work of "drainage should be adjudged,* and none other "person or persons, should within the said Levell "have such and the same power and authority as "commissioners of sewers, authorized by act or "acts of parliament heretofore made and enacted, "and then in force, had or might have, *within "the said Level"* They were also invested with power to lay and levy taxes for the upholding, repairing, and maintaining the works; with fur ther power to make such by-laws and orders as by and according to the laws and customs of Roni ney Marsh were provided or used. As the go vernment of the Company was afterwards formed upon the basis of these laws and customs, and as the general Drainage Act, passed 15 Charles the 15 Car. 2.

Second, also conferred upon the corporation full APP-p-392 power to use and exercise such laws and customs, it may not be considered quite foreign to the pur pose of this work to give some information upon a subject not generally understood in the Bed ford Level.

We are informed by Lam bard, that " Romney *J J*

Marsh.

Marsh is famous throughout the realm, as well for the fertility and quantity of the soil and level, as also for the ancient and wholesome ordinance there used for the preservation and maintenance of the banks and walls against the rage of the sea.

"It containeth (as by due computation it may appear) 24,000 acres. For the taxation of Romney Marsh only (not accompting Wai land Marsh, Guilford Marsh, &c.) amounteth to fiftie pounds, after the rate of one half-penny per acre; and it is at this day governed by certain lawes of sewers, that were made by one Henry Bathe (a justice and commissioner for that purpose) in the time of Henry III.

"Of which his statute's experience in time hath begotten such allowance and liking, that it was afterwards not onlv ordered that all the low grounds between Tanet in Kent and Pensey in Sussex should be guided by the same, but they are also now become a patern and exemplar to all the like places of the whole realme, whereby to be governed. The place hath in it sundry villages, although not thick set nor much inhabited; because it was, at the period this author wrote, (1656,) evil in winter, grievous in summer, and never good, as Hesiodus (the old poet) sometime said of the country where his father dwelt; and therefore very reasonable in their conceit, which doe imagine that Kent hath three steps, or degrees, of which the first (say they) offereth *wealth without health;* the second giveth both *wealth and health;* and the third affordeth *health* only, and little or no *wealth.* For if a man minding to pass through Kent towards London, should arrive, and make his first step on land in Romney Marsh, he shall rather find good grass underfoot, than wholesome air above the head; again, if he steps over the hills, and come into the Weald, he shall have at once the commodities *call et soli,* of the aire and of the earth. But if he pass that, and climb the next step of hills that aie between him and London, he shall have wood, conies, and corn for his wealth, and (toward the increase of his health) if he sicke, he shall find a good stomach in the stone field. No marvel it is therefore, if Romney Marsh be not greatly peopled, seeing most men be yet still of Porcius Cato his mind, who held them stark mad that would dwell in an unwhole some air, were the soil never so good and fertile.

"And hereof it came to pass, that King Edward the Fourth (in the beginning of his reign) granted, and each prince sithence hath confirmed, that the inhabitants of all the towns within the limits of Romney Marsh should be incorporated by the name of bayliffe, twenty-four jurats, and commonaltie of Romney Marsh in the countie of Kent, having a court from three weeks to three weeks, in which they hold pleas of all actions, real and personal, civil and criminal; having power to choose four justices of the peace yearly amongst themselves, besides the bayliffe, who is armed with the like authority, having moreover the return of all the prince's writs, the benefit of all fines, forfeits, and amerciaments, the privileges of leet, law-day and tourne, and exemption from tolle and tare, scot and lot, fifteen and subsidie, and from so many other charges as no one place within the realme hath. All which was done (as it appeareth in the Charter itself) to allure men to inhabit the Marsh, which they had before then abandoned, partly for the unwholesomeness of the soil, and partly for fear of the enemie, who had so often brout and spoiled them. And whereas this princely policie hath found such prosperous success, as the like did in the citie of Alexandria, builded by Alexander the Great, and in Newhaven, founded by Francis the French king, that is chiefly to be imputed to the incommoditie of the place, the which (besides the inclemencie of the aire itself) affordeth no one good haven or creek for enjoying the benefits of the sea. To conclude, the court of all this libertie, together with the records thereof, is kept at Dymchurch, in a place then lately built for that purpose, and thereof aptly called Newhall."

The work of William Lambard, from which the foregoing particulars are taken, is not only a very curious volume, but is also extremely scarce, and a copy is with difficulty to be obtained. It was published in 1656; and although, doubtless, many improvements have taken place in Romney Marsh since that period, the author of the present work preferred giving to his readers an account coeval with the times of which he was treating, considering any modern improvements quite foreign to the purpose.

The Honorable William Thomas Twiselt.in Fiennes, the eldest son of Lord Saye and Sele, is one of the conservators of the Corporation of the Bedford Level. It appears by Lambard, that John Fynes, one of his Lortlship's ancestors, was created by William the Conqueror the first warden of the Cinque Ports, and constable of Dover Castle, *by gift of inheritance.* These offices continued in the family *by succession,* during the lives of his son James, who died at Folkston, and his grandson John. For some time afterwards they fell into other hands, but were restored by King Henry II. to Allen Fynes, from whom they descended to his eldest son James Fynes. They afterwards passed out of the family; but were revived in the person of James Fynes, Lord Saye, who was beheaded by Jack Cade. After the termination of disputes between the houses of York and Lancaster, James Lord Saye again held these honors, which, however, ultimately vested in the crown. This family is of great antiquity; and, being blended with the most important periods of our history, a memoir of them would form a very interesting volume.

"How long since, or by whom (says Sir Wil-Dugdnie, p. ie. liam Dugdale) this fruitful and large tract, containing no less than 24,000 acres, was won from the sea, there is no testimony left to us from any record or historian that ever 1 could discover; which defect doth strongly argue, that the first gaining thereof was a work of the greatest antiquity." Dugdale ultimately conjectures that the drainage was the work of the Romans.

In forming a government for the Fens, the Earl of Bedford was guided by the directions of the act of parliament passed in 1649; and indeed he had no other rule by which he could carry into effect his most anxious and praiseworthy desire of establishing the Company upon some firm and proper basis. The principles of the laws and customs of Romney Marsh were, after much discussion, finally adopted, as will appear from the following interesting proceedings:

"At an assembly and meetinge at Ely, the "nine and twentieth day of September, in the "yeare of our Lord one thousand six hundred "fifty and six, of the participants and adven"turers for dreyning of the Greate Levell of the "Fennes, extending itselfe into the countyes of "Northampton, Norfolke, Suffolke, Lincolne, "Cambridge, and Huntingdon, and the Isle of "Ely, or some of them, then present,

'William Earle of Bedford,

'Oliver S' John, Lord Chiefe Justice of the Court of Common Bench, at Westminster,

"Edward Russell, Esq.
"Richard Gorges, Esq.
"SrWalter S'John, Baronett,
"Sr Edward Partheriche, Kn',
"Francis S' John, Esq.
"Robert Castle, Esq.
"Thomas Chitchley, Esq.
"John Marsham, Esq.
"Robert Henley, Esq.
"Robert Hampson, Esq.
"John Trafford, Esq.
"John Carrill, Esq.
"Doctor Denton,
"William Weston, Esq.
"Richard Blackwall, Esq.
"John Knight, Gent.
"John Trenchard, Esq.
"Marke Bradley, Gent.
"William Drurye, Esq. "Samuel Fortrey, Esq. "Michael Selby, Gent. "Baldwyn Arthur,
   Gent. "Edward Partheriche,
   Esq. "Anthony Hamond,
   Esq. "William Underwood,
   Esq. "Francis Underwood,
   Esq. "Valentyne Walton,
   Esq. "Benjamin Henshawe,
   Esq.
"John Latch, Esq. "Alexander Jones, Gent. "William Crane, Esq. "Hamond Ward, Esq. "Thomas Juxon, Esq. "John Holgate, Gent. "John Sayer, Gent. "Robert Lane, Esq. "Jonas Moore, Gent. *It* George Keete, Gent. "George Gascoigne,
   Gent.

"It was unanimously and without the dissent "of any one ordered, by the said Earle, partici"pants, and ad venturers,- that the like lawes and ' customes of

Romney Marsh, in the county of "Kent, shall be in force, exercised, and used "within the said Greate Levell, for the safe guard "and conservac'on of the same, and uphoulding, ' repaireing, maintaiueing, and amending of the "workes for and conduceing to the dreyneinge "and preservation thereof."

"It is ordered by the said Earle of Bedford, Lords elected. "participants, and adventurers, that "The Right Hono'ble William Earle of Bedford, "The Right Hono'ble Oliver S'John, Lord Chiefe

"Justice of the Court of Common Bench at

"Westminster, "The Right Hono'ble John Thurloe, principall

"Secretary of Estate, "The Hono'ble Richard Gorges, "Sr Walter Sl John, Baronett, "Sr Gilbert Pickering, Knight and Baronett, "Sr Edward Partheriche, Knight, "Francis S' John, Esq., "Robert Castle, Esq., "John Trenchard, Esq., "Major Generall Edward Whaley, "Major Generall William Goaffe, "Thomas Chitcheley, Esq., "Anthony Hamond, Esq., "John Marsham, Esq., "Andrew Henley, Esq., "Robert Henley, Esq., "William Underwood, Esq., "Valentyne Walton, Esq.,

Vol. i. x
Steward.
Register.
Bailiff.
Jurats.
Benjamin Weston, Esq.,
Arthur Evelyn, Esq.,
Mathew Long, Esq.,
Benjamyn Henshawe, Esq.,
bee, and are constituted and ordained to bee,
lords of the said Greate Levell of the Fennes;
Arid are to have, use, and exercise, within the said Greate Levell, all and every the powers,
priviledges, and authorities, as the lords of
Rumney Marsh, in the county of Kent, have,
'Wse, or exercise, or lawfully may, within the said niarsb."

"It is ordered, that John Earle, Esq., be steward, and of standing councell unto the government established within the said Greate Levell of the Fennes."

"It is ordered, that Thomas Bland, Gent., be register and clarke unto the said government established within the said Greate Levell of the Fennes."

"It is ordered, that Francis Underwood, Esq.,
be bayliffe of the said Greate Levell of the
Fennes; And is to have, use, and exercise,
within the said Greate Level!, all and every the powers, priviledges, and authorities, as any bayliffe of Rumney Marsh, in the county of Kent, hath used or exercised, or lawfully might,
within the said marsh."

"It is ordered, that
Alexander Blake, of Peterborough, Esq.,
Samuel Fortrey, of Hoggington, Esq.,
Anthony Hamond, of Wilburton, Gent.,
"Edward Barber, of Denver, Esq.,
"Randolf Taylor, of Ely, Esq.,
' John Gibson, of Mildenhall, Gent.,
"George Gascoigne, of Chartress, Gent.,
"Richard Crane, of Maneu, Gent.,
"Jonas Moore, of Sothery, Gent.,
"John Bridgman, of Wicken, Gent.,
"John Child, of Coveney, Gent.,
"Henry Hampson, of Ely, Gent.,
"Edmond Welch, of Emley, Gent.,
"Gabriel Ellyot, of Peterborough, Gent.,
"John Potterne, of Stoney, Gent.,
"Henry Atkins, of Witlesea, Gent.,
"Henry Whetstone, of the same, Gent.,
"John Plomley, of March, Gent.,
"Humphrey Rowland, of Standground,
"John Savery, of Salter's Loade, Gent.,
"Jefferay Hawkins, of Ramsey, Gent.,
"William Batterne, of Thorney,
"John Gyles, of Thorney Abbey,
"Samuel Hockley, of Reach,
"be jurats for the said Create Level I of the
"Fennes; And are to have, use, and exercise, *f* within the said Levell, all and every the pow

"ers, priviledges, and authorities, as any the ju

"rats of Rumney Marsh have used or exercised,

"or lawfully might, within the said marsh."

"It is ordered, that the owners for the time Lords. "being, of the severall parcel Is of fenny and late "surrounded grounds hereinafter mentioned, "parte of the 95,000" in the acte of parl't for "dreyneing of the said Create Levell, shall be "lords within the said Greate Levell, viz.,

"That the Right Hono'ble William Earle of "Bedford, owner of 500 acres, part of 4000% the "20th lot lyeing in Knare Fenn, in Thorney, in "the Isle of Ely, and county of Cambridge, being "that part of the said 4000" abutting eastward *11* upon the common of Wisbech, called High "Fenn, and southward upon the north banke of "Moorton's Leame, his heires and assignes there"of, shall be one of the lords within the said "Greate Levell."

"Oliver St. John, Lord Chiefe Justice of the "Court of Common Bench at Westminster, owner "of 500% parte of 940", in Fassett common, in "the county of Huntingdon, being that part of "the said 940» lyeing next unto Witlesea Meare, "his heires and assignes thereof, shall be one "other of the lords within the said Greate Le"vell."

"The Right Hono'ble John Thurloe, principall "secretary of estate, owner of 500" in the com"mon Fenn called Burrowe Moore, in Dod"dington, in the said Isle of Ely, and county of "Cambridge, in the 14th lott, abutting upon Ran"some Moore and the river Neane, his heires "and assignes thereof, shall be one other of the "lords within the said Greate Levell."

"The Right Hono'ble Edward Whaley, major "generall, owner of 500", that is to say, 300a in "Helgea and Sotherey Common, in the county of "Norfolke, in the 8th lott A., adjoyneing upon Sr "Henry Willowbye's draine, and abutting upon "the river Ouze, and 200" next adjoyneing, be"ing part of 300" in the same commons, in the "9th lott B, his heires and assignes thereof, shall "be one other of the lords within the said Greate." Levell."

"The Right Hono'ble William Goaff, major "generall, owner of 500", that is to say, 400a be"ing that part of 473" in Wisbech High Fenn, iu "the said Isle of Ely, and county of Cambridge, "in the 18th lott C, next adjoyneing unto 313s in "the IS'Mott B, and 100% part of the said 313', "next adjoyneing unto the said 400", his heires "and assignes thereof, shall be one other of the "lords within the said Greate Levell."

"The Right Hono'ble Richard Gorges, sonne "and heire apparent of Edward Lord Gorges, "owner of 500" in Pulver Fenn and Turke Fenn, "in the said Isle of Ely, and county of Cambridge, "in the 15th lott F, lyeing west, on the West"water, and about St. Bennett's Crosse, his "heires and assignes thereof, shall be one other "of the lords within the said Greate Levell."

"The Right Hono'ble Benjamyn Weston, Esq., "owner of 500", that is to say, 100a in Flegg "Fenn and Flegg Croft, in Witlesea, in the said "Isle of Ely, and county of Cambridge, and 400" "in the same Fenn next adjoyneing, his heires "and assignes thereof, shall be one other of the "lords within the said Greate Levell."

"The Right Honorable Sir Gilbert Pickering, "Baronettj owner of 200a in Londoner's Fenn, "part of the 10th lott, his heires and assignes "thereof, shall be one other of the lords within "the said Great Levell."

"Sir Walter St. John, Baronett, owner of 500% "part of 932", in Eastree Fenn, in Witlesea, in "the said Isle of Ely, and county of Cambridge, "being that part of the said 932", abutting upon "the south bank of Mooreton's Leam, his heires "and assignes thereof, shall be one other of the "lords within the said Greate Levell."

"Sr Edward Partheriche, Knight, owner of "500", that is to say, 350" in Litleport, whereof "135" is part of 200"in the third lott; 100",part "of 400" in the sixth lott, Westmore east D; 45", "Hawkins and Crouchmore in the 13th lott; 70% "next Priest Houses, A, in the 13th lott; and 150"in Whelpmore, in the 12th lott, in the said Isle "of Ely, and county of Cambridge, his heires and "assignes thereof, shall be one other of the lords "within the said Greate Levell."

"Robert Castle, Esq, owner of 500", that is to "say, 250, the moytie of 500", in Greate Met"lam, in Soham, in the said county of Cam"bridge, in the 17th lott B, and the remaining "250" of the said 500", his heires and assignes "thereof, shall be one other of the lordes within "the said Great Levell."

"Valentine Walton, Esq., owner of 500", that is "to say, 333" in Somersham common, in the 12tfc "lott E, in the said county of Huntingdon, ad"joyneing upon the common, and abutting, th'one "end upon the Hards, and th' other upon Fenton's u Loade; and 167-, part of 300, in the 5th lott D "next adjoyneing, his heires and assignes thereof, "shall be one other of the lords within the said "Create Levell."

"Francis St. John, Esq, owner of 500", part of "632, in the Fenn grounds of Yaxley, in the said "county of Huntingdon, being that part of the "said 632 next adjoyneing unto WhitleseaMeare, "his heires and assignes thereof, shall be one "other of the lords within the said Greate Le« vell."

"Thomas Chitchley, Esq., owner of 600», part "of 569", in Greate Metlam, in Soham, in the " said county of Cambridge, in the 18th lott C, "being that part of the said 569' lyeing next the "river, his heires and assignes thereof, shall be "one other of the lords within the said Greate "Levell." Anthony Hamond, Esq., owner of 500", that "is to say, 300" in Downham common, and se"veralls, in the 12th lott, in the said Isle of Ely, "and county of Cambridge, abutting upon Down"bam common; and 88" in Cow Fenn, exchanged "by the com" for 88" in Downham aforesaid, and "112', part of 152' in Pyemore, in the llth lott, "next adjoyneing unto the said 300", his heires "and assigns thereof, shall be one other of the "lords within the said Greate Levell."

"John Trenchard, Esq., owner of 500» in the "county of Suffolke, that is to say, '200" in La-" kingheath, &c., H. in the 8th lott; 200" in "Towne-moores, in the 4th lott D; and 100% part "of 200», in the 7th lott G, next adjoyneing unto "the said 200", his heires and assignes thereof, "shall be one other of the lords within the said "Greate Levell."

"Arthur Evelyn, Esq., owner of 500a in West"more, south of Bedford Old River, in the said "Isle of Ely, and county of Cambridge, that is to "say, 400" lyeing on the south side of the said "river, in the 4th lott B, and 100% part of 400", in "the 5th lott C., next adjoyneing, his heires and "assignes thereof, shall be one other of the lords "within the said Greate Levell."

"Andrew Henley, Esq., owner of 500" in Byall "Fenn, in the said Isle of Ely, and county of "Cambridge, his heires and assignes thereof, shall "be one other of the lords within the said Greate "Levell."

"Will iam Underwood, Esq., owner of 500% part .' of 600a in Lakingheath aforesaid, in the said :" county of Suffolke, in the first, second, and

"third lotts, being that part of the said 600" lye

"ing next unto the towne of Lakingheath, his

"heires and assignes thereof, shall be one other

"of the lords within the said Create Levell."

"Robert Henley, Esq., owner of 500" in Bur"rowe Greate Fenn, in the county of Hunting"don, his heires and assignes, owners thereof, "shall be one other of the lords within the said "Create Levell."

"John Marsham, Esq., owner of 500" in Sto"ney and Blocke Fenn, in the said Isle of Ely, "and county of Cambridge, that is to say, 400" "in the 12th lott D, and l()0a, parte of 400% in the "third lott C, being that parte of the said last "mentioned 400", and next adjoyneing unto the "first mentioned 400% his heires and assignes "thereof, shall be one other of the lords within "the said Greate Levell."

"Mathew Longe, Esq., owner of

500% in Neate"more, in Upwell, in the said county of Nor"folke, that is to say, 250" in the 11th lott A., and "250" next adjoyneing the 13th lott B., his heires "and assignes thereof, shall be one other of the "lords within the said Greate Levell."

"Benjamyn Henshawe, Esq., owner of 500" in "Methwold, in the said county of Norfolke, that " is to say, 488" in Methwold common, in the "11th lott F. , and 12% out of 400% nextadjoyne"ing in the 7th lott, being that part of the said "400" next the river Ouze, his heires and assignes "thereof, shall be one other of the lords within "the said Greate Levell."

"And that the said lords, and their heires and "assignes, for the time being, of the severall por"tions of land aforesaid, shall, from time to time, "for ever hereafter, have, act, use, exercise, and "performe, all and every the like powers, privi"ledges and authorityes, within the said Greate "Levell, as the lords in Romney Marsh, att the "time of the making of the said act, have, did, "may, or of right ought to use, exercise, or per"forme within Romney Marsh."

"Resolved upon the question,"

"That there be one expenditor for the Greate
Levell of the Fennes."

"That there be two serjeants for the Middle
Levell."

"Two serjeants for the South Levell."
"One serjeant for the North Levell."

"Ordered, that Mr. George Dalton be expenditor for the Greate Levell of the Fennes."

"Ordered, that George Hall and Christopher
Bird be bayliffs for the Middle Levell; George
Barnes and Thomas Moore for the South Levell;
and Edward Baker for the North Levell: who are to use and exercise within the said Levell the powers as the serjeant of Romney Marsh doth or may lawfully doe."

"Ordered, that all persons heretofore setled and established by order of the Company, concerning the stateing and takeing accompts, be continued with their sallarys; and nll things in relation to such accompts are to continue as now they be untill further orders."

"Ordered, that all officers nowe employed in any workes, be continued in their severall places and employments as now they are, and until further orders."

"Ordered, that Mr. Dalton, the expenditor, doe prepare a schedule of all taxes now in arreare,
and upon what lands, and to present the same at twoe of the clock this afternoon unto the
Company, to the end the lands may be sold for the taxes arreare."

"Ordered, that Mr. Bayliffe Underwood be al"lowed twenty shillings *per diem* for his travelling "charges, when and soe often as he shall be em"ployed, or meete the jurats upon the publick "businesse of the societie; And to have and re"ceive to his owne use all such fees and allow'" ances within the said Levell, as the bayliff of "Romney Marsh, in the said county of Kent, "useth to take or receive, or lawfully may."

"Ordered, that Mr. Bayliff doe elect a fitt per*u* son to be his clarke, to attend him att his "meetings with the jurats of the said Levell, "to make entryes in a booke of their acts and pro"ceedings, who is to have twenty pounds per an"num for his sallary paid unto him by the ex"penditor."

"Ordered, that every jurat for the said Greate "Levell of the Fennes be allowed five shillings "*per diem* for his travelling charges, when and "soe often as any of them shall singly, or with "others, make a view of the workeg within the "said Levell; and six shillings eight pence *per* "*diem,* when and soe often as they, and every of "them, shall meete Mr. Bayliff upon the pub"lique business of the said society."

"Ordered, that every serjeant of the said "Levell, be allowed three shillings foure pence *"per diem* for his travelling charges, when and "soe often as he shall be employed by Mr. Bay"liff alone, or by Mr. Bayliff and the jurats upon "the publick businesse of the said society;

And "the said serjeants are to have and receive all
"fees used and accustomed to be received by the "serjeant of Romney Marsh."

"Ordered, that Sr Edward Partherich, Knight, "John Latch, Anthony Hammond, William Crane, "and Samuel Fortrey, Esqre8, be a committee to "prepare instructions for Mr. Bayliff and the Ju"rats of the said Levell: And when the same are "resolved upon, they are desired to deliver them "unto the register and clarke, to enter the same, "who is to send coppyes thereof unto Mr. Bay"liff."

"Ordered, that Mr. Earle be allowed one hun"dred pounds per ann. for his fee of being stew"ard and councell, and to be paid by the expen"ditor halfe yearely."

"Ordered, that Mr. Bland, the register and "clarke, be allowed for his extraordinary paines "and travelling charges this summer upon the "Company's businesse, the summe of thirty pounds, "to be paid by the expenditor, Mr. George Dal"ton."

"Ordered, that Mr. Eland's former sallary be "continued; and that Sr Edward Partherich, "Knight, John Latch, Anthony Hammond, Wil"Ham Crane, and Samuel Fortrey, Esquires, be a "committee, to consider of and direct his em"ployment as register and clarke, and what they "think fitt to allowe him for his attendance there"in, and the way and manner of raiseing the "same; and the certificate of the said committee, "is to be entered, and to be performed and pur"sued."

"*The Committee's certificate for the Register "and Clarke's employment, 1st October,* "16,50."

"1st. To attend the governour, deputy governoar, "bailiffs, and commonalty, at all their meetings."

"2. To record all their orders and decrees, and "inroll all the leases and conveyances made by "the corporation, in a book to be kept for that "purpose.''

"3. To doe all other matters and things which "any way may concerne the businesse of the said "corporation, as register and clarke."

"4. To attend the lords att their publick "meetings of session, and to prepare their de"crees, enter and inroll the same, and all their "orders."

"5. When there shall be occasion fora publick "meeting of the bailiff and jurats, upon notice "thereof from Mr. Bailiff, to give attendance "there, and to enter and inroll their proceed"ings."

"6. To extract unto the serjeants all the fines "and amerciaments sett and imposed before the "lords att their sessions, and by the said bailiff '' and jurats, at their meetings."

"7. To enter and.inroll all the proceedings "transmitted from the bayliff and juratts."

"All which proceedings are to be entered and "inrolled in several bookes, to be prepared for "that purpose."

"8. To inroll all deedes whereby any estate of "freehoukl is conveyed of any part of the 95000

"acres in a booke to be prepared for that pur*fl* pose; And to have and receive such and the "like fees as have been accustomed to be paid."

"9. To make an entry of all leases of any part "of the said 95,000" in a booke to be prepared "for that purpose; and to receive for such entry "twoe shillings six pence."

"10. The bookes are to be prepared at the "Companye's charge."

"11. To be allowed a yearely sallary of fifty "pounds, to be quarterly paid, for his attendance "as register and clarke unto the said corporation "and lords att their sessions, and to be allowed "reasonable travelling charges, when imployed "about the publick affaires of the Company."

"12. All the bookes of entryes and inrollments "to be delivered unto the said register and clarke ' by indenture."

"Edward Partherich,
"Anthony Hamond,
"John Latch,
« William Crane."

"And lastly, it is ordered, that none of the 11 orders made att this general 1 assembly and "meeting, nor any of the matters in them con"teyned, concerning the government of the said "Levell by the charter of incorporation under "the greate scale of England, bearing teste att ""Westminster, the thirteenth day of March, in "the tenth yeare of the reigne of the late King ". Charles, the lords, bayliff, and jurats, and their "successors, and the lawes and customs of Rom"ney Marsh, nor noe other matter or thing con"cerning the government of the said Levell by '' the officers and persons aforesaid, and their "successors, according to their severall jurisdic"tions and autboritves limited unto them, estab"lished and setled, shall be reversed, altered, "changed, or suspended, but by the consent of the "governour, deputy-governour, bayliffs, andcom"monalty, participants, and adventurers, have"ing fifty-five thousand acres att the least of the "said ninety-five thousand acres."

Tlie system of government thus arranged was perhaps the best that could have been devised under all the pressing emergencies of the case. It did not, however, " work well," and was soon discovered to be utterly inefficient for the purposes required. Taxes were imposed; but there was extreme difficulty in obtaining payment.

The government of Cromwell had now attained an acknowledged stability. He had conciliated many of the ancient nobility. A parliament had been elected by the people. The Earl of Bedford never shrunk from any exertions that were likely to promote and benefit the grand object of his life, a complete drainage of the Great Levell.

At a meeting of the company, held at the chambers of Lord Chief Justice St. John, in Lincoln's Inn, on the 26th January, 1656, appear the fol-A. u. n;r;. lowing orders: -" Ordered, that Mr. Gorges, unto whose care "the sole management of the companye's affaires

"are committed, be desired to advise with Mr.

"Serjeant Fountayne, or other counsell, to pre

"pare a petition to the parliament, and an act

"whereby the 95,000" may for the future be taxed

"by themselves, and apart from the several coun

"tyes and parishes wherein the same doe or are

"supposed to lye upon all future taxes and pub

"lick charges; And alsoe, that the said 95,000"

"may be exempted from payment of tythes in

"kind unto any of the impropriators, rectors,

"parsons, or vicars, or any other charges or as

"sessments, unto the parishes wherein the said

"95,000" doe or are supposed to lye; And that in

"recompence thereof, the said 95,000s may be

"-charged yearely to pay a reasonable summe of

"money unto the Commonwealth, to be imployed

"in maintenance of preaching ministers, or other

"wise as the state shall direct, until there shall

"be churches and chappells built within the

"Greate Levell of the Fennes, according to the

"power given by the charter of incorporation

"of the late King Charles, or in such other way

"as councell shall advise to be most convenient."

"Ordered, that Mr. Gorges be desired to ad

"vise with Mr. Serjeant Fountayne, or other

"councell, to prepare a petition to his Highnesse

"the Lord Protector, for granting letters patents

"of incorporation unto the lords, bayliffs, jurats,

"and coi'alty of the Greate Levell of the Fennes,

"or as participants and adventurers, as councell

"shall advise; And for granting such jurisdic

"tions, priviledges, and immunityes, as may be "convenient and necessary; And to incorporate

"the towne of within the said Greate

"Levell, with a mayor, aldermen, and coi'alty, one "markett every weeke, and two fayres yearely; "And to prepare and frame a draught in paper "for such letters patents, or in such other way ' as councell shall advise, and effectually to pro"secute the same."

"Ordered, that Mr. Gorges do purchase, or

"cause to be built, att the towne of,

"a convenient house, with necessary accomoda"tions, for the publique meetings of the lords, "bailiffe, jurats, and coi'alty, and for theire re"ceipt and entertainement, and to fitt and prepare "the same att or before their next meeting in "Easter weeke, if it may be, att the charge of the "Company."

The Company afterwards met at "Mistris Hen"ley's house" until the 18th of April, 1657, when the Honorable Richard Gorges, having succeeded to the title of his father, and become Lord Gorges, was desired to provide chambers in the Temple or elsewhere, at the Company's charge, and to fit and prepare the same for their public meetings. On the 15th of May following, the Company appear to have met for the last time at the Lord Chief Justice's chamber; at least there are no records of any further proceedings until the Restoration.

The first meeting at the Fen Office in the Inner Temple appears to have taken place on the 20th of June, 1660.

A succession of misfortunes at this time ocVol. i. v cut-red in the family of Cromwell, which terminated in the death of the protector, and finally in the extinction of his government, and of the Commonwealth, and contributed to the restoration of King Charles the Second. Cromwell died on the 3rd of September, 1658, the anniversary of his victories of Dunbar and Worcester. Although his son, Richard Cromwell, was nominated his successor, it *was* clearly discernible that the protectorate government would expire with the mighty genius by which it had been created and consolidated. By this event new and arduous duties devolved upon William Earl of Bedford. Well was it for the Great Level that that incomparable nobleman possessed such an inexhaustible store of patience, zeal, and perseverance.

CHAFFER XIII. *Causes of the Restoration.—Situation of the Earl of Bedford, his participants, and adventurers.—Desertion of Saint John.—Lord Gorges.—The Earl of Bedford's return to parliament.—The Restoration.—State of the Level.—First temporary act.—Earl of Bedford's petition, and order thereon.—Second temporary act.—King's proclamation.—Commission of Sewers.—The State of parties in the Great Level.—Further parliamentary proceedings.—The General Drainage Act. g*

The restoration of Kins' Charles the Second

Restoration.

completely changed the aspect of public affairs throughout the kingdom. The defection of Monke, the commander of the army, and the intrepidity of Montagu, the commander of the navy, conduced to hasten that important event. "The nation, too, (says Godwin, in his History "of the Commonwealth,) was grown tired of a "perpetual uncertainty, and panted for a perma ' nent and substantial settlement. Various sys' tems had been started, some brilliant, some "full of generous sentiments of liberty, and of £ high and noble aspirations, but they had all *f* failed." The feelings of the English nation are determinately monarchical. It required, and it will ever require, great oppression, long system of misrule, as well as unfeeling indifference to the interests of the people, before this country can be made the scene of those tremendous convulsions which, in other nations, shake thrones and destroy dynasties "England, (continues the same historian,) "through every successive period of her history, "has had a king. The prejudices of the great "mass of her inhabitants are in accord with that "form of government. It is interwoven with all "her statutes. The very lawyers can scarcely see "a single step before them without the idea of "such an office, as the pole star of their proceed"ings. The tenure of every inch of land in the "country is either directly or indirectly feudal; "that is, involving in it the idea of the supreme "leader of an army, dividing the soil in great or "smaller parcels amongst his followers. Take "away this idea, and you almost wholly unsettle "all the notions of property that have been en"tertained, and our judges and courts would "scarcely know how to determine any question "of conveyance, entail, or inheritance, that came "before them. We cannot expect suddenly to "raise mankind to any standard of visionary per"fection; we must accommodate ourselves to

"their preconceptions, and take advantage even "of their prejudices, in the attainment of practi"cal benefits. The English people are habitually "a calculating and reasoning race."

It was clearly foreseen that the distractions of the country, arising from religious and political strife, would end, as they ultimately did, in the restoration of its ancient form of government. Whatever effect this event might have upon public affairs, it was a measure that must in its very nature sensibly affect the interests and the proceedings of those who were embarked in the great measure of the general drainage of the Fens, and who had already difficulties of no ordinary nature to contend with. The situation of the Earl of Bedford, at the death of Cromwell, was most embarrassing. Although he had taken no part whatever in the public proceedings of the long parliament, or of the Protector; nor is he mentioned as one of those noblemen who were courted by Cromwell, and became members of the House of Lords established by his government; still many, very many painful recollections, grievous misgivings, and fearful anticipations, must have perplexed and harassed the mind of this exalted nobleman. His illustrious father hadenrolled himself amongst that band of patriots, whose determined opposition to the arbitrary measures of an infatuated prince, led to those scenes which terminated in the civil war, and the extinction of monarchy. William Earl of Bedford, his son and successor, had also fought in the same glorious cause, against overweening prerogative; but although he soon retired from the service of the Parliament, as well as from all interference in political affairs, yet it cannot be denied, that when the happiness and property of thousands of the people were at stake, he readily stepped forward to accomplish that for others which his noble and disinterested nature prevented his doing for himself. The drainage act of 1649 was passed by the Long Parliament upon his request; the final adjudication of drainage was delivered by the judges of the Commonwealth; the confirmation of all the proceedings of the Earl and his participants and adventurers had taken place during the accession of Cromwell; and that confirmation was afterwards formally ratified under the parliament convoked by his authority. Princes and courtiers are not a forgiving race: they are (when it suits their purpose) endowed with long memories.. It was fair to suppose that the exiled monarch, on his return to his native land, and to the possession of the high destinies from which he had been so long expelled, would not only feel anxious, but that sound policy would induce him, to conciliate a man of the high station, the great wealth, and the extended popularity, of William Earl of Bedford. The situation of this nobleman, however, was by no means enviable; and a man of less moral courage, less perseverance, less energy of character, and less benevolence of disposition, would, long before the present conjuncture, upon many previous momentous periods of this great undertaking, have retired from the cause in disgust and despair. The difficulties of his situa-Desertion of tion were greatly augmented at this period of peril, by the desertion of St. John, his friend, his counsellor, and his coadjutor. The Lord Chief Justice had been too deeply involved in the late memorable proceedings, not to feel that his only means of safety consisted in an abandonment of that country which he had served with so much zeal and ability; but in which, he plainly foresaw, by the course of events, the improbability of his still continuing to fiad a secure asylum. Saint John retired to a foreign country; and, notwithstanding he returned some time afterwards, and effected a reconciliation with his sovereign, yet never again did he interest himself in any measure connected with the drainage of the Level. His fen estates were sold for nonpayment of the taxes on the 14th of March, 1657; and although two subsequent meetings of the Company took place in his chambers,on the 18th of April, and on the loth of May, 1657, he does not appear to have been present; nor have we any further record of his interfering in the affairs of the Company.

The loss of Saint John at this eventful crisis was a subject of most serious regret to the Earl of Bedford.; but it was in some degree compensated for by the accession to the interests of the Company of Lord Gorges, a nobleman who for many LrJ Gorges, years had taken a most active part in all the proceedings relative to the drainage of the Great Level. Richard Lord Gorges was the grandson pf Edward Lord Gorges, named in the indenture of fourteen parts, as one of the original participants with Earl Francis. This family had for many years taken great interest in the drainage of the Fens; and Richard held the very important office of surveyor-general, from the time of the establishment of the corporation to the period of his death. In his attention to the interests of the Fens he was indefatigable. The Earl of Bedford placed great reliance upon his judgment, and entertained the highest opinion of his integrity. Upon the death of Lord Gorges (the subject of these remarks) the title became extinct.

No proceedings whatever appear to have taken place between the last meeting of the company, on the 15th day of May, 1657, and the period of the restoration; at least, no record of any such Proceedings of proceeding is discoverable. The government (If it may be so called) during the short period the death of Crom-gUpreme authority was vested in that weak and irresolute person Richard Cromwell, was in a state of distraction. The parliament convened by him met only to give way to the reassembling of the remains (or, as it was then facetiously called, the rump) of the long parliament. Their deliberations continued until the 6th of March, 1660, when they dissolved themselves, and thus put a termination to that most famous assembly.

The interval between the death of Cromwell and the restoration, was passed in mere squabbles for power between the several leaders of the army, the remains of the old republicans, and the chief partisans of the numerous religious sects which had arisen during the Commonwealth, especially the presbyterians. The people looked on with indifference: the result was easily anticipated. On the 25th of April, 1660, a new parliament assembled, and the lords (in defiance of a promise made by General Monke to exclude them) again took their seats in the upper house, and made choice of the Earl of Manchester as their speaker. Immediately after the meeting, they ordered the Earl of Manchester to write to the Earl of Bedford to take his place in their house; which the latter accordingly did. The Earl of Bedford ThcEariof had too much penetration not to foresee, that the tirnisto pTrleaders of parliament designed the restoration. On liamcDt Friday, the 27th of April, 1660, the lords desired a conference with the house of commons, "to "consider of some way and means to make up all "the breaches and distractions of the kingdom." The Earl of Bedford was one of the lords appointed to manage the conference. The commons chose Sir Harbottle Grimstone as their speaker. Both houses confirmed General Monke's commission of Captain General, and the members emulated each other in expressing their abhorrence of the execution of the late King, and in reflecting on the memory of Cromwell. This was a prelude to the restoration. Charles was proclaimed on the 8th of May, 1660, and arrangements were instantly made for his unconditional restoration; but not without an ineffectual attempt on the part of that eminent and distinguished statesman and lawyer, Sir Mathew Hale, to impose certain restrictions upon the return of the king. Montagu was despatched to attend his majesty to England; and the monarch was restored to his dominions and throne amidst the most general demonstrations of joy. The presbyterians, however, who had mainly contributed to bring about this event, were ere long taught by oppression not to rejoice over the humiliation of the republicans. No idea was ever more erroneous than that Charles and his friends acted mercifully towards their adversaries: in truth, they proceeded as far as they durst, and even pursued by assassins some of those who had sought refuge in foreign climes. The king's undisguised encouragement of every species of profligacy, reflects disgrace on the age that could tolerate such conduct. His violation of the law, and his designs against religion, evince that (like princes in general) he had neither profited by experience, nor improved by adversity.

On the 15th of May, 1661, (a week after the proclamation,) the Earl of Bedford was appointed one of the peers "to view and consider of what w ordinances had been made since the lords aud "parliament were voted useless, which now pass "as acts of parliament; and to draw up and pre"pare an act, to present to the house, to repeal "what they think fit; and the Lord Chief Baron "Weld and Mr. Serjeant Mallet to assist them."

The important charge thus committed to the Earl and his learned colleagues was performed with great circumspection. A bill was introduced into the house of lords, and after passing that house and the commons, it received the royal assent. By this act it was provided, "That the izcar.2. "parliament begun and holden at Westminster, "the third day of November, in the 16th year of "the reign of the late King Charles of blessed "memory, should be fully dissolved and deter"mined." All acts of parliament passed during the interregnum, not reenacted after the restoration, were subsequently declared null and void.

Let us here consider the fearful situation of the Great Level, and the difficulties by which the Earl of Bedford was surrounded. Our readers will recollect, that by the original contract in the Lynn law, 12,000acres were given to the crown App. p. 109. in return for its support to the measure of drainage.

King Charles the First had granted 2000 acres, part thereof, to his lord treasurer, Jerome Earl of Portland . The remaining 10,000 acres continued in the crown until the time of the king's death. In the pretended act, (as it must now be called,) passed 1649, no mention whatever is made, either of the 2000 acres vested in the Earl of ToTtlaod, or of the 10,000 acres then lately vested in the crown. The whole 95,000 acres (as set out by the St. Ives Law) are vested in the trustees appointed by the act of 1649, for the benefit of the Earl of Bedford, his participants, and adventurers. Ante, p. 173. Mr. Weston, on the part of the Earl of Portland, This nobleman resided in great privacy during the commonwealth, at Whittlesey, in the Isle of Ely; but history gives no record of his public life beyond what is stated in a note in the Appendix to this work, page 388.

it has been already stated, agreed with the Company to *pay pro raid* the taxes generally imposed upon the whole Level, and then continued in possession. Upon the restoration, those who had shared inthe misfortunes naturallyexpected to participate in the prosperity of the king. The Great Level being now drained, and the works completed, it became evident that the crown, which had at this juncture so many favourites to reward, and so many interests to conciliate, would not forget its claims upon this large proportion of the Level. The claim was in effect made, and ultimately substantiated. Many of the old adventurers had been ejected from their lands during the commonwealth, in consequence of their taxes being unpaid; and sales were made from time to time, while the owners (in consequence of their adhesion to the royal cause) were either residing abroad, or suffering under the most painful deprivations at home. *Fas aut nefas,* they claimed restitution. The hostility to the measure of drainage, which had never entirely ceased, now broke out in violent threats. Tumultuous assemblies took place, and serious apprehension was felt that the works, which had been raised with such unceasing care, labour, and perseveran-

ce, would be utterly destroyed. The efforts of the discontented seemed particularly directed against the great bank between Over-Cote and Earith. This expected disturbance was the more fearful, from the state of the laws, and the powerless situation, in this respect, of the Earl of Bedford, and the participants, and adventurers. The laws of the restoration had abrogated those of the commonwealth. The Earl of Bedford found himself situated as he had been at the death of his noble father. Neither his spirit It has been stated, upon the authority of Clarendon and other writers, that this distinguished nobleman died of the small pox; but this is doubtful. The author, since writing that part of his work which refers to this melancholy event, has discovered a See ante, curious document, which may be interesting, not only as a p' specimen of style of composition, but also because it relates to Francis and William Earls of Bedford. The document is entitled, "The Earle of Bedford's Passage to the Highest Court of "Parliament, May the ninth, 1641, about tenne a'clock in the "Morning, observed by his lordship's phisician, Doctor Cade"man. London, Printed for Hugh Perry, 1641."

"*The Earle of Bedford's Passage to the Highest Court of "Parliament." "*Upon the sad newes of the death of Master Francis Russell "at Paris, his father, my most honoured Lord of Bedford, told "me that foure faire oakcs of his were lately blowne downe "as it were altogether; of which subject my lord made so "moving a discourse, as it seemed to mee their extirpation "tooke deepe roote in his thoughts. Shortly after, my lord "sent for me againe, and then complained that he found his "owne health somewhat shaken: wherefore, to lesson the "maintenance of a future sicknesse, he desired to resume a "vomit, which the last yeare had gently cured him of churlish "sicknesse in the countrey: but in this, both my lord and my"self were willing to aske the counsell and consent of Dr. "C'raige, as well a true friend as a faithful phisician to his "lordship. Hee frnding him the next day in a feverish dis"position, inclined to the letting of his lordship's blood first, "which as it was learnedly proposed, so it was presently exe"cuted. Afterwards, seeing my lord continue sicke by an op"pression of choller in his stomacke, consented to give him a ". vomit. When that had done working, as it often happens, nor his activity shrunk one moment from difficulties, however appalling. The Lynn law was still in operation, and the general statute of sewers, (23

"nature being discharged of one burden, herselfe shakes off "another, like *Gallen's* asse, that was too weak to winch off "two snckes, would never bear one, there flourished in divers "parts of his skin some red spots, which my noble Lndy "Brooke, my lord's daughters, and Misteris Roberts, his dili"gent servant, first observed; whereupon my lord, who ever "considered other's safety before his owne content, with ex"traordinary earnestnesse, forced his dear lady and children, "much against their wills, to leave him.

"This yeare, that hath been fertile of wonders, many strange "eruptions have beene made in the skin that have resembled "the small poxe, when it proved otherwise, even to the de"ce'rving of the best phisicians; no dishonour to the profes"sion. The clearest knowledge of mankind is clouded with "errors in all employments. *An medicina an non putanda et,t "quam tamen mutta fallunt. "*My lord being thus parted from his dearest lady and chil"dren, as a tree, without a barke and branches.

"Out of the great zeale, the influence of my lord's favours to "me, hud kindled in my heart, put me into passion, which, if "it makes us blind and unable to see things present, much "more it does obscure things farre off, and to come. All that "I could doe for that time to comfort my lord and myselfe was "to say, I believed it was but a simple boyling of blood, which "he had often formerly had, and had neither the infection nor " the perill of the small poxe. I endeavoured to be very eheer"ful with him, having ever found that the speeches of the "phisician as good and bad aspects do govern and raigne much "in the hearts and thoughts of the patients, and much more "with their passions, heighten or lessen the power of their "sicknesse.

"Some recover of the plague, because they never knew they "had it; others dye of a fit of the ague, because they thought Hen. 8. c. 5.), as well as the general drainage act of App. *f. m.* Queen Elizabeth (43 Eliz. c. 11.), were still valid and existing laws. The Earl felt the necessity of

"it the plague: nlwaise the small poxe comes soonest out, "when 'tis not thought of within, to the great security of them "that have it: for amongst all good signs in that disease, that "is the best, that they breake forth together and quickly; how"soever, all exanthemata and eruptions to the skine require the "same cure and government, except some are pursued and "chased out with lcsse severitie.

"There are plants thrive best in the shades, and others "better on any hills; my lord's body was so subtile, as he "could scarce endure to bee covered up a whole night in hte "bed. We can take up coales in their embers, but flames "never.

"A faithful servant of his told me, hee was so wearie of his "bed, as hee feared it would be his grave, by these words, / "*foole away my life to observe the physicinns;* and, in my hear"ing, when he was denied to rise, he sighed out this profes"sion of obedience: *well then, I will die to observe the physi"eiant.* If I were now upon my death bed, and to declare "what my lord died on, I should say hee died of too much of "his bed, and not of the suialle poxe: tillSaterday night I am "sure hee had no signe of danger, as I am sure that then there "was no hope of life, nature having given over the field to de"votion, which came in so armed and so invincible as I never "saw the like, though I have waited upon many who had no "other businesse in life than to die well; his breath was spent "before his eies and hands ceased to be raised to heaven, as if "his soule would have carried his body along with it.

"Thus, though he commanded his body to bee buried with "decency, but not pompe, yet I could not but publish the glo"rious manner of his death. Those that knew the obligations "I had to this great and good lord will, I presume, pardon his "lordship's constant honourer, T. C."

It would seem that the above very curious document was restoring tranquillity in the Level, before any steps could be taken to enable him to carry into effect or assume the power and authority even of the existing laws. Accompanied by Lord Gorges, he left London for the Great Level. The greatest number of discontents were in the South Level, particularly in the neighbourhood of Swaffham Reach, Swasesey, and Over. Indeed, the inhabitants of those parts of the Level had never generally concurred in the measure of drainage. The Earl sought out the leaders; he heard their complaints, and promised them redress. His appearance amongst them, the urbanity of his manners, and the recollection of his long and faithful services, appeased their anger, and quieted their hostility. He felt it prudent, however, to employ persons to Watch the great works both day and night, until affairs should arrive at a more settled state; and these judicious arrangements being completed, the noble lords returned to London. It was obvious to the Earl of Bedford, that amongst so many conflicting interests and passions, no general measure of legislation could immediately be expected. The Earl had a most difficult task to perform. His caution was equal to bis perseve written purposely to disprove a report that the Earl died of the small-pox: and hence we may infer, that such a death was rather a disgrace, and that the prejudice and horror excited by this disease existed at that period in the greatest degree j and we all know that those feelings are scarcely eradicated in the present day, notwithstanding the "march of intellect," with JLawyer Brougham's "schoolmaster abroad."— 1829.

ranee. He presented a petition to parliament, stating fully all the facts of the case, and praying for leave to bring in a bill for settling the drainage of the

Great Level of the Fens. Leave was given, and the bill was introduced in the month of May, 1660; but it will be seen presently, that this proceeding instantly set in motion all the conflicting interests, thereby convincing the Earl that a long time must elapse before any general measure could be adopted. Therefore, without arresting the progress of the general bill, or interfering with the proceedings of the litigating parties, his lordship, on the 31st of August, 1660, introduced the following temporary bill.

"*An Act for the necessary maintenance of the "work of dreynlng the Great Levell of the "Ferns." "*Be it enacted, by the king's most excellent First tempo"majestie, by the advice and with the consent of rary "the lords and commons assembled in purliu"ment, that for maintenance and preservation of "the Great Levell of the Fenns, extending itselfe "into the countyes of Northampton, Norfolke, "Suffolke, Lincolne, Cambridge, and Hunting"don, and the Isle of Ely, or some of them, and "for layeingand leavying of taxes, and secureing "the said Levell from drowning only, that all "taxes already made and assessed, or to be made ' or assessed, only upon the ninety five thousand "acres given by one pretended act of parlia"ment, of the twenty ninth day of May, one

Vol. i. z

"thousand six hundred forty-nyne, unto William "Earleof Bedford, Edward Russell, Esq., Robert "Henley, Esq., deceased, and Robert Castle, Esq., "and their heires and assignes, in trust for the "saidEarle, his participants, and adventurers, for "dreyning of the said Great Levell before the "twenty-ninth day of May next comeing, by co"lour of, or according to the intent of the said "pretended act, shall stand in force, and shall w and niay be collected and gathered, soe as the said taxes to be hereafter sett upon the said "nynety-five thousand acres exceede not three *v*-shillings the acre; and that all arreares of rent "already incurred upon or out of any part of the "said nynety-five thousand acres, or that shall "incurr or grow due before the said twenty-ninth "day of May next comeing, upon any contract "or lease of the premises, or any part or parcel ' thereof, shall be received and recovered as if the-' said pretended act had been a good and effec tuall act; and the possession of the nynety-five "thousand apres is setled and quyeted as the "same now is, untill the said twenty-ninth day of "May next, any thing to the contrary thereof "notwithstanding. Provided allwayes, and it is "further enacted and declared, that this act, nor "any thing therein conteyned, shall extend, or be "construed to extend, to preclude the king's ma"jestie, or any other person or persons, from and *fl* after the said twenty-nyntli day of May, one "thousand six hundred sixtie one, from any right, "tytle, claymCj or interest, which his majestic, or "any other person or persons had, hath, or may "have, or pretend to have, to any part of the said "nynety-five thousand acres mentioned in the "said pretended act; but that all such right and "title shall be preserved to his majestie, and to "all such other persons, after the expiration of "this act, as fully as if this act had not beene "made, or according to such determination as "shall be thereof made by the parliament, before "the said twenty-ninth day of May, one thou"sand six hundred sixtie one. Provided alsoe, "that this act shall not be construed or made use "of to countenance or confirm any sales, for"feiture, or other dispositions, conveyances, or "estates of lands, made for non-payment of "taxes and assessments, or otherwise, or to make "good any act or thing whatsoever that hath "been, or shall be done, in pursuance or by co"lour of the said pretended act, after the said "twenty-nynth day of May, one thousand six "hundred sixtie one; but that all persons con"cerned, and all things and estates, shall be "and remayne in the same state and condition "from and after the said twenty-nynth of May, "as if this act had never beene made. Provided "allways, and be it enacted by the authority "aforesaid, that all such differences as now are "or shall arise betweene the former adventurers "and the said Earle of Bedford and his partici"pants, and all things in difference and dispute "between the said Earl and participants, and "the countreys within or bordering upon the

"said Le'vell, are not att all concluded or over1' ruled by this act, or any thing therein conteyn"ed*;* but all the said differences are left to be *41* determined according to law and equity. Pro' vided alhvayes, and be it enacted by the autho!' rity aforesaid, that if, by occasion of tbeadvcn"turers' workes, the water shall be raised highei4 "on the auncient banekes then formerly, to the *u* damage of the countrey; that then the lord '' chauncellor, lord treasurer, the judges of the ',' one bench and other, and barons of the exche"quer, or any two of them, or the judges of the "assizes in the respective countyes, are hereby "impowered, upon heareing of partyes andjudg"ment of the cause or causes, to award damages, "open sluices, and to apply such remedyes as"shall be just. Provided allwayes, and be it fur' ther enacted by the authority aforesaid, that "Arthur Annesley, Esq., Sir William Playters, "Sir John Hewett, Barronett, Richard Fyenes, '-' Samuel I Sandys, Robert Phillipps, William Ter ringham, William Dodson, and Anthony S ' John, Esq", claymeing a fourth part of the said "nynety-five thousand acres, be and are constif tuted comissioners to joyne with the Earle of "Bedford and his participants, for the more or(derly support and carrying on the worke of "the said Levell dureing tlie continuance of this! act." i3SoPt.i6«o.

' On the 13th of September, 1660, this bill received the royal assent, and gave time for the Earl to reconcile, if possible, all opposing partiesSoon after the passing of this act, the parliament was dissolved; but upon the meeting of the new parliament, the following order was made by the house of commons, upon a petition presented b the Earl of Bedford, bis participants, and adventurers:

"*Die Sabbath!, 18 Maij,* 1661.

"Upon reading the petition of William Earl EariofBcd"of Bedford, participants, and adventurers, for "dreyning the Great Levell of the Fenns, shew"ing, that the said Level having been drained at "the petitioners' charge, for the recompense of "95,000 acres; and that by an act of the last "parliament, possession of the 95,000 acres is "setled and quieted as the same then was until "the 29th day of May instant, within which' "time it was conceived another act of parliament "would have passed for a perpetual settlement "of that business, which being not effected, and "the time neer expiring, some attempts have "been lately made, by cutting of bankes, to en"danger the drowning of a great part of the "said Levell; and it is conceived, that further "attempts will be made after the said twenty"ninth of May instant, if it be not timely pre"vented, which is endeavoured to be done by "presenting a bill to the commons house of par"liament, which is now in agitation there; It is "ordered by the lords in parliament assembled, ' that all unlawful forces, ryotts, and assemblies,

"within the said Levell and parts adjacent, and "the cutting of any banks, sasses, sluices, or other "works made for drayning of the said Levell and "preservation of the same, are hereby straightly "forbidden; and that the quiet possession of the "said Great Levell of the Fenns,and the workes for "the drayning of the same, be continued in the "possessions of the said Earl of Bedford, partici"pants, and adventurers, and their assignes, as "now they are, until the parliament shall take "farther order therein, or an eviction be had by "due course of law: Provided nevertheless, that "nothing in this order shall be in any wise preju"dicial to the King's title, nor to aney claiming "from his majesty, but that the King may enjoy "his rights: And hereof all mayors, sheriffs, bay"lifts, constables, and other his majesty's officers, "are to take notice for the keeping of the peace, "and quieting the possession of the premises as "aforesaid: And lastly, that this order being pub"lished in the several parish churches and chap"pells in and about the said Levell, all persons "are to take notice and yeeld their obedience "hereunto, as they will answer the contrary at "their perills."

"Jo: Brown, *Cleric. Parliamentorum.*
"

"*Die Luna,* 20 *Maij,* 1661. "Ordered by the lords in parliament assembled, that this order shall be printed and published."

"Jo: Brown, *Cleric. Parliamentorum*"

Soon after this order, the Earl again introduced the general bill; but still there vere so'many matters requiring investigation, so many contending interests, and such contrariety of feeling, that this session also was closed by postponing the general bill, and bypassing the following temporary act:

"*An Act for confirming and continuing an Act* Second tempo"*'fw the necessary mayntenance of the worke of* "*dreyning the Greate Leveli of the Fenns*"

"Dee it enacted by the king's most excellent "majestie, by the advice and with the consent of "the lords and commons assembled in parlya"ment, that one act made or mentioned to hee "made upon or since the five-and-twentieth day "of Aprill, in the twelfth yeare of the raignc of "the king's most excellent majestic that now is, "by his sayd majestie, by and with the advice "and consent of the lords and commons assembled "att Westminster, upon the said five-and-twen"tieth day of Aprill, and then continued untill "the nyne-and-twentieth day of December then "next following, and then dissolved, hereinafter "perticulerly expressed by the tytle thereof, (that "is to say,) 'An Act for the necessary mainte"nance of the worke of dreyneing the Great Le"veil of the Fenns,' shall bee, and is hereby con"firmed and continued, and shall stand and bee "in force untill the-first day of May next ensueing, "and not longer: Provided allwayes, and be it "enacted, that his majestie's title and possession "unto and in the tenn thousand acres, parcell of "the ninety-five thousand acres, in the sayd Great "Levell, formerly assigned unto his majestic, "shall not, by vertue of the sayd act, bee any "way impeached; but that his Majestie and his "now lessees of the sayd tenn thousand acres, "bee and are hereby setled and vested in the quiet "and peaceable possession of the sayd teun thou"sand acres." Daring the progress of this bill, the following vote pas§ed the House of Commons:.

"*Die Mercurii, quin. Januar.* 1661."

"Resolved upon the question,

"That the committee to whom both the bills concernrng the "Great Leveli of the Fens, called Bedford Level, are coin"mitted, do consider of both bills, and provide that the works "may be maintained; and do insert the names of Coll: Sandys "and Sir William Terringham, and the other persons who have "the like claim, into the bill; and do preserve their rights; "and do erect a judicature, to give recompence where they "shall see cause."

"That, by the bill, Coll: Sandys and Sir William Terringbam "may be put into possession of such part of the Leveli as was "set out for the lot of Sir Miles Sandys and Sir Thomas Ter"ringham, according to their several interests under the four"tcenth part deed."

The following session the general drainage bill was again presented, and underwent great discussion and opposition. The discontents were increased by these repeated delays; and the Earl of Bedford, still finding no chance of the general bill passing, applied to parliament for its more immediate aid in quelling the disturbances which had arisen; and, in consequence, the following order was passed by the house on the 19th of May, 1662.

"Whereas by reason of the time several bills i?'i May, "now depending in parliament cannot be dis"patched this session, it is therefore ordered, by "the lords spiritual and temporal in parliament "assembled, that the lord treasurer, the Duke of "Buckingham, the Earl of Bedford, and the Lord "Bellasis, do forthwith attend the King, and re"commend unto his majesty the preservation and "maintenance of the works made for the Great "Level of the Fens, for which bills are nowpend"ing, and for quieting and settling the possessions "as they now are, until the parliament can pass "an act on that behalf; and that his majesty will "be pleased to hear and settle the differences be"tween the adventurers of Francis Earl of

Bed"ford and William Earl of Bedford. "

This order was followed by the King's proclamation.

« By the King." *"A Proclamation for the preservation of the* Eing's ProcU *"Great Level of the Fens, culled Bedford Le"vel, and of the works made for the dreinhig "of the same"*

"Charles R."

"Whereas the Great Level of the Fens, called "Bedford Level, extending itself into the coun"ties of Northampton, Norfolk, Suffolk, Lincoln, "Cambridge, and Huntingdon, and the Isle of "Ely, or some of them, hath been dreined by our "right trusty and wel- beloved cosin William "Earl of Bedford, participants, and adventurers, "for dreining of the said Great Level, at their "very great costs and charges; and ninety-five "thousand acres of late surrounded grounds, par"eel of the said Great Level, have been assigned "and set forth for the recompense of dreining "and maintaining the said Great Level, whereof "twelve thousand acres then belonging to us, our "heirs and assigns, and are now enjoyed by us "and our assigns, and the residue of the said "ninety-five thousand acres are enjoyed by the "said Earl, participants, and adventurers; the "which work being of publick concernment and "great advantage, benefit, and profit, to the whole "nation, an act was made by us, with the advice "and consent of the lords and commons, assem"bled at Westminster, the five and twentieth day' "of April, in the twelfth year of our reign, inti"tuled ' An act for the necessary maintenance of "the work of dreining the Great Level of the "Fens,' whereby the said Earl, participants, and "adventurers, were enabled as well to levy taxes "then formerly imposed upon the said ninety-five "thousand acres, as then after to be imposed by "vertue of the said act, and the possession of the "said ninety-five thousand acres setled and qui"eted as then it was, which said act did expire "the nine and twentieth day of May, which was "in the thirteenth year of our said reign; And

"whereas in the parliament begun at Westmin"ster the eighth day of May, in the said thir"teenth year of our reign, by one other act, inti"tilled ' An act for confirming and continuing an "act for the necessary maintaining of the work of "dreining the Great Level of the Fens,' the said "former act was confirmed and continued until "the first day of May instant; And whereas a bill "was preferred and prosecuted in our house of "commons by the said Earl, participants, and ad"venturers, for maintaining and preservation of "the said Great Level, and of all the rivers, dreins, "cuts, banks, sasses, sluces, tonnels, and other "works made, whereby to prevent future inun"dations, and had proceeded therein to settle and "agree the greatest part thereof, but could not, "in regard of shortness of time, perfect the same; "and therefore both our houses of parliament "have severally, by their order, made the nine"teenth day of May instant, recommended to our "princely care the preservation of the said Great "Level; and more particularly by the order of the "house of peers, is further recommended to our "care the works there made, and quieting and "settling of the possessions as then they were "until further order; And whereas some attempts "have been lately made by cutting of banks and "forcible and unseasonable opening of sasses "and sluces within the said Great Level, to the "endangering of the drowning of a great part "thereof: We, therefore, in pursuance of the said "recommendation of both our houses of par

"liamcnt, and much minding the publick peace "and safety of this kingdom, and to give all "just and lawful countenance and encourage' ment to so publick a work, and *foe* support "and preservation thereof, have already for the "government and maintenance of the said Great "Level, and for laying and levying of taxes "as well to be hereafter set as now in arrear, "upon the said ninety-five thousand acres, caused "a commission of sewers to be issued under the "Great Seal of England for that purpose; and "that so famous a work may not now miscarry, "we do hereby publish and declare our pleasure "to be, That the said commissioners do lay taxes "and assessments upon the said ninety-five tbou"sand acres onely, for support and maintenance "of the works made for dreining of the said Great "Level, and upon no other part of the said Level; "and we do streightly forbid, under pain of our "displeasure, and such punishment as is due to "contemners of our royal commands, all future "attempts, disturbances, interruptions, entries, "forces, riots, assemblies, or any other unlawful "act or acts, tending to the disturbance of the "publick peace within the said Great Level, or "parts adjacent, or the interruption of the said "William Earl of Bedford, participants, and ad"venturers, their tenants and assigns, or of us or "our assigns, in the quiet possession and enjoy"ment of the said ninety-five thousand acres, or "any part or parcel thereof, or of or in any of "the rivers, dreins, cuts, banks, sasscs, sluces,

"tonnels, or any other works made for dreining "of the said Great Level, or interruption, moles"tation, or disturbance of any of their officers, "agents, or workmen, in any of their works of the "said Great Level, or collecting or levying any "taxes, or arrear taxes, in order to preserve the "said Great Level until further order. And all "our justices of the peace, mayors, sheriffs, and "other ministers of justice, and all other our "officers military and civil, and all our lov"ing subjects, are hereby required to be aiding'' and assisting to the said commissioners of "sewers, and such as they shall appoint, to see "our royal commands, hereby published, duly "observed, as often as occasion shall require, as "they will avoid our royal displeasure."

"Given at our Court, at Hampton Court, the

"thirtieth day of May, 16(52, in the four

"teenth year of our reign."
"God save the King."

In order to give effect to the proclamation, and to enable the Earl of Bedford, his participants and adventurers, legally to meet for the purpose of carrying on the drainage, a petition was pre-

sented to the high court of chancery for a commission of sewers, under the authority of the 23 lien. VIII..which was accordingly issued, directed Commission of . Seven.
to the following persons:
"Edward Earl of Clarendon, Lord High Chan"cellor of England,
"George Duke of Albemarle,
"Jerome Earl of Portland, and others of his ma
"jestie's privie counsell, "William Earl of Bedford, "The Justices of both Benches, and Barons of the
"Exchequer,
"The Justice of the Isle of Ely, "Rob'. Lord Brookes, "Thomas Chicheley, "Thos. Lord Culpepper, Esq., "Richard Lord Gorges, "Edward Digges, Esq., "John Russell, Esq. "Edward Russell, Esq., "Benj". Weston, Esq, "William Russell, Esq., "Sir Ralph Verney, Bart.,
"Sir Thomas Willis,
Bart., "Sir John Marsham,
Bart., "Sir Andrew Henley, Bart.,
"Sir Walter S'. John,
Bart.,
"Sir Thomas Dorrcll,
Knt.,
"Sir Allen.Appsley,
Knt.,
"Sir Thomas Thynn,
Knt.,
"John Fryer, M. D.,
"WilliamDenton,M.D.,
"Robert Henley, Esq.,
"Edmund Berry Godfrey, Esq.,
"Samuel Smith, Esq.,
"Samuel Fort rev, Esq.,
"William Crane, Esq.,
"John Spilman, Esq.,
"Francis S«. John, Esq.,
"Robert Hampson,
Esq.,
"Joseph Ayloff, Esq., "Michael Holman,
Esq.,
"Francis Crane, Esq., "Edward Partherich,
Esq.,
"SamuelSpalding,Esq.,
"John Adams, Esq.,
"John Child, Esq.,
"William Drury, Esq.,
"William Hamond,

Esq.,

Under the authority of this commission, and the provisions of the statute of sewers, passed 23 Hen. VIII, and those contained in the general drainage act of Queen Elizabeth, the Earl of Bedford, his participants, and adventurers, carried on the business connected with the drainage of the Great Level until the general drainage act passed in the 15th year of the reign of Charles the Second.

We may now direct our attention to the parliamentary proceedings concerning the disputed claims of all the litigating parties: and these claims may be arranged under four heads;—first, the claims of the crown and its assignees to the 12,000 acres granted under the provisions of the Lynn Law, secondly, the claims of the participants of Earl Francis, called the "Old Adventurers;" thirdly, the claims of the adventurers under the pretended act, called the "New Adventurers;" and fourthly, the claims of those who represented the navigation. It will be recollected, that the 95,000 acres had been originally divided into 20 lots. The division was as follows:

The twenty lots in the first book of lots allotted to fourteen persons, and by them subscribed,
"Francis Earl of Bedford,-3, 9, II, 14, 20.
"Sir Philibert Vernatti,--1.
"Sir Miles Sandys, junior,-2.
"Sir Miles Sandys, senior,-10, 13.
"John Tirringham,---4, 6.
"Robert Henley,----5, 6, 13, 17.
"Edward Lord Gorges,--6, 15, 17.
"Sir Robert Devil,---7.
"William Sams,----8.
"Oliver Earl of Bullingbrooke, 9.
"Anthony Hammond,--12.
"Sir Francis Crane,---16.
"Henry Lord Maltrevers,-18, 13.
"John Latch,----19." The mark thus shews the lots wherein these persons were sharers with others.

These six were sharers only in the 6, 12, 13, and 17 lots;—
"Arthur Ingram,---6
"Arthur Annesley,--6
"John Marsham,---12
"Samuel Spalding,--13
"Oliver Sl John,---17

"Robert Castle,---17"

No sooner had the restoration been effected, than the following petition was presented by the old adventurers:

"To the honourable the knights, citizens, and "burgesses, assembled in parliament:—
"The humble petition of Sir William Play-
"ters, Knight and Baronet, Sir John Hew-
"ett, Baronet, Col: Samuell Sandys, Col:
"William Terringham, Col: Robert Phil-
"lipps, Col: William Dodson, and others,
"claiming under the original adventurers
"of the Great Levell, called Bedford Le-
« veil,—
"Sheweth,

"That your petitioners, or those from whom "they claim, were by letters patents, dated 13 "Marcii, 10 Carol! Primi, incorporated as the "originall adventurers for the dreyning of the "said Great Levell, which accordingly, after the "expence of 200,000/. by those from whom they "claim, was dreyned, and so adjudged; and Vol. i. 2 A

"thereby were lawfully seized of 32,500 acres "and more, besides bis majestie's proportion of "10,000 acres, being near a moiety of the 95,000 "acres allotted to the said adventurers.

"That by reason of the commotions of the peo"pie, and by a pretended act of parliament, ob"tained by Oliver Sl John, Valentine Walton, "William Say, John Lisle, Robert Titchburn, "Edward Whaley, William Goffe, Francis Un"derwood, John Thurloe, and others, in 1649, "both his Majesty and your petitioners were dis"seized of 42,500 acres at least.

"And whereas in the last session of parliament "a restitution of all his Majesty's lands was "enacted (whereof the said 10,000 acres is in"eluded) as your petitioners conceive.

"Your petitioners humbly pray, That the said "pretended act of 1649 may be disannulled; "and that your petitioners may be also "restored to their rights and possessions, or "what they justly claim in their shares of "the said 32,500 acres, against all unjust "intruders and disseisors since the said "corporation; and if the corporation may "be fixed according to the said letters pa"tents, which was, by a governour, a deputy "governour, two bayliffs, and twelve com"moners, whose names your petitioners have "hereunder subscribed in one colume, and in "the opposite colume, the names of such as "your petitioners humbly conceive have the "right of succession or continuance, being

"persons which your petitioners hope no
"interest can except against, whom your "petitioners humbly desire may continue
"for one year, and then to proceed in future
"elections, according to the modell of the
"aforesaid corporation.

By which speedy settlement, agreeable to the
"original government, this beneficial work
"may receive an happy composure, the ad-
"jacent counties pacified, all just interests
"quieted, and this honourable house eased
"of many applications.

"And your petitioners shall ever pray, &c."

"The old governours as they "The new governours as they "are named in the said pa-"are desired. t«nt.

"*The Governour.* "*The Governour.* « Francis E, of Bedford, then "William Earl of Bedford. "Governour, deceased.

"*The Deputy Governour.* "*The Deputy Governour.* 11 Sir Miles Sandys, senior, Samuel Sandys, Esq.
"Knight and Baronet, De-
"puty Governour, deceased.

"*The Bayliffs.* « *The Bayliffs.* "Sir Thomas Tirringham, « William Tirringham, Esq., "Knight, deceased, "Sir John Hewett, Baronet.

"Sir Miles Sandys, jun., "Knight, bayliffs, decd.

"*The Commoners.* "Oliver Earl of Bulliugbrook,

"deceased,
"Henry Lord Matrevers, decd, "Edward Lord Gorges, decd, "Sir Francis Crane, knight,
"decd, "Sir Robert Lovett, knight,
"decd, "SirPhilibert Vernat, knight,
"decd, "William Samms, Doctor of
"Law, decd, "Oliver St. John, Esq. , "Anthony Hammond, Esq., "Samuell Spalding."

"*The Commonert.* "Anth: St. John, son to the
"said Earl of Bullingbrook,
"Sir William Playters, Knight "and Baronet,
"Richard Lord Gorges,
"Arthur Annesley, Esq.,
"John Lord Culpepper,
"Robert Phillipps, Esq.,
"Hublin, Esq,
"Col: William Dodson,
"Anthony Hammond, Esq.,
"Samuell Spalding."

Another petition was also presented by the new adventurers, and the following statement was also laid before parliament:

'THE SEVERAL INTERESTS CONTROVERTED CONCERN"ING THE GREAT LEVEL OF THE FENS."

"*Old Adventurers under Francis, late Earl of* "*Bedford, in the drayning of the Great Level* "*of the Fenns, or deriving under them, not at* "*all concerned in the disputes upon the title of* "*sales for nonpayment of taxes.*" "William Earl of Bedford,
"Col. John Russell,)
« Edward Russell, of the said Earl,
Francis Lord Brooke,
Richard Lord Gorges,
Benjamin Weston,
"Esq.,
Sir Thomas Thynn,
Sir Henry Hene,
Sir Thomas Dayrell,
Sir Gilbert Gerard,
"junior,
Robert Henley, Esq.,
John Adams, Esq.,
William Crane, Esq.,
John Carrill, Esq.,
Dr. William Den ton,
Ser« Fountaine,
Dr. John Fryer,

Roger Jenyns, Esq.,
John Munns, Esq.,
John Spilman, Esq.,
Richard Spencer,Esq.,
"Sir Tho: Stanley,
"Sir John Marsham,
"Sir Andrew Henley,
"Sir Thomas Willis,
"Tho: Chichley, Esq.,
"William Hammond,
"Esq.,
"Joseph Ayloffe, Esq.,
"John Cropley, Esq.,
"William Drury, Esq.,
"Samuel Fortrey, Esq.,
"Robert Ham pson, Esq.
"Matthew Halworthay,
"Esq.,
"George Keate, Esq.,
"Samuel Smith, Esq.,
"SamuelSpalding,Esq.,
"Humphry Sholcross,
"Esq.,
"Robert Yarway, Esq.,
Tho: WToodward, Esq.,

"And about one hundred and threescore other persons, not concerned in the disputes aforesaid, owners of about 64,000 acres, part of the 95,000 acres allotted for draining of the same Levell. *Several proportions of the said 95,000 acres, sold* "*for nonpayment of taxes; the countrey being* "*then under water, no man in possession, and* "*nothing to sequester or distrain; with the names* "*of the then supposed oivners, and those that* "*now pretend to claim under them as old adven*"*turers or their assigns.*"

"Sir Myles Sandys, who was not only a com"mittee-man, but a principal actor in pro"curing the Rump Act, claimed about "10,000 acres, whereof he conveyed un"der the pretended act of May, 1649, to "several persons about 7000 acres; 2700 "acres being the remainder, was sold for "nonpayment of taxes, 22d April, 1650. "Collonel Sandys claims underSir Myles, "who joyned in sale of other men's lands "for non-payment of taxes, and of the "King's 10,000 acres... . 2700

"Henry late Earl of Arundel acted under "the said pretended act, paid taxes, was "present at several meetings, and by his "own direction his proportion was sold. 5700

"Sir William Tirringham pretends to claim "under Sir Thomas or Sir John Tirring"ham; he was also present at divers "meetings under the said act, and the "proportion was sold.... 5000

"Sir John Hewet pretends to claim under "Sir Robert Bevi), who was also present "at divers meetings, and was sold. 3700

"Earl of Bullinbrook had 2000 acres, and "was sold, claimed by Francis St. John. 2000

"Sir Robert Gorges (now claimed by Collo "nel Philips) was sold... 1000 "Sir Charles Harbord was sold.. 0800

"Earl of Anglesey was present at divers "meetings, and was sold.. 0833

"Collonel Dodson purchased of Sir Myles "Sandys under the act of 1649, 256 acres, "the which was sold for nonpayment of "taxes, and he afterwards released to the "purchaser....-

"Lord Culpepper claims under his father "250 acres, which was sold for taxes. 250

"Francis Hoblyn pretends to claim 3000 "acres under Sir Francis Crane, who is "neither his executor, administrator, or "assignee. The 3000 acres was sold to "Mr. Crane by consent of Sir Richard "Crane's executor, who also conveyed to "him.....

"Henry Dearham was a participant for "about 1500 acres, which was sold, and "he after released to the purchasers.

"These proportions above mentioned, are those "which were sold for nonpayment of taxes, with "the names of the supposed owners, who had not "at any time the actual possession of any part of "the same.

"The 95,000 acres being under water, and in "possession of the countrey, and the 100,000/. ex"pended in the first undertaking totally lost, the "old adventurers were necessitated to procure "some authority from the powers then in being, as "well for the getting of the possession against the "countrey, as for encourageing and carrying on "this second undertaking; and also to sell the "land of the defaulters for nonpayment of taxes, "according to the equity of the first agreement, "without which it had been impossible to have "effected the work.

"Under which title we, or those under whom "we claim, became purchasers from the old ad"venturers:

"Thomas Chichley, Esq., "*Dr* William Denton, "Edward Digges, Esq., "William Hammond, Esq., "Robert Henley, Esq., "Edmundberry Godfrey, Esq., "And about threescore other persons, some being "widows, infants, a.nd others now beyond the

"Say and others attainted of treason became "purchasers of about 6250 acres for default of "taxes, the which being vested in his majesty by "the act of attainder, is since granted to his grace "the Duke of York."

The Earl of Bedford did not take part on either side. It is gratifying to find that his conduct was neither impugned, nor impugnable. He merely furnished *the facts* required by the king and the parliament, to enable them to arrive at an equitable conclusion. His lordship's object, during these contentions, was the preservation of the works of the Level, and the ultimate accomplishment of some definite form of government. He pursued the even tenor of his way, each hostile party alternately seeking the aid and influence of his counsels, and the protection of his great and good name. His situation, notwithstanding this neutrality, must have occasioned intense anxiety to his feeling and honourable mind. On the one hand, some of the parties had been the companions, or the representatives of the companions, of his noble father; their property had been sacrificed, and their prospects destroyed: on the other, the Earl had been present, and had concurred (under the sanction of one of the most eminent and learned judges that ever graced the annals of legal history,) in those proceedings, and those sales, which had vested in the new adventurers their right and title, and without which proceedings and sales the work of drainage could never have been effected. It was indeed a most painful dilemma, not only for the Earl of Bedford, but also for the crown and the parliament; the latter indeed were naturally desirous to confirm friends and to conciliate foes. The parliament experienced much difficulty upon the question, and endeavoured to impose upon others the task of an adjustment of the various existing differences. They referred the consideration of the case to certain lords of the council, who were requested to act as referees between the parties. This reference produced the following order:

"*At the Court at Whitehall, the 24th of October,* "1662." "Present,
"The King's most Excellent Majesty,
"His Royal Highness the Duke of York,
"His Highness Prince Rupert,
"Lord Chancellour,
"Lord Privy Seal,
"Duke of Albemarle,
"Marquess Dorchester,
"Lord Chamberlain,
"Earl of Portland,
"Earl of Saint Albanes,
"Earl of Sandwich,
"Earl of Carlisle,
"Earl of Lauderdaile,
"Lord Wentworth,
"Lord Seymor,
"Lord Hatton,
"Lord Holies,
"Lord Ashley,
"Sir William Compton,
"Mr. Treasurer,
"Mr. Vice Chamberlaine,
"Mr. Seer: Morice,
« Mr. Bennet."

"Whereas, upon the humble petition of the ad"venturers for draining the Great Levell of the "Fenns, called Bedford Levell, representing that "both houses of parliament had, by their order of "the 19th May past, humbly recommended to "his majesty to be graciously pleased to hear and "settle the differences between the said adventu"rers; And thereupon his majesty, by his refer"ence of the 6th of July last, was graciously "pleased to appoint the hearing of the matters "contained in the petition this present 24th of "October; at which time many of the adventu"rers appearing, and council learned being heard "both on behalf of such of the new adventurers as "had, by virtue of a pretended act of parliament "made by the usurpers, anno 1049, sold and dis"posed of 35,000 acres of land belonging to other "adventurers, for nonpayment of taxes, in pur"suance of the said pretended act, and also of the "part of other adventurers, who by that means "had, since the making of that act, been dispossest "of their several shares in the said 35,000 acres. "After serious consideration of the whole matter, "and of the best means to compose and settle the "differences between the said adventurers, it was "ordered by his Majesty present in council, that "the lord chancellour, the lord treasurer, the lord "privy seal, the lord chamberlain, the Earl of "Portland, Saint Albanes and Carlisle, the lord "Holies, the lord Ashley, and the two secretaries "of state, or any four or more of them, calling to "their assistance such of the judges as they shall "think fit, should be a committee to hear, exa"mine, and compose (if they can) the differences "between all the said adventurers; And to that "end it was also ordered, that the new adventurers "do prepare the accompt of the charges they have "been at in draining and improvement of the "35,000 acres, since the making of the said pre"tended act, anno 1649, together with the yearly "value thereof; as also that the other adventu"rers, who have been dispossessed of the said "35,000 acres by virtue of the said pretended act, "do likewise prepare their accounts since that _. "time (if they have any), with estimates of the "mean profits of the said lands, together with "their charges, and to make such defalcations "as they can from the new adventurers' said ac"counts: And when either party shall be ready, "that they give notice to the clerk of the council "attending, who thereupon is required to adver"tize the lords of the committee thereof, that so "their lordships may appoint some fit time and "place to receive all such accounts, charges, and "defalcations, and thereupon to endeavour to "compromise differences between the said adven"turers (if possibly they may), or otherwise to re"port to his majesty the state thereof, and what "they conceive fit to be done therein.

"And it was further ordered, that the petition "and paper of Colonel Robert Philips, this day "likewise read at the board, be referred to the "said committee.

"Edw. Walker."

In pursuance of the above order, the new adventurers delivered in the following statement, which the old adventurers answered, by a counter-statement, both of which will appear in the following pages.

The New Adventurers' Account, given in by them according to an order of the 24M *of October,* 1662, *at the Council Table. "*An account of money expended for draining "and improvement of the lands purchased for "non-payment of taxes since May, 1649.

"Every lot of 4000 acres, parcel of the 95,000 "acres allotted for draining the Great Level of "the Fennes, is (debtor) viz.

Draining. £ s. d. s. d. "1. That part of the said "Level, lying on the north "side of Bedford River, "was adjudged drained, "and the taxes then paid "came to 12. 6d. per acre, "the which for one whole "lot of 4000 acres came to 2500 0 0

"2. The other part of the "said Level, lying on the "south side of Bedford "River, was adjudged "drained, and the taxes "then paid, from the 26 "March, 1651, the first "adjudication, came unto "*ll. Os. lUd.* per acre, the "which for one whole lot "of 4000 acres came to 4191 13 4

The Answer of the Parties dispossest. "As to the new adventurers' accompt, for "moneys expended upon each lot of 4000 acres, "for draining, &c., contained in six paragraphs *Draining.* "That the new adventurers have not performed your lordships' order, of the 24 of Octob:; (nor pursued the preamble of their own account, which declares their account to be an account of moneys expended for draining and improvement); for they onely make their charge out of the tax-roll, of what hath been imposed upon the lands, but not out of the ex-penditor's book, of what was laid out in draining or improvement."

£ i. d. "6. The draining taxes imposed "upon every whole lot of 4000 acres, "from Michaelmas, 1653, till Lady"day, 1663, amount to 25. 3d. per "acre, which comes to.. 5050 0 0 *Improvement.* 1. Charges of hasockK ing and burning of every "whole lot of 4000 acres, "to make it fit for culture, "costs.. . 1000 0 0

"2. Interest for the same "for nine years and half, from Michaelmas, 1653, "to Lady-day, 1653. 540 0 0 1540 0 0

"3. The sub-dividing of every lot "of 400 acres into 50 acres pieces and "under by ditching... 500 0 0 u 4. The planting of quicksets, "oziers, and other wood, upon every "lot of 4000 acres... 400 0 0

"5. The buildings erected for habi

"That the new adventurers have not "performed your lordships' order, of the "24 of Octob:; (nor pursued the pream"ble of their own account, which declares "their account to be an account of moneys "expended for draining and improvement); "for they onely make their charge out of "the tax-roll of what hath been imposed "upon the lands, but not out of the ex"penditor's book, of what was laid out in "draining or improvement." *Improvement.* "1. As to the charge of hasocking (or taking of "the uppermost grass,) and burning of the lands, "is a charge born by the under-tenants and occu*u* piers of the land, and redound to their advan"tage, but to the parties dispossest is a great prejudice, and therefore ought not to be allowed. "Nor was the hasocking or burning useful to all "lots, but only in some private grounds, accord"ing to the discretion of the under-tenant, so it "was no publick charge, nor to be allowed by "the parties dispossest.

"2. As to the interest, as well in the fourth and "fifth paragraph foregoing, as in this, they an"swer, that the cause being taken away, the effect "ceaseth: no principal no interest.

"3. As to sub-divisions, they were performed "in every lot by the first adventurers, under whom

£. S. f/.

"tations, barns, stables, and other ac"commodations, upon every lot of "4000 acres.... 800 0 0

"6. For gates, posts, rails, and pales, "to sever the grounds and bridges for "passages, for every lot of 4000 acres 200 0 0

"7. Taxes and assessments for arms "and other public charges, at *3d.* per "acre, imposed by the late pretended "authority, and since his majesty's "happy return, upon every lot of 4000 "acres per annum 50/., for eight years, "comes to 400 0 0

"8. Bayliff's wages and travelling "charges, to let and dispose of every "lot of 4000 acres, at 50/. per annum, "for nine years and half, ending at "Lady-day, 1663... 475 10 0

"1. The totall charge upon every "lott of 4000, is... 22192 13 4

"Toward which is to be discount"ed by profits received.. 4750 0 0

"Rest as a clear charge upon every lot 17442 13 4 "the parties dispossest do claim; but possibly some "sub-divisions of those sub-divisions were made "by the new adventurers since 1849; but they *t* are also to be considered as the acts of sub-ten' ants, being of private not of public use.

Thus in the original document j but evidently a mistake.

"4. As for planting, &c., it is the work of sub"tenants, and very rare to be seen in that Level; "(it may be) upon a part of some one lot, but not "generall upon every lot or sub-divisions, and not "publick.

"5. As to buildings, &c., they were not allowed "when the parties were dispossest, and they have "no reason now to allow them upon reposses"sion. But those are rare also to be seen in any "lot, and those that are, are according to the "nature of the tenancy, so, being private and "not publick, cannot be allowed.

"6. As to gates, posts, &c., for those of publick "use there is toll paid; for those of private use "they cannot be brought to publick account, be"cause most lots are of different nature, and em"ployed to different use.

"7. As to state taxes and armes, in obedience "to the act of oblivion, and not otherwise, the "parties dispossest do not make any objection "to the allowance, but suspend it.

"8. As to wages, &c., the parties dispossest will "allow all just salaries when they are brought "into account, but not extravagancies.

£. . d.

"1. As to the totall charge (ac"counting mean profits at 4750/) "they say the whole charge is. 17442 13 4

"2. And after that rate to be computed for "every greater or lesser quantity, the persons "that complained to be grieved by sales for non"payment of taxes, making out their titles un"der the fourteenth part indenture to the respec"tive proportions by them claimed."

"4000 Acres Creditor.

"3. After severall adjudications there were "great disputes as well between the countrey "amongst themselves to the proportions allotted "out of every town, as between the country and "adventurers, whereby the possession was de"tained from the adventurers, and the 95,000 "acres was a long time in severing from the coun"try, and dividing into lots and proportions.

"4. And although part of the 95,000 acres, "which was in the first adjudication, was posses"sed before Michaelmas, 1653, yet that part "which was in the second could not be possessed "till 1694, and therefore by a medium the pro"fits received are charged to commence from "Michaelmas, 1653, for the whole lot of 4000 "acres, at 2. *Gd.* per acre per annum, comes to "500/. per annum, and for 9 years and a half, "to be determined at lady day, 1663, makes « 4750/." £. *i. d.* 'To which the parties dispossest "answer, that we conceive they "mean by the totall charge, either "a bare imposition or conjecture; "for who paid it, or who received "it, or who expended it, doth not "appear. If it were upon a pub"lick account, it may be made "publick; if upon some particular "lots, and not upon every lot, it "ought not to be allowed as a rule "to the rest. But admit it were "(as they say) yet it will be evi"dent by the subsequent 'account, "that the old adventurers' charge "(accounting interest as they do) "up to the year 1663, for each lot "the charge is.... 28764 12 0 "(and no mean profits) so that the "old adventurers do out-balance the "new, both in the totall summe, the "equity, and in law.

"2. As the title, it is sufficiently set forth in "the following Narrative .

"3. As to the 4000 acres creditor, and the "disputes of the countrey, that also is fully set "forth in the ensuing Discourse .

Owing to their extreme length, the Narrative and Discourse are not transcribed.

In addition to the above objections to the new adventurers' statements, the old adventurers also delivered in the following document.

"*The Old Adventurers or parties dispossest, their Account, stated two wayes.*

"The first way.

£. *s. d.*

"1. It is evident, that the old ad"venturers' account was stated in De"cember, 1637, at 186956/. *I6s.6d.* , "the single interest of which to our "Lady-day, 1663, makes the charge "of each lot to be 2S764/. 12. "but accounting no further than "December, 1649, it is but. 16486 8 0

"4. As to the value of the lands at 2. *6d.* per "acre, we cannot admit that low value.

"First—Because it is lesse than the draining "taxes inserted in their account, Fig. 1, 2, and 6, "and so not probable.

"Secondly—It is contrary to the 7 paragraph "of their account, for improvements, where they "say, that the publick tax came to *Sd.* per acre, "whereby it is evident that the country valued "those lands at 10. per acre, the publick assess"ment not usually exceeding 6*d.* in the pound "upon the yearly rent.

The New Adventurers' Account. £. *s, d.*

"The utmost summe which the "new adventurers do charge upon "each Jot (as appears in their ac"count, to which there are suffi"cient reasons for defalcations of "the greatest part) is but..22192 13 4

"Which compare "with either.. 30006 8 0 "Or with.. 28764 8 0

"As on the other side of this ac

"Between December, 1649, and "December, 1653, the lands of the "old adventurers were sold at more "than 2/. per acre (besides taxes), "which surplusage of sales (by "their pretended act of 1649) was "to have been restored to the own"ers, so that upon each lot of 4000 "acres sold at 2/. per acre, there "was raised.... £. 5. d.
8000 0 0

"The single interest whereof, "accounting from December, 1651, "(being the medium of four years, "between 1649 and 1653,) to our "Lady-day, 1663, amounts to. 5520 0 0

"So the totall charge of each lot "thus accounted, is... 30006 8 0

"The second way,

"2. The originall charge of each "lot (as above said) is.. 16486 8 0

"The mean profits of 4000 acres, "at 6. per acre, is 1000/. per an"num; which being accounted from "December, 1651, (the medium as 11500 0 0 "aforesaid) to our Lady-day, 1663, "at single interest for the same "time amounts to... 690 0 0

So the totall charge of each

"lot thus accounted is. 28676 8 0

"count, it is evident, that the old "adventurers' charge is greater by 7813 14 8 "or...,. 6571 14 8 "(for each lot of 4000 acres) then "the new adventurers can pretent "to by their own account (if ad"mitted)."

They also delivered in the two following statements, as specimens of individual cases, "which "two differ from all the rest in bulk and equity, "and yet give a great light to the whole."

"*As to the Earl of ArundeVs Case.*
'The first way of account.
£. . (/. "The Earl did settle his shares in

"Bedford Levell upon Sir William "Playters, and other trustees, for the "payment of debts, (which trust is 'since transferred to Sir Richard "Onslow for the same uses,) and ac"cording to the common charge of "the old adventurers, from Decem"ber, 1637, to December, 1649, the "charge of each lot, upon single in"terest,did amount to 16486/.8.y. (W., "so that the Earl's charge for one lot "and a half was then at.. 24129 120

"Paid in taxes by the said Earl, "from 1649 to 1661, at 1 Is. 3d. per "acre, according to the new adven"turc-rs' account, for 6000 acres. 3368 00

"The single interest of which, from "December, 1649, to our Lady-day, "1663, is 2232 10 0

"The surplusages of the sales of "his 6000 acres, which ought to have "been restored to him is., 12000 0 0 £. 5. d.
'The single interest of which, from December, 1651, to our Lady-day, 1663, is..... 8-250 0 0

"Or thus:

"The rent of the said lands, "per acre, amounts to.. 17250 00

"The single interest for the year's « rents is.... 1030 0 0

"So that the Earl for his 6000 "acres, according to the 1st way of "accounting (with the taxes paid, "from 1649 to 1651,) his charge is 49862 0 0

"Or, according to the second way "of accounting (including taxes paid "between 1649 and 1651), his charge "is- 47897 0 0

"*As to Collonel Sandys fits Case.*

"It differs from the former, for the Earl's title "is derived from mediate original adventurers; "but Sir Miles Sandys, the father, being an ori"ginal adventurer, Sir Miles Sandys, the son, liv"ing in the Isle of Ely, (the heart of the Levell,) "by their credit, interest, and hospitality to all "the old adventurers and their dependants, (for "many yeares at a great charge,) gave the first "life and continuance to this great work; and "thereupon the father was made deputy gover"nour, and the son, one of the bailiffs, under "Francis Earl of Bedford, the governour thereof; "to support whose credit and that work, Coll: "Sandys became engaged with the father and son, "in at least 50,000/., principal debt; whereupon "all their shares, consisting of 10,375 acres, were "conveyed to trustees for indemnifying Coll: "Sandys, from such debts as he did or should "stand engaged with Sir Miles.

"Now Sir Miles, the son, being survivor, be"tween the years 16-19 and 1653, (at which time "he died,) did, with his trustees, sell and mort"gage severall parcels of the said 10,375 acres "and that which Collonel Sandys aims at, in de"manding the whole, is but to distinguish be"tween real sales and mortgages; and such as are "really sold by Sir Miles and his trustees, upon "view of their evidence, he is ready to confirm, "and for such as are mortgages he desires to ac"count (as to their debts,) and redeem, and as "for the rest he hopes for a great repossession.

"Now Coll: Sandys being cousin, next heir, and "administrator to Sir Miles, the survivor, and left "under the pressure of so great a debt, (besides "his own,) I was so instrumental, that between "1655 and 1660, by help of Sir Miles's estate, C. "Sandys' estate, and mine own, that I paid and "discharged of Sir Miles's debts 39,150/., and of The first person is preserved, as this is an extntct from a letter sent by John Fetturs, one of the lords referees.

"C. Sandys' debts 24,150/. But although there is

"paid and discharged full 63,031/. debts, (besides

"all charges incident to the dealing therein with

"102 creditors,) yet there is a very great debt be

"hind, both of Sir Miles and Coll: Sandys, though

"in truth the debts, both what is paid and be

"hind, may justly be termed debts contracted

"upon publick concerns; for as to Sir Miles's

"debt there can be no doubt but it was upon the

"Fenne account: and as to Coll: Sandy's debt, it

"is well known that a little before the wars he

"was a purchaser of 8000 pounds worth of land,

"(without borrowing,) and in the wars, at his

"own charge, he raised two regiments of horse,

"and two of foot, and eight score dragoons, (be

"sides accidentals,) without any pay during that

"time (save as he was governour of Worcester).

"By which public disbursements, and thereby "diminution of his fortunes, he hath no other "means left (in respect of ancient settlements) of "doing justice, but receiving it.

"Now that Sir Miles's charge in this particular "may be the more evident, be pleased to peruse "the following account:

"The first way— £ . d. "According to the common charge "of the old adventurers, the charge "of each lot, upon single interest, at "December, 1649, did amount to "16486J. 8. 0d., so that Sir Miles's "charge for 10,000 acres is.. 41216 0 0 £. S. it. "Paid in taxes, by Sir Miles, from "Dec. 1649 to Dec. 1651, for) 0,000 "acres, at 12. 6rf. per acre.. 6250 0 0

"The single interest thereof. 3750 0 0

"The surplusage of sales which "ought to have been restored to Sir "Miles, (out of which whatever hath "been justly sold by Sir Miles and his "trustees is to be deducted,) but ac"cording to the rule of 4000/. for 2000 "acres, the surplus is... 20000 0 0

"The single interest whereof, from "Dec. 1651, to ourLady-day, 1653, is 12900 0 0

"The second way—or otherwise.

"Accounting, at 5. per acre, for "10,000 acres, and for 375 acres, be"ing his share of 3000 acres, set aside "for contingencies, deducting as "aforesaid, is.... 29828 0 0

"The single interest of which yearly "rents amounts to... 1725 0 0

"I. So that accounting according "to the first way, in the old adven"turers' account, Sir Miles's charge is "for two lots and a half..8411600

"2. Or accounting according to "the second way, in the old adven"turers' accounts, and then his charge "for his share is.... 82769 0 0

"So his lowest charge is.. 82769 0 0 £. 5. (/.

"Besides, the adventurers did owe "to Sir Miles, for money expended by "him before 1650, as appears by bills "then given in by him, 603/., the single "interest whereof from 1650 to 1663 "in total is 1068 0 0

"The totall charge of Sir Miles, "wherein Coll: Sandys as heir, ad-mi"nistrator, and creditor is concerned, "and was (among other considera"tions) a just ground for the vote for "his repos-session, amounts to. 85184 0 0

The above documents having been delivered in to the lords' referees, they appointed a meeting to be held on the 14th of November, 1662, when the following order was passed. Jf

"*At Whitehall, the* 14 *o/Novemb.* 1662.

"By the lords, the referrees appointed by the "board,about the Great Bedford Levell of Fennes;

"It was this day ordered, that the new adven"turers of Bedford Levell of Fennes, do forth"with deliver unto the other party, or their soli"citor, their accounts, to the end both parties "may be prepared and be ready to attend the "said lords referees at the lord chancellor's "house, upon Monday, the four and twentieth

Vol. i. 2 c

"of November instant, in the afternoon, at three "of the clock . "Richard Brown."

The conflict continued unabated during this session, embittered, no doubt, by the recollection on both sides of past events. It cannot be denied, that in some cases the demands of the old adventurers were most nefarious. We will instance the case of the Earl of Arundel, who had voluntarily relinquished his lands, had refused to pay Lis proportion of the taxes absolutely necessary, and, as already stated, had even sent his agent to authorize the Company to make sale of those lands. In violent revolutions and convulsions of states, justice generally marches in the rear, and arrives at bead-quarters, when the leaders are somewhat exhausted. The time that elapsed between the prorogation and the assembly of parliament was passed in numberless attempts on the part of the Earl of Bedford, and other persons in the confidence of the crown, to reconcile the several jarring interests. Their efforts were not ineffectual. Probably the old adventurers did not receive from the government the determined support which their too sanguine feelings had led them to expect. The parties all appeared before the lords' referees, were heard by their respective counsel, and a general bill drawn up under their authority was agreed to be presented to parliament in the following session. Memorandum.—The aforesaid order of council mentions 35,000 acres: the parties dispossessed claimed at least 5:5,000 acres.

On the 16th of May, 1663, appears the following entry in the lords'journal.

"Read a second time, ' An act for settling the "drainage of the Great Level of the Fens, called "Bedford Level.'"

Several petitions were then presented to the house from divers persons, desiring to be heard by their counsel at the bar before the passing of the aforesaid bill.

"Upon the second reading of the bill, intituled "'An act for settling the drainage of the Great "Level of the Fens, called Bedford Level,' and "several petitions exhibited concerning the mat"ter of the said bill, it is ordered, by the lords "spiritual and temporal in parliament assem"bled, that all parties herein concerned, as well "those that have petitioned, and such others as "shall petition, are to be heard by their counsel to and witnesses at the bar (if they desire it) on "Tuesday next, the 13 July, at 10 o'clock, upon *u* the matter contained in the said bill, at which "time the several parties in this cause are to at"tend accordingly."

On the 14th of July, a further order for hearing counsel was passed, and on the 15th of the same month " the counsel and witnesses of the old ad"venturers and new adventurers were heard at "the bar upon the matter contained in the bill for "draining the Great Level of the Fens, called Bed"ford Level, and afterwards it was committed."

The labours of this committee were incessant.

i Every one was patiently heard both by himself and his counsel; every interest was discussed till (something like the proceedings upon the first Ean Brink Bill in 1795) the obduracy of parties gave way, it being clearly foreseen that the bill would ultimately pass. At length, on the 24th of July, the bill was reported with some alterations, and passed, and sent to the commons desiring their concurrence in some amendments and some provisions that had been inserted.

The great struggle had been previously made in the house of commons. Never perhaps did any parliamentary proceeding undergo so protracted and patient an investigation. It ended at last (as will be seen when we come to analyse the act itself, and notice the proceedings under it,) in mutual compromise and general discontent of the conflicting interests, and probably without affording satisfaction to any of the disputant parties. It has, however, been said to be one of the most perfect instances of the wisdom and abilities of the legislature that the extensive statute laws of this General Drain-country can furnish. On the 27th of July, 1663, 27, use's, this celebrated act received the royal assent; and thus, after the most unparalleled struggles, was established the corporation of the "Bedford Level," a title well deserved, and which the author hopes will form for ever an indissoluble bond of union between the House of Russell and the Great Level of the Fens.

CHAPTER XiV. *Continued exertions of William Earl of Bedford. — Attempts to abridge the power of the commonalty of the corporation. — The project defeated. — Court of appeal. — Proceedings of the corporation. — Colonel Dodsons design. — Sandy's Cut. — Further application to parliament. — The Tax Act passes. — Its utility. — The clause for general enclosures throughout the Bedford Level considered. — The clause repealed by the statute of James. — The death and character of William Earl of Bedford.*

William Earl of Bedford might now have reposed continued npon the laurels he had so dearly earned, and re-juT &nriof' tired once more into privacy, followed by the prayers, the blessings, and the gratitude, of the people resident within the Great Level, whose welfare he had finally consummated, and whose personal interests he had firmly established. He acted a far more noble part. His conduct was founded upon the admirable motto of the philopher of other days, "*Nil actum reputans si quid*

Attempt to abridge the powers of the commonalty.

superesset agendum" thinking nothing accomplished while aught remained to be achieved. A corporate body, it is true, was legally and firmly constituted; but its materials were discordant and inharmonious. Painful recollections were yet indulged, and party feelings had not subsided. It required the dignity, energy, and popularity of this disinterested and indefatigable nobleman, to preserve order and regularity, to sooth conflicting interests, and even to calm and to check vulgarity and violence.

The first meeting under the general drainage act took place at the Fen Office in the Inner Temple, on the 1st day of August, 1663. It is the author's intention, before he considers the powers conferred by this act of parliament, or the proceedings under it, as well as the relative duties and practice of the corporation, their legal rights and functions, to pursue those historical details which will put his readers into full possession of the *materiel* upon which their knowledge of the Bedford Level must be founded, and their judgment ultimately guided.

Although the select body of the corporation consisted but of the governor, six bailiffs, and twenty conservators, and although the proprietors of 100 acres only could interfere in elections, yet it must be remembered, that *every owner of any part, however small,* of the 95,000 acres, was and still is a corporator, and entitled to be present at the public meetings of the corporation. Probably these meetings were not marked by that order, regularity, and decorum, which peculiarly distinguish the meetings of more modern times; feelings were more diversified; interests more conflicting; objects more difficult of attainment. Many of the new adventurers, who, upon the parliamentary compromise, had been admitted as members of the select body of the corporation, were not enured to the previous mode of conducting fen business: their courtly habits could ill brook the honest bluntness of the ingenuous fen man, boldly asserting, and courageously, if not courteously, maintaining his rights and privileges. These courtiers had too much at stake to withdraw from the corporation, however their disgust might be excited, or their more delicate feelings wounded. They pursued a different, but not more honorable course. Their party was strong amongst the members of the select body of the corporation; and, although opposed by the ever watchful Earl of Bedford, as well as by Lord Gorges and others, under pretence of amending the general drainage act, they carried a resolution for an application to parliament, which measure, if successful, would have greatly curtailed, and probably annihilated the powers of the commonalty. In the ensuing session (relying upon their courtly interest) a petition was actually presented for leave to bring in a bill involving this nefarious purpose. The hbuse of commons acted justly: they had not forgotten the struggles of the last session. The prayer of The project the petition was refused. The following counter petition was presented by the commonalty, which was accompanied by reasons why the prayer of the first petition should not be granted.

"To the honorable the knights, citizens, and "burgesses, in the commons house of par"liament assembled;

"The hdmble petition of the commonalty of "the corporation of the Great Level of the Fens, "called Bedford Level, consisting of about four"score persons:

"Sheweth,

"That at the last session of this parliament, "upon a long and mature consideration, there "passed an act for the settling of that great and "advantageous work of draining the said Levell, "by which act the said adventurers, their heirs "and assigns, were made a corporation, consisting "of one governour, six bailiffs, twenty conserva"tors, and commonalty.

"That your petitioners are informed, that some "particular persons, seeking their own private "advantage more than the publick, upon pretence "of explaining the said act of parliament, do en"deavour to get another act, whereby, amongst " other things, your petitioners, being the com"monalty of the said corporation, might be ex"cluded from being any part of the said corpora"tion.

"That it would be your petitioners' utter ruin,-" if the disposing of moneys, and appointing of "officers, and other affairs relating to and con"cerning the said Level, should be transacted by "the said governour, bailiffs, and conservators, or "any five of them, without the privity, know"ledge, or consent of any of your petitioners, be"ing by far the greatest and most considerable "part of the said corporation; and have always, "since the first undertaking to drain the said "Level, been consulted with, and had votes in "disposing the said affairs of the said Level; And "there being no reason at all (unless the private "gain of a few persons, that labour to set up their "own single interests to your petitioners' undo"ing,) why your petitioners should be excluded "from being of the said corporation;

"Your petitioners therefore humbly pray, that "your honours will be pleased to review the "last act, and then your petitioners will be "confident you will find no cause to alter the "bill already passed this honorable house, "but that the commonalty may enjoy all "their powers and authorities thereby given "them, with the rest of the twenty-seven per"sons therein named, as governors, bailiffs, "and conservators.

"And your petitioners shall pray, &c.
"

"Reasons humbly offered why the commonalty of "the corporation of the Great Level of the "Fens ought not to be excluded from the rest "of the corporation, contrary to the act of par"liament passed the last session.

"1. That the twenty-seven persons named as "governor, bailiffs, and conservators, may not "have above seven thousand acres by the propor"tions allotted them by the said act, so that the "residue of the 83,000 acres will rest in the com"monalty, and so consequently they must pay so "much the more for taxes; and thereupon they "ought to give their assistance and advice in the "ordering of the affairs of the said corporation, "and in choosing of officers, who receive and pay "their money, make their contracts, and order "all their works, as the said commonalty have "always done from the first undertaking, and as "they may yet doe by the said last act of parlia"ment, they having a hundred acres or more "a-peece.

"2. That by said act of parliament, the com"monalty, although they have an hundred acres "a peece, yet they are excluded from acting as '' commissioners of sewers, or laying of taxes with "the said governor, bailiffs, and conservators; "but for otherwise acting and advising, the par"liament did conceive it just that the common"alty should be part of the corporation, in the ordering of affairs of the said Level.

"3. That the Great Level consists of three Le"vels, and the works of one have no dependence "on each other. Then, if the commonalty have "no other vote than for the election of the 27 per"sons, (if all the commonalty should not attend at "the time of election,) such persons may be chosen "for the said 27 persons as may have all their in"terest lye in one Level (at least wise the major "part of the 27 persons), and then they may or"der and direct what moneys they please, and "expend the same to what works or concernment "of their own they please, to the mine of all other "parts of the Levell without controule.

"4. That no persons will ever purchase any of "the said lands, unless they maybe sure of being "of the number of the 27 persons; for otherwise, "they must be continually paying their moneys, "and never know what shall become of it or of "their estates.

"5. That several persons have purchased under "the last act who were encouraged thereunto "upon that interest which the commonalty had "in the corporation; so that if that power be "taken away, the purchaser will be much preju"diced in his bargain.

"6. That the commonalty alone cannot, by the "said act, order, direct, or dispose of any thing "concerning the said Great Level, unless by and "with the consent of the governor, or two of the "bailiffs. Nor are the governors, bailiffs, or con"servators, excluded from acting or ordering any

"thing without the commonalty (if they be not "present at their meetings."

The brevity of language and simplicity of statement used by these poor and humble suitors, must excite our sympathy and admiration. They had the sanction and support of the considerate and humane William Earl of Bedford, whose name and influence thwarted a design so evidently unjust. It was natural that the petitioners should receive this sanction and support. The house of Russell ought to be the cradle and asylum of liberty, and its representatives the firm and undaunted advocates of the unalienable rights of the people. Those honorable distinctions were dearly earned by the self-devotion and disinterested conduct of Earl Francis; they were established by the benevolence, the unparalleled perseverance and inextinguishable zeal of Earl William; alas! they were finally consummated upon the scaffold by the blood of their heroic descendant. Conn of Ap-In the act of 15 Car. II. it is recited, that " parApp.'p.405. "ticular persons and parties did alledge, that the "draining of one place hath drowned and made "worse the lands in other places, and that divers "other persons did alledge and complain, that the "said 95,000 acres in many places are not indif"ferently set out or allotted, according to the "law made at Lynn, in the 6th year of the reign "of the late King Charles, nor according to agree"ment made with the country, but in many places "greater quantities have been taken from the

"owners, commoners, and townships, than ought

"to have been, and that some lands have been

"taken, as belonging to one parish and county,

"which in truth belonged to another; and in

"many places, the allotments have been taken

"very inconvenient for the townships,

which "ought not to have been by the said agreement:

"And whereas the draining aforesaid, and future

"maintenance of the said Great Level ought to

"be without prejudice to navigation; and because

"all complaints which have been made, and all

"prejudices which have been or shall be done to

"particular persons, parishes, and places, cannot

"be sufficiently provided for by the act, certain

"commissioners are nominated and appointed by

"the act, for the several counties of Norfolk, Suf-App.p.40.

"folk, Cambridge, Huntingdon, Northampton,

"Lincoln, and the Isle of Ely, to hear and deter

"mine complaints upon these several matters."

These commissioners were invested with very extensive powers, and might be considered as a kind of board of control. There is no record of their ever meeting. They became defunct for want of succession; which circumstance was fortunate for the corporation, whose rights and privileges would have been greatly narrowed had this commission continued to exist; and this would have been the case, had it not been for the vigilance of the Earl of Bedford, whose foresight and wisdom seem never to have abandoned him. It was moved in the committee upon the bill, in the house of lords, that the vice-chancellor for the university of Cambridge, the mayor of the town of Cambridge, and the mayor of King's Lynn for the time being, should *ex officio* be three of the commissioners. The Earl foresaw that these appointments would give perpetuity to the commission, and that all its inquisitorial powers might in future times be called forth to the annoyance of the corporation. He moved and carried a proposition for their being struck out of the list of commissioners, in their official capacity, which was accordingly done; although, singularly enough, their names are, by a clerical error, omitted to be erased in another part of the act. Many ineffectual attempts have been made to renew this commission; but the corporation were fortunate in having a perpetual guard over their interests like the Earl of Bedford. The shadow without the substance of power would have been left to the corporation, had the powers and authorities of this commission been rendered capable of perpetuity. The Earl of Bedford was a constant attendant at the meetings of the board, (an appellation then assumed and still continued by the select body,) and of the corporation at large. The select body were not unanimous, and the plans of drainage adopted under the sanction of the pretended act were by no means heartily approved of. The system had, however, proceeded too far to be remedied without an entire revolution, and at an expense which neither party was inclined to incur. Still a strong desire of Improvement prevailed, and in the year after the establishment of the corporation, Colonel Dodson, who had been many years Colonel nodin the service of the adventurers, being called upon, delivered in a design for a better drainage, to which the reader is referred, as fully set forth in the Appendix: the perusal will amply repay App.p.420. him for the time bestowed upon it. An estimate App. p.472. accompanies this design; and the author pauses one moment, to draw the attention of his friends in the South Level (and he trusts he has many and *sincere* ones) to that part of the estimate which relates to the making of Sandy's Cut.;.

"The making of Sandy's River from Ely to "Littleport chair, at I/. 15. a pole, will cost "1680/. M!"

By the way, this river is now called " Sandall's Cut;" but its original name was "Sandy's Cut," being (according to the fashion of using the names of persons generally adopted in these days) named after Colonel Sandys, who was one of the most influential members of the corporation, and who invariably took a very active part in the proceedings of the board and of the corporation.

No alterations in the system of drainage took place in consequence of this design. It seems to have been an abortive attempt at improvement.

The act of 15 Car. II., with all its excellencies, was not free from imperfections; all human laws are liable to them, and those institutions only are the best, which possess the fewest; but it must be said, that these defects were such as could not be foreseen: they were to be discovered only by TmAct, experience. The 15th of King Charles II. had given the corporation a general power of taxing, without prescribing the form or manner in which that power was to be executed. Under that act, the tuxes were imposed by way of an acre tax, so that the same specific tax was laid for every acre. This was found to be a tax of great inequality; for, as the lands differed much in value, whilst the produce of the best lands enabled the owners to pay the taxes, the worst were taxed nearly to the extent of (at that period) their intrinsic worth. This did not escape the vigilance of the Earl ofBedford. The tax was altered to a gradual acre tax of five different sorts, and the lands were taxed in proportion to their relative value; but this remedy was not equal to the evil complained of, inasmuch as the different value of the lands was not ascertained, and five sorts were by no means sufficient in number to procure the desiredj effect, namely, equality of taxation. The corporation, under the sanction and influence of their governor, the indefatigable Earl of Bedford, applied again to parliament to arrange this difficult matter, and to make some few further amendments in the policy of their constitution, shewn by time and experience to be necessary. But the great object of that application was to procure an equality of taxation. The parliament had always manifested a favorable disposition towards the measure of drainage; and, throughout all the varied and dif ficult proceedings, had acted with great deliberation and inflexible impartiality. The application was kindly received; and the legislature rendered the corporation the assistance required.

It will be recollected, that the 95,000 acres were originally divided into twenty lots or shares, each lot containing lands in various parts of the Level. The 95,000 acres still continued divided in these lots amongst the several owners, and were then, and still are, distinguished as the "Adventurers' Lands;" the remaining part of the Level being denominated the "Free Lands." The tax act was ApP. p.«4. passed 20 Car. II. (1667J, and commissioners were thereby appointed from amongst gentlemen of the country, to view and survey the adventurers' lands, and afterwards to sort, divide, and rate them not under the number of seven sorts and degrees. The 12,000 acres granted to the crown, and which were then, and now are, called the "King's Lands," were to be taxed at a medium; for instance, when the whole 95,000 acres are taxed at 6HO/. 7. *iy.,* the 12,000 acres were to be taxed at 1. *3d.* per acre, and so in proportion. The commissioners proceeded in the work with great unanimity and despatch. They did not disturb the several proportions, as they were set out in the twenty lots or shares; but finally assorted them into eleven different degrees or sorts, commencing the first or inferior sort of land at *4d.* per acre, and so advancing gradually *4d.* per acre each sort, until they arrived at the highest or superior land, which was of course taxed eleven fourVol. i. 2 D pences, or 3. 8rf. per acre. A more full and particular account of these taxes, and of the lands from which they arise, will be found detailed in a subsequent part of this work. The difficulty of the task thus imposed upon these commissioners was perceived by the parliament; and accordingly it was enacted, that all parties who were dissatisfied. 479. *pth* the judgment of the commissioners, should have the power of appealing to the governor, bailiffs, and conservators; and in the event of the governor, bailiffs, and conservators, not giving relief to the parties so dissatisfied within forty days, they had then the power of appealing to certain commissioners named in the act. To the honour of the commissioners appointed to value and assort the land, it ought ever to be borne in remembrance, that such was the discretion and impartiality shewn in the execution of this most arduous task and important trust, that although several appeals were made to the governor, bailiffs, and conservators, yet five alterations only took place in consequence of those appeals, and the court of *dernier ressort* was never called upon to exercise its functions. The proceedings of the commissioners have been confirmed by the judgments and opinions of all men who have had any concerns within the Level; and even at this distant period there is not in general any surer way of determining the intrinsic value of the lands in the Bedford Level, than by an application to. p. 486. that survey, where their relative values are almost exactly ascertained. By the valuation and assortment affixed by these commissioners, the adventurers' lands continue to be taxed until the present time. A more judicious or more equitable mode could not have been adopted.

The act of the 15th of King Charles the Second, General sure clause.
had invested lords of manors and commons with APp. p. 4os. a power to divide and inclose their commons. This was perhaps well meant for the improvement of the country; but the best intentions may be perverted to the worst of purposes. In pursuance of this power, many of the lords did inclose and divide their commons, and the several commoners had their respective shares allotted to their commonable houses .
The division of commons and wastes, says a writer of that period, was prejudicial to the country in general, and to the adventurers in particular. To the country in general, as it enabled people to sell their estates by piece meal, and leave their families paupers. To the adventurers in particular, because, by such division, the inclosed adventurers' lands sunk in value; for while property of the country consisted in a right of common, the stock was supported upon commons in summer, and upon inclosed ground, or the product of it, in winter.

In ancient as well as modern times, the people These inclosures took place under decrees, all of which are inrolled in the Petty Bug Office, in Rolls' Chapel, Chancery Lane. It was the earnest defire of the author of this work, in order to render it as complete as possible, to have extracted a list of those decrees, but he found the expense attending it far beyond any reasonable expectation of remuneration.
at large have always been averse to inclosures. The natural and social disposition of the English nation leads to a community of interests. The bond of onicn is broken by the separation of a mutual, and the acquirement of an individual interest. A paternal government, seeking the comforts, the happiness, and the moral rectitude of its subjects, promotes those natural feelings of union and community of interests, and receives for its reward the unflinching loyalty, the unbounded cheerfulness, and the sturdy independence of those who have the happiness to live under its guidance, animated by feelings at once so amicable and at the same time so politic. Alas! in our times the converse of this conduct has been ruthlessly pursued by those who have wielded the powers and energies of England. The rich have been enabled, amidst the semblance of a prosperity, in reality only fictitious, to lay house to house, and field to field; to heap up riches, reckless of the parties by whom they may ultimately be gathered. The link which gradually connected all ranks and classes of society, has been torn asunder and this once happy, proud, and generous people of England, left without their natural leaders, have become a nation of splendid and squalid paupers, paltry hucksters, and heartless avaricious moneylenders; while crime and immorality stalk throughout the land, and stain its annals with the most appalling scenes and the most unblushing profligacy. Palaces and gaols, hospitals and workhouses have, during all "the vast improvements of the age," arisen in frightful contiguity; and while the scaffold groans with its victims, the cries of the patriot and the people are drowned in hollow promises of economy and reform, or forgotten in the revels of

thoughtless dissipation and extravagance. Such has been the result of the boasted increase of inclosures; such has been the result of depriving the population of their natural share in the soil that gave them birth, and ought to have A. D. isso. given them bread. The feelings of the author sometimes overcome the more sober dictates of his judgment. To proceed:

It was found out in time, that this provision for permitting general inclosures, and the use to which it was applied, instead of improving, tended greatly to distress the country. Once more the Earl of Bedford stepped forth as the friend and advocate of the interests of the people. The corporation, under his auspices, made application to parliament, and obtained an act for the repeal of this most injurious clause. The recitals in that App. p. sis. act of repeal demand the serious reflection of the statesman, the philosopher, and the philanthropist. They are as follow:

"And whereas the taking and cutting of the App. P. 520. "said commons and wastes into small pieces is "since found to be very prejudicial to the owners "and country, being a great waste of ground in "division, which are hard to be kept as fences "between party and party; the road-ways and pas"sages through such commons, as set forth, being

"very low, and generally in bad ground, not

"passable, or well to be amended, whereby such

"divisions are of little value: And whereas it oc

"casions great diminution of stock, and decay of

"houses, many persons selling their shares of com

"mon from the house it belongs unto, *to a greater "impoverishment and increase of the poor"* ,, The act of parliament, while it repealed the power of making further inclosures, confirmed those inclosures and divisions which had been then already made, on particular conditions. This was the last amendment made in the constitution of the Bedford Level Corporation, during the lifetime of William Earl of Bedford, and concludes the history of those events and those interests which he with so much spirit, perseverance, and benevolence, had advanced, patronized, and protected, during the long and honorable career of fifty-one years.

Death and cfca-I' would be unjust to the memory of this illusiEarUfl" trious nobleman to close the history (feeble, it is Bedford. true,) of his exertions, without some tribute to his memory, some recollections of his virtues, some tears of sympathy for his sorrows, some expressions of gratitude for his unparalleled exertions. The language of adulation cannot reach the confines of the grave; but the energetic language of truth stimulates to exertion and to imitation. The author trusts, and firmly believes, that the day will never arrive, when the house of Russell will require any stimulus to exert itself in the sacred cause of its country and its fellow citizens.

The Earl of Bedford sedulously and almost constantly attended to the affairs and interests of the board and corporation, from the first meeting, which, as already stated, took place upon the 1st of August, 1663, until the 30th of May, 1683, from which time he appears to have absented himself until the 12th of November, 1685: and he was well entitled to do so. He retired in privacy, to indulge the sorrows of a parent, and the agony of a wounded mind. The Earl had exerted himself in forwarding the restoration. He had wisely and disinterestedly counselled his King in times of peril and difficulty. Of his exertions in behalf of the people, the author has given already signal proofs. But withal, it pleased Providence to visit him, even in the decline of life, with heavy domestic afflictions. In short, he was doomed to know, that on the 21st of July, 1683, his son, his brave, generous, patriotic, and gallant son, the Honorable William Russell, perished upon the scaffold. The lacerated feelings of a parent prevented his appearance for nearly two years, even to promote the welfare of that country, for whose best interests the greater part of his valuable life had been so meritoriously and so beneficially spent. The latter days of his noble father were clouded by domestic sufferings. He, too, had to deplore the loss of a beloved son, and to endure the mortification of beholding another son form ties and connections utterly hostile to his wishes. He also had to undergo the bitterest disappointments and the basest ingratitude. Yes! Francis Earl of Bedford had cause for sorrow; but his griefs sunk almost into insignificance, when compared with those which must have wrung the heart of his generous and high-minded son, William Earl of Bedford. Time, the alleviator of sorrow, healed, in some degree, the wounds of this admirable man; and we find him again engaged in the concerns of the corporation from the 12th of November, 1685, until the 3rd of June, 1696, which was his last attendance at their meetings. On the accession of the Prince and Princess of Orange to the throne, he was sworn one of their privy council; and, at their coronation, carried the Queen's sceptre with the dove. On the 10th of May, 1689, his lordship was constituted Lord Lieutenant of the counties of Bedford and Cambridge; and on the 1st of March, 1691, Lord Lieutenant and *Gustos Rotulorum* for the county of Middlesex and liberty of Westminster.

He sought for no other honors or employments; but their Majesties, on the 21st of May, 1694, (5 W. and M.) created him Marquess of Tavistock and Duke of Bedford; and for bestowing these honors, it is set forth,—

"That this was not the least, that he was the "father to the Lord Russell, the ornament of his "age, whose great merits 'twas not enough to "transmit to posterity; but they were willing to "record them on their royal patent, to remain in "the family, as a monument consecrated to his "consummate virtue; whose name could never "be forgot, so long as men preserved any esteem "for sanctity of manners, greatness of mind, and "a love to their country, constant even to death. "Therefore, to solace his excellent father for so "great a loss; to celebrate the memory of so "noble a son; and to excite his worthy grandson, "the heir of such mighty hopes, more cheerfully "to emulate and follow the example of his illus"trious father, they intailed this high dignity "upon the Earl and his posterity."

The venerable William, then Duke and Earl of Bedford, departed this life in the 87th year of his age, on the 7th of September, 1700, in the maturity of age, and the plenitude of honor. The author of this work would in vain attempt to do justice to a character so benevolent, so patriotic, so disinterested, and so exalted, as William Duke of Bedford. Alas! what pen is capable of a task so fruitful in subject, and yet so difficult in execution! Fortunately, the reader will find the Duke's character delineated, and his just eulogy pronounced, by one far more competent than the author of these sheets, to do that justice to the subject which it so amply merits.

His grace was buried at Chenies, in the county of Bucks, the burial place of the Russell family, where a most noble monument is erected to the memory of him and his countess. The King directed one of his own chaplains, the Rev. Doctor Freeman, to preach a sermon upon the occasion; which sermon was afterwards printed by royal command, and is dedicated to the Duke's grandson and successor, Wriothesly, second Duke and sixth Earl of Bedford. In this dedication the reverend preacher takes leave to lay before his grace what all his friends and all good men expect from an heir of the Bedford family:—" That you'll make it your chiefe "study to promote the glory of God, to whose "bountiful goodness you are indebted for so many "great and uncommon blessings, by your autho"rity and example, crushing profaneness and vice, "and maintaining the true religion and virtue; "that you'll be a faithful supporter of the mo"narchy, a true friend to your country, a liberal "patron and benefactor to the church, a great "encourager of learning, and an invincible cham"pion of the Protestant Religion."

The text is taken from 1 Cor. ix. 25:

Now they do it to obtain a corruptible crown, but we an incorruptible.

The reverend preacher speaks of the deceased "As an illustrious example indeed, yet made the "brighter by shining *in a dark place,* in a loose "and degenerate age, where greatness and good"ness so seldom meet together."

He then proceeds to portray the character of this illustrious nobleman, in the following terms:

"I shall not here take notice of the nobleness "of his extraction, and the greatness of his de"scent; nor travel the many ages back in the "leafs of time, to discover the spring of this very "ancient and renowned family: These are little "things, not to be named with the admirable en"dowments of his mind, and the manifold gifts of "the Holy Spirit wherewith his soul was adorned. "Who can sufficiently admire or fully imitate "the sweetness of his temper and the benignity "of his nature? The greatness of his birth made "him the more humble; the height of his con"dition did not exalt his mind; there was no"thing of pride and fastidiousness in his conver"sation; 'twas all condescension, without being "mean and cheap. That man had a great deal "of demerit in him indeed, that was wholly re"fused admittance into his presence, and none "ever went uneasie out of it whose requests were "reasonable, and their persons not unworthy: no"thing but sin had his frown; the good actions of "men had his praise, their weakness his excuse, "their afflictions his pity, and their distresses his "succour.

"His piety towards God was sincere and unaf"fected; his devotion in the closet, daily; in "publick, constant, uniform, and regular; he had "indeed a charitable opinion of all good men who "did not come up in all points to the church of "England, but he utterly dislik'd schism and se"paration; his religion was inward, in reality and "substance, not plac'd on externals; he was very "much for unity and peace in the church, but "his opinion was, that they might be preserv'd "by a mutual forbearance in matters of cere"mony, without a rigid imposition of them; and "he was wont to say, that he thought it equally "superstitious to shew too much zeal either for "or against them. But whilst he made known "his moderation unto all men, and bestowed his "favors too upon many whom he judged con' scientious, tho' of a different perswasion, he "ever in his practice kept close to the church of "England. You might see him, unless prevented "by sicknesse or other necessary occasion, every "Lord's-day at church, and there behaving him"self with the greatest devotion, strictest atten"tion, and humblest reverence, especially at the "blessed sacrament, communicating frequently, "always on his knees, and with most ardent af"fections, and ever expressing a great uneasiness "and dissatisfaction when unexpected accidents "kept him (as he used very sensibly to call it) "from the food of his soul.

"Here was the family wherein not an oath nor "a prophane jest could be heard; where sobriety "was habitual, virtue and religion triumphant, "and the worship of God daily and devoutly per"formed; and so highly conducive did he think "the publick worship of God to be for the glory "of God and salvation of souls, that he gave such "orders for the affairs of his family on the Lord's"day, that most of his servants were at liberty "timely to attend upon it, and none of them "wholly let and hindered from it. The concern "also he h'ad for God's house was answerable to "the veneration he had for his worship; he was "always ready to promote any design for the "erecting chapels and churches where there were "none, and encreasing the number of them where "they were thin. In time of the civil war, when "every thing almost of order and decency was "called superstition, as he was passing by where "the possest souldiers were pulling down part of "a church, and the ornaments of it, and ask'd of "him to give them something to encourage the "work, he said to those about him, 'My father "and I have built several churches, and by the "help of God I'll pull none down.'

' His beneficence and his alms were of the "same piece with his piety; he was never back"ward to forgive; always ready to distribute; "his charity, like that of God's, was universal, "not confin'd to sects and parties, but flowing "abundantly towards all men, yet discreetly "plac'd and proportioned, according as men's "needs and capacities presented, giving most "where it was most wanted, and where it might "be to the best purposes. He loved good Chris"tians, of what denominations soever, many "of which subsisted by his bounty; and for "others, whose virtue was suspected, and their "conversation of no good report, whilst he hated "hiprocrisie and vice, he relieved their persons, "shewing himself a true friend to mankind, and "a benefactor to the human nature.

"I need not mention that mighty zeal he had "for the Protestant religion, for the interest of

"his country, its laws and liberties, and his never "to be shaken faith and affection to our invin"cible monarch, who so generously, in spight of "all hazards and oppositions, came over for the "rescue and deliverance of them. They are too "flaming to be hid. In the late times of difficulty "and persecution, he was a strenuous defender of "them, and an hearty supporter of those who "ventured far in that cause. The great Lord "Russell, his son, was a martyr, and died for "them; and its no wonder that such heroicke "actions begat in the breasts of all an honorable "esteem of him, gain'd him the distinguishing "love of his prince, and the particular regard of "Heaven.

"The whole nation no doubt are very sensible "of this irreparable loss, and there's great reason "for it, to the peace and welfare whereof he so "highly contributed by his counsel, by his estate, "by his example, by his prayers, and by his cha"rity, the which arc styled in scripture sacrifices, "to signifie, in a high degree, their acceptable"ness to God, and the great power they have "with him to avert judgments, and to draw down "blessings upon a kingdom. But the several "counties, over which, under the king, he pre"sided, ought to be most affected with it, who "lived under the healing influences of his care, "and reapt the fruit of his wise and steady ad"ministration; more especially, we of Saint "Paul's, Covent Garden , who, next to the in The precincts of Covent Garden were erected into a parish

"finite goodness of God, our Maker, have rc"ccived from him the opportunities of worship"ping God, and of making ourselves easie in this "world and happy in the other.

"It pleased God to bless him with a numerous "offspring, and that he liv'd to see his children's "children to the third generation; all in condi"tion suitable to their birth, and highly beloved "and honoured for their own and their father's "sake.

"His servants have lost the best of masters, the "poor a liberal benefactor, the church a bounti"ful patron, the government a potent friend, and "religion a sure protector.

"In the midst of all, there is one consideration "left to alleviate our sorrows and support our "minds; what is our's, the nation's loss, is his "infinite gain: Therefore, while we feel and be"wail the heavy dispensation, let us, with our "disconsolate thoughts, mix those joyful ones of "his salvation. We may weep for ourselves, but "he's at rest, above the reach of evil.

"It was his daily prayer, that, next to the par"don of his sins, God would give him an easie "passage; and God was pleased to hear his "prayer: never did any person leave the world "with greater inward peace, a more resigned "mind, with less struggle and diseompo-sure, and by act of parliament, passed in the reign of Car. II., and called "Saint Paul's, Covent Garden." The parish church was erected at the expense of Earl William, was burnt down sonic few years since, and the present church erected upon the site thereof.

"with more assur'd hopes of a joyful resurrection, "than he did. His lamp of life was not blown "out; the oyl wasted by degrees, and the flame "went out. Nature was quite tired and spent, and "he fell asleep. But whilst his body sleeps in the "grave, his soul is returned to God, that gave it, "there to receive the end of his faith, the fruits "of his piety and charity, ever an incorruptible "crown of life and glory. *They do it to obtain a "corruptible crown, but we an incorruptible"*

Thus terminated the mortal career of William Earl of Bedford, one of the most exalted, amiable, and benevolent characters that have adorned this, or any other age or country.

Francis and William, Earls of Bedford, have long slept within the narrow limits of the tomb; but the services they have rendered to the Bedford Level have left impressed upon the hearts of fen-men an imperishable sense of gratitude and affection, which the author hopes will descend from generation to generation.

CHAPTER XV. *Phenomena of the Fens. —The Soil. — Nature of Turf.—Plants and natural productions. — Opinion of De la Pryme.—System of drainage.— Mills and steam engines.—Mode of cultivation. Decoys.— The Meers.*

Before we proceed to inquire into the laws and customs of the Bedford Level Corporation, the duties imposed upon its members, or the works more especially intrusted to their care and management, it will not be unentertaining to the readers of this work, more especially to those who do not reside within the precincts of the Fens, to notice some particulars of a country so little known, and yet so important to the interests of the kingdom at large.

Many theories have, at various times, been advanced, as to the actual condition of the Fens in the early and middle ages; but in fact, there is no record, no history, that can tend to elucidate the subject; nor can any satisfactory reasons be assigned for certain phenomena peculiar to this country.

Vol. i. 2 E

The soil of the One remarkable feature of the Great Level is, that very large tracts were, and still are, covered with a thick crust of turf. Several thousand acres were in this state; but the improvement of drainage has, in many places, altered the nature of the soil, and induced considerable change in its cultivation.

Nature of turf. The turf consists of a congeries of the roots and fibres of about forty different species of plants, mixed with earthy matter. In some places it is several yards in depth, in others only a few inches. When the turf is removed, a natural mould Is discovered, partaking of the nature of highland; and persons who have watched the progress of the labourers in the Fens, aver, that they have seen the land beneath the turf lying in ridge and furrow, as if, before the turf collected upon it, it had been submitted to the highest operations of husbandry. At an early period, the turf in its natural state was so soft as to be incapable of supporting the weight of a human being. A pole might with ease be thrust into it to the depth of several feet; and, indeed, in times of more recent date, it has been difficult, owing to the softness of the ground in certain parts, for horses to work the plough.

It is a property of turf water, to preserve from decomposition substances deposited in it. The labours of the inhabitants of the Fens, in digging amongst the turf, are often rewarded by the discovery of the trunks of large trees in a perfectly sound state. Firs measuring thirty yards, and oaks measuring five feet and a half in length, and trees of other descriptions, as well as large quantities of fir apples and hazel nuts, have been found. In the moor beds, animal substances are also preserved. When deepening the Wisbech River, in the year 1635, the workmen, at eight feet below the then bottom of the river, struck on another bottom, hard and stony, and there discovered, at different distances from each other, and overwhelmed with silt, seven boats; which, no doubt, had remained thus bedded for many ages past. And at Whittlesey, in digging through the moor, at a depth of eight feet, the labourers came to a perfect soil, and swaths of grass lying thereon, as if it had been newly mown.

The circumstance of the roots of trees (found, as before-mentioned, in great numbers, in most parts of the Level.) standing in firm ground at considerable depths under the moor; and the circumstance of the causey extending from Denver to Peterborough, being covered with a moor from three to five feet in depth, shew, that the surface of the Level is now much higher than formerly.

And when the foundation for setting down the sasse at Salter's Lode was being excavated, the silt was observed to be ten feet deep: immediately next below that, the workmen found firm moor of three feet in thickness; then bluish gault, which they judged to have been silt originally, because, being dry, it not only crumbled, but contained within it the roots of reeds: below that they perceived moor of three feet thickness, in quality much firmer and clearer than the other; and lastly, they found a whitish clay, supposed to have been the original natural bottom soil.

The famous antiquary, Sir Robert Cotton de Bruce, making a pool at the skirts of what was then called Connington Down, in Huntingdonshire, found what was at that time conjectured to be the skeleton of a large sea fish, nearly 20 feet long, lying in perfect silt, about six feet below the superficies of the ground, and as much below the present Level of the Fens. And, strange to say, the skeleton, by continuing so long in that kind of earth, had become quite petrified.

And at the setting down of Shirbeck Sluice, near Boston, a smith's forge was found, at 16 feet deep, covered with silt, together with (as some who were present have affirmed) all the tools, horseshoes, and other things, belonging to the smith. To which may be added, that in driving the piles for securing the foundation of the Great New Sluice set down at the mouth of the New Cut, a little above Boston, in Lincolnshire, in the year 1764, at about 18 feet deep, under the then pasturage surface, were found the roots of trees standing as the trees had grown, some of which were obliged to be chopt through, to afford a passage to the piles. In some other parts of the pit dug for laying the same foundation, at about an equal depth, small shells were observed, lying in the same manner as they are now often seen to lie at the bottoms and sides of the marsh creeks.

Even in modern times, many subjects of curiosity have been discovered during the progress of the works in the Bedford Level. In excavating the rivers under the authority of the Middle Level River Act (passed in 1810), hazel nuts and fir and other trees were perceived at some feet below the original bed of the river, particularly in a river near Sawtry, called Monk's Lode. In other rivers in the Middle Level were found spears, shields, and military weapons; andin deepening the river near Ely by the South Level commissioners, so lately as last summer, a very antique sword was found in a perfect state of preservation. This sword is now in the possession of Thomas Archer, Esq., of Ely; and the articles discovered in the Middle Level rivers are preserved by Mr. Cambers, of Whittlesey. Several human bodies have also been disinterred, the remains perhaps of unfortunate persons lost in attempting to cross the fens while in their nndrained state.

The turf moors are covered with such plants as the heath, ling, and fern. The *mytica gale,* plants, and natural productions, and a grass with a beautiful white tuft, called the cotton grass, are found in abundance.

With respect to the trees that have been found Opinion of Dc la rryme. in the turf beds, De la Pry me, the celebrated antiquary, already mentioned, entertains a double hypothesis. Some of these trees have their fibrous roots attached; others have been cut or burnt down; some have been squared; others bored through; wedges of stone or iron have been found in some, and near them the heads of axes have been discovered. For these reasons De la Pryme is of opinion, that most of them have been purposely cut down, and that the fall of those trees was the proximate cause of the formation of the turf. For lying along the ground, they obstructed the course of any little stream which might be near them, and also the reflux which might collect from the overflowing of the great rivers; and whatever earthy matters those waters brought with them would remain, and form a soil more congenial to the less useful plants, than to those which might minister to the wants of man or beast. These plants, flourishing and decaying in regular and unobserved succession, would form, with fresh accessions of earthy matter, yearly additions to the bed of turf, till it arrived at the state in which it is now seen.

His second hypothesis is, that the destruction of the forest (for the trees are, in parts, so numerous, that they must when standing have formed what might well be called a forest) was the work of the Romans. It is supposed, that they were cut down to deprive the Britons of the shelter they afforded, and to destroy the fastnesses from which the natives were accustomed to issue in their attacks upon the Roman stations. Whether this opinion can be sustained, or not, it is evident that the destruction of these trees must be referred to a very remote period; and if the above statements of the existence of the marks of tools upon the trees, and of the presence of the instruments themselves, can be relied on, we may very fairly infer, that the forest did not perish by natural decay. Few trees, if any, were planted here, or indeed any where, in the middle ages of our history; yet Doomsday Book shews us, that there was in the fens, as in other parts, that species of country denominated *sylva pascua*.

A country like this, as might be expected, was better adapted for the sports of the field than for the regular operations of husbandry. The opportunities it afforded for enjoying the pleasures of hunting, fowling, and fishing, were unrivalled. The fisheries were then cultivated, more perhaps for profit than for pleasure. At a time when, owing to the strictness of a religious rule, the consumption of fish was much greater than at present, the fisheries, whether on the coast or the inland lakes, became an object of important consideration. Of fowling we have fewer particulars; yet it is evident, that aquatic birds must have delighted in a region like this; indeed, most of this species of the feathered tribe yet abound throughout the Level, although their numbers are greatly decreased by the progress of draining. It is not, however, to be supposed, that the whole of this district, before the drainage, was either rendered inhospitable by the turf and the water, or devoted to the mere amusements of the chace. There were many fertile spots, producing grass and corn; and even as early as the time of the conquest, a considerable population was employed, as well in agricultural pursuits as in the fisheries.

It being intended that this work should be of a practical, rather than of a theoretical character, to prosecute these inquiries further has been deemed unnecessary. Indeed, the author has neither the requisite time nor talent. He is anxious only to avoid the sin of omitting any subject connected with the country of which he treats: and in justice to himself he must remark, that many discussions have already been introduced, less with a view of offering his own opinions, than of inciting others better qualified for the task, to a more minute investigation of subjects at once so interesting and instructive. System of To proceed. The system of drainage has undergone, from time to time, very beneficial improvements. Some time after the passing of the general drainage act, 15 Car. II, the Bedford Level was in a lamentable state, and in imminent danger of being once more reduced to the condition from which it had been reclaimed by the unparelleled exertions and perseverance of Francis and William Earls of Bedford. The board of the Bedford Level corporation have had to encounter the severest trials and difficulties. Debts accumulated; taxes became in arrear. Their attention, however, to the multifarious and arduous duties intrusted to their charge did not relax; but their burthens became ultimately too weighty to be borne, without calling upon the Level at large to exert its every energy to relieve them from the load of perplexity and danger by which they were likely to be overwhelmed. The funds of the corporation were not at any time more than adequate to maintain and support the great works of drainage, such as the several sluices, bridges, and great barrier banks; but to these expenses, and the annual salaries of its officers, was soon added the interest of the debt. The minor works throughout the Level, it is true, were then, and still continue to be, App. P. 100. under the jurisdiction and control of the corpo-388-396ration.

By the Lynn Law it is directed, "that the system of "owners of the adventurers' lands shall divide App'.np?H4. "and sever their lands one from another, unless "they shall rather desire to lie undivided, by such "sufficient partition, dikes, and fences, as shall be "necessary to convey or carry away the rain water "towards the great drains, and that such parti"tions and fence dikes, *if any such should be made,* "shall be made by them in such an uniform man"ner as may best conduce to the perfecting the "whole work." The contract of Francis Earl of Bedford extended no further than to make the lands of the Level "summer lands;" and, therefore, little notice appears to have been taken of this direction. In fact, the adventurers can scarcely be said to have had possession of the proportions intended to be set out as a recompense for the general drainage. By the pretended act (1649), the App. p. 371. original contract was much enlarged. The lands were to be made "winter grounds." The adjudication of the commissioners at Peterborough and Ely, Ante. p. 210. legalized the Saint Ives Law, by which law the adventurers' lands had been set out to the several adventurers. Individual interests now arose; sales and purchases began to take place; and cultivation assumed a more settled feature; and had the ad venturers fortunately adhered to a natural system of drainage, there can be no doubt, that the full and complete execution of the contract of William Earl of Bedford would have been apparent at the present day. But retrospects are painful. The natural rivers were unimbanked; the artificial ones began early to grow up; their banks were perfectly inefficient. In short, the fallacy of the Vermuyden system was discovered when it was too late to retrace the steps of those who had been deceived by the Dutch adventurer. The system was therefore pursued; and as Mahomet would not go to the mountain, the mountain was obliged to come to Mahomet. The corporation continued to struggle under the most appalling difficulties.

Drainage by In the year 1678 it appears, that in consequence of the following order, made at the April meeting at Ely in that year, their attention was first directed to the artificial system of draining by mills:

"Ordered, that for the better and speedier "cleansing and scouring of draynes, the four sur"veyors of the Level do forthwith buy each of "them a mill, made for that purpose, and pay for "the same out of the money allotted for their "respective Levels."

The mills here alluded to were probably small horse mills, set upon lands nearest the river. It does not appear that this measure was productive of any great good, although perhaps it gave rise to the general expedient of artificial drainage afterwards resorted to by the owners and occupiers of the Bedford Level. Yet this expedient was not adopted for some time; for in the year 1699, a petition was presented by the inhabitants of Chatteris, setting forth the damage occasioned by the erection of a mill, by one Green, near Slade Lode, and such mill was ordered to be presented by the court of sewers. The idea of draining by mills had however excited too much attention to be easily eradicated; and accordingly, in the year 1703, we find mills erected by Sylas Tytus, Esq., of Ramsey, (the then owner of the estates now possessed by William Henry Fellowes, Esq.,) John Delaney, the Earl of Torrington, and others; which mills were likewise presented at a court of sewers as nuisances, and ordered to be pulled down. The consequence was, these parties resorted for relief to a court of equity. Bills were filed against the corporation *ex officio,* and against several of its component members. The following answer to those bills must be interesting, as it clearly points out the grounds of the dispute.

"The joint and several answers of Sir Roger "Jenyns, knight, John Jenyns, Henry Ox"burgh, John Walsham, Malbon Caryll, "esquires, and William Cole, gent., six of "the defendants to the bill of complaint of "Sylas Tytus, Esq. , John Delaney, the right "honorable the Earl of Torrington, *Sec., com*"plainants.

"These defendants saving, &c. They severally "answer and say, that the several mills in the bill "mentioned, and the several parcels of land "whereupon the same are therein likewise men"tioned to be erected, are and do lie within the "compass of the Great Level of the Fens, called "Bedford Level, as in the bill is charged. And "these defendants do severally believe, that the "several complainants may be severally interest"ed in the said lands and mills, as in their said "bill of complaint they have set forth; and that "they have erected the said mills or engines on "their said lands, to throw off water from the "same, which in working do throw or cast out "the waters in such manner, and into such drains, "rivers, cutts, and outfalls, by name, belonging to "the governor, bayliffs, and commonalty of the "company of conservators of the Great Level 1, and "to be kept and repaired by them, as in the said "bill is sett forth: But as to the late or present "conditions thereof, these defendants, for greater "certainty as to the truth thereof, do severally "crave leave to refer themselves to the answer of "the said company of conservators, defendants, "in like manner in this cause, and in which "said answer these defendants were all included, '" (except the defendant Henry Oxburgh) as mem"bers of the said company of conservators, and "have therein and thereby more particularly set "forth the same. And these defendants do fur"ther severally say, that they know not how far "the said complainants are interested in the said

"lands or mills, or of what estates they are seized; "nor do these defendants, or any of them, know "whether the complainants, or any of them, have "a right to erect on their said lands any such "mills or water engines, or any mills or water en"gines at all, as by their said bill is pretended; "but do conceive, that in case the complainants "have a liberty of building and erecting such "mills and water engines, yet they, the said com"plainants, ought not by any means to work or "use the same in such manner as they have lately "done, to the prejudice or drowning of their "neigh-

bours' lands adjacent, on pretence of se"curing their own; but that they ought to be "content with the usual way of draining by the "said company of conservators of the said Great "Level, and commissioners of sewers for the same, "constituted and established (amongst other "things) for that purpose by the act of parliament "of the loth year of King Charles the Second, in "the bill and hereinafter mentioned, and to ac"quiess in their judgments, and submit to such "orders as they shall think most fit and necessary "to be made for or concerning the preservation "of and public good of the said Great Level: And "the rather, for that by the said act of parlia"ment, in the bill set forth, and intituled 'An act "for settling the draining of the Great Level of "the Fens called Bedford Level', the adventurers "and undertakers of that great work of draining "are made a body politic and corporate in deed "and name, and to have succession for ever by

"the name of the governor, bayliffs, and common' alty of the company of conservators of the Great "Level of the Fens; which said governor, bayliffs, "and twenty conservators, duly elected and chosen "out of the said commonalty, or any five or more "of them, whereof the said governor, bayliffs, and "their successors, or any of them, to be two, are "also thereby empowered to act as commission"ers of sewers for the said Level, exclusive of all "other commissioners of sewers for ever; and, as "commissioners of sewers, to judge of and deter"mine which drains and outfalls are most neces' sary for the public benefit, and preservation of "the whole Great Level in general; as by the said "act of parliament, to which for more certainty "these defendants do severally refer themselves, "more fully may appear. And these defendants "further severally say, that they do believe, that ' if the complainants would use their said lands "for pasture or summer crops only, as well as "others who have estates thereto adjoining do, "and would have patience to let the waters run "off by the common drains of the corporation, "their said grounds would be as well drained as "the grounds of these defendants, or any others "within the said Great Level; and there would be "no such necessity for their erecting or working "of their said mills (as in their said bill they pre"tend there is); neither do these defendants know "or believe the said complainants are under any "necessity at all of erecting or using their said "mills; nor have these defendants given the com

"plainants any occasion so to do (as in their bill "is suggested); nor ought the complainants, or "any other owners of lands within the said Great "Level (as these defendants conceive and are ad"vised) to erect or make any works for draining, "at their own wills and pleasures, their own lands, "to the damage of the public draining, and the "prejudice of other lands adjacent, upon any pre"tence whatsoever; for should they be permitted "so to do, it would be impossible for the commis"sioners of sewers, or the said corporation, (as "these defendants do conceive and believe,) whose "business and charge it is to preserve the whole "Great Level, to answer the great trust reposed "in them for that end and purpose; for the doing; "whereof great sums of money are yearly raised "by the said governor, bayliffs, and conserva"tors of the said Great Level, by virtue and "authority of the aforesaid act, in every year; "and which said sums of money do some years "amount to the sum of upwards of 5000/., and "in other years to upwards of 6000/., as these "defendants do believe; all which sums of "money these defendants believe are duly and "fairly applied to the public use of the said Great "Level, and in or about other the matters requi"site and necessary to the support and preserva"tion thereof; but for more certainty therein, "these defendants crave leave likewise to refer "themselves to the answer of the said corpora"tion, other defendants in this cause, and in "which these defendants are likewise included

"as aforesaid, and also to the books and proceed"ings of the said corporation in relation thereto,." to which the complainants may have resort "whenever they please. And these defendants "further say, that, there having been great riots "committed within the said Great Level, in or "about the year of our Lord 1698, chiefly occa"sioned by the complainants working their said "mills, to the great damage of the owners and "land-owners of the lands adjacent, (the people "in general being very much incensed thereat,) "these defendants, Sir Roger Jenyns, knight, "John Jenyns, then and yet bayliffs of the said "company of conservators, and these defendants, "John Walsham, Malbon Caryll, and William "Cole, then and yet conservators and members of "the said company, and this defendant, Henry "Oxburgh, then, but not at this time a conserva"tor or member of the said company, together "with the other defendant, Richard Marryott, "then and yet conservator, and the other defend"ant, Edward Woodward, then, but not at this "time, a conservator, together with Ralph Pier"son, Esq., then and yet bayliff of the said com"pany, and Lionell Walden, Esq., deceased, then "a conservator, then being all commissioners of "sewers for the said Great Level, did meet and "act at the town of March, in the said Great "Level, on the 26th day of March, in the year "of our Lord 1699; at which court Reginald "Mitchell, gent. , Edward Smith, and others, ju"rors, were duly returned and sworn to enquire "of and concerning the works within and with"out the said Great Level, which said jurors were "duly elected out of the six neighbouring coun"ties, and were men of great ability and worth, "having most of them estates of inheritance "within the said Great Level, and having little or "no adventure lands, but were summoned from "all or most parts of the said Great Level, and "charged upon oath, to enquire of all nuisances, "and other grievances committed within the said "Level, enquireable before commissioners of "sewers; and they the said jurors being so im"pannelled, charged, and sworn, did (amongst t" other things) present, that there then was, and "for four years last past had been, a certain "windmill or water engine, standing near to a "certain drain or river, called Whittlesea Dike, "then in the occupation of Mrs. Frances Keat, "widow, (one of the complainants,) within the "said Great Level, which had raised waters, silt, "slough, and other matters, into the said Whit"tlesea Dike, being one of the public drains in "the said Level, so that by reason thereof the "same drain then was and had been landed, silt"ed, and filled up, to the great injury of the said "Level, by drowning adjacent lands, the hind"ranee of navigation, and the continual nuisance "of the land owners having right to drain their "waters by the said drain and rivers. And this "defendant, Sir Roger Jenyns, for himself fur"ther severally saith, that he hath not, nor ever "had, any lands near Whittlesea Dyke, in the bill Vol. i. 2 F

"mentioned, or that parte of the said Bevill's

"Leam that adjoins thereto, as in the said biH

"is untruly suggested, or within ten or twelve

"miles of the place complained of in the bill, to

"be stopped up by a sluice in Bevill's River. And

"all these defendants do severally deny, that the

"said sluice was not so sett up in Bevill's River,

"for the bettering only of some or any of these

"defendants' lands, as in the said bill is untruly

"suggested; for that the same was so done by,

"the order of the said corporation, about twenty

"five years ago, and not by the order or direction

"of these defendants, or any of them these de

"fendants, nor any of them being then members

"thereof; To which said order of the corpora

"tion, and the answer concerning the same, these

"defendants crave leave to refer themselves. But

"these defendants do severally say, that they

"these defendants, so far as they have been con"cerned, have, to the utmost of their abilities and "powers, used all proper means for preserving the "said Level, pursuant to the great design and in"tent of the said act of loth of King Charles the "Second; and have done every thing to the best "of their judgments, skill, and power, for the "common good of the said Level, in discharge of "the trust reposed in them by the said act, with"out having any respect to their own private in"terest, or preservation of their or any of their "own lands more than the lands of others. And "these defendants severally deny, that they, or any "of them, have had any other shares or allotments "out of the said Great Level, other than part of "the 83,000 acres vested in the said corporation "by virtue of the aforesaid last mentioned act of "parliament, and under whom these defendants "claim as participants, or otherwise. And these "defendants do believe it may be true, but with "all do conceive and are advised, that it is not at "all material whether the waters issued by the "said complainants' said mills did first pass "through the complainants' own lands, since that "the same have been found by lawful and good juries, upon their oaths, to be nuisances, and "prejudicial to the lands adjacent, and otherwise, "as aforesaid, by overflowing the same. And these "defendants further severally say, that they do "not know or believe, that there have been any "offers made to them, or any of them, before the "exhibiting the said bill of complaint, to try ' whether the complainants have such right to "work and use their said mills, as in and by the "said bill is pretended: However, these defend"ants conceive and are advised, that they are no *u* wise obliged to try the same; nor do they know "that they ar« concerned, as private persons, "whether the complainants have such right or *f* no. And these defendants severally deny, that "they have ever misapplied any sums of money, "at anytime raised pursuant to the directions of "the said last mentioned act of parliament, or "otherwise, for the preservation of the said Le"Tel, nor do they know of any misapplication "thereof. And further, all these defendants do "severally deny all the combination and confe"deracy unjustly charged upon them by the said "bill; and humbly pray to be hence dismissed, "with their reasonable costs and charges, in this "behalf most wrongfully had and sustained. "

This document has been selected, as detailing more fully than the official answer of the corporation, the motives and rules of action in relation to this important subject, by which the board was actuated, in concurrence doubtless with the country at large.

The termination of the suit was favorable to the corporation; and for some time the system of draining by mills appears to have been abandoned.

After many struggles, the Level became so inundated by the choking up of the interior drains, the defective state of the rivers themselves, and the neglect to improve the outfalls to sea, that the corporation found it impossible to resist the importunity of the country to resort to an artificial system of interior drainage; and accordingly, at a board held at Ely on the 9th of April, 1726, the following entry appears upon the books:

"Upon reading the petition of the inhabitants "of Haddenham and Wilburton, in the Isle of "Ely, setting forth that the Hundred Foot Bank, "above and below Earith, being so low that it "can't contain the land floods within the Wash, "and that the said banks were overflowed twice "last year, to their great damage; and that they "are apprehensive the whole Level is in danger "of loosing its outfalls to sea; and hearing of "a project carrying on for turning the Hundred "Foot River, which, besides the great charge "thereof, would he so far from answering the "proposed end, it would contribute much to "make it worse; and pray that the said banks at "Earith may be raised to their due height; and "that such method may be used for regaining a "general outfall as shall be thought convenient."

This petition was soon followed by the suggestion of a plan of private drainage by legislative enactment. An application was made to parliament in the ensuing session, and gave rise to the first private district act within the Bedford Level. First private It is entitled, " An Act for the effectual draining J' and preserving of Haddenham Level, in the Isle of Ely." From this period may be dated the plan of Drainage by draining by water mills, apian which has been brought into universal operation throughout the Level until nearly the present period. The state of the corporation funds at this period led to a measure, the adoption of which could scarcely have been contemplated; namely, the formation of each of the three Levels into an isolated government, with powers, independent of the corporation, of appointing its own governors and officers, raising taxes, and expending its amount in internal works of drainage, with power also of borrowing money upon credit of those taxes. It must, however, be always remembered, that notwithstanding these local acts, the entirety of the rights of the Bedford Level corporation is preserved in as ample a manner as if those acts themselves had not been passed; and consequently, the general control of the corporation is not in any degree abridged. But the measure itself relieved the corporation from considerable liabilities... 755. The artificial system of drainage, under the authority of local district acts, by the means of water engines, may be thus explained:—Certain proprietors of any given quantity of land, agree to apply to parliament for a local act (which was originally considered to be a measure in aid of the funds of the Bedford Level corporation). The boundary is set forth, and subdivision dikes are made, for draining the estate of each owner. These division ditches empty themselves into a main drain, cut at the general expense of the owners, (commonly called the Mill drain,) and run through the whole district, which is embanked all around by a mound of earth, raised at a height proportioned to the quantity of water required to be excluded. The mill drain termi nates at one end, near a river, upon the banks of which the water mill is erected, and thus, by means of a circular wheel, the water which has found its way into the mill drain, is thrown from thence into the river, whence it passes to the outfall, and onwards to sea. The number of mills in each district depends of course upon its extent, and the head or quantity of water required to be discharged. This artificial system has continued for many years; but in modern times, the great improvement in the general or exterior drainage of the country, (the particulars of which will be noticed hereafter,) has led to many practical advantages. The first plan adopted in this respect, was the erection of what are termed "Double Double Hft». lifts;" that is, first, one large mill is erected near the main river, and then a smaller one at some distance behind: the one mill, by first raising the water from the mill drain a certain height, and in certain quantities, lessens what is called the head of water to be thrown by the first mill, and finally greatly facilitates its operation.

Within a short period, a still further improve-Drainage by ment has taken place, by the erection of steam su""11"-"" engines. Their capability of throwing out water at all times when required, gives them an advantage over water engines, which cannot work without wind, and of course very serious consequences may occur before a favorable wind can be ensured. Water mills are very numerous throughout the Level; but only five steam engines have been hitherto erected; one in Borough Fen, near Thorney, in the North Level; one in West Fen, near March, in the Middle Level; two in Littleport Fen, near Ely; and one in Swaffham and Bottisham district, upon the banks of the Cam, near Clayhithe Sluice; the three last of which are in the South Level. A general opinion prevails, that the system of draining by steam engines will continue to be prosecuted; but this will necessa rily depend much upon the finances of the respective districts. Many intelligent fenmen, however, indulge the hope of acquiring a natural drainage, when the operation of the great works of drainage now undertaken, in a greater or less degree in all the three Levels, can be fully ascertained. The author cannot rank himself among the number of these sanguine personages. Nature, once abandoned to the intricacies of art, never resumes her empire to her wonted extent.

Having thus endeavoured to explain to the inexperienced and non-resident fen-man, the way in which the interior drainage of the country is carried on, we will now proceed to some remarks upon the mode of cultivation.

cuitivationof Of late years, owing to the great improvement in the general drainage of the Fens, the mode of cultivation has undergone considerable change, a change highly beneficial both to owner and occupier. Formerly oats and cole-seed were the chief productions of the Fens; but nothing can afford more satisfactory evidence of the great alteration for the better, effected in this important country, than the fact, that wheat is now regularly sown throughout the Level, instead of spring cropping. In the neighbourhood of Upwell, nearWisbech, the cultivation of flax and hemp was very general, but has lately been on the decline. It cannot be expected, that the author should lay down any specific rules for cultivation: like other lands throughout the kingdom, the mode varies according to the quality and nature of the soil. His object is, to give strangers an idea of so important a subject. The ancient method of management of black fen land, or turf moor, was, to divide the farm into five or six fields: In the first year to pare the land with a plough, place the earth in small heaps, burn those heaps, spread the ashes, (which act as a powerful manure,) plough the whole over, and sow the land with rape or coleseed, which the cultivator sometimes allows to stand for seed, but more generally feeds off with sheep. The second year, the land is sown with oats; the third, with wheat, and laid down with proper seeds; and then continues three or four summers in grass, according to the number of fields into which the farm is divided; after which it will be again fit to undergo the course already stated. Some persons permit a third of the whole farm to be under plough; others, a greater proportion. Some poor lands are burnt, and sown with wheat upon the ashes; then with barley; and laid down with seeds, comprising generally certain quantities of rye-grass, and red and white clover, lamb-tongue, and tresfoil; the quantity sown depending upon the quality of the land. This plan frequently produces a good herbage the first year. But of course the reader understands, that the mode of cultivation must inevitably vary with the different natures of the soil throughout The great and exterior works of drainage under the control and direction of the corporation, will be explained when we consider the effect of the works belonging to that body. the Fens; sometimes, for instance, beans or coleseed continue for a crop in lieu of oats.

The great improvement in the general drainage has introduced the system of summer fallows. An entirely new plan of management is now becoming cuying tho very general, namely, what is termed "claying the land." This mode of management is so very modern, that the author finds some difficulty in giving an accurate description of its singular process. The land is dug into pits about three feet three inches wide, and two feet deep, more or less, according to the discovery of the clay; and these pits are about eleven yards distant from each other. The top soil is laid by the side of the pit; the clay is then dugout, and thrown over the surface of the land; after which, the pits are again filled with the top soil, and the whole field ploughed over, and put into a state for cropping. The cost of this mode of cultivation is extremely heavy; but very sanguine expectations are formed of the most successful results. The charge varies, of course, according to the depth of the clay below the surface: at the distance above stated, we may state it to be 2/. per acre. The pbject is to give solidity to the land; but it is for experience to prove, whether the heavier soil will not force itself back before the industrious owaer cau reap the reward of the expense he has thus unavoidably incurred. One beneficial effect, undoubtedly, arises from the measure,—the employment ef the poor. The following letter, which has recently appeared, is inserted in this work *verba tint,* without regard to its literary merits, as it throws some light upon this novel and interesting subject.

"Sir,

"As work for the poor forms one of the most "important considerations of the day, a subject "unquestionably deserving the best attention that *lt* can be given; no one need fear submitting his "ideas; because the subject is at once laudable "and praiseworthy, even if carried only to anex"tent local circumstances and means the country "in which we live, possess.

"We have long, too long, witnessed the nature "of, and unsatisfactory employment of the poor "man, the patience with which he works and re"ceives the miserable dole for his labour, only "marking discontent by a pensive glance, and "calculating with unerring, but fearful correct"ness, how the wants of his poor family are to "be sustained during the ensuing week. Here, "necessity keeps back the sixpence which for"merly he would spare, forming, with others, "alike mindful with himself, the fund towards "which he could look with confidence and plea"sure, and draw from it comfort in distress. Ex"eluded thus by poverty (the original inventor) ' from institutions reputable to a British labourer, "he is obliged to send his poor supplicating wife "to the parish overseer for relief, scantily given; "the support he requires is withheld, continuing "him still upon the bed of sickness.

"I am not a theory man, drawing fancied pic"tures: as a practical man do I speak, and can "prove, if proof is required, the truth of what is "stated; but to produce a different order of things "with reference to the subject, and improve the "poor man's condition, is the object, and my aim. "I should like to see introduced a system of em"ployment, that, not like a road disencumbered "of the snow; is again immediately covered, and "no trace left of what had been done: a descrip"tion of labour new in its kind, and benefiting "the employer and the employed; the neighbour"hood improving the habits and degenerated mo'rals of the poor, rendering poaching, by re"ducing the cause, far less tempting. With those "advantages, another will consequently follow, "and has taken place in a parish in Hunting"donshire; a considerable reduction of the poor"rates, the poor carrying the smile of content"ment, meeting those with respect and esteem "whom Providence has placed above him; feel"ing that reciprocal obligation towards each "other, which mark the cheering hope, and "brings to mind days that are gone. But to "the point. From drainage,— and here let me "thank those zealous promoters who have done "so much service to a country, which may be "said, and I believe very justly, to rank with-" many counties more favoured by nature,— "we have a generous soil, requiring, it is true, "some attention; good roads, fair rivers, and, last "not least, a mine of wealth below, or, speak"ing more fen-man-like, a bed of clay, of which "twenty-five years back we knew nothing. It is, "sir, to this rich and wealthy bed of clay I am so "earnest and anxious to draw the care and atten"tion of the agriculturist: nature seems to have "laid it for our use, and at a time when to relieve "the distress that pervades the country, is cer"tainly most inviting. It is almost needless to say "to my brethren, clay is found in every part of "the fens, at the depth of 3, 4, 5, and 6 feet, "which, when mixed with the poorest soils, pro"duce an increased quantity, and greatly im"proved quality, of every kind of corn, particu"larly wheat. I venture to assert, that on any "given number of acres, double the quantity of "the latter may be grown, than if it had not "been clayed. The grass seeds generally sown "on wheat are improved beyond calculation, "both as respects quality and ability to carry "stock, and in the same ratio adds generally to "the benefit of the farm. Claying is done by "cutting parallel trenches, 10, 11, and 12 yards "from each other; 36, 40, and sometimes 48 "inches wide; out of which, after sinking down, "is cast, equally divided, two draws or two feet "of clay, giving about 400 cart loads to the acre; "for this work is paid 40, 50, and 60. per acre; "(may I ask, can an acre of land be manured for "less?) enabling the labourer to earn 12. to 14. "per week, besides what his wife and family may, "by spreading the clay. Its weight and texture, "mixed with the fen soil, gives what it wants,

"solidity, and reduces the moor. By an adop"tion of an employment which I have endea"voured but faintly to explain, of the beneficial "results there can be no doubt. It improves the "interest of the landlord, the property of the "tenant, and condition of the poor man. Thus ' actuated have I ventured in giving these re"marks, with an assurance that your readers will M not attribute to me motives of a different cha"racter.

"I am, sir,

"Your very obedient servant, "H. W."

The process of turf digging will be adverted to in a subsequent part of this work.

Decoys. Amongst other subjects of curiosity, we must not omit some notice of the "Decoys," or receptacles for catching wild fowl. There are four of these places, namely, one in Borough Fen, near Thorney, the property of Sir Culling Smith, Bart.; another in Holme Fen, near Stilton, the property of the trustees of the late Captain Wells; and a third at Lakenheath, in the county of Suffolk, the property of William Eagle, Esq. It is supposed, that decoys were in former times much more numerous. One was originally formed in the edge of the Fen at Chatteris, but no vestige of it remains, except the wood by which it was surrounded, and which is called " Coy Wood" at this day. These decoys are generally formed by pools, surrounded by wood, and branching off from them are small channels or ditches, called " Pipes." At the time of catching the fowls, these pipes are covered over with nets, which rest on hoops, and are terminated by a drawing net. Into these the wild fowl are enticed by various devices; but the usual mode is by means of a decoy duck, trained for that purpose. This bird is taught to obey the whistle of the decoy-man, who tempts it to swim up the trapping tunnel, when he sees a number of wild fowls; these following the tame one, and being led into the channel, are then inclosed, and ultimately taken by the net. Sometimes, however, from their extreme shyness and caution, the tame duck does not succeed in trepanning others: in such cases, the decoyman employs a small dog, which, by swimming about amongst the rushes and reeds, and alarming the wild fowl, drives them up the mouth of the net. The decoy should be surrounded by not less than forty or fifty acres of land, well planted, in order to preserve the place quiet. The general season for working the decoy is from the end of the month of October to the month of February. These decoys are considered very lucrative concerns; indeed, the quantities of fowl sometimes taken almost exceed belief.

At the time of the original drainage, under the Meers. Lynn Law, it was enacted, "That meeres, meer "grounds, poles, and lakes, and such grounds as "shall according to art, and by the approbation "of the commissioners, be left for forelands and "receptacles of waters, shall not be accounted to "be such grounds, as the said Earl, by his agree"ment, should drain, nor shall be accounted any "part of these grounds by or out of which he is "to have recompence from the said work." This was certainly a most injurious system, and fraught with great danger, inasmuch as it always placed the country at the mercy of aHarge quantity of water, at considerable distances from the outfalls; although it cannot be denied that, by acting as reservoirs, upon pressure of flood, the meers have sometimes, (but not of late years,) presented a breach of bank; particularly when all the district mills were pumping the waters into the rivers connected with the meers, the sluices below being prevented from running by the pressure of the upland floods down the Hundred Feet River.

There were originally many of these meers in different parts of the Level; several are now drained, and become firm land: for instance, Benwick Meer, near Ramsey, now the property of Mr. Isaac Ibberson; and Soham Meer, now belonging to the very respectable family of the Grangers, of Streatham, near Ely, by whom the same was purchased from the trustees of the late Marquess of Townsbend.

Amongst the meers that yet remain undrained, Whittlesey Meer is the most extensive. This most spacious fresh water lake in the southern part of Great Britain, on which have been exhibited several regattas and ice-boat sailings, is about six miles from the town of Whittlesey, situated at the extremity of the county of Cambridge, and on the north side of the county of Huntingdon, about thirty-eight miles west of the German Ocean, six miles down the Nene, from the city of Peterborough, and two miles and three quarters east from Stilton. Its surface covers 1570 square acres, and it is eight miles and three quarters in circumference. It abounds in a great variety of water fowl, and the following species of fish, (viz.,) pike, perch, carp, tench, eels, bream, chub, roach, dace, gudgeons, minnows, &c. In the summer months this lake is visited by many of the nobility and gentry from various parts. At times it is said to be violently agitated without any visible cause. It is fed by the surplus waters of a vast tract of upland country on their passage to the sea. An attempt to trace the origin of this beautiful and extensive piece of water would prove fruitless, and at best would terminate in conjecture and obscurity; but its antiquity and importance are shewn by the authority of Doomsday Book, and by its having, so early as A. D. 664, been granted by Wolphere, king of Mercia, to his new founded monastery of Medehamstead (now Peterborough). This monastery, on its destruction by the Danes, in 870, reverted to the crown.

Doomsday Book mentions, that the abbot of Ramsey had one boatsgate in his own right, and a second boatsgate, which he held of the abbot of Thorney, with two fisheries and one virgate of land. The abbot of Thorney had two boatsgates.

In 1507, Henry the Seventh granted the office of Vol i. 2 o keeper of the swanery on the meer of David Cecil, for the term of seven years.

In 1662, Charles the Second granted to Edward Earl of Sandwich the office of master of the swans within the whole kingdom, and also the office of bailiff or keeper of Whittlesey Meer. The lord of the manor has a right to summon the fishermen (or fenny ferries) to his two courts, holden at Holme; when presentments are made, and his bailiff proves the nets with a brazen mesh pin; and on being found under-sized, he is at liberty to take a fine, or destroy them: the lord is also entitled to fines and forfeitures, with other manorial rights.

The present rights of fishing are as follow:

The trustees of the late William Wells, Esq. lord ofGlatton, with Holme, eleven boatsgates.

Lord Say and Sele, lord of Farcett, one, and a private fishery.

The church of Peterborough, two.

The late Earl of Carysfort, one.

There are other small meers in the neighbourhood, as Brick Meer, Ugg Meer, Ramsey Meer, &c., which belong to William Henry Fellowes, Esq., and also a small meer in Yaxley, which belonged to the late Lord Carysfort.

Mr. Golborne, in the year 1777, went through Whittlesey Meer, and on sounding it, found the bottom in general very even, with four feet and a half of water, and two feet of mud under it. Nothing can be more easy than the complete drainage of this meer.

The contents of this chapter will perhaps be considered somewhat miscellaneous: the author can only repeat, that he is desirous not to omit any subject of interest, curiosity, or instruction, relating to the Bedford Level; and when he treats of matters foreign to his habits and acquirements, he throws himself upon the indulgence of his readers.

CHAPTER XVI. *Boundary of the Bedford Level.—Constitution of the corporation. —Distinction between corporations by statute and by charter.—Constituent parts of the corporation.—The select body, from the foundation to the last election.—The election of the Corporation.—Their power to purchase, hold, and dispose of lands.—Their corporate assemblies.—Meetings of the select body.—Corporate documents.—Evidence.*

Boundary. The boundary of the Bedford Level, as set forth in the general act, (15 Car. II.,) is readily traced at the present day. It extends over more than 300,000 acres of land; and, as already stated, is situated in six counties, viz., Northampton, Norfolk, Suffolk, Lincoln, Cambridge, and Huntingdon, and in the Isle of Ely.

Constitution. It is a remarkable feature in the constitution of the Bedford Level corporation, that, differing from the generality of corporations, it is founded by statute, *i. e.*, by the three estates of the realm, and not by charter, and the fiat or favour of royalty only.

The distinction between the two kinds of cor-Diitinction between corpora porations is important. When it is mtended to iions by statute .... and by chiirter.

establish a corporation, and to mvest it with powers or privileges which, by the principles of the common law, cannot be granted by the king's charter, recourse must be had to the aid of an act of parliament; as if it be intended to grant the power of imprisonment, as in the case of the Eyd., Voi.l.' college of physicians; or to confer an exclusive p' right of trading, as in the case of the East India Company; or to erect a court, with power to proceed in a manner different from the common law, which is the case of the vice-chancellor's court in the two universities. But it has been well observed, that most of those statutes which are usually cited, as having created corporations, either confirm such as have been previously created by the king, as in the case of the College of Physicians before mentioned, which was erected by charter in the tenth year of Henry the Eighth, and was afterwards confirmed in parliament by the act of the 14th and 15th of the same king; or they permit theking to erect a corporation/N/ulure, with such and such powers; as in the case of the Bank of England, and the Society of the British Fishery; so that the immediate creative act is usually performed by the King alone, by virtue of his royal prerogative. Corporations have seldom been constituted by parliament, the power of conferring on a body of men a corporate capacity having always been considered a flower of the crown. When, however, the legislature creates or confirms a corporation, the assent of the persons incorporated or confirmed is not necessary, on account of the plenitude of the power of parliament. And a corporation once established by a statute either wiicoTon creative or confirmatory, cannot be altered by any

Corporations,.....,.,,....

P.25. mferior authority, even in the regulation of its forms.

App-p. 120. The corporation of the Bedford Level had, it *is* true, a charter granted by King Charles the First, which is duly referred to in the recital of the sta-, tute of 15 Car. II.; yet it is evident, upon the perusal of that statute, that the very extensive powers intrusted to the corporation, particularly the power of taxing the lands of the subject *ad libitum,* of arbitrarily selling lands in default of payment, the power of general inclosure of lands, and the constitution of a perpetual commission of sewers, could not, and ought not to be exercised solely at the instance of the prerogative of the Sovereign. The exalted character of the corporation of the Bedford Level; the individual rank and respectability of its opulent and distinguished members; the extent of its corporate qualifications; its ample powers; and the extent and importance of its jurisdiction, combine to render it unrivalled, and entitle it in great truth and moral justice to be (as it always has been) considered the first corporation in the United Kingdom.

App.p.i20. The question whether the charter granted by King Charles the First, is now a valid and existing charter, has repeatedly been agitated. Of the fact of its being still available for the exercise of any right or power then granted to the corporation, not a shadow of doubt remains in the mind of the author. In the first place, the charter is recited and acknowledged in the act 15th Car. ApP. p. 386. II.; and secondly, supposing the corporation to have been dissolved for want of succession, and the statute to have created an entirely new charter, or even to have revived (with additional powers) the old one; or even supposing it to have been a charter of restitution; the corporation became entitled to its former rights and franchisee, and subject to all its former obligations. It seems *Kyi.,* Vol. 11. indeed, that a corporation which has been dis-p " solved or suspended by the loss of the governing members, may be revived under a name different from that by which it was formerly known, and may still preserve its identity and former wiicox, p. se. rights. Another curious circumstance connected with the statute of the 15th of Charles II. is its exemplification under the great seal.

The select body of the corporation, usually The select called " The Board," consists of one governor, six bailiffs, and twenty conservators, annually chosen, in manner to be presently mentioned; and as the most eminent men of the ages in which they lived, have from time to time been members of this important corporation, the author has taken the pains to extract their names from the order books; and has added such remarks and observations as he considered might be interesting to *his* readers.

1663. *List of the several Members of the Board, from the passing of the Act of* 15 *Car. II. to the Year* 1929, *inclusive. Governor.* William Earl of Bedford. *Bailiff's.*

Richard Lord Gorges,
Sir Richard Onslow, Knt.,
    Sir William Terringham,
Knight of the Bath, Samuel Sandys, Esq., Thomas Chicheley, Esq.,t Samuel Fortreys, Esq.

Conservators.
Sir Gilbert Gerard, Jim.,
   Knt.,†
William Denton, Esq.,
William Crane, Esq.,
   N.B. The foregoing by the act of 15 Car. II
   Edmond Berry Godfrey, Esq.,
   Arthur Evelyn, Esq.,
   Samuel Smith, Esq.,
   Roger Jenyns, Esq.,
   Robert Castle, Esq.,
   Robert Hampson, Esq.,
   Josh. Ayloffe, Esq.,
   Thomas Lord Culpepper,
Sir John Hewett, Bart.,
Arthur Onslow, Esq.,
Robert Phillips, Esq.,
Anthony St. John, Esq:,
Sir Oliver St. John, Knt.,
Sir Charles Harbord, Knt.,
Francis Hoblyn, Esq.,
Samuel Sandys, Jun., Esq.,
Robert Terringham, Esq.,
members were nominated The fifth Earl, afterwards created Duke of Bedford. Hie Grace continued governor 37 years.
f.Formerly proprietor of Wimpole, the splendid seat of the present Earl of Hardwicke, K. G.
   J Sir Gilbert Gerard's father was M. P. for Middlesex in the long parliament.
   § This title became extinct in 1719. An ancestor of the present Earl of Suffield. He was surveyor general to the crown, *temp.* Car. I. Captain William Harbord, a younger son of Sir Charles, married Catherine, daughter of the Honorable Admiral Edward Russell.
Sir John Denham, (elected a bailiff, *vice* Sir Richard Onslow,)
   John Casburgh,
(elected a conservator, *vice* Samuel Smith.)
Governor.
   William Earl of Bedford, re-elected.
Bailiffs.
The Right Honorable Arthur Earl of Anglesey,
Thomas Lord Cnlpepper,
John Lord Berkley,
Sir John Hewett, Bart.,
Robert Phillips, Esq.,

Joseph Ayloff, Esq.
Conservators.
Sir Gilbert Gerard, Knt.,
Sir John Denham, Knt.,
Samuel Sandys, Sen., Esq.,
Francis Hoblyn, Esq.,
   Sir William Tyrringham, Knt.,
   Sir John Shane, Knt.,
Griffith Bodunda, Esq.,
Samuel Sandys, Jun., Esq.,
Sir Charles Harbord, Knt.,
Robert Hampson, Esq.,
Roger Jenyns, Esq.,
John Casburgh, Esq.,
Terringham Stephens, Esq.,
Arthur Onslow, Esq,
William Hamond, Esq.,
Cornelius Vermuyden,
   Esq.,†
   Robert Tirringham, Esq.,
Michael Holman, Esq.,
Sir Thomas Littleton, Knt.
1664.
1665. same book, the name of Robert Hewett, Esquire, appears, in addition to the above. *Governor.*
The Right Honorable William Earl of Bedford.
Bailiffs.
The Right Honorable John Lord Berkley,
Richard Lord Gorges,
Thomas Chicheley, Esq.,
Colonel Samuel Sandys,
John Casburgh, Esq.,
Robert Hampson, Esq.
Conservators.
   The Right Honorable Thomas Lord Culpepper,
   The Honorable John Russell,
   Sir Andrew Henley, Knt. and Bart.,
Governor.
   The Right Honorable William Earl of Bedford.
Bailiffs.
Thomas Lord Culpepper,
Richard Lord Gorges,
Sir William Terringham,
Sir Gilbert Gerard,
Robert Hampson, Esq.,
Roger Jenyns, Esq.
   Sir William Tirriugham, Knt.,
   Sir Charles Harbord, Knt. Sir Gilbert

Gerard, Knt., Sir Robert Henley, Knt., Sir Thomas Littleton, Knt., Sir John Hewett, Bart., William Denton, Doctor in
   Physic,
   Nicholas Pedley, Esq., Robert Phillips, Esq., Samuel Fortrey, Esq., Francis Underwood, Esq., William Crane, Esq., Hoger Jenyns, Esq., Michael Holman, Esq., Francis St. John, Esq., George Underwood, Esq., John Bradborne, Esq.
Conservators.
Arthur Earl of Anglesey,
.'ohn Lord Berkley,
Lord Bellasses,
Sir Charles Harbord, Knt.,
Sir Robert Henley, Knt.,
Sir John Shaise, Knt.,
Sir Thomas Littleton, Knt.,
Thomas Chicheley, Esq.,
William Atthburuham,Esq.,
Sir John Hewett,
   John.CasBurge, Esq., William Denton, Doctor in
   Physic,
   Nicholas Pedley, Esq.,
Joseph Ayloff, Esq.,
   Samuel Fortrey, Esq., Francis Underwood, Esq., Michael Holman, Esq., Richard Marryott, Esq., John Bnidborne, Esq.
Bailiffs.
John Lord Bellassis, Michael Holman, Esq., (elected bailiffs in the stead of—
   Thomas Lord Culpepper,
Sir Gilbert Gerard.)
Conservators.
   Sir Thomas Willis, Knt., Sir Gilbert Gerard, Knt., Samuel Sandys, Esq., Robert Hewett, Esq., Matthias Taylor, Esq., George Underwood, Esq.,
   David Offley, Gentleman, (elected conservators in the room of— Lord Bellasses, (elected bailiff,)
   Sir John Shaise, Knt.,
Sir Thomas Littleton,
Knight,
William Ashburnham,'
   Esq.,
   Joseph Ayloff, Esq.,
Francis Underwood, Esq.,
Michael Holman, Esq.
(elected bailiff.) *Governor.*
   The Right Honorable William Earl of

Bedford.
Bailiffs.
The Right Honorable Arthur Eail of Anglesey,
   The Right Honorable John Lord Berkley,
   The Right Honorable Richard Lord Gorges,
   Michael Holman, Esq.,
   Roger Jenyns, Esq.,
   Robert Hampson, Esq.
Conservators.
The Hight Honorable John
   Lord Bellasses, Sir Thomas Willis, Bart., Sir Andrew Henley, Knt. and Bart.,
   Sir John Bernard, Bart.,
Sir Charles Harbord, Knt.,
Sir John Shaw, Knt.,
Sir William Terringham,
   Knt., 1668.
1669.
   William Hamond, Esq., (elected a conservator in the room of John Bradborne, Esq.) The celebrated Honorable William Russell, (one of the sons of William Earl of Bedford,) who was beheaded in the reign of Car. II. (A. D. 1(583.) In the subsequent reign, when his Majesty's brother, King James II., found himself in the greatest difficulties, he applied for assistance to the venerable Earl of Bedford, who fearlessly answered him by this cutting expression:—" I had a son, sire, who could have served your Majesty."

This celebrated personage is sometimes styled William Lord Russell, at others, Lord William Russell; but both these appellations are erroneous. He was only the second son of an Earl, and died previously to his father's elevation to the dukedom; consequently he was only "the Honorable William Russell;" but his lady, having survived the dignity conferred upon her husband's father, is very properly styled Lady William Russell.
1677. 1678. *Governor.*
The Right Honorable William Earl of Bedford.
Bailiff's.
The Right Honorable Arthur Earl of Anglesey,
   The Right Honorable

Richard Lord Gorges,
   The Right Honorable Sir Thomas Chicheley,
   Robert Hampson, Esq.,
   Roger Jenyns, Esq.,
   Samuel Fortrey, Esq.
Conservators.
The Right Honorable Thomas Lord Culpepper,
   The Honorable William Russell,
   Sir John Hewett, Bart.,
Sir Thomas Willis, Bart.,
Sir Gilbert Gerard, Knt.,
Sir Nicholas Pedley, Krit.,
Sir Lyonell Walden, Knt.,
Dr. William Denton,
Silius Tytus, Esq.,
John Marsham, Esq.,
William 11 uniond, Esq.,
Anthony Hamond, Esq.,
Edwin Sandys, Esq.,
Richard Marryott, Esq.,
George Nicholas, Esq.,
Thomas Wright, Esq.,
John Holuian, Esq.,
Hugh Underwood, Esq.,
George Keats, Esq.,
Christopher Cratford, Gent.
   Sir John Chicheley, Kut., Edward Woodward, Esq., Mr. Robert Mingay, elected conservators in the room of
   The Right Hon. Thomas Lord Culpepper, Sir John Hewett, Bart., William Haniond, Eaq.
Governor.
The Right Honorable William Earl of Bedford.
Bailiffs.
TheRight Honorable Arthur Earl of Anglesey,
   The Right Honorable Richard Lord Gorges/
   The Right Honorable Sir Thomas Chicheley, Knt.,
   Sir Lyonell Walden, Knt.,
   Robert Hampson, serjeant at law,
   Roger Jenyns, Esq., (in the place of the celebrated Honorable William Russell).
Conservators. Sir Thomas Willis, Bart., Sir Henry North, Bart., Sir John Hewett, Bart., Sir Nicholas Pedley, Knt., Sir John Chicheley, Knt., Sir Thomas Fitch, Knt., Dr William Dcuton, Silius Titus,

Esq., Ralph Widdington, Esq., Richard Marryott, Esq., George Nichohis, Esq., Thomas Wright, Esq., Samuel Fortrey, Esq., Lyonell Walden, Esq., Edward Woodward, Esq., John Firicham, Esq., John Jejiyns, Esq, Mr. Christopher Cratford, Mr. William Bagnall, Mr. Robert Mingay.
The Right Honorable Tho mas Lord Culpepper,
   Thomas Pinfold, doctor of the civil law, (elected con servators in the room of 1685. Sir John Hewett, Bart., Sir Nicholas Pedley, Knt.) 1689. *Governor.*
The Right Honorable William Earl of Bedford.
Bailiffs.
The Right Honorable Richard Lord Gorges,
The Right Honorable Sir Thomas Chicheley, Knt.,
Sir Thomas Willis, Knt.,
Sir Lyonell Walden, Knt.,
Roger Jeiiyns, Esq.,
Lyonell Walden, Esq.,
Conservators. Sir Henry North, Bart., Sir Henry Bedingfield, Bart., Sir John Chicheley, Knt., Sir Francis Pemberton, Knt,
Sir Thomas Pinfold, Knt.,
Dr William Denton,
Silius Tytus, Esq.,
George Nicholas, Esq.,
Thomas Wright, Esq.,
Richard Marryott, Esq.,
John Fincham, Esq.,
John Jenyns, Esq,. Malborn Carill, Esq.,
Ralph Pierson, Esq., James Fortrey, Esq.,
   Anthony Hamond, Esq., Mr. Christopher Cratford,
   Hugh Underwood, Esq., Mr. John Milbourne.
   Roger Jenyns, Esq.,
   Edward Woodward, Esq., 1690. (elected a conservator in the room of Thomas Wright,
   Ralph Pierson, Esq, (elect-Mr. John Wolfe, (elected 1691. ed a bailiff in the room of conservators in the room SirLyonell Walden, Knt.) of Sir John Chicheley,
   Dr. William Denton,
   Sir Lyonell Walden, Knt., Ralph

Pierson, Esq.)

Thomas Mulsoe, Esq.,

Only nineteen conservators were elected at this meeting; and an order was passed that a new conservator should be elected in the room of Edward Woodward, Esq., upon the hist Thursday in the then next term; but no such election ever took place.

William Fortrey, Esq., of Sir Francis Pcmberton, 1692.

John Willys, Esq., (elected Knt., conservators in the room Edward Woodward, Esq.)

At a meeting held at the Fen Oflice on the 23rd 1693. Vol. i. 2 H of March, 1693, Lord Gorges acquainted the corporation, that by reason of the badness of the ways, and their illness, neither Lord Bedford, his Lordship, or Sir Thomas Chicheley, could attend at their next meeting at Ely in April next, for the sale of lands forfeited for nonpayment of taxes, and for raising of taxes for carrying on the works; and that Mr. Jenyns the elder, surveyor-general, being taken violently ill, could not possibly go down neither; and that there might be no failure for want of a bailiff to make a court, Sir Thomas Chicheley made it his request, that he might surrender up his place as bailiff, as accordingly he did: And thereupon the court proceeded to make a new election; and did nominate and appoint John Jenyns, Esq., one of the conservators, to be a bailiff, until a new election at Whitsuntide then next, who was sworn in accordingly: And Sir Thomas Chicheley chosen a conservator.

At the Whitsun Meeting,

John Jenyns, Esq., again elected a bailiff, and The Right Honorable Sir Thomas Chicheley, Knt., elected a conservator.

The board, in other respects, continued the same as in 1692.

1693. At a meeting held at the Fen Office on the 26th of October, 169.3, Anthony Hamond was elected a bailiff in the room of Roger Jenyns, Esq., deceased.

It does not appear that any person was elected a conservator in the room of Mr. Hamond.

April 26th, Richard Marryott, Esq., acquainted 1694. the corporation, that the commonalty requested that the elections might be held at Ely for the ease of the electors (by reason of the majority residing in the country): It was ordered, that it be debated at the last meeting of the then term, whether the election of the corporation should be kept at the Fen Office as usual, or at Ely.

On the 17th of May, 1694, it was ordered, that the next election should be kept at the Fen Office, the usual place.

Governor. John Jenyns, Esq., 1694.
His Grace William, First Lyonell Walden, Esq.,
Duke and Fifth Earl of Ralph Picrson, Esq.,
Bedford. Anthony Hamond, Esq.
Bailiffs. Conservators.,
The Right Honorable Rich-The Right Honorable Arard Lord Gorges, thur Earl of Torring
Sir Thomas Willys, Bart., ton .
Arthur Herbert, Earl of Torrington, was the son of Sir Edward Herbert, attorney-general to King Charles I., afterwards lord keeper of the great seal, who was banished for his steadfast loyalty to that prince.

This Arthur was bred up to maritime affairs, and in the reign of King Charles II. was employed by that King, in the command of a fleet before Tanglers; and afterwards against the

The Right Honorable Sir Roger Jenyns, Esq.,
Thomas Chicheley, Knt., Williiim Fortrey, Esq.,
Sir Henry North, Bart., Thomas Mulso, Esq,
Sir Henry Bedingfidd, Bart., Edward Woodward, lisq.,
Sir Lyonell Walden, Knt., John Willys, Esq.,
Sir Thomas Pinfold, Knt., Henry Oxburgh, Esq.,
Silius Titus, Esq., Christopher Cratford Esq.,
George Nicholas, Esq., Malborn Carill, lisq.,
Richard Marryott, Esq., John Wolfe, Gent.,
Hugh Underwood, Esq., John Milbourne, Gent.

Algerines; but because he would not comply with the measures of the reign of King James, he was deprived of all commission. Whereupon, betaking himself to Holland, (at a time when many of the English nobility and gentry went over to the Prince of Orange,) he returned with that prince to England, as admiral of his fleet; and was soon after sent back to fetch the Princess of Orange.which service he performed according to his trust.

Being afterwards, upon their accession to the crown, constituted their Majesties' admiral, he went in April, 16H9, with a squadron of ships to the Irish coast, to intercept a French convoy, bound thither with men, provisions, arms, and ammunition, for the Irish rebels. He met them in Bantry Bay, where he engaged them some hours at great disadvantage; but the conflict ended in a drawn battle. Next summer, 1600, he fought the French fleet off Beac-hy Head, who were indeed much superior in strength and number of ships; when suffering a defeat, he was charged with the miscarriage of the battle, thrown into the Tower, and at length brought to trial for such miscarriage, but acquitted. However, he lost his commission, and had no command afterwards. This noble lord married two wives; tirst, the widow of Pheasant, Esq.; and secondly, the widow of Thomas, late Lord Crewe; but by neither had he any issue. Upon his lordship's death, in 1716, the tit'e became extinct; but his real estates were devised to Henry.Earl of Lincoln, as hereafter mentioned in a notice of that title. The Earl of Torrington, after his disgrace at court, became one of the most eccentric men of the nge in which he lived,!;» I.

SirFrancisPemberton, Knt., the room of Sir Lyonell 1695. (elected a conservator in Walden, Kilt.

The Right Honorable Ad-a conservator in the room 1696. mirol Russell, (elected ofSirHenryNorth,Bart.)

Cambridge; Viscount Barfleur, in the duchy of Normandy; and Earl of Orford, in the county of Norfolk. In *May,* 1701, he was impeached in the House of Commons. His trial commenced 23d

June, when he was unanimously acquitted of the articles exhibited against him. His lordship died without issue, 26th Nov. 1727, when the title became extinct. He inherited the estate at Chippenham, near Newmarket, from his father the Honorable Admiral Edwurd Russell.
Conservators. William Fortrey, Esq.,
The Right Honorable Ar-Hugh Underwood, Esq., thur Earl of Torrington , Thomas Mulso, Esq.,

The Right Honorable Ed-Edward Woodward, Esq., ward Earl of Orford, Henry Oxburgh, Esq.,

The Right Honorable Rich-David Rowlands, Esq., ard Lord Gorges f, Nicholas Malabar, Esq.,

Sir Thomas Willys, Bart., Christopher Cratford, Gent.,

Sir Thomas Pinfold, Knt., Malborn Carill, Gent.,

Silius Titus, Esq., John Walsham, Gent..

Richard Marryott, Esq., John Brownell, Gent..,

Lyonell Walden, Esq., William Cole, Gent.

Nov. 7th. "It was ordered, that the register do 1700. summon a corporation, and such of the commonalty as were in or near town, to appear that day fortnight, at the Fen Office, to elect a new His Lordship died in 1716, when the title became extinct, He devised all his real estates to Henry Fiennes Clinton, seventh Earl of Lincoln, an ancestor of the present Lord Say and Sele, alleging as a reason, that he had so done from Lord Lincoln's political conduct during the party struggles that disgraced the latter end of the reign of Queen Anne. The estates were sold by the trustees of Lord Lincoln, in 1764, to Sir Sampson Gideon, Hart, afterwards created Lord Eardley upon whose death in 1824, without male issue, one third of those vfiry estates became vested in the Honorable W. J. Twiselton Fiennes, the eldest son of Lord Say and Sele, by his lordship's marriage with one of the three daughters and co-heiresses of Lord Eardley; and thus, after a lapse of more than a century, have the estates returned to a descendant of the original possessor, Henry Fiennes, Lord Lincoln. t His lordship had sold part of his estate, which sale disqualified him for the office of bailiff. He was created Viscount Dundalk, in the kingdom of Ireland, by King James the Second -, and upon his lordship's decease, in 1712, the title became extinct. governor, in the place of William Duke of Bedford, deceased." *Nov. Qlst.* The corporation met, and unanimously elected Wriothesley, second Duke of Bedford , governor, being (as expressed in the order book) very sensible that his Grace's predecessors had been great benefactors and supporters of the corporation and the works of draining; and a committee of the board was appointed to wait on his Grace the next morning at 11 o'clock, to acquaint him therewith. The common seal was directed to be affixed to the above order. Wriothesley, second duke and sixth earl of Bedford, was the grandson of William, first duke and fifth earl. He was married the 23d of May, 1695, to Elizabeth, only daughter and heir of John Rowland, of Stretham, in the county of Surrey, Esq., by Elizabeth, his wife, daughter of Sir Josiah Child, of Wansted, in Essex, bart.; which John Howland was the last surviving son of Jcffery Howland, of Stretham, Esq., and died 2d Sept. 1686, leaving his daughter, the said Elizabeth, ihcn an infant, who being heir to a very great fortune, his Grace, soon after his marriage, and in his father's lifetime, was, on the 12th of June, 1695, created Karon Howland, of Stretham. After his marriage he travelled into France and Italy; and on the 7th of Sept., 1700, succeeding his grandfather, became Duke of Bedford. Soon after he came of age, 27th June, 1701, he was constituted lord lieutenant of the counties of Bedford and Cambridge, and lord lieutenant and custos rotulorum of Middlesex, and one of the gentlemen of his Majesty's bedchamber. On the accession of Queen Anne to the throne, he was sworn one of the privy council; and was lord high constable of England, on the coronation, 2:)d April, 170'2. He was elected knight of the most noble order of the Garter, and installed at Windsor, 13th March, 1702 3. He died of the smallpnx, 2(ith May, 1711, in the 31st year of his age, leaving issue by his duchess, (who died at Stretham, 29thJuly, 1724,) two sons and two daughters. His Grace had great natural talents and qualifications, which were much improved by travel and conversation; but in the hitter part of his life he chose retirement; and died generally lamented. He was governor of the corporation eleven years.
Francis Pemberton, Esq., Abraham Hiss, Gent.,

Henry Fleming, Esq., William Cole, Gent.,

John Walsham, Esq., John VVakelin, Gent.,

John Jenyns, jun., Esq., Captain Martin Lacy,

John Brownell, Esq., Thomas Jenkinson, Gent,

Clayton Milbourne, Esq., — Brockett, Gent.

William Underwood, Esq., *21st June.* The court was informed, that Wrio- 1711. thesley, second Duke of Bedford, the governor, was dead; and thinking it very needful to choose another forthwith, in his room, to support the interests of the corporation, did, (upon due notice given of the election,) unanimously choose the most noble Wriothesley, third Duke of Bedford, his son, governor for the year ensuing.

The court was informed, that Mr. Brockett, His Grace was then a minor, being only three years of age. He was born in the year 1708, was married on the 23d of April, 1725, to the Lady Anne Egerton, only daughter of Scroop, Duke of Bridgewater, by the Lady Elizabeth Churchill, his first wife, third daughter and co-heir of John Duke of Marlborough, by whom he had no issue. His Grace, labouring under an ill state of health, was advised by his physicians to visit Lisbon; but in his passage he was so ill that he was obliged to be put on shore, at the Groyne, in Spnin, where he departed this life, 23d of October, 1732; and his body being brought to England, was interred at Cheneys, the burial place of his ancestors. He continued governor of tha corporation twenty-one years. His Grace evinced his regard for the interests of the Bedford Level,

by the following bequest, extracted from his will, dated the 30th April, 1730: "Item, to the Corporation of the Great Level of the Fens, called Bedford Level, I leave all that they owe me on bond." This sum was upwards of 2000/. elected conservator at the then last Whitsun Meeting, was not duly qualified, he having no adventurers' land; and it was resolved, that bis election was therefore void; and thereupon David Rowlands, Esq., was elected a conservator in his stead. 1712. *Feb. Tlh.* The court being informed that An thony Ilamond, Esq., one of the members, had gone to Spain, and by reason of his service for the government of that country, he could not attend the meetings of the corporation, did think fit, until his return, to remove him, and elected Mr. Henry Saffery in the room of the said Anthony Hamond. 1712. At this election there was a strong opposition against several members of the board; and upon a scrutiny taking place at the close of the election there appeared,
For the Duke of Bedford as For John Jenyns, sen., Esq.,

Governor, as one of the bailiffs.

Good votes 15 Good votes 18

Against him, good votes 15 Against him 12 "but no bailiff." This opposition probably would not have arisen, but from the circumstance of the Governor being an infuiil. t These words appear in the Order Book.

For Sir Roger Jcnyns, Knt.
Good votes 17
Against him 11
For John Chicheley, Esq.,
as one of the bailiffs.,

Good votes 14
Against him 12
For John Washall, Esq., as one of the conservators,
Good votes 16
Against him 11
For Mr. Henry Saffery, aa one of the conservators,
Good votes 15
Against him 12
For. William Underwood,
Esq., as one of the conservators,
Good votes 13
Against him 14

but no bailiff.
For Mr. William Cole, as one of the conservators.
Good votes 15
Against him 12

At this election, seven persons appear to have voted against each of the above members; two of which electors had not registered their conveyances, and five had no land: they are not, therefore, included in the above numbers.

At the close of the elections, the board remained the same as at the election of 1711, except as to the alterations mentioned as having taken place on the 21st June and 7th February; and except that William Fortrey, Esquire, was elected a bailiff, in the room of James Fortrey, Esquire; and the said James Fortrey, Esquire, was elected a conservator, in the room of the said William Fortrey, Esquire.

July 3rd. A committee of the board was appointed to confer with counsel about prosecuting Thomas Carter and others, for their misbehaviour at the election day, and proceed therein as they should be advised. Upon which occasion, the fol 1712. lowing very curious affidavit was intended to be filed in the Queen's Bench, but no subsequent steps appear to have been taken:—
"Joseph Hope, gentleman, register of the cor"poration of the governor, bailiffs, and common "alty of the company of conservators of the Great "Level of the Fens, called Bedford Level, maketh "oath, that the said corporation, being on Wed"nesday the eleventh of June last, assembled to"gether as usual, at their office, called the Fen "Office, in the Inner Temple, London, to elect a "governor, bailiffs, and conservators for the pre"sent year, pursuant to their act of incorporation "made in the 15th year of the reign of King "Charles the Second; and his Grace the Duke of "Bedford, governor, elected for the last year, and "the same bailiffs and conservators elected for "the said year, being declared elected again for "this year; two of the said bailiffs and five con"servators were thereupon sworn, and then the "court adjourned to six of the clock in the even"ing of the same day, to swear such others of the "said members so elected as aforesaid, as might "then come in and demand to be sworn; and ac"cordingly the court did meet again at the said "adjourned time, and did swear another of the "said bailiffs so elected as aforesaid, and did en "quire if there was any more to be sworn: At "which said second meeting, Thomas Carter, "William Anderson, Benjamin Howlet, Roger "Friend, John King, Robert Read, John Read, "sen., John Papworth, Thomas Brassitt, and

"John Curtis, being of the commonalty, (and "who had been admitted to vote at the said elec"tion,) together with Thomas Hurst, John Read, "jun., Miles Carter, jun., and Andrew Rolfe, "persons not appearing qualified to vote at the "said election, and who had nevertheless taken "upon them to vote at the said election, did ap"pear again in the said office in a riotous and "tumultuous manner, and gave great disturbance "there; whereupon the said court did break up "and adjourned to a further day: And, notwith"standing the said Robert Carter, William An"derson, Benjamin Hewlett, Roger Friend, Tho"mas Hurst, John King, Robert Read, John "Read, sen., and John Read, jun., John Pap"worth, Miles Carter, jun. , Andrew Rolfe, Tho"mas Brassitt, and John Curtis, were told they "had no business there at the said adjourned "meeting, the election of members being over, "and that they might be gone about their busi"ness; they did nevertheless continue in a tumul"tuous manner to keep possession of the said "office, and refused to depart at this deponent's "desire, pretending they were dissatisfied with "the election of the Duke of Bedford for go"vernor, and of some others of the members then "elected; and they then did, in a very indecent' "and disorderly manner, take upon them to pro"ceed to elect a governor, three bailiffs, and five "conservators, by themselves, and without a bai"liff with them, declaring they hud a right so to "do. And this deponent further saith, that the "said Thomas Carter did, in this deponent's pre"sence, put up the Right Honorable the Earl of "Orford for their governor, who was elected as "such by them, in this deponent's presence and "hearing. And then this deponent went out of "the said office, and left them there, proceeding ' in like manner to elect the said three bailiffs "and five conservators; and they detained this "deponent's son with them."

The following note is attached to the above affidavit:—

"These were a poor, sorry, insignificant parcel "of persons, brought up to town by some dis"carded officers of the said corporation, who had "been turned out some short time before for ill "practices, and were brought in upon the gen"tlemen at the election by surprise.

"And these proceedings of those people have "been so dispersed abroad the country, and such "ill use made of them, that diverse persons have "been so much influenced, that they refuse to "pay taxes to the corporation, and threaten to "try it at law with them. This will be of ill "consequence to the public if some remedy can"not be had to punish the insolence of these "fellows, which if it can be done by an infonna"tion in the Queen's Bench, we know all the rest "will submit, and most of these squeak, if once r

"an information be granted against them, which "is hoped shall be obtained on these affidavits."

In another affidavit made upon the same occasion by Thomas Hope, the son of the above mentioned Joseph Hope, the register, it is stated, that they subscribed a paper declaring the Lord of Orford governor elected; and another paper declaring Dr. Wright, clerk, Sir Comport Fitch, and

Mr. Robert Hewitt, bailiffs, and Coventry',

Edward Partheriche, Joseph Taylor, Esquires, and the said William Anderson, and Benjamin Howlett, conservators; and that it was past nine o'clock at night, before they would go out of the office; all which time the deponent was forced to stay with them to take care of the office.

... i *Nov. 13th.* 1712.

The Right Honorable Ed-the room of Richard Lord ward Earl of Orford,

Gorges, deceased.) (elected conservator in *April 8tft*. William Fortrey, Esquire, stated, 1713. that in consequence of his not being able to attend the meeting so often as a bailiff ought to do, he desired that he might resign his place as a bailiff, which was agreed; and James Fortrey, Esquire, his brother, elected in his stead.

William Fortrey, Esquire, was then elected conservator, in the room of his brother, James Fortrey, Esquire.

John Jenyns, Esq., stated, that for the same Vol. r. 2 i 1713.
1714. 1715. 1717. 1718. reasons, he also desired that he might resign his place as bailiff, which was agreed; and John Brownell, Esq., elected in his place.

John Jenyns, Esq., was then elected conservator, in the room of the said John Brownell.

1716. John Hill Esq., (elected a James Jenyns, Esq., (elect bailiff in the room of
Dr. John Wright.)
The Right Honorable Henry
Earl of Lincoln,

William Underwood, Esq., ed conservators in the room of
The Earl of Torrington,
John Wakelin, Gent.,
John Jenyns, Esq.)

This is not the William Underwood who was a member previous to this election; so that there were at this time two gentlemen of that name members of the board.

James Fortrey, Esq.,
Charles Blunt, Esq.,
John Brownell, Esq.,
Francis Penvberton, Esq.
Conservators.
The Right Honorable Henry
Earl of Lincoln,
The Right Honorable Arthur Earl of Anglesey,
The Right Honorable Edward Earl of Orford,
The Honorable Sir Thomas
Hanmer, Bart.,
John Jf iiyns, Esq.,
William Fortrey, Esq.,
Thomas Mulso, Esq.,
James Jenyns, Esq.,
John Walsham, Esq.,

Henry Coventry, Esq.,
John Hill, Esq.,
John Wright, Esq.,
Clayton Milbourne, Esq.,
Edward Partheriche, Esq.,
Richard Drury, Esq.,
William Underwood, Esq.,
John Le Pla, Esq.,
John Walsham, junr.,Gent.,
Henry Saffery, Gent.,
William Cole, junr., Gent.

George Keate, Gent., Jacob Hiss, Gent., (elected conservators m the room of
Thomas Mulso, Esq.,
James Jenyns, Esq.
1719.

The question having been previously put, as to the re-election of James Jenyns, Esq., there appeared 17 votes for him and 32 against him.

July 22wJ. At a meeting (at which none of the commonalty appear to have been present) John Jenyns, Esq., signified to the court (by Sir Roger Jenyns) his desire to resign, which was accepted; and James Jenyns, Esq., was elected conservator for the remainder of the year, in his stead. 1719. 1720. John Walsham, Esq., Edward Harrison, Esq., (elected a bailiff in the (elected conservators in room of the room of
James Fortrey, Esq.) John Walsham, Esq.,

James Fortrey, Esq., James Jenyns, Esq.) 1720. *Nov.Jth*. William Underwood, Esq., (elected a bailiff in the room of Charles Blunt, Esq., deceased.

The court was informed, that John Jenyns, Esq., was discharged from being a conservator, by a misrepresentation made to the meeting on the 22nd day of July, 1719, by which means his brother, James Jenyns, Esq., was elected in his room; and there being a vacancy by the election of William Underwood, Esq., as a bailiff, the court.. thought fit to elect the said John Jenyns a con servator in his place.

1721.. No further alteration.

A bill was brought into parliament, on the petition of several of the commonalty, to compel the elections of the board to be taken in the country; which bill was opposed by the board; and, on a division in the house of commons, it was thrown out by a great majority.

1722. Nathaniel Green, Esq., the room of

Nathaniel Kinderley, Gent., Richard Drury, Esq., (elected conservators in Henry Saffery, Esq.)

John Wright, Esq., (elected a bailiff in the room of John Waisham, Esq.)

John Walsham, Esq.,

Sir John Barnard, Bart.,

John Skrymshire, Gent.,

Edward Bearcroft, Esq.,

(elected conservators in

the room of John i Wright, Esq.,

William Fortrey, Esq.,

John Hill, Esq.,

Edward Partheriche,

Esq.) 1723.

and 56 against hi m; but there not being the concurrence of a bailiff with the majority, he was declared continued. 1725.
Governor.
The Most Noble Wriothesley Duke of Bedford.
Bailiffs.
The Right Honorable Henry Earl of Lincoln,
Edward Harrison, Esq.,
Sir Cecil Wray, Bart.,
James Jenyns, Esq.,
Robert Lightfoot, Esq.,
William Underwood, Esq.,
Conservators.
John Wright, Esq.,
The Right Honorable Arthur Earl of Anglesey,
Sir Francis St. John, Bart.,
Sir Thomas Hanmer, Bart.,
Joseph Kettle, Esq.,
Henry Coventry, Esq.,
Clayton Milbonrne, Esq.,
Thomas Dixon, Esq.,
George Keate, Esq.,
Nathaniel Green, Esq.
William Thomson, Esq.,
Thomas Underwood, Esq.,
John Hagar, Esq.,
James Fortrey, Gent.,
Thomas Holt, Esq.,
John Le Pla, Gent.,
Mr. John Smith,
Sir John Barnard, Bart.,
John Skrymshire, Gent,
Edward Bearcroft, Gent.

1725. *June 5th.* A meeting was held for supplying the defects in the last election, it appearing since, that several of the members were not duly qualined, and— The ancestor of the present worthy and honorable representative of that family, now resident in the seat of his ancestors, at Somersham, in flic county of Huntingdon, for which county, and Cambridgeshire, he served the office of high sheriff in the year 1026.
, L

Francis Pemberton, Esq., the room of Lord Mic i Samuel Shepheard, Esq., klethwaite,

John.Wyldbore, Esq., Thomas Dixon, Esq., (ejected conservators in John Le Pla, Esq.)

At this election a poll was taken for William Underwood, Esq.; 49 votes for him, and 39 against him. For Thomas Dixon, Esq., a bailiff; 44 votes for him, and 39 against him. For James Fortrey, Esq.; 47 votes for him, and 34 against him. For Mr. Richard Saffery; 40 votes for him, and 34 against him. These four members were therefore declared duly elected.

1728. *Nov. 21st.*
Joseph Kettle, Esq., (elected conservators in (elected a bailiff in the the room of Joseph room of the Earl of Kettle, Esq., elected

Lincoln, deceased.) bailiff,

Mr. Thomas Underwood,

David Greenhill, Esq., resigned.)

Mr. Peter Brookes,

1729. *March 25th.* Joseph Kettle, Esq. , who was elected a bailiff on the 21st November, not being then duly qualified, and being since duly qualified, he was upon the question put, elected a bailiff.

1729. *Whitsun Meeting.* The following entry appears in the order book of the corporation:

"The Duke of Bedford and several conservators, with a great many of the commonalty, assembled at the Fen Office, in order to proceed to the election as usual, and being informed that Mr. Dixon and all the rest of the former bailiffs (except Mr. Harrison) were at Brown's Coffee House, in Mitre Court; the governor sent several messages to them to attend, to proceed to election: but they returned for answer that they understood that they were to be turned out, and that they would, not give his grace any trouble, but that he might proceed as he pleased. His grace, however, with the rest of the body then assembled at the office, waited two hours for their coming; but upon recollecting that the Duke had not been sworn into his office, and a doubt arising whether he could proceed to election unless so sworn, his grace, attended by the register and two of the conservators, (viz. Mr. Keate and Mr. Pemberton) went to the coffee-house, and entered the room where the bailiffs were, and the Duke demanded to be sworn, whereupon those gentlemen rose up in a great hurry, and made the best haste they could out of the room, (being a room up stairs, and not the public coffee room;) but before they could get out the register administered the oath of office to his grace, in the presence of most of them, before they could leave the room, and his grace thereupon kissed the book, and publicly said, 'Take notice, gentlemen, J am sworn, and am now ready to go The Duke had only then attained his majority.

to election.' His grace then returned to the office, and acquainted the members present of his having taken the oath, and they proceeded to the election; but before they did so, Edward Harrison, Esq. , sent in his resignation in writing."

"The Court resolved that the several bailiffs should be first elected; and the question being put separately, as to the election of each of them, it passed in the negative,and other gentlemen were elected in their places. After the bailiffs were elected, five of them being present, were sworn, and the conrt then elected the most Noble Wriothesley Duke of Bedford their governor, who was also sworn,when they proceeded to the election of the several conservators; and at the final close of the election the board consisted of the following members: *Governor,*

The Most Noble Wriothesley Duke of Bedford.
Bailiffs.

Sir John Bernard, Bart., (in lieu of Lord Viscount Mk-kfethwaUe,)

Francis Pembcrton, Esq. (in lieu of Sir Cecil YVray,)

George Ke;itc, Ueq., in (in lieu of Edward Harrison,Esq., resigned,)

Edward Partheriche, Esq., (iii lieu of William Underwood, Esq., resigned,)

John Brownell, Esq.,(in lieu of Thomas Dixon, Esq.,)

William Cole, Esq., (in lieu of Joseph Kettle, Esq.) *Conservators.*

The Earl of Anglesey,
Sir Thomas Hanmer, Bart.,
Sir Francis St. John, Bart.,
The Honorable Edward
Harrison, Esq., (in the room of Francis Pembefton,Esq.,elected a bailiff,)
James Fortrey, Esq.,
John Skrymshire, Esq.,
James Jenyns, Esq.

Sir John Barnard resigned his office of bailiff, and Humphrey Smith, Esq., was elected in his room; Richard Drury, Esq., was elected a conservator.

Governor.
The Most Noble Wriothesley Duke of Bedford.
Bailiffs.
The Honorable Edward Harrison, Esq.,
Sir John Bernard, Bart.,
Francis Naylor, Esq.,
Dingley Askham, Esq.,
Thomas Dixon, Esq.,
John Brownell, Esq.
Conservators.
The Earl of Anglesey,
Thomas Underwood, Esq.,
Joseph Kettle, Esq.,
Sir Thomas Hanmer, Bart.,
The Honorable Henry
Coventry, Esq.
Edward Partheriche, Esq.,
An ancestor of the present chairman of the board. Mr. Jenyns was a lord of trade, and represented the borough of Cambridge in parliament several years. He was a scholar, a wit, and a statesman. His works were collected and published by the late Charles Nalson Cole, Esq., heretofore register of the B. L. C.

f At this meeting Lord Viscount Micklethwaite (late one of the bailiffs) was removed from the situation of surveyor-general. The receiver general and serjeant at mace were also removed. 1730. 1731. 1732. 1733. At the April meeting: The Most Noble John, 4th Duke of Bedford.!

Afterwards John fourth Duke and eighth Earl of Bedford. t Elected Gotenor on the death of his brother Wriothesley, 3rd Duke and 7th Earl. John Duke of Bedford was an eminent statesman j he was born 30th Sep. 1710; and married llth Oct.,

The Right Honorable Mr. Thomas Carter, (elect-1733.

Charles Lord Lynn, (elect-ed conservators in the ed a bailiff in the room of room of

The Honorable Edward The Duke of Bedford (late

Harrison, Esq.,deceased.) Lord John Russell,

Henry Smith, Esq., Edward Partheriche,Esq.) 1735. The Right Honorable Lord Francis Nailour, Esq.,

St. John ofBletsoe, Owen Fann, Gent. , (elected

John Brovvnell, Esq., conservators in the room (elected bailiffs in the of the Right Honorable room of Sir John Bernard, Bart., John Lord St. John, Brownell, Esq.

Francis Nailour, Esq.,) Hickson Wright, Esq.

Sir John Bernard, Bart., 1736. William Cole, Esq., (elected David Greenhill, Esq., a bailiff in the room of Francis Pemberton, jun.,

John Brownell, Esq.,) Esq.,

Nathaniel Day, Esq., Daniel Descow, Gent.,

Keeper of New Forest in the county of Hants j and on tb« l:3th Feb., 1747-8-, his Majesty was pleased to nominate his Grace to be tme of his principal Secretaries of State. In October, 1748, he was chosen one of the Governors of the Charter House. On the 22-atl June, 1749, at a chapter of the most noble order of the Garter, held by his Majesty at Kensington, his Grace was elected one of the Knights Companions of that most noble order, and was installed tit Windsor July 12th, 1750, and placed in the 12th stall on the Prince's side. On the 13th April, 1751, he was constituted Lord Lieutenant and Gustos Rotulorum of Devonshire, and of the city and county of Exeter; and in June follotung, resigned the seals of one of his Majesty's principal Secretaries of State. His Grace was one of the Lords Justices, during his Majesty's absence in his German dominions in the years 1-745, 1740, and 1750. His Grace was also Lord Lieutenant and Governor of Ireland in 1737; and on *the* 4th Sept., 1762, was appointed minister plenipotentiary to the Court of Versailles; and on the 3rd Nov. following, signed atFontainbleau, the preliminary articles of ptaue with France and Spain; and, lOth Feb., 1763, subscribed the ratification of a definitive treaty of peace between the belligerent powers-of Great Britain, France, Spain, and Portugal. His Grace, upon his return from France, vaa mado President of the Council.

This eminent statesman died on the 14th Jan., 1771, having continued Governor of the Corporation nearly 38 years.

His Lordship held the post of Master of the King's Stag The Earl of Sandwich, Matthew Wyldbore, Esq., (elected conservators, in the room of
John Walker, Esq.,
Mr. Robert Gill).
No alteration.
Governor.
His Grace The Most Noble John fourth Duke of Bedford.
Bailiffs.
The Right Honorable The
Earl of Lincoln,
Coulson Fellowes, Esq.,
Francis Nailour, Esq.,
Soame Jenyns, Esq.,
Henry Partridge, Esq.,
William Cole, Esq.

Upon the question, that Dingley Askham, Esq. should be re-elected a bailiff, it was resolved in the negative; and a poll being demanded and taken, there appeared for him, 21; against him 30.

Peter Standley, Esq.,
Thomas Revell, Esq.,
William Thomson, Esq.,
Conservators.
The Right Honorable The
Earl of Sandwich,

Sir Francis St. John, Bart.,
Sir John Bernard, Bart.,
Sir Thomas Drury, Bart.,
William Greaves,Esq.,B. B.,

Hounds, from which he retired upon the accession of the Grenvilleand Whig administration, in 1806; and upon their retirement he was appointed to the lucrative situation of Post Master General. He was certainly a man of very moderate talents; and yet possessed that useful kind of knowledge, which enabled him,

durmg a long political career, to secure to himself good situations under government, and also whenever he could, to quarter his creatures and dependents upon the public purse.

VOL. I. 2 K
1746.

1747. 1748. Mr. Cole was elected Register oF the Corporation in 1757. The last edition of DugdaVe's History of Draining and Imbankitig, was published by Mr. Cole, at the request and expense of the Corporation.

John Partherich, Esq., (elected a conservator in the room of Henry Reade, Esq.)

MatthewR obinsnn Morris, Esq., (elected a bailiff in the room of The Earl of Sandwich.)

William Greaves, B. B., Esq.,
John Leaford, Gent.,
John Gardnerf, Gent.,
(elected conservators in the room of Matthew
Robinson Morris, Esq.,
John Wyldbore, Esq.,
John Partherich, Esq.)
1753.

1754. 1755. 1756. 1793. Afterwards created Lord Rokeby. t Grandfather of the present Marchioness of Townshend, and great grandfather of the Enrl of Leicester, her eldest son bom after her marriage with the present George, third Marquis of Townshend.

John Drage, Esq., (elected a conseivator in the room of
Sir Thomas Peyton, Bartv resigned).

The Most Noble Francis
Marquess of Tavistockf,
(elected a bailiff in the room of Robert Butcher, Esq.)

The Honorable Sir George
Warren, Knt. of the Bath, late George Warren, Esq., Robert Butcher, Esq., (elected a conservator in the room of The Rev.

Thomas Neale, clerk).
He served the office of high sheriff for the counties of Cambridge and Huntingdon. . + This nobleman had the misfortune to be killed by a fall from his horse on his return from hunting, and consequently never succeeded to the dukedom.

Mr. Robert Walsham, Gent., (elected a conservator mthe room of Maximilian Walsham, Esq., deceased.)

Matthew Wyldbore, Esq., (elected a bailiff in the room of Matthew Robinson Morris, Esq.)

Thomas Waddington, Esq.,
John Hagar, Esq., (elected conservators in the room of Henry Symons, Esq. ,
Matthew Wyldbore, Esq.)

The Right Honorable Lord Viscount Townshend, (elected a bailiff in the room of The Right Honorable the Earl of Lincoln).

Robert Palmer, Esq.,
M r. Peter Descow,
(elected conservators in
No alteration.
Mr. Thomas Moore, jun.,
Mr. John Gardner, jun.,
(elected conservators in the room of Sir George
Warren, Knt.,
Henry Robinson, Esq.)
the room of Mr. Thomas Moore,
Robert Butcher, Esq.)

Sir Sampson Gideon, Bart., (elected a bailiff in the room of
The Marquess of Tavistock).
Then M. P. for the county of Cambridge. He had become the purchaser of the extensive property devised to the Earl of Lincoln by the Earl of Torrington; and was elected a bailiff without having been previously chosen a conservator.

William Fellowes, Esq.,
John Thomson, Esq.,
David Burges, Esq.,
(elected conservators in the room of James For trey, Esq.,
Mr. John Gardner, sen.,
The Rev. Mr. peniberton).

William Fellowest, Esq.,
Robert Palmer, Esq.,
(elected bailiffs in the room of Coulson Fellowes, Esq.,
Soame Jenyns, Esq.)

Soame Jenyns, Esq., Thomas G round J, Esq., (elected conservators in the room of William Fellowes, Esq., Robert Palmer, Esq.)

Sir Thomas Hatton, Bart., (elected a 'conservator in the room of Thomas Waddington, deceased).

1771. The Most Noble Francis 5th Duke of Bedford§. (elected governor in the room of his grandfather, John Duke of Bedford). The ancestor of the present Thomas Burges, Esq., whose family have been for upwards of a century resident at Benwick, in the Isle of Ely. Mr. Thomas Burges served the office of high sheriff for the counties of Cambridge and Huntingdon in 1820, in a manner suitable to his ample fortune and fen possessions. f Father of W. H. Fellowes, Esq., the present M. P. for the county of Huntingdon. Mr. Fellowes, the father, represented the borough of Andover, in Hants, in parliament, several years. $ Mr. Ground served the office of high sheriff for the counties of Cambridge and Huntingdon.

§ His grace was then a minor of the age of five years; and continued governor thirty-one years. He was born on the 2'2nd of July, 1665, and died unmarried, universally regretted, on the 2nd of March, 1802. The reader is referred to the ad .J mirahly and eloquently drawn character of this distinguished and amiable nobleman, by the late Right Honorable Charles James Fox, in n speech delivered to the house of commons upon the occasion of moving for a new writ for the borough of Tavistock, in the room of his brother Lord John Russell, who had succeeded to the dukedom.

Henry Dashwood Peyton, Esq, (son of George Dash wood, Esq., of Peyton Hall, in the county of Suffolk, by Margaret, second daughter of Sir Sewster Peyton, Bart., and sister of Sir Thomas

Peyton, at whose decease the baronetcy (which was created in 1684) expired, having assumed by act of parliament, in obedience to the testamentary injunction of his uncle, the said Sir Thomas Peyton, the surname of Peyton,) was created a baronet, 18th Sept. 1776 Sir Henry married Frances, eldest daughter of Sir John Rous, of Henham Hall, since created baronet of Stradbrooke. Sir Henry was M. P. for the county of Cambridge, and died in *i* Mr. Heatheole resides at Cumington Castle, in the county of Huntingdon. He sat several years in parliament for the borough of Ripon, in Yorkshire. He has also served the office of high sheriff for the counties of Cambridge and Huntingdon. Being in the possession of the greater part of the estates of the learned antiquary Sir Robert Cotton de Bruce; he and his descendants (upon a vacancy) will have great claims to be appointed one of the Cottonian trustees of the British Museum. At any rate, his claim rests upon equal, if not superior right, to those who now fill the situation. t His lordship was Lord Lieutenant of Ireland, 1795, for a very short period; and to his ill-advised recall, the horrible events of the three subsequent years have been justly attributed. Hia lordship was appointed president of the council during the short administration of Lord Grenville and Mr. Fox, in 1806. The author (turning aside from all political feeling) records with unfeigned pleasure and delight the pre-eminent virtues and generous feelings which form the character of this munificent and benevolent nobleman, who lives justly revered in the hearts *at* his grateful and admiring fellow citizens.

George Waddingtoi), Esq., room of John Heathcote, 1778. (elected conservator in the Esq.)

Charles Gould, Esq., this year styled Sir Charles Gould. 1779.

He was many years judge advocate general, and M. P. for the county of Brecon, and one of his majesty's most honorable privy council. t Now Earl of Hardwicke, K. G., and then M. P. for the county of Cambridge. His lordship is lord lieutenant and *ctuivs rotulorum* of the same county, and high steward of the university of Cambridge. His lordship was lord lieutenant of Ireland in the year 1800. He also holds the honorary situation of surveyor-general to the corporation. He became the purchaser of the extensive estates belonging to the family of Cotton, of Gidding Grove, in the county of Huntingdon, the ancient scat of the celebrated antiquary Sir Hobert Cotton de Bruce, which estates were conveyed for sale to the Rev. Dr. Annetsley, of Heading, Berks, and George Booth l'yndele, Esq., merely *us* trustees for sale; and yet ihcec two gentlemen *(mirabde itictu)* are the present family Cottoniun trustees of the British Museum, Arthur Anneidey, Eq, was M. *If.* for Reading. The father of Jonathan l'nge, Esq, now a memlier of the board, a magistrate for the Isle of l-!ly, and higheherifi for the countirs of Cambridge and Huntingdon, in the year It) 14. t The present liarl of licsborough. 1789. 1790. Sir Sampson Gideon, Bart., Right Honorable Lord is this year styled the Eardley.

1792. William Fellowes, jun., Esq., (elected a conservator in the room of Thomas Gotobed, Esq., deceased.)

Sir Charles Gould, Knt., is this year called Sir Charles

Morgan.

1794. No al te rati on.

Lord Viscount Duncannon, is this year styled Earl of

Besborough.

1795. No alteration.

1796. No alteration. 1797. Lord John Russell,t Samuel Wells, Esq.,J Thomas Page, Esq., (elected conservators in the room of

J. Waddington, Esq.,

deceased,

Thomas Page, Esq., deceased,

Christopher MilbouniCj

Esq., disqualified.)

At this meeting the whole of the business was finished without an adjournment of the board; and it was the first time such a circumstance had occurred since the passing of the act 15 Car. II.

t The present Duke of Bedford.

I The father of the present register: he died in the year 1817, and is interred in the north nisle of the cathedral church of Peterborough.

The Rev. George Jenyns, (elected a bailiff in the room of the Right Honorable Lord St. John).

The Right Honorable Lord St. John,

Charles Morgan, Esq., (elected conservators in the room of

The Rev. George Jenyns, elected bailiff,

The Rev. Henry Green, deceased.) 1798.

William Fellowes, Esq., this year styled William Henry

Fellowes, Esq.

1799.

Governor.

The Most Noble Francis Duke of Bedford.

Bailiff's.

The Most Hon. George

Marquess Townshend,f The Right Honorable Lord

Eardley,

William Fellowes, Esq.,

Sir Charles Morgan, Bart.,

John Gardner, Esq.,

Rev. George Jenyns.

Conservators.

The Right Honourable Lord

St. John,

Rev. Jeremiah Pemberton,

John Wing, Esq.,

William Wells, Esq.,

Arthur Annesley, Esq.,

The Right Honorable Lord

Brownlow,

The Right Honorable Earl

Fitzwilliam, The Right Honorable the Earl of Hardwicke, Thomas Ground, Esq., 1800.

M. P. for the county of Huntingdon. t His Lordship was lord lieutenant of Ireland in the year 1780; and was also lord lieutenant and *cuxtos rolulorum* of the county of Norfolk. He was the grandfather of the present George Marquess Townshend, whose present Marchioness was only child and heiress of William Dunn Gardner, Esq., by Sarah, the only surviving child and heiress of John Gardner Esq., of Chatteris, in the Isle of Ely. Now Sir Charles Morgan, Bart., M. P. for the county of Monmouth. f Mr. Yorke represented the

county of Cambridge many years, during which time he was one of the most useful and efficient county members that ever entered the house of commons; and by his sedulous attention to the private business of the county and Isle in parliament, be rendered great services to his constituents, who in return gave him the most unbounded confidence, abstracted from all political considerations. Mr. Yorke filled the important situation of first lord of the admiralty, secretary of state, and secretary at war. lie retired from the representation of the county upon being appointed one f the tellers of the exchequer, and was succeeded by Lord Francis Godolphin Osborne, the present member. The eldest son of the Earl of Hardwicke, who was unfortunately drowned. + The eldest son of Earl Fifzwilliatti, and M. P. for the county of York. His lordship is the representative of Frances, -*only* daughter oad child of Sir Robert Cotton tie Bruce, who mar
William Dunn Gardner,
Esq., (were elected conservators in the room of
   Sir Charles Morgan, elected a bailiff,
   Rev. Jeremiah Pemberton).
1808. Thomas Page, Esq., (elect-John Edes, Esq., ed a bailiff in the room of the Marquess of Towns hend, deceased).
The Honorable Sampson
Lord Eardley,
John Wil mot, Esq.,
(elected conservators m the room of
Thomas
Page, Esq., bailiff,
Lord Brownlow, deceased,
Lord Royston, deceased).
1809. This was the first Whitsun Meeting held at Ely, the election having heretofore invariably taken place at the Fen Office in London.
JohnThurlow Bering, Esq.,
Robert Bevill, Esq,
George Maxwell, Esq.,
Richard Orton, Esq,
Thomas Skeels, Esq.,
(elected conservators in the room of Arthur Annesley, Esq., removed for non-attendance).
ried Sir Thomas Proby, and had one daughter, who married Charles Wentworth, Esq., of Harrowden Hill, in the county of Northampton, afterwards first Marquess of Rockingham, who had no male issue; but one of his daughters married William Earl Fitzwilliam, father of the present earl. Being the personal representative of the lust heir direct of the family of Sir Robert Cotton de Bruce, the famous antiquary, it is presumed Lord Milton is entitled (and so on in succession) to be one of the Cottonian family trustees of the British Museum.
  Earl Fitzwilliam, disqualified,
  Henry Pointer Standley, £aq., disqualified,
  The Earl of Besborough,
resigned,
  Admiral Thomas Wells,
now employed on actual service).
  No alteration.
  No alteration.
  Mr. Bevill and Mr. Skeels were both opposed; but upon polls being demanded and taken, the numbers appeared, for Mr. Bevill, 18; against him, 13; for Mr. Skeels, 16; against him, 15.
1810. 1811. 1812. 1813.
  No alteration.
1814. 1815. 1816. John Thurlow Bering, Esq., (elected conservators in (elected a bailiff in the the room of John Thur rooin of Thomas Page, low Dering, Esq., elect
  Esq., ed bailiff,
  William George Adam, Esq., William Adam, Esq., dis-
William Wells, Esq., qualified).
  At this meeting there were five candidates proposed, viz: William George Adam, Esq., Samuel Farmer, Esq., Jonathan Page, Esq., William Wells, Esq, and John Shearing, Esq.; and the votes being taken, there appeared 25 for Mr. Adam; 25 for Mr. Wells; 16 for Mr. Page; 5 for Mr. Farmer; and 3 for Mr. Shearing.
1817. Jouathan Page, Esq., well Esq., deceased,
  William Roberts, Esq., Samuel Wells, Esq., de-
John Fryer, junr., Esq., ceased,
(elected conservators in Thomas Jay, Esq., deceathe room of George Maxsfid).
  At this meeting two other candidates were proposed, viz: John Hibbert, Esq. , and Thomas Spooner, Esq.; and the votes being taken, there Wm. Wells, Esq., was a post captain of the royal navy; and married Lady Elizabeth, the youngest daughter of John Joshua late Earl of Carysfort. He died a short time since; and in the year 1818, was nominated (without his concurrence) as a proper person to represent the county of Huntingdon in Parliament; but was unsuccessful after a poll of four days' duration, at the trifling expense of less than 100*l*. A singular instance of virtue and constitutional feeling and proceeding, on the part of the freeholders, well worthy of imitation, and redounding to their immortal credit.
4 appeared 61 for Mr. Page; 33 for Mr. Roberts; 33 for Mr. Fryer; 29 for Mr. Hibbert; and 27 for Mr. Spooner.
  No alteration.
  Tycho Wing, Esq., (elected a conservator in the room of The Rev. John Wing, resigned).
  No alteration.
  Sir Henry Edward Bunbury, Bart.,
  Charles Jenyns, Esq., (elected conservators in the
room of William Wells,
Esq., resigned,
  Thomas Skeels, Esq., deceased).
  At this meeting George Pryme, Esq. , was also proposed; and a poll being taken, the numbers appeared, 48 for Mr. Jenyns; 44 for Sir Henry Edward Bunbury; and 38 for Mr. Pryme.
  Richard Greaves Townley, Esq., (elected a conservator in the room of his father, Richard Greavea Townley, Esq., deceased).
1818.
HenryJamesNicholls.Esq., nathan Townley, resign-1819. (elected a conservator in ed). the room of,The Rev. Jo
1820.
1821. 1822. 1823. 1824. George Pryme, Esq., the room of John Edes,
  John Angerstein, Esq., Esq., (elected conservators in The Honorable Mr. Eard ley Eardley).
  Thomas Barges, Esq., was also pro-

posed, but no poll was demanded.

1825. Thomas Orton, Esq., (elected a bailiff in the room of The Right Honorable Sampson Lord Eardley, deceased.)

John Fryer, jun., Esq., was also proposed; and upon a poll taken, there appeared for Mr. Orton, 29; and for Mr. Fryer, 22.

Thomas Spooner, Esq., elected conservator.

The Honorable William Rowley, Esq., de

Thomas Twisleton Fien-ceased, nest, Thomas Orton, Esq.,

John llibbcrt, Esq., elected bailiff, (elected. conservators in Sir Henry Edward Bunthe room of Ousley bury, Bart, deceased).

Mr. Thomas Richardson and Sir CullingSmith, Bart, were also proposed; and a poll being taken, there appeared for Mr. Spooner, 49; Mr. Fiennes, 44; Mr.Hibbert, 32; Mr. Richardson, 32; and Sir Culling Smith, 22: but neither the governor nor a bailiff having voted for Mr. Richardson, the governor, who was present, decided the election to have fallen on Mr. Spooner, Mr. Fiennes, and Mr. Hibbert.

He hnd served the office of high sheriff for the counties of Cambridge and Huntingdon. t The eldest son of Lord Say and Sele.

John Hibbert, Esq., (who had not taken his 1826. seat at the board in consequence of his election in Ih25 being subsequently considered void) was again proposed, and unanimously elected a conservator.

John Fryer, Esq., (elected a Esq., (elected conserva-1827 bailiff in the room of tors in the room of

Sir Charles Morgan, Bart., John Fryer, Esq., elected resigned), a bailiff,

Admiral Sir Joseph Sidney The Honorable Charles

Yorke, Kut., Yorke, resigned,

Sir Culling Smith, Bart., William Roberts, Esq.,

John Wulbanko Childers, resigned).

John Hemington, Esq., (elected a conservator in the room 1828. of Thomas Spooner, Esq., resigned).

No alteration. 1829.

Since the last election, a vacancy has been occasioned by the death of Sir Culling Smith, Bart. Sir Culling Smith married one of the daughters and co-heiresses of Sampson last Lord Eardley; and in the year 1828 served the office of high sheriff for the county of Hertford. But under the advice of counsel, it was subsequently understood, that the election, as fur as regarded Mr. Hibbert and Mr. Richardson, was a void election. APP. p. 397. The board, or the select body, are directed to be yearly elected upon Wednesday in Whitsun week. This election formerly took place at the Fen Office in London, until the year 1809, when the same was very properly removed to Ely. In order to make a valid election, the governor or one of the bailiffs must be present. From the wording of the clause in the act of parliament, it has (as already mentioned) sometimes been considered, that where two candidates are proposed, and upon the poll, one of them has not the vote of the governor or one of the bailiffs, such candidate cannot be elected. In a recent case, this point was mooted, and the election determined in favor of the candidate (both being equal in numbers) on whose side the governor or bailiff had voted; but doubts having arisen as to the propriety of this decision, the governor, anxious for the due administration of justice, and actuated by a sincere desire (which it is hoped will ever influence the house of Russell) not to infringe the privileges of the electors, stated the following case for the opinion of the present attorney general (Sir James Scarlett). CASE,

As to the Election of the Board.

15th Charles II, c. 17. By an act of parliament then passed, "An act for settling the drain ing the Great Level of the Fens called the Bedford Level," it was enacted, that William Earl of Bedford, son and heir of Francis Earl of Bedford, and the adventurers, and participants of the said Earl Francis and Earl William, or either of them, their heirs and assigns, in such manner as therein contained, should be a body politic and corporate, in deed and in name, and have succession for ever, by the name of the governor, bailiffs, and commonalty of the company of conservators of the Great Level of the Fens, which corporation should consist of one governor, six bailiffs, twenty conservators, and commonalty. And that the said William Earl of Bedford was to be the governor, and certain persons therein named, the six first bailiffs, and the first conservators. And the said governor, bailiffs, and conservators, to continue until Wednesday in Whitsun week, in the year of our Lord 1664, and from thenceforth until new elections by the said corporation, or the major part of them which should be then present.

Sect. Id. And for the continuance of the said corporation in succession for ever, it was further enacted, that the said governor, bailiffs, conservators, and commonalty, upon Wednesday in Whitsun week/yearly, should, at a public meeting to be holden for the said corporation, by the greater number then present, (whereof the said governor, or one of the bailiffs, to be one,) elect a new governor, bailiffs, and conservators, respectively.

Doubts having occurred upon the last mentioned question,—

Your opinion is requested, whether, in the event of there being two candidates for the office, either of hailiff or conservator, and each candidate having an equal number of rotes, in case the governor, or one of the bailiffs, should be among the voters for one of such candidates, such one can be considered duly elected, notwithstanding the equality of votes.

Opinion.

"It appears to me, that in the case here supposed, there would be no election."

"J. Scarlett." "Temple, July 14th, 1825.''

Probably this opinion will be acted upon in future, should no circumstances arise to require the interposition of a superior court. By the act of parliament it is provided, that none be capable to be, *or continue* governor or bailiff, that hath not /pp. p-397. 400 acres or more of the 95,000 acres; nor to be conservator, that hath not 200 acres or more of the 95,000 acres; nor any of the ctonmonalty, that hath not 100 acres or more of the said

95,000 acres. The qualification of the electors has, upon many occasions, given rise to difference of opinion; and as the board have recently taken advice upon this subject, and at the last election for the office of register acted upon that advice, the case and opinion then taken are now inserted, it being considered, as in the former instance of the election of the board, that the advice here given will be adopted until its propriety shall be controverted by judicial decision.

CASE, *As to voters at elections.*

By statute, 5 Charles II., c.17, the adventurers engaged in draining the Great Level of the Fens, called Bedford Level, are incorporated by the name of the governor, bailiffs, and commonalty of the company of conservators of the Great Level of the Fens; and by the second section of the act, the corporation is empowered to appoint a register and other officers.

By the eighth section of the act it is enacted as follows:

"And be it further enacted, that aH convey"ances by indenture of the said 95,000 acres, or "any part thereof, entered within the said regis"ter, in a book to be kept for that purpose, shall "be of equal force to convey the freehold and in"heritance of the said 95,000 acres, or any part "thereof, as if the same conveyances by inden"ture were for valuable considerations of money, "enrolled within six months in one of the king's "courts of record at Westminster; and no lease, "grant, or conveyance of, or charge out of or "upon the said 95,000 acres, or any part thereof, "except leases for seven years or under, in pos"session, shall be of force, but from the time it "shall be entered with the said register as afore"said; the entry whereof being endorsed by the "said register upon such lease, grant, convey"ance, or charge, shall be as good and effectual "iu the law, as if the original book of entries "were produced at any trial at law, or otherwise."

Mr. Bevill, who held the office of register to the corporation, is lately dead.

In his life-time, several conveyances of lands, forming part of the 95,000 acres allotted to the corporation, were left at the Fen Office in London, where the register books and other documents of the corporation are deposited, and where the business of the registry is always transacted, for the purpose of being registered. At the time of his death, many of these conveyances had not been entered in the registry books, nor was any indorsement of the register put upon them. The corporation are about to proceed to the election of a successor to Mr. Bevill; and a question has arisen, whether the conveyances thus deposited, and not entered, can be so far considered as registered, as to entitle the purchasers to whom the estates are conveyed by them, to vote on the election, provided they become entitled through such deeds, and any others previously registered, to the quantity of land required by the act for their qualification on elections (100 acres).

Your opinion is requested on the point on behalf of the corporation. And if you should think that the purchasers are not entitled to vote, you will be pleased to say, whether the vendors of such estates, in case the conveyances to them were duly registered, are entitled to vote, notwithstanding they have ceased to have any interest in the estates.

And you will be pleased also to advise the corporation on the following points, likely to arise at the election.

Whether the devisees under wills passing corporation lands, are not entitled to vote, although the wills may not be registered; the clause before stated appearing only to require conveyances by indenture to be registered.

Whether a mortgagee in possession of corporaration land, under a mortgage, either in fee, or for a term of years, is entitled to vote in respect of such mortgaged property; and if not, whether the right of voting remains in the mortgagor.

Whether a trustee or guardian of corporation lands, appointed by deed or will, and in the receipt of the rents and profits on behalf of any other person, is qualified to vote, or whether the right of voting rests with the cestui que trust; and whether a feme covert, or her husband in her right, is entitled to vote in respect of property belonging to her.

The only cases we find in the books respecting the registration of deeds by the corporation are, the King *v.* the Corporation of Bedford Level, East, Vol. 6, p. 536. Hodson t;. Sharpe, East, Vol. 10, p. 350.

Opinion.

"I am of opinion, that those purchasers whose conveyances have not been entered with the register in the book kept for that purpose, have no voice in elections, because it cannot be said, that that such persons have an interest, when conveyances have been previously declared to be of force, but from the time of registration. Whether proprietors from whom such purchases have been made, still retain the right of voting, seems to me a different question, and I am aware of no authority applicable to it; but I incline to think they do not, because they have done all that in them lies to divest themselves of their interest; and in effect have done so, as between themselves and their assignees, according to the case in the JOth East.

"2. It may be argued, that a devise is a grant, and so within the words of the 8th section; but I am of opinion, that the whole of it, taken together, applied to conveyances only, and that a devisee may therefore vote without registration of the will.

"3. I think it clear, that a registered mortgagee in fee or for years, being in possession, has a right to vote.

"4.1 think the cestui que trust, not the trustee, entitled to vote; and the guardian during the ward's minority. But if land be devised to trustees, with discretionary powers to deal with it for the benefit of others, I apprehend such trustees would be considered as owners, and entitled to vote.

"The husband seised in right of his wife, may vote in respect of her property.

"T. Denman."

"Lincoln's Inn, October 1st, 1824."

Let us now consider the mode in which the corporation at large, and the select body, respectively assemble for the prosecution of the business of the Level.

In almost all chartered corporations it is absolutely necessary, that a majority of the select body should be present, in order to give validity to an election; but the statute of incorporation of the Bedford Level expressly provides, that the "governor, bailiffs, conservators, and commonalty shall, at a public meeting for the said corporation, *by the. greater number then present, (whereof* App-p. 397. *the governor or one of the bailiffs to be one* ,) elect a new governor, bailiffs, and conservators respectively.

The said governor, bailiffs, and conservators, App. p. 388. were, in the first instance, to continue until the then next Whitsun week, and thenceforth until new elections by the said corporation. In the event of an election not taking place, either by One of the majority of the corporation present; not one of the electors on either side...
reason of the non-attendance of the governor, w one of the bailiffs, or any other accidental cause, the old members of the board would continue until a fresh election, which may take place at any time during the year, although their office would expire at the then next Wednesday in Whitsun week.

App. p. see. The corporation of the Bedford Level, by the constitution, are enabled to sue and be sued, and without license of mortmain, to purchase manors, lands, tenements, and hereditaments, not exceeding 200£. per annum, and goods and chattels, and to dispose thereof in the name and to the use of the said corporation. This limited power of purchasing has been exceeded by almost all corporations. From peculiar and local circumstances, the Bedford Level corporation is now possessed of considerable freehold property, consisting almost entirely of public houses; and doubts have arisen whether the corporation have the power of selling such freehold property, or indeed of aliening any of their possessions. This point has, however, been settled long since. All civil corporations, such as the corporate companies of trades in cities and towns, *and all corporations established* KyO,

108. *by act of parliament* for some specific purpose, unsid. 162. less expressly restrained by the act by which they are established, or by some subsequent act, have, and always have had, an unlimited control over their respective properties, and may alien in fee, or make what estates they please for years, for life, or in tail, as fully as any individual may do with respect to his own property.

Two public meetings of the corporation at large are held annually at Ely; the one (as already stated) on the Wednesday in Whitsunweek, and the other in the month of April. The latter meeting was appointed by the statute, 20 Car. II. , to be held at Ely, on the Wednesday, App. p. 477. Thursday, or Friday, after the first Sunday in April. This was, however, altered by the Style Act, and directed to be held eleven days later. 24Geo.s.c.23. The rule for finding the April meeting is already set forth in the Appendix to this Work, but for App. p. 522. convenience is now repeated.

Rule for finding the day on which the Annual April Meeting of the Corporation at Ely is to be held.
Take the first eleven days out of April; look for the first Sunday after the eleventh day, and the Wednesday after that Sunday will be the first day of the April meeting. For example, for the year 1830, the first Sunday after the llth falls on the 18th of April; the Wednesday after that Sunday is the 21st, which will be the first day of the April meeting for the present year.

The board has *the sole power* of imposing the tax, which must be done at the April meeting at Ely, on one of the days before mentioned. The board has also the general direction of the works, and the management of the revenues of the corporation, and they likewise pass all the accounts' abstracts of which are always printed for the inspection and observations of the commonalty. Perhaps, legally speaking, the Aboard is intrusted by the corporation at large with a power, in this respect, beyond the exact letter of the statute; but the convenience and advantage resulting to the Level from the exercise of this assumed power must be at once obvious to the country, when we consider the indefinite number of the commonalty; and it undoubtedly tends greatly to facilitate the business, while the controlling authority still remains in the body at large.

The board assembles at the April meeting on the Tuesday evening; and at ten o'clock precisely on the following morning the serjeant places the mace upon the table. The oath of office is then administered by the register to those members who were not sworn at the time of their election, or in the interval between that time and the then meeting; after which, the minutes of all the proceedings that have taken placeduring the year are readover; and after the question put by the chairman, and no objection taken, such proceedings are confirmed. The board then proceeds to the general business of the country; such as passing the officers' accounts, ordering new, and repairs of old works, ami hearing petitions from the country, until the whole business is concluded; the several adjournments being always entered from time to time. The business generally lasts until the Friday. At twelve o'clock precisely on the Thursday in the The mace wns presented to the corporation in 1663, by William, then Earl, and afterwards Duke of Bedford,

April meeting, the board adjourns to the Shire Hall at Ely, preceded by the serjeant, bearing the mace, for the purpose of holding the public meeting for the election of officers: the board then proceeds to the sale of lands forfeited for arrears of taxes; after which they return from the Shire Hall.

After the election, all the officers are sworn by the register, in the presence of the board, to the due, faithful, and diligent discharge of the duties of their respective situations.

At the Whitsun meetings, the board assembles on the Tuesday evening, and proceeds to business on the following morning at ten o'clock precisely; and (with the exception of the time the members are engaged at the Shire Hall in holding the corporate meeting for the election of the board) continues to transact general business, which consists chiefly in hearing petitions and disposing of matters left for consideration from the April meeting. The business is generally concluded on Thursday evening, and sometimes earlier. Immediately upon the return of the board, after the election, the several members are respectively sworn, both as corporators and as commissioners of sewers. The former oath is as follows:

"Ye shall swear that you will faithfully and impartially execute the office of—governor, bailiff, or conservator, as the case may be, without. fear, favor, or affection;

"So help you, God."

The oath of commissioners of sewers will be in Vol. i. 2 M serted in that part of the work which treats of the select body in that capacity.

The oath is always administered by the register.

The board is extremely averse to originate any measure, or order any expenditure, except at the April meeting; on which occasion a large attendance of members of the board and the country is generally ensured. This appears by the following standing orders or bye-laws:

"Upon a debate had relating to the taking up money under the corporation seal, it was thought convenient that, for the future, no money should be taken up but by the direction and privity of the major part of the seven and twenty; It is therefore ordered, that the same be observed as a rule for the future, only excepting such order or orders for taking up money as shall be made at the corporation's general meeting at Ely, being at time and place, by act of parliament, when and where the whole seven and twenty may and ought to be present. That then money may upon emergencies be taken up by a fewer number."—23rd June, 1681.

"Application was made to the board, under very urgent circumstances, by the commissioners under an act for scouring out, &c., the rivers and drains in the Middle Level, to have the Tongs Drain deepened, without which the country could not obtain the full benefit of cleansing their rivers; and the board having ordered one-half of the expense, amounting to about 600/., to be paid, the following resolution was made:

"Resolved, that although the members attending this meeting have made the above order, yet they feel the importance of requiring that all applications for works of such a nature, should be made at the April meeting, where there is a general attendance, and where the arrangements are made of the money concerns of the corporation for the year then commencing. Ordered therefore, that the April meeting be, for the future, the only time for making orders for all works requiring any material expense, except works subject to accidents, and which are of such a nature as indispensably require immediate execution."—21st June, 1817.

All the orders of the corporation, and of the board, (except those relating to the accounts which are prepared by the auditor,) are drawn up by the register, and then read over and passed by the board, after which they are entered in the minute book, and subsequently faircopied into what is called the order book. The orders of the auditor are delivered to the register, and entered in like manner. By an order of the board passed in 1819, the meetings of the board in April are held at the Lamb Inn; and in Whitsun week, at the White Hart Inn.

It should be stated, that although the sale of lands forfeited for non-payment of taxes, takes place in the Shire Hall; it is under the direction App.P.392. of the select body only, and not of the corporation at large.

The select body are empowered not only to lay App. p. 388. the tax, and to sell for non-payment thereof, but they are empowered, "all other things to do in order to the support, maintenance, and preservation of the said Great Level, and works made or to be made;" by virtue of which provision the board always directs the execution of the future works, and generally regulates the affairs of the Level.

It has been questioned, whether either the board itself, or even the corporation at large, possesses the power of making bye-laws. It is said, that when a corporation is created by act of parliament, for a particular purpose, and a power of making byelaws relative to the object of the institution is even expressly given, (which is not the case with the Bedford Level corporation) this neither enlarges nor abridges the power they would have had inde

Eyd.2,p.in pendently of such an express clause. The Bedford Level corporation has power to erect new works, as well within, as without the Great Level; and the members may meet in their corporate capacity, when and where they please; but as commissioners

App. p. 391. of sewers, they can only sit and act *within* the Level The parliament that assembled upon the restoration, consisted by no means of a flexible set of men, meeting only to impose taxes upon the people, and register the edicts of the crown or its menials; on the contrary, they adopted very decisive measures to protect the general interests of the Community; and, until their dissolution, were mainly instrumental in restraining the furious zeal, and bitter animosities of those who sought to benefit themselves by the heedless destruction of such persons as had been inimical (as the courtiers calfed it) to the interests of their master. The wary and considerate conduct of the, parliament has been already shewn, in their proceedings with reference to the disputes in the Level; but their regard to the rights of the people is particularly evinced by the clause which enacts, " That the lessees of the King's Majesty, his heirs and successors, of the 10,000 acres, or of any part thereof, and the assigns of such lessees, and every or any of them, shall be capable to be elected and chosen into the office or place, offices or places of governor, bailiffs, and conservators aforesaid; and to vote in such elections and choice, and in all other matters,

I as fully to all intents and purposes as any other members of the corporation, owners of any part of the said 9. 5,000 acres, may be elected and chosen to vote in such election and choice, or in any other matter; so as such lessees and their assignees respectively, have and be lessees or owners of double the quantity or number of acres, parcel of the said 10,000 acres, as by virtue of this act is required to qualify any person to be elected and chosen into the office or place of governor, bailiff, or conservator respectively, and to vote in such elections and choice, or in any matter touching the said Level; and so as such leases or assignments they claim by be entered with the register."

It was foreseen by the ever watchful Earl of Bedford, that the 10,000 acres thus restored would be granted out to some favourites of the crown; and being subdivided might greatly influence the elections in future times. He therefore, very properly obtained from the parliament this concession, and also another of a very important nature; namely, that if any breaches should happen in any of the banks, saases, sluices, tunnels, or other works within the said Great Level, or in any of the works made without the said Great Level, for carrying the waters of the said Great Level to sea, by reason of some inevitable accidents, the same should be repaired and made good in convenient time, by and at the charges of the said corporation and their successsors; *but no other charge* should be laid upon the said corporation or their successors, for or in respect of such breaches, nor for or in respect of any breaches that had happened theretofore in any of the said banks, sasses, sluices, or other works; nor should the said corporation be enforced to give to any other person any recompense for any loss or damage which had or should happen by reason of their making necessary and sufficient banks for the defeuding of the said Level from being overflowed, and for the leading of the waters of the said Level in their channels, as they then ran into their outfalls at sea. It should not be omitted to state, that in order to maintain the peace and good government of corporations, and to secure their adherence to the purposes of their institution, the law has appointed a tribunal to inspect the conduct of their internal affairs, to whose decision all disputes arising within them must be referred.

This tribunal, in the case of eleemosynary and ecclesiastical corporations, is in general that of a private visitor; and of all other corporations, the Court of King's Bench. The latter exercises its visitorial jurisdiction in two different ways; namely, by writ of mandamus, or by information in the nature of a quo warranto.

In modern legislation it is almost always pro-corpolate vided, that the books of proceedings of the parties carrying the intention of the legislature into effect shall of themselves be evidence. The statute of 15 Car. II. has made no such provision; we must therefore consider this very important subject with reference to the law established by judicial proceedings in regard to corporations in general.

Corporate documents are of two kinds, those *Evidence.* which are the records of the municipality, relat-Lvh. BL ing only to the members of the body politic and Marriage» persons under its government, which are of a pub-Ju'3B' lie nature, and evidence in all questions among mt''2I£b£n themselves, and also in questions of a public right, w-, as that of swearing and admitting freemen; and i7How.st.Tr.

810 those of the other kind, which relate to the corpo-Moore's c»., 17 How. St. Tr. rate rights in respect of strangers, and are as s»4. much private writings as the title-deeds of any individual.

When corporation books have been kept pub-R. ",.. Motberlicly as such, entries made in them by the proper sc' '93' officer have been generally admitted to be given in evidence. And of similar authority are entries made by another proper person during the sickness of the officer, or on his refusal to attend; but in the latter case, the reason why they were not made by the officer ought to be shewn. R. . Lord Where the original document is of a public na ture, and would be evidence if produced, it is not 405. necessary to shew the document itself, for it may be required in many places at the same time; for that reason an immediate sworn copy made by the proper officer will be admitted. custody. The custody of corporate documents belongs 2 Bur. 7tiTMm more particularly to the chief officer; but they 2Kenyon,486! ought to be kept in the usual depository. R. *v.* Ipswich, *If* tne custdy of their documents belong to one i2J8rdRaym of their officers in virtue of his office, the corporation cannot compel him to deliver them up, but may require that he submit them to their inspection whenever they think proper. inspection. Every corporator has, as such, an interest in the tieYstM223 documents of the corporation, and a general right Rd» shciicy insPect them upon all proper occasions; and if R1!-' Babe's uPon Application for that purpose, the officer who T. R. 580. jias the custody refuse to shew them, the court

R. n. Tower, 4M.&S. ir2. wiu grant a mandamus to enforce his right.

Rogers, v.' jone,5D.& A corporator has a right to inspect these docuR. *v.* Tmvan-ments, to obtain information as to his rights, whe nion, 2 Chit..

Rep. 366, n. ther m a dispute with a foreigner, or the corpora

R. *v.* Che.ter,,...,-r.

i chit. Rep. tion itself, or any of its members.

"' "The mayor, bailiff, sheriff, town clerk, or other officer of any corporation, having the custody of or power over the records of the same, shall, upon R.25Geo. 3. c. the demand of any person, being an officer or me,m58. s. 4. ker of such corporation, on the payment of one shilling, permit such person, on any day or days, except Christmas Day, Good Friday, and Sunday, between the hours of nine in the morning and three in the afternoon, to inspect the books and papers, wherein the *admission* or swearing in of the freemen, burgesses, or other members or officers of such corporation, shall be entered, and to have copies or minutes of the admission, or the entry of swearing in of any one or more of such freemen, burgesses, or other members or officers, upon paying sixpence for every one hundred words for writing the same. And if such mayor, bailiff, sheriff, town clerk, or other officer, shall refuse or deny to anyrperson hereby entitled to demand it, the inspection of such books or papers, or to have copies or minutes thereof as aforesaid, such mayor, bailiff, town clerk, or other officer, shall, for every such offence, forfeit and pay the sum of 100/., together with full costs of suit, to him, or her, or them, whoshall inform aad sue for the same within one year after such offence committed, by action of debt, bill, plaint, or information," &c.

It has been already stated, that the Court of writ of mandamus. King's Bench is the visitor of all corporations, where the charter has not appointed that officer. Therefore, the writ of mandamus is a prerogative writ, by which the Court of King's Bench exercises its supreme jurisdiction over all public bodies, and officers in the administration of justice, when the law has not provided another specific and adequate remedy. It has been peculiarly applied to the regulation of corporations, for the purpose of compelling them to observe the ordi nances of their constitution, and to respect the rights of those who are entitled to participate in their privileges.

The author has thought it necessary to insert these particular points, because they may occur in the ordinary transactions of the corporation; but the learned reader will readily perceive, that much more extended inquiry will be necessary when more abstruse questions shall come in issue.

The author has thus briefly laid before his readers the constitution and powers, as well of the corporation at large, as of the select body; in doing which he has endeavoured

"Nothing to extenuate,

"Nor to set down aught in malice."

He is a public servant. He has neither partialities nor prejudices to indulge. His sincere and earnest wish is, to perform his duty faithfully, impartially, and diligently, to the satisfaction of the board, the corporation, and the country at large.

CHAPTER XVII. *Officers of the corporation, — How appointed.— Their election,—Salary.—Duties.—Regulations on the death of the Register.—List of persons who have from time to time held the several offices under the corporation.*

By the general drainage act, (15 Car. II.) the cor-Appointment .,.. of officers. poration at large are to use a common seal; and they have also power to appoint a register, re-App. p. 387. ceiver, one or more serjeants at mace, and other officers, and allow them salaries, and remove them, and make new at their pleasure. An invariable custom has obtained for the corporation to elect their officers annually at the April meeting, although the statute does not direct them so to do. It is a wholesome practice, and will always stimulate to exertion; it has, indeed, been thought hard, inasmuch as an officer might be ousted, either without due notice, or from private pique or malice; but should such an event occur, the officer would have redress by applying to the court of king's bench to exercise in his behalf its visitorial powers. All the officers are directed to be sworn; and the corporation has power to demand and receive an account from all and every the officers, agents, and servants, their executors and administrators. *The Surveyor General.*

The office of surveyor general is not mentioned in the statute of incorporation; but it has existed from the commencement of the corporation. The office, although it has been always held by noblemen and persons of consideration, was formerly one of much labour and responsibility, it being the duty of the officer, at earlier periods, not only to submit to the corporation the works necessary to be executed for the general drainage of the Level; but afterwards to attend to their execution. In the infancy of the corporation, in order to execute the office with satisfaction to the corporation and the country at large, not only was a considerable knowledge of the principles of drainage required, but an intimate acquaintance with the local interests and feelings of the Level was likewise indispensable. After the works of drainage were settled, this office became less practically efficient; and its more important duties were transferred to, or rather divided amongst, the subordinate officers of the corporation. The surveyorgeneral was originally paid a large annual salary for his services; but the office is now considered honorary; although it has been the practice occasionally to address this officer upon any great works intended to be made. He may be regarded in the light of a visitor to the corporation. The surveyor general's office is annual; and the election takes place at the April meeting. The situation is now helil by the amiable and venerable Earl of Hardwicke. His extensive possessions in, and intimate connections with the Fens, would at once furnish an apology (were any required) for the insertion in this work of some biographical notices of this nobleman, who justly possesses the kindest feelings of gratitude and respect of all fen men. The Earl of Hardwicke, at all times, from youth to manhood, and from manhood to old age, has exerted himself for the interests of the Bedford Level; advancing, by personal exertion and pecuniary aid, every measure projected for the improvement of the country. His lordship, in the year 1780, (then the Honorable Philip Yorke,) became a candidate for the representation of the county of Cambridge; Lord Robert Manners, uncle to the present Duke of Rutland, and the late Lord Eardley, then Sir Sampson Gideon, Bart., being also candidates: and, after a severe contest, at the close of the poll, the numbers were— Lord R. Manners,---1741 The Honorable P. Yorke,--1455 Sir Sampson Gideon,--1038

The first two were consequently declared duly elected.

The history of this contest, which excited the most intense interest at the time of its occurrence, is deserving of notice, particularly from those who feel curiosity as to the events of " other days. " At this period (1780) the nation was smarting under the effects of the unjust and atrocious war against the American colonies, which had been carried on against the known and declared sense of the people, with an obstinacy that amounted to infatuation. It was this sensible difference between the parliament and the people, and the heavy burthens so wrongfully imposed upon the nation, that originated the clamour for a reform in the representation, and greater economy in the expenditure of the public money. County meetings were generally held, to petition parliament. The county of Cambridge was not then less forward than at the present day in the discharge of its public duty. A requisition was numerously signed, and presented to the high sheriff (Thomas Rumbold Hall, Esq.), who declined to convene a meeting. It was, however, held, and petitions were voted for reform and economy. The two members, Sir J. H. Cotton and Sir Sampson Gideon, refused to present the same to the house of commons; and the consequence was, a determined opposition to their return upon the dissolution of parliament, which took place soon after. Sir J. H. Cotton retired (unable to face the storm); but Sir S. Gideon, relying upon his constant kindness and attention to the county, and particularly to the Isle of Ely and the Bedford Level, in which he was the owner of vast property, resolved to wait the result of the poll. The following summary will shew the prevailing feeling among the freeholders.

"*General state of the poll.*"

At this period, the late Mr. Pitt was brought forward as an avowed advocate for reform; and after a vehement struggle was returned for the university of Cambridge, which he continued to represent until the time of his death, in 1800, having evinced his sincerity in the cause of reform, by increasing the national debt from six to sixty millions.

Mr. Yorke continued in the representation of the county until the death of his uncle, in 1790; when he succeeded to the title of Earl of Hard wicke. His lordship is lord lieutenant and custos rotulorum of the county of Cambridge, and high steward of the university of Cambridge, to which latter post he was elected in 1806, upon the demise of the Right Honorable William Pitt. His lordship was also lord lieutenant of Ireland in 1800.

The following noblemen and other persons of consideration have held this office, from the passing the general drainage act, 15 Car. II., to the present period:

The Right Honorable Lord Gorges, 1663
Roger Jenyris, Esq., 1686
John Jenyns, Esq., 1694
John Chicheley, Esq., 1717
The Right Honorable the Earl of Lincoln, 1725
The Right Honorable Lord Micklethwaite, 1729
Edward Harrison, Esq.,. 1730
The Right Honorable Charles Lord Lynn, 1733
The Right Honorable Charles Lord Viscount Townshend, 1739
The Right Honorable Henry Earl of Lincoln, 1744
The Right Honorable Francis Marquess of
Tavistock, 1764
The Right Honorable Lord Viscount Townshend, 1767 The Right Honorable The Earl of Hard wicke, 1809 *The Register.*

The Register is considered the chief paid officer The Register, of the corporation, and the appointment has always been justly held to be one not only of honor, but of great responsibility. He is the organ of communication between the board, the corporation, and also the several owners and occupiers of lands interested in the drainage of the Bedford Level. He is elected annually at the April meeting at Ely, and is subsequently sworn to the due execution of his office: the oath is administered by the governor, or one of the bailiffs. Being a sworn officer, the duties must be transacted by the register himself, and not by deputy, except in cases of sickness, or on some other extraordinary occasion; and then the deputy must be appointed and allowed by the board. This was ordained by the corporation so long since as the year 1692. The salary annexed to the office is 200/. per annum: but in consideration of the various duties that have devolved of late years upon the register, such as keeping up the lot books, making out the annual tax roll, (formerly the duty of the receiver and expenditor general,) the late register (whose services in general, and more particularly in forming and completing a correct lot book, were most essentially beneficial to the corporation) was allowed an annual gratuity of 100/. in addition to his salary. Upon an attentive examination and serious consideration of the continued increased

Vol. i. 2 N duties of the office, a committee of the board reported the propriety of allowing the present register a gratuity of *70l.* per annum in addition to his salary, during the pleasure of the board, which report has been confirmed; and the payments have 'been punctually made to the present period. The additional labour of preparing an annual rent roll and particular of all the property of the corporation, and transmitting copies thereof in the month of February to the receiver and expenditor general and t» the auditor, has been recently imposed upon the register.

The duties of the register are numerous and important; from which naturally results great responsibility. Whenever a public or private meeting of the board or corporation is held, he attends as the register of the court, in like manner as the register of the Court of Chancery, or the Court of Admiralty, or any other court of record to draw up the minutes of the proceedings. These minutes he first enters in a rough minute book, each order being previously read and approved. The orders are afterwards fairly transcribed into another book, called "The Order Book," containing all the proceedings both of the board and of the corporation. After each meeting, he transmits to the several members, the offices of the corporation, or other parties interested, copies of such orders as may be necessary to be promulgated for the purpose of carrying the same into execution.

He keeps all the records, muniments, and papers, belonging to the corporation, in the public office, called the Fen Office, (until recently situate in Tunfield Court, in the Inner Temple, London, and *now* at No. (5, Serjeant's Inn, Fleet Street,) which is open to the public on Mondays, Wednesdays, and Fridays, between the hours of ten and two, except during the weeks of the April and the Whitsun annual meetings, when the register and his clerk are occupied in their attendance upon the board and the corporation at Ely. Every conveyance, mortgage, lease, (ex-App. p. sso. ccpt leases of seven years or under,) and all other instruments affecting any part of the adventurers' lands, must be registered in books provided by the corporation, and kept in the Fen Office, in London; and as no deed can have any legal effect until it is so registered, and a certificate thereof endorsed and signed by the register upon such instruments, it is an important duty that all the deeds left at the office for entry be faithfully and accurately registered and endorsed, and that the books into which they are copied be preserved with care and in good order. Should the original deed be lost, there can be no doubt that the entry in the registry books would be evidence in a court of law, particularly as the clause requiring registration states, that "the entry of registration being en-App. p. 393. "dorsed by the register upon such lease, grant, "&c., shall be as good and effectual in the law as "if the original book of entries were produced at "any trial at law or otherwise;" the term " as good and effectual" making either the one or the other evidence. Wills, and certificates of descent and heirship, when the owners of adventurers' lands die ApP. P. 39.1. intestate, are also required to be entered in books to be kept for that purpose. Probably the statute of 15 Car. II. does not go to this extent; but a standing order of the board directs these measures, as tending to the continuance of a correct lot book.

The register prepares the sale conveyances of adventurers' lands forfeited and sold for non-payment of taxes, and all leases and conveyances of the corporation estates and property.

He procures all moneys on the corporation creApp. p. 612. dit, (the same being ordered to be raised under the great seal of the corporation); and he has to report to the board such of the old creditors as may have given the legal notice required for the repayment of their money. He prepares all bonds for money borrowed, either for the exigences of the corporation, or in exchange for old bonds, which any of the creditors are desirous of delivering up.

It is his duty also to make out copies or extracts of any deeds of conveyance or wills that may be wanted from the registry, at the expense of the parties requiring the same. He produces the registry books to persons wanting to search for security of a purchaser's or mortgagee's title, or otherwise; but he is not permitted to shew to any person (except the governor, bailiffs, and conservators, individually or collectively,) the order books of the board, or of the corporation, or to furnish copies thereof, without a special direction from the board. Every owner of any part (however small) of the adventurers' lands, is a corporator, (although not entitled to vote at elections, unless possessed of 100 acres and upwards,) and is therefore entitled to inspect the books of accounts; but the register cannot give or permit extracts to be taken therefrom by the publie, without the special direction of the board or of the corporation.

It is likewise his duty to keep with accuracy the lot book of the corporation, which contains APp. p. 253, the names of the respective owners of each por- 48C'692. tion of the several twenty lots or shares into which the 95,000 acres were originally divided amongst the adventurers and the crown. From this lot book he is enabled to make out for the receiver and expenditor general the annual tax roll, containing the names of all the owners, according to the registry books; and by this means the receiver and expenditor general is enabled to make out the several tax receipts correctly.

The register attends and regulates the triennial lettings of all the corporation estates and property, except such parts as may have been let under the authority of the board, upon improvable leases for a longer term. These lettings are now ordered to take place at Ely, in the month of April.

The registry, minute, order, and lot books, and other necessary books and stationery, are provided by the register, the costs of which are defrayed by the corporation.

It is expected, that the register be acquainted with all the records and acts of parliament relative to the Great Level, the law of sewers, the laws relative to the registry of deeds, and the laws connected with corporations in general; that he may be ready to answer any question proposed to him by the board, or by any member of the corporation.

Every private act of parliament in any degree affecting the drainage, inclosure, or improvement of lands, rivers, bridges, or other works within the limits of the Bedford Level, is, by the standing orders of the board, directed to be hud before the register, that he may consider whether any of its clauses or provisions interfere with the rights of the corporation, or are injurious to drainage or navigation; and that he may see that the clauses fully and absolutely reserving the rights of the corporation are duly inserted, in the form directed by the standing orders of the board.

It would be impossible to detail the various duties attached to the important office of register. He is the legal organ of the board, and of the corporation; and it is most material that he should possess (besides the requisites already stated) a thorough knowledge of the locality of all parts of the Bedford Level, and the operation and effect of all the rivers, drains, hanks, bridges, sluices, and works erected therein, or having influence upon the outfalls to sea.

As the prosperity of the Level is so intimately connected with the faithful discharge of the duties of the register, the electors will best consult their own interests by instituting a strict scrutiny into the qualifications of the persons who may from time to time offer themselves as candidates for this arduous situation. Under a board less vigilant, less attentive, and less informed than the present, the security of the Bedford Level itself might full a sacrifice, should an inefficient or inattentive register be elected.

The register must not be disappointed if he finds himself incapable of giving general satisfaction to the board, the corporation, or the country, nor on that account relax his utmost exertions in their service; his duties are too complicated,and the several interests too conflicting, to afford a hope of his total escape from censure. By some the register will be considered too active, by others, too supine; by some, too economical, by others, too extravagant; some will accuse him of inclining too much to the board, others, of leaning to the corporation at large. Let him, however, discharge his duties fearlessly and impartially, and he will always have the proud satisfaction of knowing, that he holds the most responsible and valuable office that any statutable corporation in the kingdom has iu its power to bestow.

Register's Fees.

Exclusive of his annual salary of '200/., and the gratuity of 70/., the register is entitled to the following fees:

Searching each register book—one shilling; general search—two guineas.

General search of lot or account books —two guineas. Single registry fees—one shilling for the first 100 words, and sixpence for every subsequent 100 words.

N. B. Deeds not enrolled within six months from the date pay double fees.

Certificate of enrolment of each deed—two shillings and sixpence. Copies or extracts—eightpence per folio, of 72 words. Abstracts of title— ten shillings each brief sheet.

The register is paid five guineas by the promoters, and the register's clerk receives five shillings, for affixing the great seal of the corporation to all private bills in parliament; and also a fee for perusing the drafts of such bills, according to their length.

For affixing the seal to any instrument, at the instance of private parties—one guinea; five shillings to the register's clerk, and coach-hire to and from the keepers of the seal.,

For each attendance at either house of parliament—five guineas.

The register is paid all his travelling expenses, and an allowance of one guinea per day for his personal expenses.

Leases, conveyances, &c., are paid for according to their length.

For procuring money and preparing bonds for the corporation—seventeen shillings and sixpence each bond, exclusive of the stamp.

Two shillings are paid to the register for every letter written for payment of taxes in arrear.

Regulations on the Death of a Register.

"Ordered by the board, that upon the death of the present or any future register, the office and all the papers in it be locked up; and that no one be admitted to make searches, or to have any access thereto for any purpose of business, until the necessary directions have been given."

"Ordered, that the clerk or other person having the care of the office, under the register, do give the earliest notice of the death of the register to the governor or surveyor general; or if either of them is not in town, to any one of the bailiffs; any or either of whom is hereby required to call a meeting of the board; and until such meeting, the governor, surveyor general, or bailiff is hereby required to give such directions, and do such acts as the occasion shall appear to require. But as the mixture of the private papers of the register with the papers of the office is almost unavoidable,"

"Resolved, That until the election of a new register, no papers, although they are the private papers of the register, be removed, but in the presence of one or more members of the board, who, before they are taken away, will be satisfied that they do not concern the corporation." *List of persons who have Jllled the office of Register since, the passing of the General Drainage Act,* 15 Car. II. *, to the present period.* 1663. Thomas Bland, Esq.

Mr. Bland had previously held the situation of clerk to the company of adventurers, under the pretended act, passed 1649.

1692. Joseph Hope, Esq. 1717. Joseph Hope, junior, Esq., sworn duputy register. 1720. William Plaxton, Esq, elected and sworn deputy register, iti the room of Joseph Hope, junior, who was discharged for neglect of duty. 1723. William Plaxton, Esq, elected register on the death of Joseph Hope, sen, Esq. 1745. Benjamin Woodward, Esq. 1757. Charles Nalson Cole, Esq. 1803. William Safffery, Esq.

Upon this occasion, Edward Christian, Esq., a Barrister at Law, and Chief Justice of the Isle of Ely, was also a candidate; and the members on the poll being nearly equal, a scrutiny took place, and the numbers were ultimately: Saffery, 82; Christian, 81; but in consequence of several conveyances having been registered by Mr. Gotobed, who had for some time acted as deputy to Mr. Cole, the appointment of Mr. Saffery was resisted, and gave rise to an application to the Court of King's.Bench; but Mr. Satfery's election was ultimately confirmed .

The following is the result of the application to the Court Bench. had been obtained, calling upon the governor, buicommonalty of the company of conservators of the the Bedford of King's Bench. fi East, 356.' A rule had been obtained, calling upon the governor, bui 1812. Robert Bevill, Esq.

Upon this occasion, Thomas Mortlock, Esq., Barrister at Law, was also a candidate; and upon the close of the poll the numbers were: Bevill, 115; Mortlock, 53. Majority for Mr. Bevill, 62.

Great Level of the Fens, to shew cause why a writ of mandamus should not issue to them, commanding them to admit and swear Edward Christian, Esq. , into the place and office of registrar of the said corporation.

By stat. 15 Car. II, c. 17, s. 2, the Earl of Bedford and others, who had commenced the drainage of the Great Level, were incorporated, by the name above mentioned; and the corporation was to consist of a governor, six bailiffs, twenty conservators, and commonalty, who were to meet together " when, where, and as often as they please, and appoint a registrar, receiver, one or more serjeants at mace, and other ollicers, and allow them salaries, and remove them and make new at their pleasure." By sec. 15, the governor, bailiffs, and conservators, are to be elected yearly, upon Wednesday in Whitsun week. By sec. 8, all conveyances by indenture within the Level, "entered with the same registrar in a book to be kept for that purpose, shall be of equal force to convey the freehold and inheritance, &c., as if enrolled, &c. j and no lease, grant, or conveyance, &c., shall be of force, but from the time it shall be entered with the said register as aforesaid; the entry whereof being endorsed by the said register upon such lease, &c., shall be as effectual in law as if the original book of entries was produced at any trial," &c.; and by sec. 14, " the governor, bailiffs, conservators, register, receiver, or other officers nominated as aforesaid, and every other, from time to time, into any of the respective offices to be chosen," shall take a certain oath of office. It was stated in the affidavit, that for above a century back a deputy register had at intervals been elected, as it seem'ed by the corporation, though the act of parliament did not 3 Nov. 1824. Samuel Wells, Esq.

Upon this occasion, Charles Jenyns, Esq., barrister at law, was a candidate, and at the close of the poll (after a scrutiny conducted before the board) the numbers were: Wells, 68; Jenyns, 66; Majority for Wells, 2.

mention any such officer in terms; and thirty-seven instances were stated of such annual elections of the same or different persons, at the times when the annual election to other offices was made. In 1757, Mr. Cole was elected register for the first time, and was annually re-elected till his death, in December, 1804. A few years before Mr. Cole's death, the corporation, at the request of the registrar to choose a deputy register, elected Mr. Gotobed deputy register, without a salary; and he also had been annually re-elected since that time. The minute of his election stood entered in the books:—" The corporation then proceeded to the election of officers for the year ensuing;" and then followed the list of names of officers elected, amongst which is that of "T. Gotobed, deputy register." After Mr. Cole's death, in December, 1804, Mr. Gotobed continued *de facto* in the exercise of his office, in registering titles at the usual place, and in the same form and manner as he had done in Mr. Cole's life time. Of 130 titles registered by' Mr. Gotobed, since his appointment as deputy, of which the registers were signed in his own name as deputy, and not in the name of the principal, 60 of them were registered after the death of Mr. Cole. The election of a new register in the room of Mr. Cole, took place on the 17th of April, 1805, when Mr. Christian and Mr. Saffery appeared as candidates; and the former having 81, and the latter 82 votes, Mr. Saffery was declared duly elected, and was accordingly admitted and sworn into the office by the corporation. It was, however, objected on the part of Mr. Christian, that some of Mr. Saffery's voters (said to be 13 in number) had their titles registered by the deputy register, after the death of his principal, four of whom had their titles so registered on the 13th of April, only four days before the election, when they had certain knowledge of the death of Mr. Cole. But the affidavits on the other hand stated, that the first person to whom the objection, if any, applied, who proffered his vote at the election, tendered it for Mr. Christian, and was accepted by the corporation as a good vote, with full knowledge by all the parties present of the circumstances under which the title was registered. *The Receiver and Ejcpenditor General.*

This officer is also annually elected by the The Receiver members of the corporation, possessing not less than 100 acres of adventurers' land, assembled at the Shire Hall at Ely, at the April meeting.

The duties of this officer are various and considerable. He receives the tax laid upon the whole of the adventurers' lands in the Level, at the times of payment appointed by the board at the April meeting, which tax is invariably ordered for the months of June and November. He also receives all the rents due to the corporation from their estates, and the whole of their revenue; and by him are paid the salaries of the officers, and the interest on the corporation bonds. He also pays the superintendents of the works their respective allotments for carrying on the necessary works according to the orders of the board.

The case was argued at considerable length, and the court deferred their judgment, which Lord Ellenborough, C. J., on the next day delivered as follows:

"The only point made in this case on which the court entertained any doubt, was, whether Mr. Gotobed, in acting as a register after the death of Mr. Cole, was to be considered as an officer *de facto,* whose acts would give effect to the conveyances registered by him during that period; and we think he cannot be so considered. On these affidavits he must be taken as a deputy and assistant to Mr. Cole; and as the necessary consequence of the death of the principal was putting an end to his authority as deputy, the question is, whether, according to the cases respecting the stewards of manors, he had such colorable authority, into which the purchasers of lands could not examine, as to induce them to register their deeds with him, from their having a fair ground to infer that a registration by him would be good and sufficient to eflecluate their conveyances. An officer *defacto* is one who has the reputation of being the officer he assumes to be, and yet is not a good officer in point of law; 1 Ld. Raym. COO. In this case, Gotobed was never more than deputy; and therefore, after the death of his principal, he never could have had the reputation of being more thnn deputy; but such reputation must necessarily have ceased with the knowledge of the death of his principal. When that fact was notorious to the owners of land in the Level, no one could have registered his deeds with him under a belief that he was acting as the assistant of one, who, by the course of nature, had ceased to fill the office, in the execution of which he was to be assisted by the deputy. In this case Cole died in December, and the greater part of the conveyances objected to were registered some months after, on the election. The case pressed upon us from Moore, 112, on being considered, is not, we think, an authority against this opinion; where Manwood, C. B., says that' There is a diversity between copyhold grants by a steward who has a color, and no right to hold a court, and one who has neither color, nor right: for if one who has color assemble the tenants, and they do their service, the acts are good which he does as the under-steward, when the head steward is dead.' But this must be understood of acts of the under-steward after the

In short, all the money affairs of the corporation pass through his hands. The receiver formerly kept a lot book of the whole quantity of the 95,000 acres of adventurers' land, according to the ancient division into 20 lots or shares at the time of the first undertaking of drainage, by which he apportioned the tax chargeable on each proprietor's land, according to the several degrees or sorts; for which purpose, the changes of pro-T.ixnrt,2oc«r. perty occasioned by deaths, conveyances, &c., were!P'' from time to time transmitted to him by the register. The duty of keeping the lot books containing this information, is now transferred to the register, who prepares an annual tax roll, comprising particulars of the quantity of land, and the death of his principal, nnd before his death is known; for if that were known to the tenants, what color could he hive to act? It Ib said in that book, that the nets of such steward (t... a steward *de facto*) are-good, because the suitors cannot examine his title: but when his authority has notoriously ceased, no such reason obtains. This doctrine of Mamvood's seems no more than what was the law in the case of all judicial officers, when the interest of the officers determined on the demise of the crown; for though in consideration of law the commissions of the judges, &c., immediately determined on such demise, yet their intermediate acts, between the demise of the crown, and notice of it, were good. 2 Hale's P. C. 24, Cro. Car. 79, Sir Randolph Crew's case. We wish to be understood as saying nothing as to the registration of conveyances by *Mr.* ' Gotobed in Mr. Cole's life; and as it does not appear that any registrations have been m.ide by a deputy after the death of w principal before the present occasion, we do not apprehend that any ill consequences will result from this our opinion, which is confined to such registration."

Rule absolute.

amount of tax of each owner, and transmits the same to the receiver.

The latter officer used formerly to receive the bulk of the tax at Ely; but for the accommodation of some of the proprietors of adventurers' land, who resided in London, he was permitted to appoint a deputy, who kept a book there for that purpose; and after having received the tax of such proprietors, transmitted an account thereof to his principal, before the time of his return of forfeitures. This plan being inconvenient, an order was made by the board, in the year 1820, prohibiting the receipt of any part of the taxes in London. It should be stated, that at the period of his first election, Mr. Evans, the present able and attentive receiver, voluntarily offered to attend in the months of June and November, at the towns of Chatteris, March, Whittlesey, and Ramsey, for the purpose of receiving the taxes from the proprietors in those districts. The remainder of the tax is paid at the receiver's office at Ely. This plan is still adopted, and has proved of essential service to the country.

The receiver is also directed to forward to the auditor, in the first weeks of July and December, a correct list of all persons in arrear, in order that the auditor may be enabled to charge them with. the penalties upon the taxes so in arrear.

Annually, on the first day of February, the receiver furnishes the register with a fair engrossed roll or schedule on parchment, containing an account of all the arrears of taxes and penalties then unpaid; which, after being examined by the latter, is certified under his hand and the seal of the corporation, and returned by him to the receiver, in order that the same may be publicly affixed to the door of the Shire Hall, according to act of parliament. The receiver places the said App. p. 396. schedule (usually denominated the arrear roll) on the doors of the Shire Hall at Ely, on the three several market days (Thursdays) immediately preceding the public meeting in April, to notify to the defaulters that their lands will be forfeited and sold at such meeting, unless the taxes and penalties be sooner paid. The extreme,

though necessary severity of the law in this respect, has induced the board to take every precaution, consistent with the due discharge of their important duties, to prevent oppression, not only by direct, ing that the arrear roll shall be advertised in the provincial papers two weeks previous to the April meeting, and that letters shall be written by the register to the several persons in arrear, but also by framing the conditions of sale so as to enable the board to interfere in eases of mere accident or particular hardship.

The ancient, opulent, and most respectable firm of Messrs. Child & Co. at Temple Bar, have been bankers to the corporation ever since the first undertaking of the drainage of the fens, and the chief cash account is kept there; but for the convenience of the receiver, cash accounts to a limited extent are also kept at the banks at Wisbech and Ely.

The receiver annually brings the whole charge VOL. I. 2 O and discharge, with the proper vouchers, before the auditor; and the receiver and auditor attend the board at the April meeting, when the whole accounts are ultimately examined and finally allowed; after which, a full abstract thereof is immediately printed and circulated amongst the owners of the adventurers' lands, and the book containing a full statement of the various items of expenditure for the year, as soon as completed, is sent for their inspection to the office of the receiver, where it remains until the first day of February yearly, and is then returned to the Fen Office to be deposited with the records.

The payment of the annual interest due upon the corporation debt, is also under the control of the receiver and expenditor general, who, invariably, before the fifth days of January and July, transmits to the Fen Office the warrants for the half year's interest due on the corporation bonds, directed to Messrs. Child & Co., signed with his own hand; and with such warrants he sends up a list of the creditors, with the amount of the interest due to them respectively.

The mode of obtaining payment by the creditors upon these warrants, and the regulations APP. p.M2. adopted upon their receipt by the register, will *29 Geo. 2.* c. 9., ,,,-,,, ..,..,., be found more fully detailed under the heads of "Corporation Debt," and " Duties of Register."

The receiver and expenditor general, at the time of his appointment, enters into a bond with two sureties approved by the board for the due performance of his office.

He likewise takes an oath, immediately after his election, for the due and diligent discharge of his duties; and he is always in attendance at all public meetings of the board or the corporation.

He has a salary of I20/. per annum, with an allowance for stationery, and an ancient fee of sixpence, called "an acquittance," upon every receipt exceeding ten shillings, for his trouble in making out the same. He gives security, to the corporation, in the sum of I0,000/., for the faithful discharge of the duties of the office.

The following is a list of the several persons who have filled this responsible situation, from the passing of the act, 15 Car. II., to the present period:

Robert Mingay, Esq.,-1663
Roger Jenyns, jun., Esq.,-1689
Sir Roger Jenyns,-1699
Edward Partheriche, Esq.,-1725
Robert Lightfoot, Esq.,... 1728
Edward Partheriche, jun., Esq.,-'-1728
William Cole, Esq.,----1730
Francis Pemberton, Esq.,-1731
Humphrey Smith, Esq.,--1738
Gotobed East, Esq.,-1743
Whetham Robinson, Esq.,-1750
John Drage, Esq.,-1751
John Waddington, Esq,-1760
James Golborne, Esq.,-1790
Hugh Robert Evans, Esq.,--" 1819

The Auditor.

The Auditor. The auditor is annually elected, at the April meeting at Ely, by the owners of not less than 100 acres of adventurers' land. It is his duty to examine carefully all bills and accounts sent to him by the receiver and expend!tor general, the register, or the superintendents, and to correct errors, and disallow improper charges; and his allowance, testified by his signature, is necessary previously to payments being made, unless they be for sums specifically ordered by the board. In the first week in the months of July and December, the receiver and expenditor general provides a list of all unpaid arrears of taxes for the auditor, who thereupon charges the receiver and expenditor general with the gross amount of the several penalties incurred by the non-payment of the taxes in the preceding months of June and November, when they are payable.

The receiver and expenditor general having, previously to the April meeting, transmitted to the auditor the statement of all the accounts for the year, they are carefully examined and compared with the vouchers by the auditor, and a detail of the particulars thereof is drawn out by him and entered into a book, and, at the April meeting, submitted to the board, with such observations thereon as he may think necessary.

The accounts being finally examined and passed by the board, it becomes the duty of the auditor to enter the particulars thereof in a parchment-covered book, which book is produced to the board at their Whitsun meeting, and is then left (as already stated) at thje office of the receiver and expenditor general at Ely, for the inspection of the owners of adventurers' lands, until the 1st. day of February following, when the same is to be removed to the Fen Office, and deposited with the other records of the corporation. On the examination of the accounts, the vouchers are delivered by the receiver and expenditor general to the auditor, who, after the Whitsun meeting, deposits them in the Fen Office.

It is also the duty of the auditor annually to prepare and print a perfect abstract of the accounts, and to distribute the same amongst the several owners of adventurers' lands, before the Whitsun meeting.

With regard to the duties of the auditor, the following orders have, at different times, been made by the board; and it is his province to see them duly performed by the proper parties.

Each superintendent is yearly to make out, by the 1st of March, the whole account of his receipt and expenditure for the year then ending, or as near thereto as can be, including the balance at the beginning and end of the year; and immediately after that day to send the same to the auditor, with all the bills and vouchers.

Each of the superintendents is to keep a cash book, and enter therein every receipt and pay mcut on account of the corporation, day by day as they occur; and the same is to be produced whenever it is required; and a copy of the account of each month is to be sent to the auditor during the first week of the month following.

No part of the allotments for the banks, nor any money, is to be paid by the receiver and expenditor general to the superintendents, without the direction of the auditor, except money for subsist for the bankers for a month or six weeks, and for days' work and jobs, and for bills not exceeding five pounds.

All other bills are to be sent to the auditor to be audited by him before they are paid, and are not to be paid by the receiver until so allowed by the auditor.

The account of every measuring up of banking work of every description, with an account of the subsist paid and the balance due to each contractor or gangman receiving subsist, is also to be sent to the auditor, before the balance is paid, and such balance is not to be paid by the receiver until the account be allowed. ' "

The auditor is not to receive any monthly account, except it be made according to the regulations, and contain an account when and for what every payment is made, together with the amount of every receipt of money, and the time when received.

The auditor takes an oath immediately after his election, for the due and diligent performance of his office, and attends at the general April and Whitsun meetings, and at any other of the public meetings, either of the board or of the corporation, at which his presence may be required. He has a salary of 100/.

per annum, with an allowance for stationery, travelling charges, and ofher disbursements.

The following is a list of the several persons who have held the situation since the passing of the General Drainage Act, 15 Car. II., to the present period: 1663. Richard Marryott.
1703. Upon the death of Mr. Marryott, it was ordered, that the auditor should not be in one person, and two conservators were appointed for this year only. 1704. Ralph Pierson, Esq. 1711. John Chicheley, Esq. 1717. William Fortrey, Esq. 1723. Francis Pemberton, Esq. 1726. Nathaniel Green, Esq. 1729. Thomas Dixon, Esq. 1730. Francis Pemberton, Esq. 1731. John Brownell, Esq. 1736. It was ordered, that the office of auditor should be extinguished, and the duties annexed to those of the register, then held by Mr. Plaxton. 1745. Upon the death of Mr. Plaxton, the register, the offices were again divided, and Mr. Owen Fann elected. 1749. Mr. Fann declined the office, but no auditor was appointed. 1752. No auditor was appointed till this year, when Mr. Woodward the register was appointed. 1757. Charles Nalson Cole, Esq., auditor and register. 1805. William Saffery, Esq., ditto. 1812. Robert Bevill, Esq., ditto. 1824. Upon the death of Mr. Bevill, the offices were again divided, and Francis King Eagle, Esq., was appointed. 1825. Steed Girdlestone, Esq. mace. *The Serjeant at Mace.*

The serjeant at This officer is elected annually at the April meeting, by the majority of owners of not less than 100 acres of adventurers' lands, at an annual salary of 10/. 10. Immediately after his election he takes an oath for the due and faithful discharge of his office. The act of the 15th of Car. II., sect. 10, makes the persons to whom sales have been made of lands forfeited for taxes in arrear and penalties, lawful purchasers. And the act of 20 Car. II. directs the serjeant at mace to put the land into their possession by precept, under the seal of the corporation, in the nature of a writ of *haberc facias possessionem* at common law.

No directions appear upon the proceedings of the corporation relating to the manner in which this duty (doubtless the most important of his of fice) is to be executed; but for such regulations as have from time to time been made, the reader is referred to the chapter which treats of the mode of selling lands forfeited for nonpayment of taxes.

Besides the duties vested in him by the act of 20 Car. II., as to setting out and delivering possession of lands sold for arrears of taxes, the serjeant at mace is often called upon to set out boundaries between contending parties, and between the corporation and different owners, both of free and adventurers' lands.

This office, to be executed with fidelity and impartiality, requires considerable local knowledge of the situation and value of all the different lots of the adventurers' lands: and it is but justice to say, that the register has witnessed instances in which the present serjeant at mace has displayed considerable skill both in setting Out lands sold for nonpayment of taxes, and in ascertaining boundaries in dispute. Indeed, few persons in the fens possess more extensive local information than the present serjeant at mace.

When the board act as commissioners of sewers, to this officer belongs the duty of summoning the jury, under precept from the commissioners, and of levying amerciaments and fines directed by the court of sewers.

The mace, which was presented to the corporation by William Duke of Bedford soon after the enactment of the 15 Car. II., always continues in the custody of the serjeant, who places the same upon the table immediately before the commencement of business by the board. He also precedes the board and corporation, when they attend at the April and Whitsnn meetings, to hold public courts of the corporation at the Shire Hall at Ely, for elections, sales of lands, and other purposes.

The fees payable to this officer for setting out and delivering possession of land sold for nonpayment of taxes, have been regulated by an order of the board, made at the Whitsun meeting, 1822, which allows him one guinea a day for his time, together with the charge for horse-hire and expenses, and all reasonable sums paid to the surveyors, when (as must generally happen) be finds it necessary to call in their assistance.

He is also entitled to certain fees for the duties discharged by him, when acting under the authority of the commissioners of sewers; but these fees are adjusted by the board as occasion requires.

The following is a list of persons who have held the situation from the passing of the act of 15 Car. II. to the present period:

Mr. George Barnes,-1663
Mr. William Browne,-1667
Mr. William Turkington,-1701
Mr. Sheffield Stubbs,-1711
Mr. Gotobed East,-1724 Mr. Gotobed East having purchased some adventurers' land sold by the corporation for arrears of taxes, Mr. James Robinson was appointed serjeant at mace, specially for the purpose of delivering possession to Mr. G. East.

Mr. James Ralph,----1726
Mr. Miles Rook, 1730
Mr. Gotobed East,----1736
Mr. John Bailey,-----1744
Mr. Thomas Gotobed,----1751
Mr. William Marshall,----1781
Mr. James Golborne,-1797
Mr. James Golborne, jun.,-1801
Mr. William Marshall,----1812 *The Engineer.*

Upon the resignation of the late Mr. Golborne, Tuc engineer, who held the office of superintendent-general of the works of the corporation for a great number of years, the Middle and South Levels were subdivided into several portions, and the works were placed under the charge of a certain number of superintendents. But owing to the effect produced by the Eau Brink Cut, which had been made near the harbour of Lynn, for the improvement of the outfall, it became apparent that a very heavy expenditure would sooner or later be required from the corporation. The Hundred Feet River was directed by the original Eau Brink Act (35 Geo. III. c. 77.) to be scoured out by the corporation; and, indeed, it is impossible to avoid stating, that although the funds of the corporation, by the liquidation of their debt, became in a flourishing condition, yet the state of the great works of the

Level by no means kept pace in repair and security with the improvement in their financial circumstances. It was clearly the policy of the then members of the board to place themselves in a position to meet these claims, which they foresaw must inevitably come upon them, as soon as the effect of the proposed new cut should be fully ascertained.

The board have always evinced much anxiety that their outlay should be managed with liberality and judgment, but, at the same time, should be confined within its.proper limits. They can have but one object in the discharge of the weighty duty confided in them, namely, to provide as economically as possible for the security of the country, and to give satisfaction to their constituents; it not being forgotten, that the members of the board, from their extensive property, are also greatly interested in the result of their own proceedings.

In order, therefore, that they might have, when the time should arrive (and soon it did arrive) for this heavy expenditure, a person on whose skill and ability they could rely, the board took steps to obtain the assistance of a resident engineer who could devote his time and talents exclusively to their service. Upon the special recommendation of the late John Rennie, Esq., Mr. John Dyson, the present able, intelligent, and assiduous engineer, was, in the year 1824, appointed engineer to the corporation during the pleasure of the board. Mr. Dyson's conduct has hitherto justified the good opinion entertained of him by his patron and the corporation; and the woj-ks erected and executed during the period he has held his situation, will hand down his name and skill with credit to after ages.

The duties of the engineer are to report from time to time the state of the several works of the corporation; to advise as to their repairs, renewal, situation, and effect; and finally to carry into execution such orders as may be given by. the board. He has an annual salary of 250/., including all charges whatever connected with the works of the corporation. He has lately been allowed one, and sometimes two assistants, in consequence of the heavy works carried on under the sanction of the corporation. He is to reside at Downham, or where the board may from time to time direct. At the period of Mr. Dyson's appointment, the board ordered, that the whole of the works and duties of the superintendents and officers should be executed by them with his concurrence; and, ultimately, the whole of the works of the corporation were placed under his *general* control, although under the immediate charge of the several officers of the corporation.

. *The Supermtendents.*

Four superintendents are elected annually, at Thesnperinthe April meeting, by the majority of owners of not less than 100 acres of adventurers' land, *foe* the carejxnd protection of the several divisions of the Middle and South Levels, namely, 1st. Superintendent of the north division of the Middle Level, and of the works and purposes within and attached thereto; of which division Mr. John Little, of Eldernell, near Whittlesey, is the present superintendent, with an annual salary of 65/.

2nd. Superintendent of the south division of the Middle Level, and of the works and purposes within and attached thereto; of which Mr. John Owen, of Mepal, near Chatteris, is the present superintendent, with an annual salary of 40/. 3rd. Superintendent of the east division of the Middle Level, and of the works and purposes within and attached thereto; of which division Mr. Joseph Sedgley, of Welney, near Wisbech, is the present superintendent, with an annual salary of *50l.* 4th. Superintendent of the South Level, and of the works and purposes within and attached thereto; of which division Mr. Joseph Little, of Eldernell, is the present superintendent, with an annual salary of 100/.

Each superintendent has the care of all the property and works of the corporation, within or attached to his division.

To him belongs (subject to the directions and concurrence of the engineer) the general execution of the orders of the board relating to such works or property. He ought once, at least, during each year, to view all the public rivers, drains, banks, bridges, sluices, tunnels, and other works within or attached to his division, whether the same be or be not made or maintained by the corporation.

He is to report to the register from time to time all encroachments on the banks, and impediments to the passage of the waters to their outfall, within or without the Level, and whatever appears likely to affect the drainage, or the security of the country, or the interests of the corporation.

Whatever work is to be executed under his control, and whenever money is to be expended, the superintendent has to see to the completion of that work, and the moderation of the charges, the amount of which he is specially ordered to transmit monthly to the auditor. The engineer or superintendent alone has authority to set men to work, to order work to be done, to enter into contracts, and to incur or subject the corporation to any charge or debt. The superintendent is to be watchful, that there be no waste of materials, loss of time, or charge for what is not pet-formed. It is his duty personally to view, examine, and measure up the banking work, which the board have specially ordered to be done, every fortnight. He is responsible that there be no imposition upon the corporation, as far as can be within the reach of his utmost activity and vigilance.

As to all occurrences arising in the execution of works, for which the orders of the board have not provided, and for which a committee shall not be appointed, the superintendent is required to apply to any three or more members of the board, resident in his vicinity, and to follow the directions of such three members acting as a committee, the same being reduced into writing. When the expense is likely to exceed the authority given to three or more members of the board, and in all cases of doubt or importance for which no order is made or direction given, the superintendent is to apply to the register, who, should he think it necessary, is to call a meeting of the board; or, should that be inconvenient or impracticable, such of the members of the board as can be convened by summonses, shall be a committee; and the directions which (for want of a board) such committee, attended by the register, shall give, shall be followed by the superintendent. But when the case is so urgent that there is not time to apply to the register, nor to summon a board or committee, the responsibility must rest upon the superintendent, and he must decide whether it is not an expenditure which the board will sanction.

Each superintendent has also to serve all notices, and to do whatever may be necessary in the business of the corporation arising within his division, or relating to the works attached to it, whether he may have to go out of his division or not. The superintendents are also to attend at the April and Whitsun meetings of the corporation, and such other meetings of the board, or of any committee of the board, as may be required. They are allowed fifteen shillings a day for their charges while attending the board; which sum includes the expenses of their horses, &c.

Every sluice-keeper and resident labourer is wholly subject to the directions and control of the resident engineer, and of the superintendent of the division to which he is attached. He has no authority beyond that of obeying and carrying into execution their directions; but it is the duty of the superintendents to see to the execution of whatever is directed to be done by the persons under them.

A list of questions, relative to the state of the corporation works and property, and on other subjects immediately connected with the duties of the several superintendents, is annually sent by the register to each superintendent, who is required to answer and return the same before the 1st day of April in each year; which list is examined by the register, and, if necessary, the whole, or particular parts thereof are submitted to the consideration of the board.

It is also part of the duty of the superintendents to see that all the houses, cottages, buildings, and fences belonging to the corporation are kept in proper repair; and when the repairs which ought to be made by the tenants to the corporation are neglected, the superintendents should give the parties notice, and should they still fail, report their neglect to the register. The fences and milestones on or across the banks are also under the care of the superintendents.

It is a very important part of the office of the superintendents to observe that the waters have a free passage to their outfalls at sea; and that lighters Vol. i. 2 P and boats be not allowed to remain in such places as may occasion any obstruction to the drainage, in particular at or near the sluices and bridges. Whenever any wears or fishing places are made or continued, by raising earth or placing faggots between the river and the banks, so as to narrow the passage of the waters, and thereby prejudice the drainage by holding back the water, it is the superintendent's business immediately to remove such obstructions, and to report the same to the register; and this he should do, whether it be in an ancient river, or in any of the rivers or drains made by the corporation. Whenever any nets or eel-grigs, or other devices for catching fish, are so used and placed in any ancient river as to obstruct the waters and injure the drainage, the superintendents should report the same to the register; and in the rivers or drains made by, or belonging to the corporation, the superintendent should take up such nets, eel-grigs, and other de, vices for catching fish, whenever they obstruct the drainage; 'and if the offence be repeated, he is to destroy the same, and report his proceeding to the register.

The weeding of the rivers and drains requires the frequent attention of the superintendents, in order that the weeds may be so cut, that, at the seasons when a clear passage for the waters is required, the weeds may be no impediment.

Each superintendent is to provide and keep, in the corporation store-houses, or in such other places as may be most convenient, a sufficient stock of every bill a certificate that the work was well executed at the times mentioned, and according to the charges, and that they are fair and reasonable.

Each superintendent, immediately after his election, is sworn to the diligent and faithful performance of the duties of his office. The oath is always administered by the register in the presence of the board.

Sluice-keepers. keepers. Sluice-keepers are also annually elected for the principal Sluices, by the members of the corporation possessing not less than 100 acres of adventurers' land, assembled at the Shire Hall at Ely, at the April meeting.

Each sluice-keeper acts under the direction of the register, the resident engineer, or of the superintendent to whose division the sluice is attached; and when any thing of importance occurs, it is his duty to report it immediately to the superintendent.

The sluice-keepers, when the passage of the waters is required for the purposes of drainage, should use their utmost diligence both by day and night, that the doors be opened as soon as, and as long as, a run can be obtained; and when the ebb doors are required to be closed for keeping up the navigation, it is their duty to take care that they are kept shut. The si nice-keepers, however, are not allowed, on any occasion, to admit waters into the rivers without a written order from the engineer or superintendent.

It is also the business of the sluice-keeper to do all in his power, without committing a breach of the peace, to oppose any person who shall attempt to pass through any of the sluices at a time or in a manner which may occasion any injury thereto, or who shall force open the doors, or draw the lighters in by horses, or force the lighters in before the doors are properly open, or leave any barge, &c., either in the sluice, or so near thereto, as to prevent the opening, shutting, or using thereof; or, when the same is open for the dramage of the fens, who shall place, or continue, a barge, lighter, &c., so as to obstruct the passage of the waters draining through the same, or who shall attempt to do any other injury; and he is to communicate all that happens to the superintendent, that the offenders may be immediately prosecuted by the corporation.

These officers, at Denver Sluice and Salter's Lode, are required to keep a daily account, from the 1st day of November to the 1st day of June in every year, of the greatest and lowest height of the waters above the cill of their own sluice on both sides, distinguishing when the height is occasioned by a flood, and shewing how many hours the water ran through; and if any particular flood or tide should happen during any other part of the year, a similar account is to be kept.

Denver Sluice, Saiter's Lode Sluice, and the Old Bedford Sluice, being contiguous to the tidal river, require the constant care and presence of the sluice-keepers: it is consequently their duty not to be absent therefrom, for any purpose whatever, without the consent of the engineer or superintendent; and when that consent is given, the absence is to be as short as possible.

It is also a part of the sluice-keepers' business to keep their respective sluices in good order, and, particularly when necessary, to croome, dydle, or remove the sands in the' sluice, or at the backs or fronts thereof; and when there is ice, to break it, and to do any thing consistent with their duty as sluice-keepers, as the engineer or superintendent may think requisite on the part of the corporation.

Each sluice-keeper is sworn, immediately after his election, to the diligent discharge of the duties of his office. The oath is always administered by the register, in the presence of the board.

The following is a list of the present sluicekeepers, with their respective annual salaries: £. t. d.

George Stevens, Denver Sluice,--45 0 0 John Pinnock, Saiter's Lode Sluice,-40 0 0 David Bowker, Standground Sluice,-20 0 0 John Ayres, Hermitage Sluice,--400 Abraham Le Pla, Welche's Dam Sluice, 220 Thomas Baker, Sixteen Feet Sluice,-5 0 0 £ t. d.

John Owen, Sutton Wash Sluice,-500 William Winters, Welmore Lake Sluice,) # James Custance, Seven Holes at Earith,) By the provisions of the Wash Act (52 Geo. III. c. 145.), the Wash commissioners are bound to contribute a moiety towards the repair of these sluices, and pay forty shillings per annum for the salary of the sluice-keepers.

CHAPTER XVIII. *General commissions of sewers.—Provisions as to sewers works in the Bedford Level.—Lynn Law.—Charter.—Saint Ives Law.—Pretended act.— General drainage act.— The select body of the corporation appointed commissioners of sewers.— System of puddling.—Advice of Lord Tenter den.*

General com-Commissions of sewers have existed from time mission o sew-immemorial; they are coeval with the common law, from which they emanate, although aided by the App. p. Ib. provisions of the general sewers act, 23 Henry VIII, c. 5, as well as by other statutes, passed both before and after that enactment, which is considered at the present time as the regulation and guide of the laws and practices of commissioners of sewers throughout the realm.

provision «»to But before we notice the law of sewers in genesewers works., i, « « in the Bedford ral, let us consider the same in relation to the Bedford Level. By the Lynn law, (an act of the then commissioners of sewers,) the *old* rivers and cuts continued in the proprietors; but the *new* rivers, cuts, and drains, to be made by.the Earl of Bedford, and his assigns, and the banks thereof, A. p. Iog. and the foreland on the inside of the banks, not exceeding 50 or three-score feet at the most in breadth, were agreed to belong to the Earl and his assigns, in respect he or thgy were to maintain the same; he and they also paying for the *several* lands of any particular owner thereof, such recompense as the commissioners of sewers then contracting with App.p. uo. the Earl should think fit. The charter gives to the corporation then con-The charter. stituted, power to make laws and ordinances for the support of the works of drainage; and also the conservancy of *all waters and banks,* within the App. p. 132. fens and marsh grounds of the Level, as well those that then were, as those that should thereafter be made, and with power to inquire by jury, and to fine and imprison.

By the St. Ives law, Francis Earl of Bedford was saint ives law. declared to have drained the Fens according to App. p. 2-14. the intent of the Lynn law; and the 95,000 acres were thereby decreed and set out to him, with all and every the water-courses, rivers, drains, weardikes, forelands, not exceeding 60 feet in breadth, banks, sluices, and works of draining within or upon the said Great Level, or any parts thereof, by the said Earl or his assigns made or erected. The Earl had also the power to make new works &c., App. p.251. according to the Lynn law, bat under the control At the period of the undertaking by Francis Earl of Bedford,.by far the greater part of the Level consisted of open undrvided commons. See Hnyword's Survey, Apj). p. 141.

of six or more of the commissioners of sewers: the ancient rivers and drains were to remain to the right owners. The pretended The pretended act went yet further in this res net pect, for it enacted and ordained,, that no commissioner or commissioners, by virtue or colour of any commission in that behalf, should at all interfere in App. p. 373. the Level, to interrupt, disturb, or molest William Earl of Bedford, his participants, or adventurers. The Earl was also empowered by that act, to make any new, or enlarge any old cuts, sasses, sluices, drains, banks, receptacles, or other works necessary or conducive to and for the said draining, through or upon the grounds of any person or persons within or without the Level; and for that purpose he was to have free passage, ingress, egress, and regress, by and through such grounds, or any part thereof, paying or tendering to the owners of, and parties interested in the said grounds, for all such cuts, sasses, sluices, drains, banks, receptacles, or other works made or to be made in and upon the *grounds without or within* the

Level, such reasonable recompense as by the owners and patties interested should be agreed upon; or if any difference should happen, the same was to be settled by the commissioners of appeal and judicature named in that act. Thus we find the whole of the new rivers, banks, and sluices themselves, actually vested in the Earl, but he had only the conservancy of all the old rivers; the right of soil and fishing continuing the property of the former owner. By the Lynn law, if the Earl took *several* lands, he was to make satisfaction according to the commissioners of sewers; but by the pretended act, this compensation was to be for *all* lands cut and used for the works, and was to be settled by the commissioners named in that act. Now, as both the commissioners of sewers, and the commissioners of appeal and adjudication, have become legally defunct, these means of compensation cannot of course be resorted to by the corporation. But we now arrive at the provisions of the gene-General drainral drainage act, which enacts, that the 83,000 agea" acres, remainder of the 95,000 acres, (after deducting the King's 12,000 acres,) with the ways, passages, new rivers, cuts, drains, banks, and forelands, are absolutely vested in the corporation; In trust, nevertheless, for William Earl of Bedford, and the adventurers and participants of Earl Francis and Earl William. The corporation was em-
App. p. 394. powered to execute estates, that is, to sign and seal conveyances of any proportionate part of the 95,000 acres that were claimed, and such claim substantiated, by any of the new adventurers and participants. The corporation had also power to erect, App. p. 396. from time to time, any new works *within* the Great Level, *or without* the Great Level, for conveying the waters of the said Great Level by convenient outfalls to the sea; so always, that if they cut any *several* grounds, they should give full recompense It was omitted to be stated in a former part of the work, that this act was duly enrolled and exemplified in the high court of Chancery.

and satisfaction for the same; which damage was to be awarded by the commissioners of appeal appointed by that act; but these commissioners being also defunct, no legal provision remains at this period for making compensation in any of the modes suggested by those several documents. The Earl of Bedford, and those who prepared the general drainage act, anticipated not only this difficulty, but also the absolute necessity of arming some proportion at least of the corporation with ample, summary powers, as well for the purpose of making compensation for injury sustained by any act of the corporation, as for the protection of the rivers, banks, sluices, and general works of drainage, which were so continually liable to unforeseen accidents and rue select hostile attacks, either by the effect of floods, or by "tne attempts of malice. Accordingly, it was provided» that the select body of the corporation for tne time being, or any five or more of them, where

App. p. 391. f J of the governor or bailiffs for the time being were to be two, for maintainance and preservation of the Great Level, by convenient outfalls to the sea, should for ever thereafter be, and were thereby made and constituted commissioners of sewers, *for and of the said Great Level of the Fens,* It has always been a matter of doubt, whether commissioners of sewers could originate and execute any *new uorlts.* This question is quite immaterial, as regards the Bedford Level sewers; because the *corporation* is empowered to make any new works, as well within, as without the Great Level; but the question is important, as regards commissioners of sewers in general. See Cullis on Sewers, p. 114. Dugd. 371.

and were thereby enabled from thenceforth to use and exercise the power and authority of commissioners of sewers, *within* the said Great Level of the Fens, and of the works *made or to be made* without the said Great Level, for conveying of the waters of the said Great Level by convenient outfalls to the sea, touching all matters and things whatsoever happening to be executed or done *within* the Great Level, or the said *works without* the Great Level. All the powers vested in commissioners of sewers at large, were also given to these App.p. 393. fen commissioners, and no other commissioners of sewers were to intermeddle.

The select body, in their character of commissioners of sewers, cannot sit and act *without* the said Great Level, for which *only* they are appointed; although they have full power and control over any works made or to be made hi/ the *corporation without* the Great Level; such, for instance, as the care and conservancy of the rivers and banks of the Tongs Drain, and Saint John's Eau, both of which works were made by the corporation, and are *without* the Great Level; but the act does give them power over works under the control of other commissioners of sewers.

In the early periods of the corporation, the operation of the commission of sewers was indispensably requisite, in order to enable them to make compensation to parties for any injury sustained, This must be construed to moan, works made or to be made by the Bedford Level Corporation.

as well as to preserve and protect the works of drainage by summary process. The exercise of this important function, however, after some years, fell almost into disuse.

System of At length a strong desire to improve the forma

"plddlDg tion of the barrier banks arose in the country, and the system of what is named "Puddling" became generally adopted, not only by the corporation, but also by the district commissioners, and by individuals. This system consists in cutting through, or rather opening, the top of the bank three or four feet, according-to its height, and inserting into such opening strong gault or clay, obtained from the highlands adjoining the Level. The heavy particles sink to the base of the bank, making the seat or bottom firm and solid, and also preventing that soakage of water through the bank, which the porous nature of the Fen soil had previously rendered almost unavoidable.

For want of a mode of making compensation, considerable difficulty existed in obtaining highland earth. Persons were either incapacitated for conveying their estates, or indisposed to afford the accommodation required. Many encroachments had also taken place in the Level, upon the works and property of the corporation, occasioned in some degree by the lapse of time, and relaxation on the The corporation have five places reserved for obtaining highland earth; two in Whittlesey field; one at Horseway, near Chatteris; one called Branghill Pits, near Sutton in the Isle of Ely; and one called Roswell Hill pits, near Ely.

part of some of the officers of the corporation. These circumstances induced the board, in the year 1816, to revive the court of sewers. They felt, however, some difficulty as to the mode of proceeding. To put the machinery into motion was found to be both difficult and expensive; they wisely sought for and obtained the advice and direction of him who now fills and adorns the eminent station of Chief Justice of England, with an assiduity and ability highly honorable to himself and beneficial to his country . Long, long may it please Divine Providence to continue the able and unceasing labours of this learned, upright, and indefatigable judge, for the benefit of his admiring and grateful countrymen 5 Woe be to the people of England, should the judgment-seat of this revered nobleman be filled by One Man, whose tongue proclaims liberty, and his heart oppression;—who clamours for the freedom of the press, and buries its talented advocates in the darksome dungeon;—who shouts for reform with one class of patrons, and becomes the willing instrument of oppression with another class! Heaven forefend the people of England, should the career of this One Man *progress* beyond its present undeserved elevation

In consequence of the advice of Mr. Abbott, two courts of sewers were held at Ely, the one on the 27th of August, 1816, and the other on the 22nd of July, 1822, the proceedings of which are fully recorded in the order-books of the corporation; and a

Lord Tenterden (then Mr. Abbott). precept or warrant was issued by two of the bailiffs, and four of the conservators, commissioners of sewers, under the common seal of the corporation, and delivered to Mr. Marshall, the serjeant at mace, for summoning the jury; and the serjeant at mace having returned the precept, with the panel of the jury by him summoned, twenty-one of them appeared and were sworn.

From the period of holding the above mentioned courts, the select body have always been sworn after their election as commissioners of sewers; and entries have always been made in the order book, of their proceedings as commissioners of sewers, as well as a minute that the select body assembled and adjourned in that capacity.

Having thus brought before the reader the peculiar circumstances connected more particularly with the select body of the Bedford Level, in their character of commissioners of sewers, it was the intention of the author to have proceeded to the consideration of the very important subject of commissioners of sewers at large: the obsoleteness of their practice, the paucity of correct information, and the general ignorance that prevails in this respect, induced him to investigate the matter with some pains, labour, and research; but this investigation, from its extent and complexity, must be at present deferred, with the assurance of the author's intention to undertake the task at as early a period as his numerous avocations will permit.

The oath (of which a form will be found in the Appendix, p. 24,) is always administered by the register.. CHAPTER XIX. *Registration of Deeds t*

It is much to be regretted, that the various law reports afford but little information on this division of our labours. The books are indeed scanty, without precedent, on a subject so important; the following case being the only one they contain concerning the registration of conveyances of lands under the-jurisdiction of the corporation of the Bedford Level:.. A

Hodson v. Sharpe, 180$.—10 East, 350. "The defendant to an action of covenant for The want of« .. gistration under not repairmg certam premises demised to bun the Bedford by the devisor of the plaintiffs, for the term of c»r. u. c.'i7., only postpones eleven years, pleaded, that the premises were part the priority of " of the 95,000 acres mentioned in the statute not"avoid them u 15 Car. II. c. 17., for draining the Bedford Level, prti e

"and then averred that the lease had not been en-sclves"

"tered with the register for the time being, ap-

"pointed by the corporation, in manner required

"by the said act, by reason of which the inden-

' ture was of no force.

"But the court held, that after the lessee had "had all the benefit which he could derive under

Vol. i. 2 Q

"the lease, he should not be permitted to object that "it was not registered. They said, that the object "of that clause in the act on which he relied, was "to take away the priority of the party whose title "was not registered, with respect to subsequent "claimants whose titles were registered; but it "never was intended to operate between the par"ties themselves, so as to enable a lessee who had "enjoyed under it to dispute the lease.

"Judgment for the plaintiff."

The decision in the above case seems to have been regulated by reasoning particularly applicable to the relative characters of the parties to the action, the plaintiff being the lessor, the defendant the lessee.

App.p.393. As doubts are continually arising on the *practical* operation of the 8lh section of the act of the 15th of Charles II, with respect to the regis'tration of deeds, where common recoveries are suffered; in the absence of all express authority to direct the judgment, the following observations are submitted with much deference, and it is hoped, will be indulgently received. In practice, it frequently occurs, that a tenant in tail, suffering a common recovery of lands within the BedfordLevel, omits the registration of the deed creating" the tenant to the *prcecipe* until after the term in which the recovery lias been suffered. Other analogo us cases are of daily occurrence with respect to deeds omitted to be registered until after their operations have been controlled by subsequent .1...-/ deeds; but the case of a recovery is selected, from its great importance to the most extensive titles in the Fens.

The question arises, whether a subsequent registration is sufficient, by retrospective operation, to constitute an effective deed to make the tenant to the writ of entry. This point has often been agitated, but has never been judicially determined. Let the subject then be considered with reference to other statutes of a similar nature: 1st, may be briefly noticed the effect of an enrollment (under the statute of enrollment, 27 Hen. VIII, c. 16) of a 27 H. 8, c. *is.* deed to make a tenant to a *prcecipc,* subsequent to the period of suffering the recovery; and, 2dly, the effect under the Middlesex Registry Act; and then may be inquired how far an analogy exists between these acts and the one now under discussion.

By the rules of the common law, provided there was a seisin at the time when the writ of entry was sued, that seisin would have supported the recovery, although the seisin was defeated after judgment given, by a condition, or evicted by an older title. Now the words of the statute of en-27H. 8, c. 16. rollment are: "That no manors, lands, tenements, or other hereditaments, shall pass, alter, or "change from one to another, whereby any estate "of inheritance or freehold shall be made or take "effect in any person or persons, or any use there-' "of to be made by reason only of any bargain and Prcst. Convey. 38, cites I Kcb. 7155.

"sale thereof, except the same bargain and sale be "made by writing indented, sealed, and enrolled "in one oT the king's courts of record at West mi n"ster, &c., within six months after the date of the." same writings indented, &c." This statute indeed differs from the Bedford Level corporation act. It says that no hereditaments shall pass by bargain and sale, unless enrolled within six months; and thus it follows, that if the bargain and sale be enrolled in six months, it is good *ab initio,*

But the 15th Car. II. says, " that no grant, &c. „. shall be offeree but from the time of being en tered;" consequently any act done between the execution of the deed and the time of its entry, is done when the deed is *not in force;* and if the power of doing it is created by the deed, such power is not legally in existence at the time when it is attempted to be exercised.

. With reference to a bargain and sale, a celebrated writer has observed, that on account of its peculiar properties, the recovery will be void,

or rather voidable, unless the bargain and sale shall be enrolled in due time, namely, within six

lunar months. For although he says, it is nov agreed that the bargain and sale operates *instun*

ter on the freehold, yet this operation is subject to an implied condition that the grant shall be void

ab initio, unless the enrollment shall take place within the limited time. This point certainly appears an anomaly in law, and is the result of the

Preston on Conveyancing, p. 38..

provisions of the statute of enrollment, and not of the rule of the common law.:

The modifications under which the tenant takes the freehold by means of the bargain and sale before enrollment is still open to controversy. Vari-r ous notions have prevailed, and hypotheses enteiv tained on the subject, which it is not necessary to discuss in this place. Suffice it to say, that however irreconcilable are the opinions on the particular point, it is universally admitted that the enrollment will have a relation back to make good the recovery of the bargainee against whom the *prcccipe* was brought before enrollment.

This construction of the effect of the enrollment of bargains and sales has been by some thought to sanction a similar doctrine with regard to the registration of instruments under the 15 Car. II. A comparison, however, of the language of the two acts will tend, it is apprehended, to refute such a conclusion.

The words of the former we have seen; those of the latter, in the 8th section of 15 Car. II., are as follow:—It is enacted, "that no 15far.ii.c.17. "lease, grant, or conveyance of, or charge out of "or upon the said 95,000 acres, or any part there"of, (except leases for seven years or under in "possession,) shall be offeree but from the time "it shall be entered with the said register as afore"said." Now, if the deed is by this clause to take See Bncon on Uses, edit, by Rowe, note 106, p. 169; 2 Sanders on Uses, p. 5i, 2d edit.; Pigott on Recoveries, pp. 56—7. effect only from the period of registration, it follows that until registration it must be utterly ineffective; and it seems equally clear, that against adverse claimants a good tenant cannot be made by a registration after the recovery suffered; for the tenant never had the freehold in respect of which alone he could he tenant, nor is it probable, even where there is no adverse claim, that a title depending on such a recovery could be recommended with safety.

A stronger resemblance, it is submitted, exists between the Bedford Level act and the statute which requires the registration of conveyances of lands in the county of Middlesex . It is thereby enacted, "that all deeds and conveyances con"cerning any honors, manors, lands, tenements, or '. hereditaments, in the county of Middlesex, shall '" be adjudged fraudulent and void against any

Sec *cases* on tins act. Doe "subsequent purchaser or mortgagee for valuable v. AUsop, "considerations, unless a memorial thereof be reAid."i42.an "gistered in the manner by the act directed, before triii, 2 fiiigh "the registering of the memorial of the deed or "conveyance under which such subsequent pur"chaser or mortgagee shall claim."

Under this act, whatever equity a purchaser may have, that he cannot take a legal estate of freehold until his deed be entered in the register's books, is proved by the circumstance that a subsequent purchaser without notice, having his deed first registered, has both at law and in equity the preferable title.

7 Anne, c. 20. e. 1. . The distinction

would therefore seem to be, that in the case of the bargain and sale, under the 27 Hen. VIII. c. 16., the deed has an immediate efficacy, subject to be defeated by neglect of enrollwent in six months; and in the cases of the 15 Car. II, c. 17. , and the 7 Atme, c. 20., the registration is a necessary ingredient in the first instance o constitute an effectual deed against opposite interests. At all events it would be highly imprudent, where no obstacle to the registry exists, to dispense with the entry of the deed in the register books before the suffering of the recovery, upon the assumption that the instrument by which the tenant to the *proecipe* is made, may be rendered valid by a subsequent registration. ', If the foregoing reasoning be correct, in the absence of all legal decisions bearing immediately upon the point (except the case of Hodson w.Sharpe, already quoted), it would seem, that no deed can have any legal operation until after it is entered with the register, and his endorsement of the entry placed upon the instrument so entered; and that no subsequent registration can give effect, so as to destroy the operations of any deed previously registered, and deducing a title from the same source as the unregistered deed; for if the registered deed be made by a person claiming under the *unregistered* deed, and the unregistered deed be invalid, it follows that the registered deed must also fail, for want of a legal foundation. However adverse may be the effect of the subsequent deed so previously registered, although subsequently dated; inasmuch as the original deed was inoperative until registration, the party had no legal power (until registration) to give effect to the uses of such subsequent deed.

The author has naturally felt great 'anxiety upon this subject: he could not be insensible to its importance. His opinions have been fortified by several to whose judgment he is always happy to defer; still the subject is presented to his legal readers in great humility. One good effect must necessarily result, namely, a due consideration by all parties interested in the subject, either professionally or otherwise, of the propriety, and indeed absolute duty, of an immediate registration of all deeds affecting adventure lands; and probably, circumstances may arise to induce the corporation to apply to the legislature.

Another question has been mooted under the words of the clause directing the registration of deeds, namely, whether the books of entries are evidence, in the event of a deed being lost. Upon this point the better opinion appears to be, that if the deed be lost, the book of entries, which is of itself evidence of the registry, would also be evidence of the deed itself and its contents. *The following standing orders or byelaies, now in full operation and effect, have been made, at various periods, by the board, to induce, a currect registration of deeds.* 1st. The register laid before the board the returns of the conveyances registered, by which it appears, that a considerable proportion do not contain the lot or number of the land conveyed, and that many of them do not state whether the land described is adventurers' land or not; and the want of such particulars appearing to this meeting to be one of the causes of the defects in the names of the owners in the taxbook; Ordered, —that no conveyance be registered without an order from the board, if executed after the 29th day of September next, unless the land conveyed is described as adventurers' land, nor unless it contains the quantity, or reputed quantity of the land conveyed, and the lot and number in the lotbook of the corporation. Whitsun meeting, 1816. amounting to eleven or twelve in number, except one, being brought to the office; resolved, that such members of the board as are members of parliament, do communicate with the speaker of the house of commons, whether any course can be devised by a standing order of the house, as to drainage, navigation, and inclosures, within the Level, by which bills for these purposes would require applications to the register, for the consent of the corporation, or under which, at least, notice might be given of such bill to the register. 2nd. Ordered, that no conveyance be registered, unless it specify the lot, number, and part conveyed, with such certainty as will enable the register to transfer it from the quantity owned by the grantee; and proper entries of such transfers are hereby ordered to be made by the register in the office books, called the description or title books, the quantity books, and the name books. April meeting, 1820. 3rd. Ordered, that every person succeeding to the possession of any adventurers land, as heir at law to the former owner, send to the register, signed by himself, or his attorney or agent, a certificate or letter, saying that he is in possession, as. heir at law of his father, or of A. B., his uncle, as the case may be, who died at such a time, of so many acres, roods, and perches, in Lot,, No. ——, Part,;and of so many acres, roods, and perches, in other lots, as the case may be, so described as will enable the register to make the necessary transfer to the name of such heir at law. April meeting, 1820.

4th. Ordered, that every person who becomes the owner of any adventurer's land under a will, send to the Fen Office the probate, or an attested or other copy, to the satisfaction of the register, to be entered by him in a book to be kept for that purpose, together with such a description of the land so devised, as to lot, number, part, and other particulars, as will enable the register to transfer the same to the name of such new owner. April meeting, 1820. 5th. No fees are to be paid for the entry of certificates or of wills. The fees for the registration of conveyances and wills remain as they were settled in 1751. 6th. Ordered, that for all conveyances not entered at the Fen Office within six months after the day of its date, double the present fees be received by the register; that by a speedy registration, the account of the owners of each lot and number may be more conveniently kept.

Fen office, May 15, 1817.

On the 23rd day of the same month, Lord Viscount Milton, then and still a member of the board, communicated to the board, then sitting, "that he had applied to the speaker of the house of commons, in compliance with the request contained in the resolution of the board, made at the last meeting; and that upon his lordship's motion, a standing order upon the subject had been made by the house: after which communication, it was ordered I hat the thanks of the board be given to his lordship for his attention to the interests of the corporation upon this occasion.

In consequence of this motion, the house passed the following standing order;—

"That when any application is intended to be made to the house for leave to bring in a bill, for inclosing, draining, or improving, or for altering or amending any act of parliament for inclosing, draining, or improving lands within the Great Level of the Fens, commonly called the Bedford Level, a further notice of such intended application shall be given in writing to the corporation of the Bedford Level, in the months of August or September, or either of them, immediately preceding the session of parliament in which such application is intended to be made."

The following resolutions were made at a meeting of the board, holden at the Fen Office, on the 11th day of June, 1814.

Resolved, that upon all occasions relating to Bills;n P»riithe parliamentary business of the corporation, a""'"t' when it appears to the register desirable to consult a committee of the board, without calling a special meeting of that body, that any two of the members of the board who are also members of either houses of parliament, constitute such committee, whose directions on such occasions are to be followed by the register.

The board having taken into consideration the different clauses for saving the rights of the corporation in drainage and inclosure acts within the Level, and the representation made by the register upon the legal effect of each; and also having taken into consideration the provisoes and saving clauses prepared by him, and inserted hereafter; Resolved, that the same be entered amongst the proceedings of the corporation, and that the register use his endeavours that no drainage or inclosure bills within the Levels pass without their behig inserted. This time is now extended to the months of October and November in each year, for all notices.'

Resolved also, that the register, upon all occasions when it shall appear desirable, call special meetings of the hoard for the purpose of considering the hills in the house; and that once during the sessions of parliament, a meeting of the board be called and advertised, that as much as possible the parliamentary business of the corporation may be taken into consideration at a full meeting of the board; and when the parties interested in such bills may, if necessary, have an opportunity of attending.

It appearing to the board that there can be no drainage, ami scarcely an inclosure bill within the Level, where the commissioners do not take some authority over some part of the banks, rivers, and drains, vested in the corporation; these banks, rivels, and drains, are the absolute property of the corporation; and as no such bills can be obtained without an application to the other proprietors, the corporation have at least as great a right to be applied to for their consent as any individual, and to insist that without such an application to the corporation, the standing orders of parliament have not been complied with. Resolved, that applications for all such consents be sent to the register, and, if granted, that the same be under the seal of the corporation: And that all bills for which the consent of the corporation shall not be applied for, be opposed by the corporation; and that the register do take such steps, by petition or otherwise, for opposing the same, as shall appear to him necessary; and that the expenses of such applica

"Provided always, and be it farther enacted, that nothing in this act contained shall extend, or be construed to extend, to invalidate, lessen or diminish, alter or take away any of the rights, powers, and authorities vested in the said governor, bailiffs, and commonalty of the company of conservators of the Great Level of the Fens, called Bedford Level, or in the said governor, bailiffs, and conservators of the Bedford Level corporation, by virtue of an act of parliament made in the fifteenth year of the reign of King Charles the Second, intituled ' An act for settling the drainage of the Great Level of the Fens called Bedford Level,' or by any other act, statute, or charter, law of sewers, or otherwise howsoever; but that all rights, powers, and authorities, which are now vested in the said governor, bailiffs, and conservators, and in every or any of them, shall for ever hereafter remain, continue, and be, in the said go. vernor, bailiffs, and commonalty, and in the said governor, bailiffs, and conservators and every of them, as fully and amply to all intents and purposes as if this act had not been made." Proviso in Resolved, that the following proviso be inserted luclosure Acts......

in mclosure acts, after the clause givmg general powers to the inclosure commissioners:

"Provided always, and be it further enacted, that nothing herein contained shall extend, or be construed to extend, to authorize and empower the said commissioners to allot, set out, or divide, any part or parts of the banks now vested in, possessed by, belonging to, or under the care or authority of the governor, bailiff, and commonalty of the company of conservators of the Great Level of the Fens, called Bedford Level, or the governor, bailiffs, and conservators of the said corporation, or any part or parts of the front and back forelands of such banks adjoining, or lying open to the said commons and waste grounds, or any part or parts thereof, or to intermeddle with, or to make any order relating thereto; but that the said banks, with the front and back forelands thereof, shall be deemed and taken as not being any part or parts of the said commons and waste grounds, and shall remain and continue in the said governor, bailiffs, and commonalty, and in the said governor, bailiffs, and conservators, in the same manner, and subject to the same rights, as if this act had not been made.

"Resolved, that the following general saving clause in inclosurc acts be inserted in the usual place:

"Provided always, and be it further enacted, General Saving Clause in that nothing in this or the said recited act con-inclosurc Acts. tained, shall extend, or be construed to extend, to relieve, exonerate, or discharge, any part or parcel of the lands or grounds containing 95,000 acres, called Adventurers' lands, from the payment of all or any of the taxes to which the said 95,000 acres of Adventurers' lands, or any part or parcel thereof, are now subject or liable, or to which they may hereafter become subject or liable, by virtue of an act, of parliament passed in the 15th year of the reign of his majesty King Charles the Second, intituled 'An act for settling the drainage Vol. i. 2 R of the Great Level of the Fens, called Bedford Level,' or of an act passed in the 20th year of the reign of his said majesty King Charles the Second, intituled ' An act for taxing and assessing of the lands of the adventurers within the Great Level of the Fens;' but that all and every part and parcel of the said 9. J,000 acres of Adventurers' lands shall for ever hereafter remain subject and liable to all such taxes, and powers of taxing, imposing, charging, and assessing the same, and of levying and recovering of such taxes, as are now by virtue of the said two last-mentioned acts, or otherwise, vested in the governor, bailiffs, and commonalty of the company of conservators of the Great Level of the Fens, called Bedford Level, or 5u the governor, bailiffs, and conservators of the said corporation; and that nothing in this or the said recited act contained, shall extend, or to be construed to extend, to empower the saidcommissioners,or any of them, or any other person or persons whomsoever, to.. have, use, or exercise any power or authority over, or to alter, obstruct, or intermeddle with any of the sluices, tunnels, bridges, or other works, or with the rivers, sewers, drains, wear-dykes, or the banks, or the front and back forelands thereof, that now are, or hereafter shall be vested in, possessed by, belonging to, or under the care or authority of the said governor, bailiffs, and commonalty, or in the said governor, bailiffs, and conservators of the said corporation; or to invalidate, lessen, or diminish, alter, or take away, any of the rights, powers,and authorities, vested in the said governor, bailiffs, and commonalty, or in the said governor, bailiffs, and conservators, by the said last-mentioned acts of the 15th and 20th years of the reign of his said majesty King Charles the Second, or by virtue of any other act, statute, or charter, law of sewers, or otherwise howsoever; but that all rights, powers, and authorities, which are now vested in the said governor, bailiffs, and commonalty, or in the said governor, bailiffs, and conservators, or in every or any of them, shall for ever hereafter remain, continue, and be, in the said governor,bailiffs, and commonalty, and in the said governor, bailiffs, and conservators, and every of them, as fully and amply to all intents and purposes, as if this act had not been made." CHAPTER XXI.

Particulars of the 95,000 acres of Adventurers" lands.—The Cut Land Roll. —Turf Act.—The revenues of the corporation.—The annual taxes. —The or rear roll.—Particulars of the lands charged with each sort of tax.—Amount of tax in each Level.—Public houses. —Tolls.—Hermitage sluice, and Bridge toll.—Banks andjisheries. —Cottages,and regulations thereof.—The expenditure of the corporation Barrier banks.--Minor banks.— General orders for expenditure.—Extra expenditure.— The debt of the corporation.— First and second Bond act.—Payment of interest. —The Fen office. THE ADVENTURERS' LANDS.

It has been already stated, that Francis Earl of Bedford, the original undertaker of the drainage, and his participants, had 95,000 acres of land allotted to them under the provisions of the Lynn. p. 103 law, as a recompense for draining the whole Level; of these 95,000 acres, 12,000 were allotted to the king for his patronage; and his majesty afterwards granted 2000 acres, part of his proportion, to Je-No£8toApp. rome then Earl ef Portland. THE CUT LAND ROLL.

The following particulars are given, in order to make the reader better acquainted with the local situation and distribution of those lands.

. *The Adventurers' Lands in the different Levels.*

A. It. P.

In the North Level 11,627 2 0

Middle Level 46,536 2 0

South Level 36,836 0 0

"83,372 2 0 _ *The Adventurers Lands in the different Counties, and the Isle of Ely.*

A. R. P.

In Norfolk-9,888 0 0

Suffolk-'--5,350 0 0

Cambridge-7,832 0 0

Isle of Ely,-54,758 0 0

Huntingdon 13,552 0 0

Northampton-3,220 0 0.

Lincoln----400 0 0 *The Particulars of the* 12,000 *Acres allotted to the King.*

In the North Level.

A. R. P.

Number 1. Crowland--400 0 0 2. Borough Fen--2622 0 0 3. Little Borough Pea-88 0 0 4. Alderlands.--290 0 0 5. Single Sole.--4500 6. Northam and Cranmore 80 0 0 7. Furlongs--15 3 30 8. Richard Darby's-1 0 10 9. Tanholt-30 3 0 10. Oxney---26 0 0 11. Alderfen---1100 12. The Harp--420 13. Troughton's "--030 14. Butcher's--500 15. Nortbey---64 0 0 19. Whittlesey North Fen 1078 0 0 24.--Pryor's Fen 189 0 0 _ «-. "

Acres-4951 0 0 In the Middle Level.

A. R. P.

Number 15. Standground--127 0 0 16. Farcett---1102 0 0 17. Yaxley---661 0 0 18. Sawtry--218 2 0 19. Whittlesey Flag Fen 2078 0 0

Some years since, the owners and occupiers of adventurers' lands were in the constant practice of digging up land for turf, which was used or sold for fuel. In many cases, such land was rendered quite useless, and not worth the annual taxes. In some cases, there were lands that had been taken for the works of the corporation, and which had been taken out of the charge of taxation, while in other cases, the land charged with the corporation tax could not be set out or discovered. Formerly, the board from time to time, upon application of the parties, took these circumstances into consideration; and certain lands were placed upon what was then called the Cut Land Roll. A few years since, at the instance of the late very active and intelligent register (Robert Bevill, Esq.), the contents of this roll were brought under the consideration of the board, and many acres (perhaps not to the satisfaction of all parties) brought into charge. The following is the schedule of the lands in the Middle and South Levels, the taxes of which are now ordered by the board to be annually deducted.

Lot, No.
1. 23. Several of Well and Welney, A.
Part 5. In the Wash--
2. 2. Sutton, in North Fen.
Part 5. Adjoining the Twenty
Feet Drain-6. 8. Mepal Severals, A. Part 5. Formerly Whinne's and Wigmore's 9. 9. Byall Fenn, B.-15. 19. Warboy's, &c., F. 17. 22. Severals of WeU and Welney, F.
Part G. Formerly Raven's-
Sort.

TURF ACT. The Turf Act was passed 23 Geo. III. c. 25.— App. p.esz. ...,,,. 23G. 3c.25.

It was an expedient, and by no means a politic one, for enabling the corporation to lessen the enormous debt of 35,000/., which had then accumulated upon their resources within the Middle and South Levels.

The corporation are not compellable, but are App. p. 682. only enabled, to redeem the tax. The impolicy and utter inefficiency of the act, as a financial measure, was soon discovered by the board; and no taxes are now released on any pretence whatever.

The following are the particulars of the lands released under the provisions of the act.' Generally speaking, they are of a very inferior quality.

Sort. Quantity. Tax.
Lot, No. A. R. p. £. i. i. 1. 4. Westmore North, A.-3 10 0 0 0 17 6 1. 23. Do. D.-3 8 0 0 0 14 0 2. 2. Sutton, in North Fen.

Part 10. Short North Fen Drove 5 800 134 2. 15. Upwood Fen, lying next towards Ramsey-2 4620 2143 3. I. Islehatn Common, A.

Part 1. Furthest from the river 2 600 070 2. Nearest the river-3 22 0 0 1 18 6 4. 10. Grunty Fen, C.--3 10 0 0 0 17 6 5. 1. Haddenham Common, D. 5 36 0 0 550 5. 3. Sutton, South of Bedford river. Part 5. Adjoining land, called the Besons-_ 5 10 00 192 6. 1. Isleham Common, B.

Part 1. Furthest from the river 2 15 0 0 0 17 6 2. Nearest the river-3 39 00 383 7. 1. Isleham Common, C.

Part 7-Furthest from the river 2 20 0 0 134 7. 6. Methwold, &c, F.-1 900 053 8. 2. iladdenha.ni Sevcrals.

Part 8. The Nether Delphs-8 1400 354 8. 3. Sutton, South of Bedford river. Part 2. North of the Gault

Causeway--5 100 0211 10. 8. Barwell Common, A.-2 22 0 0 158 10. 19. Normoor in Chatteris, next to Honey, A. -4 16 0 0 1174 10. 20. Warboys, &c, B. -3 300 053 11. 3. Coxncsts, iu Sutton.

Pait 3. Formerly Carter's-5 03&6 026 Sort. Qu.inlity. Tax.

Lot, No. A. R. r. £.,.,1. II. 7. Coveney Scverals, D.

Part 1. Part of Hall Feu-3 14 0 0 146 11. 18. Raveky Fen--3 21 2 10 1 17 8 13. 5. Sir Robert Heath's seve ral grounds, in SoLam 2 12 0 0 0140

J3. 13. Stilton Common,-4 3000 3100 13. 1G. Upwood Fen, adjoining

Whittlesey Way 2 10 0 0 0118 14. 1. Isleham Common, D.

Part 1. Furthest from the river 2 64 3 8 3157 15. 17-Normoor in Chatteris, D.

Fart I. North of the Forty Feet 4 42 0 0 4 18 0 2. South of the Forty Feet 4 43 1 0 5 0 11 16. 12. Normoor in Chatteris, C. 4 16 0 0 1 17 4 16. 5. The remainder of Holme

Fen, from the Earl of

Portland's part-G 28 2 23 5 0 G 17- 17. Warboys, &c., 11.-3 10 0 0 0176 17. 23; Westmoor North, V.-3 10 0 0 0 17 6 19. 15. Feltwell Severals, C.

l'artS. Formerly Wace's-1 27 3 0 0 16 2£ 23. Glassmoor by the Steads 22J 500 09 5$ 27. Highway Grounds-3 200 036 28. Part of Holme Fen-6 194 1 37 34 0 8£ THE REVENUES OF THE CORPORATION. *The Annual Taxes.*

All the particulars relative to the lands allotted to the corporation and its adventurers having been noticed, it will be desirable for the reader to become acquainted with the revenues by which the works of the corporation are now maintained.

The tax is annually laid at the April meeting, by the governor, bailiffs, and conservators only,. p. 477. according to the direction of the act.

A single tax is four-pence an acre upon the lands of the worst quality, and called the first sort or degree; eight-pence an acre for the second sort; one shilling for the third sort; and so on for all the eleven sorts into which the 83,000 acres, part of the 95,000 acres, are divided. The remaining 12,000 acres were originally decreed to belong to the King. They are charged with a medium tax, which, when the 83,000 acres are taxed at a single tax, is thirteen-pence an acre . Of course, a single tax, and three-fourths of a single tax, amount to seven-pence an acre for lands of the second sort, and so on in proportion to the highest sort. And the medium tax upon the part of the 12,000 acres in those Levels, is 22/. an acre. The North Level has for many years been taxed with a single tax and onequarter of a single tax, which amounts to fivepence an acre for the first sort; ten-pence an acre for the second sort; and so on in the same proportion; and for the part of the 12,000 acres in the North Level, the medium tax, when the sorted lands pay a tax and a quarter, is 16irf. an acre.

The annual tax has varied. In 1671, the tax was laid at a tax and three fourths, having been previously only a tax and one-fourth. This increase is stated to have taken place in consequence of a debt of 10,8607. 0. 5rf., due to William, then Earl of Bedford. It was subsequently reduced to a tax and one-fourth, at which it generally continued until the year 1777, when it was raised to a tax and three-fourths, at which it has continued ever since. At that period, the corporation debt amounted to the enormous sum of 35,6007., and a considerable part of the adventurers' lands became invested (as it was termed) in the corporation, no purchasers being found for the same when forfeited for nonpayment of the taxes. The corporation let these lands by auction for arty sum they could obtain.

The annual order of the board for payment of the tax requires (for the part of the 83,000 acres of land, situate in the Middle and South Levels,) the payment of a single tax, according to the several sorts, before the end of the month of June, and of the three quarters of a single tax before the end of the month of November; and for the part of the 83,000 acres in the North Level, three quarters of a tax for the June payment, and one-half for the November payment: and for the part of the 12,000 acres, situate in the Middle and South The revenues of the North Level, as will be seen in a future part of this work, have been separated from the other two Level;. App. p. 326.

Levels, thirteen-pence three farthings an acre for the November payment; and for the part of the 12,000 acres, situate in the North Level, ninepence three farthings an acre for the June payment, and six-pence an acre for the November payment, under the penalty of three shillings and four-pence for every twenty shillings, and after that rate for every less sum that shall be in arrear and unpaid at the end of each of those months. *The Arrear Roll.*

If the tax and penalty are not paid previously to the public meeting at Ely, in the month of April, the same is placed upon what is termed the Arrear Roll, which contains the description and quantities of the land in arrear, the names of the owners, and the amount of the tax and penalty. The mode of proceeding to sale is rather curious. The register reads from the roll the full particulars of each lot, and then demands what quantity any one will take for the amount of the tax and penalty; and should any one, for instance, say he will take the tenth, the register then inquires, if any one will take less than that quantity, until he has at length obtained the amount of the tax and penalty for the smallest possible quantity.

So long since as the year 1678, this mode of proceeding was questioned, and the right of the corporation established, as will be seen from the following case: *Brown* v. *Hammond.*

"18th January, 1678.

"Tho plaintiff *set* forth, that he was seised of "300 acres of land in the Fens, which he demised "to Allison, at 50/. rent for two years, and after, "at 60/. rent. The lessee covenanted to pay all "taxes; 30/. tax was imposed, and *31.* penalty in"curred; the lessee having sufficient rent in his "hands to pay the 33/. , combined with the defen' dant, one of the conservators, to defeat him of "his inheritance, and forbore to pay the 33/. The "officers appointed to sell by the laws of the Fens, "sold 100 acres of the 300, for the 33/., to the de"fendant, a commissioner; whereas the 100 acres "were worth 400/., to be sold.

"The defendant denied combination, and plead"ed to the rest the statute of draining; and that "the sale was made according to and by virtue of "those statutes.

"The Lord Chancellor allowed the plea, for he "could not relieve contrary to an act of parlia"ins1lit: and if he should, it would destroy the "whole economy of the preservation of the Fens; "and compared it to the case of a mortgagor of "houses in London of great value, that should be "settled by the judges, according to those acts "made concerning London to be rebuilt. The "court could not examine any sale on pretence of "equity."

The quantity on the arrear roll has varied from time to time. Sometimes, upwards of 20,000 acres became forfeited for nonpayment of taxes. For several years, not one acre has been forfeited otherwise than through a mistake, and for want of money to pay the tax at the stated period. In order to relieve titles from difficulties, lands have been sometimes put up to sale, as forfeited lands, with a view of obtaining a bargain and sale under the corporate seal. Such a bargain and sale will confer an unexceptionable title. But, of course, this is a dangerous experiment, as any individual may bid, and thus deprive the owner of part of the estate.

The. Adventurer Lands, with the Particulars of the Quantity lying In the different Levels, charged at each Sort. The Particulars of the Tax, calculated when a Tax and three quarters are charged for the Middle and South Levels, and a Tax and a quarter M/km the North Level.

The single tax (including the medium tax of *3d.* per acre upon the 12,000acres originally allotted to the king.) £. . d. £. t. d.

North Level -635 7 8f

Middle Level-2771 17 H

South Level-1644 1 0 4415 1811 1,-:--r :-= ,,, 5051 6 7i

A quarter tax on the whole., 1262 16 7J

A half tax on the Middle and South Levels, being subject to a tax and a quarter only, 220" 19 5£

Total a68522 2 9 Deduct tax released under the North Level Act, 27;j

Geo. II. "-, 59 19 2

Tax released under the

Turf Act in the Middle and South Levels-93 14 9£ 153 14 oJ 734

Middle and South Level Tax, deducting tax released under the Turf Act, (page 617.) June tax-4362 7£ November tax 3271 15 8£

North Level.

£. . d. Amount of June tax, by calculation as above 440 11 3£

Amount of November tax, by calculation as above----293 14 2

Nett amount of the tax for the North Level £ 734 5

Middle and South Levels.

£. t. d. A mount of the June tax, by calculation as above-4362 7 7i Deduct for land not ascertained, (vide Cut Land Roll, p. 6J 6.)--5 15 6 *The Tax, according to the Tax Roll.*

North Level.

Nett June tax---440 12 1

Nett November tax----293 14 5 £*734* 6 7

Middle and South Levels.

Nett June tax--4356 14 10$

Nett November tax--3267 13 3£ 367624 8 U

In the tax roll many of the lots are divided into smaller quantities. In the above calculations, they are computed by the whole lots. The fractions occasion the difference.

The board, from the earliest period, have manifested great anxiety to provide proper regulations for the collection of the taxes, as will be seen from the following orders:

"Whereas it appears to this court, that divers frauds and inconveniences have happened to purchasers by the undue payment of adventure taxes at the respective days and times when they are yearly ordered and appointed to be paid: now, to the end to prevent such inconveniences and frauds for the future, this court hath thought it fit, and ordered, and doth hereby order, that the receiver to the corporation for the time being, do for the future take particular care, that he do not receive of any person or persons whatsoever, any tax or taxes due in November for a November tax, when the party or patties paying the same is or are in arrear of the preceding June tax, but that the June tax be first discharged before the November tax be received. 11th April, 1695."

"Ordered, that the receiver do not, in any case whatever, take any tax without the penalty, after the day the same is incurred, nor lay down money for any person, without an express desire in writing for so doing. April meeting, 1755."

App.p.692. The lot book of the corporation, which ought to contain the names of all the several owners of tax each owner with the quantity he actually possesses by the acre, according to the number of acres in the whole lot, although it falls short of statute measure."

«

"Resolved also, that when it is clearly made out, that a whole lot, upon being divided, falls short of statute measure; and that the first or any subsequent owner, has sold off part as statute measure, or by any other description, whereby any owner gets the whole, or an undue portion of the fall short charged to him; that in such cases, the difference of such measure be divided to each of the owners of the lot, in proportion to the laud possessed by each."

"Ordered, that the receiver make out separate receipts for each owner, according to the tax roll, in the names and quantities, and no others, whoever may pay the tax."

"When an owner conveys part of his land, and the purchaser neglects to register his conveyance, the receiver cannot divide the tax charged in the tax roll; he is therefore required to receive the whole amount or none of it: and as this is occasioned by the default of the purchaser, ordered, that if such owner tender to the receiver the amount of the tax and penalties for his part of the land, what is to be sold for the taxes in arrear and penalties, is hereby directed to be taken out of the land of such new purchaser; and if the amount of the tax and penal ties exceed the probable produce of his land, the board, before such sale takes place, will make such orders, as will be a protection against the consequence of the neglect of such new purchaser."

It may be observed in conclusion, that by a App. p. 678. specific clause in the bond act (29 Geo. II), the corporation are empowered to tax the 83,000 acres with such tax as they may judge necessary; but wJien we consider the high state of perfection which almost all the great works of the corporation have recently attained, reasonable hopes may be indulged, that if the seasons continue propitious,, the owners of adventurers' land may look forward with confidence to the discharge of their debt, and even the reduction of the present taxation, at no immeasurable distance of time.
prevent such a course, by public auction.

Public Houses.
1 Fish. 2 Anchor 3 Three Pickerills. 4 Three Horse-shoes 5 Crown 6 Crown 7 Dog and Duck. 8 Hardwicke Arms 9 Fish. 10 Three Fishes 11 Three Fishes 12 Three Tuns 13 Green Man 14 Chequer 15 Ship. 16 Plough 17 Plough & Fleece 18 Ship 19 Black Pots 20 Chequers. they are let every six years Annual
Where situate. Rent.
Sutton Chain.
Sutton Gault.
Mepal Bridge.
Oxlode.
Do...
　Welney.
Hilgay.
Hermitage.
Sutton Gault.
Welche's Dam.
Do...
　Welney..
Do...
　Purl's Bridge.
Do...
near Littleport Bridge 43
Southery...14
Denver Sluice.. 150
Horseway.. 15
Boot's Bridge.. 5
　£696
Tolls upon banks and bridges.
Tolls.
The traffic along the several banks, and over the several bridges, is now very considerable; and, with a view as well to make some compensation to the corporation for the injury received thereby, as also to preserve their exclusive ownership to such banks and bridges, tolls are taken in different parts of those banks and bridges. The tolls are let triennially, at the April meeting; and the annual income at the last letting, in April, 1825, amounted to 98/.

Since that letting, an almost entirely new source of revenue has accrued to the corporation, in consequence of the erection of the new sluice and cast-iron bridge over the Ouze, at the Hermitage; and by the scouring out the old branch of the river (called the West River) leading from Earith to Ely. The tolls of the sluice, and of the bridge over the same, were let, until April, 1828, at the annual sum of 210/., but the present rent is now 160/. An excellent and recently completed road to Cambridge, through Willingham, forms the pleasantest as well as the nearest communication between the Fens and the town of Cambridge. This communication has also been greatly facilitated, by the readiness of the parishioners of Willingham to forward the interests of the corporation; in return for which attention, they are permitted, during the pleasure of the corporation, to pass toll-free across the Hermitage Bridge, upon the payment of five shillings annually. The corporation and their officers have a right to pass toll-free through their common gate.

Banks and Fisheries. and The banks and fisheries of the several rivers fisheries.. belongmg to, and vested m the corporation, are also let in lots triennially, at the April meeting. It does not appear material to particularize this property. The present annual income amounts to *981. 7s.* for the banks; and 71/. 5. for the fisheries. *Cottages.*

In limes of flood and pressure of water against the banks, the corporation found it extremely convenient to have labourers, accustomed to the peculiar kind of work necessary to counteract any danger to the country, resident upon and near the banks; and as, in many places, space existed between the foot of the bank and the adjoining lands, and as the board has hitherto given encouragement to poor persons to erect cottages, they are now very numerous; but recently, the board has not granted leave to erect cottages, as a matter of course. This permission operates also as an inducement to poor labourers to lay by some part of their hard earnings, in the hope of being able to erect a cottage, under the sanction and protection of the corporation. Persons thus desirous of building, apply for land by petition, at the April meeting, and an order is made for the register to make out a lease accordingly. The board always pays particular attention to all who make application respectmg property of this nature; and frequently, in the case of death or marriage, acts as a court of equity. The cottages are under the charge of the several superintendents; and the annual income, from this source of revenue, amounts to 111/. 17. 6d.

Besides these revenues, there are several sums paid to the corporation for acknowledgments of encroachment upon their property, as well as for the grant of improvable leases, the amount of which, although trifling in appearance, may yet be of essential importance to the corporation at some future period. At the present time, they amount to the sum of 50/ 13.v. 5d.

It may not be amiss to add a summary of the ordinary annual income, under the varied heads already stated: — £.,. d.

The Tax 7624 8 1
Penalties 104 15 8
Public Houses.... 696 0 0
Tolls (including the Hermitage) 318 0 0
Banks and Fisheries.. 1059 12 0
Acknowledgments, &c... 50 13 5
Cottages..... 111 17 6
Annual payment from the River i j
Nene Commissioners, towards the repair of Standground, Salter's Lode, and Old Bedford Sluices.... *45 0 0*
Total average revenue of the corporation.... £ 10,010 6 8f

The EXPENDITURE OF THE CORPORATION.

Having stated the annual income and general turc. resources of the corporation, we may now turn our attention to the mode in which that income and those resources are applied, under the direction of the board, for the general benefit and improvement of the country. It must be obvious, from the peculiar nature of the works of drainage, and the great extent of the barrier banks, as well as the long course of rivers throughout the Level, that the amount of the annual expenditure must be very unequal; although (highly to the honor of the board) the greater part of the barrier banks are in a most excellent state, and nearly all the works of drainage greatly improved. It is indeed impossible to foresee consequences that may arise from adverse seasons; but it would be hard, (after the immense expense recently incurred, by making the Eau Brink Cut, and works incident thereto,) if the flood waters should rise as high, and continue as long as heretofore. Still however, hazard is inseparable from the nature of fen-property; and it will ever be politic in the corporation to look forward to, and provide for, events which may be productive of the most fatal calamities, should they unhappily occur when the corporation are unprepared.

At the annual April meeting, the board takes into consideration the state of the finances, and of the ways and means for the ensuing year. No money is voted for works, requiring any material expense, except at this meeting. *Minor Banks.*

The ordinary ways and means of the corporation, according to an estimate made upon the expenditure of the years 1807, 1808, 1809, 1810, and 1811, enabled the board at that time to allot for the Barrier Banks the annual sum of 2551/. 1.; and for the Minor Banks, including the Tongs, 787/. 6. *9tl.* These sums are made the basis of the scale by which the amount of the allotments is now fixed; and whatever increase or decrease may take place, it has been resolvetl by the board, that such increase or decrease shall be made to all the banks in equal proportion (that is to say); adding or deducting to or from each allotment, one-fourth, one-fifth, or other proportion, according to the sum which the board may annually be able to allow for the banks.

Banks of the Cam.
Per Mile.
Miles. £. i. d.
Swaffham&Bottisham District 4 at 2 10 0
Waterbeach Level----4-2 10 0 2-10 0 0

In consequence of the very heavy expense incurred in widening and deepening the One Hundred Feet River, the forming and making the Cradge bank on the wash side of the One Hundred Feet River, and the erection of new sluices at the Hermitage, Salter's Lode, Old Bedford, and Well mo re Lake, the board, at the April meeting, A. D. 1828, reduced the annual allotments oneseventh for all the banks. The whole of the works This term is well known in the Fens; it is a corruption from the word " Ridge," and means raising a small bank on the top of the old bank, to prevent the flood waters over-running into the adjoining lands.
in the One Hundred Feet River and washes being now completed, and the other general works of the corporation in good repair, the haling also entirely diverted from the great south bank of the One Hundred Feet River, to the Cradge bank, a still App. P.795. greater reduction took place at the last April meeting, (A. D. 1829). The annual allotments now stand as follow: *Barrier Banks.*

From Swavesey to Mepal

Mepal to Denver Sluice
Earith to Wetche's Dam
Welche's Dam to Denver Sluice 429
Standground Bank
Whittlesey Field to Guyhim
A 0 1 17
14
13 *Minor Banks.* Banks of the Cam.
From Swaffham to Bottisham-
Waterbeach Level
Banks of the Ouze.
Middle Fen district
Burnt Fen district
Feltvvell district
Hilgay West Fen-
v
Littleport district
Banks of the Tong's Drain
Total Minor Banks, &c.
Total Barrier Banks
8 8 7 10

The application of the money yearly allotted for the repairs and maintenance of the banks of the corporation, is left to the several superintendents, to be expended according to the annual report made by them, in their respective divisions, subject to such orders as may be made by the board; care being taken every year, that all inequalities in the height of the banks are made up, by preserving a level top, in order that the expenses of cradging in times of flood may be saved. Extra expen-The corporation have lately incurred a considerable expense beyond their annual outlay, in borrowing money, in consequence of unfortunate disputes with contractors, and parliamentary proceedings; but it is hoped those extra demands will not again occur, at least, for some time.

The remaining charges on the funds of the corporation consist in the payment of the annual salaries to the officers, repairs of public houses and sluices, and sums allowed to the register and officers for traveling, interest upon the debt, expenses of the Fen office, and of the meetings of the board.

The following is a general statement of the expenditure of the corporation for the year 1829: INTEREST paid on Bonds— £ s. d.
On 18.100/. one year, at *M.* per cent.

724 0 0
On 5,000/. ditto, at 5/. per cent.-250 0 0 SALARIES paid.—One year-
Mr. Wells, Register---200 0 0
Same, proportion of gratuity from April 1828, to February 1829, at 70/. per annum, by order of the Board-54 3 7
Mr. Girdleslone, Auditor--100 0 0
Mr. Evans, Receiver arid Expenditor General 120 0 0
Mr. Marshall, Serjeant at Mace-10 10 0
Mr. Dyson, Engineer-250 0 0
Mr. Hills, Collector of Cottage Rents 12 0 0
Mr. John Little, Superintendent-65 0 0
Mr. Owen, ditto---40 0 0
Mr. Sedgeley, ditto-50 0 0
Mr. Joseph Little, ditto---100 0 0
Mr. Stevens, Sluice-keeper--45 0 0
Mr. Pinnock, ditto---40 0 0
Mr. Bowker, ditto---20 0 0
Mr. Baker, ditto-500
Mr. Owen, ditto-500
Mr. Lepla, ditto----220 ANNUITIES, Taxes, and other Annual
Payments:—
Elizabeth Ayres, one year's annuity-30 0 0
Ann Young ditto--15 0 0
Ellen Hartley ditto--15 0 0
Lucy Carter ditto--10 0 0 VOL. I. 2 T
John Bond, yearly allowance for ser-£ . d. vices 20 0 0 Wisbech and Chatteris Turnpike
Trustees, yearly payment--30 0 0
Eau Brink Drainage Tax, one year-24 5 0
Middle Level River Tax, ditto-11 8 6
South Level River Tax, two years-2 5 10
Willingham Tithe for Holts, one year 1 0 0
Kent of Cottage for William Foreman, two years-----600 FEN OFFICE Charges:—(these of course vary every year).
General Disbursements for Fen Office,viz.—
Rent 91 15 0
Assessed Taxes,Tithes, and Insurance 32 16 3
Water Rates, Celler Rent, and Lamp trimming-.----7170
Commons---- 7 18 0
Books, Stationery, and Printing-51 7 1
Allowance for Servant---47 0 0
Coals and Candles---10 10 0
Postage, carriage, and porterage-35 10 8.
Miscellaneous disbursements--6 17 6
Register's bill for traveling expenses 111 2 0
Ditto for law charges---37 5 4,
WORKS.—Expenditure for Works as under:
CradgeBank, Messrs.Martin and Co. as by contract----3,846 5 4
Ditto, Bills and day labour-497 18 3
Ditto, Superintendent and assistants-_ 56 14 0
Old Bedford Sluice—Bills and day labour-. 1,328 10 8
Denver Sluice.—Bills--81 13 7
Public Houses.—Bills for building and £ *s. d* repairing-----277 8 8
Miscellaneous Works—Bills--226 0 85 MIDDLE LEVEL, NORTH DIVISION. *Allotments.*
Expenditure by Mr. John Little, the superintendent, in the under-mentioned works:—
The Barrier Bank----290 14 1£
The Tongs Bank----113 2 4
Sluices, Tunnels, and Bridges--23 4 11
Roding Rivers-... 14 19 0
Ouze Shores-... 1 16 0
Miscellanies-----1793
£461 3 8 MIDDLE LEVEL, SOUTH DIVISION.
Expenditure by Mr. Owen, the superintendent, in the under-mentioned works:----r.-The Barrier Bank----229 4 10 Sluices, Tunnels, and Bridges-16 7 4
Miscellanies----16 1G 11
£262 9 1 MIDDLE LEVEL, EAST DIVISION.. Expenditure by Mr. Joseph Sedgeley, the superintendent, in the undermentioned works:—
The Barrier Bank--559 15 94
Sluices, Tunnels, and Bridges-18 5 11
Roding Rivers----14 12 8
Miscellanies-520 597 16 4
————».—-——TM»— SOUTH LEVEL.
Expenditure by Mr. Joseph Little, the

superintendent:.,v. /.
The Barrier Bank, Upper Division-176 15 9
Ditto Lower Division-1,475 0 9
Cradge Bank-52 4 2
Sluices, Tunnels, and Bridges-56 17 1
Roding Rivers----66 15 8
Planting Holts-32 5 6
Miscellanies----136 19 Oh
1,996 17 MINOR ALLOTMENTS:—
 Swaffham and Bottisham District- 000
  Waterbeach Level---51 8 6
  Littleport and Downham District-170 1 5
  Middle Fen District---0 0 O
  Burnt Fen District---124 9 8
  Felwell District-80 3 2
  Hilgay West Fen----17 2 10
  River Wissey.... 000 MISCELLANEOUS DISBURSEM ENTS:
 Mr. Baker, for surveys and plans- 113410
Board and Committee meetings— expenses 235 1 10
 Bills for advertising, printing, and stationery
  Attendants, messengers, &c.-
Auditor, for disbursements by him-
Expenditor-General, for ditto by him
Bankers for interest, postages, &c.-
Small bills and disbursements
OUTSTANDING BONDS. £ s. rf.
 Bonds at 4l. per cent, interest-- 18,100 0 0
 Ditto at 5l. per cent, interest-. 6,000 0 0
 Total amount of Bond debt-£23,100 0 0 FOR THE NORTH LEVEL. ARREARS of Rents remaining unpaid 5 10 0
INTEREST paid—one year on 8,300/. at 5l. per cent.-... 415 Q 0 SALARIES paid—one year:.
 Mr. John Burdock, superintendent-70 0 0
 Mr. John Williams, ditto--20 0 0 WORKS.—Expenditure for works aa under:—
Mr. John Burdock, superintendent, balance of last year due to him-6 19 3
 ---expenditure by him on the Moreton's Leam, North 146 5 11 153 5 2
 Mr. John Williams, the superintendent, expenditure by him on the Welland Bank----128 16 3

THE DEBT.

From the nature of the works of draining, the The debt, annual sum necessary for their ordinary support (after they are completed) may be nearly calculated; but no calculation can be made, with any degree of certainty, of the expenses that may arise from the extraordinary accidents to which those works are liable. The enemies to contend with, are the elements of wind and water. When the rivers glide gently in their course, wafted by kind and favorable breezes to their outfalls at sea, the corporation may look on with pleasure and security; yet they cannot always indulge in this gratifying prospect. Floods and tempests arise: the strongest banks areleveled: and in a moment,asitwere,whole districts are laid waste, and not a vestige remains of the industry of man, or of the improvements effected within the country from generation to generation. The melancholy catastrophes to which all artificially drained countries are liable, make it impossible to compute, with certainty, the disbursements that may be required; and therefove, whenever the fund for these expenses is stated and fixed, it must happen, that the repairs rendered unavoidable by accidents will require sums of money, which the ordinary course of the revenue will not supply. To this must be added, that, as the art of draining derives great assistance from experience, new and expensive works, in the course of time, are deemed necessary, and consequently render the general expenditure more uncertain. Neither the Lynn law, the pretended act, nor the general act of the 15 Car. II. , enables the corporation to anticipate their resources by borrowing money upon credit of their taxes and other revenues. Considerable sums, however, were borrowed from time to time, but chiefly for specific works, in different parts of the Level, and from individuals more or less interested in those works. The Russell family were ever ready to aid the necessities of the corporation; and there can be no doubt of their having greatly impaired their paternal inheritance, by the frequent advances that wej'e made from the period of passing the Lynn law in 1631, to the enactment of the general drainage act at the restoration, and indeed long afterwards.

Soon after the act of the 15 Car. II. was passed, the corporation having by that act a common seal, made use of that seal for borrowing money, either for repairing of breaches in their banks, or for such new works as the judgment of the corporation, or the select body thought necessary. They gave bonds to the creditors, and paid the interest out of their annual taxes. Those bonds were paid off, when required, by new loans from new creditors, to whom fresh bonds were made, and the old ones cancelled. The provisions of the act of 15 Car. II., it is true, authorize the corporation to im-App. 1)t424, pose an acre tJix upon the whole of the adventur- 4a5' ers' lands; but as the legal estate in the lands on which the taxes were to be laid for the maintenance and support of the Level, were, by such conveyances as the act of parliament directs, vested in the respective members of the corporation, to whom they were conveyed in their natural capacity; considerable doubts arose, whether the several creditors could obtain any satisfaction for their debts at law, beyond the goods or lands of which the corporation were actually seised; although the question, considered on principles of equity, appears more favorable on behalf of the creditors.

The money borrowed by the corporation under their common seal, had been applied to the support and preservation of the Level; and the proprietors of the 95,000 acres had their ordinary taxes raised to that amount, instead of having a distinct tax imposed on them for liquidating that debt; for, doubtless, the creditors might have applied to the court of chancery to oblige the corporation to execute the powers they had by that act of taxing the 95,000 acres by laying a tax thereon for the payment of the full amount of such debts, so borrowed and applied. Thus, even in the infancy of this corporation, no provisions being made, their credit became somewhat problematical, and serious consequences might have ensued from this defect; but they were indebted to some, well attached to the undertaking, for such sums as were wanted. In process of time, those who remembered, and had been personally interested in the original undertaking, being dead, and that credit which was founded on their partiality being also at an end, the corporation were forced, as it were, to go into the world with their credit. Great sums were at different times paid for procuring money, and heavy expenses were incurred by the constant exchange of securities, occasioned by the want of such a credit as was assignable at market. On a review of the necessities of the corporation, and the nature of their credit, one cannot help wondering how that credit has been supported, under the many trials it has undergone. It could only have been sustained by the influence of the illustrious personages, who were governors, and members of the select body, and also of the corporation. The house of Russell particularly, was at all times most ready, when called upon, with such sums as were necessary for the pressing exigencies and demands of the corporation. Large sums have been advanced by that family, the times and manner of payment of which were so arranged, as best to suit the finances and convenience of the corporation . Instances of the protection of these noble benefactors occur frequently in the journals of the proceedings; and Wriothesley 3rd Duke and 7th Earl of Bedford, remitted by his last will (as a noble mark of his affection for the Great Level) a large debt due to his Grace from the Middle and South Levels. He died in the year 1732, at an early age, having been only four years governor of the corporation; but by this instance of his bounty, he displayed a benevolent regard for the country, and a strong desire to imitate the example of those illustrious ancestors from whom he was descended.

Such at that time was the general state and nature of the corporation credit. By the act passed 29 Geo. II, the revenues of the North Level were App. p. 526. separated from those of the other two Levels. The proportioned share of the general debt of the corporation, which the proprietors of that Level By an order of the board, made A. D. 1734, the bonds of the corporation were assimilated to those of the East India Company.

ought to sustain, is settled, and a fund created for the payment of it, and the proprietors of that Level stand totally discharged from the remainder of the debt then owing, or which should afterwards be contracted, on account of the other two Levels » which are in like manner, discharged from the past and future debt of the North Level.

In the year 1755, the debt of the corporation, amounting to 27,44Q/., the revenues of the corporation, and the state of their finances, underwent a thorough investigation, as well as a review in parliament; and although the security of the original creditor had been narrowed with his own consent, by passing the North Level act, the corporation thought it highly proper, that all former doubts concerning their credit should be removed, and their debt receive a parliamentary sanction, and have the advantage, in common with 'other public bodies, of being assignable. On these principles of tenderness to the creditors, and good policy to the constitution of the corporation, a bill was brought into parliament, and passed in First BondAct, the 29th. Geo. II, called " the First Bond Act", by 29Geo.2,c.9. 'J

App.p.632. which it is enacted, that during such time as any

App.p. ess-, (jgbj. or sum of money should be due and owing from the corporation, all the lands should be taxed with a single tax; and the corporation was also empowered to lay a further tax if necessary; thus amply providing a fund, for the due discharge of all its engagements. By this salutary act, a guard is placed against the corporation ever extending its credit, beyond the proper limits of the fund available to answer it.

The debt of the corporation, for the services of the Middle and South Levels, cannot exceed 32,000/.; notwithstanding the annual amount of the tax is upwards of 7000/. The debt for the North Level cannot exceed 5000/.; while the amount of the annual income,applicable to the discharge, is upwards of 600/.

The amount of the debt, since the passing of the first bond act, has of course, greatly fluctuated; but owing to repeated breaches in the great banks, and the tax roll containing many thousand acres of land in arrear, the debts had arrived at a sum beyond that which the corporation were enabled legally to borrow under the first bond act. At this period, the state of the funds of the corporation was truly deplorable; and it was found absolutely necessary to apply to parliament to enable them to surmount the difficulties by which they were environed.

In the year 1772. the act called "the Second The second Bond Act,

Bond Act" was passed. By the provisions of that 2 o«o. 3, c. 9.

r App. p. 669. act, the corporation are enabled to borrow further sums, upon security of the taxes of the Middle and South Levels; so as, by such further borrowing, the debt (including the then existing bond debt of 30,700Z.) do not exceed the sum of 44,000/. This additional sum could only be borrowed in case of the actual breach of the great banks, to which purpose only it is to be specifically applied. Provision was made, for its annual discharge; so that, except in case of actual breach in the great barrier banks, this act is perfectly inopcrative; and most sincerely it is hoped, the painful necessity of resorting to its enactments will never recur; should it however unhappily occur, these provisions may be called into effect.

In the year 1825, the debt of the corporation, as far as regarded the Middle and South Levels, was reduced to the sum of 3000/.

The board had resolutely adopted the plan of reducing the debt, in contemplation of being called upon by the country to carry into effect very extensive, as well as very expensive, measures in the One Hundred Feet, or New Bedford River, occasioned by the opening of the Eau Brink Cut; App.p. 772. the corporation being under an engagement by the original act, passed in 1795, to scour out, widen, and deepen that river.

Perhaps the importance of this great work had prevented a due consideration of the state of the sluices throughout the Level. Be this as it may, the corporation were compelled to rebuild nearly the whole of the sluices, and also to carry ou works to a great extent in the One Hundred Feet River. To meet the required disbursements, the corporation were compelled to create a new debt, which at this period amounts to 23,400/.; but considering the improved state of all the great banks, the entire re-erection of the sluices at Saiter's Lode, Old Bedford, Wellmore Lake, the Hermitage, and Standground, the relief occasioned by widening and deepening the One Hundred Feet River, and forming the Cradge Bank on its Wash side thereof, and the ample resources of the corporation, the country may, it is hoped, should no untoward events occur, confidently look forward to its reduction, at no distant period.

Nothing can exceed the regularity with which the interest of the debt is paid to the creditors. It has already been stated, under the head of the duties of the office of " Receiver and Expenditor General," that that officer universally, before the 5th daya of January and July, transmits to the Fen Office the warrants for the half year's interest, directed to the corporation cashier or banker (Messrs. Child and Co., Temple Bar). The creditors call at the Fen Office for these warrants; the register delivers them to the person for whose use they are drawn; and Messrs. Child and Co. pay the interest on sight of the warrant.

In taking means to pay off the debt incurred up to the year 1824, the board resorted to the expedient of a sinking fund: this mode of operation is somewhat complicated, and in a great degree connects the corporation with the fluctuating state of the government funds and securities. When next the board are enabled to take measures for the liquidation of the debt, the propriety of continuing this mode will be seriously considered, and possibly some other more eligible plan adopted.

It should be stated, that the corporation can only borrow sums not exceeding 100/. each, to be secured by their bonds, which are duly numbered and entered in books kept at the Fen office; and when any creditor requires payment of any one or more of his bonds, he gives six months' notice in writing to the register at the Fen office, who lays the same before the board; and directions are given to the receiver and expenditor-general to discharge the same at the expiration of the notice.

The bonds of the corporation are assignable; but all such assignments must from time to time be entered into the bond-book kept at the Fen office, for which a fee of *12s. 6d.* is payable to the register. The bonds were originally assignable by indorsement, without stamps, in the nature of an exchequer bill.

It is impossible to imagine a more desirable in-vestment for money, than placing it out upon the bonds of the corporation; the smallness of the amountof the bonds(100/. each) makes themalmosl negotiable for the purposes of private life; the regularity of the payment of the interest half yearly, renders them equal in convenience to the public funds; while their *real* value is not bottomed in delusion, but rests on the solid foundation of a landed revenue, equal to the full discharge of the debt in less than four years, even should the corporation be under the necessity (which is now most improbable) of borrowing to the extent allowed by parliament. Hence it is, that the corporation seldom find any difficulty in raising money. It is well therefore, that they are prevented from borrowing beyond a certain amount, lest the facility of procuring loans should induce them to disregard a system of economy, honorable alike to the board, and advantageous to the country.

THE FEN OFFICE.

It may perhaps be interesting to some persons TUeFcnOfficc. to be acquainted with the history of the place in which the records of the corporation are deposited, and in which are kept the books of registration of all transfers of adventurers' lands.

There are no documents to prove where the adventurers met to carry into effect the original undertaking under the Lynn law. These records were probably destroyed in the great fire of London, which happened in the year 1666.

On the day following the passing of the Pretended Act, nine of the adventurers met at Lord Whitelock's house (then one of the keepers of the great seal of England), near Temple Bar, and agreed to pay, and did then contribute, forty shillings a piece for discharging the clerks' fees of the parliament, for passing and engrossing the act. The adventurers then appointed every Monday, Wednesday, and Friday in the week, and the same place, for their future meetings; from which circumstance it is presumed arose the practice of having the Fen Office open to the public only upon those days, between the hours of ten and two; although for the general accommodation of the publie, the registers have not been very strict in the observance of this ancient custom.

From this period to the year 1657, the adventurers appear generally to have held their meetings either at the chambers of Oliver Saint John (then Lord Chief Justice of the Common Pleas), in Lincoln's Inn, or at the house of Mr. Henley, near Temple Bar, who had been appointed treasurer to the company.

In the year 1657, Lord Gorges (the then surveyor general) was desired to provide chambers in the Temple, or elsewhere, at the company's charge, and to fit and prepare the same for their public meetings; and thence,until the restoration in 1660, the adventurers seem to have assembled in the chambers in the Temple; except when they sat as commissioners of sewers, or proceeded to the sale of lands forfeited for non-payment of taxes, in which cases they uniformly met at Ely. Some of the prebendaries of the cathedral church (particularly Doctors Moyle and Beaumont) from time to time complimented the board with the use of their respective houses in the college, " for their better accommodation."

After the enactment of the statute 15 Car. II., the adventurers continued to hold their London meetings at the Fen Office, until the year 1665, when it appears from an entry in the order books, that the corporation adjourned to meet the first Thursday in the then following Term, at the Fen office; but no meeting was held, " in regard of the plague which raged in London;" they, therefore, again adjourned to meet at Oxford; and a court of the corporation was held on the 2'2d November, 1665, in the Philosophy Schools of the University of Oxford. A second meeting was also held in the same month, and at the same place, when they adjourned to meet at the Fen Office, on the first Thursday in the then following term; but there is an entry that such meeting was not held, " in regard of the continuance of the plague in London." The next meeting took place at the Fen Office, on the 13th February, 1666.

In addition to these inconveniences, the corporation were fated to sustain a most serious calamity; for on the 2d September, 1666, occurred the great fire in London; by which, not only were the Fen Office chambers destroyed, but it is also supposed that most of the original documents, relating to the proceedings of the adventurers under the Lynn law and the pretended act, and, probably, many other papers which would have thrown considerable light upon the earliest history of the Fens, perished in the conflagration. Lord Gorges (then surveyor. general) appears, by an order made at the first meeting of the corporation, to have removed some of the "evidences and accompts;" but these, it is presumed, were only the book of entry of proceedings; for, with the exception of a box, containing some public papers relative to the Lynn law, no document of importance, connected with the concerns of the company previous to the proceedings under the pretended act, is now discoverable in the Fen Office.

The following entry relative to the great fire is found in the order book of the corporation:

"Mr. Hampson's chambers, where the Fenn Vol. i. 2 u office was kept, being burnt in the most dreadful fire, which began in Pudding-lane, on the east side » of New Fish-street, upon Sunday morning, about two o'clock, being the C2d of September, 1666, and consumed all the buildings from thence into the Temple church, and Inner Temple hall, and the greatest part of the city of London, the corporation was at a straite for a place to meet at, and made choice of Mr. Moyle's chambers, in the Inner Temple lane, London."

In the year 1667, the chambers, situate on the ground floor of No. 3, Tanfield Court, Inner Temple, were purchased of Mr. Hampson, who had erected them upon the site of the old chambers; and from their adjoining the Temple-hall, it would appear, that the great fire terminated in one point at this place, and in another, at the Temple church opposite. They were held under the society of the Inner Temple, for one life, heretofore renewable upon payment of a fine, the amount of which on the last renewal (the death of Mr. Justice Le Blanc, when Charles, the son of the late register, Robert Bevill, Esq., was nominated,) was 1000/. The society afterwards came to a resolution not to renew any of their chambers, but to let them to tenants at will. The annual outgoings of the chambers (including insurance of Mr. Bevill's life) for taxes, commons, water, and cellar rent, laundress, &c., amounted to about *35l.*

The Fen Office has, however, been lately removed to No. 6, Serjeants' Inn, Fleet-street. This circumstance was occasioned by the dilapidated state of the building in which the business was previously transacted, and the demolition by the society of the Inner Temple of the range of chambers of which the Fen Office formed part. A most beautiful building has since been erected updn the terrace fronting the garden and the river.

The corporation received the sum of 1600/. for their interest in the chambers The sum of 1S0/, was paid for the unexpired term of nineteen years (from lady day last) in the lease of the present Fen Ofiice,subject to the annual rent of 90/., and other small outgoings.

The Fen Office is the most ancient register office in the kingdom. The object of it originally was to furnish information to the board and the corporation, who were the proprietors of the adventurers' lands, liable to the payment of the corporation tax. But it was soon discovered, that it answered all the other purposes for which registry offices have been established in Middlesex and Yorkshire. The public are therefore enabled by inspection (at the times already noticed) of the register's books at the Fen Office, to ascertain the existence of any statement or encumbrance affecting any of the adventurers'lands proposed to be sold, settled, or encumbered.

It may be proper to state, that schedules of all books, papers, and muniments of title whatever, relating to the corporation, are carefully preserved in the Fen Office, and are from time to time, when considered necessary, examined by a committee of the board. Upon the election of a new register, this duty is never omitted.

CHAPTER XXII. *Division of the Three Levels.—The North Level: its several ancient and modern works of drainage, and internal economy.—Thorney Church, and Crowland Abbey. —Private Acts.—Kinderley's Cut.—Tidd and Newton Act.—Nene Bridge and Outfall. —Lord William Bentincke.—The intended improvement in the North Level drainage.*

It has already been stated that so long since as the year 1697-8, the corporation came to the resolution of partitioning the whole Level into three divisions, to be thereafter distinguished by the names of the North Level, the Middle Level, and the South Level. This plan was no doubt well intended by those who suggested it, but its policy is extremely questionable. Nature had so intermingled the respective interests of the Levels by their connecting links, the natural rivers, as to render their independence on each other impracticable. Art added greatly to this physical impossibility. For instance, the security of the south bank of Moreton's Leam will always be more or less affected by the state of the water in the Whittlesey Wash, and of the outfall below Wisbech. The North Bank is affected in the same way. A like remark may be made as to the relative positions of the Old Bedford and the One Hundred Feet barrier banks. To these local causes may be added, that as in larger communities, names often give birth to parties, so in this lesser range, somewhat similar consequences ensued. When that which had hitherto been called the Bedford Level,—a name comprehending the whole country,—was cantoned into the three districts, with distinct boundaries and appellations, ideas of separate interests were engendered, and the proprietors of lands in each division began to consider the advancement and improvement of their own, as distinct from and unconnected with the other districts. This was a grievous mistake, and originated only in a difference of denomination; for the three levels were all children of one common parent—Drainage, and have and ought to have but one common interest. This work would scarcely be deemed complete without some practical details of the general etate of these several divisions, THE NORTH LEVEL.

This district contains all that part of the 95,000 The North acres which lies between the north side of More-vc'ton's Leam and the south side of the river Weiland.

In the year 1728, the debt of the corporation amounted, for the whole Level, to the enormous sum of 17,ISO/. Wriothesley second Dukeof Bedford was then in his minority, having for his guardian the most noble William Duke of Devonshire. At this period an agreement was entered into between the Duke of Devonshire, on the part of his ward, and Henry Earl of Lincoln, (being the principal proprietors of the lands within the North Level,) and the corporation, by which the revenues of the North Level were taken from the control of the corporation, and applied by those two noblemen to the services of that Level. Things continued in this state until the year 1753, when the first North Level act passed. It appeared from a statement of the account at that period, that the Middle and South Levels were indebted to the Duke of Bedford and Earl of Lincoln, on account of the North Level, in a sum exceeding 18,000/.—an amount, however just the demand, much beyond the ability of the corporation to discharge. John Duke of Bedford inherited the anxious and earnest wishes for the prosperity of the Fens, which had so eminently marked the characters, and guided the conduct of his illustrious ancestors. His grace perceived the fatal effects of this heavy and still increasing encumbrance, and the possibility of its bringing the utmost ruin on the other two Levels. He perfectly understood the disease, and therefore readily devised the remedy. In the. vear 1753, under the sanction and protection of

App. p, 543.

John Duke of Bedford, the corporation applied to parliament; and an act subsequently passed, entitled " the First North Level Act." The sum of 14,750/. was then due to the Duke of Bedford, and 3150/. to Henry Earl of Lincoln; both of *t* which sums were most generously remitted, and the securities cancelled. This statute contains app-P-543a very full narrative of the whole transaction. The several accounts between the Levels themselves, and between the Levels and the creditors of the corporation, are settled, and such provisions made as will entirely prevent a recurrence of any thing of the same kind, it being provided, that the lands of the North Level should be completely discharged from payment of the residue of the debt of 14.300/., owing in the year 1728, and from the debt of 13,000£, contracted since that period, as well as other debts then owing from the corporation, in respect of works of the North Level. It was also properly provided, that the North Level App. p. 547. should not be subject or liable to the payment of any debt contracted by the Middle atid South Levels; and that those Levels should not be subject to any debts contracted on account of the works of the North Level.

The owners of the required proportion of adventure lands are still qualified to become members of the select body, and to vote at elections, and upon all other occasions, except where money is to be borrowed on account of the Middle and South Levels; on which occasion they are particularly restrained from voting. The adventurers' taxes are paid to the corporation receiver, and may be expended under the sole control and order of the corporation, in manner particularly directed by the act of 1753, and by another act passed in 1771, called the " Second North Level Act;" by APP.P.644.

which latter act an additional tax was laid, and was made applicable by the corporation to certain works specified therein.

The officers of the North Level are annually appointed at the April meeting; and, in short, their separation from the other two Levels may be regarded rather as a pecuniary transaction than as an actual severance.

The North Level is divided into five districts; and power is given to raise taxes for their several internal drainages. The plan of disposing of the taxes was unfortunately practised by the corporation in this Level to a considerable extent some years since, by which means, this part of the annual income of the corporation has been greatly reduced. It is hoped that this pernicious system will not be again resorted to.

The North Level being considered by many of the proprietors of the Middle and South Levels as a kind of *terra incognita,* the author has been anxious to furnish his readers with such minute particulars as may convey a proper knowledge of that part of the Bedford Level .

The North Level and Portsand (which last district, by the act 27 Geo. II, is united with the North Level drainage,) are divided into five districts, and contain 39,622a. *r. 3Gp.* of taxable lands, viz.--: For these details the author has to thank his friend Tycho Wing, Esq., of Thorney Abbey, one of the Conservators of the Bedford Level Corporation.

t The whole of the North Level contains about 48,000 acres; of which Newborough, 5,276 acres; Flag Fen, Sutton St. Edmund's Great and Lrttlc Commons, about 2,500 acres; are exempt from the general North Level taxes. Vide 27 Geo. II. A pp. p. 526. 554.

The *First* contains 4489a. lr. 14p.; and is bounded on the west by the high lands of the Soke of Peterborough, from which it is separated by an ancient Roman drain, called the CanDyke; on the North, by the river Welland, and part of a drain called the Old South Eau; and on the east and south, by a ridge of high land, running from a place called the Black Horse, in the town of Eye, where this ridge crosses the Carr Uyke.

The *Second* district contains 3,643a. 3r. 22.; and is bounded on the north-west side by the high lands at Eye and the Carr Dyke; on the east and north, by Catswater and Thorney Dike; and on the south-west by the Counter Drain and north bank of Moreton's Leam.

The *Third*, or *Thorney Lordship*, contains 17,5880. 0r. 9p.; is bounded on the south-east by Thorney Dike; on the north-west, by the Old South Eau; on the south-west, by Catswater and the above-mentioned ridge of high land; and on the north-east, by Gold Dike.

The *Fourth* district contains 6,449a. 3r, 3p. It is separated from Thorney Lordship by Gold Dike, and from Wisbech hundred by the old South Eau. On the south-east it abuts against the Counter Drain and north bank of Moreton's Leam; and the opposite side, against part of the old South Eau.

The *Fifth* and last district is called Great Portsaud. It contains 7,451a. lr. 28p.; is bounded on the south by the Old South Eau; on the north, by Asendyke; on the west, by the river Welland; and on the east, by Sheppy Bank.

The water from the above five districts is conveyed to a place called Clow's Cross by the Old and New South Eau, and from thence by the Shire Drain, to the river Nene, below Wisbech, at Gunthorpe sluice.

The external works of drainage are under the control of the corporation: the internal works are under the management of a committee, called the North Level Committee, consisting often commissioners, elected at an annual aggregate meeting of all the commissioners for the several districts, held at the Duke's Head, in Thorney, on the first App. P. 553. Monday in July. Two at least of the members of this Committee must be chosen for each of the several districts.

By the pretended act, the Earl of Bedford, his App. p. 373. participants, and adventurers, were restrained from meddling with the waters of the river Welland, or with the works in Deeping Fen. These restrictions were not however continued by the general drainage act, passed 15 Car. II. By the latter act, the Crown reserved certain rights as to Dowsdale bank and South Eau river.

There are, within the five districts, one steam engine, and about thirty water engines.

Banks.

The north bank of Moreton's Leam, from Peterborough fen-gate to the tollbar at Guyhirn, twelve miles and a half; repaired by the honorable corporation of the Bedford Level

The Welland bank, from Peakirk bridge to Crowland, five miles; repaired by the«said corporation.

The Welland bank, from Crowland to Brother House, four miles; repaired by Thomas Orby Hunter, Esq.

The south bank of a drain leading from the south dam at Crowland to the Lot Mill, one mile and a quarter.

The north bank of Old South Eau, from the Lot Mill to Dowsdale, two miles and a half.

The south bank of the same, from the Lot Mill to Clow's Cross, nine miles.

Shire Drain banks, from Clow's Cross to Gunthorpe sluice, eleven miles.

The bank on the east side of Catswater, from Thorney Cross to Storer's Bar, and of the drain from thence to the Counter drain, two miles and three-eighths

The north bank of the Counter Drain, from Hurt's grounds to Guyhirn, ten miles and a half.

The west bank of the Old South Eau or Thirtyfoot, from Guyhirn to Clow's Cross, four miles and a half.

The banks of the new South Eau, from GoldDike to Clow's Cross, two miles and one furlong and a half.

The banks of Gold Dike, from the old South Eau to Knarr Lake, four miles and three quarters.

These are all repaired by the commissioners of the North Level, under act 27 Geo. II.

Rivers.

The New or Smith's Leam, and Hill's Cut, from the broad water, below Peterborough Bridge, to Guyhirn Bar, twelve miles and a half, cut by the adventurers.

Moreton's Leam—the channel of the river prior to the cutting Smith's Leam. It is navigable to the Ball public house, adjoining Whittlesey field; it then crosses part of the Great Wash; thence the ancient channel is quite choked: It is the property of the corporation of the Bedford Level.

Catswater and the Old South Eau, ancient branches of the Nene.

Carr Dyke-f-, a Roman work, the boundary of the Level.

Thorney River, the navigation from the Dog and Doublet to Thorney, so called.

Both these rivers are vested in the corporation of the Bedford Level, having been cut under the contracts of Francis and Willi.im, Earls of Bedford. The navigation from Peterborough to Wisbech passes through these two rivers. A tonnage-toll is taken for all boats and barges, under the authority of the Bedford Level corporation, and the amount applied in deepening and scouring those rivers, towards the repair of the N. Bank, and in making such other works as may improve the navigation. f That part of the bank of this dyke, and of the river Welland, which is called the "Folly River," is now repaired by the commissioners, under the authority of an act passed 52 Geo. Ill, c. 143, for draining and inclosing Great Borough Fen Common, now forming part of the First District, and called Newborough, containing 5,276a. 0r. 12p. *Public Roads.*

Turnpikes.—From Peterborough to Thorney, 53 Geo. III.

From Wisbech to Thorney, 50 Geo. III.

From Eye to Crowland, 57 Geo. HI.

From Thorney lo Crowland.

From Thorney to Portsand.

Private Roads.

From Thorney to Whiltlesey (toll at Thorney). From Thorney toNewborough (toll at Catswater). From the last-mentioned to Peak irk (toll at Powder Blue). From Thorney to Gedney Hill (toll at the Lordship end). From Peakirk Bridge to the Brother House on the Welland bank (toll near Crowland, and at Brother House).

Private Drainages.

Third District.—The Duke of Bedford's 17,588a.
0r. 9p. In the fourth district. — Mr. Abraham Ulyal's (Throckenholt) 2I4a. 0r. p. In the fifth district.—Thomas Orby Hunter, Esq.'s, 6688a. 3r. 24p. In ditto.—Mr. James Whitscd (formerly Butler's) 393a. I/. 9. *Public Tolls.*
At Eye, Edgerley bar, and Thorney Causeway bar, 53 Geo. III.
At Newborough bar, 57 Geo. III.
At Boarden House bar, 50 Geo. III.

Private Tolls.

At Thorney bar, Thorney Lordship-end bar, and Catswater bar, belonging to his grace the Duke of Bedford.

At Powder Blue bar, belonging to Robert Griffin.

At Storer's Bar, Mr. John Pank's.

At Peterborough fen gate; the Dog and Doublet gate; and Guyhirn gate; on the narth bank of Moreton's Leam; and a gate on the Welland bank, near Crowland; belonging to the-honorable corporation of Bedford Level.

Brother House bar, on the Welland bank, and also a gate at the same place leading into Portsand; Blake's bar, on the road through Portsand to Whaplode Drove; and Dowsdale bar, on the South Eau bank; belonging to Thomas Orby Hunter, Esq.

A tonnage duty of one shilling a ton at the Dog and Doublet sluice, belonging to his grace the Duke of Bedford.

Sluices.

The Dog and Doublet sluice ; Wardley's sluice, near ditto; the White Hart Sluice, near Thorney; This sluice, and the drain leading thence to Thorney, were erected and cut at the sole expense of William Earl of Bedford, of North Level, and trustees of Wisbecli and Thorney turnpike-road, jointly.

Bridges (Private).

One over StnithYLeam, near Peterborough fengate; Earl Fitzwilliatn. One over the Counter Drain, on the Dog and Doublet premises. One over ditto, at Barton's. One over Thorney Dike, opposite the last mentioned. One over ditto, called the Stone Bridge. One over the Old South Eau, leading into Portsand. One over ditto, at the Lordship end; Duke of Bedford.

One over the Counter Drain (W. Bridges). One ditto (J. Watson's). One ditto (J. Wylie's). One ditto (Gull Bridge). One ditto (Wright Crane's). One over Old South Eau (Cant's Bridge). One over ditto, at Murrow.

Officers.

John Burdock: John Williams, B. L. C. The former the north bank of Moreton's Leaui; salary, 70/.: the latter the Welland bank; salary,20/.

Fcraci27Geo. John lliidkin, first and fifth districts; salary 5I. t»

Thomas Burdock, second district; 10/,

John Bradshaw, third district; 10/.

Joseph Gilby, fourth district; 10/.

The duties of the above are to estimate and superintend the repairs of the banks, and scouring out the drains, in their respective districts; to see that the drains are roadcd, tracks taken up, and moles destroyed.

Hart Buck, clerk to the commissioners; salary, 5/.,
and one gninea a day for attending meetings.

Thomas Steed Watson, treasurer; salary 40/., and
Sd. per pound as collector of the taxes.

William Pear, keeper of Clow's Cross sluice; salary, 2/.

John Pear, Keeper of Gunthorpe sluice and Hill's sluice, surveyor of Shire Drain and the banks thereof; salary, 25/.

Thomas Steed Watson, treasurer and collector; £TJlcUlu " . i (jrei. 111.
salary, 70/. Hart Buck, clerk; salary, 5I.

F'r interior works of drainage.

First district; John Williams; salary, 8/. 8s. The«esre«p-

Second district; Charles Boyce; salary, 15/.

Fourth district; Joseph Gilby; salary, 15/.

The duties of the above are to superintend the roading and scouring out the mill and other drains in their respective districts, the repairing the mills, and destroying the moles therein *Taxes* .

A tax of 6rf. per acre on the North Level and Portsand, (per act 27 Geo. IF,) which can be lowered as occasion may require; laid at the annual gene For further particulars of the Adventurers' lands and taxes in the North Level, see *ante,* p. 624, &c.

VOL. I. 2.X ral meeting of the commissioners on the first Monday in July, amount, at *6d.,* 990/. It. 2(1.

Debt.—None.

A permanent tax of *6d.* per acre on £.,. d.

the North Level, and *3d.* per acre upon Portsand, by act 11 Geo. Ill, amounts 807 8 4

Tax purchased off".

Distr. £ s. d. 1st. Lord Eeardley--77 7 3$
2d. J.Wing,nowW.Crane'slO 13 7:: 3d. Duke of Bedford-439 14 0 527 14 11

Debt, 2000/. £ 369 13 5 A permanent tax of *6d.* per acre on the North Level, and *3d.* per acre upon

Portsaud, by act 36 Geo. Ill, amount 897 8 4

Tax purchased off.

First district, Lord Eeardley---77 7 3£

Debt, 1,900/. £ 820 1 Qi

Tax laid annually by the commissioners of the first district for interior works of drainage, 1. per acre.— Debt, 507.

-laid annually by the commissioners of the second district for the like purpose, 2. *Gd.* per acre, which can be lowered as occasion requires.

Acts 13 and 15 Geo. III.— Debt, 1,260/. tr-—-laid annually by the commissioners of the fourth district for the like purpose, to the same amount, per act 40 Geo. III.— Debt,, 1,050/.

The late little common is not yet drained, for want of means of communication with the great common, from which it is separated by the New South Eau. Its drainage is, however, provided for by the above act; but it does not yet pay any tax.

There is another small tract of land,

called Throckenholt, containing about 224 acres, in the 4tb district, which discharges its waters by a private mill into the Old South Eau, under Murrow Bank, a little above Clow's Cross, and thence into Shire Drain.

The errors of Sir Cornelius Vermuyden in neglecting to alter or improve the several outfalls to sea, have already been adverted to. This grievous fault was discovered at no remote period after he had commenced operating. So long since as the year 1721, the attention of the corporation was forcibly drawn to the very imperfect state of the river below the town of Wisbech, and the matter was brought under the consideration of the board. A conference took place between the corporation and a deputation from the town of Wisbech; both parties *appeared* to concur in a plan for improving Kinderiey'i the river below that place. A new cut (now called c"fc Kinderley's Cut) was ordered to be made, for the purpose of turning the channel of the river under Shire Drain sluice, and keeping it confined within a narrower channel. It was to be two miles in length, and to begin at the river's end, about four or five miles below Wisbech. And it was also intended to carry the river, in a confined channel, two miles further, to a place then called Peter's Point, where there was a fall of five feet seven inches. Had this work been then completed, it would have been of great advantage to the river. For the more contracted it is towards the sea, the deeper and better must be the channel, and more rapid the passage of the waters. The town of Wisbech seems to have been lamentably deficient in honor and integrity in this respect, and to have fallen far short of their more worthy descendants. It appears that the corporation had only their " bare words," and not " hard and fast," or in " black and white." Accordingly, by the time the cut was nearly completed, and a dam was being made across the old river, in order to turn its course into a new channel, the Wisbech gentlemen, notwithstanding their verbal concurrence, *falsely* (or charitably speaking, *by mistake* or error of judgment) apprehending the advantage of a wide indraught over all those spreading sands, complained that this new cut was not wide enough (though it was wider than the river at Wisbech by twenty feet); and that, therefore, their harbour would be immediately choked, and their navigation lost. The opening of the cut was in consequence violently opposed, notwithstanding their original agreement to the work. They rashly endeavoured to excite the country to violence, in order to demolish the works; and afterwards applied for an injunction from the Lord Chancellor to put an effectual stop to the progress of the labour of the corporation; the effect of which proceedings was, besides the creation of considerable hostile feeling among private persons and families, a long, vexatious, and expensive law suit between the town of Wisbech and the Bedford Level corporation, and a useless expenditure by the latter of nearly 2000/. The author records this transaction with some degree of regret; it gives him, however, the opportunity of contrasting the behaviour of the then, and of the present inhabitants of the town of Wisbech. Erroneous opinions of this nature no longer govern the conduct of the intelligent people of that flourishing town and port.

The beneficial effect likely to result from this measure was not forgotten, although no further steps were taken by either party. The matter was revived in the year 1751, by Nathaniel Kindi?rley, the son of Charles Kinderley, who had been employed by the corporation in making the cut, so begun below Wisbech in 1721. At length an act was passed, called the Tydd and Newton drainage act, in which provision was made for opening the cut made in 1721, and then called Kinderley's Cut, the expense whereof was to be defrayed in

Tidj and New-manner following:— The Tidd and Newton proton Act.' prietors were to pay 1000/. out of the taxes imposed by the act: the corporation 1000/. out of the funds of the Middle and South Levels; and whatever further sums should be required to complete the work, the same were to be provided by the commissioners of the North Level, by whom the work was to be executed. The old channel of the river and the bare sands were by this act vested in the corporation; but the annual rents arising . therefrom were to *be* applied to the repair of the New Cut, and the overplus (if any) was directed to be paid to the North Level commissioners.:

It does not appear that Kinderley's Cut was opened, or the sums mentioned in the Tidd and Newton act advanced, until the year 1773, when the proprietors of Tidd and Newton proposed to advance 1000/. towards opening *a part only* of Kinderley's Cut, from the West Marsh to Buckworth's Drain sluice, and continuing such cut from Duckworth's Drain sluice through the Greea Marshes to the outfall at New Gunthorpe sluice; which was estimated at 1,415/. 4.v. *4d.,* but was expected greatly to exceed that sum. The board resolved, that if the commissioners of the North Level would take upon themselves the execution of the plan, and bear the expense thereof, the corporation would co-operMe with all parties by advancing the sum of 1 ()()()/., and no more, towards the expenses thereof, which sum was to be borrowed under the corporation seal, upon security of the taxes raised for the use of the Middle and South Levels. The work was performed, and the money advanced by the corporation; nor was its application injudicious, as the improvement of the river below Wisbech tended essentially to the security of the south bank of Moreton's Lcam, which is the great protection of the Middle Level,

This improvement, although highly advantageous to the quicker passage of the upland waters to sea, was not of sufficient extent to make tha outfall complete. In addition to which, the rivers between Wisbech and Peterborough were in a very imperfect state, *as* well for the purposes of drainage as of navigation. In the year 1783, frequent meetings of the country were convened, to take this important subject into consideration; a draft of a bill was prepared, and the corporation agreed to advance the sum of 500/., on the part of the Middle, and 500*l*. on the part of the North Level, and one shilling an acre was to be laid upon the wash lands, together with a tonnage toll, and other regulations. The plan, however, led to no practical result, and ultimately proved a failure. Again and again was the matter agitated; but the several interests were too conflicting to enable the parties to arrive at any definite measure. The North Level continued to evince considerable anxiety for an improved drainage. Great sums had been wisely expended in heightening and strengthening the great barrier bank, on the north of Whittlesey Wash, under the vigilant and neverceasing care of the late John Wing, Esq.; still the internal drainage was obviously in a most defective state. In 1809, the late John Rennie, Esq., made a report as to the drainage of the first district within the North Level; and some few years afterwards he was employed to view the whole of that Level, the adjacent countries, draining their waters into the Wisbech river, and also the outfall to sea. A very luminous report followed, projecting extensive plans of improvement, both as regarded the internal drainage of the North Level, South Holland, and the hundred of Wisbech, the Whittlesey washes, and the outfall to sea, as far as Crabb Hole. His schemes, however, were too stupendous, and the sum required too alarming for immediate realization. Alas! restricted currency, free trade, national faith, and agricultural distress, had begun to make most rapid strides and fearful ravages, amongst the industrious and virtuous classes of the community. The general plan was not persevered in, although it was by no means finally abandoned.

Some biographical notices of ihis very eminent engineer will be found in a future port of this work, under the head of "The Eaji Brink Cut."

Lord William Bentincke, the brother of the present duke of Portland, and now governor-general of India, a nobleman of high rank, distinguished talents, great influence', and indomitable perseverance, had "for some time become the proprietor of considerable property in the country, called Marsh Land, lying between the two outfalls to sea of Wisbech and of Lynn. His lordship had for many years represented in parliament the county of Nottingham, where his brother resided, and had great possessions; but at the last general election he resigned that seat, and was unanimously elected for the ancient borough of King's Lynn. It is but justice to his lordship to say, that no man ever felt a greater desire to advance the general improvements of the country. His manner, perhaps, was *sometimes* too *decisive,* and his plans too gigantic for the more confined views of fen-men in general.

Be this as it may, his lordship was indefatigable, being aided in his designs by his friend and neighbour, Thomas Hoseason, Esq., whose career in the fens has been scarcely less brilliant and persevering than that of his noble friend. Of his *disinterested views* he has himself, upon various occasions, enabled his hearers to form a very *correct* estimate. Prior to the making of the Eau Brink Cut, near Lynn, there was no regular communication between the eastern and north-west parts of the kingdom; but no sooner was the great bridge, with a temporary bridge adjoining it, erected across the cut, than Lord William Bentincke and his ever watchful coadjutor foresaw the ulterior advantages that might accrue to the kingdom at large, if communication could be made by means of these works. Dilatoriness was not his lordship's reproach. A plan was formed, and estimates were None Bridge made, for the erection of a bridge across the river Act. Nene, at Cross Keys, otherwise Sutton Wash; and an embankment was to be formed at each end of such bridge. The amount of the estimate for the bridge, embankment, and works, was speedily raised in 100*l*. shares, and the payment of the principal and interest guarantied by the tolls for crossing the bridge. The bill for effecting these purposes was introduced into parliament; its provisions, however, did not escape the vigilance of those who were interested in the drainage of the North Level; they foresaw that the contraction of the stream by the arches of the bridge and its united embankments, might, in the then state of the river, be attended with very serious consequences to the security of the Fens. Although opposed, the bill ultimately passed into a law, receiving the royal assent on the 26th of May, 1826; but with a specific clause that the bridge and embankments should not be made until after the then next session of parliament; a restraint imposed for the avowed purpose of giving the North Level proprietors an opportunity of adopting some feasible plan for improving the river below Wisbech and the outfall to sea. Without doubt this statute contributed to hasten a plan of a more general practical improvement.

This bridge has been recently erected, and the embankment completed, under a contract with Sir Edward Banks, and the superintendence of the present John Rennie, Esq. The bridge over the Eau Brink Cut, that over Sutton Wash, and the one previously erected over Fossdyke Wash, below Spalding, make a complete communication between the east, and north, and north-west parts of the kingdom.

After a variety of meetings, and much discussion between the parties concerned, a bill was passed, entitled "An act for improving the outfall of the river Nene, and the drainage of the Jands discharging their waters into the Wisbech river, and the navigation of the said Wisbech river, from the upper end of Kinderley's Cut to the sea, and for embanking the salt marshes and bare lands lying between the said cut and the sea .

By this act, the corporation of the Bedford Level reserved entire their right as commissioners of sewers, but relinquished their property in the marsh lands and the sands then vested in them by the Tidd and Newton act. The value thereof (with contributious from various districts and public The following case has been judicially decided under this act, although not as yet authoritatively reported. Some of th.e points raised may perhaps be not inapplicable hereafter, under other circumstances: bodies) was applied to raise part of the ways

Michaelmas Term, 10 Geo. IV., Oct.

27, 1329. The Kixo *v.* rns Commissioners Of The Nene Outfall. *Tithes—Private Acl of Parliament— Compensation. A private act of parliament, wliick directs a compensation to be made to the several persons interested "in any lands, sandt, tenements, buildings, or other hereditaments," used for the purposes of the act, "or for any damage which shall hare been done thereto, or to the parties interfiled therein," does not tntitle a* ticar *or Icy iinpopriiitor to a compensation, in respect of titheable lands taken for the purposes of the act, and thereby rendered incapable of producing tithe*

This was a rule calling upon the commissioners for putting in execution an act of parliament, 7 & II Geo. IV., c. 68, intituled "An Act for improving the Outfall of the River Nene, and the Drainage of the Lands discharging their Waters into the Wisbech River, and the Navigation of the s;iid Visbech River, from the upper End of Kinderley's Cut to the Sea; and for embanking the Salt Marshes and bare Sands lying between the said Cut and the Sea," to shew cause why a writ of *mandamus* should not issue, commanding them to issue their warrant to the sheriff of the county of Lincoln, to empannel a jury to assess a sum or sums of money to be paid by the said commissioners to the Rev. Thomas Leigh Bennett, as a satisfaction or compensation for the damage done in the execution of the said act to the rectory and vicarage of JLong Sutton, in the county efforts at improvement recorded in the Fens; and uo doubt can be reasonably entertained of its ulti buildings, or hereditaments respectively, or for any damage which shall have been done thereto, or to the parties interested therein respectively," &c.

By the 37th section, it is enacted, that the several verdicts which the juries shall give "concerning the compensation to be made for the value of any lands, sands, tenements, buildings, or other hereditaments, and for any injury sustained, or to be sustained, shall be distinct-. and the said juries shall distinguish the sum or sums of money to be paid for the value of anysnch lands, &c., from the sum or sums of money to be paid for any such injury or damage as aforesaid, separately and apart from each other; and also shall settle what shares and proportions of such several sums of money shall be allowed and paid to any tenant or tenants, or other person or persons, Laving a partial estate, term, or interest in the premises, for his or their interest, or respective interests therein."

By section 39, it is enacted, "that the parties sustaining any real or supposed injury or damage shall give a notice in writing to the commissioners, &c., within the space of two calendar months next after the time when the same shall have been sustained; which notice shall state the particulars of such injury or damage, and the amount of the compensation or satisfaction claimed in respect thereof."

The Rev. Thomas Leigh Bennett, at whose instance this rule was obtained, was, at the time of passing the act, and still is, lay impropriator of the parish of Long Sutton, in the county of Lincoln, and also vicar of the same parish; and as such lay impropriator and vicar, entitled to the great or rectorial tithes, and also to the small or vicarial tithes, of the same parish.

According to the map or plan, and the schedules of reference alluded to in the act, as ascertaining the course of the proposed new cut or channel, that new cut or channel will pass through the titheable lands of the rectory and vicarage of Long Sutton,.which have hitherto produced corn and grass, from whence mate utility. Sonic new amendments were made in the act, during the last session of parliament,

Mr. Bennett and his predecessors have been accustomed to take and receive great and small tithes. According to that plan, upwards of two hundred acres of such titheable lands will be taken for the purposes of the commissioners, and cut away for the making of the new cut, and the surface destroyed and rendered incapable of bearing corn and grass.

Before the application for this rule, the commissioners, by their workmen, commenced the cutting away of the titheable lands aforesaid, in the direction of the proposed cut, and according to the map or plan j and Mr. Bennett, at the request of the parties to whom the tithes were leased, made a reduction of *as.* per acre in the rent at which they were then demised throughout the parish. Upon this, Mr. Bennett made to the commissioners a proposal for a certain amount of compensation, to be made to him in respect of the premises, which was declined by the commissioners, on the ground that he had an interest only in the produce of the soil, and not in the soil itself; and that they were, therefore, not liable to make any compensation for the loss of the tithes.

Mr. Bennett has, within the proper time, required the commissioners to summon a jury, under the 36th section of the act, to inquire of, assess, award, and give a verdict for, a sum of money to be paid by them to him, as a compensation or satisfaction for the damage which he will sustain by reason of the premises, and has complied with the other requisitions of the act preparatory to such proceeding. The commissioners and their committee have refused to summon such jury, upon the ground that Mr. Bennett is not a party entitled to any compensation within the meaning of the statute. Upon this refusal, the present rule was obtained.

The question for the opinion of the Court was, whether Mr. Bennett, as lay impropriator and vicar of the parish of Long Button, was, under the act above cited, 7 & 8 Geo. IV., c. 85, entitled to compensation, in respect of the titheable lands of the parish being taken and cut away for the purposes of the act, which cannot be matter of wonder, considering the great variety of objects embraced in its numerous provisions.

and the damage he would sustain:i9 such lay impropriator and vicar, or in either character, thereby. If the Court should be of opinion in the affirmative, a peremptory *mandamut* was to issue: if in the negative, the rule to be discharged. *Mr, Taifourd,* in support of the rule.—The right of the present applicant to compensation depends upon two questions:— first, whether he is a party interested in the two hundred acres of titheable land, which have been taken by the commissioners for the purposes of the act; or, secondly, whether he has sustained sut'h damage or injury thereby as will on that ground entitle him to set up such a claim. It is contended, that he is interested in respect of the tithes, which, although not expressly mentioned, may be comprehended under the general term, "other hereditaments," which occurs in all the clauses of the act applicable to compensation. The term "interested" is not to be construed strictly, but as referable to other cases of compensation, and to the intention of the legislature, which, no doubt, was to make an allowance in respect of tithes; since, otherwise, all the titheable lands in the parish might be taken by the commissioners, and the tithe-owners thus be deprived of their whole produce. But, supposing he is not on this account "interested," yet he is within the meaning of the statute as a party injured; because the land, as stated in the case, has been rendered unproductive as titheable land.

Mr. Justice Bayfey.—Suppose the owners of this land had voluntarily given it up to the commissioners, would the parson then have been entitled to a compensation for the loss of his tithes?

Perhaps not; but the fact being otherwise, it is to be presumed that the commissioners contracted for the purchase of the land, as being liable to the payment of tithes; or that the circumstance of that liability reduced the compensation awarded to the proprietors.

The works arc now in progress under the superintendence of the present John Rennie, Esq., a *Mr. T. Ctarkson,* contra, was stopped by *Mr. Juttice Bayley.*—This act must be construed, like all such acts, in the same manner as we should construe a private agreement between the parties. The first clause stated in the case, provides for cases where the parties legally interested in the soil make an agreement with tha commissioners for the disposal of that interest j and the next, which is the 36th, as well as other subsequent clauses, for those in which they cannot agree. In order to bring the present claimant, who is the vicar, within these latter clauses, it is contended, that he was "interested" in these lands, or, at least, it is said-he has received damage; and, in either event, is entitled to be compensated. It is said, that the interest he has in the tithes is an interest in "other hereditaments," which is one of the interests provided for: but he is not interested in the soil, nor has he any interest in the tithes until the subject-matter of them arise. The former owners might have used this land so that it should not produce titheable matter; the commissioners, the present owners, *by* applying it to the purposes of the act, have done no more, and have done only what, by law, they have a right to do. The vicar, then, having had no legal right, can have received no legal prejudice. The argument, that the whole parish may thus be taken away, is an argument to be used to the legislature.

Mr. Justice Littledale.—This is the first application of this kind that has ever been made, although so many canal acts have passed, the operations of which would probably be the same as is here complained of (1). It is attempted to support (1) In the acts of parliament for the Grand Junction Canal Company, and the London Dock Company, a compensation is directed to be made to persons entitled to tithes: in the former, by estimating the value of the tithes immediately before the taking and using the lands; and in the latter, by referring to the average price of corn during a certain number of year's. VOL. I. 2 Y contract for the same having been entered into with Sir Edward Banks . They are expected to be completed in about a twelvemonth, should no unforeseen accident occur.

How many able generals have obtained signal victories in detail, who never dared to venture a general engagement! The North Level, and other parties interested, found that the scheme of the late Mr. Rennie was of too grand and expensive a scale; but there can be no reasonable doubt that the plan itself will he ultimately effected by detachments, instead of a *coup de main,* or a general engagement. A bill is now pending in parliament, for improving the drainage of the North Level, by changing the course of the waters to the improved this, by supposing, that the word "heredftaments" was intended to comprise tithes; but I cannot understand how the word "heir" can here apply. As to any damage sustained by the claimant, although he may have experienced some loss, his damage is not such as the law will recognize.

Mr. Justice Parke.—I concur in the construction given to this act on both grounds. The claimant is not a person interested in the land, nor has he received any damage to entitle him to compensation. It appears to me, that, whenever a sale of land takes place under this act, whether voluntary or forced, the vicar will stand in the same situation as if it had been sold to a private person, who would be at liberty to use it as he might think proper, either for titheable produce or not. *Rule discharged*. The reader will find some biographical accounts of this most extraordinary man, this second Sir Cornelius Vermuyden, in a future part of this work, under the head of "The Eau Brink Cut." outfall; which bill, in all probability, will receive the sanction of the legislature. The measure for improving the drainage and navigation between Wisbech and Peterborough, including the great Wash, will certainly follow. May John Duke of Bedford live to behold the unskilful errors of those who had undeservedly won the confidence of his illustrious ancestors corrected and amended, for the benefit of the present and of all future ages! The progress of these measures of improvement proves, that the spirit which animated the house of Russell, in other times, in the service of the Bedford Level, hath not yet departed.

CHAPTER XXIII. *The Middle Level.—Boundary.—Its three divisions.—Their boundaries.—Early dissensions between Drainage and Navigation.—River Nene Act.—Tongs Drain.—Sir Thomas Hares transaction. — Wisbech Canal Act.—Ashlines Sluice.— Middle Level and Barrier Banks Acts.— Works generally in the Middle Level.—Private Tolls.*

Boundary of The Middle Level comprehends all that part of Level.' the Bedford Level which lies on the north side of the Old Bedford River, and the south side of Moreton's Leam. It is the largest of the three Levels, and contains upwards of 150,000 acres of fen land; and is defended from the upland waters by the great barrier banks of Moreton's Leam, and the Old Bedford River, the former extending about 12, and the latter 21 miles in length.

Divisions of tke The Middle Level has been, for some time, Middle Level.

separated mto three divisions, called the North, South, and East Division; and their respective works have been placed under the care of a distinct superintendent for each of those divisions. This has been done by order of the board, and is of great practical utility, the respective duties of each superintendent being clearly denned, and his responsibility apparent. The whole Level is partitioned into numerous private districts, for the convenience of drainage; which districts, being under the regulation of their respective commissioners and proprietors, present no subject of interest to the reader. The author, therefore, confines himself to a general description of the three divisions of the Level, and of the works under the immediate management and control of the corporation.

THE NORTH DIVISION OF THE MIDDLE LEVEL.

It was resolved, that the following be the North Divi sion, Middle southern and eastern boundary of the North Di- Level,

vision of the Middle Level. From the end of the

Forty Feet River near Ramsey, along that river to the Sixteen Feet Drain; from thence along the

Sixteen Feet Drain to Popha-m's Eau at the Black

Sluice; from thence along Popham's Eau to Well

Creek; and from thence along Well Creek to the river Ouze, at Suiter's Lode Sluice; and that whatever concerns the corporation on the east side of the Onze, and northward and westward of the above boundary, and westward of Ramsey

Town, whether within the Middle Level or out of it, be considered as within or attached to the

North Division of that Level; including Moreton's Leam Wash, and the outfall to sea through

Wisbech, so far as the Middle Level is interested

therein; together with the Tongs Drain, and the bank of the Ouze apportioned to the corporation at the east end of that drain.

The following are the principal works at this time in charge and maintenance of the corporation, situate within and attached to this division: *Banks.*

Banks. The Barrier bank on the south side of More ton's Leam, to the Ball public-house, called the Strandground bank; the same from Basingbally corner (the highlands of Whittlesey field intervening between Strandground bank and that place) to Tower-house, near Guyhirn, including Horsecroft and the Five Mile bank. This bank

Ante, p 73. was originally made by Bishop Moreton, *temp.* Henry VII.

App. p. 779. N. B. The great bank adjoining Waldersey, and extending from Guyhirn to Wisbech, is a public turnpike road, and is repaired, partly by the trustees of the turnpike (9 Geo. IV, c. 73.), and partly by the Waldersey proprietors (9 Geo. IV, c. 19.). The corporation of the Bedford Level has hitherto contributed *30l.* per annum towards its support.

The two banks of the Tongs Drain or Marshland Cut. Also, the portion of the great bank of the Ouze at the east or sea end of the Tougs Drain.

N. B. The corporation receives a certain annual sum from the Haling commissioners under the Haling Act (30 Geo. Ill, c. 83.); and also for another part on the west bank. These sums are paid by Mr. Smetham, of Lynn, and Mr. Lemnon, of Downham Market.

The bank between the Old Bedford and Well Creek.

Sluices.

Standground sluice, near Peterborough. sluices.

Saiter's Lode sluice, near Downham Market, Norfolk.

The sluices at the top and bottom of the Tongs Drain, between Nordolph corner, in Upwell, and Stow bridge.

The Black sluice, at the end of Popham's Eau, near Upwell.

Bridges.

Pond's bridge, over Bevill's Leam, between Bridges. Ramsey and Whittlesey.

The Three Holes bridge, over Popham's Eau.

The bridge over the Black sluice.

The bridge over the Tongs Drain, at Nordolph, is repaired by the commissioners of the Wisbech and Downham turnpike road (9 Geo. IV, c. 73.).

Rivers annually leaded, i.e. *the weeds cut, by the*

Superintendents.

The river Nene, or Whittlesey Dike, from Rims, &c. Standground sluice by Ravenswillow, and Conquest Lode, to Whittlesey Meer.

See some remarks as to the repair of this bridge by the corporation, in a future part of this work, under the article "Bridges."

The Nene, from Whittlesey Meer, by Ugg Meer and Ramsey Meer, and Benwick, to Flood's Ferry.

Ramsey Lode.—Bill Lode.—Hook's Lode.— Monk's Lode.—Burbeach Stream.—New Dike.— Raveley Drain. —Bevill's Leam, from Whittlesey Meer to Whittlesey Dike.—Whittlesey Dike. — The Nene, from Flood's Ferry by Outwell to Well Creek.—Well Creek, from the Nene to Salter's Lode sluice. —The Tongs Drain.—Popham's Eau. —The Sixteen Feet, called Thurlow's Drain. —The Twenty Feet, called Moor's Drain, including Hobb's Drain3 from Bevill's Leam to the river Nene— Bevill's Leam, from Duncomb's Corner to the Counter Drain.—The Cut or Drain between Moreton's Leam and Horsecroft and the Five Mile Banks.

THE SOUTH DIVISION OF THE MIDDLE LEVEL.

south Division, It was resolved, that the boundary of this divi

Middle Level. sion be from the end of

the Forty Feet River, near Ramsey, where it joins the river Nene, along the Forty Feet River, to the east side of the drain in the Wash, called the Delph or Thirty Feet; and from thence to the east side of the Old Bedford River, and along that side of the Old Bedford to Earith town, including the site of the old bank on the Wash side of that river, with the Forelands, be the southern and eastern boundary of the South Division of the Middle Level; and that whatever concerns the corporation, south and west thereof, up to the hard lands east of Ramsey town, be considered as within or attached to the South Division of the Middle Level: and that the causeways across the Wash at Earith-and Mepal, and the great dike and sluice opposite the Gault Pits at Branghill in Mepal, be considered as attached to that division.

The following are the principal works in charge, within and attached to this division: *Banks.*

The Barrier bank on the north side of the Old Bunks. Bedford, from Earith to the boundary line at Welche's Dam, called the Upper Division.

The Forty Feet bank, from the corner of the Sutton and Mepal Districts, to Welche's Dam.

Sluices.

Welche's Dam sluice.

The sluice at Mepal, at the end of the great siuiccs. dike, leading from the Old Bedford to the pits at Branghill Closes.

Bridges. The bridges over the Old Bedford at Sutton Badges.

Gault and Mepal.

Welche's Duiu bridge, over the Forty Feet.

The Forty Feet bridge, near Ramsey.

Puddock bridge.

River to road.

The Forty Feet river. River to road.

THE EAST DIVISION OF THE MIDDLE LEVEL.

It was resolved) that the following be the boundary of the EastDivision of the MiddleLevel: From the point on the east side of the drain in the Wash called the Delph or Thirty Feet, where the line of the South Division turns southward, along the Forty Feet River to opposite the Sixteen Feet Drain; and from thence along the Sixteen Feet Drain to Popham's Eau; and from thence along Popham's Eau and Well Creek to Salter's Lode sluice; and from thence along the west bank of the Ouze to the One Hundred Feet River; and along that river to Wellmoor Lake; and from Wellmoor Lake, including the drain, to opposite the corner called the Thorn Tree; and from thence along the south side of the drain in the Wash called the Thirty Feet or the Delph, to the East Division of the South Level; and that whatever concerns the corporation lying within the above boundary, and not included in the North Division, be considered as within the said East Division of the Middle Level; and that the care of the dam at Wellmoor Lake, and the discharge of the waters of the Wash through that lake, be considered as attached thereto.

The following are the principal works in charge, within or attached to this division: *Banks.*

The barrier banks, from opposite the Forty Feet River to the Thorn Tree.

The bank from the Thorn Tree to the One Hundred Feet River.

The bank from thence, by the side of the One Hundred Feet and the Ouze, to the Old Bedford sluice, so far as it belongs to the corporation.

The whole is called the Lower Division of the Barrier Bank.

Sluices and Tunnels.

The Old Bedford. siuicesand

Welney tunnel. Tunncls

The new tunnel, through the bank near Earith.

Bridges. The bridge over the Old Bedford, at Welney. Bridges.

The bridge over the Old Bedford, at Welche's

Dam.

Boot's bridge.

River to road.

The Old Bedford from Welche's Dam to the River to road, river Ouze.

.

Such are the works now repaired by the corporation within the Middle Level. Let us proceed to give some account of the improvements that have taken place from time to time in this extensive part of the Bedford Level.

We have already stated, that from the first Earlydisaenaccounts of draining the country, a mutual and Drainage and unnatural jealousy has existed between those con-avisatlon. cerned in carrying on the navigation through the Great Level, and those whose immediate object was the work of drainage. Those whose business and livelihood arose from being carriers by water, were never satisfied with, nor ever thought they would have enough of their favourite element; and seem to have been afraid that the rivers themselves would be reduced to dry land; whilst those who proposed the recovery and preservation of the country, meant only to confine those rivers within their proper bounds; but always suspected, that the navigators would, to the extent of their power, prevent the ultimate success of these designs. Hence the struggles that unfortunately took place in obtaining the several legislative enactments, and hence the provisions in favor of navigation, which form part of these enactments.

Perhaps the cause of their jealousies, like many others, had no real and substantial foundation, and originated in a natural alarm-on the part of the drainers, at measures, the result of which, from their novelty, it was impossible for the most ingenious to calculate, or fully to comprehend.. No doubt exists that there is a natural alliance between drainage and navigation: it is founded in reason, and cemented by the strongest ingredient that can render alliances permanent,—Unity of interests. A navigation it is true, had existed through the several natural rivers, having their course through the Fens, long, very long, anterior to the projects of drainage contemplated in the seventeenth century; but it must have been very uncertain, very expensive, and most imperfectly conducted. There were no banks to be used as haling ways; and in general, the success of the voyage depended on the winds, and the manual labour of the navigators; a dependence which those who are the least acquainted with the nature of an inland navigation must readily admit would prevent its being carried to any great extent. But there is a question, which may be fairly asked, and to which it will be difficult to give such an answer as may refute the doctrine of reciprocity of interests. For what purposes could not navigation be carried on, beyond the confined commerce of a few towns, requiring only fuel and other inconsiderable articles of commerce? The drainage of the Fens opened a new and extensive mart.

The inhabitants,, whose lot was thrown in this then miserable country, had few wants, as their means of siipplying-them were very scanty. luxury was an idea they had not acquired and their wishes never earned tbem beyond a d«sire of those things, without which life cannot subsist. But when the adventurers had drained the country; when, in consequence of that, it was peopled; when the labour and industry of the inhabitants, in tilling the gronDd, was rewarded by bounteous harvests; when, in the sublime language of sacred writ, *I/us. great valley stood so thick with corn, that it did laugh and &i»g;* when the prophetic part of the charter of iocorporatLoiu granted, by King Charles I, was fulfilled, "that in those places, which lately presented nuthi ng to the eyes of the beholders but great waters, and a few reeds, thinly scattered here and there, under the Divine mercy, would be seen pleasant pastures of cattle and kine, and many houses belonging to the inhabitants;"—then it was, that Navigation might have perceived the advantages that arose from its alliance with the landed interest, whose object was draining; that navigation was then first employed in carrying the riches of this country, either into the inland parts of this kingdom, or to their sea ports, from whence it was carried all over the globe. The returns that were made for what was carried out, produced plenty at home: that plenty soon introduced a sort of luxury, which was no longer contented with the necessaries of life; and this established commerce, a large share of the advantage of which, accrued to those who carried on the navigation. Then too it was, that the adventurers beholding the several little fleets, that traversed the different parts of this country, freighted with its produce, should with wonder and gratitude have acknowledged their obligations to those, by whose kind assistance they first became, as it were, a commercial people, and, without whom, in vain had they drained the country, in vain had they tilled the ground. Such might have been, such ought to have been, the kind dispositions of these two interests towards each other; but Prejudice interfered. Obstinacy, that constant attendant on Prejudice, lent her aid; and the suggestions of Reason passed by unnoticed. But however unnoticed Reason's suggestions were, yet length of time and experience, those grand specifics for the cure of all prejudices, have convinced the several parties concerned, of the truth of what hath been above advanced. Draining and navigation at last have found out the natural connxion that subsists between them; they have found out and acknowledged their mutual dependence. Whatever mechanical advantage the navigation of this country had received from the works of the adventurers; though the rivers by being contained within their banks, had in some places been so much deepened as to admit the passage of vessels of greater burthen than had before been used; though these banks were of the greatest advantage, serving as roads by the sides of rivers, for the horses which draw the boats along to pass; though sluices had been built for draining, which much improved the navigation; yet no tolls had ever been paid, no acknowledgments made by the navigators, for the assistance which they received from the great and expensive works of the adventurers. The equity and justice, as well as the legality of such tolls, were sufficiently understood, and were fully established and settled by the charter of incorporation granted by King Charles I. App. p. 137.

There is a very considerable navigation carried on through the Great Level from the port of Lynn, up into Huntingdonshire and Northamptonshire, by which the inhabitants of these and the adjacent counties are furnished with many of the necessaries as well as luxuries of life, owing to a coasting trade and foreign commerce. This navi gation is earned on through the river Nene. That part of it which lies within the boundaries of the Great Level, was in many places filled up and decayed, so that it was with great difficulty and expense that the voyages were performed. Those who carried on the navigation, and those who used this river as a drain to carry off their waters, applied to the Bedford Level corporation to deepen and scour it out. That corporation saw the necessity of the work, acknowledged the utility of it, but at the same time confessed their inability to undertake it, at *so* great an expense as such a work must amount to, which would either exhaust the provisions made for the maintenance of their general works, or engage them in contracting a large debt, which in the end would be of dangerous consequences to the other parts of the Great Level. In this situation were things, when a treaty was set on foot by John Duke of Bedford, between the Bedford Level and those who carried on and were principals interested in the navigation. The corporation of Lynn took the lead on behalf of the merchants-, and were assisted by the Honorable Mr. Horace Walpole, afterwards Lord Walpole, of Wolterton, and Sir John Turner, Bart., at that time their representatives in parliament, who manifested great intelligence, candour, and diligence in the part they acted for the common good. Plans, memorials, and papers of different kinds, passed between the two-corporations; but there were some points of nicety and difficulty which, notwithstanding the good dispositions that both parties brought with them to this treaty, remained unsettled. To surmount these difficulties, the Duke of Bedford himself went down into the country, and, with other members of the Bedford Level corporation, in the summer of the year 1753, met a committee of the Lynn corporation at Huntingdon, where all the matters in difference were maturely considered, and the general outlines for an act of parliament were drawn. The several parties interested, well pleased with each other, agreed to apply to parliament at the ensuing session, to obtain their sanction for what they agreed would be so much for the mutual benefit of draining and navigation. In pursuance of which, at the meeting of the parliament, a bill was brought in, and was carried through both houses with the greatest unanimity and success. This act of parliament T is called the Nene Act. The policy of that law is, by tolls laid on the navigation, to raise a fund, for scouring out and deepening the river Nene in such a manner, that both the ends of draining and navigation may be thereby answered. For this purpose, the corporation of the Bedford Level renounce the general powers they had over this river and its banks by the 15th of Car II., and the duty of making and maintaining a haling way, is placed under the care and management of commissioners. And such commissioners are appointed for carrying the act into execution, as, from their several interests therein, may be supposed to be the most able and Vol. i 2 z zealous in advancing the ends for which it was obtained.

At first, this undertaking bore the appearance of ultimate success; but it was soon obvious that the resources of the commissioners were inadequate to the expenses incurred in the execution of the works absolutely necessary. The river extended over a space of nearly one hundred miles. Bridges were necessarily required where fords were destroyed. App. p. 614, The erection of sluices became indispensable, the setting out and maintenance of haling ways, costly; the tonnage toll was only *3d.* per ton at each of the two sluices (Standground and Salter's Lode). In short, a debt of 10,000/. was contracted: the revenue became for many years incapable of discharging any part of the interest; the rivers grew up; the navigation was only partially preserved; and, until the year 1810, all was gloom and despair with those who had embarked their money in forwarding a measure so apparently propitious. Before, however, we enter upon those events which imparted a hope of the improvement of the Nene navigation, let us consider some of the measures to which this act necessarily gave rise. Soon after the act was passed, an attempt was made by the inhabitants of Denver, in the county of Norfolk, to assess the tolls taken by the commissioners at Sutton Lode sluice (which is situate in that parish) to the poor rates. This attempt was resisted, and ultimately gave rise to the following judicial decision, which it is right, for the information of other times and other persons, to place upon record.

The King v. *The Commissioners of the Navigation* App. p. 597. *of Sailer's Lode Sluice to Standground Sluice,* 1792, K. B. 4 Term Rep. 730.

A poor-rate, by which the defendants were assessed to the relief of the poor, in the parish of Standground, for the tolls of a sluice, was confirmed at the Ely sessions, subject to the opinion of this court on the following case.—In that part of the parish of Standground, which is within the Isle of Ely, a certain sluice was erected in the year 1640, called Standground Sluice, and was supported by the corporation of the Bedford Level as a work of drainage only, across a navigable river, called the river Nene, to prevent the waters running down the said river, and to turn the same down a new cut, called Moreton's Leam. In the year 1753, it was found necessary to apply to parliament for an act to improve the navigation of the river Nene; and, accordingly, in the 25 Geo. II., an act was obtained for improving and preserving the navigation from Salter's Lode sluice, in Norfolk, to Standground sluice, &c.; in which certain tolls were made payable at the said sluice, in the parish of Standground, by every person who should carry or convey any goods through it, up or down the river. The tolls are collected at the sluice by an officer resident there, and appointed by the commissioners under that act; and they are by the said act vested in the commissioners, and directed to be applied and disposed of for the several uses and purposes of the said act, and to no other use or purpose whatsoever.

Lord *Kenyan, C.* J., delivered the opinion of the court in the following terms:

"It is not sufficient to point out property within the parish, in order to shew that it is rateable to the poor; but there must also be some person or persons in the beneficial occupation of it. I say *persons,* because corporations may unquestionably be rated, though it was once thrown out by Yates, J., that they could not. Now, in the present case, there is property which is the subject of a rate; but there is no occupier of it. The trustees have a bare naked trust, not coupled with any interest. If any interest resulted, either to the commissioners or to the owners of the adjoiningland, after the public purposes of the act were answered, these tolls might have been rated. But it is admitted, that all the money, which is collected under this act of parliament, must be expended for the purposes of the act; and therefore upon the ground upon which the court proceeded in *Rex v. St. Lukes Hospital;* namely, that there was no occupier, these commissioners are not liable to be rated." Tongs drain. The Marshland Cut, or the Tongs Drain-f-, as it 2 Burr. 1053.

+ The river obtained this appellation from its original form having been in the shape of a pair of tongs. Two river were first cut, which have been subsequently united. Downham, or Saint John's Eau, being one straight cut, has been frequently called the " Poker." is more usually called, was cut by the adventurers in 1653, under the authority of the Pretended act. The design of it was to obtain for great part of the Middle Level a nearer outfall for its waters to the river Ouze, and so to the outfall, than could be procured by the more circuitous course through Well Creek and Salter's Lode Sluice, the latter being frequently unable to run in times of floods, in consequence of the pressure of the highland waters descending by the Hundred Feet River. Not only have the persons interested in the preservation of the navigation always viewed this auxiliary drain with great jealousy, but even those who were concerned in the drainage have not been without their apprehensions on the same subject, although the motives of the parties were essentially different. The navigators feared that the waters in the rivers might run so low as to impede navigation; but the alarm of the drainers arose from an idea, that the too frequent and too continued use of this Tongs might silt up Well Creek; and that the waters being diverted from their passage through Salter's Lode sluice, the great river Ouze would lose the benefit of the scour arising from the whole of the Middle Level waters. The Tongs should be run as low as possible in the winter, and as seldom as possible in the summer months. But how is this happy medium to be carried into execution? An attempt was made by a provision in the River Nene Act to reconcile contending interests. By one of the clauses it is enacted, "that the drain, called the

Marshland Cut, or the Tongs Drain, shall not at any time be run, unless upon a breach of bank, or in case of *imminent* danger thereof, or unless the waters in the said rivers be raised more than one foot *above the level of the soil of the lowest lands in the Fens,* nor in any of the said cases, without an order in writing, signed by ten of the river Nene commissioners, whereof five to be commissioners for the said corporation of the Great Level of the Fens, or for the borough of King's Lynn, and the other five to be commissioners for the city of Peterborough, or the places aforesaid." Nothing can be more indefinite or unsatisfactory than this proviso. Who is to discover or ascertain in what part of the Level the lowest lands of the Fens are situated? Who is to determine this debatable point? For some time after the act was passed, an order for running the Tongs was always obtained from five of the board, at the April meeting, by the vigilance of some of the country members interested in the welfare of the Middle Level; and such order was subsequently signed, when required, by the other commissioners. This plan, however, ceased for some years, and the control of running the sluice was left in a great measure to the discretion of the superintendent of the corporation, with an understanding that he should from time to time consult those members of the board, who resided in the neighbourhood more immediately affected by the measure in question.

The members of the select bodies of the corporations of the Bedford Level, ami of King's Lynn, arc, *ex-vfficio,* commissioners under the River Ncnc Act. Aip. p. 598.

Thus matters continued, until, complaints having been made to the board, it was referred to Mr. Hugh Wandly, (one of the most experienced and intelligent fen-men in the Level,) first, to ascertain where, in his opinion, the lowest lands of the Fens were situated; and then for him and Mr. Dyson, the engineer to the Bedford Level corporation, to devise some satisfactory mode of running the Tongs sluices; and it was Mr. Wandly's opinion, that the gages, or land marks, to ascertain this point, should be fixed at Mr. Searle's, or Mr. Wandly's farm, in March West Fen; at Mr. Fisher's farm, on the east side of the Sixteen Feet river, near Boot's Bridge; and at the Chapel, or Four Hundred Acre farm, near Benwick.

It should be mentioned, that previously to the rebuilding of Salter's Lode sluice, in 1828, the cill of which was then lowered four feet six inches, the water was considered by the board at the height stated in the proviso, when it was at the four feet water mark on the old cill of that sluice; but, of course, this can no longer be considered a criterion. Much discussion has recently been excited by this very important subject; and at the last Whitsun meeting the following order was made:

The board proceeded to take into consideration that part of the engineer's report, which related to the running of the Tongs; when, after full deliberation, and having examined Mr. Hugh Wandly,

Mr. Atkins, the officer of the Bardolph-fen drainage, and the engineer, thereon, it was ordered, that at all times, when the water in Well Creek should stand nine feet on the threshold of Salter's Lode, the upper doors of the Tongs Drain should be immediately opened, for the purpose of passing the water to sea by the said drain, and that the same should be so regulated by the opening and closing of the lower ebb doors, that a depth of five feet six inches might be kept upon the thresholds thereof; it being, however, understood, that in case of great emergency, the officer should have a discretionary power, upon his own responsibility, to deviate from the higher gage, submitting afterwards to the board his reasons for so doing."

This must be considered merely as an experiment; and most sincerely does the author vish that this or some other final-arrangement may be made that will satisfy all parties; but he fears that the matter must always be left more or less to the discretion of those who, by their directions, will render themselves responsible to the board and to the country.

The state of the Tongs Drain came under the consideration of the board in the year 1807, in consequence of a proposal to the board, from the proprietors of lands in the Middle Level having their drainage by that cut, that the two rivers should be abandoned, and one cut only made throughout the whole line, of sufficient width and depth, and the banks thereof compressed, heightened, and strenghtened. The corporation agreed to advance the sum of 1000/., and the proprietors 2000/.; which being done, this most beneficial improvement was fully carried into effect, under the superintendence of the corporation.

A further improvement of this drain took place in the year 1807, when the Middle Level commissioners united with the corporation (the latter advancing the sum of (500/.) towards the execution of the work, which was effectually executed under the superintendence and control of the commissioners acting under the Middle Level river.

Before, however, the author quits the subject of the Tongs Drain, he feels a very strong inclination to submit to his readers some remote transactions in relation to the history of this river, which, he considers, reflects any thing but honor upon *some* at least of the parties to that transaction.

The original drains were cut through lands of sir T a very porous and swampy nature, and being at times much surcharged with water, the same ouzed through the banks, and inundated the adjoining lands, then the property of one Sir Thomas Hare; in consequence of which, violent disputes arose between the adventurers and Sir Thomas; till at length the parties effected a compromise; and the adventurers became, in 1686, the purchasers of Sir Thomas Hare's estate adjoining, containing 339 acres, for the sum of 500/., which was paid to Sir Thomas, and 50 broad pieces were also then paid to my Lady Hare, and the estate was conveyed to trustees, for the benefit of the adventurers. After the passing of the General Drainage Act, 15 Car. II., the corporation, relying upon this contract, made considerable alteration in the width and depth of the two drains, and also in the height and strength of the banks; and continued quietly in possession under the conveyance from Sir Thomas, until the year 1737, when the then Sir Thomas Hare, having succeeded to the title and estates of his ancestor, set up a claim to the lands so purchased, asserting (what was indeed the fact) that his ancestor had no power to sell, having only an estate for life. This claim was objected to by the corporation, and a reference to arbitrators was proposed, which in the end did not settle the rights of the parties. In the year 1739, Sir Thomas brought an ejectment against the tenant of the corporation to recover possession of the estate so purchased of his ancestor, and paid for. This ejectment was tried at Norwich, by a special jury, at the summer assizes in that year, when Sir Thomas obtained a verdict. The corporation were afterwards advised to file a bill in the Exchequer against Sir Thomas, which, on a hearing in that court, was dismissed.

The corporation, thus convinced that there was no possibility of supporting their title, yet sensible of the importance of these rivers to the preservation of the Middle Level, were compelled to enter into an agreement with Sir Thomas, then in the full possession of a victory. Of course, the terms of the agreement were most disadvantageous to the corporation. A committee of the board was appointed to carry on the treaty; and after various propositions on the part of the corporation, and counter propositions on the part of Sir Thomas Hare and his agents, from the superior advantage of Sir Thomas, it was finally agreed between all parties, that SirThomas Hare, in consideration of 600/., nearly the same amount having been already paid to his ancestor, should convey to the corporation in fee, "all those 339 acres of fenny land or marsh ground, more or less, called the Tongs Wash lands, lying and being within two twenty foot drains, from Stow sluice near the west end of Stow Town, or Podyke bank, and Well creek, at the Clow of Nordelphbank, with all ways, watercourses, easements, &c." And, that after such conveyance executed, the corporation should grant Sir Thomas a lease for the term of 500 years, at the reserved rent of five shillings, of "all those 339 acres of fenny land or marsh ground, called the Wash Lands in the parish of StowBardolpb, between the two drains, or twenty feet drains, leading from Stow sluice, near the west end of Stow Town, or Podyke bank, into Well Creek, or the Clow of Nordelph; and also all their drains or cuts in the parish of Stow Bardolph, in or near the said wash lands; that is to say, the two forty feet drains, the thirty feet drain, the two twenty feet drains, and also the two twelve feet drains; and also all their right of fishery in the said drains; excepting two messuages in the occupation of William Nurse and William Wells; also excepting to the corporation full and free liberty, from time to time, and at all times, to run the waters through the said wash lands as usual, and to make any new cut for the benefit of draining, and to come upon the said demised premises, or any part thereof, to scour, reed, cleanse, and mend any of the said banks and drains, and to take earth out of the said wash lands for the repairs of the same."

These were the terms of the agreement, which, after four years spent in negociation, references, and expensive law-suits, were in 1742, carried into execution. On the ninth of June in that year, Sir Thomas Hare, in consideration of 600/., executed the conveyance in fee to the corporation, and the corporation executed the lease to Sir Thomas Hare, whose descendants have been ever since in possession of the estate, retaining the two sums of 500/. and 600/., (not forgetting the fifty broad pieces to my lady,) and paying only the trifling rent of five shillings per annum to the corporation.

Since the present register has had the honor of holding his office, he has, under the direction of the board, taken advice as to the legality of this transaction; but it seems that the Hares, of Stow Hall, were, at that time, too cunning for the corporation of the Bedford Level.

There can be no doubt that the sum of 500/. originally paid was then the full value of the land purchased. It is now snid to be worth the annual sum of 100/.

The sluice of the Tongs Drain at Nordelph was substantially repaired some short time since, and the cill thereof lowered. A new sluice is now A.d. isao. being erected by the corporation at the lower end of the drain, under the superintendence of Mr. Dyson. The cill is intended to be lowered four feet, which will then be about two feet two inches below the cill of Saiter's Lode, and three feet four inches and a half below the navigation cill of Denver sluice.

But to return to the consideration of other events connected with the Middle Level:

In the year 1793, an act of parliament was wisbecii canal passed for making a canal from Wisbech, to unite' with the river Nene, at Outwell, being a distance of about six miles. The corporation and the country were induced to consent to this measure, from an idea, that in times of pressure, the waters of the Nene might be run through the canal to the Wisbech outfall, and a clause to that effect forms part of the act of parliament. This was once attempted App. p. 774. in time of great pressure of water in the Middle Level; but the canal company, to the great surprise of the corporation and the country, required a sum of money to be paid to them for the accommodation: it being intimated in no very measured terms, that no " right" existed to have the advantage of such accommodation. The corporation and the country then saw the error into which they had fallen; and the clause itself may now be considered a dead letter. It may be mentioned, that several regulations are contained in this act relative to the placing of gages, &c., to the App. p. 774.

satisfaction of the corporation of the Bedford Level.

By this statute, several important and also very intricate provisions are inserted, which materially affect the interests of the riverNene commissioners. It is almost impossible to convey to the reader a perfect idea of the complicated machinery introduced into the act for effecting these intended purposes. Each of the two bodies is to elect six trustees, to be called the Canal and Nene trustees, who are to receive an additional toll of three-pence per ton beyond the Canal and Nene tolls, of which a separate and distinct account is to be kept, and after paying the officers' salaries, &c., and *100l.* to the Nene commissioners for maintaining the navigation of the river Nene, the remainder is to be applied to preserving and supporting the navigation between Outwell and Salter's Lode sluice, in manner specified in the act, to which the reader is more particularly referred. The trustees are annually appointed by the Canal and Ne'ne commissioners; and the accounts are also annually examined and audited. But the funds of the Wisbech canal company afford little prospect of the joint fund being rendered available to the extent that Was probably contemplated by the ingenious promoters of the measure. Messrs. Gridlestone, Wing, and Jackson, are the clerks to the canal company; and Steed Gridlestone, Esq., the clerk and treasurer to the Nene and Canal trustees,

The Wisbech canal act has always been considered as a measure which escaped the nsusal vigilance of the corporation and the country. Whether this be so or not, the promoters have not much enriched *themselves* by their dexterity.

A sluice had been erected prior to passing the Asi.imc-s River Nene act. at a place called Ashline's Gravel. sluue' ,, r 'App. p. 615.

near Whittlesey, the head of which is directed not to be raised higher from the threshold than five feet nine inches, being the then height of such sluice. The proper management of this sluice will always be important to the Middle Level, as it regulates, in a great degree, the supply of fresh water in dry seasons.

The river Nene commissioners pay to the cor-App. P.623. poration of the Bedford Level the annual sums of 20/. towards the repair of Salter's Lode, and 15/. towards the repair of the Old Bedford sluices.

The debt still remains at 10,000/., and interest has been ordered to be paid to the creditors up to the year 1804. The following are the officers of the river Nene:

Annual Sal.iry.

£. s. d.

Treasurer and clerk, Samuel Wells, Esq. 36 0 0 William Cambers, of Whittlesey-220 William Elliott, of March 220 John Hopkins, of Upwell-2 2 0 Samuel Bowker, Salter's Lode--40 0 0 James Read, Standground--20 0 0 John Woodcock, Horsey Sluice--5 5 0 Ashline's Sluice-550

Surveyors,

Middle LfTd Tlic profligate expenditure of the country during' the war, coupled with an unrestricted paper currency, had so raised the price of all the productions of industry, that a spirit of improvement arose among public bodies as well as individuals. This spirit did not fail to impart its influence to the industrious inhabitants of the Bedford Level. The state of the river Nene, (the main artery of the Middle Level,) and of the several artificial rivers, had long been a subject of general complaint; so much so, that a respectable alderman of Lynn facetiously observed, that he regularly attended the river Nene meetings, until he saw on his way thither, persons making hay in the bed of the river; after which, he thought such attendance perfectly unnecessary. In the year 1805, a plan was suggested for imposing a tax

upon *all* the lands within the Middle Level, to be applied in scouring out and improving *all* the rivers and drains within that level; but owing to thegreatdiversity of interest, this scheme was not accomplished. A project, however, upon a more limited scale, was attended with greater success.

.10 c,eo. a.c. In the year 1810, an act was passed, usually called "the Middle Level River act," by which, certain commissioners were empowered to impose a tax of one shilling per acre upon certain parts of the Middle Level, to be expended in scouring out and deepening the following rivers:— 1st.— Well Creek, from the Tongs Drain to Popham's Eau. 2nd.— Popham's Eau, from Nordelph corner to the

River Nene.

3rd. The said River Nene, from Outwell church to the westward end of Popham's Eau. 4th. The Sixteen Feet River, otherwise called Thurlowe's Drain. 5th. The said River Nene, from Popham's Eau, through the town of March, to Flood's Ferry.

Gth. The Old River Nene, from Flood's Ferry to Ramsey Mere.

7th. Wlrittlcsey Dike, from Flood's Ferry to Angle Bridge. 8th. Bevill's Leam, from Angle Bridge to Whittlesey Mere. 9th. The Twenty Feet River, otherwise called Moore's Drain, together with the two parts ofBevill's Leam that adjoin it; that is to say, Bevill's Leam from Moore's Drain to the Counter Drain; and Bevill's Leam, from Moore's Drain to the end of that part that is now open, upon, at, or near Duncomb's Corner, in Whittlesey aforesaid. 10th. The Counter Drain, under Moreton's Leam bank, from Whittlesey field to Bevill's Leam. 11th. The said Old River Nene, by the side of Ramsey Mere aforesaid, to Ugmere. 12th. The said Old River Nene, by the side of Ugmere aforesaid, to Whittlesey Mere. 13th. Whittlesey Dike, from AngleBridge.through Whittlesey, to Raven's Willow. 14th. The said River Nene, from Raven's Willow aforesaid to Standground Sluice. 15th. The said Old River Nene, from Raven's Willow by Farcett to Conquest Lode.

Vol, i. 3 A 16th. Conquest Lode.

17th. Yaxley Lode. 18th. Pig Water, from' Yaxley Lode to the said

Old River Nene. 19th. Caldecott Dike. 20th. Holme Lode, provided that the same be not done without the consent of Thomas Wei Is, Esq., his heirs or assigns, in writing. 21st. New Dike, Hook's Lode, and Burbeach

Stream, or the New Cut, all leading from the

Hard lands of Holme to Ugmere. 22d. Monk's Lode. 23d. Raveley Drain. And, lastly.—Bill Lode and Ramsey Lode.

The commissioners had also power to improve the Tongs Drain. These works have been executed at the cost of about 70,000/. The shilling tax has ceased, and the tax of three pence per acre, directed then to be laid for keeping up the works, is now only imposed. This latter tax amounts to about 1200/. per annum; upon the credit of which, the commissioners have power to borrow the sum of 3000/. Never was there a more popular measure than the one in question. Never was a tax more cheerfully paid. The author of this work is not accustomed to use the language of adulation; but he delights in the performance of an act of justice. No one will deny that the progress of these works was greatly facilitated, and many conflicting interests happily reconciled, by the vigilance, promptitude, and judgment, of Thomas Orton, Esq., of March, one of the bailiffs of the Bedford Level corporation, and a very active magistrate for the isle of Ely. His conduct, as chairman of the meetings of the commissioners, has given universal satisfaction.

About the same period, two other acts were Earner passed for improving the state and security of the two great Barrier Banks; by imposing a tax, to be expended by certain commissioners in heightening and strengthening those bulwarks. The tax for the South Bank of Moreton's Leam has ceased, although it may be renewed, when necessary. The tax for the Old Bedford Bank still continues. The commissioners have expended (exclusively of the annual corporation allotment) the enormous sum of 22,647/. 1. 9d. A plan is now in agitation, and it is to be hoped will be carried into effect, for erecting a sluice at or near Oxlode, and cutting a drain across the great wash, so as to enable the corporation and the barrier bajik commissioners to obtain silt from the One Hundred Feet River, and also strong earth and gault from Branghill Pits, near Sutton. A similar plan was adopted lower down the river, near Mepal; and has been attended with great advantage.

The River Nene is the only natural river within Rivers. the Level. The artificial ones are the Old Bedford, the Forty Feet or Vermuyden's Drain, the Sixteen Feet or Thurlowe's Drain, Popham's Eau, Conquest Lode, near Farcett, and several other tributary streams, conveying the waters from the highlands.

Sluice. *fiSalter's Lode Sluice* was originally erected in 1630. It has recently.(in 1828) been re-erected by the corporation, under the superintendence of Mr. John Dyson. Upon making the foundation, three several floors were discovered, one under the other. The present cill has been lowered 4/3?. 6/»., which is one foot beneath the lowest of those three floors.

Old Bedford Sluice was also erected in 1630, and has been recently re-erected under the same management. The cill of this sluice is *3ft.* 6m., which is *ft.* 4% *in.* below the navigation.cill of Denver Sluice. *Standground Sluice* was erected originally by Bishop Moreton, to force the waters down Moreton's Leam; it has been recently re-built under the same superintendence, by the trustees of Smith's Leam navigation; the corporation of the Bedford Level having subscribed the sum of 300/. The other sluices in the Level are not of any very great importance.

Private Toils. There are several private tolls in the Middle Level, all of which were placed in lieu of ancient ferries. One crosses the deserted river of the Ouze, fromEarith to Benwick; another crosses the Carr Dyke at Horsey, between Whittlesey aiid Peterborough; another, the Old Craft River, in the parish of Upwell, called the Half-penny Toll, which formerly ran from Littleport Chair to Wisbech; another at Bodsey, near-Ramsey; and another at Mepal, in the isle of Ely; but as for this last toll, the author could never discover why or wherefore it was established. The subject of the repairs of bridges in this Level will be referred to in another part of this work, in conjunction with those of the South Level.

It would be highly desirable to have some plan of drainage for the whole of the Middle Level, to be carried into execution by a general graduated tax, and an increase of the Nene tonnage tolls; the present imperfect state of the Old Bedford river, and Forty Feet river, being any thing but creditable to the country. Besides which, from the nature of the soil, and the improvements that have taken place in lowering the cills of the several sluices, as well as from the operations of the Eau Brink Cut, there can be no doubt, that the whole of the Middle Level rivers, must sooner or later be again excavated. The waters of the Old Bedford river, at times, actually pass down the Forty Feet river, and so along the course of the Nene" to Salter's Lode, being an extended distance of more than 50 miles beyond the place of their proper discharge at the Old Bedford sluice.

The author has filled the situation of clerk to the Middle Level commissioners, ever since the act was passed. The wealthy and highly respectable and respected firm of Messrs. Gurney, Peckover, and Co., bankers, of Wisbech, are the treasurers; and Mr. William Cambers, of Whittlesey, the superintendent to the commissioners.

The author cannot permit himself to close this long, and, he fears, too prolix account, without stating that it was in one of the parishes in the

Middle Level, he first drew breath. To Chatteris, his native place, he owes a deep and indelible debt of gratitude, for its strenuous exertions in his favor, when he succeeded to the highly honorable and important situation of Register to the Bedford Level corporation.

CHAPTER XXIV. *The South Level and its boundary.— Corporation works.—The Washes.—The Wash*

Sluices, and Cradge Bank. — Saint John's Eau. — Denver Sluice. — Labelyes scheme.—Doctor Mawson, Bishop of Ely.-The Suspension Bridge.

The South Level constitutes one of the three The south Lcdivisions of the Bedford Level, and contains about 12,000 acres of fen land.

It has been ordered by the Board, that the passage of the waters of the river Ouze, and the outfall to sea of St. John's Eau, and the rivers discharging themselves into the Ouze above Denver Sluice; and also the passage of the waters above the Hermitage bridge; the passage of the waters of the Wash, through or over the Wash or Cradge bank above Wellmoor Lake, into the One Hundred Feet River; and whatever concerns the works of the corporation, not included in the divisions of the Middle Level, whether within or out of the Bedford Level, be attached to the duties of the superintendent of the South Level.

The following are the principal works belonging to, or maintained by, the corporation within this Level.

Banks.

The Barrier Dank and forelands thereof, from the highlands above Overcote, near the parish of Swavesey, in the county of Cambridge, to Denver Sluice.

N. B.—It is divided into two Divisions.

From Swavesey to Mepal, is called the Upper Division.

From Mepal to Denver Sluice, is called the Littleport and Downham Distrigt Division.

The banks and forelands of Sandy's, otherwise Sandall's Cut, given by the South Level Commissioners in lieu of the bank, forelands, and channel, of the Old River Ouze.

The Cradge Bank of the Hundred Feet River above Mepal.

N.B.—The Minor Banks within this Level, although under the control of the corporation, are repaired by the several district commissioners, aided by an annual allotment of money from the corporation, *Sluices and Tunnels.*

The Hermitage Sluice.
Denver Sluice.
Wellmore Lake Sluice.
Upwere Sluice.
Swaffham Sluice.
Bottisham Sluice..

N. B.—There is a sluice at Earith town's end, s2Gco. 3. 1812 which was built, is repaired, and the salary of the sluice-keeper paid by, the Wash commissioners. The sluice-keeper is appointed by the corporation. The sluice is called the Seven Holes, and was erected to let small floods into the Washes, down the Old Bedford River, to preserve the Cradge bank by the side of the Hundred Feet River.

Owen's Sluice and Drain, across the Wash near Mepal, erected for boating silt and high-land earth from Branghill Pits, near Sutton, for the repair of the banks on the opposite side of the Wash.

N. B.— It is proposed to make a similar sluice and drain at Oxlode, for the like purpose.

Bridges.

The Hermitage Bridge. Bridgcs

The Bridge over the One Hundred Feet River, at Sutton Gault.

The Bridge over the same at Mepal.

By an order of the board, made July 1821, these three sluices were directed to be discontinued as works under the charge of the corporation, being considered as belonging to the commissioners of the adjoining districts j but a legal inquiry is now proceeding as to the liability of the corporation to repair or rebuild the navigable sluice at Upwere.

Roswell Hill Bridge.

N. B.—The bridge over the Old River Ouze at the Hermitage, being on the public highway, leading from St. Ives to Ely, belongs to the county of Huntingdon and the isle of Ely.

Rivers.— (annually roaded, i. e., the weeds cut by the superintendents.)

Rirers. The One Hundied Feet River.

The Cam, from Clayhithe to Harrimeer.

The Ouze and Old West River, from the Hermitage to Denver Sluice, including Sandy's or Sandall's Cut.

The Miklenhall River.
The Brandon River.
The Wissey.

Sam's Cut Drain, near Southery, Norfolk.

The Washes. Again and again,-has the author of this work had to deplore the errors of Sir Cornelius Vermuyden, in no respect more conspicuous than in that part of his artificial plan for leaving upwards of 5000 acres of land, called the Washes, for the highland floods to bed in, instead of giving them *impetus* by contraction.

The great body of water from the counties of Buckinghamshire, Bedfordshire, Huntingdonshire, and parts of Cambridgeshire and Northamptonshire, pass through the New Bedford or Hundred The great bridge at Ely is repaired by the Dean and Chapter.

Feet river, (a work most imperfectly executed by the adventurers, under the pretended act, passed during the commonwealth, in 1649,) to the River Ouze, at Denver Sluice, and from thence by that river to the outfull at Lynn. On the south side is the great barrier bank,protecting the South Level; and on the north side, (the great Wash left as a reservoir for the floods, intervening,) is the Old Bedford River, cut by the original adventurers under the Lynn law, (passed 1630,) on the side of which last river runs the other great barrier bank, which protects the Middle Level.

The New Bedford River, and the Wash lands lying open to the great river Ouze, at Denver Sluice, were, of course, subject to inundation by the tides, and also by every flush of highland water; to prevent which, the proprietors of the Wash lands were permitted by the corporation to obtain originally so long since as the year 1753, and subsequently, acts of parliament to enable them to App. P. 795. form a small cradge bank on the north side of the New Bedford River, and to make a dam at a place called Wellmore Lake (the extremity of the Wash), to keep out the spring tides and small floods. Of course, at the time of high floods this dam necessarily required to be cut through: this was done merely by opening a space in the centre, sufficient to enable the flood to wear the dam away; during which operation the barrier banks had to sustain all the pressure of the waters in the Wash; and, after the floods had subsided, the dam was, at considerable expense, again made up, occasioning to the corporation a continued but unavoidable expense; otherwise every spring tide would of course have flowed into the Washes. The reader will smile at such a system of drainage.

Such, however, was the state of things, when an ssoeo. in.c. act of parliament was obtained, in the year 1795, "' 7?2 for improving the outfall at Lynn, by making what is now called the Euu Brink Cut, by which means, the circuitous course of the Ouze was avoided, and a quicker discharge to sea obtained for the passage of the flood waters of the Middle and ApP. P. 773. South Levels. This act contains a clause requiring the corporation to scour out, deepen, and widen the New Bedford River; but no definite period is stated within which this work is to be executed. The cut was opened in July, 1821. As soon as this event had taken place, the board foresaw that no long period would elapse before the corporation would be called upon to perform the task imposed upon them by the original act; but the country could not in fairness call for this performance until the complete operation of the cut was ascertained,—the great desideratum being to obtain the full flow of the waters of the Wash in time of high flood, which could not be effected until the passage of those waters (in the narrowest part of the New Bedford River) was made equal to the capacity of the Ouze; while in like manner the capacity of the Ouze must naturally or artificially become equal to the powers of the Eau Brink Cut.

The corporation had employed the late Mr.

Rcnnie, so long since as May, 1812, to view the New Bedford River, and works connected therewith, in order to obtain an opinion of that engineer as to the best mode of making the necessary improvements, against the period when the corporation would be called upon to carry into full effect the duty imposed upon them by the original Eau Brink act. Mr. Rennie made a report to the board in December following, which report was the foundation of the ultimate proceedings of the corporation.

In the year 1823, a considerable expenditure was incurred in deepening the One Hundred Feet River, above Mepal.

At the April meeting, 1824, a petition was presented to the board by several of the most considerable proprietors of lands on both sides of the New Bedford Level, praying the board to take immediate measures for improving the discharge of the waters in the Washes; and in consequence, a view was directed to be taken by the board, which took place in the month of June following.

In consequence of this view, at a meeting of the board, held on the 8th of July following, a resolution was unanimously adopted: "That the New Bedford River ought to be made of the width directed in Mr. Rennie's report of the 7th December, 1812; and that the bank on the Wash side ought to be made as directed in that report, except that it should be four feet wide on the top, that it may be used as a haling bank to relieve the bank on the Littleport district side from the wear occa sioned by the haling on that side: That an effectual sluice ought to be made at Wellmore Lake, not only for the drainage of the Wash when it is within the Wash banks, but of such dimensions that, at the highest waters, it may, with the water of the Hundred Feet, supply all that the Ouze below is capable of passing."

The board met at Ely on the 10th of December, 1824, when the following proceedings took place:

Reports of the late Mr. Rennie, as to the improvements in the Hundred Feet River; and also the report and estimate of Mr. John Dyson, the present engineer of the corporation, as to the works now proposed to be done for the improvement of the drainage of the country, in pursuance of the order of the board, were read. The board were afterwards attended by Mr. Hugh Robert Evans, Mr. B. Vipan, Mr. distance, and others, (on the part of the Wash commissioners,) who, after stating the situation of their finances, offered to advance out of their funds the sum of 500/., the same to be paid by four annual instalments, with current interest thereon; the first instalment on the first of June then next. The board were also attended by Messrs. GaleTownley, (clerk.) William Lee, Whiting, and others, on the part of the Barrier Bank and Well Fen commissioners; and Messrs. William Martin, J. Smith, and others, on the part of the Littleport and Downham district; when Mr. Dyson's report and estimates were again read, and his plans examined. The board were then asked if the intended works were to be completed in one greatly improved; but perhaps not to the extent that the operations of the Eau Brink Cut may ultimately require.

These improvements have greatly tended to the security of both the great barrier banks; and particularly, as the haling is now carried upon the cradge bank, to the great relief of the Littleport barrier bank. The advantage of a sluice at Wellmoor Lake, instead of the operation of cutting the bank, must be obvious to every one acquainted with the subject. At the same time, as these improvements were carried on, an entirely new sluice, with a cast iron bridge, was erected at the Hermitage, and the Old West river scoured out. The Earl of Hardwicke generously contributed 50/. towards the erection of the bridge, which would otherwise have been built with wood.

st. John's Eau. From the benefits conferred on the Middle Level, by cutting the Tongs Drain or Marshland Gut, it was natural that a similar improvement should be attempted for the South Level; and, ac

Ante.p. 199. cordingly, as already stated, a large river was cut, one hundred and twenty feet wide, and ten feet deep, extending from near Denver sluice to Stow bridge, for conveying to sea, with greater facility, the flood-waters descending from the several rivers into the South Level.

This work does not appear to have answered the expectations of its projectors; at least, the use of it was soon abandoned by the corporation. Perhaps it was never completed, or perhaps great injury was occasioned to the main river, by diverting the waters into this channel. Many attempts, hovrever, have been made to restore the operation of this work; and so recently as the year 1812, it was proposed to apply to parliament to restore the river to its original purposes. Many communications took place between the board and the South Level proprietors; and the late Mr. Ronnie was employed to view the river, and report his opinion as to the propriety of the measure. The following is an extract from that report:

"The advantages which have arisen to the Middle Level by making the Tongs Drain, have been used as an argument in favor of this project; and it is said, that similar advantages will arise to the South Level from opening St. Johns Eau. The cases, however, appear to me quite different, and the arguments derived therefrom do not apply to the case in question.

"The Tongs Drain is not used for the purpose of running off the floods of the Hundred Feet River, but for that of the downfal water; and for this it serves two purposes, namely, as a reservoir to contain a large quantity of the downfal water, while the river gates are shut, and by these cuts the length of the drain is shortened: the former it does to a great extent. The reservoir being large, and the land low, a large quantity of water therefore accumulates near the sluice, and it runs off quickly when the water in the river subsides; and the distance being much shorter, the fall of a mile

Vol. i..'J B is thereby increased in a greater ratio than it will be by St. John's Eau.

"As a reservoir to contain flood-water from the Old Ouze, St. John's Eau is scarcely worth naming; though, in its present state, it answers the purpose to a considerable extent for the waters from Roxham Drain, and from the lands near Downham; and as it is never intended to be used except when the water rises to full 10 feet 6 inches above the cill of the pen doors, at Denver Sluice, I fear, at that time, its mouth will be over-rode by the Waters of the Hundred Feet.

"From the arguments I have stated, I am inclined to think the advantages to be derived from this scheme will be found by no means adequate to the expense, and other disadvantages which I have enumerated."

In consequence of this opinion, the board came to the resolution, that such report presented an insuperable obstacle to scouring out St. John's Eau, as a separate measure of drainage; nor is it probable that the project will ever be revived. 54 Gco. s. c. A considerable part of St. John's Eau is now App.p. 792. used (under the control of the corporation) by the Stoke Ferry and Uoxham district, as a drain for running the waters of that district to the oatfall.

The banks and forelands of St. John's Eau are of considerable extent; and although some encroachments have been made, the whole line thereof, on both sides of the river, together with the fishery, is the undoubted property of the corporation.

The erection of Denver Sluice was part of the Denver sluice, artificial plan unfortunately adopted by Sir Cornelius Vermuyden, in the year 1652-3, in order to force the tidal waters in a straight course up the One Hundred Feet River, instead of allowing them to flow in their natural and more circuitous channel up the Ten Mile, or Ouze River. For nearly two centuries the erection of this sluice (with a similar one at the Hermitage) has been a source of contention between the corporation, the South Level proprietors, and the navigators.

Alas! to record the history of this unfortunate sluice, the author would be obliged to enter into the relation of one continued series of jealous and angry dispute. Upon no subject have the opinions of men of science differed more widely, than upon the merits or demerits of this much controverted work. The centre of the sluice appears originally to have been formed with a dam of earth strongly piled, having on one side two small brick sluices, for the purposes of navigation. It cannot be denied, that after the execution of this work, a considerable quantity of silt accumulated in the river below, which, being an evident injury to navigation, naturally excited animosity against the corporation. In the year 1682, various alterations were effected in the formation of the sluice: three brick arches were set down where the clow or dam stood: the middle arch was made 18 feet, and the two others 12 feet wide; doors were formed in each arch, capable of being taken off or set open to let in tides; and it was conceived, that these expedients would allow a much better water-way than formerly; and that a greater facility would be afforded to navigation, than existed before the erection of the original dam or sluice. The alteration, however, had not the effect of composing differences. Sinister attempts were made by night as well as by day to lessen the security of this dam; so mnch so, that between the years 1682 and 1686, serious apprehensions were entertained of its blowing up; and this would assuredly have happened, had it not been for the extreme care and vigilance of the officers of the corporation.

The state of the river below the sluice does not appear to have improved in condition since the erection of the sluice: so ruinous indeed became its condition, as to call for the immediate attention of those interested in the navigation. Ante, p. 397. Accordingly, in the year 1695, the corporation of App.p. 405. Lynn, in conjunction with the corporations of Thetford and Cambridge, resolved to apply to parliament for relief, by renewing the commission or court of appeal, appointed for the protection of navigation in the 15th year of Charles the Second; but which, fortunately for the corporation of the Bedford Level, through the foresight and caution of William Earl of Bedford, had been suffered to expire. Previously, however, to this step being taken, a conference was held between those parties and the Bedford Level corporation, at Denver Dam, on the 25th of August in that year, when the board desired to know what was required of the corporation of the Bedford Level, in order to the preservation and amending of the channel to Lynn. The parties made answer, that their desire was to have the sluices at Denver Dam, as well as the sluice at the Hermitage, taken up, so that the Old Ouze might run in its ancient channel; at least, as it did in the 6th year of King Charles the First, and in accordance with the provision in the act for draining, 15 Car. II., for the preservation of navigation. The reply was, that the corporation would consider of these proposals or desires at their first sitting at London the next term; and that their determination on this matter should be transmitted to the corporation of Lynn soon after; but it was intimated to the latter, that the corporation could not assent to their proposals, since it would cause the total destruction and loss of the South Level, and consequently of the whole draining;.

In the absence of all symptoms of an amicable arrangement, both the parties prepared for a parliamentary encounter. Counsel were retained by the corporation of the Bedford Level; a committee was appointed to view the river Ouze up to Bedford, and also the coasts below Lynn to Boston, in order to make themselves acquainted with the condition of the coasts for the preceding forty or fifty years; and to procure evidence of the goodness of the navigation, and the damage the country would sustain if the sluices at Denver Dam, and the Sass ai the Hermitage, should be taken up, in compliance With the demands of the town of Lynn; hhd also to ascertain what was the state of the navigation before the sixth year of Charles I., between Lynn and Cambridge, and Lynn and St. Jves; and the burthen of the boats, and price of freightage, and what stoppage formerly existed in the rirer buze towards Cambridge; and also to inform the land-owners of the counties bordering ton the Level, of the extent of damage likely to accrue to them, in order to obtain their concurrence in petitions for preventing the removal of the sluices.

A bill was presented to parliament in the session of 1696: the subject was freely discussed; and witnesses were examined on both sides; but on the question being put that the bill be committed, it was decided in the negative; and the navigators were consequently defeated.

The corporation of the Bedford Level appear to have been no more annoyed by the complaints of the navigators; but in the year 1713, they were destined to contend with an enemy whose power was resistless. In consequence of a violent tide rushing up the river, and encountering high floods descending from the uplands, the sluices and dam became deeply undermined; and finally, in that year, they were utterly blown up and destroyed j and the waters, although somewhat diverted by the effects of the Hundred Feet River, once more flowed in their natural channel.

By this disaster, the navigators triumphed, and no complaints seem to have been made to the corporation during the interval between the demolition and restoration of the sluice. What were its effects upon the South Level, can only be collected from subsequent events. After the tides had thus blown up the dam and sluices, the ebb of the Bedford waters flowed nearly two hours up the Badesiadc, 87. Cambridge River, with additional silt and sand every spring tide, and dropped most of it between Denver and Littleport; for though the tides which put up above Denver, did, in their reflux, in some measure, scour the river below Denver by Lynn to sea, yet those tides having no fresh waters to raise to a head at Harrimeer, (the Ouze being turned down the One Hundred Feet River,) there was scarcely any back water in summer time, to scour out the silt settled in this part of the river.

The state of the South Level, after the destruction of the sluice, gradually became worse; and at length, in the year 1723, a petition was presented to the board by the land-owners and others in the isle of Ely, as well as from Soham, and many other places within the South Level, complaining of the grievances they had lain under ever since the demolition of Denver sluice, and proposing a method of relief, by stopping the flux of the sea where the said sluice stood, and making navigable the two small sluices on the side of the sluice, opening and scouring out St. John's Eau, and suffering the outfall thereof to be where that Eau was first intended to be placed. The board were, however, unanimously of opinion, that the method of relief proposed by the petitioners would not answer their expectation of removing the grievances complained of; because the main cause proceeded from the great bodies of sands which then lay between German's bridge and Lynn. But the board, nevertheless, conceived hopes of obtaining an effectual relief for this Level in general, by certain methods then under their consideration, of conveying the waters of the Ouze by a nearer course to Lynn haven.

No effective measures seem to have resulted from these proceedings. Neither the navigators, nor (we may add) the proprietors of the South Level, had been well pleased at the original erection of Denver dam and sluices; yet, strange as it may appear, we shall find both parties lamenting the consequences of this demolition; for however great must have been the hopes of those who had so long and so justly been opposed to the formation of those sluices after this accident, yet they were also most grievously disappointed. In the first place, the mischief produced by the sluices, that is, by the silt depositing itself in the river Ouze, eight or ten feet in depth, and growing firm and compact by time, was not so easily removed. Secondly, the chief cause of the mischief still continued; for notwithstanding the greatest part of Denver sluices were blown up and destroyed, the solid dam or wall, eight feet higher than the original bed of the river, remained; and suffered but a very inconsiderable part of the spring tides to run up, if compared with their current before the said wall was built: and as to the neap tides, they could not reach them so high as Denver; and therefore the benefit of the admission of the tides through the ruins of Denver sluices, proved much less advantageous to the navigation than had been anticipated: and as to draining, the South Level became the worst embanked of the three; the very sink and general receptacle of the waters of the Middle Level and the uplands; for in every wet season, or land flood, the waters coming down the One Hundred Feet River, with a considerable current, and their outfall being almost entirely silted up by the action of the flowing tides, necessarily found their way to the lowest place; so that instead of running towards Lynn and the sea, they took their course in the South Level, through the remains of Denver sluices.

In the year 1726, another application was made to the corporation by the proprietors of the South Level, for the re-erection of Denver sluice, stating, that ever since the destruction of that sluice, and the free admission of the tides into their flat country, as well as the reverting of the One Hundred Feet waters, their lands were completely drowned; and they therefore requested the re-erection of the sluice. From time to time these applications were repeated, and a variety of conferences took place, not only between the corporation and the South Level proprietors, but also between those interested in the navigation, particularly the corpora tioti of Lynn. Schemes were delivered in for effecting an improved drainage, by two engineers of the name of Leaford and Smith, both of whom recommended the re-erection of the sluice; but the most important report, and that which fixed the corporation, was received from Labelye, a native of Switzerland, and then employed as the engineer in the erection of Westminster Bridge.

Id the year 1748, the corporation determined upon the re-erection of the sluice under the following plan, delivered by Labelye.

It was proposed, that Colonel RusselFs two eyes or openings should be cleared, as low as the top of the solid dam, then lying about two feet under the bottom of the Ouze, in the remains of Denver sluice; and the river so far cleared above and below, as to afford a free passage to the land-waters and the tides.

2nd. That a lock or pen-sluice should be constructed on the east side of the easternmost of the two eyes, of about 50/fr. clear in length, between the two pairs of breast gates, which were to point down the river, and about 1-3/vf. clear in width. 3rd. That in the opening of the remains of Denver sluice, and in the two other openings or eyes, there should be placed twenty-eight draw-doors, each from *3ft.* to 3/#. 6m. wide, made so as to shut close upon the top of the solid dam, and properly supported, leaving a free passage for the tides of *87ft.* in the dear, besides the 13/3?. in the lock, which is *1Q0ft.* passage for the land waters.

It is proper to state, that although Labelye, under the then existing circumstances, recommended the re-erection of the sluice, he by no means approved of the original plan of drainage unfortunately adopted by Sir Cornelius Vermuyden.

The corporation directed the sum of 3000/. to be raised for carrying this plan into execution; of *.x* Which, John Duke of Bedford advanced the sum of *50Ql.* The sluice was completed in the year 1750, and has continued in nearly the same state to the present period.

The author has, he fears, traced the history of this sluice at too great length. Perhaps, however, he may be justified by the consideration, that even at the present moment its condition is matter of deep anxiety, in consequence of the recent improvements in the drainage above and below it, and the provisions of one of the Eau Brink acts, (59 Geo. III. c. 79,) which empowers the commissioners to make certain alterations therein, under the authority and approbation of the Bedford Level corporation.

In the year 1754, a surprising spirit of improve- ment arose within the South Level, and was much stimulated, not only by the sanction of the Bedford Level board, but also by the exertions and assistance of Dr. Matthias Mawson, then Bishop of Ely. Bentimm'sHis

'l toryofEty, p.

When his lordship was translated to that see, the 213.

city of Ely, and country about it, were much on the decline; occasioned by the adjoining low lands having for several years been under water; and th«

public roads, at the same time, in so bad a state as not to be traveled with safety. Under these distressing circumstances, it was obvious that the only effectual means of restoring the country to a flourishing slate was to embank the rivers, to erect mills for draining the lands, and to open safe and free communications throughout the large and almost impassable levels, with which the city of Ely was environed; all of them works of great difficulty, and formidable in point of expense; but they were happily undertaken, under the sanction of several actsof parliament; and in consequence thereof a new and better face was soon given to the whole neighbourhood, and great advantages both of healthiness and commerce were derived to the inhabitants. Whatever praises were due (as many certainly were) to the intelligence, activity, and public spirit of other noblemen and gentlemen of that country, yet the success of the several schemes was greatly owing to the suggestions of this worthy prelate; to his advice and encouragement, his aid and munificence.

Through the perseverance of Dr. Mawson, the turnpike road from Cambridge to Ely was completed; a plan which many persons at that time considered as impracticable; but the success of which gave occasion for other like communications from Ely in all directions: added to which, no less. than thirteen private acts of parliament were passed , for the drainage of districts and lands within the South Level.

In the year 1777, both the Middle and South Levels were in a most deplorable condition, and the debt of the corporation, as well as the state of the arrear roll, most alarming.

In that year, a general scheme of drainage for the benefit of both Levels was projected, including a plan for erecting a new and enlarged sluice at Denver; but although a bill was prepared, and presented to parliament, the measure was finally abandoned. Nothing further appears to have occurred for bettering the condition of the South Level, until the opening of the Eau Brink cut, the full benefit of which, however, it must be admitted, has not yet been received by this portion of the

Bedford Level.

We may here notice a most important measure, which took place in the year 1827; namely, the passing of an act for improving the drainage of the South Level, and the navigation of the rivers flowing through it; a measure which entitles its promoters to the gratitude and thanks of the country, inasmuch as those prejudices which had existed for more than two centuries between drainage and navigation were swept away, it is hoped, for ever, and an indissoluble bond of union established between these two interests. The works under this act are nearly completed; Sandy's Cut being now open for the purposes of drainage and navigation, and the adjoining part of the channel of the old river Ouze finally closed. These works have been executed under the judicious direction of Mr. Mylne, civil engineer to the New River company.

It would also be unjust to conclude this chapter without adverting to a work, alike useful and or namcntal. In the year 1825, a beautiful suspension bridge was thrown over the One Hundred Feet river, at Welney, at the sole charge of the reverend William Gale Townley, the rector of Upwell, now residing at Beaupr6 Hall, near that place, and brother to Richard Greaves Townley, Esq., one of the conservators of the Bedford Level corporation. The structure does infinite credit to the taste of the projector. Its beauty is only equalled by its utility. This bridge forms a communication between the eastern and northern parts of the country and the communication is much facilitated by a recently-made turnpikeroad from Mildenhall, in the county of Suffolk, crossing this bridge, and proceeding to the town and port of Wisbech.

Prior to the erection of the suspension bridge, there was a ferry across the One Hundred Feet River, the profits of which belonged to the Bedford Level corporation; but they were given up to Mr. Townley, who is empowered, under a lease from the corporation, bearing date, 7th September, 1825, to demand and take certain tolls for passing over the bridge, for the term of ninety-nine years, paying to the corporation, during that period, a small acknowledgment of five shillings per annum; after which time, the right of taking toll reverts to the corporation.

Many bridges have been built throughout the Bedford Level, by the corporation, tjnd by other public bodies. It was the author's intention to have entered into a legal discussion as to the liability of parties to repair those bridges; but he finds his work already too protracted. His readers are, therefore, referred to those statutes and judicial proceedings which relate to this important subject .

It was omitted to be stated in the account of the Middle Level, that the two bridges over the River Nene, at the end of the Forty Feet River near Bodsey, and at Benwick, were erected by the Middle Level commissioners, under the regulations prescribed by the statute passed 48 Geo. Ill, c. 59.; and are consequently become county bridges.

The bridges between Chatteris and Wisbech, and also the bridge over the Tongs Sluice, are repaired by the trustees of the turnpike-road.

The great bridge at Ely is repaired by the Dean and Chapter.

CHAPTER XXV. *The Port of Lynn.—The Eau Brink Cut.—Biographical notices of the late John Rennie, Esq.; of Thomas Telford, Esq.; and of Sir Edward Banks. —Ouze Bridges.—District of Marshland.— Marshland Smeath and Fen.— Bardolph and Downham Fens.—South Holland.—Conclusion.*

The outfall of the Middle and South Levels, we have seen, was formerly below the port of Wisbech. After the desertion of the river Ouze from Littleport, (a period by no means ascertained,) the general outfall of these Levels was at the port of King's Lynn, in the county of Norfolk.

King'» Lynn. The ancient name of this place (according to Camden) is *Lhyn,* so named from its spreading waters; for so much is implied by that British word; but Sir Henry Spelman and others say, that it is falsely called *Lhyn,* its true name being *Len* which, in the Saxon language, signifies a farm, or tenure in fee; so *Fanethen,* in the German language, is the tenure of the fee of a baron; and *Len episcopi,* the bishop's farm: he further observes, that the word *Len* hath a more limited sense, and signifies church lands, as *Ter-llen,* in Welch,is *terra ecclesiae.* This town was called *Lin-episcopi,* Bishop's Linn, till the time of King Henry VIII, as being the possession of the bishops of Norwich; but that king exchanging the monastery and revenues of Saint Bennet in the Holm, and other lands, for the revenue of the bishoprick, this town, among the rest, came into the hands of the king, and so hath, with the possessor, changed its name into Linn Regis, or King's Lynn.

This large and ancient town stands towards the mouth of the great river Ouze, (the old channel of which has been recently diverted by the Eau Brink cut,) on the eastern side of an extensive tract of country, called Marshland, about twelve miles from the sea, forty-two from Norwich, fortysix from Cambridge, and ninety-eight fromLondon. It is built on both sides of the Ouze, but chiefly on the eastern bank of that river, though it is supposed to have stood originally entirely on the opposite side; and hence that part is still called *Old Lynn.* By the spirited exertions of its opulent inhabitants, great alterations and improvements have recently been effected in this town. The entrance is now wide and spacious, through rows of houses lately erected, instead of the former narrow and confined streets. It must be acknowledged, however, that much of its original character has been destroyed. The entrance into the town was formerly under two ancient gateways, called the South and East gates. The former yet remains; the latter has been removed.

Vol. i. 3 c

The haven, or harbour, *a* capacious; but the passage into it is accounted somewhat difficult, and even, without the aid of a pilot, dangerous, in consequence of the numerous sand banks, and the frequent shiftings of the channels, occasioned by the loose and light nature of the sandy and silty soil at the bottom.

The author hopes he is not too sanguine in looking forward to a great improvement, at no distant period, below the harbour, by contracting the channel and embanking the immense quantity of land now covered with water, and rendered utterly useless, but which, with a little skill and exertion, might be made highly profitable to those who would embark in the patriotic plan of producing so obvious an advantage, as well to the harbour as to the passage of the flood waters to sea. Prior to the thirteenth century, this harbour, compared with its present width, is said to have been extremely narrow, being then only a few perches across. The present exceeds the former depth of its waters, in consequence of the increased scour from the operations of the Eau Brink cut.

The spring tides flow at times to a height of twenty feet; and the river is of about the breadth of the Thames above bridge, and so extends itself about a mile towards the open sea. Until lately, a royal fortress, called St. Ann's Fort, stood on the north end of the harbour, with a platform of twelve large guns, which could easily command all ships entering or quitting it. In olden times, besides its fortified walls, the town was defended by nine regular bastions, and a ditch in the form of a semicircle. There are but few remains now left of these ancient defences.

The excellence of the situation of the town; its large and commodious harbour, capable of containing two hundred sail; and the several navigable rivers falling into it from eight counties, present conveniences for traffic and commercial purposes rarely to be met with. By these means, several capital cities and towns are provided with all kinds of heavy commodities; and an extensive foreign and inland trade maintained. Coals from Newcastle; salt from Lymington; deals and fir, timber, iron, wines, &c., are imported hither from beyond the sea; and from the inland part of the kingdom great quantities of wheat, rye, oats, coleseed, barley, &c., are brought down the rivers. Lynn has been long renowned for the wealth of its merchants, and the punctuality and extent of their commercial dealings.

The channel of the river Ouze, for about four miles above the harbour of Lynn, was very wide and circuitous, and equally dangerous to navigation and injurious to drainage.

The success which attended the execution of Kinderley's Cut, below Wisbech, naturally turned the public attention to a similar improvement on the river Ouze, near Lynn. Many meetings were held upon the subject; a variety of plans were projected; and for several years the matter was generally discussed amongst those interested in improving the drainage of the Middle and South

Levels. The plan suggested was to make a straight cut from a place called Eau Brink, near St. German's Bridge, to the port of Lynn, by that means abandoning the old circuitous channel. But interests were too conflicting to be readily adjusted. The owners of Fen-lands trembled at the costs of the measure; the persons interested in the navigation were reluctant to try so vast an experiment; and the corporation of Lynn at once avowed their decided hostility to a scheme which they supposed would send up the tides and bring down the floods with such velocity, that nothing less could occur than the destruction of the harbour and the adjoining buildings, which they considered would be swept away, and leave scarce "a wreck behind." The promoters of the design were not deficient in perseverance, and were besides strongly supported by many of the most influential fen-men of that period. At length, at a public meeting of laudowners, and others interested in the improvement of the outfall of the river Ouze, held at the Crown and Anchor Tavern in the Strand, London, on Thursday the 16th of June, 1791, it was resolved, that an estimate of every expense attending the making the proposed new cut from below St. German's Bridge, near Eau Brink, to the port of Lynn, (including the value of the lands to be cut through,) should be immediately prepared, and that Mr. John Smeaton, Mr. James Golbourn, (then civil engineer to the Bedford Level corporation,) and Mr. John Watte, should be employed to make such estimate. A report was laid before a subsequent meeting, containing (as matter of contrast to what has since occurred) a very curious document, in the shape of an estimate of the costs of carrying the proposed measure into effect. Probably at this dull period it may create a smile of incredulity; however, so it was.

An estimate of the expense of cutting a new cut from below St. Germans bridge, near Eau Brink, to about half a mile below Lynn. £. s. d. To spade and barrow work, in executing the said cut, including materials for the workmen, pumping, &c. &c.--27343 2 0

To purchase of land for cut and cover- 6025 0 0

To a dam over the present channel- 2000 0 0

To a bridge over the new cut--1500 0 0

To two piers at the entrance of ditto- 500 0 0 To a sluice to discharge the waters from the lands cut off----30 0 0

To superintendence-700 0 0 *An estimate of the expense of conveying the wafers of Marshland into the proposed new Cut. £. s. d.*

To cutting a new drain from Marshland or Islington drain, to nearly opposite St.

Mary's Gool-----587 5 'i

To purchase of Land for ditto--217 15 0

To a sluice to discharge the said waters 1000 0 0 To two bridges over the said drain, (made of old materials)---10 0 0 To deepening 643 rods of drain-48 4 6 To 12 bridges to lands (made of old materials)-------24 d 0

To a sluice at the lower end---150 0 0 2037 4 6

Deduct for materials to dispose of-- 150 0 0

£1887 4 6

The whole expense not to exceed39,985/.6s.6rf.!! We shall presently see the great accuracy and judgment displayed in the calculations which formed the above estimates.

At length the proprietors in the Middle and South Levels became so satisfied of the great utility of the project, that a bill was introduced into parliament in the session of the year 1793; but it was met in every stage by the most obstinate and determined hostility, which continued without intermission until the year 1795, when all parties, actually wearied out with anxiety, and the expense of litigation, (amounting on the part of the promoters only, to the sum of nearly 12,000/.) tacitly ended the contest; and an act was passed 35 Gco. s. c.77. for imposing a tax of four-pe_nce per acre for the period of ten years, upon all lands within the se Gco. 3.0.72 Middle and South Levels, Marshland, and other App.p 772. lands comprised within the boundary set forth in the act, together with a navigation-toll in and of such tax. The duration of the tax was afterwards extended to a further period of five years. A more imperfect specimen of legislation does not disgrace the statute-book. Indeed, all parties concluded the sum to be raised (notwithstanding the estimate) so utterly insufficient to perform the work, that they were content to see the law expenses paid, together with the sums subscribed by individuals and public bodies, and to leave the result to Providence.

Matters continued in abeyance until the year secco.s.c.sa. ,«, , i,,. 68Geo.3.e.48. 1816, when events occurred which led to the lDGco. 3.c.79. i., / i.. 2 Gco. 4. c. 74. renewed consideration of this important plan. App. p. 773. The restricted currency; the state of the unemployed labouring poor; and (strange anomaly) the facility of borrowing money by passing the Exchequer-loan act: all had their influence in reviving this consideration; and added to these causes, some very wealthy and powerful persons had be7 come resident proprietors of considerable estates in the neighbourhood of Lynn; and, from motives which afterwards developed themselves, took very active parts in promoting the accomplishment of the measure. Application was from time to time made to the legislature for increased powers, and extended taxation, until in the year 1818, an act was passed, increasing the tax to two shillings per acre, to terminate on the first of January, 1823. In 1818, the dimensions of the cut having been settled by the late John Rennie, on the part of the Eau Brink commissioners, and Thomas Telford, on the part of the corporation of Lynn, a contract for its excavation, and for other works connected therewith, was entered into with Sir Edward Banks, and the work began. Again and again has the author had occasion to recur to, and to lament the fatal negligence of Sir Cornelius Vermuyden, in paying no attention whatever to the improvement of the outfalls to sea below the Bedford Level. After a lapse of nearly two centuries, some gentlemen were introduced into the Fens, who, by their talents, their skill, their industry, and their perseverance, were destined to correct errors so obvious, even to the most superficial observer .

It may not be uninteresting to aftertimes, to have placed upon record the actual expenditure, and the sums which were further required to complete the projected works; at least the contrast between the modern estimates, and those of the year 1791, will be read in other days and other times with no little degree of surprise.

In a future page will be found some biographical notices of the eminent men referred to. EAU BRINK ACCOUNTS. *Statement of Account, made up to the* 25/A *Aug.* 1817.

Charge.

The total amount of the tax of *4d.* an £ . d.
acre for 15 years-7&724 0 0
Interest from Exchequer bills, and dividends on stock in the 5 per cents, made by investing the money paid to the Treasurer for taxes, until the same was appropriated for the purchase of the land to be used for the Cut--7,899 8 0
Amount of penalties received--90 9 9
Balance due to theTreasurer,for sums advanced by him beyond his receipts, to the 25th August, 1817---695 17 5
Total Charge-£ 84,409 15 1 DISCHARGE.
Payments previous to August, 1809.
The expenses of obtaining the first Eau
Brink Act, in 1795!!!!-11,94313 7
Ditto of the second Act, in 1796--665 6 6
Ditto of the third Act, in 1805--65815 9 £ 13,267 15 10
Costs of law suits by and against the commissioners-537 12 3
Ditto of obtaining schedules of the land to collect the tax by... 1,672 15 9
Printers---425 19 6
Expenses of inquisition, to ascertain the value of the land purchased for the Cut, exclusive of other charges to be £. *s. d.* paid, 1,217 6 7
Engineer's charges-... 1,563 7 0
Miscellaneous charges, including Clerk's bill, Treasurer's salary, and other expenses------2,4/5 13 8
Paid for part of the land purchased for the Cut 6,914 2 1O
Payments by the Treasurer since August 1809.
The costs of the proceedings to obtain, in 1809 and in 1810, amendments of the acts 155 44
Ditto of obtaining the act in 1816, for the more easy collection of the arrears 1,069 9 5
Paid for the purchase of the remainder of the land for the Cut, including the further costs of the inquisition to ascertain the value of the land purchased, and the costs paid to the owners of the land 27,719 15 1
Expense of repairing the Sea Bank on part of the land purchased, next the harbour of Lynn-737 10 9
Paid on account of ditching and separating the land purchased for the Cut from the land of the adjoining proprietors, making a road to the same, and for expenses relating thereto, as required by the act-670 0 0
Paid Mr. Letumon, the Clerk to the Commissioners, for his bills, since 1809-1,223 210
Paid charges of engineers and surveyors, the principal part whereof was incurred prior to 1809-285 0 7 £. *s. d.*
Paid Printers, and other small expenses 160 15 8 Treasurer's salary for nine years, and for his expenses attending meetings-522 9 6 Cost of 2,856/. 7. 6rf. stock, now remain ing in the 5 per cents 1,937 0 0

Arrears of taxes now due-21,446 13 4 684,001 14 11

There are some balances in the hands of the Collectors, which it is consi-/dered will amount to this sum; but/ 408 0 2 against which they have claims to about the same amount SUPPLEMENTAL STATEMENT, *Shewing the Receipt and Expenditure, between the* 25f& *August,* 1817, *and 12th ofdpril,* 1819.

RECEIPT. Produce of 923/. 13s. Srf. sold out of the £. *s. d.* 5 per cents 982 12 6 Produce of 15 Exchequer bills for 100(W.

each, borrowed under the Exchequer Bill Loan act..... 15,337 6 3 Borrowed upon the security of the tolls and taxes. .... 32,000 0 0 Cash received, in part of rent of land purchased for the Cut, and let by the

Commissioners until the Cut was ex cavated---_ , 400 0 0

Cash received for arrears of the 15 years' tax, at *4d.* per acre... 19,132 1 2

Penalties paid by defaulters--2,529 17 0

Cash received on account of the 5 years

Tax, at Is. per acre-12,715 9 1 1 Penalties paid by defaulters---47 14 1

EXPENDITURE.

Paid balance due to the treasurer upon his account, made up to the 25th of Au-£. *s. d.* gust, 1817 693 17 5

Advanced the Committee of Management at Lynn, for carrying on the works-1,000 0 O

Costa of the act obtained in 1818-- 2,909 3 1

Paid the Contractors----58,099 4 1

Paid Engineers and Surveyors--1,866 12 4j

Paid for land purchased for the drain in

Marshland 2,830 0 0

Paid Commissioners of Appeal and of Arrear, appointed under the act of 1816, and their Clerk-... 1,607 11 10

Paid Government, in part of 15,OOOZ. borrowed under the Exchequer Bill Loan act-_ ----2,250 0 0

Returned subscriptions towards obtaining the act of 1795---94 19 9

Paid Messrs. Burcham and West their bill for works relating to the new Cut 545 5 0

Paid Printers----2/9 15 1

Paid for repairing the South Marsh bank 462 5 0

Paid law charges----389 3 0

Paid Mr. Lemmon his bills as Clerk-786 4 10

Treasurer's salary, and his expenses attending meetings----73 4 6

Paid Parliamentary fees on the bill now pending in Parliament-300 0 0 74,189 6 94

Balance in the Treasurer's hands, 12th

April, 1819---£ 8,956 4 2

Christopher Pemberton, *Treasurer. Estimate of the probable Expense of the Wai-Its remaining to be executed under theEau Brink Acts.*

First.—As to the works which must be completed before the water can be turned into the Cut.

Excavating the Cut and making and pud-£ *s. d.* ling the banks----93,073 ' 0 0 Deduct money paid to Contractors, on account of this part of the work-57,740 0 0 35,333 0 0

The dam at Eau Brink... 3,960 0 0

Deepening the river at the lower end of the Cut, where it unites with the harbour of Lynn, and sloping the banks- 4,550 0 0

A Steam-engine to take out the water during the excavation of the Cut-6,050 0 0

The bridge over the Cut, and the New Roads to communicate therewith- 13,870 0 0

The Cut for the Drainage of Marshland, including all the works incident thereto, with the necessary occupation bridges tnd roads, after deducting 2,830/. paid for the land purchased for the same 8,583 0 0

West Lynn Drain and Sluice, including all the works incident thereto--5,368 0 0

Works at Denver Sluice '---2,780 0 0

Works upon the Cam, for the protection of the navigation-6,543 0 0

Works upon the Brandon River-- 2,406 0 0

Works upon the Mildenhall River- 2,620 0 0

Works for the protection of the Botti sham and Swaffham Levels, including pointing doors on Soham Lode, gates on Reach Lode, a pen sluice at Swaff bam Lode, and gates at Bottishaui &. *s. d.*

Lode 11,676 O O

Works for the protection of Waterbeach 500 0 O Compensation for Mr. Lane, as directed by the act..... 400 0 O £ 104,639 0 0 *Works to be completed after the opening of the Cut.*

Scouring, widening, and deepening the River Ouze, from

Denver Sluice to the head of the Cut---- 17,600 0 0

Dam at the lower end of the

Cut.... 15,625 0 0

Works for the protection of

Lynn harbour... 5,375 0 0

Works on the Hundred Foot and also on the River Ouze,

above Earith-3,876 0 0

Costs of supporting the works for two years-2,000 0 0 44,476 0 0 £ 149,115 0 0 *London, March 16th,* 1819.

John Rennie.

It is not the intention of the author to enter into any minute detail of the several items contained in the foregoing expenditure and estimate. They are records for posterity. In many respects, the subsequent outlay has greatly exceeded the estimate; in some items the works have not yet been executed, and in others they have been abandoned; but it will not escape observation, that no sum is mentioned, either for the re-erection or alteration of Denver sluice,—a work indispensably necessary to afford to the South Level the full advantages it ought to derive from the. operation of the Cut.

The Cut and banks (with the bridge) were completed in July, 1821, and were opened to the public in that month, amidst a vast concourse of persons assembled to witness the scene. The urbane, and, at the same time, able and judicious conduct of Admiral Sir Joseph Yorke upon that occasion, will never be erased from the memory of any individual who had the good fortune to witness it. The Cut itself is about two miles and a half in length. Sometime after its opening, the dimensions were found to be too contracted, and, in the year 1826, the area of the channel was widened, under a contract with Sir Edward Banks, for the sum of 33,000*l*. There is no doubt that the operations of the cut will ultimately lead to almost a new system of drainage. In some degree this has already.taken place; at any rate, the river Ouze, much higher than the Bedford Level, must be considerably deepened,—a measure that ought to be forthwith carried into effect, and which would, perhaps, render Saint Ives staunch unnecessary, and certainly relieve the fertile and valuable meadows adjoining the river from that continued pressure of water by which they are now so much affected. Probably, the total costs of the Cut, and of all the works connected therewith, will amount to little less than the enormous sum of 500,000f.

It is almost impossible to quit this subject without referring to the eminent men whom the project of the Eau Brink cut and works has introduced to the notice of fen-men and others interested in the result of those extensive designs. Whatever feelings the author may entertain towards Scotland as a nation, he does not extend those feelings to *every* individual Scotchman; nor can he be insensible to the merits of those (be their origin what it may) who have applied themselves to scientific pursuits. There are few public works in the united kingdom, erected under the genius and enterprise, or the spirit of speculation and improvement of the present age, that are not associated with the names of Rennie, of Telford, and of Banks.

John Rennie, F.R.S., machinist, architect, and civil engineer, was born on the 7th of June, 1761, at Phantassie, in the parish of Prestonkirk, in the county of East Lothian. His father, a highly respectable farmer, died in 1766, leaving a widow and nine children, of whom John was the youngest. The first rudiments of his education were acquired at the village school; and, as it frequently happens that some trifling circumstance in early life gives a bent to the pursuits, and fixes the destinies of the future man, so it fared with young Rennie. The school was situated on the opposite side of a brook, over which it was necessary to pass by means of a rustic bridge of stepping stones; but when the freshes were out, the only way of crossing the stream was by means of a boat,

J which was kept at the workshop of Mr. Andrew Meikle, an ingenious mechanie, well known in

I Scotland as the inventor of tlie thrashing-machine, t and many improvements in agricultural imple i ments. In passing through this workshop, which stood on Mr. Rennie's family property, young Rennie's attention was forcibly drawn to the various operations that were in progress; and a great part of his leisure and holiday-time was passed therein. The son of Mr. Meikle, and the workmen, seeing the delight which he appeared to take in examining their labours,.were in the habit of indulging him with their tools, and shewing him their various uses. His evenings were chiefly employed in imitating those models which had particularly attracted his attention in the workshop; and it is known in the family, that, at little more than ten years of age, he had constructed the model of a wind-mill, a pile engine, and a steam engine. That of the pile engine is still in existence, and is said to be remarkably well made.

After perfecting his education at Edinburgh, Mr. Rennie proceeded to London, visiting on his way the different mills and public works in and about the neighbourhood of all the great manufacturing towns in the north of England. He had not long been settled in London when the project of building the Albion mills was carried into execution, the mill work of which he constructed. From this period Mr. Rennie's character was established, until he ultimately rose to the head of Vol. i. 3n his profession. The limited space of this work will not permit the author to enter upon even an enumeration of all his great works; much less to give a particular account of them. A few of his more prominent works may however be mentioned. The Anchor forge, at the Dock-yard at Woolwich, is a magnificent piece of machinery. But it was as an architect that Mr. Rennie stood almost unrivalled. The architectural work which, above all others, will immortalize the name of Rennie, is the Waterloo bridge across the Thames; a structure which even foreigners admit has no parallel in Europe, for its magnitude, its beauty, and its solidity. That a fabric of this immensity, presenting a straight horizontal line, stretching over nine large arches, should not have altered more than a few inches (not five in any one part) from that straight line, is an instance of strength and firmness elsewhere unknown, and almost incredible. But all Rennie's works have been made for posterity; they were never of slight construction; nor would he ever engage in any undertaking where a sufficiency of funds was not forthcoming to meet his views.

Another work, from a design of his, to which for some years past he has given his attention, is now being carried into execution, namely, the new stone bridge over the Thames, as a substitute for that disgrace to the present age, the existing London bridge. His design, which was selected by a committee of the house of commons out of at least thirty that were offered, proposed the erection of a granite bridge of five arches, the centre one of 150 feet span. This will be the largest stone arch in the world, constructed in modern times. The execution of the work, now in progress under the superintendence and direction of his two sons, Messrs. George and John Rennie, will form a remarkable" feature in the future history of the capital. Of the five bridges which will then bestride the river Thames within the precincts of London, three of them, and those beyond-comparison the most magnificent, will have been built from the designs of one man .

In the year 1789, he married Miss Mackintosh, who died in 1806, leaving a family of seven young children, six of whom are now living; and on the 16th October, 1821, after a few days' illness, this celebrated man departed this life without a struggle, in the 60th year of his age.

The two eldest of his sons, George and John, are successfully following the profession, and promise to tread in the footsteps, and attain the pre-eminence of their father.

It is somewhat remarkable, that three of the very eminent engineers, who have been employed in the great works of the Bedford.Level, were also the projectors or builders of the five great bridges over the river Thames: Labelye, the builder of Denver Sluice, in 1749, was also the builder of Westminster bridge, erected about the same period: Robert Mylnc, Esq., father of the present civil engineer, and the original engineer for the Eau Brink Commissioners, was the projector of Blackfriars' bridge: and the late John Rennie, Esq., was the projector of Waterloo, Southwark, and London bridges.

Thomas Tclford, Esq., architect and civil engineer, is also a native of Scotland, being born, as the author understands, in Diimfrieshire. He has descended into the vale of years, unmarried. Mr. Telford is remarkable for the solidity of his judgment, superadded to great caution, foresight, and prudence. That he is not deficient in taste, or the great essentials of genius, is most clearly evinced by the various public and private works which have been executed under his designs, the number of which is scarcely exceeded by those of.the late Mr. Rennie. The most astonishing monument of his genius and his skill in architectural design, is the beautiful and splendid work called the Menai bridge, across the river at Bangor ferry, in North Wales. Had this been the only work executed by Mr. Telford, it would have handed down his name to posterity, as a man of consummate taste and ability. Mr. Telford is in the 73rd year of his age, and is now considered as the head of his profession.

Nearly two centuries have elapsed, since the great works of drainage, then projected in the Fens introduced Sir Cornelius Vermuyden into that country. The extraordinary efforts and undertakings of this celebrated man, shrink almost into insignificance when compared with those of Sir Edward Banks, whose fortunate lot it has been throughout all his undertakings for the improvement of the drainage of the Bedford Level, and the navigation of its rivers, to retrieve the errors which his great predecessor had so unaccountably committed.

Sir Edward Banks was born near Richmond, in Yorkshire, in the year 1770; and finding nothing in that country in accordance with his enterprizing mind, he went to sea for about two years; and in 1789, undertook sea-banking and draining in Holderness. In 1791, he became a contractor for making a canal between Leeds and Liverpool. In 1792, he married; ami in 1793, was engaged as a contractor on the Lancaster and Ulverstone canals, under the direction of the late John Rennie. In 1795, he was employed as contractor on the Huddeisfield canal, and the Peak Forest, in making a railway and canal, and forming an aqueduct over the river Mersey, and in making sundry tunnels on the Huddersfield canal, amongst which there is a tunnel four miles and a quarter long, under a hill called Stenage: and in 1797, he finished the Ashton-under-Line canal, which enters Manchester, and thereby establishes the carriage of goods from Manchester to Hull. In this year, the Huddersfield canal was broken down by a tremendous flood, which forced the vessels laden with goods into the fields adjoining; and four or five of the vessels were broken to pieces. Upon this occasion he contracted to repair the na- vigation, and completely succeeded. In the year 1800, Mr. Banks went to reside in Derbyshire, where he executed several works fer the improvement of the Nottingham and Cromford canals, as well as various railways and roads, employing not less than thirty vessels in carrying goods, coals, limestone, and other materials, to various parts of the country.

In the year 1803, he came into the county of Surry, and set out the Croydon, Merstham, and Godstone railways, which commence at the river Thames, at Wandsworth, and extend through the town of Croydon into the property of Hylton Jolliffe, Esq., M. P., of Merstham, with whom he at that time established very extensive lime and stone works, and carried on also a considerable trade in limestone, fuller's earth, and timber, between that part of the county of Surry and the metropolis. Mr. Banks was employed in making the public road from the vicinity of Croydon to Ryegate, in order to shorten the main road from London to Brighton; and in constructing a variety of other works of public utility in that county.

In the year 1807, Hylton Jolliffe, Esq. , retired from the concern; upon which William John Jolliffe, Esq., embarked with Mr. Banks, in the execution of the stupendous works in which he was then engaged. They jointly built the Croydon court house, and various other works in that neighbourhood; and in the year 1808, embanked the Cardiff and Leckworth marshes from the Bristol channel, and built a bridge over the riverRomney. In the year 1809—10, they finished theDartmoor prisons;built a lighthouse,andother works at Heligoland; and executed various extensive works at Houth Harbour, in Ireland. Under the direction of the late Mr. Rennie, at the commencement of 1811, they made a new entrance into the West India Docks. They constructed the York Building waterworks; and contracted for building that magnificent monument of the skill and enterprize of the age, the Waterloo Bridge, together with the approaches, roads,and works connected therewith. The contract was for a specific sum of money,according to plans given by the late John Rennie. In the year 1813, they contracted with the Navy Board to find materials, and perform the works at his majesty's dock-yard at Sheerness, which were not finally completed until the year 1830, These, the largest and most complete works that have been executed in Europe, were also designed by the late Mr. Rennie.

Mr. Hylton Jolliffe married (he daughter of Washington Shirley, Earl Ferrars: the lady died, leaving no issue. Mr. Hylton Jolliffe is now unmarried.

In the year 1816, they contracted to build the Southwark bridge, also over the river Thames, to find all materials, and to make the approaches and roads, for a specific sum of money. In 1819, they contracted for building the Custom House wall, of granite, the whole length,including the coffer dam, steam engine, and all materials. In the same year, they also contracted for making the Eau Brink Cut, near Lynn, for the purpose of improving the outfall of the Bedford Level and adjacent country; and also for the erection of the Eau Brink Bridge across that river, with various other works, locks, wears, and excavations, under the Eau Brink commissioners of drainage and navigation; most of which works were finished in the year 1821; the late John Rennie and Thomas Telford, Esqrs., having been the civil engineers. Previously to commencing the work, Messrs. Jolliffe and Banks offered to advance a very large sum to the commissioners, upon the faith of a parliamentary application in aid of the funds; and they actually executed part of the work to the extent of 40,000/. before they received any return whatever.

In 1817, they entered into a contract for a new entrance into His Majesty's dock-yard, at Deptford, with river walls, and other works; the whole of which were executed within cofferdams adjoining the river. They also contracted to make a river wall, the whole length of his majesty's victualling-yard, Deptford, within a coffer-dam. In the same year, they contracted to erect a new entrance, with locks, bridges, basins, and all complete, for the London Docks. They also expended the sum of 155,000/. in obtaining granite stone from Aberdeenshire, for certain public works, which were all completed in 1821.

In that year, Mr. Banks married his second wife, Amelia, one of the daughters and co-heiresses of the late Sir Abraham Pitches, of Streatham, in the county of Surrey.

Sir Abraham Pitches (besides this lady) left four daughters; namely, Julia, married to William Jolliffe, the father of Sir William George Hylton Jolliffe, Bart., who intermarried with Eleanor, daughter of the Honorable Berkley Paget, brother of the present Marquess of Anglesey; Peggy, married to George William, Earl of Coven'try, co. Warwick, and Viscount Deerhurst, co. Gloucesten, lord lieutenant and recorder of the city of Worcester, and high steward of Tewkesbury; Penelope, married to the late Sir Robert Sheffield, of Normanby, in the county of Lincoln; and another daughter, married to Colonel Boyce, whose second son, Henry Pitches, married Amelia, daughter of the late Duke of Marl borough.

Mr. William Jolliffe has also another son, Gilbert East Jolliffe, H. P. 15th Light Dragoons, who married Margaret Ellen, the daughter of Sir Edward Banks.

In 1822, Sir Edward Banks received the honor of knighthood, for the extraordinary exertions, industry, skill, and perseverance he had displayed in the execution of the Waterloo and Southwark Bridges, which are justly considered two of the finest bridges in the world. In 1822, he and Mr. Jolliffe contracted with the Ayre and Calder company to build sea locks to receive the shipping, and a basin to receive the barges. These works were built with stone, and large coffer-dams, in the river Humber, so as to render the two sea locks and wing walls complete; and a canal was made, eighteen miles long, together with a number of locks and bridges on the same. These works were all completed in 1827; andGoole, in consequence, became a port.

In the year 1821, they engaged to build the new London Bridge, according to the design of the late Mr. Rennie, which has undergone some alteration since his decease. The contract, includingthe approaches and roads,all complete, was for a specific sum. They also contracted to build a bridge over the Serpentine river, in Hyde Park, with approaches all complete,—a structure of singular elegance and beauty. The plan of this bridge was designed by the present John Rennie.

In 1827, Messrs. Jolliffe and Banks contracted for making a new cut, for improving the outfall for the waters of the river Nene, below Wisbech, effecting an entirely new course from' Kiuderley's cut to the sea,being from five to six miles in length: this work is also now in progress, under the direction and plans of Messrs. Telford and Rennie. They also erected, under the same superintendence, the new sluices, with the bridge and embankment, over the river Nene, at Sutton Wash; by which means a communication now exists between the eastern and northern parts of the kingdom. In the year 1828, they contracted to make a new outfall for the river Witham, at Boston, into the sea; and also to make a new cut, bridges, locks, and other works, to improve the navigation of the river Ancholine, and the drainage by that river.

It would far exceed the limits of this work to detail the various other works executed by Messrs. Jolliffe and Banks in different parts of the country. While they mark the intelligence and ability of the present age, they will also transmit to future generations the names of those 'eminent personages, their skill, their talent, ano their industry. In earlier times, the possibility of executing works of this immense extent, by individual exertion, would have excited feelings of incredulity. They will undoubtedly be viewed by posterity with admiration and delight. It is hoped that the indulgent reader will pardon these long digressions. Let us now proceed to the consideration of matters more connected with the history of the Bedford Level.

There are four bridges over the River Ouze be-Ouze Bridget. low Denver Sluice, of which the following particulars may perhaps be useful. The reader is referred to the provisions of the several Eau Brink acts, as to the alterations and improvements that may be enforced by the Eau Brink commissioners, in order to prevent any obstruction in the waters flowing down the river to the Eau Brink Cut.

Dotvnham Bridge.—The tolls of this bridge are let for about 240/. per annum. In addition to the tolls, there is a public house, and some land producing a rent of from 100/. to 120/. a year: all which funds are applicable to the maintenance of the bridge. The bridge and estates are under the superintendence of two bridge-reeves, appointed by the parish. *Stow Bridge,* belongs to Sir Thomas Hare, of Stow Hall, and is maintained by him. The tolls are let together with a farm belonging to Sir Thomas, and no separate rent paid for them. It is supposed that they produce about 30/. per annum. *Magdalen Bridge* belongs to the two parishes of Magdalen and Watlington, and is under the superintendence of four bridge-reeves, two appointed by each parish. In addition to the tolls, which amount to about 98/. per annum, there are about seven acres of land, the rent of which is also applicable to the maintenance of the bridge: there is a small fund in hand amounting to about 300/. *Germans Bridge* is also under the superintendence of bridge-reeves, appointed by that parish. In addition to the tolls, of the value of about 100/. per annum, there are about thirty acres of land, the rents of which are applicable to the maintenance of the bridge. A school is also supported out of the same funds. There is a small stock in hand, nut amounting to 10001.

The author abstains from making any remarks upon the state of the banks on both sides of tbe River Ouze, between Denver Sluice and the Eaa Brink Cut, as the subject of repair is now *sub lite* between the owners and the Eau Brink commissioners. The commissioners of sewers exercise a control over these banks; the state of which is, however, any thing but satisfactory. Whatever may be the result of the legal proceedings *now In* progress, it will behove the corporation and the Eau Brink commissioners not to lose sight of the power vested in the former, by the Haling acf, APp. p. 772. passed 30 Geo. Ill, c. S3, of appointing three commissioners for carrying that act into execution.

Marshland.
The Hundred of Fen bridge and Marshland comprises the following parishes:
1. Emneth.
2. Walsoken. 3. West Walton. 4. Walpole, St. Peter's. 5. Walpole, St. Andrew's. 6. Torrington, St. Clement's. 7. Torrington, St. John's. 8. Tilney, All Saints. 9. Tilney, St. Lawrence. 10. Tilney, cnm Islington. 11. Clenchwarton. 12. Wiggenhall, St. Peter's. 13. Wiggenhall, St. German's. 14. Wiggenhall, St. Mary Magdalen. 15. Wiggenhall, St. Mary the Virgin. 16. Old Lynn, or West Lynn, St. Peter's. 17. North Lynn, or Lynn Sf.

The outfall is by the Marshland new sluiee into the Ouze, a little above the Eau Brink Cut, and by the West Lynn gool into the channel, at Old Lynn. The drainage is under the direction of the Norfolk commissioners of sewers, who hold their meetings at Lynn. Mr. Whincop, of Lynn, is their clerk. The charges of drainage are levied by dikereeve and expenditor rates, laid from time to lime by the court of sewers. They vary from about 6rf.

The country of Marshland contains 37,000 acres.

I to 1. *6d.* per acre, per annum. There are several embanked marsh lands in Walsoken, West Walton, Walpole, Torrington, Tilney, and Clench warton, adjoining the Wisbech and Lynn channels and bay, which have separate and distinct drainages, partly into the Wisbech channel, and partly into the bay, between the Wisbech and Lynn channels, and partly into the Lynn channel, which the author believes are not under the court of sewers, but provide their own drainage.

There are several mills on the Old Marshland, worked at the expense of individuals, or the proprietors of certain districts, without any general system of mill-drainage.

The great leading drain into which most of the waters run, is the Marshland great sewer, or Chancellor's lode, lying south of the Old Marshland, which conveys the waters into the New Marshland drain and sluice, to the Ouze. The other chief leading drain is that which conveys the waters to the West Lynn Gool, and by that into the Lynn channel.

A road and bridge are now formed to connect Marshland with the Lincolnshire coast. This road communicates by the bridge across the Wisbech channel, at Sutton Wash, and by the embankment across the present Out marsh of Walpole, *with* the road leading from Walpole and Cross Keys to Lynn. This embankment will produce an immediate inclosure of a considerable tract of land in the Outmarsh of Walpole. The embankment and inclosure of the remainder of Walpole Outmarsh, and a large part of the Torrington Outmarsh, may be expected in a few years by the retiring of the sea, and a further accumulation of soil in the bay. These lands will be then liable to taxation, under the Nene outfall act. The large tract of land, late part of the Old Lynn channel, lying between the Old Marsh lands and the New Eau Brink Cut, now the property of the Eau Brink commissioners, may be considered as part of Marshland. This tract contains about 786 acres.

There is a district called Oldfield in Elm, in the Isle of Ely, which drains through Marshland, by the Marshland great sewer, and is under the charge of the Lynn court of sewers.

There is no debt on the country of Marshland, for the purposes of drainage, except under the Eau Brink drainage acts, to which Marshland is subject, paying, however, only a moiety of the present tax; although the erection of a free bridge over the cut near Lynn has been productive of the greatest advantage to the persons owning estates in Marshland. The lands in Wiggenhall are subject to taxes for interior works, under an act of parliament.

Marshland Smeath and Fen.
This tract of land was inclosed under an act of the 3rd Geo. Ill, and allotted in severally to the lords of manors and owners of common rights, in the seven townships, or eleven first mentioned parishes, in Marshland, who had previously rights of soil and common thereon. It was also drained under the same act. Previously to the drainage, the Fen was one waste of water. Under the Drainage and Inclosure act, power was given to the drainage commissioners to include in the drainage certain lands adjoining, called Wellmoor in Outwell, and Broad and Short Fens in Wiggenhall.

The quantities are
A. R. P.
Sincalh---1572 0 22
Fen--47(59 1 17

Well moor-236 3 8
Broad Fen 458 0 20
Short Fen--227 0 7

The drainage is by two fen mills, standing at the north extremity of Marshland fen, which throw their waters into the Smcath and fen drain, and thence by two sea mills adjoining the turnpike road leading to Lynn, between Lord's bridge and Thornton's bridge, and thence into and by the New Marshland drain and sluice, into the Ouze, above the Eau Brink Cut; by which works these lauds have been greatly benefited.

The lands in the Smeath and Fen were allotted to the lords of manors, and to the owners of 525 common rights; and the drainage taxation is not by the acre, but by the common right.

The yearly tax is generally 30-. for each common right, and one 20th part of the whole amount of the common right lax on the whole lands of the lords of manors (one twentieth part of the Smeath and Fen having been allotted to the lords). It has often been 3/. per common right; but since the opening of the Eau Brink cut, has seldom exceeded 30. The lands in Wellmoor and Broad and Short Fens are taxed by the acre, in proportion to the tax on the Smeath and Fen common rights. When the common rights are taxed at 30. each, this tax is at a certain defined sum per acre. There is no debt on the taxes of this district. The management of the drainage is under commissioners authorized by the act.

jBardolph Fen.
This district comprises lands in the parishes of Outwell, Stow, Bardolph, Wimbotsham, and Downham, in the county of Norfolk, lying between the Well Creek and the Tongs river, and is drained under an act of the 38 Geo. III.; Great and Little Sandy Fields, in Outwell drain, with Bardolph Fen.

The quantities are—
A. u. P.
Bardolph Fen --4663 0 33
Great Sandy Field-319 0 3
Little Sandy Field-253 2 4
Acres 5235 3 0

The drainage is by two principal mills, standing at the extremity of the fen next the Ouze, into which the waters are thrown, between Downham and Stow Bridge. The taxation is 3. 6/. per acre

Vol. i. 3 E under the act. There is a debt secured by the annual taxes; and annuities for lives have been granted to a large amount, also charged on the taxes raised under the authority of the act. Bardolph Fen is divided from Marshland Fen by the Old Potlike. The management of the drainage is under commissioners authorized by the act.

Downham Fen.
Downturn Fen. Comprises the district between the Tongs drain and the Ouze, and is drained under the authority of an act passed in 1802. The district contains about 1600 acres; and the tax is about 3. 6d. per acre. There are two mills erected upon the banks of Well Creek, for discharging the waters of this district through Saiter's *Lode* sluice into the Ouze; although the act does not authorize any such right of drainage, nor do the lands contribute to the repair and animal expenses of preserving Salter's Lode sluice, or the Well Creek river. It is said, both this tract of land and Bardolph Fen might be much improved by what is called "warping;" that is, admitting the tides, npon the reflux of which there remains a deposit of silt and sullage, which ultimately improves and enriches the original soil.

South Holland. south Holland. This district comprises a small part of the lands in Tidd St. Mary, Suttou St. James, and Suttoo St. Edmunds, in South Holland; and contains about 5,700 acres, lying north of Shire Drain; and discharges its waters into Shire Drain, and thence runs to its outfall at sea. The remainder drain by the South Holland drains, and discharge their waters through South Holland sluice into the Wisbech channel, a little below Gunthorpe sluice. The lands more northward discharge their waters into the Spalding river, called the Welland, and thence into the bay at Fosdike Wash.

The lands in this part of South Holland contain about 34,000 acres. These lands are under the regulation of a commission of sewers, which sits and acts at Spalding; Mr. Carter of that place, being the clerk.

Wisbech Hundred. m
The lands in Wisbech, north side, sometimes w»becii Huncalled Wisbech Hundred, including Tidd St. Giles, Newton, Leverington, and Parson Drove, contain about 17,700 acres, and are managed under a commission of sewers. Hugh Jackson, Esq., of Wisbech, being the clerk.

The lands called South Holland and Wisbech Hundred, and also the North Level, Portsand, and Waldersey, (the latter containing about 8,00!) acres,) contribute certain proportions towards the expense of carrying into execution the act for the improvment of the Nene outfall. Certain sums are also provided by the trustees of the Nene bridge at Sutton Wash, and the navigators of the port of Wisbech. The remainder of the funds that may be required for this extensive and important work, is to be furnished by the value of the marsh land expected to be recovered and improved by the measure. In the event of any ultimate deficiency in the general fund, the commissioners of the North Level have undertaken to make up snch deficiency; an undertaking, which the author of this work has always considered to indicate great courage on the part of those commissioners.

It may not be unentertaining to state, that many parts of these Fens, prior to their improved drainage, abounded with a remarkable species of reed, which appeared at a distance, in summer, like extensive fields of corn. In autumn, and at the approach of winter, these reeds are resorted to by innumerable flocks of birds called Starlings, which subsist upon the seeds of the plants, and lodge or roost among their branches, from whence, when scared, they sometimes ascend in such vast numbers as to appear in the sky like a thick cloud. The Fen-fowlers, in boats, take these birds by surprize, when numerously collected among the reeds; and with long guns make prodigious havoc, among them. Myriads are so destroyed, and afford a considerable article of food in the latter months of the year.

The reeds to which these birds resort, and from the seeds of which they for many months derive a great part of their sustenance, are no less remarkable in another respect; great quantities are ctrt down and reaped like corn in the latter part of summer, and being afterwards carefully dried and dressed, are tied up in bundles or sheaves, made into stacks or ricks, and are sold for coverings of houses; they make the best thatch, perhaps, ia the world. Great numbers of houses and barns,
and some churches even, are covered with this thatch, about the Fens and marsh land, and the adjoining parts of Norfolk. Being thickly laid on,
it constitutes a very durable as well as neat covering; and is said, with a little shaving and trimming, to last sometimes thirty or forty years. Of thatch coverings in general, and of these reeds in particular, it has been observed, that they make the coolest houses in summer, and the warmest in winter; being less pervious to heat and cold than any other material used for the same purpose.
Some parts of the Fens, especially on the Lincoln-Geese,
shire side, have been long celebrated for breeding large flocks of tame geese, of which considerable numbers are usually sent alive to the London markets. The owners of these geese have a remarkable and cruel custom of stripping the wretched birds of their quills and feathers repeatedly every year;
and thus render each of them conformable to Plato's memorable definition of man, "a two-legged unfeathered animal." The practice, however, has been by many considered barbarous and *inhuman,*
as it must put the miserable creatures to the most excruciating torture-f-; but as it is a source of
The small feathers are plucked five times a year, (about Lay-day, Midsummer, Lammas, Michaelmas, and Martinmas); and the larger feathers and quills, twice. Goslings even are not spared; for it is thought that early plucking tends to improve their succeeding feathers. Some proprietors are said to have had a stock of a thousand, and even fifteen hundred or more geese, besides the young ones.
t It has been said, that mere plucking hurts the fowls but emolument to the owners, by yielding to them a far greater quantity of feathers than could otherwise be produced, there is no great prospect of a practice so unfeeling being ever discontinued.

The improved state of drainage throughout the Fens, has greatly reduced the breed of geese. Turforpct. Turf or peat dug from the upper soil constitutes the chief fuel throughout the Fens, although another odd custom prevails in some parts, which is that of preparing cow-dung, and con verting it into fuel, by forming the matter in a wet state into th« shape of turf, and afterwards drying it in the sun. It yields a strong disagreeable smell in burning; and moreover deprives the farmer of a very *hrge* quantity of useful manure.

Details of Deeping Fen, Lindsey Level, and East and West Wildmoor Fens, in the county of
Lincoln, have not been furnished, having little oi no connection with the Bedford Level: indeed the history of their respective drainages, would of themselves furnish ample materials for a separate volume.

And here the author concludes his labours. He has endeavoured to be a faithfirt and an accurate historian and compiler. It cannot be denied, that much of the matter comprised in the foi6" little; as the owners are careful not to pull until the feathers ai ripe, that is, until they are just ready to fall j because, u ' from the skin before that time, (which would be discovered the appearance of blood at the roots,) they are of very i" value. Those plucked after the geese are dead, are «k to be of an indifferent quality.
going sheets may be already known to the practical and experienced Fen-man, but to the uninitiated the work may perhaps hereafter afford some useful information. Of the necessity and utility I of such a production, the writer has received con vincing testimony. A gentleman of influence and: extensive property in the Fens has recently re c signed the honorable and important situation of : one of the conservators of the corporation, alleg ing as a cause his thorough conviction.that it; would require the devotion of a whole life to qua f lify himself to act conscientiously in that capacity. t If, by the publication of this work, the author has *t* contributed in any degree to obviate this difficulty he trusts his name will not descend to posterity quite unhonored and forgotten. THE END. INDEX.
A.
Accounts
of corporation, power of board over, 527.
under care of auditor, 5(54.
Acenowledgments.— Sec *Encroachments.*
Acquittance.
Fee of receiver and expenditor general, 563.
Act Of State.— See *Oidinance.*
Acts or Parliament,
every private act affecting the Bedford Level to be laid before the register, 550.
Acts Of Parliament Cited on Referred To In This Voi.umi-;.
Magna Charta, c. 23, 72.
25 *Ed.* II, c. 4, 72.
43 Ed. Ill, c. 2, ibid.
21 Rich. II, *c.* 12, ibid.
4 Hen. IV, c. 11, ibid.
« Hen. VI, 71.
23 Hen VIII, c. 5, 75. 334—5.
s. 0, 108.
'27 Hen. VIII, 7fi.
c. *10,* 595.
31 Hen. VIII, 76.
13F,liz, 13.
20 Eliz., 88.
43£liz. c. 11, 84. 100. 335.
17 Jac. I, 14.
Id Car. 11,400.
c. 17. s. 8, 5!7.
16 & 17 Car. II, c. 12, 30.
20 Car. II, 400.
c. 2,624.
22 Car. II, 30.
1 Anne, c. 11, 24.
7 Anne, c. 20, 509.
Adjudication *(continued).*
petitions to commissioners of, 2-10, 279.

second and last adjudication, and proceedings relative thereto, 250, 276.
Adventurers,
distinguished from the "Participants," and "The Company," 160.
Adventurers' Lan-os,
meaning of the term, 118.
distinguished from "free lands," 401.
particulars of the 95,000 acres, 612.
in the different Levels, 618.
in the different counties, and the Isle of Ely, ibid.
particulars of the 12,000 acres allotted to the King, 614.
particulars of the 2000 acres granted to the Earl of Portland, 615.
particulars of, with the quantity charged with each sort or degree under the tax act, 624.
with particulars of the quantity lying in the different Levels, charged at each sort, 625.
/k(.ar Or Iivcre, 22.
Alfred The Great,
state of the Great Level under, 63-
Ancient Britons,
state of the Great Level under the, 55.
Animal Substances,
found in the moor beds, 419.
Annual Income (or Corporation),
summary of, under various heads, 635.
Annual Meetings.—See *Meelingi.*
Annual Taxes.—See *Taxes.*
Appeal,
commissioners of, 212.
Appeal (court Op),
powers of, 396.
defunct, 397.
conduct of William Earl of Bedford, 397.
April Meeting.—See *Meetings.*
Aristotle.
his theory of the tides, 46.
Arrear Roll, 561, 561.
mode of sale under, 622.
variation of quantity on, 623.
See also Tow.
Ashley's Contract, 32.
796
Ashley's Sluice,
account of, 719.
Assemblies.—See *Meetings.*
Auditor.
elected annually, 564.
duties, ibid,

oath of office, 566.
salary, 567.
alterations relative to the office, ibid.
list of persons who have filled the office, from 1G63 to the present period, 567.
B,
Badeslade,
opinion of, 294.
Bailiff, 306.
Baneers,
of the corporation, 561.
Banes.—See also *Encroachments.—Tol/t.*
of east division of Middle Level, 61)8.
of north division of Middle Level, *tiO-t.*
of south division of Middle Level, 097.
of North Level, 667.
of South Level, 728.
Banes, Sir Edward,
biographical notice of, 773.
birth, ibid.
contracts and works, ibid,
marriage, 77(.
knighted, 777.
Bardolph Fen,
boundary, 785.
drainage, ibid,
tax, ibid.
debt, 780.
Bargain And Sale,
of lands under corporate seal, (put up as forfeited lands)
resorted to to confer a good title, 624.
Barnard, Sir John, Bart.,
biographical notice of, 485, n.
Barrier Banes, 637, 639.
B&rrier Bane Acts,
of east division of Middle Level, 723.
Bjeales, Samuel Piceering, Esq., 218, «.
Bedford,
John, first Earl of, his appointments, 112.
Bedford, Fran-cis Earl Of,
his expenses in drainage, 97.
the friend and protector of the fen country, 103.
application of fen-men to, 100.
his noble character, ibid.
the contract with him: the Lynn Law, 107.
his participants, 111.
indenture of fourteen parts, ibid.

works of, 112.
St. Iveslaw, 118.
engagement of Vermuj'den, V20.
complaints to the king in council, 120.
King Charles's harsh conduct, 123.
Pym and Saint John, ibid.
reversal of Saint Ives law, 127.
conduct of the earl, 128..
distresses occasioned by these reverses, 130.
his death, 131, 333.
summary of his character, ibid.
marriage of William, his eldest son, 132.
Bedford, William, Earl, And Afterwarus First Duee,
retirement into private life, 141.
his marriage with Ann, daughter of Earl and Countess of
Somerset, 132.
character of, and conduct with regard to the Great Level,
139, 147.
desertion to the king's party, 141.
king's conduct, 1-13.
desertion of the king's party, 144.
assisted by St. John, 212.
first adjudication, 223.
second and last adjudication; and proceedings relative
thereto, 250, 276.
conduct of, under the protectorate, 281.
embarrassing situation of Earl, on death of Cromwell, 325.
deserted by St. John, 327.
accession of Lord Gorges to interests of the company, ibid,
return of, to parliament, 329.
disturbani-es in the Great Level, 331, B32.
conduct of the Earl, 335.
first temporary act, 337.
petition of Earl, and order thereon, 341.
second temporary act, 343.
continued distulbances, and proclamation, 345.
state of parties in the Great Level, 351.
conduct of the Earl, 360, 386.
general drainage act passed, 388.
Bedford, William, First Duee or—(continued).
estnblishment of Bedford Level corporation, 388.
continued exertions, 389.
conduct respecting court of appeal, 387.

created Marquess of Tavistock, and Duke of Bedford, 408.
death and character, 409.
burial and sermon, 409.
governor of the corporation for 37 years, 45G, *n.*
Il.: lunuii, Wrjotfiesley, Second Duee op,
biographical notice of, 47"2,n.
governor of the corporation 11 years, ibid.
Bedford, Wriothesley, Tiiiiiu Duee Op,
biographical notice of, 475, n.
his generosity to the Level, ibid.
    Bedford, John, Eighth Earl Anu Fourth Duee,
biographical notice of, 492, «.
governor of the corporation nearly 38 years, 491, *n.*
Bedford, Francis, Fifth Duee,
biographical notice of, 502, n.
    Bedford, The Present Duee Of, 508, n.
    Bedford Level,
when so named, 1.
extent of, and boundaries, 1, 2, 452.
particulars of fen-lands hi and near, .
provisions as to sewers works in, 5114.
the charter, Olio.
    St. Ives law, ibid.
the pretended act, 586.
general drainage act, 5H7.
divided into three levels, (560.
    Bedford Level Corporation. — See *alto Particular Tillet,and Table of Content.*
limit of jurisdiction,:54 *n.*
charter of incorporation, 114.
its dissolution, ibid.
Francis Earl of Bedford, the founder of the corporation.
133.
establishment of the Bedford Level corporation, 388.
attempts to abridge power of commonalty of, 31)0.
. constitution of, 45-2, 454.
governors of—See *Bedford.*
members of the board from 1663 to 1829. 436.
power to hold and purchase lands, 526.
corporate assemblies, 527.
proceedings at, 528.
power to make bye-laws, 532.
powers as commissioners of sewers, 533.
visitorial jurisdiction, 534, 535, 537.
    Bedford Levp.i, Corporation—*(continued).*
power of court of King's Bench over, 537.
by mandamus, ibid.
officers of, &c.—see *Table of Content i,* Ch. xvii.
power of, to restrain digging tuif, (SI!), debt of, 645. See *Debt.*
revenues of, 620.
expenditure of, 63(5.—And see *Revenuei.*
    Bedford River, 112.
    Bextixcee, Lord William, 681.
    Benvvice Meer, 448.
    Seville's Le.vm, 113.
    Bills In Parliament. See *Parliament.*
BIOGRAPHICAL NOTICES.
    See the respective names of the persons, and see also title *Names,* in this index.
    Board,
name of, when assumed, 398.
difficulties of the, 424.
constituent parts of the, 455.
list of members of, from 1663 to 1820, 45f.
bill to have elections of, in the country, thrown out, 484.
disturbance at election, 489.
business finished without an adjournment, first time since
15 Car. II, 508, *n.*
election of the, 518.
opinion of Sir J. Scarlett respecting, 520.
case as to voters at, 521.
oprnion of T. Denman, Esq, 524.
assemblies for, for proceeding to business, 525. 527-tJ.
powers of, 527.
directs sales of land forfeited for nonpayment of taxes, 531.
power of making bye-laws, 532.
select body of corporation appointed commissioners of
sewers, 588.
cannot sit and act out of the Great Level, 589.
sworn in that capacity, 592.
    Bonds
of corporation assimilated to those of East India Company,
049.
cannot exceed in amount 1007. each, 63.
are assignable, 650.
eligible mode of investing money, 6f 1.
    Bond Act,
first, 650.
second, 651.
    Bottisdam Lode, 23.
BOUNDARIES
set out by scrjeant at mace, 669.
ut Hardolph Fen, 785.
of Bedford Level, 452.
of Downham Fen, 786.
of Great Level, 1.
of Marshland, 781.
of Middle Level, 692.
of east division of Middle Level, 69B.
of north division of Middle Level, 00;).
of south division of Middle Level, 696.
of North Level, 6(51.
of South Level, 727.
of South Holland, 78ft.
of Wisbech hundred, 7H7.
Brandon, or Les&er River, 6.
outfalls to sea, 38.
    Brice Meee, 450.
    Bridge.
Crowland, or Croyland, 11.
Wandsford bridge, anecdote respecting, IU.
Wisbech, 21.
over West River, 27.
Uhidi.ks,—See also *Tollt.*
of the South Level, 207, 729.
public, of North Level, 671.
private, of North Level, 672.
of north division of Middle Level, 695.
of south division of Middle Level, 697.
of east division of Middle Level, 099.
suspension bridge over Hundred Feet River, 75O.
over Thames, builders of, 771, *n.* 774, 775, 777.
over the Ouze.—See *0uze.*
    Broad Fen,
tax, 705.
    Bulwares,
at Earith, 59.
    Bve-laws,
power of board or corporation to make, 632.
respecting registration of deeds, 600.
    Cam River, 6.
outfalls to sen, 6.

course, &c., 22.
neighbourhood, ibid.
 Cam River *(continued).*
navigation of, 24.
acts of parliament relating to, ibid,
cast iron bridge, 25.
 Carr, Or Conn Dyee, (JO.
CASES CITED OR REFERRED TO IN THIS
VoLUJIB'
 Brown o. Hammond, 323.
Clarehall *v.* Orvin, 67.
Doc d. Robinson *v.* Allsop, 599.
Edwards *r.* Vesey, 533.
Gibbon's case, 535.
Hodson *v.* Sharpe, 5JJ3.
London *v.* Lynn, 535.
M'Neil *v.* Ca'trill, 598.
Marriage *v.* Lawrence, 535.
Moore's case, ibid.
Rex *v.* Babb, 536.
Rex *v.* Chester, ibid.
 Ilex *v.* Commissioners of Salter's Lode Sluice to Standground Sluice, 707.
 Rext?. Commissioners of the Nene Outfall, 684.
Rex *v.* Corporation of Bedford Level, 554, «.
Rext), Debenham, 535.
Rex e. Gordon, (Lord George), 530.
Rex r. Ipswich, 536.
Rex n. Mothersell, 53-i.
Rex *v* Newcastle, 536.
Rex c. Pigram, 530.
Rex *v.* Rye, ibid.
Rex *v.* St. Luke's Hospital, 708.
Rex p. Shelley, 536.
Rex *v.* Travannion, ibid.
Rex p. Tower, ibid.
Rogers *v.* Jones, ibid.
 Charles I.
accession of, 103.
session of sewers at Huntingdon, ibid,
the Lynn Law, 107.
indenture of 14 parts, 111.
works of the Earl of Bedford and his participants. Hi.
charter of Bedford Level Corporation, 114.
its dissolution, 115.
general survey of fen lands, 117.
St Ives' law, 118.
engagement of Vermuyden, 120.
complaints to the king in council, and proceedings thereon, 120,1-21.

harsh conduct to Francis Earl of Bedford, 123.
renewal of Saint Ives law, 127.
VOL. I. 3 F
 Charles I. *(continued).*
king declared to be the undertaker of the work, 123.
works begun by him, 1'29, n.
of the affairs in the Level contributing to deprive him of
Crown, 134.
his execution, 153——See also *Table of Contents.*
 Charles II.
restoration of, 3-29.
disturbances in the Level, 331—2.
first temporary act, 387.
 Earl of Bedford's petition, and order thereon, 341.
second temporary act, 343.
continued disturbances, and king's proclamation,:1 i."».
commission of sewers, 340.
state of parties in the Great Level, 351.
parliamentary proceedings, 351.
general drainage act passed, 388.
establishment of the Bedford Level corporation, ibid,
attempts to abridge power of commonalty of corporation, 390.—See also *Table of Contents.*
 Charter,
granted by Car. L, if now valid 454.
of the corporation, powers conferred by, 585..
 Chater River,
its source, 12.
 Church,
power and possessions of, 74.
care of drainage, 75.
 Claying,
the land, signification of, 442.
cost of, ibid.
 Corporation,
distinction between corporations by statute and by charter, 453.
Corporation Of The Bedford Level, See *Bedford Level Corporation.*
Corporation Debt.—See *Debt.*
Corporation Of GoonfANCHESTEH.—
See *Godmanchester.*
Corporation Of Thetford.—See *Thetford.*
Corporate Documents.
custody of, &36.

interest of corporation in, ibkl.
right to inspect, ibid.
See also *Evidence.*
 Commissioners Of Sewers-.—See *Sewew.*
 Commonalty,
of corporation, attempt to abridge power of, 390.
 Common Recovery.—See *Recovery.*
 Commonwealth,
state of the Great Level under, 146.
the pretended act, preliminary and subsequent proceedings, 148. 155. 158.
progress of the works, 157.
the company, 160.
transactions with Vermuyden, 102. 172. 181.
distresses of the company, 173.
progress of the works, 213.
first adjudication, 223.
employment of Scotch prisoners, and proceedings relative thereto, 228.
state of the South Level under the, 246.
employment of Dutch prisoners, 250.
second and last adjudication, and proceedings relative thereto, 250. 276.—
See also *Table of Contents.*
 Company, the,
distinguished from the " participants", and "adventurers," 160.
adoption of laws, &c., of Romney Marsh by, 30'J.
See further, *Romney Marsh.*
 Conquest;
state of the Fens at the, 64.
Conquest Lode,108.
 Conservator,
resignation of office of, in consequence of difficulty of duties, 791.
 Corr, Or Carr Dyee, 6O.
 Cottages,
permission to build, not granted as a matter of course, 634.
under care of superintendents, 635.
source of revenue, ibid.
 Court Of Appeal.—See *Appeal.*
 Court Op King's Bench.—See *King's Bench.*
 Courts Of Sewers.—See *Sewers.*
 Cow-dung,
used for fuel, 790.
 Coy Wood, 446.
Cradoe,
signification of term, 638, *n..*
Cromwell,

his appearance in public life, 136.,i
Cromwell
pedigree, 136.
his conduct with respect to the Great Level, 137.
accession of, 281.
ordinance for preserving the works of the Great Level, 282.
stability of his government, 319.
his death, 322.
Crowland, Or Croyland Bridge,
when erected, 11.
Cultivation
of the fens, 4:26.
mode of, 440.
of flax and hemp, ibid.
Cut Land Roll, 616.
schedule of lands in Middle and South Levels, the taxes 01 which are ordered to be annually deducted, 617.
D.
Danes,
state of the Great Level under the, 63.
Debt Of Corporation, 645.
interest due on, under control of receiver and expenditor general, 562.
generosity of the house of Russell, 619.
first bond act, 650.
second, 651.
extent of, for Middle and South Levels, ibid.
—— --North.Level, ibid.
creation of new debt, 652.
interest punctually paid, 653.
Decoys, 446.
Deeds,
registration of, case, and argument thereon, 593.
De La Pryme,
opinion of, as to trees in the fens, 422.
Denver Sluice,
probable origin of, 162.
erection of, 739.
conference between corporations of Lynn and Bedford Level, 740.
demolition of, 742.
applications for re-erection, 745.
Labelye's scheme, 746.
Descartes,
his theory of the tides, 46.
District Act.— See *Private District Act.*

jJOCUMRNTS OF CORPORATION,
destroyed in fire of London, 657.
Dodson (colonel), 162.
his design, 399.
Domesday Book,
compilation of, 66.
Double Lifts,
signification of, 439.
adopted in the Fens, 100, ».
Downfal Waters, 45.
Downiiam Bridge, 37.
tolls, 770.
Downham Fen,
boundary, 786.
drainage, ibid.
Down-ham Eau, 200.
Dbtainaoe,
system of, 424.
private, of North Level, 609.
by mills and steam engines.—See note in *Table of Cbntents,* p. xiv. See also *General Drainage Act.*
Drainage Acts,
proviso in, 607..
general saving clause in, ibid.
Dijnbar,
battle of, 228.
Dung,
used for fuel, 700.
Dutch,
naval victory over the, 249.
employment of Dutch prisoners, 250.
E.
Eaeith,
bulwarks at, 59.
East Division or Middle Level.—See *Middle Level.*
Eau Brine Bridge, 37.
erected by Sir Edward Banks and William John Jolliflc, 775.
Eau Brine Cut,
made, 732.
new cut from, 755.
estimate of expense, ibid.
taxes, 759.
accounts, 761,
Eau Brine Cut, new cut from, *(continued).*
opened to public, 767.
widened, ibid,
costs of, 767.
made by Sir Edward Banks and William John Jolliffe,

775.
Edward VI.
state of the Great Level under, 77.
Election Of Board.—See *Board.*
Elizabeth, Queen,
state of the Great Level under, 78.
For general summary, see also *Table of Contents,* Ch. V.
Ely,
great bridge at, repaired by dean and chapter, 730, *n.*
751, *it.*—See also *hie of Ely.*
Encroachments,
on the banks to be reported by the superintendent, 575.
sums paid to corporation in acknowledgment of, 635.
Engineers,
anecdote respecting, 293.
John Dyson appointed in 1824, 572.
duties of, 573.
salary, ibid.
assistants, ibid.
residence, ibid.
all the corporation works under his control, ibid.
sluice-keepers and labourers subject to, 677.
Enrollment, statute of.—See *Registration of Deedt.*
Evidence,
what corporate documents are, 535.
entry in register's book evidence, if original deed lost, 647.
whether books of entries are, where deed lost, 600.
Expenditor General.—See *Receiver.*
Expenditure or The Corporation,
considered at the April meeting, 636.
extra expenditure, 610.
general statement of expenditure for year 1829, 641.
Extra Expenditure Ok The Corporation, 610.
F.
Fairs,
at Thorney, 675.
Fees Of Officers.—See the names of the different offites.
Fln Lands,
particular;: of, 2.
Fen Office,
in the Inner Temple, first meeting at the, 32I.
destroyed by the fire of London, 057.

where formerly held, G5!$.
where now held, ibid.
most ancient register office in the kingdom, C59.
object of, ibid.
all records kept there, 6!. 659.
where meetings originally held, 655.
chambers, No. 3, Tanfield Court, InnerTemple, hired for,
658.
now situated No. », Serjeants' Inn, Fleet Street, ibid.
Fens,
phenomena of, 417.
Ferries,
of the North Level, G71.
   FIENNBS, THE HONORABLE WILLIAM T.HOMAS TWISELTON,
one of the conservators, 302, *n.*
   Fire Of London,
destroyed records of corporation, 657.
except some papers relating to Lynn law, ibid.
   Fir Apples,
found in the soil of the Fens, 419.
   Firs,
found in the soil of the Fens, 418. 421.
   Fisheries,
of theWelland, 15.
right of, in Whittlesey Meer, 450.
source of revenue, 634.
   Fitzwilliam, Earl Of, 504, *n.*
   Flanders,
state of, with regard to drainage, 08.
navigation, ibid.
distinguished from Holland, 99.
Great Level, 100.
   Folly River, 668.
Forfeiture.—See *Taxes.*
Forty-feet Drain, 198.
   Free Lands,
distinguished from " Adventurers' lands," 401.
   French Names,
origin of the, in the Fens, 94.
   Fuel,
peat used for, 700.
turf, ibid,
cow-dung, ibid.
   G.
   Galileo,
bia theory of the tides, 40.
   Geese,
cruel practice of plucking alive, 789.
breed of, reduced by drainage, 790.

Geneeal Drainage,
hostility of fen-men to, lo.j.
   General Drainage Act, 84.
passed, 38it.
first meeting under, 390.
provisions of, 587.
   General Ijjclosure Clause.—See *hclosure.*
General Survey or Fen Lands, 117.
German's Bridge,
tolls, 780.
Glen, Or Glran River, G.
outfalls to sea, G.
its source and navigation, 7.
its connection with Bedford Level drainage, 8.
acts of parliament affecting, 8.
   GoDlfANCBBgTEK,
corporation, antiquity of, 31.
powers of, ibid.
town of, ibid.
   Gorges, Lord,
accession of, to interests of the company, P27.
biographical notice of Richard, Lord, 471, n.
   Grant, River, G.
outfalls to sea, G.
   Granta liivr.it, 22.
   Great Level,
extent of, 1.
original state of, 54,
state of, under the ancient Britons or Gyrvii, 65.
Romans, 57.
. Saxons, G2.
. Alfred the Great, G3.
. at the conquest, 64.
under William the Conqueror, 65.
Henry I, ibid.
   Stephen, ibid.
   John of Gaunt's design, G!.
state of, under Henry IV. V. VI. and VII., 71,73.
   Great Level— *(continued).*
state of, under Henry VIII, 74.
effect of the reformation on the, 76.
state of, under Edward VI, 77.
Queen Mary, ibid,
Elizabeth, 78.
commissions of sewers, 80.
meeting of commissioners, 83.
general drainage act, 84.
her death, 85.
state of,, under James 1, 86.

possessions of the crown in, ibid,
distinguished from Holland and Flanders, 100.
dislike of the people to drainage, 101
under Charles I. See *Charles I.*
under the Commonwealth, 146.
division of, 196.
under the Protectorate, 281.
ordinance or act of state for the preservation of the
works, 282.
adoption by the company of the laws and customs of
Romney Marsh, 303.
proceedings of government after the death of Cromwell, 328.
under Charles II, 329. See *Charles II.*
navigation through, 703.
See also *Table of Contents.*
Cheat Ouze River, 6.
outfalls to sea, 0.
Geeat River, 21.
Ghunty Fen Drain, 200
Guasu, River, 12.
Gvbvii,
state of the Great Level under the ancient Gyrvii, 58.
   H.
   Haltoft's Commission, 73.
Hammond's Eau, 198.
Hardwicee, Earl of, 505, *n.*
present surveyor general, 541.
biographical notice of, ibid.
Hahe,
transaction with' Sir Thomas, 713.
Haven,
of King's Lynn, 754.
Hazel Nuts,
found in the soil of the Fens, 410. *4,11*
VOL. I. 3 G
   Heathcote, John, Esq.
biographical notice of, 504, *n.*
Henry I.,
state of the Great Level under, 65.
Henry IV,
state of the Great Level under, 71.
III-IXU Y V.,
state of the Great Level under, ibid.
Hexry VI.,
state of the Great Level under, ibid.
Henry VII.,
state of the Great Level under, 73.
Henry VIII.,
state of the Great Level under, 74.
acts of parliament, 75.

Herbert, Arthur, Earl of Torrington,
biographical notice of, 407, n. 471, n.
High And Low Water, 47.
Highland Earth,
difficulty of obtaining, 691.
Hill's Cut, 113.
Holland,
state of, with regard to drainage, 98.
navigation, ibid.
distinguished from Flanders, 99.
Great Level, 100.
    HotLANDERS,
in England, 94.
settlement of, in England, 79.
    HoLYWELL,
jurisdiction of Bedford Level corporation ends near this place, 34.
    Horse Mills,
drainage by, 426.
    Huguenots,
massacre of, and consequence of, 79.
Human Bodies,
discovered in the Fens, 421.
Hundred Feet River, 30.
improvement of, 735.
suspension bridge, 750.
Huntingdon,
session of sewers at, under Charles I., 103.
Hyee River, 29.
Hycrb, or jEoAR, 22.
    I.
    Inclosueb,
general inclosurc clause, 403.
repealed, 405.
of marshland Smeath and Fen, 783.
    Ixclosure Acts,
proviso in, 608.
general saving in, 609.
    Income,
summary of annual income of corpoiation, 635.
    Indenture Of 14 Parts, 111.
    Interest,
on corporation debt punctually paid, 653.
See also *Debt*.
    Inundation,
causes of, &c., 44.
See further, *Tides*.
    Isle Of Ely,
marquess of; origin of title, 130, *n*.
    Ivel River, 29.
    J.
    James I.,

accession of, 86.
state of the Great Level under, 86.
his personal interest in the drainage, 87.
his letters to the commissioners of sewers, &e., 88.
becomes the undertaker of the work, 91.
his recompense, ibid.
invitation of Sir Cornelius Vermuyden, 92.
political embarrassments, 102.
neglect of fens, 103.
See also *Table of Contents,* Ch. v.
    Jemvxs, George Leonard, Esq., 172, *n.*
    Jenyns, Soame, Esq.,
biographical notice of, 491, n.
    John Of Gaunt's design, 69.
    Jolliffb,Hylton, Esq.,
engaged with Sir Edward Banks, 774.
marriage of, 774, n.
    Jolliffe, William John,
his works with Sir Edward Banks, 774, &c.
    Jurats, 306.
    K.
    Kepler,
his theory of the tides, 46.
    Kinderley'h Cut, 676.
    King.— See *the retpectiee names of the Kings in this Index*
For caws in which the king is plaintiff,— See *Cases*.
particulars of the 12,000 acres allotted to the, «14.
Kino's Bench, Couht Of,
power of, over corporations, 537.
by mandamus, ibid.
Kino's Lands,
how taxed, 401. 630.
Kino's Lynn,
session of sewers at, under Charles I., 103.
origin of name, 752.
site of town, 753.
haven of, 754.
commerce of, 755.
    L.
    Labelve,
opinion of, 206.
his scheme for re-erection of Denver Sluice, 740.
Labourers,
petition of, for pnyment, 228.
Lare, Oh Mildenhall River, 6.
outfalls to sea, 6. 38.

Lare, River,
its source and navigation, 38.
Lesser Ouzb, on Brandon River, 6
outfalls to sen, 6, 38.
its source and current, ay.
its navigation, ibid.
acts of parliament relating to, *ibid'.*
LEVELS.-See also *Bedford Lecel.-Grtat Level.*
each formed mto a distinct government, 437.
division of the three, 660.
Little Bill, the, 90.-
    Local Acts—Sec *Private District Acts.*
Loces,
from Hudd's Mill to East Deeping, 16.
    Londoners, The,
attempts at drainage, 101.
Lode, ibid.
Lords,
elected, 300—6.
Lot-booe,
contents of, 549.
kept by the register, 549. 550.
formerly kept by receiver and expemiitor-general, 559.
new one prepared by register, 629.
Lynn,
port of, 752.
Lynn Law, 107. 425. 584.
some papers relative to, saved from fire of London, 657.
    M.
    Mace,
presented by William, Earl, and afterwards Duke of Bedford, 528, *n.*
kept in custody of serjeant at mace, 509.
Mace, Serjeant at.—See *Serjeant at Mace.*
    Magdalen Bridge, 37.
tolls, 779.
    Mandamus.
writ of, 537.
Mareet,
at Thorney, 675.
    Mahquess Of The Isle Of Ely,
origin of, 138, *n.*
    Marshland,
contents of, 781,«.
district, 781.
outfall, ibid.
drainage, ibid.
road and bridge, 782.
debt, 783.

Smeath and Fen, 783.
inclosed, ibid.
drained, ibid.
tax, 784.
   Marshland Cut, 199.
account of, 708.
improvement of, 712. 716.
Mary, Queen,
state of the Great Level under, 78.
Medium Tax, 620.
   Meers, 447.
   Meetings,
of the corporation, 527.
rule for finding day of April meeting, ibid.
where held, 531.
   Middle Level,
works of the, 197.
made a distinct government, 437.
how taxed, 621.
boundaries, G92.
divisions of, ibid.
north division, 693.
boundaries of, ibid.
banks, 694,
sluices, 695..
bridges, ibid.
rivers waded, ibid,
south division, 696.
boundaries, ibid.
banks, 697.
sluices, ibid.
bridges, ibid.
rivers, ibid,
east division, 698.
boundaries, ibid.
banks, ibid.
sluices and tunnels, *ti'J'J.*
bridges, ibid.
river, ibid.
Nene act, 706.
cast division,
case respecting, 707.
   Tongs drain, 708.
   Wisbech canal act, 717.
Ashline's sluice, 719.
river act, 720.
barrier bank acts, 723.
natural and artificial rivers, ibid.
sluices, 724.
private tolls, ibid.
bankers, 725.
Middlesex Registry Acts.—See *Registration of Deedt.*
   MILDEXHALL, OR LARE, RIVER,

outfalls to sea, 6.
   Mills,
drainage by, 426.
presented as nuisances, 427.
proceedings in Chancery, ibid.—See also note in *Table of Conttnti,* p. xiv.
   Milton, Lord Viscount, 511, *n.*
Minor Banes, 638, G39.
Minute Booe, 531, 546.
Monasteries,
dissolution of, 73.
   Moore's Drain, 198.
   Morton, Bishop,
errors of, 202.
   Morton's Leam, 72. 113.
   Myhica Gale,
found in the turf moors, 421.
N.
Names,
origin of French names in the Fens, 04.
   Names Of Cases Cited Or Referred To.—See *Cases.*
   Names Of Persons Particularly Noticed Ob Referred To In
This Volume.
Search for the name required, (if not included in the following list,) under its proper head in this Index.
Adeane, Henry, Esq., '25.
Allix Peter, Esq., ibid.
Annesley, Arthur, Esq., 506, and n.
Arundel, Earl of, 208, and *n.*
Bath, Marquess of, 180, *n.*
Beales, Samuel Pickering, Esq., 248, *n.*
Bedford.—See *Bedford.*
Bernardin St. Pierre, 52.
Besborough, Earl of, 507, *n,*
Browne, 11.
   Burgess, Thomas, Esq., 502, *n.*
Burghley, house of, 11.
Burghley, Lord, 84.
Cecil, Sir Thomas, 84.
Cecil, Sir William, 81. 84.
Chicheley, Thomas, Esq., 456, n.
Childers, John Walbank, Esq., 92, n.
Coe, Alderman, 25.
Cole, Charles Nalson, Esq., 490, n.
D'Alva, Duke, 79.
De la Pryme, 94, n.
Downshire, Marchioness of, 188, *n.*
Drage, John, Esq., 500, *n.*
Dyson, John, (the present engineer), 572. 711.

Eardley, Sampson Lord, 92, «.
   Names—*(continued).*
   Evans, Hugh Robert, Esq., (the present receive anJ expenditor general), 560. 563.
Exeter, Marquess of, 84.
Fellowes, William Henry, Esq., 427. 502, «. 500, *n.*
Fiennes, the Honorable William ThYnias Tvriaelton, 302, *n.* 516, and n.
Fitzwilliams, Sir William, 81.
Fitzroy, house of, 40.
Gardner, John, Esq., 499, and n.
Gerard, Sir Gilbert, jun., Knt., 456, *n.*
Gideon, Sir Sampson, Bart., 501, n.
Girdlestone, Steed, Esq., (the present auditor), 503, 718.
Gorges, Lord, 181, n.
Gould, Sir Charles, 505, and *;.*.
Grangers, family of, 448.
Ground, Mr., 502, n.
Gwydir, Lord, 8.
Hale, Sir Matthew, 329.
Haltoft, Gilbert, Baron, 72.
Hardwicke, Earl of, 25. 159.
Hare—See *Hare.*
Henley, Robert, Esq., 220, *n.*
Herbert, Arthur, Earl of Torrington, 467, *n.* 471, n.
Ingle, Alderman, 25.
Jackson, 718.
Jenyns, Rev. George, 25.
Jenyns, George Leonard, Esq., 172.
Jolliffe, Hylton, Esq., 774.
Jolliffe, William John, ibid.
Lee, William, Esq., 101.
Little, John, (one of the present superintendents), 574.
Manners, Lord Robert, 98, *n.*
Marshall, William, (the present serjeant at mace), 571
Mawson, Dr. Matthias, Bishop of Ely, 747.
Montagu, Sir Edward, 81.
Morgan, Sir Charles, 505, nnd *n.* 510, n.
Morris, Matthew Robinson, afterwards Lord Rokebv 409, n.
   Morton, Bishop of Ely, 73.
Ncvill, 10.
Norwich, Earl of, 190, and n.
Orton, Thomas, Esq., 722.
Osborne, Lord Francis Godolphin, 510, n.

Owen, John, (one of the present superintendents) 574
Page, Jonathan, Esq., 507, n.
Palmer, Sir John, 10.
Peyton, Sir John, Bart., 89.
Pophani, C. J., 83.
Names—*(continued)*.
Pryme, George, Esq., 05,w.
Purchase, Alderman, 2-3.
Pym, 123.
Rennie, John, Esq., 60—See also *Rennie.*
Richmond, Margaret, Countess of, 72.
Royston, Lord, 511 and *n.*
Russell, Colonel John, 146.
Saint John, 123.155.
Sandys, Sir Edward Bayntum, Bait., 188, *ti.*
Sopcote, Robert, Esq., 81.
Sedgley, Joseph, (one of the present superintendents), 574.
Sherard, Castell, Esq., 220, n.
Smith, Sir Culling, Bart., 517.
Smith, Thomas, 15.
Sondes, Lord, 10.
Spooner, Thomas, Esq, 516, re.
Tavistock, Francis, Marquess of, killed by n fall from his horse, 500, n.
Tenterden, Lord, 591.
Tharpe, 220, n.
Thomson, Esq., 486, n.
Thurlowe, 250.
Thynne, Baron, 180.
Townley, Rev. W. Gale, 750.
Townly, R. G. Esq., 25.
Townshend, Charles Lord Viscount, 495, *n.*
Wandley, Hugh, 711.
Wells, Samuel, Esq., 508. 556.—See also *Wells.*
Wells, Wm., Esq., 514, *n.*
Westmoreland, Lord, 89.
Westerdyke.—See *(f'exterdyke.*
Weymouth, Viscount, 180.
Winchelsea, Earl of, 12.
Wing, Tycho, Esq., (one of the conservators), 664, n/718.
Yorke, Admiral Sir Joseph, 767.
Nar, Or Sandbingham Eau, River, 6.
outfalls to sea, 6.
Natural Productions Of The Fexs, 418.
Natural Rivers.—See *River.*

Navigation,
early dissensions between drainage nnd, 6!9.
through the Great Level, 703.
Navigation Act, 212, *n.*
Neap Tides, 49.
Nen, Nene, Or Nine River,
outfalls to sea, 6.
its course and biidge, 12.
Vol. r. 3 H
N«n, Nene, or Nine River—*(continutd).*
origin of name, 17.
its source and current, ibid,
the neighbourhood, 18.
navigation of, 20.
acts of parliament relating to, ibid,
property in the navigation, ibid,
tides, 2).
Nene Act,
object of, 705.
case respecting, 707.
commissioners of, 710, *n.*
how affected by Wisbech canal act, 716—7.
how elected, 718.
clerk and treasurer to trustees of, ibid.
Nene,
bridge act, 682.
outfall, 683.
case concerning, 684, *n.*
debt, 719.
officers, ibid,
bridges over, by whom erected, 751, ».
Newton,
his theory of the tides, 45.
Tydd and, drainage act, 678.
New Adventurers, 352.
New South Eau, 113.
North Level,
extent of the, 196. 661, 664, n.
works of the, ibid.
made a distinct government, 437.
how taxed, 621.
revenues of, separated from the other two Levels, 621, w. 649.
revenues of, taken from control of corporation, 662.
passing of first North Level act, 662.
accounts between that and the other Levels, 66;).
second North Level act, ibid,
officers of, 664.
divided into five districts, ibid.

their several contents and boundaries, 665—6.
water for, how conveyed, 666.
external works of drainage, ibid,
banks, 667.
rivers, 668.
roads (public), 669.
(private), ibid.
private drainages, 669.
North Level (continued).
internal works of drainage under management of North
Level committee, 666.
its ancient and modern works of drainage;
banks, 667.
rivers, 668.
public roads, 669.
private ibid.
drainages, ibid.
public tolls, 670.
private ibid.
sluices, ibid.
ferries, 671.
bridges (public), ibid.
—— (private), 672.
officers, ibid.
..- duties, ibid.
taxes, 673.
Kinderley's Cut, 676.
Tytld and Newton drainage act, 678.
Nene bridge act, 682.
outfall, 683.
case concerning, 684, *n.*
intended improvement of, 690.
water, how furnished in dry seasons, 670, n.
North Division Op Middle Level.—Sec *Middle Level.*
o.
Oaths Of Office,
administered by the register, 528. 530.
form of, 529.
Officers,
appointment of, 53!).
surveyor general, 541.
register, 045.
receiver and expenditor general, 557.
auditor, 565.
serjeant at mace, 568.
engineer, 571,
superintendents, 573.
sluice keepers, 580.-
of North Level, 672.
duties, ibid.

Old Auveni unfits, 352.
Old Bedfoed River, 112.
Old Bedford Sluice, 721.
Old Po-dyke, 60.
Oliver Cromwell.— See *Commonwealth.*
Onk Hundred Fbet River.—See *Hundred Feet River.*
Or Debs,
respecting registration of deeds, 600,
standing, as to drainage bills, 603.
Order-booe, 531. 546.
Ordinance,
for preservation of works of Great Level, 282.
Orford, Earl of,
biographical notice of, 469, n.
Outfall,
of Marshland, 781.
of Nene bridge, 083.
Outfalls To Sea,
neglected by Vermuyden, 292.—And see *'ertrivyden.*
Ou/e, River,
its course, 26.
upland waters, where emptied, 29.
navigation of, 30.
acts of parliament relating to, 30. 34.
stream of, 33.
disputes respecting, ibid.
below Denver Sluice, 36.
bridges, 37.
Ouze,
improvement of river, 755.
bridges over, 779.
Downham bridge, ibid.
Stow bridge, ibid.
Magdalen bridge, ibid.
German's bridge, 780.
P.
Parliament, Acts Of.—See *Acli of Parliament.*
Parliament,
proceedings in, oil bills relative to Bedford Level, 603.
duties of register as to bills before, 605.
Partheriche,
Sir Edward's proposal, 182.
Participants,
distinguished from the " adventurers" and " the company," 160.
Peaeire Drain, 113.
T,
used for fuel, 700.
Peyton, Henry Dasiiwood, Esq.,

biographical notice of, 503, *n.*
Peyton, Sib John, Bart.,
anecdote of, 89.
Phenomena,
of the Fens, 417.
Pipes,
meaning of, 447.
PLANTS AND NATURAL PRODUCTIONS,
of the Fens, 418.
POPHAM, C. J.,
attempt at drainage, 101.
Poeer, The,
why so called, 708, n.
Pretended Act, 155.
not now an available law, 107.
provisions of, 586.
Priority of Title,
case, and argument thereon, 593.
Private Bridges.—See *Bridges.*
Private District Act,
first, 437.
drainage under, 438,
Private Drainages,
of the North Level, 669.
Private Roads.—See *Roads.*
Private To'lls.—See *Tolls.*
Prosecution,
particulars relative to a prosecution of Thomas Carter and others, for misbehaviour at election day, 477.
Protectorate.—See *Commonwealth, Cromwell.*
Public Bridges.—See *Bridges.*
Public Houses,
source of revenue, 631.
list of, 632.
situation, ibid.
annual rental, ibid.
Public Roads.—See *Roads,*
Public Tolls.—See *Tolls.*
Puddling,
system of, 590.
Purchase,
power of B. L. C. to purchase and hold lands, 52G.
Q.
Queen.—*See their respective names in thit Index.*
R.
Ramsey Meer, 450.
Reach Lode, 23.
Receiver And Ex Pbnditor. General,,
elected annually, 557.
duties, ibid.
formerly kept a lot-book, 550.

interest due on corporation debt under his control, 662.
enters into bond with sureties for due execution of office
562.
oath of, 563.
salary, 563.
acquittance-fee, ibid,
list of persons who have held this office, from 1663 to the
present period, 563.
when subject to directions of auditor, 566.
Recovery,
where deed making tenant to the *preecipe* is not registered till after Term in which recovery suffered, if valid, 594.
Reeds,
in Fens, used for thatching, 788.
Reformation,
effect of the, on the Great Level, 76.
Register, 306.
administers oaths of office, 528. 530.
form of, 529.
draws up all orders of corporation and board, 531.
chief paid officer of corporation, 545.
elected annually at April meeting, ibid,
sworn officer, ibid.
no deputy, except in cases of illness, &c., ibid,
salary, ibid.
additional annual gratuity, ibid,
duties, 546. 559.
keeps all the records, &c., 546.
qualifications of, 549. 550.
fees, 551.
regulations on death of, 552.
list o.f registers from 1663 to the present time, 553.
Samuel Wells, Esq, present Register, 616.
duties of. as to bills before parliament, 605.
Registration Of Deeds,
case, and argument thereon, 593.
orders and bye-laws respecting, 600.
Registry Acts.—See *Registration of Deeds.*
Rennie, John, (the late),
bioglaphical notice of, 768.
works, 770.
marriage, 771.
death, ibid,

family, ibid.
Restoration.—See *Charles If.*
Revenues Op The Corporation,
power of board over, 527.
See also, *Banks; Cottages; Encroachments; Fisheries; Public-houses; Taxes; Tolls.*
Rivers,
banks and fisheries of, let triennfally, 634.
of east division of Middle Level, 699.
of north division of Middle Level, 695.
of south division of Middle Level, 697.
of the North Level, 608.
of South Level, 730.
weeding of, to be attended to by superintendents, 57».
 Rivers,
Brandon, or Lesser Ouze, 6.
Cam, 6.
Chater, 12.
Glen, or Glean, 6.
Grant, 6.
Granta, 22.
Great Ouze, 6.
Guash, 12.
Hundred Feet, 30.
Hyee, 29.
Ivel, ibid.
Lark, or Mildenhall, 6,,.
.Lesser Ouze, or Brandon, ibid.
Mildenhall, or Lark, ibid.
.Nar, or Sandringham Eau, ibid.:
outfalls to sea, ibid.
Nen, Nene, or Nine, 17.
Ouze, 26.
Sandringham Eau, or Nar, 6.
Stoke, or Wissey, ibid.
Ten Mile, 26.
Vealland, 9. 10.
Welland, 6.
 Rivers—*(continued)*.
Wissey or Stoke, 6.
For particular relative to the different river, tee their
retpecttne namet.
 Roads,
(public) of North Level, 609.
(private) ibid.
 Romans,
state of the Great Level at their arrival, 57.
the first undertakers of the drainage, 58.
vurks and fortifications., ibid.
Roainn banks, 59.

Old Podyke, 60
Carr, or Corr Dyke, ibid.
departure of the, 61.
Rovney Marsd,
account of, 299.
laws and customs of, adopted hy the Company, 303.
lords elected, 305.
steward, 306.
register, ibid.
builiff, ibid.
jurats, ibid.
lords, 307.
expenditor, 314.
serjeant, ibid.
bailiff's, ibid.
 Russell,
Honorable William, 407. 461, *n.*
Right Honorable Admiral, 469, *n.*
s.
 Saint German's Bridge, 37.
 Saint Ives' Law, 118.
reversal of, 127.
"decree under, 585.
 Saint Ives' Staunch,: 1.
 Saint John, Oliver,
prepared the pretended act, 155.
memoir of, 177, 200.
desertion of, 327.
 St. John's Eau,
origin of, 162, 736.
why so called, 191).
 Salaries, Of Officers.—*See the names of the different offices.*
 Salter's Lode,
discoveries, when excavated, 419.
Salter's Lode Sluice,.724.
Sam's Cut, 112.
Sandall's Or Sandy's Cut, 113.
 Sandrinoham Eau, Or Nar River,,
outfalls to sea, 6.
 Sandwich, Earl Of,
biographical notice of, 4!)7, *n.*
Sandy's Or Sandall's Cut, 113.
origin of name, 399.
Saxo.vs,
state of Great Level under the, G2.
 Scotch,
their resemblance to the Jews, 87.
as a nation inferior to Englishmen, 245. 768.
 Scotch Prisoners,
employment of, and proceedings relative thereto, 228.
 Seal *of* Corporation.—*See Title.*

Select Body.—*See Board.*
 Serjeant At Mace,
elected annually, 50!'.
oath of office, ibid,
duties, ibid,
qualifications, 569.
has the custody of the mace, ibid,
fees, 570.
list of persons who have held the office from 1GG3 to tl.e present period, 570.
 Sewers, Commission Of,
general session at Stamford, 14.
issued under Edward VI., 78.
13&20Eliz., 80.
meeting of commissioners, 83.
sessions of, at Huntingdon under Charles I., 103.
King's Lynn, ibid..
commission of, under Charles II., 349.
general commissions of, 584.
general drainage act, 587.
select body of corporation appointed commissioners of,
588.
power to make *new* works, 588, *n.*
revival of court of, 591.
power of Bedford Level corporation as commissioners of,
533..
VOL. I. 3 I
 Sewers, Commissioners Of,
arbitrary conduct of, 105.
St. Ive's lav, at Huntingdon, 118.
reversal of, 127.
oppressive conduct of commissioners, ibid.
 Shields,
found in the Middle Level, 421.
Shirbece Sluice,
discoveries, when made, 420.
Shire Drain, 113.
 Short Fen,
tax, 785.
 Single Tax, 620.
SIxTEEN-PEET RIVER, 108.
 Seeleton Of Fish,
found in Huntingdonshire, 420.
Sluices,
of east division of Middle Level, 699. 724.
of north divison of Middle Level, 695.
of south division of Middle Level, 697.
of the North Level, 670.
of the South Level, 729.
of South Level blown up, 742.

Sluice-eeepers,
subject to engineer and superintendents, 577.
authority of, ibid.
elected annually, 580.
duty, ibid.
to keep accounts of height of waters, &c., 581.
oath of office, 582.
list of present sluice keepers, and their salaries, ibid.
    Smith's Leam, 197.
Soham Meer, 448.
Son,
of the fens, 418.
    South Holland,
boundary of,.7R6.
drainage, ibid.
    South Level,
works of the, 199.
on the south side of Bedford River, 203.
for forelands, north side, 20j.
from Guyhirn to Peterborough, on the north side, ibid.
_ on the south side, 200.
additions by Vermuyden, ibid,
bridges, 207.
    South Level *(continued).*
proceedings with reference to the, 227.
employment of Scotch prisoners, and proceedings relative
thereto, 2-28.
state of, under the Commonwealth, 246.
employment of Dutch prisoners, 250.
second and last adjudication, and proceedings relative
thereto, 260. 276.
made a distinct government, 437.
how taxed, 621.
its boundary, 727.
corporation works, ibid.
banks, 728.
sluices and tunnels, 729.
bridges, ibid.
rivers, 730.
washes, ibid.
    Eau Brink Cut, 732.
    Rennie's report, and resolution thereon, 733.
    Dyson's ditto. 734.
    St. John's Eau, 736.
    Denver Sluice, 739.
demolition of, 742.
improvement of, 747.
    South Division Of Middle Level.—

See *Middle Level.*
    Spears,
found in the Middle Level, 421.
    Spring Tides, 49.
Standground Sluice, 724.
Starlings, 788.
Statutes.—See *Act of Parliament.*
    Stamford,
corporation of, 14.
    Steam Engines,
adoption of, in Fens, 100, *n.*
drainage by, 439.
    See *note in Table of Contents,* p. xiv.
    Stephen,
stale of the Great Level under, 65.
    Steward, 306.
    Sticelebaces,
river famous for, 12.
    Stoee Or Wissey River,
outfalls to sea, 6.
    Stonea Drain, 15)8.
    Stow Bridge, 37.
tolls, 770. -
    Superintendents,
duties of, 565. 574. 577.
under control of engineer, 573.
four elected annually, ibid.
1. of the north division of the Middle Level, 574.
2. south _ ibid.
3. east ibid.
4. South Level, ibid.
salaries, ibid.
when subject to engineer, ibid,
attendances at meetings, 576.
allowances to, ibid.
control over sluice-keepers and labourers, 577.
moneys received and paid by them, 571).
accounts, ibid,
oath of office, 580.
have care of the cottages, 635.
    Surveyor General, Office Op,
former duties of, 540.
now considered honorary, 540—1.
is annual, 541.
now held by Earl of Hardwicke, ibid,
list of persons who have held the office from 1GC3 to the present period, 544.
    Suspension Bridge,
over Hundred Feet River, 750.
Swaffham Lode, 23.
    T.
    Taxes. See also *Arrear Roll.*

difficulty of collecting, 227. 319.
gradual acre tax, 400.
power to impose, vested in board at April meeting, 527.
where received, 560.
sale of lands forfeited for non-payment of, 531.
under direction of select body, ibid.
proceedings prior to sale of lands forfeited for non-payment of, 661.
proceedings on sales, 5G8. 622.
corporation not coiupellable to redeem, 617.
schedule of lands in Middle and South Levels, the taxes of
which are ordered to be annually deducted, 617.
variations in, 620, *n.*
when and by whom imposed, 620.
single tax, ibid,
medium tax, ibid.
North Level tax, 621.
Middle and South Level lax, ibid.

    Taxes—*(continued).*
particulars of tax, calculated when a tax and three quarters
ure charged for Middle and South Levels, and a quarter
upon North Level, 026. %
according to tax roll, 627.
regulations respecting the collection of, 628.
of North Level, 673.
    Tax Act,
enactment and utility of, 400.
king's land, how taxed, 401.
conduct of commissioners, 402.
particulars of adventurers' lands, with the quantity charged
at each sort or degree under the, 024.
adventurers' lands, with particulars of the quantity lying in
the different levels charged at each sort, 625.
    Tax Roll,
prepared by the register, 559.
    Telfohd, Thomas, Esq.,
biographical notice of, 772.'
    Temporary Act,
first, 337.
second, 343.
    Ten Mile River, 26.'
    Thetfohd, Corporation Of,

power of, with respect to the Lesser Ouze, 39.
Thornet Lordship, 665.
fairs at, 675,
market, ibid.
Thurlow's Drain, 198.
Tidal Waters, 45.
Tidi And Newton,
drainage act, 678.
Tides,
Newton's theory of, 45.
Aristotle's, 46.
Kepler's, ibid.
Galileo's, ibid.
Descartes', ibid,
high and low water, 47.
spring and neap tides, 49.
Title,
to lands, (put up for sale as forfeited lands) through the medium of a bargain and sale under the corporate seal, 624.
Tolls,
of the Welland, 15.
are let tricnually, 633.
Tolls—*(continued)*.
hermitage sluice and bridge toll, ibid.
let at an annual rent, ibid.
public, of North Level, 67o.
private, ibid.
under Nene act, 705.
private, in east division of Middle Lerel, 724.
of Downham bridge, 779.
of Magdalen bridge, ibid.
of Stow bridge, ibid.
of German's Bridge, 780.
Tongs Drain,
account of, 199. 708.
improvement of, 712. 716.
use of, 737.
Townshend, Georqe Marquess Of, 509, *n*.
See also *Gardner,* under title *Names,*
Trees,
trunks of, found in the Fens, 418. 420.
Tunnels,
of east division of Middle Level, 699.
of South Level, 729.
Turf,
nature of, 418.
power of corporation to restrain digging, 619, *n*.
used for fuel, 790.

Turf Act,
object of, 617.
particulars of lands released under, 618.
power of corporation to restrain the digging of turf, 619, n.
-WATER,
qualities of, 418.
Twenty Feet River, 198.
Tyud And Newton,
drainage act, 673.
u.
Uflo Meer, 450.
Undertaeers, The, 88.
Vealland.—See *Wetland.*
Vbejiuyden, Sir Cornelius,
invited to England by King James I., 92.
his birth and parentage, ibid.
his plans, 96.
knighted, ibid.
Hatfield Chase granted him by the crown, ibid.
his marriage, and issue, ibid.
his ultimate fate uncertain, 97.
Veemuyden, Sib Cobxelius— *(continued)*.
his discourse on drainage, 07.
his contract with commissioners to drain Great Level abandoned, 103
engaged by Francis, Earl of Bedford, 120.
Hollanders engaged by him, 135.
transactions with him under the commonwealth, 160.
his demands, 164.
answers thereto, 1(15.
his reply, 1G7.
rejection of his demands, 160.
renewed negotiations, 17'2. 181.
intrigues of, 180.
triumph of, 195.
plan respecting the South Level, 227.
second and last adjudication, and proceedings relative thereto, 250. 276.
distresses and death of, 288.
errors of, 200.
last record of that family, 457, *n.*
Veemuyden's Eau, 198.
Visitorial Jurisdiction, 534. 535. 537.
writ of mandamus, 537.
Voters.—See *Board.*
w.
Waluersea Act, 91.
Wandsford Hridge,

anecdote respecting, 1!).
Warping,
signification of, 786.
Wash Act, 683.
Washes,
of South Level, 730.
Water,
how provided for North Level in dry seasons, 670,«.
Water Mills,
drainage by, 437.
And see *Table of Contents, p.* xiv. n.
Weeding,
of rivers, attended to by superintendents, 578.
Welche's Dam, 200.
D, River,
outfalls to sea, 6.
its source and current, 0.
acts of parliament affecting, 9. 13.
origin of the word, 9.
the neighbourhood, and seats, ibid.
tolls, 15.
fishery, ibid.
Wellmoor Laee, sluice at, 735.
tax, 7«o.
Wells, Samuel, Eso, (late Register), 508, «.
Wells, Samuel, Esq., (present Register), treasurer and clerk of river Nene, 710.
clerk to Middle Level commissioners, 725.
Chatteris his native place, 726. Westeroyee, 121. 162.
"consulted, and his opinion, 292.
"weston, his application to parliament for the 2000 acres 173. West Riveb, 2:).
bridge over, 27, n.
Whittlesey Diee, 17.
Whittlesey Mei-r,
origin unknown, 449.
rights of fishing in, 400. William The Conqueror state of the Great Level under, 65. Wind Mills, likely to be exploded, 100, n. Wisbech, 20. bridge, 21.
canal net, 717. commissioners of, how elected, 718.
clerks of, ibid.
WlSBECB IIrnin;n, boundary, 787.
tax, ibid. reeds, 780. Wissey, Or Stoee River, outfalls to sea, 6. 38. Wissey, Riveu, its source and current, 42. its navigation, ibid. tolls of, ibid. Wores, of the corporation, power of board over, 527.

Y.

Yaxley Meee, 450.

Yoree, Honorable C'jiaei.es, 510.

CPSIA information can be obtained at www.ICGtesting.com
Printed in the USA
BVOW07s0045030614
355237BV00008B/194/P